CHURCHILL'S MAN OF MYSTERY

The mysterious life and career of Desmond Morton, Intelligence officer and personal adviser to Winston Churchill during the Second World War, is exposed for the first time in this study based on full access to official records. After distinguished service as artillery officer and *aide-de-camp* to General Haig during the First World War, Morton worked for the Secret Intelligence Service from 1919–1934, and the fortunes of SIS in the interwar years are described here in unprecedented detail. As Director of the Industrial Intelligence Centre in the 1930s, Morton's warnings of Germany's military and industrial preparations for war were widely read in Whitehall, though they failed to accelerate British rearmament as much as Morton – and Churchill – considered imperative. Morton had met Churchill on the Western Front in 1916 and supported him throughout the 'wilderness years', moving to Downing Street as the Prime Minister's Intelligence adviser in May 1940. There he remained in a liaison role, with the Intelligence agencies and with Allied resistance authorities, until the end of the war, when he became a 'troubleshooter' for the Treasury in a series of tricky international assignments. Throughout Morton's career, myth, rumour and deliberate obfuscation have created a misleading picture of his role and influence. This book shines a light into many hitherto shadowy corners of British history in the first half of the 20th century.

Gill Bennett was Chief Historian of the Foreign & Commonwealth Office from 1995 to 2005. She has written extensively on diplomatic and Intelligence history.

WHITEHALL HISTORIES: GOVERNMENT OFFICIAL HISTORY SERIES

ISSN: 1474-8398

The Government Official History series began in 1919 with wartime histories, and the peacetime series was inaugurated in 1966 by Harold Wilson. The aim of the series is to produce major histories in their own right, compiled by historians eminent in the field, who are afforded free access to all relevant material in the official archives. The Histories also provide a trusted secondary source for other historians and researchers while the official records are not in the public domain. The main criteria for selection of topics are that the histories should record important episodes or themes of British history while the official records can still be supplemented by the recollections of key players; and that they should be of general interest, and, preferably, involve the records of more than one government department.

THE UNITED KINGDOM AND THE EUROPEAN
COMMUNITY:
Vol. I: The Rise and Fall of a National Strategy, 1945–1963
Alan S. Milward

SECRET FLOTILLAS
Vol. I: Clandestine Sea Operations to Brittany, 1940–1944
Vol. II: Clandestine Sea Operations in the Mediterranean, North Africa
and the Adriatic, 1940–1944
Brooks Richards

SOE IN FRANCE
M. R. D. Foot

THE OFFICIAL HISTORY OF THE FALKLANDS CAMPAIGN:
Vol. I: The Origins of the Falklands War
Vol. II: War and Diplomacy
Lawrence Freedman

THE OFFICIAL HISTORY OF BRITAIN AND THE
CHANNEL TUNNEL
Terry Gourvish

CHURCHILL'S MAN OF MYSTERY : DESMOND MORTON
AND THE WORLD OF INTELLIGENCE
Gill Bennett

CHURCHILL'S MAN OF MYSTERY

Desmond Morton and the world of Intelligence

Gill Bennett

Routledge
Taylor & Francis Group

LONDON AND NEW YORK

First published 2007
by Routledge
2 Park Square, Milton Park, Abingdon, Oxon OX14 4RN

Simultaneously published in the USA and Canada
by Routledge
270 Madison Ave, New York, NY 10016

Routledge is an imprint of the Taylor & Francis Group, an informa business

© 2007 Crown Copyright

Typeset in Times New Roman by
Keystroke, 28 High Street, Tettenhall, Wolverhampton
Printed and bound in Great Britain by
The Cromwell Press, Trowbridge, Wiltshire

British Library Cataloguing in Publication Data
A catalogue record for this book is available from the British Library

Library of Congress Cataloging in Publication Data
Bennett, Gill.
Churchill's mystery man : Desmond Morton and the world of intelligence / Gill Bennett.
p. cm. — (Whitehall histories : government official history series)
Includes bibliographical references and index.
1. Morton, Desmond, Sir, 1891–1971. 2. Intelligence officers—Great Britain—Biography.
3. Great Britain—Officials and employees—Biography.
4. Churchill, Winston, Sir 1874–1965—Friends and associates. I. Title. II. Series:
Government official history series.
DA566.9.M67B46 2006
327.410092—dc22
[B]
2006016243

Published on behalf of the Whitehall History Publishing Consortium.
Applications to reproduce Crown copyright protected
material in this publication should be submitted in writing to:
HMSO, Copyright Unit, St Clements House, 2–16 Colegate,
Norwich NR3 1BQ. Fax: 01603 723000.
E-mail: copyright@hmso.gov.uk

ISBN10: 0–415–39430–9 (hbk)
ISBN10: 0–203–96678–3 (ebk)

ISBN13: 978–0–415–39430–7 (hbk)
ISBN13: 978–0–203–96678–5 (ebk)

FOR HENRY AND DOMINIC

'Personally, I like reading history and biographies but I never *believe* any
of them'

Desmond Morton,
3 October 1962

The author has been given full access to official documents. The data and factual information in the report is based on these documents. The interpretation of the documents and the views expressed are those of the author.

CONTENTS

CONTENTS

LIST OF ILLUSTRATIONS

The following plates appear between pp. 134 and 135.

ABBREVIATIONS

AA	*Auswärtiges Amt*
ADC	*Aide de Camp*
AEA	Committee on Allied African Economic Affairs
AFHQ	Allied Forces Headquarters
APOC	Anglo-Persian Oil Company (later British Petroleum)
ARC	Allied Reparation Commission
ARCOS	All-Russian Cooperative Society Ltd
ATB	Advisory Committee on Trade Questions in Time of War
BAOR	British Army on the Rhine
BEF	British Expeditionary Force
BISS	British Industrial Secret Service
BMEO	British Middle East Office
BOAC	British Overseas Airways Corporation
BSC	British Security Coordination
C/CSS	Chief of the Secret Intelligence Service
CAS	Chief of the Air Staff
CCG(BE)	Control Commission for Germany, British Element
CFR	Committee on French Resistance/Committee on Foreign (Allied) Resistance
CID	Committee of Imperial Defence
CIGS	Chief of the Imperial General Staff
Cmd	Command Paper
CNS	Chief of the Naval Staff
COGA	Control Office for Germany and Austria
COI	Coordinator of Information (US)
COS	Chiefs of Staff/Chiefs of Staff Committee
CPGB	Communist Party of Great Britain
DCOS	Deputy Chiefs of Staff/Committee
DCSS	Deputy Chief of the Secret Intelligence Service
DMO&I/DMI	Director of Military Operations and Intelligence/Director of Military Intelligence
DNI	Director of Naval Intelligence

DoT	Department of Overseas Trade
DPP	Defence Plans (Policy) Sub-Committee
DPRC	Defence Policy and Requirements Committee
EAC	Economic Advisory Council
EH	Electra House
EPG	Economic Pressure on Germany Sub-Committee
FCI	Committee on Industrial Intelligence in Foreign Countries
FO	Foreign Office
GC&CS	Government Code & Cypher School
GHQ	General Headquarters
GPU/OGPU	State Political Directorate/Unified State Political Directorate (Soviet security service)
HDSE	Home Defence Security Executive
HMG	His/Her Majesty's Government
HMT	His/Her Majesty's Treasury
HO	Home Office
IARA	Inter-Allied Reparations Agency
IDC	Imperial Defence College
IIB	Industrial Intelligence Bureau
IIC	Industrial Intelligence Centre
IPI	Indian Political Intelligence
IRD	Information Research Department (FO)
IRO	International Refugee Organisation
ISI	Industrial Secret Intelligence
JIC	Joint Intelligence Committee
JPS	Joint Planning Staff
JPSC	Joint Planning Sub-Committee
LCS	London Controlling Section
MCA	Ministry of Civil Aviation
MEW	Ministry of Economic Warfare
MoD	Ministry of Defence
MUW	Ministry of Ungentlemanly Warfare (SOE)
NAEB	North Africa Economic Board
NERWA	Near East Relief and Works Agency
NKVD	People's Commissariat for Internal Affairs
NSY	New Scotland Yard
OSS	Office of Strategic Services (US)
PCO	Passport Control Office
PPS	Principal Private Secretary
PSO	Principal Supply Officers' Committee
PUS	Permanent Under Secretary
PUSC	Permanent Under Secretary's Committee
PUSD	Permanent Under Secretary's Department (FO)
PWE	Political Warfare Executive

RAF	Royal Air Force
RFA	Royal Field Artillery
SACMED	Supreme Allied Commander, Mediterranean Forces
SE	Security Executive
SHAEF	Supreme Headquarters Allied Expeditionary Force
SIC	Security Intelligence Centre
SIS	Secret Intelligence Service
SOE	Special Operations Executive
SRC	Situation Report Centre
SS	Secret Service
STD	Soviet Trade Delegation
TGC	Tripartite Commission for the Restitution of Monetary Gold
TNA	The National Archives (UK)
TWED	Trading with the Enemy Department
UKDel	UK Delegation (to the UN at New York)
UNGA	United Nations General Assembly
UNRPR	UN Relief for Palestine Refugees Programme
UNSC	United Nations Security Council
USSR	Union of Soviet Socialist Republics
VCSS	Vice Chief of the Secret Intelligence Service
WAD	*Wirtschafts Aussendienst* (Overseas Economic Service)
WO	War Office

INTRODUCTION

Desmond John Falkiner Morton (1891–1971) was an only child who never married. He destroyed his private papers, wrote no account of his personal or professional life and threatened repudiation or even legal action to anyone who contemplated including him in their memoirs or monographs. There are few family papers, and those who remember him agree that he was an intensely private person who, though sociable and even garrulous, revealed little of himself or his work. To attempt to trace his life and career is to pursue an imprint through snow that seems to have been carefully swept clear by someone in a swift sledge going before. The track may, of course, have been obscured innocently by subsequent snowfall. It is important not to see sinister shadows down every cold trail. The fact remains that research has revealed very little evidence about Desmond Morton as a man: where any documentation survives, it too often consists of (deliberately) unreliable and capricious reminiscence in correspondence written late in his life. It is fortunate that the official record reveals rather more about his career, the greater part of which was spent in or on the fringes of the 'secret world'. It is that world that forms the principal focus of this book.

Nevertheless, his early life is important. Though neither he nor his family left any record of his upbringing, education and military career, it is clear even from the impersonal factual record that all three are vital to an understanding of the kind of man he became and the way he conducted his professional life. I make no apology, therefore, for the early chapters of this book, even though Morton, the central character, leaves barely a footprint on the trail. Though a singular man in many respects, his experience – the late Victorian upbringing, the family military tradition, the indelible scar of five years on the Western Front – is representative of a generation of men who, if they survived, became the politicians and military commanders who dominated British public life and the armed forces for the next half century. An understanding of that experience is fundamental not just to the life of Desmond Morton but to the world in which he moved.

Born in 1891 at 9, Hyde Park Gate – a house later inhabited, coincidentally, by Winston Churchill – Morton progressed through Eton and the Royal Military Academy at Woolwich straight to the Western Front. A brave and highly decorated artillery officer, he suffered a severe wound in March 1917 that affected his health for the rest of his life, but by the end of July was back in France as ADC to the Commander in Chief, Field Marshal Sir Douglas Haig. He remained with Haig until April 1919 when he entered section MI1c of the War Office, by which designation the Secret Intelligence Service (SIS) was then known. There, as head of Production, he was responsible for obtaining information on foreign – principally Soviet – activities directed against Britain and Western interests, and built up a wide range of domestic and overseas contacts. He also took a keen interest in what might be called the organisational side of Intelligence, and exerted some – not always benign – influence upon the development of the British Intelligence establishment during the interwar years.

During the latter part of his service with SIS he became increasingly involved with the gathering of economic and industrial intelligence, and a rather more public phase of his career began in 1929 when he became Director of the Industrial Intelligence Centre, formed in response to the Committee of Imperial Defence's demand for information on potentially warlike preparations undertaken by foreign governments, particularly that of Germany. Morton supplied a constant stream of information on economic war preparations, obtained from both overt and covert sources worldwide, to the Committee, to the Cabinet – and to Winston Churchill, a friend since 1916 but not at that time in office. He played a major part in ensuring that on the outbreak of war in 1939 a Ministry of Economic Warfare could spring fully formed from the brow of the Treasury, and served as its first Director of Intelligence until Churchill swept him into 10 Downing Street in May 1940 to serve as his Intelligence adviser.

As one of Churchill's circle of personal advisers, in a post that was unspecified and informal but wide-ranging, Morton enjoyed the advantages of influence and access but was, unsurprisingly, widely distrusted by many in official positions. Nevertheless, his quick brain, administrative flair and seemingly inexhaustible capacity for work earned him considerable respect across Whitehall as a knowledgeable and efficient colleague (though some, like Foreign Secretary Anthony Eden, wished him 'at the bottom of the sea'). In the early years of the war Morton was very close to Churchill, enjoying his role as the Prime Minister's liaison with the Intelligence world, and continuing to intervene (some would say interfere) in the organisational turmoil that characterised the British Intelligence establishment at that time, including the formation of the Special Operations Executive (SOE) in the summer of 1940 and the development of a close relationship between British and (emerging) American Intelligence communities.

Morton's role as 'cut-out' was not restricted to Intelligence matters. There was a constant queue of people, British and foreign, military and civilian, official and opportunistic, grand and lowly, useful or sometimes plain mad, who wanted to see the Prime Minister. Those directly concerned with the prosecution of the war, or with a personal claim on Churchill, had their own channels to his presence; and of course the Prime Minister's Private Office played a central role. But Churchill trusted Morton, especially in the case of overseas visitors or those on errands of particular sensitivity, to weed out the inessential and insane, and to interview those with a serious mission before recommending whether the Prime Minister should see them. It was a role affording a certain power that Morton relished, but that tended, unsurprisingly, to increase his unpopularity with those who felt his influence to be intrusive or even malign.

In addition to his Intelligence-related work, Morton spent much of his time conveying Churchill's views (and directives) to a range of bodies from the Home Defence Security Executive to the Committee on Foreign (Allied) Resistance and the Joint Intelligence Committee. He was always careful to distinguish between the Prime Minister's views and his own: the former were more dynamic of expression, and of course authoritative, but Morton's own interventions, based on inside knowledge and experience, were, as even his enemies allowed, almost invariably well-informed and often perceptive. Also, he was an old hand at administrative manipulation; he knew who to talk to and how to get things done – a side of him later immortalised by Anthony Powell in the character of Sir Magnus Donners.[1]

Gradually, Morton's Intelligence liaison role diminished as Churchill developed closer personal contacts with the departmental Chiefs, and his influence waned generally from 1941 onwards; the evidence suggests, also, that he became somewhat disenchanted with the Prime Ministerial style. Nevertheless, he remained an important figure in the No. 10 machine, in particular working closely with the Allied governments in exile in London and with General de Gaulle and the Free French movement. Though the last year of the war saw a natural diminution in this area of activity, other tasks intervened, and 1945 saw Morton on a series of errands for Churchill, including visits to France and Greece, and involved with post-hostilities planning. At the end of July 1945, however, with Churchill out of office, and without an official position either civil or military, there was nowhere to go. The new Labour Government was keen to make a clean sweep of the 'old guard'. And Morton's personal and professional style, all too often abrasive and with a tendency to arrogance, had alienated many of those who might have considered including him in their post-war plans. The war had absorbed all his attention and time for the past six years: he had no close family left alive; he heard and saw little of Churchill, who he considered to have turned his back on him; he felt very much alone.

Whitehall, however, had not finished with him yet. The end of the Second World War left Britain victorious but bankrupt and exhausted, and with far-reaching responsibilities towards the Empire, towards a defeated Germany, towards its American and Russian Allies, and to an emerging proliferation of international institutions and financial arrangements. In these circumstances the British governmental machine found itself strained to breaking point. Men of experience and administrative ability were at a premium. So it was that Morton, despite an Intelligence man's traditional aversion to being a 'civil servant', spent the next eight years until retirement undertaking a series of trouble-shooting jobs, nominally attached to the Treasury but often working to the Foreign Office. From the Inter-Allied Reparations Agency and the Tripartite Gold Commission in

1946–49, to the UN Economic Survey Mission to the Middle East in 1949, to Civil Aviation agreements in the Middle East 1950–51, Morton cut a swathe through obstructive bureaucracy at home and overseas (even taking on the United Nations) with his usual combination of flair and outrageous disregard for the niceties of diplomatic convention. He caused trouble wherever he went: he bemused his opponents and upset his colleagues; but he got results. He would, I think, have been pleased by the following comment by Roger Makins (later Lord Sherfield), trying to smooth the ruffled feathers of the Ministry of Civil Aviation in June 1951:

> [I] think that the role of 'farceur' is one which should occasionally be allowed even in official life ... with Desmond Morton's tendencies towards the telling of tall stories and the pulling of legs, go also many qualities which make him a good negotiator, especially in the wilder and woollier countries.[2]

Morton retired from the civil service in 1953. For a while he hovered on the fringes of the official world, but suggestions that he should be drawn into various shadowy enterprises came to little. Instead, he threw himself into a different form of public service, this time on the board of the London Postgraduate Teaching Hospitals, where he served as Chairman from 1956–66, a tireless interlocutor of the Ministry of Health. He also lectured on military and strategic matters, and was a prominent member of the Catholic Laity in the United Kingdom (his devout Roman Catholicism did not prevent him from being a thorough nuisance to the Church if his sharp eye discerned inefficiency or inconsistency). Though his health, always under strain, deteriorated in these last years, he remained energetic and active until the last few months of his life. Despite his protestations of a desire for relaxation and peace, he sought neither. His death on 31 July 1971 brought the curtain down on an unremittingly active life.

Since embarking on the quest for Morton in 2000 I have had generous help from a wide range of people and institutions. My principal thanks are due to Mrs Tessa Stirling, Head of the Cabinet Office Histories, Openness and Records Unit, and to her staff, especially Sally Falk and Richard Ponman. I owe a great debt to the Foreign & Commonwealth Office for the support I received with the Morton project while serving as the FCO's Chief Historian: in particular, to Sir Michael Jay and Lord Kerr of Kinlochard, and to Mrs Heather Yasamee, for her support and long friendship; and to all my former colleagues in FCO Historians, particularly Dr Christopher Baxter. In 2002–3 the FCO kindly granted me a year's leave of absence to take up a Visiting Fellowship at Corpus Christi College, Cambridge, where the Master, Professor Haroun Ahmed, and his wife Anne, the President, Professor Christopher Andrew, and his wife Jenny, and all the Fellowship were most supportive and made me feel part of the Corpus 'family'.

I should also like to thank those members of the UK's Intelligence Agencies who shall remain nameless, but who have guided my research and writing, providing not only expert help but also encouragement at times when the search for Morton seemed to have reached yet another dead end. Without them this book would not have been written. To those I may name: John Scarlett, Chief of the Secret Intelligence Service, and his predecessor Sir Richard Dearlove; Dame Eliza Manningham-Buller, Director General of the Security Service, and her predecessor, Sir Stephen Lander; Sir David Pepper, Director of GCHQ, and his predecessor, Sir Francis Richards; I offer thanks for both personal support and practical assistance.

A full list of the archives consulted may be found in the Source Note and Bibliography. I am grateful to the Keeper and staff of The National Archives at Kew, the Director of the Churchill College Archives Centre, Cambridge, the Trustees of the Liddell Hart Centre for Military History, King's College, London, the Syndics of Cambridge University Library, the LSE Library, the Royal Artillery Historical Trust and BP Global Archive Management for permission to quote from their material. In all these archives I have received much friendly help from the staff, but should like to mention in particular: Penny Hatfield (Eton College); Allen Packwood and Andrew Riley (Churchill College Archives Centre); Sue Donnelly (LSE); Peter Housego (BP); Kate O'Brien (Liddell Hart Centre for Military Archives); Patrick Zutshi (Cambridge University Library); the Records Management staff of The National Archives at Kew, particularly Howard Davies and Stephen Twigge; and Paul Evans (Royal Artillery Museum). I am also very grateful to those in Whitehall Departments dealing with archival and review questions, in particular Penny Prior and Pat Andrews (FCO), Iain Goode and David Russell (MoD), John Green, Sue Wayland, Nick Weekes and Alan Glennie (Cabinet Office); and also to Phil Reed, Director of the Cabinet War Rooms, and his staff. Dr Peter Martland, Mr Ian Sayer, Mrs Joan Bright Astley and Mr Philip Daniel generously made available documents from their own collections.

I am most grateful for information, advice and support from academic colleagues too numerous to list. To the following I owe a special debt of friendship as well as professional expertise: Professor Christopher Andrew; Professor M.R.D. Foot; Professor George Peden; and Professor David Stafford. I have learned from discussions with Joan Bright Astley, Tony Bishop, David Burke, Andrew Cook, Philip Daniel, the late Sir William Deakin, Professor David Dilks, John Gerson, Sir Martin Gilbert, Professor Eunan O'Halpin, Dr Keith Hamilton, Professor Keith Jeffrey, Dr Peter Martland, Professor David Reynolds, Professor Patrick Salmon, Mark Seaman, Dr William Z. Slany, the Lady Soames, DBE and Professor Wesley Wark. Members of the Cambridge postgraduate Intelligence Seminar directed by Professor Andrew have offered valuable insights, in particular Chantal Auban, Victor Madeira and Paul Winter, while Harry and Percy Hayball gave helpful research assistance.

To those relatives and friends of Desmond Morton that I have been able to contact I am especially grateful. I should like to thank in particular George Franks, Michael Conyngham Greene, Angela and Peter Mynors and Mrs Gil Parker and

John Parker, all of whom have given or lent documents and photographs, as well as sharing their memories and patiently answering my questions. The Leather Family History Society, particularly Dr David Leather, provided a rich source of information on Morton's maternal family. Sally Brown and Kate Crowe helped me through the archival complexities of family and literary history.

Finally, Susie Gavin, Chris Poulton, Jane Hayball and Mark Ormerod provided essential help in looking after my cat and children while I was pursuing Desmond Morton. My elder son, Henry, designed the Morton database; while Dominic, as ever, reminds us of the important things in life.

1

ANCESTRAL VOICES

Mortons and Leathers

In August 1966, after reviewing the first volume of Harold Macmillan's memoirs[1] Desmond Morton commented in typically facetious style that he was thinking of writing his own life in nine volumes, 'one vol for each 8 years, with a tenth if I live to 80'. The first volume, he said, would begin as follows:

> I was born on November 13th, 1891 at 11 a.m. precisely. It was snowing hard. Though remembering little of this highly important event, its consequences include such phenomena as a hatred of the cold in all forms ever since, especially cold boiled mutton. That I was born in the house which, a good deal later on, became the property of Sir Winston Churchill, in Hyde Park Gate, may be regarded as a coincidence. I have always understood that this house was hired for the purpose of my arrival from the then owner, since my parents then lived at Windsor (not Windsor Castle). . . .[2]

Apart from a brief notice in *The Times* and his birth certificate, confirming his parentage, date and place of birth, this letter, written in his 75th year, is the only documentary reference that has been found to Desmond Morton's entry into the world. We must take his word for it on the reason why he was born at 9 Hyde Park Gate: it is certainly true that he hated the winter months, and Christmas in particular, all his long life. Very little is known of his parents' life at the time of his birth, but as the only child of a late marriage he was much wanted and greatly loved. His mother, Edith, had in fact been carrying twins, but the other baby, a girl, died at birth. Morton was fond of saying, in later life, 'I killed my sister'.[3]

Desmond Morton's parents, Edith Harriet Leather and Charles Falkiner Morton, had married in 1887 at the ages of 31 and 44 respectively: late, in those days, for a first marriage on each side. We do not know how, when or where they met, though since Charles – always known as Charlie – was a cavalry officer and travelled widely with his regiment, including periods in Ireland and India, theirs must have been an intermittent courtship. Again, we can only rely on Desmond to explain his parents' late marriage, though his explanation seems a plausible one. Edith's father, John Towlerton Leather, a patriarchal figure much attached to his youngest daughter, disliked and distrusted the military and did not want her to marry a soldier. Edith and Charlie had to wait until after his death in 1885. In that year Charlie was still in India, commanding the XIV Royal Hussars, whom he brought home to England in 1886. He and Edith were married on 10 February 1887.

Both Desmond's parents came from large, sprawling families of contrasting orientation. The Mortons – or rather, the male members of the family – were soldiers, lawyers and literary men: indeed, a surprisingly large number, perhaps not inappropriately, combined the profession of lawyer with that of actor, playwright or theatrical producer. Two of Charlie's great-uncles, Thomas Morton and John Maddison Morton,[4] were moderately successful Victorian playwrights, while his great-grandfather was the eminent Georgian poet and dramatist Thomas Morton,[5] who entered Lincoln's Inn in 1784 and whose works included *Speed the Plough*, containing the phrase 'What will Mrs Grundy say?', widely used long afterwards to comment on potentially shocking or scandalous behaviour. Mortons can be traced back to the 12th century throughout the British Isles and beyond: there was, for example, a family connection to Thomas Morton of Merrymount, known as the 'English adventurer in America', who left his law practice in London to found in 1625 a settlement in Massachusetts known as Merrymount, where he scandalised more sober colonists by selling rum and firearms to the natives and dancing round a maypole with Indian women; he came to a sticky end after immortalising his experiences in *New English Canaan* (1637). Desmond's branch of the family, however, had its roots in Ireland, with a strong 19th century connection to the Indian subcontinent.

The Leathers, on the other hand, were technical men and entrepreneurs: engineers, contractors, architects, surveyors. The family was firmly rooted in northern England, ranged across Derbyshire, Nottinghamshire, Lancashire and Yorkshire, though the Leathers' skills took them far and wide and their tangible legacy can still be seen in bridges, dams and canals across England. Edith's great-grandfather, George Leather (1748–1818) had been Chief Colliery Engineer to the Yorkshire 'Coal King' William Fenton. George had eleven children and at least 25 grandchildren: his three sons that survived to adulthood included a civil engineer, an architect and Edith's grandfather James (1779–1849), pro-prietor of Beeston Colliery. With a few exceptions the family remained in the North of England, many in or around Leeds, and Leather daughters married local men (particularly clergymen), the family ties still tighter when Leather sisters chose bridegrooms who were brothers. Edith's father, the eminent Victorian water engineer John Towlerton Leather, moved a section of the family further north when in 1858 he bought one of the oldest estates in Northumber-land, Middleton Hall, fifty miles north of Newcastle upon Tyne. There he adopted readily and conscientiously the responsibilities of lord of the manor, and became a prominent local philanthropist, serving a term as High Sheriff of Northumberland.

Morton's baptismal name, Desmond John Falkiner Morton, carries within it all the clues to this variegated family background. Desmond was not a traditional Morton forename, and the evidence suggests a choice based on ancestry with a touch of romantic appeal. Three months before Desmond's birth in November 1891, his mother Edith pasted into her scrapbook a cutting from a magazine concerning Lady Katherine Fitzgerald, the 'old' Countess of Desmond, who according to popular legend lived for 140 years, dying in 1604 from a fall while climbing an apple tree at her home in County Cork. Although parts of the story are certainly apocryphal – she was also supposed to have danced with Richard III – there seems no doubt that the Countess of Desmond was a remarkable woman who lived to a great age, possibly over 100. Daughter of Sir John Fitzgerald, Lord of Decies, she became the second wife of Thomas Fitzgerald, twelfth Earl of Desmond, some time after 1505, and bore him a daughter. In widowhood she retired to the dower house, the Castle of Inchiquin, apparently travelling to England with her daughter to present a petition to King James I protesting against the seizure of her estates by English settlers (they had to stop for a time on the way because her elderly daughter was exhausted by the journey). According to the *Itinerary* of Fynes Morison, the Countess continued to the end of her life to walk daily to the market town three miles from her home in Youghal.[6]

The story of the forceful and charismatic Countess may have attracted Edith, but there was also a family connection. The Desmonds belonged to one of the most ancient of Irish families, the McCartys or McCarthys, whose genealogy, according to *Burke's Peerage*, could be traced back to Heber, eldest son of Milesius, King of Spain, through Oilioll Olium, King of Munster, in the third century. The Earls of Desmond, Clancarty and Glencave all belonged to the McCarty clan, and McCarty was the maiden name of Charlie Morton's mother, Mary Geraldine, another forceful and relatively long-lived woman (1822–1904). Mary was one of the twelve children of the chieftain of the oldest branch of the clan, Justin McCarty of Carrignavar, Co. Cork, and Isabella Falkiner, grand-daughter of Sir Riggs Falkiner, MP for Castlemara, thus providing another of Desmond's forenames. Mary married, successively, two barristers with business connections in India and spent a considerable part of her married life there. She was said to have been an intimate friend of Lord Dalhousie, Governor General of India from 1848 to 1856, and to have counted Thackeray, Trollope and Fanny Kemble among her circle.

Mary's first marriage, to Thomas Charles Morton, produced two sons: Desmond's father, Charlie, and Gerald, born in Calcutta in 1843 and 1845. Very little is known about Thomas Morton: his practice was based at Belgrave Square, in London, but he appears to have had business and possibly professional interests in India and Ceylon. Thomas died in 1855, and three years later Mary married another barrister, William Brownrigg Elliot, grandson of the first Earl of Minto, who had gone out to India to sort out the affairs of his father's Bengal Indigo

Company. He and Mary had two sons, Cyril and William, born in India in 1858 and 1861, but on the death of his father he took his family back to Scotland. There William purchased in 1862 the mansion house of Benrig, on Tweedside, and settled down with Mary to fulfil his duties as Laird; also playing a prominent part in Liberal affairs during Gladstone's 1868–74 Administration. Their son Cyril died young, in 1868, but in the best family tradition the younger William became both a barrister and an actor, recording his career in *In My Anecdotage* published in 1925. 'Willie' Elliot was a prominent figure in the world of Liberal politics, but was known more particularly as a 'clubman' and raconteur in the London literary and social scene during the 1890s; he took a keen interest in the young Desmond, who recalled him fondly in later years as a favourite uncle.

When Mary Morton married her second husband in 1858 her two Morton sons, Charlie and Gerald, had already returned to England to be educated. Both boys attended Eton and Sandhurst before entering the Army. Gerald Morton[7] had the more distinguished military career, becoming ADC to the Lieutenant Governor of the Punjab in 1871 at the age of 26, and achieving great distinction during the Afghan campaigns, fighting alongside Lord Roberts during the siege of Kandahar in 1879. At the time of his sudden death, in 1906, he was about to relinquish command of the 7th Division of the Irish Command at the Curragh, though he had recently been more in the public eye as President of the Court of Inquiry into a notorious case of bullying at Aldershot among the Scots Guards.[8] Described by the *Irish Times* as 'a perfect type of the thoughtful, kingly [*sic*] gentleman, yielding no part of his duty to courtesy, but still retaining courtesy in all his duties', one newspaper also noted a nice sense of humour: commanding the Lahore district during the Boer War and alarmed by losing all his best troops to the front, Gerald returned the following response to a wire from HQ asking how many more men he could spare: 'the ten men under my command are at present playing football; I might spare one of the goalkeepers if urgent.'[9]

Charles Falkiner Morton's career was perfectly respectable though less exalted: his passion was for horses rather than staff work. Entering the First Royal Dragoons as cornet of horse in 1862, he remained with the 'Royals' for the greater part of his career, eventually reaching the rank of Lieutenant-Colonel. During this period the Royals were stationed all over England, rarely staying more than a year in one place apart from serving in Ireland from 1867–73 and again from 1880. It is not known where or when on his travels Charlie met his future wife, Edith, but it is likely to have been before 1883 when he was transferred to command the XIV King's Hussars, then stationed in India. Promoted Colonel in 1885, the following year he brought his regiment home to England. In 1887, the year of his marriage, he was appointed Assistant Director of Remounts, a post chosen by him in preference to another command in order to indulge his passion for horses. Charlie was an enthusiastic sportsman who had owned and raced horses in India, Ireland and England, both on the flat and in steeplechases. During his final three years in India Edith collected press reports of his sporting exploits: a report in *The Fusee* dated 13 August 1884, for example, records Charlie riding five of his own horses

4

in eleven races over three days, and winning five of them.* Though forced to resign his commission through ill-health in 1892, cuttings in Edith's scrapbook show that he continued to take a keen interest both in horse racing and other forms of sport, including cricket and angling; Desmond recalled being taken as a boy to Thurston's billiards hall by his father.

Until his marriage in 1887 Charlie had apparently devoted his life to horses and the Army, though what little evidence survives indicates a lively and sociable personality. In keeping with Morton tradition, both he and Gerald seem to have been involved in amateur dramatics: as early as 1860 they had played leading parts in two farces written by their great-uncle, John Maddison Morton, *Box and Cox* and *The Rifle and How to Use It* (Edith later pasted the programme in her scrapbook). Charlie was also willing to sing in public, performing 'On the Steamer' and 'The Old Brigade' at a concert held at Middleton Hall in December 1887. It would seem, therefore, that he was well able to cope with the large and gregarious Leather family. For in marrying Edith, he was joining forces not with a spinster emerging from a long subjugation to her elderly father, but with an attractive, strong-minded, relatively wealthy and well-travelled woman whose family background had made her independent and self-reliant. While she was close to her father and may have deferred marriage to please him, in adulthood she had divided her time between Middleton Hall and her father's London residence, 19 Carlton House Terrace. She travelled widely in the United Kingdom, visiting friends and members of her large extended family, and appears to have made regular trips to Europe as well.[10]

Edith was the youngest child of John Towlerton Leather, who gave Desmond his other forename. 'JTL', an interesting character who undoubtedly passed on some of his qualities and independence of mind to his youngest daughter, repays some study. Born in Liverpool in 1804, he came from a family of notable engineers, though his own father James had in fact been an accountant and colliery proprietor in Liverpool and Leeds.[11] JTL left home at nineteen with £5 in his pocket to apprentice himself to his engineer uncle George Leather in Bradford, working with him on the Aire and Calder Navigation and Goole Docks. By the age of 25 he had set himself up as a civil engineer with offices in Sheffield, where he designed and built seven dams for the Sheffield Waterworks Company, six of which are still in use.[12] Known as 'Contractor Leather' (the 'contractor' in major construction projects of this period assumed financial responsibility for the entire undertaking, including engaging labour and plant at his own expense), JTL enjoyed a long and successful career until well into his seventies as civil engineer and entrepreneur, his major projects including the Portland Breakwater and Spithead Forts and extensions to Portsmouth Harbour, as well as reservoirs,

---

* The report noted that the *Mowl Ali* Handicap on 9 August was won by 'Col. Morton's *Sailor Boy*, notwithstanding the fact that his astute owner declared the pony was lame and allowed him to go for a song in the lottery'.

bridges and railways across the country; he also founded the Hunslet Steam Engine Company and owned a colliery.

Despite his involvement in high-profile projects that attracted a good deal of public interest (and public money), Leather seems to have remained a surprisingly low-key figure. A serious, rather austere and somewhat diffident professional, meticulous in fulfilling his responsibilities, he was undoubtedly ambitious though seemingly ill at ease with social, if not with financial success. JTL was, perhaps, disinclined towards the networking and self-promotion that would have brought greater recognition of his achievements; he never quite rose to the public heights of his profession, unlike, for example, his apprentice, John (later Sir John) Fowler, who spent five years with Leather in the 1830s and went on to become President of the Institute of Civil Engineers. Nevertheless JTL enjoyed considerable financial and social success. During the 1850s and 1860s, at the peak of his career, he was able to buy two paddle steamers, the *Princess* and the *Contractor*, and a steam yacht, *Ceres*; he owned large houses in Yorkshire and in Northumberland, where his estate of Middleton Hall extended to nearly 7,000 acres; and as a London base he bought 19 Carlton House Terrace (where his neighbours included the future Prime Minister, William Ewart Gladstone, and the Duke of Newcastle), installing a housekeeper and servants. In 1859 he was also granted his own coat of arms, with the motto *Nil Nisi Quod Honestum*.*

One wonders, however, whether he had much time or opportunity to enjoy these fruits of success, since his projects required him to spend long periods on site or travelling; certainly, there was not much opportunity to spend time at home with his family. His personal life, which undoubtedly suffered from the demands of his professional responsibilities, had been touched by loss and disappointment. In 1832 JTL had, much against her father's wishes, married his first cousin, Maria, daughter of his uncle and mentor George Leather. Just twenty-one and pregnant at the time of her marriage, Maria bore JTL six children, four of whom survived childhood, but she died from pneumonia in 1849, having spent considerable periods of time living with her family in Leeds when JTL's work commitments took him away from home; in 1844 he bought Leventhorpe Hall, just south of Leeds, to please her. Despite his prolonged absences, Leather was much affected by Maria's death, which was followed a month later by the death of their youngest daughter, Catherine Rosa; within a year, both his parents were dead too. His reaction was to seek a change of scene by bidding, successfully, for the contract to construct Portland Breakwater.

JTL's second wife, Harriet Spencer Page, Edith's mother, was co-heiress to her father Isaac Spencer Page's estate at Shirland in Derbyshire, and the two families had known each other well for some time. They married in 1852 when she was thirty-three, but their evident happiness was short-lived. Their first child, a boy, lived only eighteen months; Edith was born in 1856. On 18 May 1859 Harriet was

---

* Nothing except that which is honest.

killed in an accident while driving a pony and trap with JTL's grown-up daughter Annie, three-year old Edith and two of JTL's small nieces (all unhurt). Leather was devastated: he had 'now lost two wives in their prime and four of the eight children born to him'.[13] His grief and despair are evident in a 'Christmas Box' letter written to Edith in December 1859, seven months after the death of her mother:

My little darling Edith,

The earnest prayer of thy poor bereaved father, my sweet little darling, is that you may grow up by the grace of our Lord in all goodness in the likeness and after the example of thy sainted mother – who altho' lost to us in this life, let us hope that we may meet her hereafter in that world where neither sin nor sorrow can be known.

We may one and all wish you my darling a 'Merry Christmas' for happily it is far beyond thy young mind to comprehend the bitterness of the affliction which the loss of thy dear mother inflicts upon her unhappy husband.

That every blessing of this life may be extended to you my sweet darling and that you may be received into the Kingdom of Heaven hereafter is the sincere and hopeful prayer of your Father,

J. Towlerton Leather[14]

At the time of Harriet's death JTL's youngest child by his first marriage, Arthur, was thirteen and attending Rugby; the eldest, Ellen, was already married, and Frederick, JTL's somewhat feckless heir, was twenty-four. It therefore fell to Annie, at the age of twenty, to take over the care of little Edith. Since JTL's reaction to the loss of his second wife was to throw himself into another major construction project that took him away from home, this time to Portsmouth and Spithead, Annie brought Edith up, first at Middleton Hall, and later accompanying her to London. As both grew older the relationship was more one of close friends than mother and daughter. Annie never married, but lived in Kensington until her death in 1910.

John Towlerton Leather died in 1885, leaving an estate with a net value of over £250,000 – the equivalent of at least £15 million today. As a prominent local landowner and man of substance, he had taken his responsibilities seriously and was well respected. A local memoir described him as a 'friendly and hospitable neighbour, a considerate and generous landlord and last but not least a constant employer of the working classes . . . prompt and liberal with his payments': he had built a large number of new homes and a school for tenants on the Middleton estate, served as a local magistrate and was High Sheriff of Northumberland from 1875–6.[15] Writing to Edith in August 1883 as he entered his eightieth year, he referred to his 'long and arduous struggle', regretting that he had not tried 'more earnestly to overcome the weakness and frailty that tempts one to do wrong rather than right'. Nevertheless, he felt he might fairly say that he had 'not led an idle life' and that his efforts had been 'well and bounteously rewarded with a degree of success that is by no means common'. He regretted, however, that there seemed little prospect that this 'social advance' would be continued after his death: a reference, certainly, to his dissatisfaction with his eldest son Frederick, whom he considered irresponsible and insufficiently serious.[16]

JTL's will, an extremely complex document – twenty pages of closely spaced copperplate handwriting – was a masterpiece of Victorian control *d'outre-tombe*. It made careful provision for his tenants, creating a trust from the Northumberland estate that included Middleton Hall, the whole of the Middleton township and those of Detchant, Hetton and part of Holburn. It also imposed considerable restrictions on his heir, stipulating for example that none of the properties could be knocked down and replaced with a building of greater value, ensuring that no tenants could be forced out of their home by increased rents.[17] Edith and Annie, JTL's two unmarried daughters, were given a choice for two years after his death of where they wished to live, at Leventhorpe Hall near Leeds or in London at Carlton House Terrace, and a lump sum to invest for an annual income: £30,000 for Annie, and £25,000 for Edith in recognition of the fact that she had, in 1881, inherited her mother's share of the Shirland estates.

The respect and affection felt locally for Leather was extended to his youngest daughter 'little Edith', who had grown up at the manor house and was well known and liked. The occasion of her wedding to Colonel Charles Morton on 10 February 1887 was one of great local interest and rejoicing: flags hung from windows in Belford, where the wedding took place at St Mary's Church, the railway station was festooned with bunting and thirty local girls carrying baskets of snowdrops lined the path to the church. The ceremony was conducted by Edith's brother-in-law, the Reverend William Medcalf (married to JTL's daughter Ellen), and she was given away by her half-brother Fred. Charlie's best man was Lt-Colonel Rhodes of the Royal Dragoons: the regiment presented the couple with a carriage, while the XIV Hussars sent a chest of silver spoons and forks. The *Court Journal* described Edith's dress as 'composed of a body and tunic of cream and gold brocade, trimmed with duchesse point, over a petticoat of cream satin', with a veil and diamond ornaments. Though not a 'grand' wedding in society terms, it was reported extensively in the local and national press. The list of just over 60 official guests was headed by Mr and Mrs Elliot – Charlie's mother and stepfather – but was otherwise dominated by Leathers, together with local aristocracy and dignitaries, including the Earl and Countess of Tankerville and Sir Edward Grey (the local MP).

After the ceremony there was a champagne tea at Middleton Hall (with a dinner for the tenants at the Blue Bell Hotel), and then Charlie and Edith left by train for London. Whether the honeymoon was spent in England or abroad is not recorded; nor where the couple took up residence afterwards. It is likely that, as Desmond later wrote, Charlie and Edith went to live at Windsor, since his job as Assistant Director of Remounts would have been based near the Remounts

Office at Hounslow, the source of replacement horses for the 'resupply chain' to the Cavalry. Nor is it clear for how long the house at 9 Hyde Park Gate, where Desmond was born in 1891, was rented. After Charlie resigned his commission in the following year, however, the family became established permanently in London, at the large house in Chelsea at 3 Beaufort Gardens, running between the King's Road and Cheyne Walk, which was to be home to Mortons and their relations for most of the next century; it was to be Desmond Morton's London home until 1952.

A military upbringing: 1891–1914

Almost nothing is known about Desmond Morton's life between his birth on 13 November 1891 and entering Eton College in Summer half 1905 at the age of thirteen. All that remain of his early years are fleeting reminiscences, whether in the form of family stories or of Desmond's own correspondence written towards the end of his life, undoubtedly embellished and at least suspect of accuracy. He seems to have been by nature a solitary child, fussed over though not spoiled by his parents. As a family they were comfortably off, thanks to Edith's parents, and Beaufort Gardens served as a London social hub for both Mortons and Leathers. Press notices collected by Edith of family weddings in the 1900s often read 'the reception was held at 3 Beaufort Gardens', and Gerald's daughters May and Geraldine were both married from there, Charlie giving them away in place of his late brother. There were holidays abroad – possibly property abroad, too: when Gerald's youngest daughter Geraldine married Captain Hugh Elles on 9 October 1912 they spent their honeymoon in the south of France at 'a villa lent by Colonel and Mrs Morton'.

Edith, competent and decisive, ran a tight ship and ruled husband, son and domestic establishment with a kind but firm hand. Very little can be discerned of Charlie's character, though one gets the impression of a genial, military figure, more than happy to leave arrangements in Edith's capable hands. Although there is no record of Desmond's early education, it seems likely that he was, as was usual at the time, sent away to preparatory school. His own recollection (admittedly not always reliable) would seem to confirm this. Writing to R.W. Thompson in 1967, he explained that his dislike of Christmas – a frequent theme – dated back to his childhood:

> One came back for the holidays to home. But my good and loving parents always asserted that I should be dull, merely being at home; whereas it was the very place I wanted to be. Hence the very day I got back from school I was dragged off to stay with relations in the country – all much older than myself – who spent the time 'keeping me amused'! Being a polite child, I spent the time in a sort of dull misery, with a sickly smile, longing to get back home, where I had my own things, did not have to be dressed up every day in stuffy clothes, did not have to be

made to dash about and be taken to call on 'cousin Etheldreda', a year or two younger than myself, hideous to look on, appallingly feminine in an arty-crafty manner, 'a perfect little lady' and as insincere (poor child) as an alligator's baby.

The letter goes on to describe how at the age of eight he rebelled and threw his hated cousin into a pond, causing her to revolt in turn against feminine convention, changing her name to Jane and enthusiastically joining Desmond on rabbiting expeditions.[18] Without placing too much reliance on the veracity of this account, Desmond's lack of siblings, and indeed, lack of any family of similar age in London, points away from his being educated at home: nor does a tutor or governess figure in the 1901 census entry for 3 Beaufort Gardens.

Despite the suggestion of enforced visits to relatives, borne obediently if not willingly, a picture begins to emerge from this letter and other fragmentary evidence of what Desmond was like as a boy, and indeed, would be like as a man. Sociable but essentially solitary; friendly but ill at ease with intimacy; lively and quick-witted, but lacking (or perceived to be lacking) in empathy. None of these characteristics is perhaps unexpected in an only child surrounded principally by adults, who experienced an essentially Victorian upbringing, but in the light of what is known of Edith, and of her father John Towlerton Leather, a sort of pattern may be discerned. Both offered considerable support – social, practical, financial and even emotional – to their extended families, while retaining a somewhat formal and austere manner; for their spouses and children they held a deep, loyal but undemonstrative and not uncritical affection. In the same way, Desmond took a close interest throughout his life in other people, their characteristics and motivation: once he was old enough to read about developments in the new science of psychology he followed them closely, and despite appearances to the contrary an often impatient manner did not mean that he dismissed others lightly. But his interest was detached and analytical, rather than personal or emotional: an approach that was to be an asset to an intelligence officer, but somewhat inhibitory in terms of forming close relationships.

All this is to look too far ahead. The events of 1914–18 were also to have a permanent effect upon Desmond's character and personal style. Suffice it to say that as a small boy he seems to have preferred his own company and, even if he was sent to board at a preparatory school, lacked the experience of brutal sibling camaraderie to prepare him for Eton College. There is no way of knowing whether any friends entered Eton at the same time as he did. In any case, according to family reminiscence, he found it a shock. He was proud to be going there, following in his father's and uncle's footsteps. Like them, he was destined for a military career, and was well aware that Army Class at Eton was the route to Sandhurst or Woolwich. He was not, however, prepared for the alien ritualism of Eton or the rough and tumble of his contemporaries.

Unfortunately, no record survives of how he coped with life at Eton or what he thought about it: his school career, though successful in academic terms, left the barest ripple in College documentation and none in any private papers. Though Eton's archives are by no means complete for this period, Desmond's house for most of his school career, Tatham's, is unusual in that no House Book has survived for any of the relevant years, 1905–9; even more unusually, there is no House photograph. The Corps enrolment book, where one would expect to find details of a boy destined for Army Class, does not contain his name. The Eton Boating Book records briefly his participation in the Ante-Finals of the Novice Pulling, 1908; Conybeare's* House Football Book, 1909 judges him as a very useful 'Fly'; but he did not join the Eton Society or any well-known clubs, nor, apparently, take a prominent part in literary, artistic or musical activities.

There is no indication of who his friends were, but some of his contemporaries were to become colleagues and contacts in his military and professional life, among them Ralph Wigram, Frank Ashton-Gwatkin and Stewart Menzies, future Chief of the Secret Intelligence Service.[19] Other contemporaries included the future King Leopold III of the Belgians, Julian Grenfell (killed in 1915), Osbert Sitwell, Denys Finch-Hatton (Keeper of Wall and winner of many musical and literary prizes), the mathematician H.T.J. Norton and three of the four remarkable Knox brothers, Ronald, Edmund (E.V.) and Arthur Dillwyn ('Dilly'), who became respectively a notable theologian, Editor of *Punch* and an outstanding codebreaker in both World Wars. Half of Desmond Morton's contemporaries at Tatham's lost their lives before 1918.

Desmond's arrival at Eton in 1905 just preceded that of a new Head Master, the Hon Edward Lyttelton.[20] There were about a thousand boys in the school at that point: numbers had risen steadily during the 18th and 19th centuries, from 196 in 1698 to 987 in 1890 (there are less than 1300 today). According to the rules at that time, Desmond had to sit Trials during his second term at Eton in order to seek election to Army Class after Christmas. The four Army Classes were primarily for students who intended to go straight from Eton to the Royal Military Academies at Woolwich or Sandhurst rather than to university. Teaching was kept separate from the rest of the School, and concentrated on Science subjects, rather than the Classics; there was an additional charge of £3.10s each term, and a high level of attainment in mathematics was expected.

Morton was elected to Army Class I at Christmas 1905, one of three boys to take a Trials prize; he also took the Brinckman Divinity Prize. Although in later life he was to express regret that he had concentrated on physics rather than Greek, he clearly had an aptitude for science subjects in which he excelled, as well as in modern languages, winning the Assistant Master's German prize in 1907 (when Stewart Menzies won the Master's prize), and the Maths and Science prizes in 1909. The qualifying exam for Woolwich and Sandhurst, held in two

---

* After the sudden death of his housemaster, H.W.F. Tatham, on a reading party in Switzerland during the summer vacation in 1909, Morton transferred to the house of A.E.C. Conybeare for his final term.

parts in September and November, required high passes in English, English History, Geography and Maths, and in two subjects out of science, French or German and Latin or Greek. Twelve boys passed into Woolwich from Eton College in Michaelmas term 1909: Morton was first of his class, listed as a specialist in Science with a Distinction in Trials.

Desmond was now eighteen. During his teens he was, presumably, no longer despatched by his parents to stay with country cousins during the vacations, but it is likely that he was taken or sent abroad, to gain experience of European languages and culture. A War Office record of service dating from the First World War noted that his knowledge of foreign countries encompassed the West Coast of Norway, the North and South coasts of France, Dresden, Hanover and neighbouring regions of Germany, Northern Italy and the Canary Islands; a pattern of travel that might indicate family holidays as well as summers spent (possibly en pension) in France and Germany, a common experience for a young man of his class and education. Early in his military training he was able to pass examinations in French and German to Interpreter level (as well as preliminary Russian), suggesting that his schoolboy languages may have been enhanced by periods of immersion.

After eighteen months at the Royal Military Academy, Morton was gazetted 2nd Lieutenant on 20 July 1911 and posted to the 133rd Battery, 31st Brigade, Royal Field Artillery (RFA) in August, joining the School of Gunners at Shoeburyness in Essex on 23 September to begin the Young Officers' Artillery Course. Completing that successfully, he was posted with his brigade to Sheffield in October 1913 and promoted to full Lieutenant on 20 July 1914. Mobilisation followed two weeks later.[21] It was as if his military training had been scheduled precisely for completion at the outbreak of hostilities. Morton was now twenty-two, and had spent the previous five years learning the technical details and operational rules of artillery warfare, discipline and military leadership, lacking only experience of real combat. The forthcoming conflict was what he had trained for.

What sort of man had he become? No photograph survives from this period, but he was described as tall and dark with a small moustache, and of erect bearing. Of his inner life or social circle we know little, since he left no record and is not mentioned by those contemporaries who documented their experiences. Serious-minded, thoughtful, conscientious: probably, as he remained so all his life, despite a later carapace of brash bonhomie. An affectionate son, certainly; but independent and inclined to his own company and pursuits. He seems to have had an interest in Morton family history, drawing up embryonic family trees going back to the 12th century on which he corresponded with the Probate Registry in 1913. His academic record at school and in military training indicates drive and ambition, and a certain single-mindedness. His uncle 'Willy' Elliot tried to interest him in politics, apparently asking if he could put Desmond's name down on a list of potential Liberal Peers if Asquith carried out his threat to force King George V to create them in order to force through Irish Home Rule legislation in

1913. Desmond, however, noted that although he and his uncle were 'good pals', he himself was not a 'good Liberal' at that time or any other: 'I was much too busy trying to become a good soldier.'[22] The success of his efforts was to be put to an immediate test.

On 17 August 1914, now transferred to 42nd Brigade RFA at Bulford, he embarked for France with the 3rd Division of the British Expeditionary Force. Like many 'young officers', he was probably enthusiastic at the prospect of putting his training into practice, and stimulated by the British Government's decision to declare war on Germany after a long period of mounting tension: as Professor Hew Strachan has pointed out, in 1914 even the most non-military rationalists found themselves unprepared for 'the emotional force of the war's outbreak'.[23] From a military point of view, the troops felt well trained and ready for combat, the war expected to be over by Christmas: there was a sense of excitement and confidence.[24] If these were Morton's emotions, they were soon to be tested to the extreme. Apart from a few short periods of leave, he was to remain on the Western Front until April 1917.

2

PROPHESYING WAR

The Western Front, 1914–17

The 42nd Brigade Royal Field Artillery, 3rd Division, British Expeditionary Force embarked at Southampton in four ships on the night of 17/18 August 1914. During the next three days the 3rd Division concentrated near Rouen, before proceeding by train and on foot towards Mons where it was intended that, as part of II Corps, they should form the left wing of French forces in Northern France. Instead of the French, however, they found the Germans: General von Kluck's First Army, which had passed through Brussels on 20 August and swept on to Mons. Neither side expected to meet the other there: von Kluck believed that the British would be coming from a different direction, having landed at Ostend, Dunkirk and Calais rather than Le Havre and Boulogne; and the British Commander-in Chief, Sir John French, had refused to heed the warnings of the head of Intelligence at GHQ, Colonel (later Lt-General Sir) G.M.W. Macdonogh, that the Germans were pushing to the west and threatening to envelop the BEF. Nevertheless, by 23 August both I and II Corps of the BEF, under Generals Haig and Smith-Dorrien,[1] were engaged in sudden and violent conflict with an enemy superior in numbers and firepower, and Morton's brigade was plunged quickly into action. During the next few days II Corps was to lose nearly 8,000 men, and although Morton's own battery, the 41st, and indeed the 3rd Division, escaped relatively lightly, the experience must have been both confusing and overwhelming.

Morton's brigade first saw action at 3 a.m. on 24 August, near Nouvelles. Ordered to withdraw by the Mons-Maubeuge road later that morning, they engaged further with the enemy near Blairon before withdrawing again, joining the 7th Infantry to provide the rearguard of the 3rd Division. At 7 a.m. on 25 August they were again in action near Solesmes. By this time Sir John French, still at GHQ in St Quentin and out of touch with the action (as well as at odds with the French Command)[2] had ordered a general withdrawal, hoping to be able to put some natural obstacle between the BEF and the German forces before a battle. Chaos ensued on the roads around Mons and Maubeuge as the Divisions of II Corps attempted to obey this order with the German army close on their heels. Amid the confusion 41st Battery became detached from 42nd Brigade and found itself joining the rear party of 2nd Royal Irish Rifles, thus arriving last at Le Cateau on the morning of 26 August, though by chance in a good artillery position for the great battle that took place that day.

Early on the morning of 26 August 1914, when his Corps had been marching for more than 24 hours, Smith-Dorrien decided that they must make a stand on the line Le Cateau-Quarries-Moulin d'Esnes (a distance of about 13 miles), even though the 'rolling billowy nature of the country and the numerous deep valleys made the position one that was difficult to defend'.[3] He sent the following message to GHQ: 'Inform French Cavalry Corps that Second Corps is not retiring today, and ask for their cooperation on our left flank.' Neither the French Cavalry nor the BEF I Corps was in any position to help. The story of the ensuing battle of Le Cateau on 26 August, when the German forces were halted and indeed turned back, though at terrible cost to the BEF, passed swiftly into the training manuals for instructive study by officers, and has a special resonance even today in British military history, though opinion remains divided as to whether Smith-Dorrien took the right decision. French considered that Smith-Dorrien 'should not have fought at Le Cateau and that the action had effectively broken II Corps': in fact the Corps, despite 7,812 casualties, retained its cohesion.[4] But upbeat early accounts of the battle took the view that Smith-Dorrien was a hero: Le Cateau, it was said, had dissipated the myth that the German army was invincible; and in Smith-Dorrien's 'eager grip the sword bit deep into the German host'.[5]

No record has been found of Morton's own view of the battle, though he certainly had a good vantage point: arriving at 9 a.m. on 26 August, his battery took up a position east of Tronquoy in a small copse from which they were able to bring effective fire to bear on the Germans trying to advance on the west side of Caudry; as the battery commander noted, 'The action was in full swing, and our position was spread out in front of 41 like a great map'.[6] Third Division artillery was generally better situated than that of other divisions at Le Cateau, and suffered correspondingly fewer casualties;[7] they were thus able to withdraw after the battle in relatively orderly fashion, free of German pursuit, although the official account describes a 'rudderless horde' of men making their way south in pouring rain: 'no one who took part in it could ever forget that Wednesday night.'[8] In his official report on the battle French noted that he deplored deeply the serious losses suffered by the British Forces: 'but they were inevitable in view of the fact that the British Army – only two days after a concentration by rail – was called upon to withstand a vigorous attack of five German Army Corps.'[9] He did not acknowledge that his own refusal to believe intelligence received, and his inability to liaise effectively with the French, played any part in the plight in which the BEF found themselves.

Le Cateau highlighted important organisational and operational weaknesses in the BEF that became even more apparent during the next few months: poor communications at all levels; a lack of coordination, particularly between battalion and artillery commands; underestimation of the importance of firepower (showing that in future greater efforts must be made to knock out enemy guns, and to make British artillery more accurate and proactive); a lack of flexibility in interpreting field regulations; and insufficient appreciation of the importance of aerial observation. The lessons to be learned from Le Cateau were increasingly pressing as it became clear that a long and indecisive conflict was in prospect: as Sir Michael Howard puts it, 'by the end of 1914 the short war for which Europe's armies had been preparing for the previous forty years was over, but nobody had won it'.[10]

The battles of 1914 carried particular lessons for the use of the Royal Artillery. The Regimental history, though naturally partial, makes the point neatly:

> No other part of the Army can meet the severe demands of the principles in war as successfully as can the gunners . . . nothing is more surprising than the sudden, unexpected arrival of tons of high explosive on an unsuspecting target.[11]

The Commanders of the BEF were to discover the truth of this only too soon, and to realise that their own Artillery, though they fought bravely, were achieving neither surprise nor sufficiently impressive firepower. In August 1914 the Royal Artillery comprised 4,083 officers and 88,837 Other Ranks, yet surprisingly little thought appears to have been given to how they could best be employed by the BEF. The 3rd Division, of which Morton's brigade formed part, consisted of about 15,000 men at full strength: three infantry brigades of four battalions each; a Field Company of Royal Engineers; and the Divisional Artillery, comprising two field brigades, the 40th and 42nd, each with three batteries of six 18-pounder guns (firing mainly shrapnel with a range of up to 6,500 yards), and one of six 4.5" Howitzers (capable of firing heavier projectiles, and at a higher angle). The other five BEF Divisions – the largest force that could be mustered in the summer of 1914 from troops in the British Isles, since half the infantry were serving overseas[12] – were similarly constituted. Yet decisions on strategy and tactics, attack or withdrawal were made by Divisional and Battalion Infantry Commanders with little or no consultation with the Artillery commanders on whom they depended, assuming their support in advance and in retreat, but with little regard to the artillery's intrinsic value as an instrument of attack or defence. The Regimental history's description of Artillery officers – of whom Morton was one – as falling into 'the socially acceptable gap between the pure warrior who fought with his hands and the military technician',[13] was both telling and indicative of the underlying problems.

The dogged attrition of the 1915 campaigns showed that the placing of batteries, accuracy of registration (ascertaining the position and type of an enemy target) and the success of a barrage were more often the result of good fortune than design, unless proper aerial observation had been possible. Correspondence later in the War, including with Churchill when he was Minister of Munitions, shows that Morton took a keen interest in the technical side of artillery warfare and was appalled by the manufacturing and technical defects revealed by the early campaigns; his experiences laid the foundation for closer attention to armament and ammunition manufacture, both in Britain and overseas, in the interwar period. By 1916 the importance of command, control and logistics was better appreciated, but real improvements did not come until late in that year when it was recognised that the Battle of the Somme had placed an intolerable strain on the Gunners.

The Artillery were relied upon to destroy enemy emplacements: to cut wire, and clear the way for infantry advance; in support of an attack, or to cover withdrawal; to obstruct the enemy and ambush his reinforcements; and, since the number of batteries was always insufficient to cover the line and there was no artillery reserve until mid-1917, they had to do this in response to requests not just from their own brigade but from other brigades or even other Divisions as required. Although the Infantry generally had a much more unpleasant time in the line, enduring worse conditions and suffering greater casualties, they also had more frequent and longer periods of relief than the Artillery, who tended to be always on the move and often got detached from their Divisions: 'the Gunners could never really rest, day or night, answering calls for fire incessantly.'[14]

Nevertheless, life as an Artillery officer, though hard, had its compensations. Despite the horrors of the trenches and frequent marches, there were periods of quiet between battles. According to a memoir by Lieutenant A.E. Robinson of 42nd Brigade, rations were good and abundant, and whisky 'more plentiful than soda' at 3s 6d a bottle for officers, who played bridge, poker and *vingt-et-un* and made much use of the mess gramophone; if they were lucky, 'civilised' billets were obtained in local *estaminets* where champagne and wine flowed, good meals could be ordered and there was the possibility of a game of golf. Robinson also noted with amazement that 'the Battery frequently moved from one Army to another over long distances, but our mail always seemed to catch up with us promptly', bringing his mother's daily letters.[15] It would be nice to think that Edith Morton wrote to her son daily, too, but if she did no letters survive.

This description of an officer's life on the Western Front reflects that in many other contemporary accounts and memoirs: Robert Graves's *Goodbye to All That*, for example, evokes unforgettably the flavour of mess life, lurching between unbearable tension and high comedy. In view of his forthcoming close association with Morton, it is perhaps relevant to note also the experiences of Winston Churchill,[16] who following his resignation as Chancellor of the Duchy of Lancaster in November 1915 spent several months in Flanders commanding a battalion of the 6th Royal Scots Fusiliers.[17] He gave his officers a slap-up dinner of oysters and champagne the night before they advanced, and faced with worrying insouciance the dangers of the front line, telling his wife that 'It is one long holiday for me'.[18] Rejecting the much-hated bully beef, he requested food parcels from home containing ham, cream and stilton.

It is impossible to know how congenial such a life was to Desmond Morton. His military training would of course have prepared him for it, and like the majority of officers he doubtless adopted at least a carapace of conformity. One is tempted to wonder, however, whether Morton's experience might have resembled that of his near-contemporary, Lieutenant (later Major-General Sir) Edward Louis Spears,[19] who served as liaison officer between the British and French head-quarters from 1914–17 and, like Morton, struck up a close relationship with Churchill during the First World War that was to last for many years:

> His solitary youth had not prepared Spears well for human contact. He could be tactless and his quick intelligence ruthlessly pierced weak argument. The ideals of the mess were those of courtesy and effortless amateurism, neither of which he adopted. An outsider from the start, he stayed one all his life.[20]

Judging by their later careers and personal fortunes, Morton was little better at 'courtesy and effortless amateurism' than Spears, and there are indications that neither man found intimate comradeship easy.

Morton left no record of his experiences in the First World War, and little would be gained from recounting in detail all the battles and campaigns in which he took part: it is, perhaps, sufficient to say that he fought in all the major campaigns on the Western Front until April 1917, including the Marne, the Second Battle of Ypres and the Somme, and survived. He was a brave and successful soldier. Although his name appears rarely except for movements and promotions, his record was a distinguished one: by the time he was wounded in March 1917, marking the end of the first phase of his First World War career, he was commanding the 41st Battery with the rank of Acting Lieutenant Colonel, had won a number of decorations including the Military Cross and *Croix de Guerre*, and had been twice mentioned in despatches. He had also gained experience of staff work, having been appointed on 25 January 1915 ADC to General Haldane at Divisional Headquarters, returning to the 42nd Brigade on 4 August that year as Adjutant (he left behind a rare trace of himself at this point: parts of the Brigade's War Diary are in his handwriting, in the blue pencil that was later to characterise his interventions at SIS). In November 1915 he was promoted to Staff Captain, 3rd Division Artillery, and returned to the 41st Battery, then at Alquines, on 17 February 1916, taking command on 25 April, as a Temporary Captain, RFA.

If his own later account was correct, as told to Sir Martin Gilbert in 1967, it must have been shortly after this that Morton first met Churchill. The 6th Royal Scots Fusiliers, over whom Churchill had taken command on 4 January 1916, were responsible for a sector of the line near Ploegsteert (naturally re-named Plug Street), just north of Armentières and south of Ypres. The Battalion's advance HQ was at Laurence Farm, about 100 metres behind the British front line, where they usually spent twelve days out of every twenty-four, interspersed with six days in support and six days' rest. While at Laurence Farm, Churchill liked to set up his easel and paint in the courtyard, although it was pitted with shellholes. According to Gilbert, this is how Morton described their first encounter:

He told me that he had first met Churchill on the Western Front, when, as a major [*sic*] in the Royal Artillery, he was told to visit a particular battalion commander to arrange an artillery barrage. On asking a private soldier the way to this particular battalion headquarters, Morton was told, 'You will find that one in the middle of no man's land' . . . Morton found Churchill busy painting. They discussed the proposed barrage, which Churchill intended to be a heavy one. Morton suggested, respectfully, that before the bombardment began, Churchill should consult with his brigadier, but Churchill replied, 'I have no faith in brigadiers'.[21]

This encounter probably took place between 20 March (when Churchill returned to Laurence Farm after a short period in London, where he had made an unwise Parliamentary speech that left him humiliated politically)[22] and 7 May 1916, when he resigned his commission and returned home to resume his political career. From the end of March until 12 April the 42nd Brigade RFA was engaged in heavy shelling of the German front line around the St Eloi trenches, just north of Ploegsteert, capturing, losing and re-taking Crater No. 5: it is quite likely that Morton would have been sent to make contact with Churchill's battalion.[23] There is no suggestion, however, that they had any further contact until 1917, when Churchill visited the Front as Minister of Munitions and Morton had become ADC to the Commander-in-Chief of the BEF, Field-Marshal Sir Douglas Haig.

Much has been written about the traumatic effect that military service in the First World War had on the generation of young men who survived it. Vivid accounts, both autobiographical and fictionalised, evoke all too clearly the atmosphere and conditions of the Western Front. But without personal recollection or third party evidence it would be foolish to speculate on its impact on any individual. For Morton, all that it is possible to say with any certainty is that the First World War imparted three enduring legacies: a deep commitment to the Roman Catholic faith to which he converted in 1916; poor health (a legacy that he embraced with typical determination and insouciance); and a military-style taste for the exercise of authority and imposition of order that was to characterise his civilian career and was liable to cause as many problems as it solved.

Morton's conversion to Roman Catholicism was, apparently, both shocking and unwelcome to his family, and in particular to Edith, a staunch adherent of the Church of England whose family included several members of the Anglican clergy. It must have taken a strong resolve for him to announce his decision and carry it through against her opposition. Nothing is known of when he formed the determination to seek instruction: the fact that he won several Divinity prizes at school may indicate a certain early intellectual interest in theological matters, though he later claimed that Eton's religious education classes consisted of 'an occasional pi-jaw on obvious morals' and of translating sections of the Greek New Testament, with very little reference to 'God, Christ or the Church'.[24] In later life he was inclined to attribute his change of religious allegiance to a more general dislike of 'the Establishment', whose 'obvious faults' he blamed on 'the waffling and failures of the Anglican form of Christianity',[25] but it seems dangerous to place too much credence on the attribution of motives by a man in his late sixties to his younger self at twenty-five.

It is possible that his decision was influenced by encounters with Roman Catholic chaplains on the Western Front: though relatively few in number, they were noted for their determination to be with the troops in the front line, and respected and admired for their bravery and spirit. They also met a very real need: the rituals of sacramental confession and extreme unction were comforting to men in constant contact with death, and even to non-Catholics 'there was something commendably professional about the Catholic Padre'.[26] As one Anglican wartime chaplain put it, 'The Church of Rome sent a man into action mentally and spiritually cleaned. The Church of England could only offer you a cigarette.'[27]

Robert Graves wrote that he and his fellow officers had little respect for the Anglican regimental chaplains, who were 'under orders to avoid getting mixed up with the fighting and to stay behind with the transport', whereas the Roman Catholic chaplains:

> were not only permitted to visit posts of danger, but definitely enjoyed to be wherever fighting was, so that they could give extreme unction to the dying. And we had never heard of one who failed to do all that was expected of him and more . . . Anglican chaplains were remarkably out of touch with their troops. The Second Battalion chaplain, just before the Loos fighting, had preached a violent sermon on the Battle against Sin, at which one old soldier behind me grumbled: 'Christ, as if one bloody push wasn't enough to worry about at a time!' A Roman Catholic padre, on the other hand, had given his men his blessing and told them that if they died fighting for the good cause they would go straight to Heaven or, at any rate, be excused a great many years in Purgatory.[28]

At the beginning of the war only seven Roman Catholic Chaplains accompanied the BEF to France, though many more volunteered later; altogether eight hundred and ten served in the conflict, thirty-six of whom were killed. One of the original Chaplains was the distinguished priest Monsignor William Keatinge, who had served in the Boer War and was recalled from Cairo to travel to France with the 3rd Division, where Morton may have encountered him. A charismatic figure who became Senior Catholic Chaplain to the British Army on the Western Front, Keatinge was also known for his sense of humour and as a 'born raconteur,' qualities much appreciated by Morton in later life at least. Another impressive figure was the Benedictine Dom Stephen Rawlinson, who began the war with the 2nd Royal Irish Rifles (where Morton could have met him on the retreat from Mons), then succeeded Keatinge as Senior Chaplain when the latter went to Mesopotamia in 1916, and became responsible for directing the efforts of all Catholic Chaplains to British Forces in France and Flanders. There would also have been a Chaplain attached to Morton's own Brigade, possibly Father Luke Bellanti SJ, who had been a master at Stonyhurst before the war. He was certainly serving with the Brigade in 1917 when Lt. Robinson, who joined 42nd Brigade after Morton had left, wrote of him as 'a wonderful chap loved by us all and as brave as a lion',[29] while a former pupil, Air Vice-Marshal J.C. Nealy, said that Bellanti would 'crawl into no-man's land to succour the dying'.

Whether or not Morton was influenced personally by any of these men, it seems likely that he found the example set by Roman Catholic chaplains inspiring during his long period on the Western Front: their commitment won the respect of both troops and Army establishment for 'their courage, endurance and leadership in addition to their priestly devotion'.[30] According to a report in *The Tablet* in 1918, there were forty thousand conversions to Roman Catholicism during the war in France alone.[31] Many people have, of course, found that close and concentrated experience of warfare tends to polarise their religious convictions towards rejection of all faith or to a deeper level of belief. Spears, in his journal for 5 January 1915, complained that it was 'horrid to believe in nothing & just do one's duty because it is one's duty as I do', noting that 'all Frenchmen have become v. religious since the war & the priests fight best'.[32] Whatever the origins of or influences on Morton's decision to convert to Roman Catholicism, his commitment was lifelong, and the Roman Catholic faith was to be the cornerstone of his principles and beliefs until his death.

According to War Office medical records, Morton's health first began to suffer late in 1916, probably as the result of the prolonged strain of three years almost solidly on the Front. After assuming command of the 41st Battery in April of that year, Morton's role was to provide artillery support to the 3rd Division of XIII Corps in preparation for the joint offensive that had been planned by the Allied High Command at the Chantilly conference in November 1915.[33] Meanwhile French and German forces fought a grim battle of attrition around Verdun, creating 'a nightmare landscape such as the world had never seen' with more than half a million men killed.[34] The Royal Field Artillery played a key role in Haig's ambitious assaults on the German front, intended to relieve pressure on the French in the north and to establish a continuous British line stretching from Ypres almost to the Somme. It was during this period of preparation for the Somme offensive that Morton won his MC, awarded on 3 June 1916. The Brigade's War Diary records the decoration rather than the occasion for its award: his own retrospective account of the episode in question is, predictably, a facetious one:

> I got my MC in the first world war for getting my troop stuck in the mud. As we could not move the guns, nor get away fast enough on foot, we had to stay where we were in the face of a lot of battle-minded Germans who were busy over-running French trenches in front of us during the battle of the Somme. We had lots of ammo, so shot it all off. Since the range was short we could aim straight and did not, I think, kill any Frenchmen. But the Germans who thought we were all dead, or hoped it, were much discommoded and had to retire up a steep slope pursued by

the shells of my enthusiastic battery and the loud curses of the irritated French, whose commander thereafter embraced me on both cheeks. I got the MC actually for submitting to his caress.[35]

With French forces badly depleted by Verdun, it was British troops who now took up the main burden of the campaign.[36] At the end of May 1916, 42nd Brigade had a rare, short period of rest and training before the Allied offensive, due to begin on 1 July. After moving from Eecke to Dieckebusch and then to Lumbres during the second half of June, on 2 July they received orders to proceed immediately to Amiens, and by 7 July were in action in earnest covering the 18th Division on a line from Bazentin-le-Grand to Longieval. The following day one of the Brigade's other two Battery commanders, Captain Mackenzie of the 29th, was killed; on the 13th, the Commander of 45th Battery was wounded and had to be replaced. On 14 July the 3rd Division was in action on the right flank of the attack against the German front at Bazentin Ridge, pressing through to Delville Wood in what Liddell Hart called 'the bloodiest battle-hell of 1916'.[37] The bitter fighting over the next four months saw the Allied forces advancing only ten miles and losing more than half a million men.

It is not surprising that during the terrible battles of the Somme, after three years' more or less continuous service on the Western Front, the strain was beginning to tell on Morton, who had received his substantive promotion to Captain on 8 August and was promoted again to Acting Major on 24 September. In the latter month, when early autumn rains had turned the ground into a swamp through which it was almost impossible to move the heavy artillery, he began to have feverish attacks; by October, when the exhausted troops were still being urged forward by Haig against a seemingly impregnable German defence, he was coughing up blood and losing weight. Pronounced 'run down' by the medical authorities at the Front, after the brigade had participated in the major attack launched on the Germans at Ancre by II, V and XIII Corps on 13 November, he was granted leave to the UK from 29 November until 9 December. He was soon back in the field, however, now with temporary promotion to Acting Lieutenant Colonel. The carnage of the Somme had now been succeeded by a period of confusion and intermittent engagement that brought its own physical and mental strains.

The first three months of 1917 were a period of retrenchment and realignment on both sides of the Western Front. The whole strategic balance of the war was in the process of alteration, with the rejection in early January of the German peace plan of 12 December, the ensuing German declaration of unrestricted submarine warfare against Britain, and the decision by the United States first to break off relations with Germany and then, after the Zimmermann telegram, to declare war themselves.[38] The Allied military strategy in France and Belgium, agreed at a Conference held in Rome in January (attended by the new British Prime Minister David Lloyd George who had replaced Asquith on 11 December 1916), was broadly to try and exhaust the enemy forces by renewing the Somme offensive across a wider front. Behind this general objective, however, lay deep disagreement between the French and British on issues of command, tactics and timing.

Haig and the new French Commander in Chief, General Nivelle, now in overall command, argued their way through a series of conferences in February and March, while Ludendorff ordered a general withdrawal of German forces to a shorter Hindenburg Line, twenty-five miles to the rear. In their retreat the Germans carried out a devastating campaign of slash and burn that left livestock dead and property destroyed. While their Commanders disputed, British forces pursued the withdrawing German forces through the death-filled desert they left in their wake and prepared as best they could for the forthcoming Arras-Vimy offensive that Haig had determined would be launched in April, directing the greatest British strength there while keeping back a reserve either to exploit success east of Arras or to reinforce the Second Army in Flanders.

During the first three months of 1917 the 42nd Brigade was in intermittent but regular contact with the enemy, supporting the Infantry of various Divisions as well as their own. After a brief period of rest in early February for cleaning and training, they marched into action at Wanquentin on 26 February, supporting a successful raid by the 36th Infantry Brigade, 12th Division.[39] On 5 March they supported a raid by the 1st Gordons: between 6 and 12 March, a raid by 14th Division; on 17 March, a raid on enemy trenches by 35th Infantry Brigade. The Germans then retired behind the Hindenburg Line, but on 20 March they retaliated, sending out a force that was repulsed twice and forced back by the British barrage. On 28 March, near Arras, following two days of heavy German shelling, Morton was hit by a machine gun bullet, revealed by X-Ray to have entered below his left shoulderblade, passing through his lung before becoming lodged between his fourth dorsal vertebra and the arch of the aorta, which it narrowly missed penetrating. He escaped death by a fraction of an inch. The Brigade War Diary noted merely: 'Captain P.W. Lee takes command of 41st Battery vice Major Morton, wounded.'[40]

After a short period in a Field hospital Morton was invalided back to the UK on the hospital ship *Newhaven* on 5 April 1917. Two days later he was admitted to the 'Russian Hospital', a private house in London owned by Count Muraviev-Apostol,[41] a Tsarist exile, who converted it to a hospital for officers during the war. On 19 April Morton appeared before a medical board at Caxton Hall, which rated him unfit for general or home service for four months, noting that he still experienced difficulty and pain with breathing:

> He has lost flesh 1½ stone since the war began. He has been out in France all the war & is feeling the combined effects of this long continuous stress added to his present grave wound.[42]

The position of the bullet meant that it was far too dangerous to attempt to remove it. The Board granted him leave until 20 July 1917 and awarded a gratuity of

£100. On 7 May he was admitted to the Private Convalescent Home for Officers at Lennel Coldstream in Scotland. Although he continued to experience shortness of breath and pain, his wound healed, no hint of TB was found, and he made steady progress, though still weak. Before he could appear at another Medical Board, however, he received the following letter, dated 14 July 1917:

> My dear Morton,
>
> I hope that you are getting on all right and are fit again (this is private). The C. in C. is thinking of having a Gunner ADC and I was asked. I have said that you were the most desirable person I knew in the Regt. As you have been seedy the job should suit you and would give you a useful connexion. I don't know of course that you will be offered it. But if you are fit I expect so – it might be worth thinking of.
>
> Yours sincerely,
>
> H.D.O. Ward, VIII Corps[43]

No trace of Morton's reply has been found, but on 23 July he attended another Medical Board, who had received a letter from the Adjutant General's office, and agreed 'that although under the circumstances he is not fit for full general service, he is fit for an appointment at GHQ, France'. Two days later he was on his way back to France, where he took up his appointment (now reduced to his substantive rank of Captain) as one of four *Aides de Camp* to Sir Douglas Haig on 26 July.

Writing to Sir Basil Liddell Hart many years later, Morton said that although Haig 'always said he disliked Gunners' he had accepted Morton's nomination as ADC by his Artillery adviser, Sir Noel ('Curly') Birch, who warned Morton that Haig was 'a rum 'un'. In the same letter Morton also commented that he had been 'told by the medicos' that he was 'officially no longer capable of active service', and 'had only three years or so to live. They were wrong on both counts.'[44] Given the seriousness of his wound and the fact that the bullet was lodged so close to his heart ('seedy' would seem an understatement for the state of his health), his decision to take up Haig's offer does seem a brave one, if not foolhardy. In November 1948 the *Sunday Despatch* carried an article about Morton, noting that he had just celebrated his 57th birthday although he 'should have died on a Flanders battlefield 31 years ago'. Allowing for the tendency of both Morton and journalists to hyperbole (the article alleged that he had been told 'he must never ride or take any violent exercise again', but went on to ride '7,000 miles over the battle area'), the final sentences ring true nevertheless:

> If I had literally carried out the doctor's instructions life wouldn't have been worth living. So I decided to carry on normally.

A Gunner ADC, 1917–19

The period immediately following Morton's return to France was one of the most disastrous and dispiriting of the war for the Commander in Chief he had come to serve, and indeed for the Western Allies in general. In the East, Russian forces were crumpling before the German attack; the Italian front was in imminent danger of collapse; American forces had yet to arrive, and the third Battle of Ypres, otherwise known as Passchendaele and described as 'the last scene of the gloomiest drama in British military history'[45] began on 31 July, five days after Morton's arrival at GHQ. Haig was convinced that the only way to defeat the Germans in the West was to wear them down through the tactics of attrition, pushing on from Ypres towards the Belgian ports. Despite some early successes, the BEF was soon bogged down by rain, mud and fierce German resistance. Both sides lost heavily (more than 200,000 men each by November), but although little ground had been gained, Haig had in fact inflicted considerable damage not just on German troops but on morale in Germany as well.

However, when Haig's next attack at Cambrai, beginning on 20 November 1917, led to the German forces retaking all the ground they had lost, 'he 'lost his last vestige of credit with his political masters'.[46] At an Allied conference at Rapallo on 5 November, Lloyd George and the new French Prime Minister, Georges Clemenceau, set up the Allied Supreme War Council, comprising political leaders supported by military advisers, with the aim of directing military policy, the allocation of forces to the various theatres and the organisation of supplies. This naturally reduced the influence and freedom of action of the military commanders: in February 1918 Lloyd George further undermined Haig's authority by replacing Sir William Robertson with his own protégé General Sir Henry Wilson as Chief of the Imperial General Staff: 'In both France and Britain civilian control of strategy was now complete.'[47]

It is less easy than might be supposed to estimate the effect that all this had on Haig. He was, naturally, dispirited by the lack of progress made by the BEF, by the fact that the Germans had not yet collapsed as he expected them to do, and of course by the losses suffered by his troops. However, the evidence indicates that he still believed his tactics to be correct (a consistency of judgement that was to be at least partly justified in the second half of 1918), and was not overly concerned by political interference in military affairs except in so far as it concerned his own personal position.[48] Morton's comment on this aspect of Haig confirms those of other contemporaries:

> I found him interested politically in nothing that did not to his mind directly affect the possibility of himself superseded in command. Since, by that period, he had weathered the most serious storms, and knew it, there was very little in which he was really interested. He understood nothing of politics, economics or of governing a country![49]

Morton was by no means the only person to find Haig hard to understand: commentators remain divided as to his personality, military abilities and contribution to Allied victory. Morton's views are interesting, however, in view of the fact that he spent the last eighteen months of the war more or less constantly in Haig's presence, riding with him and taking his turn in his private office, yet claimed that despite being treated by him with 'intimacy and trust' Haig remained 'no little of a mystery'. Their relationship might also be considered to shed some light on Morton's personality as well as Haig's.

Although we have little contemporary evidence of Morton's experiences as Haig's ADC,[50] his account to Liddell Hart, written in 1961 in response to an article by the latter in the *Sunday Times* entitled 'The Enigma of Haig', is a measured one, as Liddell Hart acknowledged: 'I only wish others who had worked with him could be anything like as objective as you are.'[51] Though not uncritical, Morton was always loyal to 'the Chief', whom he had respected and who, indeed, helped to further Morton's own career. While Haig may have distrusted Gunners, Morton testified that he had always been treated with the utmost courtesy, in the same way as the other ADCs who had been with Haig throughout the conflict. Haig had a reputation in Whitehall and in senior military circles for being difficult and obstructive, but in Morton's view this stemmed from his intense personal ambition:

> He was very fair and just and kind to his subordinates and loyal as well; though a holy terror to his equals, superiors and possible competitors. The private soldiers in his regiment, when they knew him, adored him, as did younger officers. He had a strict sense of what was apt and fitting for a gentleman to do and how such should behave . . . He had trained himself never to show outwardly, by word or deed, any great emotion. He never shouted nor swore, nor raised his voice in anger, which last he also never showed outwardly. Self-discipline was his guide . . . [52]

Morton respected gentlemanly behaviour, self-control and courtesy and, like many men (especially military men) of his generation, distrusted the outward show of emotion. He also respected physical and moral courage, with which he considered Haig to be highly endowed. But Haig's well-known inarticulacy, and unwillingness to talk about military matters, made working with him difficult:

> He could talk – he never chattered or even chatted – freely on <u>certain</u> subjects which had nothing to do with the war or military affairs, and also on his past experiences as a soldier; but what he was thinking about the war as it stood on any particular day, no one, not even his Chief of Staff could fully make out. He gave his orders quick enough, but never explained them. Moreover, men say he was tongue-tied. If it came to public speaking that was abundantly true. He was anyway a 'silent' man. But such silence was babbling compared with what he said when he gave

an oral instead of a written order. You had to learn a sort of verbal shorthand, made up of a series of grunts and gestures.

Although his staff work had already offered some experience of administrative
duties, and of the importance of order and efficiency, Morton's service as ADC to
Haig afforded him the authority and opportunity to develop the somewhat
aggressive style – what would today be called a proactive management style – that
was to characterise his later career. Record keeping, the arrangement of appointments and meetings, making and exploiting useful contacts, getting things done
the way he and his Chief wanted: all these skills Morton developed not just with
ease but with relish, clearly enjoying the work. He also learned a lot, as he later
acknowledged to R.W. Thompson:

> It is interesting for me to realise that even Harold Macmillan and Charles
> de Gaulle, both within a year of me, were only regimental soldiers and
> Captains in the first world war, whereas I had the enormous interest of
> a mind without too many prejudices and quite ignorant of things, AND
> by sheer luck in a very subordinate capacity to be at least a personal
> observer in the bung-ho centre of the staff of the British Commander in
> Chief.[53]

There is no doubt that the chief benefit Morton derived from his service with Haig
(apart from administrative *savoir-faire*) was the opportunity to establish lasting
connections with many of the prominent politicians and statesmen of the
day, as well as the military commanders. Many visitors to the Front, including
Lloyd George, Churchill and Sir John Simon,[54] as well as French leaders such as
Foch and Clemenceau, were looked after and shown round by the ADCs; Haig,
who disliked most political visits in principle, frequently asked Morton to look
after his distinguished visitors and report afterwards if they had said anything
interesting (i.e. that related to him). Morton was also sent back to England with
messages on various occasions, when Haig asked him to call on his wife, too.
King George V made several visits to the Front (he and Haig often corresponded
on the conduct of the war): Morton described showing him around and 'over-
hearing conversations at Mess not meant for me'; the King, he said, was
'remarkably indiscreet at times', making no secret of his great dislike for Lloyd
George to whom he referred with a Germanic accent as 'Thatt Mann'; in Morton's
opinion the King 'could not bear L.G. largely because of his extremely rude and
uncultivated manner in private dealings'.[55]

In addition to distinguished visitors, of course, Morton also developed close
links with other members of Haig's staff, such as his Private Secretary Phillip
Sassoon, and also with Spears, who in May 1917 had moved to Paris to act as
liaison between the War Office and the French Ministry of War – what Lord Esher
called 'the most difficult and dangerous job in Europe';[56] Spears continued to visit
the Front and to act as interpreter and liaison officer at important Anglo-French

meetings. More importantly, Morton made his first real contacts with the Intelligence world.[57] Many Intelligence strands intertwined at GHQ, and as ADC to the Commander-in-Chief Morton had the opportunity to observe, whether first-hand or on paper, the efficiency of their methods and personnel. He commented later on Haig's disastrous choice of Brigadier John Charteris as his Intelligence chief to replace Macdonogh:

> He hated being told any information, however irrefutable, which mili-tated against his preconceived ideas or beliefs. Hence his support of the desperate John Charteris, incredibly bad as a DMI, who always concealed bad news, or put it in an agreeable light.[58]

Morton would also have been party to information about and from the competing intelligence networks run in France and Belgium by GHQ, by the War Office and by Morton's future Chief, the former Naval Commander Mansfield Cumming,[59] head of the foreign intelligence section of the Secret Service Bureau created in 1909.[60] Another of Morton's future Chiefs, Stewart Menzies, was also working in Intelligence at GHQ, to which he had moved in December 1915 after serving in the Second Life Guards where he had been awarded the DSO and MC during the Second Battle of Ypres;[61] even if he and Morton had not come into contact with each other at Eton, they must have done so now. Menzies was also a close friend of Archibald Sinclair,[62] who had introduced him to Churchill (Sinclair had become friendly with Churchill while both were learning to fly, and had served as Churchill's second in command at Ploegsteert); and Sinclair was also a close associate of Spears. With all these, and many more officers who were to surface in or around the Intelligence world after the war, Morton now became familiar.

His burgeoning relationship with Churchill merits special attention. After his appointment as Minister of Munitions in July 1917 Churchill, who always enjoyed visiting the front line and now had legitimate business to take him there, made many visits to France, nearly always staying at Haig's headquarters (until he set up his own personal HQ at the Chateau Verchocq in May 1918). He and Morton now renewed the acquaintance made at Ploegsteert in 1916: Morton would certainly have been included in many of Churchill's discussions and dinners with Haig and his staff, as Churchill later described in *World Crisis*:

> When I became Minister of Munitions in July, 1917, I frequently visited the front as the Commander-in-Chief's guest, and he always sent his trusted Aide-de-Camp, Desmond Morton, with me. Together we visited many parts of the line. During these sometimes dangerous excursions, and at the Commander-in-Chief's house, I formed a great regard and friendship for this brilliant and gallant officer . . .[63]

The two undoubtedly got on well: Churchill had a habit of taking up brave young officers, particularly if wounded or highly decorated (Spears was another example), and his tribute to Morton in *World Crisis* was a sincere one. But in addition to friendship and good company, with both Morton and Spears, Churchill sought a sounding board for his ideas, as well as a source of information, advice and indeed practical help on matters where they had more opportunity (or time) to provide it. For Churchill, friendship was always an interactive process. The relationship between Spears and Churchill at this stage hinged largely on Spears's contacts in Paris, both with the French and with the White Russians who began to gather there in the wake of the Bolshevik revolutions in February and November 1917. With Morton, their early relationship and correspondence centred not on political but on more technical matters. Despite Haig's avowed aversion to 'new ideas' and 'mechanical contrivances', shortage of fighting manpower, increasing industrial mobilisation in Britain and developments in weaponry and ammunition brought him, and other commanders, to an increasing acceptance of the 'dominant technological imperative' espoused so passionately by the Minister of Munitions during his frequent visits to GHQ.[64] Morton was well placed to participate in these discussions and learn more about an area in which he had been interested since his early days at Woolwich.

Churchill and Morton shared a deep concern at the technical weaknesses of artillery and ammunition that had been revealed in the war (though considerable improvements took place between 1914 and 1918). They also shared a particular interest in the development of the tank: Churchill had been agitating the War Office on the subject of 'caterpillars' since January 1916 (Morton witnessed their first appearance on the Somme later that year),[65] and continued to press for an increase in production and in the number of men allocated to the Tank Corps, whom he described in September 1918 as 'the most profit-bearing we have in the army'.[66] Curiously enough, Morton had some family connection with the Tank Corps: its commanding officer from 1916–19, Lt. Col. Hugh Elles,[67] had married Geraldine, youngest daughter of his uncle Sir Gerald Morton, in 1912; and after her death married her elder half-sister May Franks, a widow, in 1923.

Very little correspondence between Churchill and Morton survives from this period, but an example is a letter written by Churchill to Morton on 12 May 1918, regarding what had clearly been a previous exchange on the subject of 'prematures', shells that exploded too early. The correspondents had already established a habit of confidentiality: the letter, asking for further details of defective shells, concluded: 'These papers are sent to you privately. You should not show them to anybody, and needless to say I shall not quote your name or involve you in any way.'[68] Later, on 22 July 1918, he wrote the following letter to Morton, containing a typically creative Churchillian suggestion:

My dear Morton,

Arrangements are being discussed to provide for a better liaison between M[inistry] of M[unitions] & the Army on Inventions & devices of all kinds. It has occurred to me that perhaps you might like & the C in C might be willing for you to assume a dual function of ADC & liaison with us on this class of work. Thus you will move about the Army & collect ideas & pass them on to us keeping yr chief au fait at the same time.

It is possible there will also be another officer so that the work wd not be too heavy & in any case of course yr liaison work wd come after yr present duties. I thought it might amuse you.

Will you let me know what you think of the plan, & how I had best proceed & if there are any particular 'snags' to avoid . . .[69]

What Morton, or indeed Haig, might have thought of this suggestion is not revealed, but there is no sign that the idea progressed any further.

During 1918, in any case, Morton would have had little time to investigate 'inventions and devices'. It was a year of desperate military struggle, when the deadlock of attrition was finally broken and the US forces were at last able to play a key role. The first part of the year was dominated by the Ludendorff offensive in March, attacking first the British forces on the southern part of their line east of Amiens, and then the French on the Aisne, approaching near enough to Paris to begin bombarding it with heavy artillery. But from the Allied counter-offensive in July, assisted by forty-two American divisions, the tide turned and the Germans began to retreat; by October the forces of all the Central Powers were beginning to collapse and Germany was swept by internal revolt. Still, however, German military discipline held firm and it seemed as if the war might go on for some months. But all of a sudden the end was imminent: the armistice was signed at 5 a.m. on 11 November, and at 11 a.m. the war came to an end. Although Morton left no record of his feelings, it is surely permissible to assume that they must have included relief, exhaustion, bitterness and sadness for the enormous loss of life of the past five years. Perhaps also an element of pride of achievement, for the Allies, for British Forces, for Haig, even for himself? In retrospect, Morton tended to disparage his own contribution, and his view of Haig's achievement was measured:

> One has to recall that he did get his way, he did end as Commander of the victorious British Army in France. But God! at what a cost in lives at the time and the consequential alteration of the society he longed to preserve, and the beginning of the destruction of the whole economy of this country; a matter of which he had no sort of understanding whatsoever.[70]

Although the war was over, for Haig, and therefore for Morton, there was much work still to do. Haig remained Commander-in Chief, and apart from brief visits to the UK both men remained in France until 5 April 1919, spending much of their time in Paris where the Peace Conference had opened in January. At that stage, Morton still seemed destined for a postwar career as a professional soldier:

he had recently been mentioned in despatches again, and on 9 February 1919 was recommended by Haig for accelerated promotion and appointment to the Staff College, receiving the rank of Brevet (honorary) Major shortly afterwards. His health, however, remained problematic. Since his wound he had been frequently troubled with chest complaints, as he was to be all his life, though there is no evidence he allowed this to impair energetic performance of his duties. On 9 January 1919 he had written to the Adjutant-General applying for a wound pension, stating that he had recently been re-examined: 'fresh X-Ray photographs of the bullet have been taken and fresh complications have been disclosed.' A medical board held in France on 11 March, when Morton was convalescing from influenza in the Michelham Home for British Officers, heard that he complained of occasional attacks of faintness and pain in the chest after exertion. The Board agreed that there was 'no doubt that he suffers from a certain amount of disability as a result of his wound', and rated him unfit for general service for three months.

Meanwhile, however, Morton's destiny had changed. Statesmen, politicians and senior figures from the diplomatic, military and intelligence worlds had converged on Paris: Lloyd George was there, as were Churchill, Spears and Sinclair; so were the new DMO&I, General Sir William Thwaites; the Permanent Under Secretary to the Foreign Office, Lord Hardinge;[71] Sir Maurice Hankey,[72] the powerful secretary to the War Cabinet; also Menzies, on the staff of Basil Thomson, handling security for the British delegation; and more shadowy figures later to feature in Morton's professional life, such as the spy Sidney Reilly. High-level conversations were held and agreements reached. On 23 April 1919 Morton took up a post in War Office section MI1(c), at the grade of GSO3; on 1 August, in accordance with an arrangement made in Paris between Lord Hardinge and General Thwaites,[73] he was formally seconded to the Foreign Office 'for special reasons of secrecy'. He had joined the Secret Intelligence Service.*

---

* SIS evolved through many designations that can be confusing: in the 1920s, for example, MI1(c), was used both for SIS and for the War Office liaison section that dealt with it. For the sake of simplicity I have used SIS throughout until after 1938–9 when the designation MI6 was used interchangeably.

3

MAJOR MORTON OF SIS: 1919–22

Desmond Morton joined SIS as Head of Production at a salary of £73 14s 4d per month (about £26,000 per annum at current values): the third highest salary after Sir Robert Nathan (£83 6s 8d, about £30,000) and 'C' himself (£104 3s 4d, about £37,200). His official starting date was less than a week after returning to England from France with Haig at the beginning of April 1919, and he took a scant two weeks' leave before beginning a period of handover with his predecessor on 23 April. During these two weeks he presumably returned to his parents' house at 3 Beaufort Gardens, but no record or correspondence survives to suggest what he did, or how he felt on finally returning home for good after nearly five years. During that time he had experienced a disabling wound, and sustained severe physical and psychological pressure in a military career that had kept him almost incessantly on the move since August 1914. Though neither he nor his family appear to have recorded their experiences, we know from many other accounts that such homecomings were frequently traumatic for all concerned. His parents were, presumably, pleased and relieved that their only son had come home; but for Morton the transition to a domestic environment after the harsh routine of the Western Front, followed by a heady period accompanying Haig to Allied Supreme Council meetings and attending Peace Conference discussions in Paris, must have been at least disorienting.

Joining SIS, Morton was not demobilised formally but remained on the War Office books (they did not give up hope of retrieving him for further service until he finally retired from the Army in January 1937). Rare photographs show a tall, trim, military figure, sporting 'the toothbrush moustache that was then almost part of a Royal Artillery officer's uniform'.[1] A closer examination suggests a certain tension and anxiety in a rather drawn face, despite his habitually cheerful, if formal smile. He was now twenty-seven, and had spent all his adult life in the Army. There had been little opportunity, even if he had so wished, to marry or establish any sort of close relationship in the preceding ten years. He had come into contact, particularly since 1917, with a wide range of acquaintances, but the little correspondence that survives gives no indication of close friendships. In fact, there is no evidence that he ever had an intimate relationship, with woman or man, throughout his long life.

Many years later, he told his cousin that there had been someone during the First World War, possibly a nurse, to whom he might have been close, but that she had died. He also said that this person was one of 'only two or three' in his entire life that he might have wished to marry: and that of these, 'two had died and one became a nun'. If this is true, it is rather a poor record, and begs the question whether the women in question were ever aware of his interest. The surviving evidence indicates a general wariness towards, and awkwardness with women in general, apart from family members and domestic servants. It has been suggested that he did not consider it would be right to marry, given his precarious state of health; Lady Soames, Sir Winston Churchill's daughter, describes how as a teenager she and her friends used to watch Morton playing tennis at Chartwell, wondering whether the bullet lodged near his heart might one day cause him to 'blow up'.[2] He has also been described, by male friends, as a 'typical old-fashioned bachelor'. It is this description that seems to suit his character most nearly, however suspect it may seem to a contemporary readership accustomed to revelations and secret scandal. Not a whiff of dalliance, sexual intrigue or passion has been detected in a close study of Morton's life. He remained sociable, but essentially solitary, until his death, and his emotions were closely guarded. In this he was not unusual of his generation: he was by no means the only frontline survivor of the First World War who found close relationships and intimacy difficult, if not impossible. His response to what would now be called post-traumatic stress was also a common one; to throw himself into work.

The scanty nature of the surviving documentation means that any chronological division of Morton's early SIS career is to some extent arbitrary. This chapter deals with the first three years, from the summer of 1919 until roughly the summer of 1922, a period in which Morton was learning his trade and SIS was developing its sources for its primary commitment, obtaining information on Bolshevik Russia and on Republican Germany. Though new to the practical organisation of Intelligence, it did not take him long to express himself confidently on everything from agents' cover stories to the way to write reports. The aggressive energy with which Morton charted his course, both personally and professionally, led him (not for the last time) into conflict with colleagues and superiors, including Cumming himself. The years 1919–22 are illuminating of SIS's organisational development as well as of Morton's career: both experienced uncertainty and considerable change. Before telling their story, however, it is important to understand what sort of a Secret Intelligence Service Morton joined in April 1919.

SIS in 1919

During the First World War the British Intelligence establishment was expanded and distorted rather like the inflation of a giant balloon, assuming unexpected shapes and inspiring in its rise some hot air but also a burning blast of energy that turned it into a highly mobile and far-reaching instrument. Distinctions between agencies, between military and civil authorities (the former necessarily dominant), between channels of communication and sources of information, became blurred and intermingled in the interests of the war effort. A common sense of purpose overrode (generally) administrative and operational rivalries. When peace came, however, bringing reordered political priorities and the necessity for sharp economies to reduce an £8m national debt, the balloon was rapidly deflated, and inevitably failed to regain its original shape. All parts of the civil and military administrative machine found the transition from war to peace difficult, unpredictable and disruptive. 1919, the first year of peace – indeed, the year of peacemaking – was a year of readjustment, redirection and retrenchment. There was a great deal of what would today be called 're-engineering' or 'modernisation'. It was an uncertain time in which to embark on a career in Intelligence.

Both before and during the war, short-term military secondments into the Intelligence branches were common practice. At the time Morton joined SIS, many officers who had been absorbed into the organisation during the war were leaving, both voluntarily and as a result of post-hostilities retrenchment, either to rejoin their branch of the armed services or to return to their pre-war occupations. Some had gone even before the Armistice: Frank Stagg, for example, the naval commander whose recollections of Cumming are quoted in Alan Judd's biography, had left in June 1917, while the actor Guy Standing, lent to SIS from the Royal Naval Volunteer Reserve, had departed to the Ministry of Information in December 1917.[3] After November 1918 there was severe and irresistible pressure on all Intelligence services to cut back. Cumming told Lord Hardinge in March 1919 that he had lost fifty-eight staff already that year, though he estimated that SIS's commitments had increased by three hundred percent over the previous year.

'C' was only too well aware of plans afoot to amalgamate his service with others, to hive off areas of responsibility to other agencies and to restrict his independence. Nevertheless he remained remarkably, yet as will be seen rightly confident, determined to ignore the temporary storms and get on with the work with which he had been charged in 1909 when the Secret Service Bureau was established. The original objectives of the Bureau created in October 1909, following the recommendation of the Haldane Committee that a secret government department should be set up to deal with espionage and counter-espionage, were geared towards countering foreign – specifically German – activities hostile to Britain. They have been summarised neatly in Cumming's biography:

> First, in conjunction with the Home Office, to take necessary counter-espionage measures, including the use of agents within Britain. Second, to act as a screen between the War Office and the Admiralty on the one hand and foreigners willing to sell information on the other; third, to deal on behalf of the War Office and the Admiralty with agents spying for Britain abroad.[4]

The emphasis was on counter-espionage, the province of that section of military intelligence known since 1916 as MI5 and run by Colonel (later Sir) Vernon

Kell.[5] The idea of a parallel organisation dedicated to acquiring information overseas through the use of agents was, however, a new one, and Judd and others have described at length the difficulties that Cumming experienced in carving out a role and obtaining resources for his part of the Bureau, and the problems caused by the anomalous relationship between what became known as the Secret Intelligence Service, the Foreign Office (responsible for political intelligence) and naval and military intelligence (regarded by the War Office as the only authorities properly responsible for such matters).[6]

From the start, however, Cumming seems to have had a clear idea of what he wanted to do, and in the few short years before war broke out had begun to carve out the sort of Intelligence organisation that he considered was required. Though forced to work within a military framework, frequently frustrated and often overruled, starved of resources and even ignored, between 1909 and 1914 he laid nevertheless the foundations of an essentially twentieth, rather than nineteenth century intelligence service, civilian, rather than military. The sort of agents he attempted to engage; the kind of cover he wanted them to operate under; the idea that agents based in one country should supply information on another; his attempts to widen the scope of information gathering by the use of open source material and by harnessing new technical developments like aerial reconnais-sance;[7] all laid a preliminary but innovative and solid foundation for the post-war agency, though many of his ideas had to be suspended or subsumed in the wider realms of military intelligence until after the First World War.

To understand the organisation that Morton joined in 1919, it is worth noting certain particular features of Cumming's pre-war Service, which comprised a handful of employees and was dominated by the personality of its Chief. These can already be discerned in his report of April 1910 on the first six months of the Secret Service Bureau,[8] and are directly relevant to Morton's later career. One was Cumming's unswerving determination to keep his own counsel on his activities and intentions and those of his staff: he would, he said, 'prefer to keep my plans, assistants, methods and meetings entirely to myself, as secrets shared with anyone else, cease to be secrets'. It was a principle he instilled in all who worked for him, and characterised the post-1919 Service as well as the prewar; and it was followed by Morton, as by Cumming, all his life. Though a logical precept for those running an Intelligence service, when carried to extreme lengths it could also have counter-productive consequences for both intra- and inter-agency cooperation.

A second important, and innovative feature was Cumming's early emphasis on the importance of acquiring information from businessmen, whether as agents or as sources. He realised that both British and foreign industrialists were often best placed to discover details of overseas military and commercial develop-ments. Indeed the first known Intelligence report from SIS, dated 18 January 1910, contained information on the German armaments manufacturer Krupp.[9] Senior industrialists were also likely to have links with governmental and official sources overseas. They had a legitimate reason – as well as the resources – for travelling widely and visiting industrial enterprises in other countries, and were often able to speak several languages. In addition to these peripatetic sources of information, after the First World War a number of prospective long-term SIS agents overseas were given commercial cover in the country concerned (the use of Passport Control as cover was by no means exclusive). The activities of foreign commercial organisations also came under close scrutiny by SIS, and intelligence obtained about them provided convincing evidence of their use by foreign governments for espionage directed against the British Empire.

Cumming's diary contains a number of cryptic references to possible business contacts and prospective agents. During the First World War he welcomed warmly SIS recruits of military rank from the commercial world, such as Lt Col F.H. Browning, 'everyone's idea of the ideal man-about-town',[10] a director of the Savoy who left SIS in December 1919 but continued to maintain a close connection with the Service. Another example was Sir William Wiseman, a British baronet with pre-war business interests in the US, Canada and Mexico, taken on by Cumming in 1915 and whose wartime liaison role between the British Foreign Office and the American President Woodrow Wilson with his adviser Colonel House has been well documented.[11] Wiseman was only one of a number of international businessmen, drawn onto the fringes of the Intelligence world during the 1914–18 war – another notable example was the Canadian W.S. Stephenson[12] – who went on to develop in peacetime commercial intelligence networks for their own purposes that were tapped into profitably by SIS and, in some cases, merged almost seamlessly into the Intelligence establishment again during the Second World War.

This was an area of activity that was to prove of particular interest to Morton and influence the course of his career. The latter part of his time in SIS, after 1926, was dominated by his involvement with Section VI (the Economic Section), and led on logically to his work on economic and industrial intelligence in the 1930s, and as Director of Intelligence in the Ministry of Economic Warfare from 1939–40. Here, too, he was following in Cumming's early footsteps. During the First World War Cumming worked closely with the War Trade Intelligence Department (later the Ministry of Blockade), obviously appreciating the synergy of their and SIS operations.[13] In May 1916, for example, he wrote to Samuel Hoare,[14] whom he had sent to Petrograd to take over the British Intelligence mission there:

> I wish you to enquire into all matters with Enemy Trading, and these enquiries will of course include questions affecting the improvements of our own trade, which would otherwise be taken by the enemy. In the first instance, you will work on the lines suggested by the questionnaires supplied by the War Trade Intelligence Department, but I have no doubt that you will find the subject will broaden out, and it may very likely, towards the end of the war, become a matter of supreme importance.[15]

The importance of protecting UK trade in any future conflict and of denying the enemy access to raw materials remained a sub-text of British economic policy throughout the interwar years, and the Intelligence community, as Cumming (and later Morton) realised, had an important part to play in collecting the information on which the planning and execution of economic warfare was based.[16]

At the end of the First World War, however, it seemed for a while as if all Cumming's pre-1914 hopes and plans for his new service would evaporate. Indeed, immediately after the Armistice in November 1918 SIS appeared close to collapse, since the majority of its personnel were temporary officers who could not be replaced owing to the uncertainty of the future of the organisation. There were those in British official circles who felt that in peacetime there was no further need for an overseas intelligence service, or that if it survived it should be absorbed into one of the Service intelligence departments, a more 'natural' home. The international situation, however, remained menacing: the Allied Supreme Council, despite its name, had competing priorities and concerns, and the Paris Peace Conference, hopelessly bogged down in detail, declined in authority and momentum as it extended in time. Meanwhile, a new German Government was struggling to define and exert its authority, particularly over the military, many of whom did not seem to accept that the war had ended in their defeat; and over-stretched Allied occupation forces faced a German population suffering economic hardship and internal unrest. Most of all, the Soviet Russian regime, regarded by Western governments as both dangerous and profoundly alien, continued to defy confident predictions of its imminent demise and threatened to embroil already war-weary countries in continuing struggle and expense.

The world was not secure enough for the British Government to dispense with secret intelligence from overseas. On 28 December 1918 Hardinge agreed to Cumming's 'going ahead and arranging for a peacetime S[ecret] S[ervice] on the basis of £30,000 a year' (a considerable reduction from wartime funding levels); and on 31 December the Director of Military Intelligence, Major General Sir William Thwaites, instructed Cumming to send civilian agents to unoccupied Germany and 'establish themselves for a permanent service'. Meanwhile, how-ever, Thwaites was simultaneously seeking the amalgamation of SIS, MI5 and other Intelligence branches under the control of the War Office.[17] Within weeks, another threat to SIS was posed by the Secret Service Committee appointed by the War Cabinet in January 1919, under the chairmanship of Lord Curzon,* to enquire:

(a) what is being done at present by the Secret Service Branches of the several Departments

---

*   Curzon, then Lord President of the Council, assumed the chair of the Committee in the absence of the Foreign Secretary, Arthur Balfour, in Paris. He and Balfour exchanged jobs on 23 October 1919.

(b)   how this work can best be coordinated with a view to the necessary
      action being taken with the utmost promptitude.[18]

In fact, the Committee was convened to consider the question of counter-
intelligence directed against organised labour unrest, rather than secret intelligence
in the SIS sense. At the beginning of 1919 British policy makers saw Germany
in chaos, most of Europe seemingly under the shadow of Bolshevik revolution,
independence movements challenging British rule in Egypt and India, Sinn Fein
triumphant in Ireland and a tide of industrial unrest at home. A wave of strikes
in the engineering and other industries was exacerbated by the Government's
demobilisation policy: in January 1919 the Triple Alliance of miners, railwaymen
and transport workers was revived, and 5000 British troops in a camp near Calais
staged a mutiny against demobilisation delays. Churchill, newly appointed
Secretary of State for War and Air, 'feared that widespread disobedience would
encourage Bolshevism in Britain',[19] and was forced to consider plans for military
forces to come to the aid of the civil authorities in the event of a national strike.
Pressure for higher wages and shorter hours, however, had to be set against strong
Treasury pressure to balance the budget; and pressure for demobilisation against
the need for a strong occupation force in the newly defeated but already restive
Germany.

   In these circumstances it is small wonder that the Committee paid little attention
to secret Intelligence, about which its members knew little and understood less.
Two early documents taken by the Committee, a memorandum for the War
Cabinet by the First Lord of the Admiralty, Walter Long, dated 16 January 1919,
together with a complementary memorandum of 23 January by the Home
Secretary, Edward Shortt, illustrate this. Long referred to the 'Director of Secret
Service', by whom he clearly meant Kell, and urged the importance of an efficient
civilian system to alert Ministers to the dangers of Bolshevism; Shortt, while
agreeing with Long that 'serious attempts are being made to disseminate
Bolshevist doctrines in this country,' averred that there was no such person as
the Director of Secret Service, referring instead to the diverse anti-subversion
responsibilities of Basil Thomson and Special Branch. Neither mentioned foreign
intelligence.[20] Although the Committee's report contained a paragraph describing
correctly the structure and functions of Kell's and Cumming's organisations, it
was clear where their preoccupations lay.

   The Committee's report issued in February 1919 paid tribute to the wartime
efforts of the secret service, which had placed at the disposal of the British
Government information 'equal, if not superior, to that obtained by any other
country engaged in the War', but observed disapprovingly that:

   There is no doubt that as a result of the general extension of the secret
   service organization there has been overlapping of activity and responsibility, and the large sums of money required for all these operations
   have not always been expended economically or to the best advantage.

Cases were quoted to the Committee of agents employed and paid separately by more than one branch of the intelligence service and of information by the same agent being given to different branches, with the result that one report appeared to confirm the other though both really came from the same source. Such a duplication of effort is perhaps inseparable from Secret Service work, but is nevertheless to be deprecated and with experience ought to be reduced to a minimum.[21]

Despite this stern admonition, the Committee concluded that it was 'convenient to maintain the distinction between military and civilian intelligence', and Cumming and SIS were barely affected by their recommendations, which were focussed upon the creation of the ill-fated Directorate of Home Intelligence under Basil Thomson, Assistant Commissioner of Police at Scotland Yard, and on the need for organised anti-Bolshevik propaganda.[22] SIS's budget was reduced: in April 1919 Cumming's estimate of £250,000 per annum (compared with £80,000 per month at the end of the war) was approved. But as an organisation SIS was left intact, and indeed its remit expanded: Cumming reached agreement with Thomson in April to take on all overseas anti-Bolshevik work, and by August 1919 he had been commissioned to maintain a peace time skeleton organisation in all foreign countries, with no other department permitted to operate overseas. By September 1922 the only secret overseas organisation not under SIS control was the intelligence branch of the Army of the Rhine.[23]

Cumming's survival has been attributed to strong support from the FO, personified by Hardinge, Balfour and Curzon. It is certainly true that all of these, and Churchill, supported Cumming, defended his budget estimates and opposed SIS's amalgamation under a War Office umbrella.[24] They were valuable supporters at a time when swingeing cuts in defence expenditure were in the offing.[25] There were, however, other factors at play that increased SIS's chances, and it is likely that Cumming's apparent insouciance was founded on a shrewd calculation that if he kept his head down all would be well. The episode confirmed his belief that there was everything to gain by maintaining a strict policy of need to know about his Service's activities. Nevertheless, although the existence and independence of his organisation may have been safeguarded, the reduced number of SIS officers was a matter of serious concern.

In June 1915 Cumming had listed his staff at home and overseas as forty-seven (not including all agents); by October 1916 the total had reached one thousand and twenty-four, including sixty at Headquarters.[26] As Cumming told the second meeting of the Secret Service Committee on 7 February 1919, he accepted that reductions were inevitable at the end of the war.[27] However, if SIS were to undertake a serious programme of intelligence-gathering on Bolshevik activities, not to mention keeping a close eye on what was going on in Germany, his drastically reduced headquarters staff was insufficient to deal with the necessary recruitment and handling of agents and with the collection and dissemination of information from a wide range of countries. Although Cumming was the dominant driving force in what remained a highly personalised service, he could not do all the work himself, and the haemorrhage of experienced staff after the Armistice inflicted severe damage on SIS capability.

Recent organisational changes had made the shortfall even more apparent. Following a landmark agreement in 1917 between the then DMI, General Macdonogh, and Lord Hardinge, constituting the first official acknowledgement that secret service activities would cover requirements outside the military field,[28] SIS HQ had been divided from late that year on the basis of types of intelligence (eg naval, economic, political), rather than geographically as before. Though all under C's umbrella, each Requirements section included staff from its customer departments (for example, from the FO for political intelligence), and dealt directly with its agents in the field, whose reports were prefixed by the relevant designation (e.g. CXP for political, CXA for aviation). They then passed information on to the appropriate Ministry. According to Captain Somerville, RN, the first head of the Naval Requirements section, the new system effected immediate improvements: he claimed that from the beginning of the war until October 1917, two hundred and sixty naval documents had been filed, whereas eight thousand were filed between November 1917 and November 1918.[29]

Cumming had little choice but to accept these changes, intended by Macdonogh to strengthen War Office control over SIS, though in fact they strengthened its independence by forging stronger links with non-military departments. The reorganisation proved an enduring basis for SIS HQ operations for the foreseeable future, and a number of the 'embedded' liaison officers moved permanently from their parent departments into SIS: Menzies, for example, the future Chief, began his SIS career as a Military Intelligence liaison officer in the Military Requirements section, transferring formally to the SIS establishment in April 1923. A further reorganisation in 1919, involving the functional division of SIS Headquarters into Production (dealing with operations and organisations abroad) and Circulation (passing information to and from government departments) accentuated the need for a strong central staff.

In 1917 Macdonogh had promised, according to Cumming, to provide 'a good, strong character officer' for the organisational side of SIS,[30] but it seemed that until 1919 none could be spared. Was this intended to be Morton's role? Macdonogh and his successor Thwaites, as well as Haig, were all aware of Morton's administrative abilities; as indeed was the new Secretary of State for War, Churchill. Where better to put an officer of proven organisational skills and a reputation for getting things done, familiar with the military intelligence establishment, with a distinguished military record but of less than robust health? And from Morton's viewpoint, turning aside from a military career but seeking another outlet for his ambitions and abilities? The Intelligence world, always imbued with an enticing air of mystery, may well have appealed. Without documentary proof it is impossible to be certain, but it must be at least possible that in his sponsors' eyes he was intended to be the 'strong character officer' for whom a need had been identified two years earlier.

Certainly, it seems that Morton was looking to the longer term rather than a temporary attachment. We do not know who approached him with regard to joining SIS, what he was told his duties would be or what was discussed by Hardinge and Thwaites in Paris when they arranged his secondment. However, the only two accounts of his move from the Army to SIS, although scarcely objective (emanating from Churchill and from Morton himself), may hold the answer. Churchill, in *The Gathering Storm*, did not hesitate to take responsibility:

> In 1919, when I became Secretary of State for War and Air, I appointed him [Morton] to a key position in the Intelligence, which he held for many years.[31]

Morton's version, as recorded forty years later, is typically more grandiloquent, and attributes his change of career to the Prime Minister:

> Returning from the war with a bullet lodged in his heart he was appointed by Lloyd George to start the Foreign Intelligence Service with the emphasis particularly on Bolshevist Russia (and soon on Germany also, the Balkans, etc).[32]

Cumming, had he lived long enough, would certainly have been outraged by the latter account (though perhaps, familiar with Morton's style, unsurprised). However, in April 1919, faced with a diminishing Headquarters staff and a growing workload, it is hard to imagine that he did not welcome Morton's arrival, whatever the long-term prospects.[33]

If Morton thought of himself as a new broom, sweeping the untidy remnants of wartime intrigue from the SIS corridors and imposing military discipline, he must have been swiftly disabused. He soon found he had entered an environment very different from the ordered military life he had led for the past ten years, and dealing with very different people. SIS Headquarters was at this point based in Whitehall Court in Westminster, where Cumming lived as well as worked, thus inspiring irresistible images of his descending the stairs on his backside or negotiating the corridors one-legged on a child's scooter.[34] At the end of 1919 Cumming and his central staff, presumably including Morton, moved to 1 Melbury Road in Kensington:[35] convenient for Beaufort Gardens though less so for the gentlemen's clubs where Morton and his colleagues lunched regularly. Though he presumably visited other SIS offices in central London, Morton would have spent the majority of his time at the Kensington headquarters until SIS moved to Broadway Buildings in 1925.

Cumming ran SIS with a generally effective but somewhat chaotic mixture of hands-on control and inspired improvisation. His senior staff at HQ, such as Nathan, Browning, Claude Dansey and 'Paymaster' Percy Sykes, were, however capable, undoubtedly individualistic of approach; some of the agents and sources with whom Morton had to deal were, as we shall see, even more colourful. This may have added to the attraction, or at least the interest, of the job. Morton was more impatient with the lack of properly formulated office procedures. Compared to MI5, for example, SIS had little in the way of a developed bureaucratic system: no figures survive for 1919, but by 1922, when Morton had ten staff in his Production section and the Political Requirements section alone numbered a further ten, there were still only eight staff in the SIS central Registry (Cumming had had to fight in 1920 to retain any at all) and six typists. A slim administrative machine had its advantages: colleagues could be consulted easily and reports passed swiftly to those who needed to see them; but the lack of a clear hierarchical system, combined with Cumming's obsessive secrecy, was irksome to the young officer accustomed to the well-oiled wheels of the Commander-in-Chief's GHQ. It seemed to offer some scope for 'putting things in order' and Morton lost little time in attempting to institute administrative changes. 'Organising the office' was an area where he felt confident. He knew far less, however, about the chief focus of his job as head of Production, or 'Prod': organising the collection of information from overseas.

Since 1918 SIS had been building up a network of representatives, grouped under 'Regional Inspectors', in countries adjacent to Soviet Russia, such as Poland and the Baltic States, and in Scandinavia where the Bolsheviks transacted a great deal of political and commercial business, including with Germany.[36] Particularly important were SIS stations in the Baltic: by 1920 a station had been opened in Helsinki, supervised by a Regional Inspector in Stockholm; by 1921, stations were operating in Tallinn, Riga and Kaunas, with a number of sub-stations, and business was so brisk that the head of Tallinn station was made Inspector General of the whole Baltic area in early 1923. These representatives controlled their own sources within the target country: SIS representatives in Latvia, for example, controlled in their turn sources in Moscow, including some placed at the heart of Bolshevik bureaucracy.

The basing of representatives outside the target country was a deliberate tactic. One of the operational principles laid down at the time of the 1919 SIS reforms and observed generally at this period, stipulated that intelligence on an important target country should be obtained by representatives working from a neighbouring country, rather than from within the country itself, attracting less attention and increasing security. In the same way, SIS stations in Paris and Brussels supplied information on Germany (and also on Turkey, where Constantinople was a notorious intelligence *entrepôt* and German intelligence known to be active), while details of the activities of secret monarchist groups dedicated to the restoration of the Hohenzollern dynasty in Germany were supplied by sources in Switzerland.[37] The fact that a great deal of important material on the Bolsheviks was obtained through SIS agents in Poland and the Baltic States was a sign that the system was working, rather than the opposite.

There were, naturally, problems with this approach. Arms-length handling of sources was difficult, and open to abuse, both by the sources themselves (one source, from Moscow Military District, was found to have fabricated completely reports of Soviet fortifications on the Finnish island of Seiskari); and by some SIS representatives who found it rather too easy to shift the blame for their own inactivity. It was also very difficult, as the Zinoviev Letter affair was to show in 1924,[38] for SIS to assert effective quality control. It is certainly true that accurate information on the working of the Bolshevik regime was hard to obtain at this period; it is also true that, at times, SIS was guilty of relying with too great a degree of credulity on sources that were inherently unreliable, such as competing White Russian opposition groups, Anglo-Russian exiles and returning military men whose service on the Russian borders in the fight against Bolshevism had left them with a somewhat excitable view of the potential for radical change. Reliable information on Germany was in some ways easier to obtain, although the waters were muddied by the competing and often contradictory activities of different parts of the German Government. By the end of 1919, however, Morton's Production section was receiving useful information from the majority of European countries.

The quality of this information was inevitably uneven. Although some SIS representatives, such as R.L. Tinsley in Rotterdam, had begun to work for Cumming during the First World War and were tried and tested,[39] others, like Frank Marshall who had worked for MI5 during the war and succeeded A.L. Hudson in Copenhagen in August 1919, were new recruits to secret service overseas. It took some time, therefore, for them to establish themselves and their cover, whether as Passport Control Officers, businessmen or accredited journalists, and to develop the contacts that would enable them to acquire useful information. Some found the process difficult, as Morton's correspondence reveals. The problems experienced by Marshall, by no means unique, provide a useful example. Transferred to Warsaw in February 1920 after clashing with the Danish Foreign Minister, Marshall was criticised in a letter from Morton of 16 May 1920 for providing reports that were taken from the local Polish press:

> What we want . . . is absolutely <u>inside</u> information or none at all . . . I know how hard it is to produce what is wanted, and it is equally hard to criticise in this general way, but if you will start with the idea that nothing that ever appears in a newspaper is of the least value, I am sure everything will be all right.

Marshall accepted the reproof, but complained of the difficulties of his task:

> Information is extremely difficult to obtain here, as my agents are scarce and of very little use as they are all men who have worked in the Russian or German secret service, and are more dangerous than profitable, and furthermore absolutely untrustworthy.

Morton's response was not unsympathetic, and he suggested to Sir Robert Nathan on 14 May 1920 that 'in view of the fact that one or two of his recent reports have contained a gem of the right sort of stuff, I could quite well write back and encourage him to some extent'. Nathan agreed, also suggesting that Paul Dukes, who was about to visit Warsaw under an assumed name travelling as 'secretary' to Rex Leeper of the Foreign Office, might be able to help steer Marshall in the right direction. Meanwhile Morton assured Marshall on 28 May that the Foreign Office had praised two of his more recent reports, though he stressed the importance of giving his sources as 'the value of a report is always increased by fifty per cent if we know exactly how the information was obtained'.

As these exchanges with Marshall show, after little more than six months as 'Production' Morton was already confident in his evaluation and criticism of incoming reports and had adopted the somewhat patronising – some said arrogant – style that was to irritate many who came into professional contact with him. In contrast to his Chief, who committed little to paper and preferred to brief his representatives in private and informally,[40] Morton favoured a more codified approach. His arrival in SIS was followed quite swiftly by an increase in the circulation of what he would have called 'office orders': he was always inclined to spell out procedures and methods, sometimes in what appears excessively pedantic detail, though he would have argued that it was better to leave no room for doubt as to what was required. A set of instructions drawn up at this period for the officer who was to open the SIS station in Riga, stressing the importance of an orderly and rigorous approach to his duties, illustrates this. Though unsigned, they emanate from Morton's section and bear the unmistakable hallmarks of his style. Production urged the new arrival, as soon as he had settled in, to:

> allot numbers to every source from which you obtain information, whether that source is a paid, unpaid agent or even an unconscious source which you constantly tap . . . we shall require full particulars of any other agent or source that you make use of in order that we may card them up for reference in PROD . . . you should send the name of the individual, his nationality, social position, abbreviated past history, probabl[e] qualifications for employment, what lines he may be likely to be best on, and why, etc. In sending in these particulars, all names and other information likely to lead to the identification of the individual in case your letter got into the wrong hands should be put into code. We should like to get this list at the very earliest opportunity so that when your reports [come] in . . . we shall at once understand who the author or authors are . . .

The instructions from Circulation (also Mortonesque in style), though headed 'brief hints on the form of reports', comprise a detailed step-by-step guide to their compilation, for example:

> At the head of your report put your serial number, the town from which it is written, and the date. In the centre of the page underneath put a

concise title explaining the substance of the report. On the left hand side put the number of the source who obtained the information. Commence by stating how the information was obtained, or if this does not fit in with the remainder of the report attach a covering letter explaining this. At the end of the report type-write, or write . . . if you are the final authority responsible. At the end of the report at the bottom left hand corner [set] out the distribution, so far as you are concerned.

A catalogue of similarly specific instructions concludes by enjoining the representative to 'get the report typed out in paragraphs in as clear a manner as possible'. Whether the recipients of these instructions were grateful or irritated is not revealed, but they give the flavour of Morton's early organisational efforts. An account of SIS's anti-Bolshevik activities between 1919 and 1922 is similarly revealing.

Reds, Whites and Blues,* 1919–22

The Bolshevik Revolution of November 1917, the formation of a Soviet Russian government that signed a peace treaty with Germany, the massacre of the Romanov family and, most of all, the continued survival of a regime with the avowed purpose of fomenting world revolution, had administered a profound shock to the British Government and its allies. At the conclusion of five years' hostilities with Germany they realised that unless they fought what was in effect another war, they faced the unpalatable alternatives of Bolshevik or German hegemony in Eastern Europe and the Baltic states. Within the Allied Supreme Council, however, there was little appetite for continued military involvement. Western troops had been sent to Russia to try and secure her as an ally in the war against Germany: once that effort had been negated, those troops had been drawn increasingly into the Russian civil war in a role neither sustainable by their governments nor acceptable to public opinion.

Lloyd George's general policy during 1919 was to withdraw military support for attempts to overthrow the Bolshevik regime, while maintaining a commitment to support bordering states if they were attacked by the Bolsheviks. This policy was subject to some modification as the fortunes of the anti-Bolshevik forces of Admiral Kolchak and Generals Yudenitch and Denikin waxed and waned, and as the Allied Supreme Council took a more or less bold view of the situation. However, the Prime Minister's priorities were clear, as he had told the House of Commons on 16 April 1919:

---

* The phrase derives in this context from Russian forger *par excellence*, Vladimir Orlov; according to him, the Blues were the Russian Monarchists in Berlin, who would reconstruct the old Russian white, blue and red flag by taking up their stand between the Reds (Bolsheviks) and the White Russians.

> Russia is a country which it is very easy to invade, but very difficult to conquer . . . I share the horror of all the Bolshevik teachings, but I would rather leave Russia Bolshevik until she sees her way out of it than see Britain bankrupt.[41]

This was, in the end, the view of all the Western Allies, however strongly they supported the anti-Bolshevik cause. Even had the political will to continue the fight been present, resources after five years of war were insufficient for the task: Curzon estimated in August 1919 that by the end of the year the total cost of the British Government's intervention in Russia would have reached £94 million.[42] Moreover, the weight of evidence as 1919 drew on indicated not only that the anti-Bolshevik forces could not win, but that more and more of the Russian population, utterly weary of war, did not want them to. Some people living in areas 'liberated' from the Bolsheviks found conditions worse than before. Oliver Harvey, a new recruit to the FO, summed up the pragmatic official view:

> It is impossible to account for the stability of the Bolshevik Government by terrorism alone. A handful of violent men may terrorise a city, or a small and compact country, but they cannot infuse ardour into farflung armies or hold down millions . . . We must admit the fact that the present Russian Government is accepted by the bulk of the Russian people.[43]

The Russian situation, it became increasingly clear, must be left to 'sort itself out', while the provisions of the peace treaty could be used to force Germany to withdraw from the Baltic States and deter her from too close an involvement, friendly or hostile, with the Bolsheviks.

Lloyd George's views were not shared by all his Ministers – Churchill, in particular, urged constantly that money, men and arms be sent to support the anti-Bolshevik cause[44] – nor by all of the multifarious British official representatives in and around Russia at that time. While there was no accredited mission in Moscow, there was nevertheless a confusing array of diplomatic and other official missions operating in the area: what Curzon termed 'Allied Missions despatched in every direction . . . to produce something like order out of the prevailing chaos'.[45] There were, for example, British diplomatic missions in Siberia at Vladivostok, and in North Russia at Archangel, with a British GOC (General Officer Commanding) in charge of the military side in each case; examples from a long list of other missions, military, economic and political, were a special mission to Transcaucasia, despatched in July 1919 under Mr Wardrop, formerly Consul General at Moscow; an economic mission under Colonel Macalpine on behalf of the British section of the Supreme Economic Council, attached to General Denikin's headquarters at Ekaterinodar; and a British Supply Mission at Murmansk, headed by Mr. Lambert.

All these, and many more, were busily sending reports (and opinions) back to London.[46] Diplomatic, military and economic activity in relation to the Bolshevik regime and its opponents was also intense at all the Baltic capitals, where fear of potential or actual Bolshevik attack led added urgency to appeals to the Allied and Associated Powers for support and protection; and in Paris, Berlin and Warsaw, where White Russian groups (and, consequently, the foreign department of the *Cheka*) were especially active.[47] Finally, important information on the Soviet Union reached London from other capitals, such as Paris, Constantinople and Peking, where diplomatic missions were used for the traffic of confidential information, or meetings between representatives of many countries, including Russians, Red and White.

The range of information reaching the British Government from these 'open' sources has been described at some length because of its relevance to Morton's job at SIS, for two reasons in particular. Firstly, at a variety of levels – Ministerial, departmental and personal – a large amount of information was being received daily which then had to be fitted together into a sort of jigsaw puzzle to represent what the Government, and in particular the FO, knew about Soviet Russia; it was for SIS to supply, from secret sources, the missing pieces, and for Morton to arrange for the collection of the information, gather it in, and pass it on. Secondly, the multiplicity of diplomatic and fact-finding missions in or around Russia created a large pool of potential contacts and informants with direct experience of Bolshevik and anti-Bolshevik activities. The majority of officers joining SIS immediately after the First World War did so on the basis of their knowledge of Russia and its language, and other 'Russia hands' embarked on or resumed professional, academic or commercial careers. Their shared experience of the Russian civil war proved a powerful common factor, and within the relatively narrow social circle that produced senior officials, industrialists, lawyers or newspaper proprietors there was a rich seam of experience, knowledge and support. To put it shortly, Morton and his colleagues knew a lot of influential people who had served in or around Russia, nearly all of whom retained a decided prejudice against Bolshevism.

However, SIS also needed up to date, reliable information from agents in the field, and in 1919 these were thin on the ground. The messy collapse of the so-called 'Lockhart Plot' against the Bolshevik regime in August 1918[48] meant that the elaborate (if confused) information-gathering machinery established in Russia during the war – described as 'a mixture of intelligence-gathering, disruption, sabotage and assistance to British military forces'[49] – had ceased to function, its Missions closed down and its representatives forced to leave Russia. If, as seemed increasingly likely, the Bolsheviks were about to defeat their opponents conclusively, accurate information on the Soviet regime would be at a premium and the securing of reliable long-term sources a priority. To supply the short-term need for operational intelligence, Cumming despatched agents to Russia on a series of fact-finding missions, some of which have become well-known as 'adventures' within Bolshevik-controlled territory, including the daring exploits under multiple disguises of the charismatic Paul (later Sir Paul) Dukes and the extraordinary antics of a group of young naval volunteers despatched from Osea Island in Essex to destroy the Russian Baltic Fleet.[50] Such enterprises, much enjoyed vicariously by Cumming, could, indeed, only be embarked upon by 'young men given clear overall directions and a loose rein'.[51] They did not address the problem of long-term intelligence gathering, which had to be tackled more slowly and methodically: this was part of Morton's job.

It is appropriate that the earliest surviving piece of SIS correspondence in Morton's name is dated 3 October 1919, and concerns Sidney Reilly,[52] not because of the more colourful and dangerous exploits of the 'Ace of Spies', but because of his rather less well-known professional activities on behalf of SIS during this period. A complex, unpredictable and undoubtedly self-serving individual mired in deception and conspiracy, Reilly was nevertheless capable of taking a hard-headed and perceptive view of the Bolshevik regime, described by him as 'the worst form of autocratic tyranny known to history'.[53] First taken on by Cumming in March 1918 and deeply implicated in the 'Lockhart plot' that led to his being sentenced to death by the Bolsheviks *in absentia*, Reilly had undertaken a further mission for SIS to South Russia in December 1918 together with George Hill, returning in February 1919.[54] He spent most of 1919 travelling between London and Paris on SIS business, reporting on the plans of Boris Savinkov[55] and other White Russian activists, and gathering useful information on events in Russia while continuing to campaign in favour of positive action against the Bolsheviks. When in London, he met up with like-minded 'Russia hands', including agents who had served in Russia during the war, and others, like J.D. Gregory of the Foreign Office, who remained professionally involved in Russian affairs.[56]

It is not known exactly when Reilly and Morton first met: it is possible they had already encountered one another in Paris even before Morton joined SIS. By the autumn of 1919, however, they were in regular contact and Reilly lost no opportunity of giving Morton the benefit of his views and experience of intelligence-gathering in regard to Bolshevik Russia. Though Morton left no record of his initial impressions of Reilly, there seems no doubt that he was impressed by the latter's knowledge of Russia, and possibly a little beguiled by his flamboyant style. A letter written to Reilly on 4 January 1920 gives something of the flavour of their relationship, hinting also at the extent to which Morton, after only six months at SIS, had assumed the mantle of 'Intelligence man'; Assuring Reilly that 'C' was 'very just to everybody who works for him', Morton wrote:

> You are quite safe, or ought to be now, after the numerous efforts that have been made by various swells to apply the boot. I expect when you get pushed away you will not go alone, as all our nefarious past will by that time have come to light, in which case I think we had better club together, buy an island in the West Indies and start a republic of our own.

You may be President if you will give me the job of Chancellor of the Exchequer.[57]

Though soon to become disillusioned, in early 1920 Cumming still regarded Reilly, despite his larger than life *persona*, as capable of serious and systematic intelligence work,[58] and involved him in an ambitious information-gathering exercise designed to improve the quality and quantity of SIS reporting on Russia by trying to coordinate the intelligence activities of all governments concerned with combatting Bolshevism. This scheme, which involved Morton closely, was launched despite the fact that in February 1920 Cumming's annual expenditure had been reduced to £65,000, and that on 15 March he had been instructed to close down stations in Athens, Christiania (later Oslo), Copenhagen, Helsinki, Madrid, Stockholm, Trieste and Warsaw.[59] Though the latter order was counter-manded ten days later, money remained tight: a minute by Morton of 15 March 1920 referred to marking time 'until we see if we are going to have any money for Warsaw or not'. Cumming, characteristically, refused to be derailed by Whitehall belt-tightening but pressed ahead with his plans.

On 22 April 1920 Cumming sent a message to Constantinople to the effect that Malcolm Maclaren – described by Bruce Lockhart as an ex-merchant navy man wearing gold earrings that 'gave him the look of a pirate'[60] – who had worked for SIS in Russia since 1918 and had just managed to escape through Baku to Turkey, was required home urgently by SIS 'to take complete charge of our affairs in Northern Europe'. Maclaren's immediate brief on his arrival in London was to give the benefit of his experience and advice to SIS on the situation in Russia and the best way of acquiring accurate information on the Bolsheviks. In London he re-established contact with Reilly, with whom he had worked previously in Russia, and the two men set about devising parallel schemes involving an extensive fact-finding European tour that would also set up channels for the future exchange of useful intelligence with other governments and groups.

Maclaren's original scheme was, apparently, too ambitious for Cumming, who preferred one drawn up by Reilly, and was prepared to commit SIS funds to it. Following discussion with Morton and Reilly, Cumming, who also interviewed Vladimir Orlov[61] (just arrived from Paris) on 19 August 1920, agreed to authorise payment for all four men (Reilly, Orlov, Maclaren and Paul Dukes) to travel through Europe in the last quarter of 1920 gathering information.[62] (One might be forgiven for thinking that the fact that these four rogues were all involved in the planning and execution of the scheme should have been enough to consign it immediately to the realms of fantasy and intrigue.) On 20 August Morton wrote to Maclaren, explaining Cumming's preference for Reilly's scheme, and noting that Reilly had invited Morton and Maclaren to lunch with him at his rooms in Albany on 23 August to discuss details. Meanwhile, financial arrangements were set in train by SIS to settle the personal affairs of both Maclaren and Orlov: money was advanced to help the former's wife and son, who had managed to escape from Baku to Tiflis, to return to England; and Morton was charged by Cumming with making arrangements to pay the passage to England of Orlov's wife and two children, currently in a camp at Tel-el-Kebir in Egypt (Foreign Office help was needed in the latter case).

Maclaren, Reilly, Dukes and Orlov left London separately. Maclaren set out for Warsaw via Danzig on 23 September, and a week later sent 'Major Stanley' (Morton's alias) an account of an interview with Savinkov, described as 'the recognised political chief of the Russian anti-Bolshevik movement in Poland'. He then travelled to Riga to interview Klembovsky, a military adviser to the Bolshevik delegation negotiating peace with Poland. On 6 October he was back in Danzig, reporting the establishment of a 'secret intelligence centre' designed to include members of foreign missions; by 16 October Maclaren was back in Riga, 'still alive and going strong', from where he travelled to Stockholm and thence, at the end of the month, to Berlin. Reilly, after a visit to Paris at the beginning of September (where he was spotted wearing naval uniform, leading to a complaint from the Admiralty to 'C'),[63] followed Maclaren to Poland on 20 October. There he met up again with his former comrade in arms, Paul Dukes: Marshall wrote to Morton on 28 October that the two men were 'happy as a pair of "sand boys" constructing a perfectly good new Russia', adding on 4 November that they were 'still rebuilding the Russian Empire in the direction of Minsk, unless they have already been chased out by the Poles'.[64] Orlov seems have gone back to Paris in September and thence to Berlin, although there are references to his being in Riga with Maclaren. All four of them were clearly enjoying themselves.

During their travels in the autumn of 1920 both Reilly and Maclaren corresponded regularly with Morton, letting him know their movements and plans; if Dukes also sent reports to Morton, they have not survived. Communication with Orlov was always less direct. Sometimes, when their paths had coincided, Reilly and Maclaren reported on Orlov's plans and movements: but they also sent messages and material to Morton for onward despatch to Orlov, usually via the SIS station in Berlin. In the early autumn, Morton's response to all these reports was generally brief but encouraging. As the 'tour' progressed, however, and the four adventurers appeared increasingly to be pursuing their own (unrealistic and expensive) agenda, he became more critical. On 17 November he complained to Maclaren, then in Berlin (where it must have been cold, since he asked Morton to send him a winter overcoat), that their recent reports contained nothing new or of value. In December, sending Sir Robert Nathan an account of the work done by Maclaren and Orlov, Morton commented that 'though it shows they have worked very hard, I do not see that the story is exactly our affair but more their own'.

By the end of 1920 the travellers, too, evidently felt that they had done as much as they could, and were anxious to pursue their own enterprises. On 3 December Reilly, Maclaren and Orlov met in Paris and agreed that a 'tremendous amount of spadework' had been done. Reilly wrote to Morton after the meeting that:

> everything now depends upon how it will be utilized. Even if no official arrangements are made with the G[ermans] we are assured of the full

benefit of O[rlov]'s work with them . . . we will, I feel sure, be better informed on Russia than ever before provided we have somebody at the office who will be able to digest and summarise the whole thing. This seems to me the whole crux of the matter.

In a report dated 17 December 1920, Maclaren set out what he and his colleagues thought they had been trying to achieve:

we had as our aim the investigation of the possibility of forming an anti-Bolshevick [*sic*] intelligence service which should be able to work at the highest possible pressure of all those engaged by the intelligence services of the governments interested in the combatting of Bolshevism and yet be run at a minimum cost. Before doing so we studied the Bolshevick system of agents scattered all over Europe, likewise the main moves of the Bolshevicks in their efforts to organise a general European social revolution . . . we endeavoured to convince all those who were at the head of the intelligence services that the episodic character of the struggle with Bolshevism which was being carried on today by each government independently without any coordination between the activities of their anti-Bolshevick service and those of others . . . was absolutely harmless to the Bolshevicks, as each government independently cannot determine the main thing – the Bolshevick system of world work . . .

Maclaren reported that the heads of the intelligence services contacted were unanimous in agreeing with this analysis, and in supporting in principle the idea of a coordinated effort. However:

for various reasons [they] could not decide on their own initiative to officially enter into an agreement with us. At the same time, they are quite willing to assist us to the best of their ability, putting at our disposal the whole of their espionage and counter-espionage organisations with the following provisions: (1) they are to receive in exchange . . . similar material from the intelligence services of other governments, (2) they are to be allowed certain funds for the development of their network of agents, the maintenance of couriers, stationery and other expenses . . .

The report went on to list contacts, their positions, the sort of information they could provide and on what conditions. There is no evidence to suggest that Cumming ever contemplated providing funds for foreign intelligence services to cover their expenses in providing the required information. It is likely that he was sceptical from the first of the potential for any formal inter-governmental co-ordination of intelligence. Nor did he have much patience with reports of elaborate plans hatched by Savinkov and reported with enthusiasm by Reilly and

Maclaren. Nevertheless, it seems both Cumming and Morton considered that the autumn peregrinations of their four headstrong representatives were worthwhile, for the more limited purpose of gathering information from countries bordering on Russia, to gauge the strength and depth of enduring anti-British feeling, and to set up useful channels for the future exchange of intelligence.

The end of the 1920 expedition did not conclude Morton's involvement with Maclaren, Reilly and Orlov,[65] though it marked the beginning of the end for all three men's association with SIS. Tracking their movements over the next two years provides a useful snapshot of Morton's work in SIS, as well as illustrating developments within the organisation itself. In the case of Maclaren, a more personal dimension of Morton's career is also revealed. Maclaren left Paris in January 1920 to take over from Marshall as SIS representative in Warsaw. His original cover was commercial (he planned to set up an engineering business), but by February he was writing to 'Stanley' (Morton) to ask whether he might also be accredited as correspondent to 'one of the British middle class papers', which he felt would give him better access to information and possible recruits (accreditation to the *Morning Post* was later arranged by Menzies, who was friendly with the paper's owner, Lord Apsley). Although the reports on his exploits with Reilly, Dukes and Orlov were assured and even tended to the swashbuckling, Maclaren seemed much less confident in a resident's job. Like his predecessor, he found it hard to break into the right Polish circles, and as early as 5 March 1921 apologised for the poor quality of his work so far, adding that 'should I fail to get really good results within the coming month I am afraid you will be fully justified in cancelling our present arrangement'. Morton wrote back encouragingly, assuring him that the FO was finding his material 'exactly what was wanted'. Maclaren was grateful, writing on 23 March:

> You can be assured that I shall do everything possible to justify your good opinion of the work I am trying to do and hope that in the near future the quantity as well as the quality will meet all your requirements. When I have managed to get things to that stage I shall begin to be satisfied in my mind that I am not a parasite but a live portion of the great machine being directed by you.

Maclaren's next exchanges with Morton, however, reflect a crisis in the latter's career, which must be viewed in the context of renewed financial difficulties faced by SIS in the spring of 1921. At the end of March 1921, Morton reacted with surprising violence to a request from Maclaren for some stamps, writing at length about the problems such requests caused the SIS paymaster, particularly if the money were not sent in advance. A somewhat sourly repentant letter from Maclaren, enclosing a cheque for £1, elicited an apology from Morton – 'sorry if I made an idiot of myself' – but a false note had been struck. Although further exchanges in early April seemed normal, at the end of the month Maclaren was told by Bertie Maw, who had worked for SIS in Bucharest during the war and had recently joined Production, that he, not Morton, would be his SIS contact in future, as Morton himself confirmed in a letter of 30 April:

> This is partly because I am going away for a few days and partly because I have taken on rather more than I can manage at present. I write this in case you should think your last letters to me have sent me into a padded cell at Hanwell. I am still in the office and propose remaining here until fired out, which, under the present course of events, may not be very long.

Maclaren, not surprisingly, was alarmed by this letter, replying on 15 May that on receiving Maw's letter he had:

> thought thoughts but certainly nothing like the ones you suggest . . . I do not like the last two lines of your letter and hope for all our sakes that you are absolutely wrong in supposing that to be the case. Wishing you the best of luck.

During May and early June Maclaren reported to Maw, telling him that one of his agents, codenamed 'Sparkling', had been arrested and that he himself was under suspicion. Then, on 16 June, Maclaren wrote again to Morton, who replied on 1 July; it was Maw, however, who informed an angry Maclaren at the end of the month that the SIS station in Warsaw was to be closed down as the result of an earlier turf war between Marshall and the British Legation. Though his employment with SIS terminated officially in August 1921, Maclaren remained in business in Warsaw and in periodic contact with Maw and Morton until 1924.

Meanwhile, Morton had also been dealing with the reports submitted from Vladimir Orlov in Berlin. Armed with a blueprint for an intelligence network based on Berlin with contacts throughout Europe, Orlov, now with the SIS designation Z/51, had left Paris at the end of 1920 to set up an office in Berlin (housed and financed by the German *Polizeipräsidium*). As agreed with Cumming when the latter had handed over £500 in August 1920, the intelligence Orlov collected was his to dispose of, but copies were to be passed to SIS (who later learned that the German authorities, too, demanded copies in return for their facilities). By mid-1921 he was supplying regular reports on Bolshevik activity outside Russia, Soviet internal affairs and Russian Monarchist activities: General Wrangel, who was also involved in the establishment of Orlov's intelligence office, arranged for him to receive copies of all reports by White Russian military attachés. At first Orlov's product was rated highly by SIS who, according to one report, subsidised Orlov's bureau to the tune of £5,000 per year. Orlov's knowledge and experience, particularly of Russian personalities, was encyclopaedic (after all, he had worked for many of them). When in February 1921, for example, he asked SIS for permission to travel to Constantinople to make further arrangements for acquiring information, Morton assured him that 'his movements are absolutely his own affair, and that we give him the freest hand possible in all matters, including the matter of funds placed at his disposal so long as those funds go on'.

Only a few months later, however, Morton was complaining that Orlov's reports contained 'shoals of long political appreciations of the kind we don't want in addition to the real meat', and there was a growing suspicion that the information he provided was drawn from his own knowledge and from casual contacts, rather than from secret sources. In addition, Orlov's increasingly close relationship with Russian Monarchist organisations in Paris and other dubious contacts (his chief agent in Berlin was known to work for the *Cheka*) reduced his credibility with SIS. They also suspected that some of the material he supplied was produced by a well-known forger, Bernhard von Uexkull, who ran a political news bureau, *Ost Information*, known to have links with German Intelligence and the powerful industrialist Hugo Stinnes.[66] When Orlov reported on the activities of this 'band of adventurers' in May 1921, commenting that the demand for forged Soviet documents was so good that 'several enterprising people are making a good living out of them', SIS wondered whether Orlov was not himself one of these enterprising people, and instituted elaborate enquiries (including stealing some documents from *Ost Information* to check against Orlov's productions). A detailed report received from Prague in December 1921 was not reassuring, concluding that it was 'impossible for anyone but the fully initiated' to tell what were genuine and what were fakes.

In 1921–22, however, Orlov had supplied a steady stream of useful information, and when SIS decided to sever their connection with him in January 1923 Maclaren was not the only one who complained that Orlov's information was 'too good to lose'. Morton's view was that much better and more reliable material was now being received from other sources, such as Riga (some of whose material, was, however, later shown to have originated with Orlov), Paris and the SIS station in Berlin. Orlov, he complained, never divulged his sources or the provenance of the documents he supplied, and was suspected of selling the same document to all his paymasters. Nevertheless, contact was maintained for some time after Orlov ceased to receive payment from SIS and, as the Zinoviev Letter affair was to show, his ongoing activities in Berlin made it impossible to sever the link entirely.

Finally, what of Reilly, who had admitted to Morton in November 1920 that he had 'not had a minute's time for anything outside Russian affairs'? He remained deeply involved with Savinkov and his anti-Bolshevik schemes throughout 1921, thereby incurring the displeasure of Morton and Cumming, who had no wish for SIS to be embroiled in such conspiracies. When Savinkov was banned from basing his operations in Poland under the terms of the Soviet-Polish peace treaty in March 1921, and shifted his base to Prague, Reilly accompanied him.[67] Reilly's arrangements later that year to bring Savinkov to London, submitting in advance a long report that he wished copied to the Prime Minister's private secretary, Rex Leeper, and to Winston Churchill, further alienated not just SIS but the FO as well.[68] In April 1921 Reilly had also met Spears (who described him as 'rather seedy but really quite nice'[69]), who was already in close contact with Savinkov. At Reilly's urging Spears entered into a number of more or less hopeless business ventures with him, visiting Prague in July 1921 to discuss the production of radium with the Czech Finance Ministry. By August 1922, however, Spears too had become disillusioned with Reilly's methods and broken contact.[70]

It is less clear if and when Morton himself severed contact with Reilly. Although by the end of 1921 Reilly had no further official connection with SIS, and Cumming certainly wanted nothing more to do with him, the evidence indicates some continuing informal contact. Reilly was certainly not welcome at Headquarters: as he wrote to Maw of Production section on 23 January 1922, 'Morton may perhaps have told you just now it is healthier for me to keep away for a while'. A minute from Morton to Maw of 31 January, however, advising him on terms of a reply to a request from Vienna as to Reilly's reliability, sheds an interesting light both on their relationship and on Morton himself:

> Reilly is not a member of our office and does not serve C in that he is not receiving any pay from us. He worked at one time during the war in Russia for C's organisation and is now undoubtedly of a certain use to us. We do not altogether know what to make of him. There is no doubt that Reilly is a political intriguer of no mean class, and therefore it is infinitely better for us to keep in with him, whereby he tells us a great deal of what he is doing, than to quarrel with him when we should hear nothing of his activities . . . he is at the moment Boris Savinkoff's right hand man. In fact, some people might almost say he is Boris Savinkoff. As such he has undoubted importance. In addition to the above, Reilly is of course a very clever man, indeed with means of finding out information all over the world. Whatever may be Reilly's faults, I personally would stake my reputation that he is not anti-British, at the moment at any rate, and never has been. He is an astute commercial man out for himself, and really genuinely hates the Bolsheviks. That is about all one can say of him.

This minute says rather a lot about Morton and is an early example of a style of writing that he was to adopt, with increasing skill, throughout his career. It makes clear that Morton, as a loyal representative of the organisation, adopts an entirely proper (and detached) attitude to the subject in hand ('Reilly is not a member of our office . . . we do not altogether know what to make of him'), and that any interest in Reilly is purely professional ('it is infinitely better for us to keep in with him . . . he has undoubted importance'); it implies a degree of inside information ('he tells us a great deal of what he is doing . . . a very clever man, with means of finding out information all over the world') and invites respect for the writer's superior judgement ('I personally would stake my reputation' . . .); it concludes by implying that if all comes to grief, it will not be the fault of the writer who has done his best to warn/inform/deter ('That is about all one can say of him'). Morton became a past master at reporting events or conversations in which he had been personally involved – particularly when there were unfortunate or damaging consequences – in such a way as to indicate that responsibility could not conceivably be attributed to him; that he had given due warning but had not been heeded; or (in sorrow rather than anger) that the capricious judgement of others could not be foreseen.

The above constitutes an observation rather than a condemnation. Morton did not shirk responsibility in his professional life, and though he certainly made mistakes, he was an acute observer who learned quickly, and acquired a well-deserved reputation as an 'operator' with a good deal of common sense, much given to dispensing good advice even if much of it was, inevitably, ignored or rejected. He valued efficiency and was impatient of disorder. Morton also had the professional soldier's talent for keeping his head down and out of the line of fire, and a healthy instinct for self-preservation. If a bad situation could not be improved, he distanced himself from it (the use of third person was always indicative) and was disinclined to accept blame for what he regarded as the mistakes of others. Essentially a loner, he did not unburden himself to others, except in the Confessional, and sought no sympathy. If the buck was passing, he did not intend it to stop with him.

These were not characteristics that inspired popularity, and relations with his SIS colleagues, if generally cordial, do not seem to have been close. This may, however, have been more his doing than theirs. An exchange of correspondence in early 1921 with Major W.L. Woollcombe, who joined SIS from the War Office in February of that year, is revealing in this respect. As a postscript to a letter of 1 January 1921 to Woollcombe concerning the latter's starting date, Morton remarked in jocular fashion that Woollcombe and his wife had 'cut him dead' when they passed him near Hyde Park underground station the previous Sunday: 'possibly you did not recognise me in a top hat, and thought I was either a Member of Parliament or a War Profiteer!' Woollcombe, apologising for his rudeness in a letter of 5 January, expressed the hope that Morton would visit him and his wife, later extending a specific invitation to dinner ('we wd. be delighted to see your wife too . . .'). Morton however, quickly withdrew into his shell: he was, he said, just about to take a week's leave and would be out of town on the appointed date. Few examples of such invitations survive: all were declined. Morton preferred to do his socialising in an all-male environment, usually his club.

As the exchanges with Maclaren show, Morton clearly experienced some sort of crisis, personal and professional, in 1921. No further evidence has been found to explain what happened to him, for how long (or to where) he went away, or whether there really was any serious prospect of his leaving SIS. SIS's financial crisis, however, is well documented. On 21 February Otto Niemeyer of the Treasury had warned his Permanent Secretary, Sir Warren Fisher,[71] that the estimate of £475,000 for the Secret Service vote in 1921/22 'does not look at all pretty' and was bound to be challenged by the Financial Secretary, making it 'almost impossible . . . to maintain the suppression of detailed information about the expenditure'. He recommended revising the estimate down to £300,000 and establishing a committee to consider the whole question of secret service expenditure. The Chancellor of the Exchequer, Austen Chamberlain, approved Fisher's recommendation on this basis, and the Cabinet on 22 March 1921 reconvened the Secret Service Committee, this time comprising Fisher, Sir Eyre Crowe[72] (who had replaced Hardinge as Permanent Under Secretary at the Foreign Office) and Hankey. It met first on 27 May 1921 and held four further meetings in May and June, issuing its report on 27 July.[73] Cumming was summoned to the third meeting on 2 June, also attending a separate meeting with Crowe and the Director of Naval Intelligence, Rear-Admiral Hugh Sinclair, on 9 June.

Although, as in 1919, the Committee did not direct its strongest criticism at SIS – Basil Thomson's Directorate of Intelligence and the War Office, who would 'admit no diminution of their demands', bore the brunt – all branches of the Intelligence establishment were put under severe pressure to cut back. Cumming explained that SIS supplied information to the Admiralty, War Office, Air Ministry, Colonial and Foreign Offices, Department of Overseas Trade and to the India Office (sharing some agents with Indian Political Intelligence), as well as to Sir Basil Thomson. Nevertheless, he volunteered 'by suppressing certain branches' to make savings which would reduce his expenditure from £125,000 to £87,500, with the possibility of a further £10,000 reduction in the following year. He added that:

> Further economies would be facilitated if he were in a position to assure continuity of employment to the members of his staff who felt considerable uncertainty about the future.

At that time, job security in SIS was non-existent: contracts were unknown, and both officers and clerical staff were employed on the understanding that they could be dismissed at short notice with no financial compensation. Although the Committee thought it would be difficult to address the problem, Crowe agreed to 'consider the possibility of giving some limited assurance to the senior officers concerned'. Though Cumming did not, of course, give details, his statement raises the possibility that Morton might have been one of the 'senior officers'; perhaps after two years in the job, at the same salary, he may have been concerned about his future. No details were given, though Morton did receive a pay rise from £884 per annum to £900 in October 1921.

The Secret Service Committee were again sympathetic to Cumming and to SIS, particularly when other departments, such as the Admiralty, stressed their dependence on his secret intelligence. Their report stated that they had been 'unable to discover any point at which the secret intelligence organisation encroaches upon, or is encroached upon, by any other', and stated that they had found no signs of culpable extravagance or mismanagement. Most of their recommended economies were found from military intelligence, from transferring certain activities to the public vote, and from abolishing Thomson's Directorate (established only two years before), whose work was considered to overlap too far with that of the police and MI5. The record does not make clear exactly what cut SIS was required to bear, but as the reduced overall estimate of £300,000 stood, some economies must have been necessary.

Nevertheless, the Committee's recommendations constituted in some sense a reprieve, and Morton's letter of 1 July 1921 to Maclaren is full of relief, though whether on his own or SIS's behalf is unclear:

> Our stocks are beginning to rise to a degree which I would hardly every have thought possible. I gather that the new chiefs of ZP [the Foreign Office] are making people there work very hard and have successfully pointed out that the attitude of that office, namely, that they know everything and nobody could help them at all is absurd. Anyhow they have at last begun to study to some small extent at any rate and have discovered that we are the only people they are in touch with who can produce such details as they need. For the moment therefore our stocks are probably high all round and things are moving. I feel like touching wood as this office goes up and down to such a remarkable degree.

An interesting light on Morton's reference to a 'new' attitude on the part of the Foreign Office is shed by a circular letter sent out in February 1921 by the PUS, Crowe, to all British Embassies and Legations in Europe. Crowe pointed out that the postwar re-establishment of the barriers between diplomacy and Secret Service, undermined during the recent War, seemed to be causing some difficulties. Some of Her Majesty's Representatives abroad, he said, appeared to harbour 'a feeling of jealousy and suspicion regarding what may be going on behind their backs', impeding the mutually beneficial exchange of information. This suspicion, Crowe assured them, was unnecessary:

> Today the old type of Secret Service has disappeared and melodrama has given place to a more sober style of enquiry from which the diplomat need no longer, as he was very properly required to do before, withdraw the hem of his garment. It is largely concerned with subterranean revolutionary movements and individuals, and instead of spying on the military defences of individual countries, devotes itself principally to detecting tendencies subversive of the established order of things, irrespective of whether these are directed against the United Kingdom or are International in character. Enquiries are greatly assisted by the fact that in most countries our Passport Control officer is in direct communication with the Chief of Police, for the purpose of his ordinary and ostensible duties; for it is through the Passport Control Officer that

agents' reports are forwarded to headquarters, and in the course of his enquiries about individuals he can occasionally pick up useful pieces of general intelligence.

Crowe said that he had already taken steps to establish closer contact between the Secret Service and Foreign Office Heads of Department; now he wanted to extend that cooperation overseas, so that the two services felt free to exchange views on the spot. With Curzon's approval, he now asked every diplomatic representative to nominate a senior member of his staff who would discuss with the PCO the secret information the latter received (other than naval or military information), and be free to ask for more detail if required. The Head of Mission would then be free to utilise such information in his official despatches. It is hard to believe that Crowe's vision of diplomats and SIS representatives freely comparing notes was implemented successfully at many overseas Posts; but these instructions may have contributed to a greater degree of mutual regard. In any case, by mid-1921 Morton clearly felt that the FO was now treating SIS in London with increased respect; he also appears to have overcome his own personal demons.

Although by July 1921 Morton was back in the Production saddle, his position in SIS, though outwardly secure, seems to have undergone some subtle change during the second half of the year. It may be merely because he now had more staff to whom to delegate (Maw now conducted much of the Production correspondence); possibly, also, because of the uncertainties created by the financial situation in 1921; he may also have felt that his upward progress through the organisation was insufficiently swift. Whatever the reason, his relations with his Chief (whose own health seems to have suffered during 1921–22)[74] seem to have deteriorated. In diary entries for 11 and 12 January 1922 Cumming expressed himself forcefully about what he called 'the influence constantly brought by this officer to set me against my superiors':

Maj. M. came in to protest against the letters sent by Treasur[er] to all P.C. branches notifying them of the reductions ordered. He said that the sending of these without reference to him was another proof that the Paym[r] was 'inefficient'. I declined to accept this criticism as not being true or any part of his business & reminded him that he had taken the opportunity when I was sick [to] issue 3 long memos on procedure to the office which he had not troubled to submit to me for approval nor even to show to me on my return to work. His manner though cautiously correct as to words was very hostile & to that extent objectionable & he criticises freely & improperly both his superiors & mine, so that I can not but believe that he is working not with & for me but against me. He is hardworking & zealous but has formed the unfortunate opinion that he is the real vital spark of the organisation which only began to function when he came here & that therefore his opinion ought to be accepted & acted upon without question. I think my illness raised a hope that he might soon be able to take charge of the office & this has upset his balance.[75]

A few weeks later, discussing the choice of a successor as 'C' with Nevile Bland of the Foreign Office, Cumming ruled out Morton's candidature, writing later that Bland said neither 'DM' nor 'SM' would be acceptable (the latter apparently a reference to Menzies, interestingly already in the frame though not yet a full SIS officer).[76] We should not read too much into Cumming's jottings. No doubt Morton had been taking too much upon himself, and irritated his Chief. Equally, Cumming's intensely personal and private style of leadership must have seemed destabilising to his ambitious subordinate. Nevertheless, the two continued to work together closely until Cumming's death in June 1923, and whatever the state of Morton's mind or of his relationship with Cumming, there is no doubt that he remained 'hardworking and zealous'.

While considerable detail has been uncovered about Morton's professional life between 1919 and 1922, nothing has been found indicative of his home life with his family, his social habits or leisure activities. There is no reason to suppose he led a secluded life (although he certainly worked long hours), but whatever company he kept, he kept to himself. Nor is there any evidence during these years of contact with Winston Churchill, although in view of their previous friendship (and Churchill's close interest both in Intelligence matters and in Bolshevism) it seems likely that they continued at least to correspond during this period, and probably to meet.[77] Always a private person, with his new career Morton had even more reason to maintain the habit of secrecy. As the next chapter will show, however, in pursuit of his professional activities he had made a number of acquaintances, if not friends, who were to lead him in a number of unexpected, and even eccentric, directions.

4

THE OCCULT OCTOPUS,*
1923–26

During his first three years in SIS, Morton had directed his energies towards learning the Intelligence trade, while endeavouring to stamp his personal and administrative imprint upon the SIS organisation itself. In the first of these objectives he was successful in so far as was possible in a small agency dominated by the personality of its Chief, who was not given to consultation or informing his Headquarters colleagues of decisions in advance. Morton's role, in Cumming's judgement if not his own, was to implement those decisions and direct the follow-through, as in the case of the fact-finding mission on which Cumming despatched Reilly, Dukes, Maclaren and Orlov in 1920. When Cumming changed his mind, or decided that an agent had outlived his usefulness, it was also Morton's job to pick up the pieces. Morton had rather more room for manoeuvre in administrative matters (in which Cumming took only spasmodic interest), and had some success in instituting new procedures and reforms, though his attempts to take the organisational reins in his own hands led to some friction with his Chief.

By the end of 1922, however, the situation was changing in a way that was to affect the rest of Morton's SIS career. Cumming, whose health had been deteriorating for some time, decided to retire, and in January 1923 Rear-Admiral Hugh Sinclair ('Quex'), the former Director of Naval Intelligence, was chosen to succeed him, taking over on Cumming's death in June 1923.[1] Sinclair and Morton already knew one another, and got on well; his advent did not, however, herald any advancement to Morton's career. Like Cumming, Sinclair regarded Menzies, rather than Morton, as his informal deputy. It seems that both Cumming and Sinclair saw Morton as a useful and dynamic officer, but lacking, perhaps, the steadiness of judgement and political sensitivity essential to the running of an organisation that relied upon discretion and secrecy, and was always vulnerable to Whitehall intrigues and cost-cutting exercises. One might argue that Morton, under the shadow of two highly idiosyncratic Chiefs, never had the chance to prove his true worth; it is undeniable, however, that he could not be relied on not to upset people, and that unlike other colleagues such as Menzies, he was disinclined to keep his head down and his mouth shut.

* A phrase coined by Sidney Reilly to denote what might today be called global capitalism.

It seems likely that Morton was well aware of these internal dynamics, though it is impossible to know whether he recognised in himself those characteristics that inhibited his ambition. Though he did not relinquish that ambition, he determined to carve out a niche for himself by expanding his activities as 'Production' into more widely-cast and less familiar sources of information on Soviet Russia and Germany. Whether this was a deliberate decision on his part, or influenced by the friendships and contacts he made at this time, is difficult to say. What is clear is that from late 1922 onwards Morton began to build up a network of domestic contacts, in official and non-official circles, to complement SIS's overseas sources; thereby involving himself in some of the more esoteric and eccentric movements prevalent in public life in the 1920s.

While his professional activities and connections cast a certain light on Morton's personality, information on his personal life at this period is scant. There was, however, one important development. In 1923 he bought a house, Earlylands, at Crockham Hill near Westerham in Kent: less than three miles from Chartwell Manor, which Churchill had bought in the summer of 1922 for £5,000.[2] Earlylands was (and is) a small but picturesque house, long but shallow, with extensive grounds enjoying panoramic views over the Weald of Kent, though the property is well shielded by trees. A brick inscribed 'D.M. 1923' on the right of the original doorway seems to indicate that Morton added an extension as soon as he had bought the house, probably to allow for the accommodation of a modest residential staff. The garden now encompasses thirteen acres but was at that time even larger. Morton was to become a keen gardener, establishing copses and waterways, and even planting a vineyard, making, bottling (and drinking) his own wine.

Morton's purchase of a house so close to Chartwell must be more than coincidence. In later life he used to claim that Churchill had bought Chartwell after his own purchase of Earlylands. This is not correct, although it is possible that Morton had already decided to move to the area, or even selected the house, before Churchill's decision to buy Chartwell; it is certainly true that Morton bought Earlylands before Churchill ever spent a night at Chartwell, since the extensive renovations to the latter property took until 1924. Morton himself appears on the electoral register for Crockham Hill from the autumn of 1924. It is impossible to be sure of the chronology. There seems little doubt, however, that from the mid-1920s onwards Morton was a regular visitor to Chartwell, which was within easy, and scenic, walking distance of Earlylands: to play tennis, to dine, to drink and talk after dinner, and to walk the estate with Churchill. In turn, Churchill may have visited Earlylands, though local legend, according to which the two men used to sit talking in the garden, occasionally throwing an empty bottle into the well that stands outside the front door, seems somewhat fanciful.[3] Neither man recorded their discussions at this period, and certainly not whether they discussed Intelligence-related matters. It does not seem presumptuous, however, to assume that their shared antipathy to Bolshevism would have provided absorbing subject matter for their walks on the Chartwell estate, and their after dinner conversations that went on long into the night.

We should not get carried away by this vision of a confidential rural idyll. Neither Churchill nor Morton can have spent much time in Kent at this period: as Chancellor of the Exchequer and a key member of Stanley Baldwin's government from November 1924, Churchill was kept in London most of the time, as indeed was Morton, working long hours in SIS. Morton still spent most of his time, at least during the working week, with his parents at Beaufort Gardens, where his mother maintained a regime of benevolent domination through what the family have called 'decent formal structures'. Although it might have been expected that a bachelor in his thirties (Morton was thirty-two in 1923) would have taken London rooms of his own, it was understood that Edith, whose own childhood had been marked by loss, wished her only son to live at home. There he was well looked after, but there were limits to his independence: he was never given his own door key, although a servant would stay up to let him in at any hour. Meanwhile his mother's maid, the faithful 'West' (who had been a seamstress in the Royal Household under Queen Mary), fussed over his health and welfare: according to the family, 'West would have breathed for Desmond if she could'. (She later moved to Earlylands and, with Morton, to Kew Green, remaining in his service until her death.)

It all sounds rather claustrophobic, but it is unlikely that Morton spent a great deal of time in the house. He worked long hours, and rarely took holidays. In later life he is said to have been fond of the ballet, opera and concerts, and it is possible that these interests were developed in the 1920s. Nor is there any evidence of close friendships. Indeed, the only reference found to any form of personal contact, outside the professional sphere and his parental home, is to his visiting at boarding school Brian (later Sir Brian) Franks,[4] son of Morton's cousin, May Franks, the widowed daughter of Gerald Morton who became Hugh Elles's second wife in September 1923. Writing to R.W. Thompson in 1976, Sir Brian Franks recalled with pleasure these visits, and his enduring (rather than close) friendship with Desmond:

> He was always delightful & always amusing – full of anecdotes and fun.
> Never once did he give me an inkling of his job between the wars.[5]

The scope of the current chapter, from 1923 to 1926, covers roughly the period between the death of Cumming and the death, in 1926, of Sir George Makgill,[6] one of Morton's principal contacts with the world of the 'Occult Octopus'. This was a period that saw a considerable upsurge in Bolshevik activities directed against the UK, both in propaganda and in espionage, and consequently the expansion of SIS operations to gather intelligence on those activities. It has become fashionable to dismiss widespread fears of a 'Red Menace' during the 1920s as at best over-reaction, and at worst paranoia on the part of the British Establishment. Yet the fears of politicians, military commanders and Intelligence officers were not ill-founded, even if those authorities charged with responsibility for counter-subversion, such as MI5, could at times react to the threat of internal dissent in a way that was exaggerated and even hysterical. There was an active and aggressive campaign of Bolshevik propaganda, subversion and espionage, directed against the British Government and its institutions, carried on both overtly and covertly in the UK and from continental Europe.

The signature of the Anglo-Soviet Trade Agreement in March 1921 had appeared to herald a period of somewhat improved bilateral relations, with increased opportunities for information gathering through the reopening of diplomatic and other overt channels into the Soviet Union. By the spring of 1922, however, the Comintern (the Third Communist International, the Soviet body responsible for overseas propaganda) was supporting revolutionary movements in the West with renewed vigour, including in Britain and, throughout the British Empire. Both SIS and the Government Code and Cypher School (GC&CS) were supplying the Foreign Office with evidence of subversive activities undertaken by members of the Soviet Trade Delegation. Within Russia itself, a series of what Mr. Hodgson, head of the British Commercial Mission in Moscow, called 'executions and insults',[7] increased the indignation and frustration felt by Lord Curzon and many of his Cabinet colleagues. This culminated in the 'Curzon ultimatum' of May 1923 to the Soviet Government, threatening to terminate the Trade Agreement – and compromising British cryptographic operations, not for the last time, by referring openly to the interception of Russian traffic.[8] Though rupture was at that point avoided, and the advent of the first Labour Government in Britain in January 1924 and its early *de jure* recognition of the Soviet Union again heralded a period of partial and superficial rapprochement, the illusory nature of any 'improvement' in Soviet behaviour became clear during the Zinoviev Letter affair in 1924, and further evidence of subversive activities continued to emerge during 1925 and 1926.

During this period Morton's work continued to focus principally on the efforts of the Bolshevik regime to spread world revolution, aided or opposed by various countries, organisations, interest groups and individuals. In counterpoint to this struggle, and providing a rich potential source of information to SIS, were the efforts of what was often called 'international capital', representing business interests on every level from government downwards, to combat the subversive influence of Bolshevism. To complicate further an already complex picture, some foreign governments (notably that of Germany) and industrial interests were discovered to be supporting both Bolshevik and anti-Bolshevik activities at the same time. These pervasive links between domestic and foreign commercial interests blurred the jurisdictional boundaries within the British Intelligence establishment. So, for example, SIS might receive valuable information from overseas sources about plans by an international organisation to foster industrial unrest in a British industry; while information from British businessmen might cast valuable light upon foreign espionage activities overseas. Cross-fertilisation between the agencies enabled a large body of useful evidence against Bolshevik and other targets to be compiled, and facilitated a number of successful operations. Morton was in regular correspondence with his counterparts in the domestic agencies, exchanging information of mutual interest, though each agency tended to pursue its own lines of investigation, inevitably leading to confusion.

To supply the necessary Intelligence context to these developments, this chapter begins with a description of SIS in 1923, an organisation that, like Morton's role, had evolved since 1919, surviving further attempts to cut its budget and limit its activities. The second section, 'Stanley and Fyfe', takes its name from the aliases adopted by Morton and Makgill in their correspondence, both with each other and with the network of informants they used, for their separate and joint purposes, to supply information on Bolshevik activities, in Britain or overseas, directed from within the UK or from abroad. Finally, the political maelstrom of the Zinoviev Letter affair, connected squarely to the Occult Octopus, illustrates only too clearly the potential results of confusion between domestic and foreign intelligence-gathering, and of a clash of conflicting vested interests.

SIS in 1923

Although SIS had emerged intact, if with a reduced budget, from the scrutiny of the Secret Service Committee in 1921,[9] the financial horizon soon darkened again. Between December 1921 and February 1922 the Geddes Committee on National Expenditure, appointed in August 1921, produced a series of reports recommending wide-ranging cuts in defence spending,[10] and eliciting howls of protest from the Service departments. The Secret Service budgets were not neglected in the attack: the Geddes Committee took the view that there was scope for a reduction in the 1922–23 estimates from £200,000 to £180,000, since secret operations in Ireland were surely unnecessary in view of the Anglo-Irish Treaty in 1921, and Basil Thomson's resource-intensive Directorate of Home Intelligence had been wound up. The Treasury thought this fair:

> it is essential that economies should be effected on Secret Service as on other Services, and . . . it is not reasonable to ask that every risk should be guarded against . . . It is not reasonable to maintain 3½ years after the Armistice an organisation far more elaborate than was found sufficient in pre-war days.[11]

Out of the £180,000 the FO would be allotted £147,300, of which £65,000 would go to SIS, rather than the £100,000 originally proposed. Before the Cabinet had a chance to consider these proposals, however, Churchill (who chaired a committee appointed to examine the Geddes defence proposals), leapt to SIS's defence, arguing that War Office requirements could not possibly be met by a grant of less than £125,000:

> Even with the £125,000 grant it was not possible to maintain a SIS service in all countries . . . Though war no longer exists the situations all

over the world are so complex that greater vigilance on the part of SIS is required than in 1914. If the grant is reduced to £65,000 it means that the whole of the system will have to be re-cast, and it will happen that the spade work already put in will be completely lost and the money previously spent on it thus wasted. It is considered vital that the money available for SIS should remain constant: if agents get the idea that they may be thrown over at any moment, we cannot expect to find them, while to confine SIS activities to certain limited areas only so impairs the general efficiency and reliability of the SIS as to render it to a large extent ineffective.[12]

Cumming must have briefed Churchill in the preparation of his memorandum, supplying the figures set out in two tables appended to it, spelling out the regional implications of a £150,000 grant[13] and one of £65,000: the latter figure would mean reductions of 33 per cent at Headquarters, 40 per cent in the Near East, 33 per cent in Russia, 66 per cent in Germany and 90 per cent in Holland, while SIS branches in twenty-three countries – including those such as Latvia, Lithuania and Poland, supplying information on the Soviet Union – would have to be closed. In addition, all SIS counter-espionage work on behalf of MI5, the Department of Overseas Trade and the Colonial Office would have to be wound up.

The opposing views of the Treasury and War Office were considered on 20 February 1922 at a conference chaired by the Prime Minister: among the six other Ministers present were the Chancellor of the Exchequer, Sir Robert Horne, Churchill, who had changed jobs on 13 February 1922 and was now Secretary of State for the Colonies, and his successor as Secretary of State for War (but not Air), Sir Laming Worthington-Evans. Also present were Fisher and Niemeyer of the Treasury. Hankey's note of the conclusions of the conference stated that in the course of discussion the view was expressed that:

> the country got an inadequate return for expenditure on [the Secret] Service, that it would be preferable to spend the money on reliable infor-mation as to the economic, financial and industrial conditions in countries like Germany; that other and less elaborate and costly means of obtaining intelligence were available and that in any case the present system involved a certain amount of waste and overlapping.[14]

The conference agreed that the aggregate amount to be inserted in the 1922–23 estimates for Secret Service should be £200,000, and that the Committee on Secret Service that had examined the question in 1921 (ie, Fisher, Hankey and Crowe – the 'three biggest guns in Whitehall, without whose support no inde-pendent intelligence service could hope to survive'[15]) should be reconstituted and asked to report to the Cabinet on the best way to allocate this sum, taking into account what essential services would have to abandoned or drastically curtailed.[16] The Committee met three times, on 4, 24 and 27 March 1922: at the second meeting, attended by Cumming and by Menzies (the latter representing the War Office), the possible effect on SIS of a grant of £65,000, £85,000 and £150,000 was discussed. Cumming explained that £65,000 would also mean dismissing two agents paid from Headquarters, and abolishing the Political Section. Menzies gave him strong support, warning that even if the £85,000 figure were agreed, it would mean drawing on the Contingency Fund to pay the salaries of officers operating in the Rhine district, and that SIS services would be insufficient for safety both in the Near East and in respect of the USA (thought to have its own 'good espionage service in Great Britain'), where the Air Ministry and Admiralty felt it extremely important to 'keep a close watch on naval and aeronautical developments'.[17]

It is clear from the minutes (which carry a hint of backstairs horse-trading) that the Committee was again well-disposed towards Cumming, and inclined to squeeze other departments to increase SIS's portion, rather than to enforce cuts that on any interpretation were presented as swingeing. In their report of 4 April 1922, they announced that their investigations had had two objects in view, the first being 'to augment so far as might be requisite the sum designated to foreign intelligence', and the second to raise the reserve fund to a more satisfactory level. Between them the Home Office, Irish Office and War Office were willing to make reductions that enabled the release of £13,700 for re-allocation: the Committee recommended that £5,000 of this should be added to foreign intelligence funds, bringing them up to £90,000:

> we are satisfied that for £90,000 a foreign intelligence organisation can
> be provided which, while necessarily of a less elaborate character, will
> nevertheless cover all the countries contemplated under the higher scale
> of expenditure, and will involve neither the abandonment, nor unduly
> drastic curtailment, of any essential services.[18]

SIS had again escaped more lightly than it might have done, and Cumming must have been moderately satisfied with this result, losing £10,000 from his original estimate rather than £35,000. The exercise had also underlined the value of Menzies as an authoritative advocate for SIS: his lengthy statement on the importance of maintaining the level of SIS activity, though made as a representative of the War Office, made a considerable impression on the Committee, leading Fisher to speak encouragingly in SIS's favour: 'From Lt-Colonel Menzies' statement it certainly appeared that £90,000 would be a safer figure than £85,000.' Immediately afterwards Fisher referred to the 'generally accepted theory that "C" should have charge of all operations in foreign countries', and invited Cumming to put forward a concrete proposal for offering security of tenure to his principal agents, a principle which the Committee 'fully approved'.[19] Equally, the willingness of the Home Office and other departments to make cuts so that SIS could have more was representative of an increasing understanding in government of C's difficulties, and an acceptance that SIS was 'an essential part of the national intelligence machine'.

Nevertheless, the first quarter of 1922, like that of 1921, had been one of considerable uncertainty for SIS. There is no evidence to suggest, however, that Morton felt the same sense of personal crisis and threat that he had apparently experienced the previous year. He was busy and active, building up new contacts at home and overseas. There were now ten staff in Production section under his direction, including Bertie Maw, and the faithful Miss Gladys Gwynne, who was to serve as Morton's personal secretary through the Second World War and beyond. In August 1922 a new recruit, Captain Humphrey Plowden, joined Production at a salary of £700 per annum. By 1923, there were thirteen staff in Production and eight in the Political section, under Woollcombe, with smaller military, naval and aviation sections; the number of typists, noted as six in 1922, had dropped to four, earning between £16 and £19 per month. Morton himself had received a salary increase on 1 October 1922 to £1,000 per annum, a very respectable amount at that time (about £35,300 at current values): when Menzies joined the Military section in April 1923 his salary was only £400 per annum, although Major Valentine Vivian,[20] who joined SIS in 1923 from the Indian Police and spent a few months in Production before going to Cologne, was given a starting salary of £1,000. In fact, after these early increases Morton's salary, like that of other senior staff, remained at the same level until the 1930s. C's own salary remained at £1,250 per annum throughout the 1920s, but by 1930 had risen to £2,000 (about £82,000 in current values), paid quarterly in £100 notes.

During 1922-23 SIS also assumed full control over the Passport Control system, hitherto formally under Foreign Office direction but supervised by a committee including Home Office and Intelligence representatives.[21] The FO's Passport Control Department, run by Major Herbert Spencer, already operated out of SIS, and its full integration represented not only a welcome addition to Headquarters staff that was not included in the much-disputed budget estimates, but also a recognition that Passport Control Officer (PCO) cover was often the safest and most effective for SIS representatives in the field. A PCO attached to an Embassy or Consulate could report and check information without inter-ference from the local authorities, with the benefits of a secure place to store records and a regular and safe means of communication with SIS Headquarters. As Marshall and Maclaren had found in Poland,[22] lack of these facilities not only inhibited their activities but made them vulnerable to suspicion and even arrest by the host authorities.

From the Foreign Office point of view, the system also enabled diplomatic missions to keep a close eye on the activities of SIS representatives and on what they were reporting to London. On relinquishing control of the service to SIS, the FO ruled that one member of each mission should be designated to act as liaison with the SIS representative, with the aim both of creating better mutual understanding and cooperation, and of 'increasing the value' of SIS reports by allowing diplomatic representatives on the spot to comment or act on them before they were despatched to SIS Headquarters. Although the usefulness of PCO cover diminished as the 1920s progressed and more countries relaxed their visa requirements, it continued to be the primary cover used by SIS in the field for many years, despite the disadvantages from a security angle of its universal employment, and periodic attempts to find an alternative.

In taking up the post of Chief of SIS in June 1923, Sinclair perpetuated Cumming's tradition of dominating the Service with a highly personal style.[23] Like Cumming, he disdained bureaucracy and tended to keep a close personal hand on all aspects of SIS work, including engaging in direct correspondence with representatives in the field. According to one SIS commentator, Sinclair was:

> a thoroughly unorthodox and somewhat arbitrary commander. His simple and, in a way, logical method of tackling any emergency was to select whichever officer he considered at the time best equipped to deal with the situation and country in question, regardless of whether the officer concerned was in any way responsible for that particular matter or area.

A good impression of his management style is given by the record of a meeting he convened of SIS Regional 'Inspectors' (those directing the activities of a number of SIS representatives in a certain area) on 11 January 1924, six months after becoming Chief. He was not, he said, satisfied with the Inspectors' performance. Their posts had been 'specially created in order to relieve the pressure of work on Headquarters, and to prevent information of little or no importance being forwarded'. They were supposed to visit their Representatives frequently, offering advice and assistance, urging them to devise new ideas for obtaining 'really inside information'; they should also be communicating regularly with each other. As C's direct Representatives abroad, 'Commanders in Chief of their respective areas', they enjoyed 'the most complete freedom of action' and 'his complete support in any action which they might think fit to take, provided it was for the good of the Service'.

Despite this, they seemed reluctant to act. In particular, he felt that they were neglecting one of their most important duties:

> to prepare a scheme for maintaining their services and communications in their respective areas, in the event of war. It was explained that it was desired to maintain a nucleus organisation in each country which bordered on any of those which were likely to go to war, even if it was only a single agent in any country. This nucleus should be kept up to date and revised frequently.

The Inspectors had, however, failed to live up to expectations, producing little 'really secret' information, and displaying a marked reluctance to come up with new ideas or even to communicate with each other or with their own agents, despite the fact that 'naval, military and Communist information of a secret nature was urgently required'. This would not do: Sinclair warned them that:

> although from a point of view of organisation the maintenance of such posts was desirable, yet it was doubtful if the financial situation would permit of these posts being continued unless better results were obtained, and unless it could be shown that the maintenance of such expensive luxuries actually relieved the Headquarters of a corresponding charge.

The Inspectors must raise their game, obtain 'inside agents capable of furnishing secret information, preferably documentary', pay special attention to counter espionage and make full use of all channels of communication. Sinclair's exhortations were specific as well as general: the Inspectors must, he said, exchange telegraphic addresses and pseudonyms before they left London to return to their Regions.

This record leaves no room for doubt about Sinclair's determination to lick SIS into shape. As a former Director of Naval Intelligence, he brought to his new job firm ideas about the direction of British Intelligence as a whole. Put simply, this was that the existing agencies should be directed by a single chief, preferably himself. His experience at the Admiralty had also given him a particular interest in cryptography and a firm belief in its importance. In September 1923 he assumed formally the title of Director of GC&CS, thereby quelling to some extent the discontent felt by the Service departments at the perceived Foreign Office monopoly over cypher communications.[24] On 3 November 1923 he wrote to Crowe, asking for an interview to discuss a reorganisation of SIS 'which should be more efficient, and what is more important, should provide a basis for a war organisation'. He had heard there was an enquiry proceeding into the overlapping between the functions of Scotland Yard and MI5: this should be proceeded with as soon as possible, 'so that we can have it and have done with it'; he had proposals for GC&CS he wished Crowe to consider; he also wished to discuss illicit arms dealing by the Soviet Government, who were trying to buy up the stock of arms from the Disposals Board, arousing fears in the military authorities that they were intended for use against Poland or to assist Germany.[25] This letter gives a clear indication of how Sinclair's mind was working only a few months after taking over as C, although no record has survived of an early meeting between Sinclair and Crowe and the issues raised by the former were ventilated fully only in 1925.

In his desire to reform, and indeed to strengthen SIS, Sinclair would surely have had Morton's support: he showed a fondness for the kind of bureaucratic rigour favoured by Morton, issuing orders about the kind of reference material to be kept in the Central Registry, for example, and forming a Mobilisation Committee at Headquarters to examine a set of draft orders drawn up by Vivian. There is nothing to suggest that Morton did not welcome Sinclair's advent as C, nor his ideas. Indeed, Morton's activities during the period 1923–26, which from one perspective could be construed as designed to boost his own role within SIS, can also be seen as offering direct support to Sinclair's plans.

Stanley and Fyfe

Writing to R.W. Thompson in December 1960, Morton stated: 'I have only one enemy, International Leninism';[26] in an earlier letter, he maintained that Communism was an 'intellectual force' comparable only to Christianity as regulated by the Roman church: 'Both are absolutely definite in regard to their ethos.'[27] These opinions, refined through many years of professional interest and personal study, had their roots in Morton's work for SIS during the 1920s. In later life, he was prepared to argue objectively and without emotion against a creed he found antithetic and repellent: as a young man, whose job was to collect information on Soviet Russia, the full implications of Communism were as yet unclear, despite emerging evidence of terror, persecution (particularly of the Church) and the repression of the individual. Fear of the unknown was an important factor. In 1923 the idea of Communism as an 'infection' that the Bolsheviks were determined to spread as widely as they could had enough concrete substance to make Morton, like many others, inclined to view with suspicion any movement or organisation, domestic or foreign, showing signs of the disease.

In these circumstances it is not surprising that Morton, seeking further sources of information for SIS, was drawn into contact with individuals and groups devoted to anti-Communist ideology and activities. One such individual was Sir George Makgill. A second son, sent 'to the Colonies' as a young man to make his fortune, he had returned to England shortly before the First World War on the death of his father and elder brother, ultra-conservative in his views and full of ideas about the efficient management of labour (including a deep-rooted dislike of Trades Unionism). During the war he became Honorary Secretary of the Anti-German Union ('No German labour, no German goods, no German influence, Britain for the British') and ran the British Empire Union. To men like Makgill, the advent of a Soviet Russian Government in November 1917 threatened the very core of British Imperial capitalism and imperilled the postwar return to profitability. Industrial unrest in the UK during and at the end of the war served to increase the alarm felt by the owners of large enterprises, and to make them determined to detect incipient trouble in their own businesses and nip it in the bud. Approached by a group of like-minded industrialists, Makgill set up a private industrial intelligence service (the Industrial Intelligence Bureau, IIB), financed by the Federation of British Industries and the Coal Owners' and Shipowners' Associations, to acquire intelligence on industrial unrest arising from the activities of Communists, Anarchists, various secret societies in the UK and overseas, the Irish Republican Army (IRA) and other 'subversive' organisations.

Although organised and financed by private interests, Makgill's intelligence service had close official connections. It is clear that from an early stage Makgill had personal links with some members of MI5, and in particular with its head, Sir

Vernon Kell: it was Kell who had introduced Makgill to Morton in 1920 or early 1921. By 1923 the IIB was well established and apparently successful. Makgill had built up a network of informants, some of whom had served in British Intelligence at Dublin Castle during the First World War and were apparently put his way by MI5. Following his introduction to Morton, Makgill began to pass on information he thought would be useful, using the name 'Mr Fyfe', while Morton, writing to Makgill or to the latter's agents, used the name 'Major Stanley', though Makgill knew him by his correct name. The two men maintained a close collaboration that lasted until Makgill's death in 1926. As well as providing information, Makgill 'pooled' some of his contacts with Morton, including W.B. Findley, also known as Jim Finney, whose information was to play a key, if misleading, part in the Zinoviev Letter affair,[28] and C.H. Maxwell Knight, who had joined the embryonic British 'Fascisti Movement' in 1920 (an organisation described by SIS as being at that time 'pink rather than brown politically') but soon became disillusioned with its organisation and membership. Knight developed his own small intelligence organisation under Makgill's patronage; an organisation he was later to offer to Morton and SIS.[29]

The relationship between Morton and Makgill was a curious one. Initially at least, Morton gave the impression of having been carried away by Makgill's right-wing enthusiasms and by the wide range of his friends and contacts. Makgill was an experienced older man – over fifty when they first met – and his unofficial intelligence service appeared both impressive and productive. He was concerned with the detection and unmasking of subversion wherever it might be found, whether in the Communist Party of Great Britain (CPGB) or in a range of so-called 'secret societies', some of which look decidedly eccentric, although they were fashionable in the 1920s, as we know from the preoccupations of novelists writing about the period.[30]

Makgill sent reams of information to Morton on bodies as diverse as the British Spiritualist Lyceum Union, the Guild of Citizens Tomorrow, Rudolf Steiner's Anthroposophical Society, the German League of Oppressed Peoples (*Vereinigung Vergewaltigter Völker*), the Workers of Zion (*Poale Zion*) and the Clarté Group, said to promote a scheme by Jewish intellectuals for a Free International of European Peoples; as well as on prominent figures such as George Bernard Shaw ('certainly one of the leaders of the Revolutionary Movement in this country'), H.G. Wells ('writes a good deal of propaganda very cleverly camouflaged') and the 'Great Beast', Aleister Crowley.[31] Morton took a particular interest in the last, who claimed to have been in contact with British Intelligence while in New York during the First World War,[32] and sought further information on him through SIS channels, explaining to the SIS representative in Geneva:

> Alistair Crowley was also a theosophist, and it is a very strange thing but nearly all these theosophists and theosophical societies are connected in some way with Bolshevism, Indian revolutionaries and other unpleasant activities.

It is difficult to determine the extent to which Morton entered with sincerity into Makgill's somewhat fanatical pursuit of 'secret societies'. In their correspondence he referred enthusiastically to 'our theories' (meaning 'strongly conservative and anti-Bolshevik'), and to plans for placing articles propounding those theories in suitable journals such as *The Patriot* and the *Illustrated Review*. There are references to frequent meetings, both *tête à tête* and at gatherings of like-minded men, and they were clearly on terms of some confidence. Morton wrote to Makgill on 2 February 1923:

> There can be no talk of indiscretion whatsoever between you and me, as if we started to say that, we have both been thoroughly indiscreet, have we not? Anything I can find out is always at your disposal.

Their surviving correspondence, however, betrays no indiscretion on Morton's part: no reference to SIS activities except in the most general terms, nor to personalities except to those whom Makgill knew already. As always, Morton wrote a great deal while saying little, giving the strong impression that his motivation was professional rather than personal. Makgill is treated as a close contact, rather than a friend; a welcome lunch companion at a gentleman's club, but no greater intimacy (Morton responded to one invitation from Makgill's wife to spend a weekend at their country home, Yaxley Hall, at Eye in Suffolk, by saying that he could 'not go so far away from town at weekends'). Though generally fulsome in his gratitude for the information Makgill supplied, Morton was not always uncritical: a sharp letter of 28 May 1923 complained that a recent set of reports:

> are the reports of a little man about little things. They are the kind of reports which a policeman would put up to his inspector when told to watch people, but not one statement really carries us any further. All the names mentioned are the names of people known to be interested in Communist or Irish intrigues, and . . . there is nothing to show what these intrigues are, which is the important thing.

These sound more like the comments of an Intelligence officer than a true believer.

There is another element of the Makgill-Morton relationship that requires investigation. Makgill and his son Donald were prominent Freemasons, and it was assumed by some of their sources, shared with SIS, that Morton was one too, an allegation that has persisted in some accounts of the period. The following somewhat confusing extract from a letter written by Morton to Makgill in 1923 provides one example of why their connection was thought to be a Masonic one. Deprecating the fact that Kell, head of MI5, had referred in conversation to having helped Makgill to found 'an organisation of a secret nature somewhat on Masonic lines,' Morton wrote:

My point is this. V.K.'s statements were doubtless correct, but he is not a Br[other] so far as I am aware, and it is surely a pity that the complete secrecy of the Or[der] which we are aiming at should be jeopardised. K went on to say that a member of his office was a Br. of the Or. and so on. I have the greatest admiration and respect for K, but is it not a little unwise to say quite what he did? . . . The only reason I let you know this at all is that the conversation in question directly affects yourself and what, temporarily at least, is one of the inviolable secrets, namely the identity of the H[igher] O[fficers] . . . is it not possible that V.K. knows either too much or too little? Personally, not knowing all the facts, I would plump for the latter. He understands a great deal about the Or[der], I would say, but has not quite grasped the imperative necessity for literal and absolute secrecy on one or two points.

It is hard to know what to make of all this, and the surviving evidence is inconclusive. As an Intelligence officer, Morton may well have entered into the spirit and even the letter of somewhat dubious 'organisations', like the one indicated in this letter, for the purpose of gathering information, but it seems unlikely that he was a fully-fledged Mason. The Roman Catholic Church had first outlawed Freemasonry in 1738, and it was condemned in successive Papal Encyclicals as 'fundamentally irreconcilable' with Christianity.[33] There were, indeed, proponents of a rapprochement between the Catholic Church and Freemasonry – indeed, Makgill's son Donald's name was mentioned in such a connection;[34] nevertheless, Vatican condemnation of Freemasonry was uncompromising, and it is hard to imagine that Morton would have flouted it in this way. It seems more likely that his exchanges with Makgill on this subject were strictly professional, a judgement strengthened by the knowledge that during this period Morton was also in close contact with White Russian groups in London, Paris and Berlin, many of which were run on similar pseudo-Masonic lines.[35] He was well aware of the potency of ritualism in the world of secret societies, and what we know of his character and beliefs makes it easier to accept that his connections were professional rather than personal.

Of course, the two may have been intertwined, as indicated by the following letter, enclosing some sample reports, to Major Oswald Rayner, who had worked for SIS in Russia during the First World War but by 1923 was in the FO's Northern Department:

Herewith four of my productions which I call 'shilling shockers' . . . Two of them deal with our mutual friend [Rudolf] Steiner; one is a very brief note by a friend of mine on present day Illuminism and the last on Clarté . . . I have a number of similar other little particles on such things as German monarchist secret societies, Freemasonry and so on, which perhaps you might like to read later. Please of course treat these as what they are, namely the outcome of a private hobby of my own, grafted somewhat insecurely on my official job.

The final sentence is typically Mortonesque: such disarmingly casual admissions served to deflect curiosity and were intended to elicit information rather than comment, while Morton never took his eye off the Bolshevik ball. He was more interested in the 'octopus' financing Bolshevism than the 'occult', even if sometimes willing to embrace the latter in pursuit of the former.

A good illustration of the difficulties of obtaining reliable information on both Bolshevik and anti-Bolshevik activities is provided by the case of Captain Kenneth A. Stott, one of Makgill's principal agents, who began to supply information to Morton through Makgill in 1922. Stott had worked for Makgill since about 1920, reporting on Communist affairs in the UK, and was regarded as an authority on the British labour movement with good contacts within the more militant circles of Trades Unionism. Unlike Makgill, however, Morton was not concerned with incipient strikes: he was much more interested when Stott, who served on the Glasgow Vigilance Committee,[36] reported in September 1922 that he had been asked to act as their intermediary with a German organisation that offered funding in return for information and influence. Stott duly attended a meeting in Cologne, and discovered that the German organisation was the *Deutscher Uberseedienst*, or Overseas Service, described by Stott as a 'sort of private Board of Trade': it had, he reported, its own secret service, which sent couriers to collect information, working through extremists, Trades Unions and labour movements in general; the German Government and Secret Service were, he said, both involved. Morton wrote at the end of this report: 'Amen'. This was just the sort of information he was looking for, and he wrote to Makgill with a detailed list of questions: 'This really is business.' Stott began attending monthly meetings with *Uberseedienst* representatives in Brussels.

SIS already knew quite a lot about the *Uberseedienst* through its own representatives in Germany and France, and through liaison with the French *Deuxième Bureau*. Founded in 1916 (in agreement with the German General Staff) by a Dr Karl Bremer, together with newspaper proprietor and director of Krupps, Alfred Hugenberg, it provided a press service for German and foreign newspapers, as well as observing the activities of foreign correspondents and providing assistance to German Intelligence. After the First World War it was used by the financier and industrialist Hugo Stinnes as a media vehicle for extreme right-wing interests, as well as providing cover to agents working for the German Foreign Office, the *Auswärtiges Amt* (AA), and for the Ministry for the Armed Forces, the *Reichswehrministerium* (RWM). By 1921 it had expanded into a pervasive Intelligence service actively seeking overseas links, and was suspected by SIS of being involved in plans for illicit German rearmament.

In 1921 the *Uberseedienst* absorbed the Nuntia Bureau, an information service founded by Stinnes in 1919 to obtain information on the Soviet Union and Baltic States.[37] Morton was being supplied with information on the Bureau by his old contact Vladimir Orlov, now running his own intelligence (and forgery) service out of Berlin, and who had penetrated the Bureau at an early stage through his German police contacts. There was a further Orlov connection in that the

Uberseedienst was known to support a pseudo-Masonic organisation inaugurated by him in Berlin in 1922, known as the 'Brotherhood of Russian Truth,' billed as a 'secret terrorist society which should be supported by all true anti-Bolsheviks', though apparently used principally as a vehicle for selling forged documents. Orlov was also closely involved with General Kutepov, head of the Russian Combined Services Union (ROVS) in Paris (run on Masonic lines), who was also drawn into the Nuntia Bureau. SIS were aware that both these organisations had been penetrated by Soviet Intelligence, who were thereby enabled to lure Boris Savinkov, and later Sidney Reilly, to imprisonment and death in the Soviet Union.[38]

Morton was rightly suspicious of Orlov's reports, however well-informed: after SIS had severed their official connection with him in 1923, his information was available to the highest bidder, and he was prepared to tailor it to his audience.[39] Nor was it easy for SIS representatives to penetrate the inner ring of secrecy maintained by German official and industrial interests. In these circumstances, Stott appeared, at least for a while, to be a useful source of inside information on the *Uberseedienst* and its attendant connections. This view was shared by French Intelligence: Stott reported in March 1923 that he had received an offer from Commandant Merson of the *Deuxième Bureau* to liaise with the Germans, claiming that he had refused on patriotic grounds:

> [Merson is] a thoroughly unscrupulous man who is violently anti-British and boasts openly in France that he and his chief and the French Intelligence Services make use of the British Intelligence Services without any real return . . . His offer of £1,000 for a week's work seemed a bribe for me to do something that he knew I was likely to jib at. Otherwise the French would have offered me less . . . Had I been able to speak French when Merson was talking or to understand I would not only have refused to do his job but drop kicked him into the street.

Morton, already in close liaison with Merson himself, was unimpressed by Stott's righteous indignation, and as 1923 progressed became increasingly doubtful about 'Marmion' (Stott's code name), particularly in view of his close association with a woman suspected of being a German agent. The *Deuxième Bureau*, too, distrusted Stott, suspecting him of working both for the British and the Germans: they issued a circular notice describing him as '*dangereux au point de vue national*'. MI5 also took an interest in him: Morton had kept them informed about Stott and shared his information with both Major Alexander and Joseph Ball.[40] By July 1923, however, Alexander had concluded, as he informed Morton, that Stott's reports just did not stand up to scrutiny:

> He is badly educated, his personal conceit is enormous and his methods are unscrupulous and peculiar . . . while Stott's knowledge of the Labour movement in this country is undoubtedly very extensive and complete . . . his knowledge of foreign espionage methods seems to be sketchy and

coloured by imagination. He does not appear to realise the difference between commercial and military espionage, and when he gives the names of persons whom he suspects he appears to have no hesitation in allowing imagination and animus to have full play.

Stott's information on German agents was, in MI5's view, 'absolutely valueless'. Morton could only agree. By 1924 he had severed SIS's connection with Stott, although the latter continued to provide long reports to Makgill on the industrial situation in the United Kingdom, including reports during the 1926 General Strike.

Stott was not the only one of Makgill's agents used by Morton: with a few exceptions, it was rare for such informants to enjoy more than a brief period of credibility. Stott's case is a useful illustration of the scope of Morton's contacts in pursuit of intelligence on Bolshevik propaganda and espionage, and also of the amount of work and trouble that such contacts could involve. Initial optimism was only too often followed by disillusion and the decision to sever the connection: nevertheless, they all played their part in contributing to the overall picture built up by SIS on Soviet and German activities. Nor was Makgill's the only organisation used by Morton in this way: he received reports from a range of groups and individuals, including a commercial intelligence organisation run by an American, Wallace Banta Phillipps, in conjunction with Sir William Wiseman (now working for the insurance company Kuhn Loeb), and with Wiseman's wartime Intelligence colleague, Colonel N.G. Thwaites (no longer on SIS's books but continuing to supply occasional reports). Makgill, however, had the best domestic contacts, as well as good connections with White Russian interests, and his agents were well placed to supply information to SIS on subversive activities relevant to their Bolshevik target.

In making use of Makgill's sources, based in the UK, Morton was of course stepping outside the accepted demarcation lines between SIS, MI5 and Scotland Yard. While SIS had sole responsibility for foreign intelligence, MI5 was responsible for counter-espionage measures and for Communism in the armed forces, while Scotland Yard dealt with revolutionary organisations in the United Kingdom.[41] This division of duties was further complicated by the responsibilities within Scotland Yard of Special Branch, where, under the overall control of Sir Wyndham Childs,[42] three branches dealt with secret service matters: SS1 (formerly 'F' branch), the liaison section with SIS; SS2 (formerly 'L' branch), liaising with Chief Constables and dealing with matters relating to revolutionary organisations in the UK other than of alien or Irish origin; and a branch under Lieutenant-Colonel Carter, Deputy Assistant Commissioner, whose task was to take action on information received, liaising with Passport Control and the Aliens Branch of the Home Office, and having a large police force at his disposal. The potential for jurisdictional conflict and overlapping within this system was considerable, particularly since, as Sinclair was to tell the Secret Service Committee in 1925, it was 'impossible to draw the line between espionage and contre-espionage, for both were concerned solely with foreign activities'.[43] No one part of the machinery, consequently, felt that it was possible to receive all the relevant information from any of the others.

All sections of British Intelligence stepped across the dividing line at some point: in February 1923, for example, Morton reported information from Captain Miller, of Special Branch's SIS liaison section, that:

> Inspector MacBrien of Scotland Yard recently sent into Moscow a man whom he had been employing in this country as an agent in Communist matters . . . This was done by Inspector MacBrien apparently without Captain Miller being informed, and certainly without our being informed, which would seem to be contrary to the understanding in force whereby no one but ourselves is allowed to employ agents in foreign countries.

Morton's principal complaint in this case was that the enterprise was a waste of money, since SIS already had agents in place supplying information on the same target, the Fourth Congress of the Third International. This did not prevent him, evidently with Sinclair's agreement but without the knowledge of MacBrien, from arranging for the Scotland Yard agent to be put in contact in Moscow with one of the agents run by the SIS representative in Riga (the unfortunate police agent was later arrested and shot by the Soviet authorities).

Morton's justification for employing SIS agents within the UK was that they were providing intelligence of vital importance to SIS in checking the authenticity and content of reports received from overseas, and that this intelligence was not available from other sources. This argument was accepted at the highest level, both in SIS and in MI5. It seems clear that Morton was acting with the knowledge and authorisation of his own Chief, even if he did not necessarily inform Sinclair of the full scope or details of his domestic activities. Sinclair was certainly prepared to give full support publicly to Morton in the event of any challenge from Scotland Yard or MI5, though there are indications that in private he warned him to be more careful to observe the niceties of official cooperation. As for MI5, it was, after all, Kell who introduced Makgill to Morton, presumably because he thought that Makgill could provide information useful to SIS. In the light of the fact that two Special Branch officers were supplying information to Soviet agents at this period,[44] Kell may also have had doubts, not only about the ability of Special Branch to supply information of the same quality, but also whether they could be trusted. A comment by Morton, in a letter to Makgill in September 1922, suggests that he shared this doubt: 'I will not pass anything on to the place which has a leakage.' Nevertheless, a later note on SIS inter-war activities refers to 'an anti-Communist c[ounter]-e[spionage] organisation in England, run for late CSS by Major Morton with the knowledge of Special Branch', and there is reference elsewhere to Maxwell Knight as having run a counter-espionage network for Morton with the approval of Captain Miller of Special Branch.

Unfortunately, the evidence surviving from this period is insufficient to estab-lish the truth in any detail or with any certainty. The early to mid-1920s saw a proliferation of private groups and organisations in Britain, in response to the perceived threat of world revolution inspired by the Soviet Government, and to the more specific threat to the British Empire, particularly in Asia. SIS tapped into such organisations for information, and Morton certainly made use of their contacts, but their interaction is little documented. Nor is there any reliable evidence concerning Morton's relationship with Churchill at this period. It seems justifiable to assume that they continued to meet, if not to correspond. Churchill, however, did not need Morton to provide him with secret information. As Secretary of State for the Colonies, he had been able to insist on continuing to see the secret material he had received as Secretary of State for War,[45] and con-tinued to do so until the advent of the first Labour Government in January 1924. Although his official access was thereafter restricted, his channels of information remained good: he had long been on close terms with Sinclair, as well as with Morton. Though some accounts have hinted at Churchill's involvement with some form of shadowy, private intelligence network, no concrete evidence has been found to support the existence of such a network in the mid-1920s, despite Churchill's continuing interest in all matters secret.

The Zinoviev Letter

Morton's pursuit of the Occult Octopus, even if aimed at International Leninism, drew him firmly into the orbit of the power base of the 'Establishment': the men that ruled, financed, administered and influenced the British Empire. Though solitary by nature and by profession, he was nevertheless part of a community:

> not just the Intelligence community, but more precisely the community of an *élite* – senior officials in government departments, men in 'the City', men in politics, men who controlled the Press – which was narrow, interconnected (sometimes intermarried) and mutually supportive. Many of these men . . . had been to the same schools and universities, and belonged to the same clubs. Feeling themselves part of a special and closed community, they exchanged confidences secure in the knowledge, as they thought, that they were protected by that community from indiscretion.[46]

The members of this community, in common with Churchill, with Makgill and with Sinclair, viewed the first government formed by the British Labour Party in January 1924, under Ramsay MacDonald,[47] with suspicion, alarm and in some cases contempt. Churchill called it a 'national misfortune such as has usually befallen a great state only on the morrow of defeat in war'.[48] The fact that the Labour Government had only come to power because of a split in the Conservative ranks over free trade, made the experience if anything even more bitter. Not everyone viewed it as a disaster: former Prime Ministers Asquith and Baldwin agreed that MacDonald's politics, at least, were hardly revolutionary; but Labour's early *de jure* recognition of the Soviet Union[49] seemed nothing less than treachery to some, and unwise to many at a time when aggressive Bolshevik propaganda and subversion seemed if anything to be on the increase.[50]

Although the short-lived Labour Government was in many respects unexceptionably moderate, and surprisingly successful in both economic and foreign policy, its opponents were not only waiting for it to make a fatal mistake, but also working to undermine it in any way possible. MacDonald's bungled handling of the crisis caused by the arrest on 5 August 1924 of the Scottish Communist John Campbell, following an inflammatory article in *Workers Weekly*, proved to be the fatal mistake:[51] the Zinoviev Letter provided the opportunity to undermine a government whose electoral downfall was already inevitable. It was an episode that still rankles with the self-styled 'Labour romantics'; and Morton's role in it, if not sinister, was at least equivocal.

An extensive examination of the surviving evidence, commissioned in 1998 by the then British Foreign Secretary, Robin Cook, concluded that the letter dated 15 September 1924, supposedly addressed to the Central Committee of the CPGB by Grigori Zinoviev, President of the Executive Committee of the Comintern, and urging the Party to rouse the British proletariat in preparation for armed insurrection and class war, was almost certainly a forgery, although its precise authorship cannot be determined.[52] It also concluded that the idea of the forgery as part of an institutional campaign, directed by British Intelligence to discredit the Labour Government, is inherently improbable. There is little doubt, however, that copies of the letter, initially received by SIS from their Riga station, found their way swiftly by overt and covert means to those vested interests who could best make political capital out of it at the government's expense. News of the impending publication of the Letter in the *Daily Mail* – news first passed to the FO by SIS on 24 October 1924 – led Crowe to authorise, without MacDonald's final approval, the publication of an official protest to the Soviet Government, leading to the further humiliation of the Government and of MacDonald himself.[53]

Many details of the affair remain confused and uncertain. Nevertheless, an examination of Morton's part in it throws some light both on the role of the Occult Octopus and on his own motivation and methods. He was, in fact, at centre stage (in the Intelligence context) from the beginning. The letter arrived in SIS Headquarters on 9 October 1924 under cover of a report from Latvia (L/3900), and was passed immediately to the FO with the comment: 'The authenticity of the document is undoubted.'[54] Morton, who was responsible for its evaluation and authorised its circulation, later said that he had not thought it particularly significant when he received it. This may well be true, and although later checks on the letter's authenticity left a lot to be desired both in timeliness and thoroughness, it would not be surprising if he had accepted it immediately as genuine. The source cited in the Riga report was FR3/K, and the FR network, operating out of Riga, had been producing consistently good reports for the previous two years, with well-placed and enterprising agents in Moscow. These agents had secured copies of minutes of key Soviet bodies such as the *Sovnarkom* (Council of People's Commissars, executive arm of the Central Committee of the Communist Party of the Soviet Union), and of the Executive Committee of the Comintern: they had also obtained copies of similarly inflammatory letters written by Zinoviev to the Communist parties of other countries, including Germany, Bulgaria and the United States, as well as earlier missives to the CPGB.[55] This one looked, at first glance, much like the others.

The following day, however (10 October), the FO's Permanent Under-Secretary, Crowe, asked for 'corroborative proofs' of the authenticity of the letter before putting it to MacDonald (who held the dual portfolio of Prime Minister and Foreign Secretary), currently out of London campaigning for the forthcoming general election. Morton produced on 11 October a report based on information received at his meeting the night before with one of Makgill's agents, 'Jim Finney' (code-named 'Furniture Dealer'), who had infiltrated the CPGB. According to Morton, Finney told him that the Central Committee of the CPGB had recently held a meeting to consider a letter of instruction from Moscow concerning:

> action which the CPGB was to take with regard to making the proletariat force Parliament to ratify the Anglo-Soviet Treaty. It was decided that particular efforts were to be made to permeate the Armed Forces of the Crown with Communist agents, then to promote strikes and incite to revolutionary action so that the forces of the Crown could be called out. It is hoped this last, by reason of the Communist propaganda which will have had effect, will either refuse to quell the disturbance or join the rioters . . . the Moscow instructions received insisted on distrust of the Labour Party and MacDonald, with whom the International was disgusted in that they had shown that their policy was little different from that of a bourgeois government.[56]

On the basis of Morton's report, Crowe told MacDonald that he had heard on 'absolutely reliable authority' that the letter had been discussed by the CPGB. Finney's original report, however, did not say this. It made no mention of a letter from Moscow, stating merely that the CPGB Executive had decided to:

> do all in their power to make whatever government was in power to be the promoters of the Revolution . . . taking more effective action in promoting strikes and incitement, so that the Government in office would be compelled to bring out troops to quell disturbances.

It is hard to see how this statement could support Morton's interpretation. Later evidence confirmed that the Zinoviev Letter never, in fact, reached the CPGB:

Morton's own explanation, that Finney 'elaborated' on his written report, is therefore invalidated. It is possible that Morton conflated, accidentally or deliberately, Finney's report with the report from Latvia received the day before.[57] If accidentally, it implies a casualness that does not sit well with Morton's known *modus operandi*; if deliberately, the reason may not necessarily be sinister. Morton received a great many such reports across his desk, the majority of which were genuine.[58] He may have believed, sincerely, in the authenticity of the letter at that point. On the other hand, it might be that since he, like many of his colleagues and contacts (including his own Chief), detested the Bolsheviks and disliked the Labour Government, he welcomed the chance to throw a spanner in the works of Anglo-Soviet rapprochement. He may have been influenced, or even instructed, to do so.

The propagation of conspiracy theories is always unprofitable, as it is impossible to prove a negative.[59] There is no hard evidence to explain Morton's actions or motives, and he never revealed them (adding extra fuel to the conspiratorial fire in an interview in 1969, when he claimed that Menzies had posted a copy of the letter to the *Daily Mail* because he disliked Labour). The surviving documentation is, as so often with Morton, contradictory. By the beginning of November 1924 SIS had begun to receive reports from SIS stations that the letter was a forgery, probably originating in the Baltic States; Morton wrote to MI5 on 27 November that 'we are firmly convinced this actual thing is a forgery'. Meanwhile, however, two Cabinet Committees had been convened to consider the question of the Letter's authenticity: the first, chaired by MacDonald, reported to the Cabinet on 4 November that they 'found it impossible on the evidence before them to come to a conclusion on the subject'; it was the last act of his ill-fated Government.[60] The second, however, chaired by the new Foreign Secretary Sir Austen Chamberlain, reported on 19 November that its members were 'unanimously of opinion that there was no doubt as to the authenticity of the Letter'.[61]

Meanwhile, on 17 November Sinclair submitted to Crowe, for consideration by the Chamberlain Committee, a document, apparently drafted by Morton, containing 'five very good reasons' why SIS considered the Letter genuine. These were: its source, an agent in Moscow 'of proved reliability'; 'direct independent confirmation' from CPGB and ARCOS sources in London; 'subsidiary confirmation' in the form of supposed 'frantic activity' in Moscow; because the possibility of SIS being taken in by White Russians was 'entirely excluded'; and because the subject matter of the Letter was 'entirely consistent with all that the Communists have been enunciating and putting into effect'.[62] All five of these reasons can be shown to be misleading, if not downright false. SIS did not know, for example, the identity of the agent in Moscow said to have provided the letter, and were certainly not, as the document claimed, 'aware of the identity of every person who handled the document on its journey from Zinoviev's files to our hands'. The 'independent and spontaneous confirmation' that the CPGB had received the letter was, as has been seen, of decidedly suspect provenance, while reports of arrests in Moscow were no more than circumstantial. The claim that SIS was incapable of being taken in by White Russian forgers was more aspirational than accurate, while the final reason, that the letter was consonant with Communist policy and 'If it was a forgery, by this time we should have proof of it', may have been unanswerable, but was disingenuous in the light of reports received in the previous month.[63]

This documentary sophistry, not to say prevarication, cannot fail to arouse the suspicion that Morton, and indeed SIS, had something to hide, not just about how the letter came to be given to the Press, but also about its origin. Orlov's Berlin organisation, with whom Morton remained in touch and about which he received regular information, was identified quickly as a likely potential source of the forgery, and although the account published by the *Sunday Times* 'Insight' team in 1967,[64] alleging that one of Orlov's colleagues, Alexis Bellegarde, forged the letter begs more questions than it answers,[65] there is no doubt that Orlov had the opportunity and contacts required. It would, as one SIS account noted, have been 'easy enough for him to put in touch with a foreign intelligence service, e.g. in Riga, some well-trained agent of his own who would thereafter produce material purporting to be obtained from Moscow or elsewhere, but which was, in fact, prepared by himself'. It was part of Morton's job to pay close attention to 'expert' forgeries emanating from sources such as Orlov's service, on the grounds that:

> the information which they contain provides a check upon the authenticity of other reports . . . forgeries which emanate from any well-informed source may yield information of value, provided they are handled by an expert, since they will all contain a certain proportion of true information introduced to inspire confidence in the false.

Whatever the provenance of the Zinoviev Letter, no one, not even the Russians, ever suggested that it did not contain 'a certain proportion of true information'.

The way the letter was handled once it reached SIS, and its communication to the press, also arouses suspicion, heightened by what is now known about the activities of some of Morton's contacts: the Makgill organisation; White Russian groups at home and abroad; the head of the FO's Northern Department, J.D. Gregory, an old 'Russia hand' later shown to have been engaging in decidedly unethical (if inept) currency trading at this time in company with his mistress Mrs Aminta Bradley Dyne – whose husband was another old 'Russia hand'. Although a Treasury Committee of Enquiry held in 1928 was unable to establish any direct connection between Gregory's activities and the Zinoviev Letter, suspicions remained.[66] Similarly, doubts have been raised as to whether Morton's contacts with Ball at MI5 were politically as well as professionally motivated: and the involvement of former MI5 officer Donald im Thurn, who tried to sell a copy of the letter (which he did not possess), adds another mysterious dimension to the story;[67] the names of the former DNI, Admiral 'Blinker' Hall, and former Deputy Chief of SIS, Frederick Browning, have also been implicated.

Suspicion does not constitute proof, however, and a detailed re-examination of the documentation has produced no more conclusive evidence. The conclusion reached by the earlier investigation of the Zinoviev Letter affair remains valid:

> White Russian intelligence services were well developed and highly organised, and included the operation of a forgery ring in Berlin. It seems likely that they asked either those forgers, or their contacts in the Baltic States with similar skills, to produce a document which would derail the treaties and damage the Labour government. Because of British Intelligence links with Berlin, information about the proposed forgery could have reached certain members of British Intelligence Agencies who were on the look-out for opportunities to further the Conservative cause in Britain, and to discredit the Labour Party in the process. Anyone in that position, and with a wide net of contacts in London, was well placed not only to vouch for the authenticity of the Letter but also to encourage its dissemination in quarters where profitable – and mischievous – use might be made of it.[68]

'Anyone in that position' included Morton. He was undoubtedly in sympathy with Conservative elements in politics, press and armed forces, as well as in the Intelligence establishment. His actions and writings could be construed in that light. They could also be interpreted rather differently, in a way that does not exonerate him of political skulduggery but does fit in with what we know of him and his career. Although not susceptible of proof, this interpretation is worthy of consideration.

As we have seen, it is quite possible that Morton accepted the letter, received from a reliable SIS source, as genuine, at least initially. He prided himself on his acuity in detecting forged documents, whether slipped into the system by Orlov and his colleagues, or planted by Soviet Intelligence. SIS had received a number of similar documents obtained by agents in Moscow: they also knew, from their own sources, that the Soviet authorities were concerned that their secret documents were reaching foreign powers.[69] He may not, therefore, have thought too hard before confirming the letter's authenticity to Crowe; using Finney's report to substantiate it was merely being economical with the truth; after all, many similar letters were authentic. It soon became clear, however, that in this case SIS had been sold a pup, and what is more, that pup was likely to be used as the basis for a full-scale British protest to the Soviet Union.

This put Morton in a difficult position: professionally, he had been caught out and did not wish to maintain the authenticity of a forgery; equally, he would have been extremely reluctant to go back to the FO and admit publicly that he had been wrong. Quite apart from his personal inclination to self-justification, he would also have been forced to reveal that Finney's information about the CPGB had not been shared with, or checked by, Special Branch;[70] and that SIS had agents within the UK, a fact known to Sinclair and indeed to the other Agencies, but not to the

FO. In the light of this, it is revealing to compare the style and tone of the document produced by Sinclair containing 'five very good reasons' in support of the letter's authenticity with those of the minute Morton had written about Sidney Reilly in January 1922.[71]

While adopting a detached and professional tone, it refers, explicitly on this occasion, to the inside information possessed by SIS – not to be shared, even with the Cabinet – on agents, methods and sources; it invites respect for the superior judgement of SIS ('the possibility of being taken in by "White Russians" is entirely excluded'), and fires a final warning shot that the word of the British foreign intelligence Service must be accepted ('If it was a forgery, by this time we should have proof of it'). In other words, the document could be read as Morton 'covering his back'; more likely, it was drafted in consultation with Sinclair, and constituted a justification of the actions and judgement of SIS as an organisation. However far the tentacles of the Occult Octopus may have reached, an explanation of Morton's, and SIS's, part in the Zinoviev Letter affair based on fighting their way out of an organisational corner strikes at least as sound a note as that of conspiracy and political skulduggery. Morton might have done well, however, to recall a quotation from one of his favourite books, *Kai Lung's Golden Hours*: 'He who thinks that he is raising a mound may only in reality be digging a pit.'[72]

5

'GOD SAVE THE KING AND HIS AGENTS PROVOCATEURS!'*: 1926–28

The Zinoviev Letter affair had wide-reaching repercussions beyond its immediate aftermath. Politically, it damaged the reputation of the Labour Party and left Ramsay MacDonald and his colleagues confused and resentful, and less trustful of the Intelligence establishment. It constituted yet another setback to normalised Anglo-Soviet relations, and increased Parliamentary and public anxiety about Bolshevik subversive activities. Although Sir Austen Chamberlain, Foreign Secretary in Stanley Baldwin's Conservative Government from November 1924, strove to maintain a firm but calm response to Soviet provocation – 'no breach unless we are forced to it, no pinpricks on our part'[1] – the suspicion, even loathing of the Soviet regime entertained by some of his Cabinet colleagues was boosted by the events of 1924–1925 and led to increasing pressure for a rupture of Anglo-Soviet relations. The self-righteous and aggrieved stance adopted by a Soviet Government that felt isolated internationally only increased in British official circles the sense of mingled exasperation and alarm inspired by Comintern activities in India, Afghanistan and the Near East.[2]

Within the British Intelligence establishment, the Zinoviev affair had revealed underlying muddle and duplication, confirming Sinclair in his determination not only to reform SIS but, if possible, to impose his authority on other Agencies too. Far from seeing the episode as embarrassing or even humiliating for his Service, Sinclair saw it as an opportunity to further his own plans. As far as he was concerned, the authenticity of the Zinoviev letter was irrelevant. There was ample, genuine documentary proof to be had of Soviet perfidy and Comintern incitement. Reports continued to reach SIS daily of Soviet-inspired (and German funded) subversive activities both overseas and within the UK. To Sinclair's mind, what mattered was acquiring reliable information on these activities and coordinating an efficient campaign against them. If other departments were unwilling to take the decisive steps in this direction, SIS would. The years 1926 to 1928 saw a period of intense SIS information-gathering on Soviet espionage that the formal rupture of Anglo-Soviet relations in May 1927 hardly interrupted.

---

*   Concluding phrase of an SIS report from Moscow. Morton noted in the margin: 'Hear! Hear!'

In this activity Morton played a key role. It might be thought that the Zinoviev episode would have dimmed his star within SIS and increased doubts about his judgement and reliability. But just as Sinclair had supported robustly Morton's defence of his own, and SIS's, role in the Zinoviev affair, he now encouraged him to redouble his efforts to gather information on Soviet activities, using agents and contacts both overseas and within the UK as well. The two episodes described in this chapter illustrate the style and range of Morton's activities during 1926–28: the raid on the London headquarters of the Russian trading organisation ARCOS in May 1927, precipitating the expulsion of the Soviet Trade Delegation and the breakdown of Anglo-Soviet diplomatic relations; and the case of W.F.R. Macartney, whose attempts to secure British military information for sale to the Soviet Union were observed closely by Morton from 1926, and who was sentenced with Georg Hansen in January 1928 to ten years' imprisonment for attempting to obtain secret information and sell it to a foreign power.

As always, Morton's personal life at this period remains an enigma, and his professional life must tell the story. During 1926–28, his career once more mirrors the development of SIS: again, therefore, an understanding of the organisational development and infrastructure of SIS at this time is an essential preliminary to an appreciation of his professional activities.

SIS in 1926

Since assuming his position as Chief of SIS in 1923, Sinclair had lobbied for the amalgamation of the various elements of British Intelligence, preferably under his direction. Following his early success in securing control over GC&CS, he turned next to Indian Political Intelligence (IPI), the London offshoot of the Intelligence Bureau of the Government of India's Home Department, perhaps reckoning that the regular reports of increasing Soviet activity in India passed to IPI by SIS might persuade the former of the advantages of a closer relationship. In March 1924 Sinclair had persuaded Crowe to suggest to the Permanent Secretary at the India Office, Sir A. Hirtzel, that IPI (currently co-housed with MI5) should be absorbed into SIS. This approach elicited a firm rebuff from the India Office on 26 April:

> We have looked into this carefully but have come to the conclusion that against the positive advantage of a not very great financial saving there are definite disadvantages . . . our objects are not identical. In addition to foreign movements directed against the Empire at large we are very much concerned with relatively minor intrigues directed at Indian internal affairs which could not be expected to interest C's organisation and would be troublesome to them if they really tried to master them. Upon the whole, therefore, we should prefer to remain as we are.[3]

Thus thwarted, Sinclair saw the confusion and competition within British Intelligence revealed in the autumn of 1924 by the Zinoviev affair as confirmation of his views on the shortcomings of British Secret Service organisation. He welcomed the opportunity offered by the enquiry ordered by Baldwin in February 1925:

> The Prime Minister has decided to reappoint the Committee, consisting of Sir Warren Fisher (Chairman), Sir Eyre Crowe, and Sir Maurice Hankey, which was set up by the Cabinet on 22nd March 1921 in connection with the Secret Service. The Committee after hearing all the necessary evidence will report to the Prime Minister on the existing organisations and their relationship to one another and they will make recommendations to him as to any changes which in their opinion would conduce to the greater efficiency of the system.[4]

Sinclair lost no time in taking the initiative, writing to Crowe on 25 February 1925:

> I suggest that the first question to be put to any witnesses that may be called by your Committee is: 'Are you satisfied with the present organisation of the Secret Service. If not, have you any suggestions for improving it?' If any witnesses state that they are satisfied (which I should hardly imagine will be the case) I suggest that further questions enquiring whether they are satisfied with the cooperation and co-ordination now existing between the various branches of the Secret Service are put to them.[5]

He then went on to list the witnesses he considered necessary: apart from himself, Sir Wyndham Childs, Colonel Carter and Captain Miller of Scotland Yard; Sir Malcom Seton of the India Office, the three Service Directors of Intelligence and Sir Vernon Kell. (This was, roughly, the list of witnesses examined by the Committee, together with the Chief Commissioner of the Metropolitan Police and Colonel Eric Holt-Wilson of MI5; Major J. Wallinger, head of IPI, represented the India Office.)

The Committee met for the first time the following day, 26 February 1925. Their opening premise, that their broad aim should be 'to secure greater concentration, both administrative and geographical', of the Secret Service organisations, seemed in principle favourable to Sinclair's plans. They decided to examine the heads of all the organisations concerned, beginning with C. At the second meeting, on 2 March, Sinclair opened the proceedings by stating that in his opinion 'the whole organisation of British Secret Service . . . was fundamentally wrong':

> All the different branches ought to be placed under one head and in one building in the neighbourhood of Whitehall, and to be made responsible to one Department of State, which ought to be the Foreign Office.[6]

He went on to denounce at length the shortcomings of the present system, and to present his own recommendations for a new organisation under a single Director. Objections by Committee members were batted aside with a confidence that seemed close to contempt. He subsequently submitted in support of his arguments a document entitled 'Some recent examples of lack of co-operation, coordination and overlapping between C's organisation, MI5, Scotland Yard, IPI and the Passport Control Department', ranging from the handling of the Zinoviev letter through arms deals and postal intercepts to 'unnecessary correspondence on minor points'.[7]

The Committee made no immediate response to Sinclair's opening onslaught, although Hankey (who, as Secretary to the Cabinet, was a very influential member) expressed his reservations at an early stage, submitting a note to the Secretary, Nevile Bland, on 27 March 1925:

> I am not at present convinced that the connection between the several branches of the Secret Service and the Government Departments for whose benefit they were respectively established is not more important than their connection with one another . . . If unification took place at present I apprehend that the present control of the Foreign Office, of the Home Office, and of DMO&I (acting for the Service Departments) over the several sections of S[ecret] S[ervice] which were respectively established for their particular benefit, would be weakened and that the advantages they derive from those services might be diminished. My present inclination, therefore, is not, even as an ideal in the distant future, to go beyond doing everything we can to secure the closest coordination without altering the present balance of Ministerial and Departmental responsibility.[8]

In the face of this authoritative opinion there was little chance that Sinclair's proposals would be adopted, although the Committee's proceedings dragged on for most of 1925, delayed in part by Crowe's death.[9] By the end of June, when the Committee had held ten meetings, Fisher reported to the Prime Minister that its members found it 'impossible to submit an exhaustive report' without knowing more about the internal workings of Scotland Yard. Sir Russell Scott, Controller of Establishments in HM Treasury, was accordingly commissioned to carry out a full enquiry, reporting on 12 October.[10] The Committee met once more to consider his findings: their own report was not issued until 1 December.[11] Although this paid due deference to the views of the 'remarkably efficient Chief of the Secret Intelligence Service', it did not support them. Sinclair had, it said, been the only witness to express strong dissatisfaction with the current arrangements, and the reorganisation he proposed was too drastic for the Committee, or their other witnesses, to contemplate.

Admitting that 'if there were today no British secret service of any kind . . . we should not adopt the existing system as our model', the Committee contented itself with recommending that efforts should be made to concentrate the various secret organisations in the neighbourhood of Whitehall, in one or neighbouring buildings, using the Passport Control Offices as general cover. Sinclair – described as having 'a peculiar flair for such things' – was charged with keeping a look-out for suitable premises. The Committee also recommended that a new Assistant Commissioner should be appointed to take charge of the secret service sections of Scotland Yard, in order to defuse the 'instinctive antipathy' between Sinclair and Childs; that all sections of the Intelligence community should make an effort to cooperate more closely; and that the Secret Service Committee should remain in existence on paper, 'as it were a sleeping partner . . . to which any fundamental differences of opinion arising between the various branches could, if necessary, be referred for advice or settlement'.[12] In terms of reorganisation or reform, therefore, the Committee's recommendations had hardly advanced matters beyond the conclusions reached in 1922. Although no record of Sinclair's reactions to the Report has been found, they can only have been disappointment and frustration.

It is tempting to take the view that he largely had himself to blame. He had alarmed both his Intelligence colleagues and the Committee by his drastic proposals and intemperate manner of presenting them (he had, for example, referred to the continued separate existence of IPI as a 'farce'). Though the language of the final Report was guarded, the minutes make it clear that the principal objection of witnesses to amalgamating the Intelligence bodies was based on alarm at the prospect of concentrating so much power in the hands of one man, particularly if that man were Sinclair. There were, of course, other arguments: Kell, understandably concerned to protect his own position and organisation, had underlined the basic differences between MI5 and SIS, while General Sir William Horwood, Chief Commissioner of the Metropolitan Police, made the point that it would be much easier for a hostile government to abolish one organisation than several. The DMO&I, Major-General Sir J. Burnett-Stuart, however, was blunter: 'C already had as much as he could manage . . . he would hesitate to put too much power into the hands of so energetic and capable an officer as C.'[13] The Committee's final report was more circumlocutory:

> we admit the vast potentialities inherent in the position of the chief of a combined secret service, but the danger there lies, we think, not so much in the use to which a good chief would put his powers, but in the difficulty of ensuring a succession of officers capable of filling such a post, and in the harm which might be done in it by a man who, after appointment, turned out to be incompetent.[14]

Meanwhile, Sinclair, who probably realised from an early stage that neither his fellow Intelligence Chiefs nor the Committee were going to endorse his proposals, had launched his own programme of internal reform and reorganisation while the Committee's deliberations were still in train. The question of the 'centralisation' of departments was addressed by moving SIS headquarters during 1925 from

Melbury Road to Broadway Buildings in Westminster, opposite St James's Park tube station and in close proximity to both Whitehall and Scotland Yard. GC&CS joined them there, the two organisations occupying initially two floors of the building but gradually expanding.[15] At the same time, the SIS office at Adam Street was closed, and Sinclair instructed that from 1 November 1925 the Passport Control Office should be used as an alternative mailing address. The PCO itself, under Major Spencer, was housed at 21 Queen Anne's Gate, with a passageway constructed for direct access to Broadway Buildings. In order to disguise the connection between the PCO and SIS, Sinclair forbade his staff from entering Headquarters through the Queen Anne's Gate entrance, though he himself used the connecting passageway to get to his office from his own flat in Queen Anne's Gate.[16] Morton, too, must have found Broadway a more convenient base than Melbury Road, within easy distance of the clubs of Pall Mall and St James's Street and for catching a train down to Westerham when travelling to his house at Crockham Hill.

Another important development in 1925 was the creation of a new SIS section, Section V, to deal with counter-intelligence and counter-Communist work,[17] following a pattern of establishing independent sections, answerable directly to C, in response to specific requirements. According to an SIS Office Order issued in November 1925, Section V was to be directed by Vivian (now returned from Cologne), and would take over from Section I responsibility for liaison with the India Office and Scotland Yard, while the latter section retained its liaison role with the Foreign and Colonial Offices and the Department of Overseas Trade. Section I was also to continue to compile the Communist Review, with collaboration from V: the heads of the two Sections were to work closely together and cover each other's absences.

Sinclair had made it clear to the Secret Service Committee that in his view the distinction between espionage and counter-espionage was an artificial one, and that SIS needed access to information about domestic subversion in order to prosecute their struggle against Bolshevik activities overseas:

> It was impossible to draw the line between espionage and contre-espionage, for both were concerned solely with foreign activities, and to attempt in practice to make a distinction between the two only led to overlapping . . . MI5 looked to him to obtain abroad information relating to spies working in the United Kingdom and were then supposed to follow it up in this country; but they had no 'agents' and had to rely on informers and the interception of letters in the post . . . Sir Maurice Hankey suggested that it was the growth of communism which had so materially changed our requirements in regard to secret service since the war and C agreed.[18]

Hankey's appreciation of the problem did not, however, lead him nor the rest of the Committee to favour the amalgamation of MI5 with SIS. SIS, therefore, needed their own sources of information on the activities of Bolshevik agents and their sympathisers, to supplement that received from their overseas representatives. Sinclair had, indeed, admitted to the Committee that SIS had agents in the UK, when during the second meeting on 2 March Anderson challenged him directly:

> Did C at present employ any agents in the United Kingdom? C replied that as neither MI5 nor Scotland Yard were prepared to do so, he had been compelled to make his own arrangements in this respect for checking information received from abroad and had done so successfully.[19]

As we have seen, Morton had made it his business to build up a network of domestic sources, and the business of the new Section V concerned him closely. As SIS evolved, so did his role as head of 'Production'. By 1926 SIS head office was organised in three main groups: geographical or 'G' sections, each headed by a senior officer and responsible for the control, administration and activities of a certain number of stations in the field, allotted on a geographical basis; the circulation or liaison sections (later called Requirements), and Finance. In addition to these were the independent sections, such as Section V. Morton, as 'Prod,' dealt with both geographical and circulation sections, while the business of Section V was connected to his work on Soviet Russia and Germany. In Vivian's absence, Section V correspondence was frequently signed off by Morton, or by other members of Production such as Maw and Plowden. Meanwhile, Section V took over responsibility for Morton's network of contacts acquired through Sir George Makgill and other UK-based agents, sometimes called 'Casuals', until a major row and reorganisation led to their transfer to MI5 in 1931.[20]

While his operational responsibilities had evolved, Morton had acquired increased administrative responsibilities, leading to his assumption, early in 1926, of the designation 'C.O', possibly denoting 'Chief' or 'Controlling' Officer.[21] Although it is not clear whether he thought this up for himself, its adoption probably reflects Sinclair's acceptance that the SIS structure, as it expanded and diversified, needed a senior figure to impose some cohesion and consistency on its administrative arrangements. Section V, for example, required a central bank of information. One of Sinclair's arguments for amalgamation with MI5 had been the need for easy and speedy access to MI5's extensive card index system in order to check on suspected Bolshevik agents or pro-Communist organisations. Although MI5 and SIS regularly exchanged useful information on subjects of mutual interest, the system was not conducive to rapid cross-checking.[22] By the time SIS received an answer to an enquiry about a suspicious character, Sinclair complained, the person had long since left the country. If amalgamation were ruled out, SIS needed its own improved registry and index system in order to enable Section V (and other parts of the organisation) to operate more effectively. This led to a major reorganisation of the SIS filing system in 1926, initiating a more flexible numbering and classification scheme.

It would be wrong, however, to give the impression that Morton's time was spent in supervising filing systems. His operational workload remained heavy. The creation of Section V was a direct response to the increasing volume of reports on Bolshevik activities being received by SIS, and to an expanding demand from SIS's Foreign Office customers. During 1925–6 Morton was on the receiving end of a constant stream of reports about Bolshevik activities aimed not just at subverting the British Government at home and abroad, but also more specifically at discrediting British Intelligence itself. According to an SIS report written in July 1927, to which Morton contributed, following the Zinoviev Letter episode Soviet Intelligence had taken every opportunity to expose the British Government to what it regarded as further 'humiliation' by encouraging forgers 'to concoct documents on genuine Soviet and Comintern paper, so that they might be "planted" and subsequently denied with proof of their falsity'. SIS had obtained specimens of the special paper used for this, and in early 1926 got hold of a pamphlet published by the Soviet authorities, containing facsimiles of a number of documents purporting to be specimens of forgeries. Reports were also received that during 1925–26 the OGPU was using its penetration of White Russian organisations to distribute false information and documents. The object of this campaign was not only to discredit the documentary information communicated to the British Government, but to 'draw' the Intelligence agencies in order to discover their methods and sources.

It appeared, however, that Soviet Intelligence had quite a lot to learn. According to a copy of a GPU report, obtained early in 1927 and sent to Morton by Commander Wilfred 'Biffy' Dunderdale, head of the SIS Paris station, British Intelligence comprised four services: the 'Secret Service', run by the FO, and employing journalists and former diplomats; the 'Intelligence Office' of the General Staff; the 'Naval Branch'; and the Department of Trade, who conducted espionage through commercial attachés. Another organisation – presumably intended to be MI5 – was also mentioned, working with Scotland Yard, and 'attempting without success to do contre-espionage work'. The report continued:

> The personnel employed by these organisations is not often very efficient, but at the same time, their moral standing is extremely high, and no officer except with excellent references can be accepted . . . It is hopeless to attempt to bribe any officers of the above organisations, therefore the only method remains to compromise them, and obtain a hold over their informants or agents.

Thanking Dunderdale, Morton wondered whether this was a serious report put forward by the GPU and 'really believed in by them', or concocted for foreign consumption in the assumption – or knowledge – that it would fall into British hands. If the former, it was important, as it demonstrated that Soviet Intelligence knew 'practically nothing of value' and were 'most erroneously informed on many points'. If concocted, the implications were equally serious: what did the

Russians really know; and what did they want? Any source of information, domestic or foreign, that might provide the answers to these questions, was of interest to SIS. One important domestic source, the All-Russian Cooperative Society Ltd, ARCOS, was to be compromised comprehensively in 1927.

The ARCOS Raid

On 12 May 1927 what can only be described as a motley crew of uniformed City of London police, members of Special Branch (indeed, members of several different sections of Special Branch who failed to talk to each other) and Intelligence officers – including Morton – converged on Moorgate St underground station at 4.30 p.m. in order to launch a raid on the offices of ARCOS, which shared premises at No. 49 Moorgate with the Soviet Trade Delegation. The raid was shambolic: final arrangements were made only a few hours beforehand; no one was quite sure who was in charge; few of the searchers knew what they were looking for, nor what they were allowed to do to, or with, the ARCOS employees within; nor with the papers they found there. The documents eventually removed from the building were, when translated, inconclusive and confusing. Despite all this, however, the raid was taken by the British Government as sufficient justification for the termination of the Anglo-Soviet Trade Agreement of 1921, the expulsion of the Soviet Trade Delegation and the rupture of diplomatic relations with the government of the USSR, decisions notified to the Soviet Chargé on 27 May.

The diplomatic repercussions of the raid were far-reaching. In a memorandum for the Cabinet of 24 January 1927, Chamberlain had set out the foreign and domestic implications of severing relations with the Soviet Union.[23] British diplomatic representatives in Berlin, Rome, Constantinople and Paris argued against a provocative move that could drive countries such as Poland and the Baltic States into the arms of Russia, at a time when German infractions of the military provisions of the Versailles Settlement and arguments in the fledgling League of Nations were causing widespread nervousness in the West. In domestic terms, the Conservative Government was concerned in particular with the potentially unifying effect of rupture on a divided British Labour movement. Nor did it seem at all probable that a breach would alter Soviet policy, and in February the Cabinet decided instead in favour of a note of protest designed, as Chamberlain informed the British Ambassador in Berlin, to 'give the Soviet Government one further opportunity to mend their manners'.[24] Not surprisingly, no improvements in courtesy ensued, only a vigorous anti-British campaign waged by Soviet representatives across Europe. After the raid on 12 May, and the consequent severance of relations, all the results predicted by Chamberlain in January came about, to greater or lesser degree.

In Intelligence terms, the ARCOS raid was equally damaging. Though hurriedly planned, chaotically executed and failing in its primary objective – to recover a stolen document – it was portrayed to Parliament and to the general public as an Intelligence triumph. In fact, it was closer to an Intelligence disaster. Failing to discover (at least in the immediate aftermath of the raid) sufficiently concrete evidence of espionage or clandestine activities, the Government was forced to produce in the House of Commons, in order to justify its decision to sever relations with the Soviet Union, incriminating documents that did not come from the ARCOS raid at all but had been obtained previously by GC&CS, intercepting communications between the Soviet Mission in the UK and Moscow. The production in Parliament, and publication of these documents for all to see in a Command Paper,[25] revealed their source beyond question, leading to the immediate abandonment by the Soviet Foreign Ministry of its methods of encipherment in favour of unbreakable One Time Pad systems for its communications; thereafter no high-grade Soviet diplomatic messages could be read by the British authorities.[26] Sinclair, for one, was in no doubt that an important source of information had been thrown away needlessly:

> The value to all Departments of Government of this particular type of information and the extreme delicacy of its source of origin need no emphasis. The publication of the telegrams automatically stops their source of supply for some years at least. It was authorised only as a measure of desperation to bolster up a cause vital to Government, which had the facts been fully known at the time, needed no such costly support.

There were broader repercussions too. The raid, described (again by Sinclair) as the 'irretrievable loss of an unprecedented opportunity', cut across a number of promising Intelligence operations directed at ARCOS; it also highlighted again the innate divisions and inefficiencies of the Secret Service as a whole, presenting the Chief of SIS with yet another opportunity of arguing before the Secret Service Committee his case for a major reorganisation of British Intelligence machinery.

It is hard not to draw the conclusion from the available documentation[27] that the ARCOS raid was a half-baked idea executed hastily, with unfortunate results. But if the occasion were insufficient, the timing wrong and the result not only disappointing but damaging, it must be legitimate to ask why the ARCOS raid took place when it did, and what went wrong; questions to which the answers are by no means obvious or straightforward. As a key episode in British Intelligence history, closely involving Morton, it bears detailed examination. Although tracing Morton's involvement in the operation may not permit any conclusive judgements, it does serve to cast more light than hitherto into a distinctly shady corner, not least because he wrote a 'full' account of the raid after the event – an account that, as usual with Morton, must be handled with care. It must be remembered that both Morton and Sinclair had an interest both in justifying SIS's role after the event, and in emphasising the extent and effects of poor Intelligence coordination.

All sections of the British Intelligence machinery were very interested in ARCOS. It was the organ through which, with a family of subsidiary companies, all Soviet industrial and commercial bodies had to transact their business in the UK, and through which the STD – on terms of formal relations with the British Government, and enjoying some limited diplomatic privileges – conducted its operations. ARCOS' financial muscle, with capital of £1m and majority share-holdings affording it access to funds of between £2m and £3m, put it in a powerful position to constitute, according to one SIS report, 'the germ of the State organisation through which commerce and industry will be run in Soviet England'.

This might be considered an exaggerated, not to say alarmist view of ARCOS' role. Nevertheless, MI5, together with Special Branch, had solid evidence for suspicion of ARCOS activities in the UK and its role as an instrument of Comintern financing and propaganda activities – one report memorably described ARCOS as Moscow's 'very expensive toy'. In the same way, SIS had evidence that ARCOS was (in close cooperation with Berlin) the hub of a European financing operation for Bolshevik propaganda and subversive activities, even though its senior staff took great care, on security grounds, to distance the organisation from any overt connection with either the Comintern or with the CPGB. ARCOS was a generous employer, offering (unusually for the 1920s) both holiday and sick pay, and seeking out staff to meet its particular needs, including bilingual Russian/English speakers (such as Russian-born British subjects forcibly repatriated in 1919), Irish nationalists and disaffected police officers dismissed for going on strike.[28] ARCOS was, in short, a rich potential source of information on subversive activities, on which each Agency had its own sources of information that it did not necessarily share with the others.

In the spring of 1927 there were a number of simultaneous intelligence investigations being conducted into the activities of ARCOS, including a promising line of enquiry, being pursued on an inter-Agency basis, relating to one Jacob Kirchenstein, alias 'Johnny Walker', who was not only a senior ARCOS official but was thought to be one of the chief agents of the Third International in England and at the centre of revolutionary organisation in the UK.[29] SIS, and in particular Section V, also had its own sources of information on ARCOS. Morton himself was receiving reports through an intermediary from the former skipper of a Russian icebreaker who was employed at ARCOS to do odd jobs. MI5 were investigating reports of an espionage organisation run from ARCOS, based on the services of veteran British communists and trades unionists;[30] later adding that, at the time of the ARCOS raid, both Scotland Yard and military authorities had 'for many months' been investigating 'the activities of a group of secret agents engaged in endeavouring to obtain highly secret documents relating to the Armed Forces of Great Britain'.[31] It is, of course, possible that any or all of these investigations were being compromised by the two members of Special Branch working for the Russians at this time.[32]

SIS were certainly more than interested in finding out what really went on inside 49 Moorgate. In October 1926 they were presented with a new opportunity when an ARCOS employee, 'X',[33] described by Morton as 'a British subject of undoubted loyalty', contacted Morton's colleague Maw, who lived near X, and said he could tell him what went on in ARCOS. According to Morton, Maw consulted Sinclair, who directed that X should communicate with Scotland Yard rather than SIS: X, however, had already been in contact with the police and was unhappy with his reception; he preferred to talk to Maw. (Morton later claimed to have had no knowledge of these exchanges, but in view of his, and Maw's position in Production and work with Section V, this is difficult to accept.) For the next six months, X met Maw occasionally and passed on some information of minor interest. On 30 March 1927, however, X produced evidence provided by 'Y', a disaffected former ARCOS employee, that an official British military document had been photocopied at the ARCOS offices. Maw took the evidence straight to Sinclair, who the following day passed it to Kell. The document in question was the cover of a Signals Training pamphlet which had been distributed to Aldershot 1st and 2nd Divisions in September 1926.[34] As Sinclair later explained to the Secret Service Committee:

> The original information in the case was secured by the SIS organisation. Since, however, it concerned an act of espionage against the Armed Forces, SIS was not, according to the existing constitution, competent to lead it into concrete issues and the matter was surrendered to MI5. The latter department naturally insisted, before proceeding to action, upon satisfying itself of the reliability of the evidence.[35]

It was to take well over a month before MI5 were satisfied with the 'reliability of the evidence' passed to them by SIS. Two weeks passed while Kell had enquiries made at Aldershot regarding the document that had been photocopied. Then Brigadier Harker of MI5 insisted on seeing both X and Y, the latter of whom claimed to have been given the incriminating document to copy. For the purpose of these contacts Harker used the name 'Parker', while X – (identified for Harker's benefit as having the appearance of 'a third class clerk') – used the name 'Smith'. Elaborate arrangements were made, alarming both X and Y, who became increasingly anxious that their identities should be protected. According to Morton, Kell had to sign a sworn statement that X and Y's names would not be revealed before they would agree to see Harker; only after their meeting, on 9 May, was Harker satisfied that the story was true.

Once convinced of the reliability of the information, however, Harker and Kell moved swiftly, preparing a statement of the case during 10 May. The sequence of events on 11 May is of some importance. After consulting, at 11 a.m., the Director of Public Prosecutions, who confirmed that the copying of the pamphlet was, technically, an offence under the 1911 Official Secrets Act, Kell attempted to show his statement to Sir John Anderson, Permanent Secretary at the Home Office, seeking an appointment at noon. Anderson was, however, unavailable, as were the DMO&I and the CIGS, both of whom Kell tried next; at 12.45 p.m., he showed the statement in confidence to Sir Wyndham Childs. After lunch, Kell was on his way back to his office when he encountered, by chance, the Secretary of State for War, Sir Laming Worthington-Evans, and secured an appointment for later that afternoon. At 5.15 p.m. he showed the statement to Worthington-Evans, who referred him in turn to the Home Secretary.

Joynson-Hicks, perhaps the most rabidly anti-Soviet of Baldwin's Ministers, saw Kell at 5.40 and immediately recognised the opportunity presented by his story.[36] The fact that the document photocopied at ARCOS was of military origin was, to him, especially inflammatory. He, together, with other like-minded Ministers and officials, regarded any hint of sedition, or contact between Bolshevism and the armed forces, as a threat to the very fabric of Britain. The Home Secretary took Kell's statement immediately to the Prime Minister and found the Foreign Secretary with him: on the basis of the information presented to them, Baldwin and Chamberlain agreed that ARCOS should be raided. Kell told Childs of the decision at 6.40 p.m., and a warrant was sought from the City magistrate to enter ARCOS, search and seize 'any sketch, plan, model, article, note or document, or things of a like nature, or anything whatsoever which is or may be evidence of an offence having been or being about to be committed' against the Official Secrets Acts of 1911 and 1920. According to his own account, Kell's reaction to the Ministers' decision was one of astonishment.[37] It did – and does, indeed – appear both extraordinary and precipitate. Chamberlain had consistently expressed himself determined not to yield to 'pinpricks' from the Soviet Union; Baldwin himself was disinclined constitutionally towards hasty or provocative action. Nevertheless, they agreed, on the evidence presented by Kell, apparently on the spur of the moment, to take a step which was bound to have far-reaching consequences. Why?

One reason might be a momentary loss of patience on the part of Chamberlain, emerging from a long build-up of frustration with the policies and practices employed by the Soviet Government. The position he had adopted throughout 1926 of 'no breach unless we are forced to it' had become increasingly difficult to sustain, particularly in the light of suspected and actual Soviet financial support for the miners' strike and General Strike in that year. Nor did there seem much prospect of improvement. Contrary to the hopes or expectations of many, nine years after the November Revolution the Bolshevik regime had not collapsed and recurrent predictions of its imminent demise through financial collapse proved unfulfilled.[38] The Soviet strategy of continued pressure for financial concessions, combined with relentless covert subversive propaganda and incitement throughout the Empire and in Europe, was regarded by many politicians and officials as intolerable, even if opinions remained divided as to whether it was better to try and modify (or 'civilise') Soviet behaviour by cultivating relations, or to ostracise the Soviet regime in the increasingly vain hope that it would collapse.

In December 1926 J.D. Gregory, now an Under Secretary at the FO, had noted in a memorandum that 'the agitation for the expulsion of the Bolshevik Mission (or missions) from this country is becoming well-nigh irresistible', though concluding that a breach of relations was undesirable:

> The arguments *pro* and *con* are to some extent evenly balanced, and, though a negative policy suggests a certain paralysis, a positive policy in this case is unlikely to make things, taken as a whole, any better than they are at present. Being a leap in the dark, it might easily make things worse. The ejection of the Bolsheviks from this country would be a thoroughly pleasurable proceeding, but it would be rather the satisfaction of an emotion than an act of useful diplomacy.[39]

On 12 May 1927, at 6 p.m., urged on by the Home Secretary, Chamberlain might be thought to have satisfied his emotions, forgetting useful diplomacy. We should not, however, judge him too hastily. The evidence suggests that he did not realise – and was not informed of – the full implications of the decision; in particular, the fact that a raid on ARCOS meant, *de facto*, a raid on the Soviet Trade Delegation that was bound to be considered an infringement of diplomatic immunity (although the STD's immunity was strictly limited.)[40] In fact, he was reassured in the opposite sense: as Anderson told the Secret Service Committee on 24 June:

> Sir William Joynson-Hicks assured Sir Austen, in answer to a question from him, that on such information as he had before him he would be prepared to raid any other English company, and on this assurance Sir Austen agreed to the raid.

Tyrrell underlined the point:

> Sir Austen Chamberlain's consent only covered the raid on ARCOS: if the Trade Delegation had been mentioned Sir Austen would undoubtedly have hesitated and consulted the Foreign Office before agreeing to it.[41]

Certainly, the FO – or any of the Intelligence Chiefs, including Kell – could have warned Chamberlain of the sensitivity of ARCOS' cohabitation with the STD at 49 Moorgate. To Sinclair, Chesham House, home of the Soviet Legation in London, seemed a much more promising target, as he later told the Secret Service Committee:

> C said that he, K[ell] and Sir Wyndham Childs all knew that ARCOS and the Trade Delegation were in the same building and realised that raiding ARCOS meant raiding the Trade Delegation, which he, C, fully understood would raise serious political issues . . . ARCOS had never appealed to him particularly; moreover, it was known that all Soviet agencies abroad had had orders to burn any compromising papers.[42]

The latter was an important point. Kirchenstein was later to claim that 'about a week or ten days' before the raid the strong rooms and safes in the ARCOS offices had been cleared out, and the contents packed up and shipped off to Moscow in the Soviet diplomatic bag. He claimed that this had been done merely because of a general feeling that 'things were closing in'; and it is certainly true that nearly all the documentation found during the raid on 12 May was disappointing. This raises an intriguing question about the ARCOS raid that it has not so far proved possible to answer from the Intelligence archives. According to both MI5 and SIS accounts, the raid was decided on only during the evening of 11 May, and took place the following day. There are, however, some tantalising suggestions to the contrary.

It has been argued, for example, that a new source of telegrams, from Peking, intercepted by GC&CS, provided information that prompted the raid.[43] Even more intriguing is the suggestion of the involvement of Morton's old contact, Vladimir Orlov. On 4 April 1927 Morton wrote to Scotland Yard asking whether Orlov would be allowed into the UK; a 'very good source' had suggested that he might be coming to visit his children, at school in England. Scotland Yard reported no sign of him: but on 26 April the SIS representative in Berlin reported that Orlov had been granted a visa to make arrangements for his son's university education. Then Helsinki reported information that Orlov had come to the UK at the beginning of May at the invitation of 'the British Intelligence Service'; and on 22 June Vivian wrote to Scotland Yard that according to Dunderdale (who had an informant in Berlin keeping an eye on Orlov):

> ORLOV, on his return to Berlin, stated that he had been invited to London by the British authorities in connection with the raid on ARCOS, and had no document been found, his advice would have been taken as to how to place a suitable forgery. It is to be regretted that the opportunity of finding out more about this individual's activities and connections in the UK was apparently missed during his recent visit.

The last sentence implies that if anyone invited Orlov to the UK, it was not SIS. But if not SIS, then who? And did Morton, or Sinclair, know? If he were invited, when did he come? If he did come, it would presuppose a premeditated raid, not one arranged the night before. There are no hard facts here, and the whole story may be an illusion. If Morton knew more about it, it is not revealed in the surviving documentation. By the middle of July, he was writing to Harker about his suspicions that Orlov worked for the GPU:

> From our information it is clear that ORLOV should be regarded as a potential enemy agent, and I am positive that he would not hesitate to work sources in this country if he saw any financial gain in doing so.

In the absence of any firm information to weigh against the considerable evidence provided from MI5 and SIS sources, it is impossible to assess the possibility that the raid was, in fact, pre-planned, or that Orlov – or indeed Macartney, 'Monocle Man', who also later claimed to have had prior knowledge – were involved. The detailed accounts, and chronologies, available from these sources, though inconclusive, support the idea that the decision was, in fact, a last-minute one, and that subsequent claims resulted from a desire by certain parties to jump on the bandwagon. But it is impossible to be sure.

On the morning of 12 May, Kell and Harker visited the Chief Commissioner of Police and the Assistant Commissioner, CID, while Childs told Inspector Parker of Special Branch about the impending raid; for jurisdictional reasons, it had to be carried out by the uniformed City police, who would then invite Childs and Special Branch to take charge. Neither the police nor Special Branch officers designated to carry out the raid were warned until 1 p.m. of what was afoot, having, apparently, been given to understand that they were to stand by to visit a port 'in connection with an imaginary consignment of arms'. Inspectors Miller and Liddell of SS1, the SIS liaison section, did not hear about the raid until 3 p.m., much to their annoyance.

According to Morton, the first intimation to SIS of the impending raid on ARCOS did not come until 12.40 p.m., when he was summoned by telephone to see Childs. His account of what happened when he arrived at Scotland Yard at 12.50 is representative of his long and detailed record. It was written, in accordance with Morton's habit when distancing himself from unfortunate events, in the third person:

> When Major Morton entered, Carter [of Special Branch] had his watch out and was saying to Sir Wyndham Childs that he thought he could manage it all right, but had to go and see an agent now, how long a run was it by Tube from Westminster to Moorgate? After a brief discussion Carter left, and Sir Wyndham Childs turned to Major Morton and said 'I suppose you know what is in the wind', and explained that they were going to raid ARCOS. He invited Major Morton to accompany the raid. The latter said he would very much like to, but must get his Chief's permission first. No account was given as to the reasons for the raid. Kell, on enquiry, merely saying, 'it is the result of that man of yours that you know about'. Being obviously unwilling to say more, Major Morton could not press him, though he did not know anything of M[aw]'s man at the time.

Even taking a charitable view, this account seems scarcely credible. If – which seems unlikely – Morton knew nothing of Maw, 'X' and the subsequent investigations by MI5, his calm acceptance of Childs's startling announcement that ARCOS, an organisation in which Morton took a close interest and where SIS had informants, was about to be raided, and his unwillingness to question Kell, are not only unconvincing but would, if true, be uncharacteristically unprofessional. Morton then, apparently, went back to tell Sinclair what was afoot, but finding him at lunch, told no one else but went to lunch himself, returning to Broadway at 3 p.m. Sinclair, informed that the raid was due to take place later that afternoon, thought it would be a good idea to tell the FO about it: Chamberlain, having given permission for the raid to proceed, had not been told that it would happen the following day, and had not passed any information to his officials. Sinclair went personally to see Gregory, who informed Chamberlain, and at 4.50 p.m. – twenty minutes after the raid had begun, in London, but offering a few hours' notice to Moscow – a 'Very Secret' telegram was despatched to the Embassy: 'You ought to know that ARCOS is being raided at 4.30 this afternoon, and you will therefore take such precautions as occur to you.'[44]

Meanwhile, Morton had returned to Scotland Yard and travelled with Childs in his car to Moorgate Street tube station (a journey of only thirteen minutes, in 1927). There, together with a large number of other prospective participants – creating an irresistible mental image of trenchcoats and bowler hats – they 'stood about separately under the arcade, which was full of people, so as not to attract notice'. At 4.30 the uniformed police and Special Branch officers, followed by Childs, Carter and Morton, entered 49 Moorgate. Morton's account of the subsequent proceedings seems, on the surface, designed deliberately to provoke incredulity if not ridicule, despite its studiously neutral language.[45] Long periods of inaction interspersed by violent interludes: the inability of the searchers to read Russian, leading to Morton's being asked to bring along interpreters the following day; ignorance of which rooms to search; the confusion over whether the search warrant allowed them to remove any document except the Signals Pamphlet (which was not found); all are described by Morton in a way that makes clear his sense of frustration with the proceedings:

> Major Morton has no first hand knowledge as to what was happening elsewhere in the building during this period, but from his observation a few hours afterwards, nothing was happening. No one seemed to be in charge, there was no one to appeal to for orders or to organise the search. Carter was busy arguing with the chief officials of ARCOS regarding the opening of the safes; the City Police were on duty guarding the rooms and the rest of S[pecial] B[ranch] appeared to be wandering about and wondering what to do next. At about 8 o'clock, when all the principal documents in Room 5 seemed to have been copied, Major Morton went off to dinner, in company with Major Phillips [of MI5], whom he met in the passage way.

Morton's account of the ARCOS raid is not just an exercise in personal self-exculpation. It is clear from supporting documentation that both he and Sinclair were furious about the raid and the way it was conducted. It has not been possible to discover how much they may have known, or suspected about it in advance: nevertheless, its timing, conduct and aftermath appear to have run directly counter to SIS interests. Morton, and Section V, were running operations connected with

ARCOS, while the Kirchenstein investigation was close to bearing fruit, and could have led to widespread raids and arrests. Both Sinclair and Morton were incensed by Childs's refusal to secure the Home Secretary's agreement to the further raids that both Sinclair and Kell urged should take place immediately after that on ARCOS. To stiffen Childs's resolve, on 17 May, following a meeting at the Foreign Office, Sinclair asked Morton to deliver the following message:

> Sir Austen Chamberlain wished a message conveyed personally to Sir Wyndham Childs from him that, whereas Sir Wyndham was the servant of another Department and could therefore in no way influence his actions, he thought it might be of assistance to Sir Wyndham to know that if, as a result of the documents found in ARCOS or in raids resulting out of the first raid on ARCOS, a statement could be made clear enough to be understood by the man in the street, and powerful enough to convince the latter that the Soviet Trade and Diplomatic authorities were engaged in subversive propaganda, agitation and espionage against Great Britain he, Sir Austen, would throw his whole weight in the Cabinet on the side of breaking the Trade Agreement, and if necessary, severing Diplomatic relations as well.

The message had no effect on Childs or the Home Office: no further raids took place; according to Morton, Childs told him that the Home Secretary had vetoed them after he was told that there was no probability of finding the missing 'State document' – the Signals pamphlet – at any of the addresses it was proposed to raid. (Morton later said that he had heard from 'a reasonably trustworthy source' that both Kell and Childs considered 'it was the other official's duty to undertake the further raids'.) The situation became even worse: Morton considered the report on the raid being prepared by Captain Miller of Special Branch, for the Home Secretary to draw on in a presentation to the Cabinet, was both misleading and confusing. Bland, to whom Miller showed the draft at lunch at the Travellers' Club on 18 May, agreed. Their arguments were, however, ignored:

> Major Morton does not now think that Captain Miller understood what was being pointed out to him even at this stage, though on this occasion and on previous occasions, Major Morton himself at any rate, had quite exceeded the limits of criticism which would be possible in any ordinary Departmental conference . . .

Later that day Sinclair saw Miller's draft and was (according to Morton) appalled. He asked Morton to stay in the office overnight and draw up an alternative: the resulting document, together with Miller's report, was taken to Chamberlain by Sinclair early next morning. It clearly had little effect. By the time the Cabinet met to discuss next steps, on 23 May, the situation was beyond retrieval. The raid had already damaged Anglo-Soviet relations and handed the Soviet Government a propaganda victory, inspiring mass protests throughout the Soviet Union. On 19 May the British Embassy in Moscow had reported big demonstrations and a revival of the popular belief (now being exploited enthusiastically by the Government) in an anti-Soviet bloc organised by Chamberlain. Mr Peters added politely:

> I need hardly emphasise that in the above I am stating the matter entirely from the point of view of a British recorder of events in Moscow, necessarily in ignorance of the grounds for, and results of, the London raid.[46]

The Cabinet decided on 23 May to terminate the Trade Agreement and sever diplomatic relations. Chamberlain informed the Soviet Chargé in a note on 27 May that there were 'limits to the patience of His Majesty's Government and of public opinion here, and these limits have now been reached.'[47] An urgent personal note from Sinclair to Tyrrell on 26 May, drawing his attention to a document found during the ARCOS raid, but hitherto overlooked, that afforded 'direct proof of the participation of members of the Soviet Legation in revolutionary activities in this country',[48] arrived too late to avert the public compromising of the Government's GC&CS sources. As Sinclair later complained to Tyrrell:

> had the existence of this document been known in time, and especially if there had still been a possibility of obtaining additional evidence through further searches, it would not have been necessary to authorise the publication of the six telegrams which appeared as Part II of the White Paper.[49]

The Secret Service Committee met to consider the ARCOS raid on 24 June 1927. It had, in fact, already met on two previous occasions in 1927. At its first meeting, on 11 March, Fisher had informed his colleagues that the Prime Minister wished the Committee to be reassembled because he was 'greatly concerned regarding the state of affairs at Scotland Yard', particularly in the light of an incident at the end of 1926 when a leakage of information to the *Evening Standard* had resulted in a foreign agent cancelling a visit to the UK where he was about to be arrested. Tyrrell added that the principal source of Baldwin's concern:

> was the fear that the political work done at Scotland Yard might at any moment give rise to a scandal, owing to the Labour party obtaining some plausible pretext to complain that a government department was being employed for party politics. Home politics were tending more and more to a contest between Conservatives and Socialists, and there was grave danger that the government of the day might sooner or later turn to Scotland Yard for information needed in the party struggle. We ought,

if possible to devise a scheme whereby the government can get its information about Communist activities without having to apply for it through a paid officer of the crown.[50]

The Zinoviev Letter had clearly left its mark. Though the other members of the Committee expressed their doubts about the practicability or desirability of Baldwin's ideas – as Anderson pointed out, it would still be necessary to invoke the Home Secretary in order to act on any information, however secretly received – the Committee agreed to discuss Scotland Yard. They returned to the subject of their recommendations in previous years (never implemented), that sections SS1 and SS2 of Special Branch should be transferred to SIS. Before the second meeting, held on 22 March, Tyrell underlined his views in a letter to Fisher of 14 March:

> I feel I must place on record my view that the dangers inherent in the present system are such that no possible stone ought to be left unturned in order to separate those members of Scotland Yard, whose salaries are paid from the Secret Service vote, more definitely from an official government department than they can possibly be when they share the same building and are directed by a salaried official . . . The case calls for an operation: manipulation will at best be only a palliative, and I shall not feel comfortable – nor, I feel sure, will the Prime Minister – until this particular member has been amputated and grafted on to some obscure trunk.[51]

Then came the ARCOS raid, and although, at the Committee's third meeting on 24 June 1927, Anderson said 'he did not think the episode strengthened the claim for any radical alteration of existing arrangements', the situation had clearly changed. It was agreed that Sinclair, Kell and Childs should be summoned separately to put their own sides of the story. Predictably, Sinclair had not waited for his summons but had already put forward his views in a memorandum sent to Tyrrell on 28 June:

> The circumstances underlying the police raid on ARCOS Ltd on 12.5.27 and its subsequent developments afford a valuable illustration of certain defects, to which attention has previously been drawn, in the organisation of the Secret Service . . . It is not desired to reflect in any way upon the actions or efficiency of individual Secret Service officials. They could hardly have acted otherwise than they did in the circumstances. But it is considered that the circumstances of organisation in which these officials are called upon to act in cases like the ARCOS raid are such as to render confusion and misdirection of energy inevitable.[52]

As in 1925, he listed the deficiencies in the present system, reserving his strongest criticism for the way that the documents seized in the ARCOS raid had been evaluated, and the report compiled by Special Branch: again, he advised that 'The remedy lies in the unification' of MI5, SIS and Special Branch.

At the Committee's fourth meeting on 30 June 1927, Sinclair's account of the events leading up to the raid followed the lines of the report prepared by Morton. He supported Morton's version of events at all points, and expressed approval of his conduct. When Hankey suggested, for example, that Morton might have taken some action after his first visit to Scotland Yard on 12 May, 'C explained that he was not sufficiently familiar with the subject to grasp its full import'. This was clearly an untruth, even if Morton had not known the full history of Maw, X and Y. Sinclair's unwillingness to entertain any criticism of Morton's conduct was, however, not only in line with his invariable policy of supporting his staff and SIS as an organisation, but also reflected his single-minded approach to the Committee's work. By 30 June he, and Morton, had already conducted an internal inquest on the ARCOS raid and its aftermath. He was certainly not going to discuss its operational implications with the Secret Service Committee. His purpose in giving evidence was to press the case for institutional reform.

Once more, he was to be disappointed. The Committee's proceedings fizzled out inconclusively. Its members were disinclined to take Sinclair's lectures too seriously; possibly they did not realise the full implications of what had happened. Their chief criticisms (though still mild) were reserved for Kell: for not keeping C informed between the time when the latter handed over X's evidence and the time of the raid; but more particularly, for daring to approach Ministers directly rather than going through the proper channels. Tyrrell expressed himself 'shocked' that Kell had had direct access to the Home Secretary on 11 May, emphasising the impropriety: 'He spoke from long experience of the disastrous results arising from the omission of stages in the ordinary channels of communication with political heads of departments.' His colleagues solemnly agreed. Otherwise, they were disinclined to view the raid too tragically, concurring in Anderson's verdict that 'Cooperation had been good on the detective plane, although there had been some impetuosity higher up.'[53]

If Sinclair were cast down by yet another rejection of his ideas, he cannot have been surprised. The outcome only strengthened his, and Morton's, determination to improve SIS's own anti-Bolshevik capability and efficiency. The severance of diplomatic relations with the Soviet Union made little difference to the business of espionage and subversion. Covert operations that had been run through ARCOS were disrupted by the raid, but their direction was soon discovered to have relocated to Antwerp and Hamburg. The European travels of certain suspected spies continued to be watched closely by Morton and by Section V. A particular focus for their scrutiny was one Wilfred Macartney, also known as 'Monocle Man' or (his own favourite) 'King of the Underworld'.

'Monocle Man': the case of Wilfred Macartney

In 1933 the writer Compton Mackenzie (who had employed Macartney on secret work during the First World War)[54] referred to him in a private letter as 'that unfortunate man who is now serving ten years' penal servitude for comic opera espionage'.[55] There is, indeed, an element of the comic and even ludicrous attaching to his case, although the charges against him and his fellow defendant Georg Hansen were serious and the penalty severe. A detailed account of the case made against them can be followed in the records of the court proceedings.[56] These reveal the central role played in the prosecution case by Morton's evidence: they include a copy of the sworn statement submitted by 'Major Desmond John Falkiner Morton', though during the *in camera* proceedings on 17 January 1928 he was sworn in as 'Peter Hamilton,' the alias he had adopted in late 1925 in preference to Major Stanley. He was known as Mr Hamilton by George Monkland, his informant on Macartney. Morton's statement, though long and factual, does not quite convey either the 'comic opera' – or the sinister – elements of the affair, nor the extent or thoroughness of SIS's enquiries into Macartney's activities. They regarded him as providing serious evidence of Soviet espionage in the United Kingdom, and of the ongoing subversive activities directed by Soviet Intelligence from abroad.

Wilfred Francis Remington Macartney's history was extraordinary enough. Born at the turn of the century in Malta, in 1916 he inherited £70,000, a considerable fortune, on the death of his father who had made his money in the Malta Tramways. Meanwhile, Macartney had joined the Royal Naval Volunteer Reserve and spent an adventurous war, serving first as a Censor Staff Officer in Syria and then as Military Control Officer on the island of Zea in the Aegean (working to Mackenzie, then employed by SIS). The latter role led him to claim thereafter that he had 'worked for the British Secret Service'.[57] He ran through his inheritance like a knife through butter, and proved quite unable to modify his spending habits when it melted away: by his own admission, he went 'completely wrong' after the First World War, floating a series of bogus companies and taking part in numerous creative financial swindles. By 1925 he was almost bankrupt and claimed to be a convert to Communism, although he seems to have regarded it as a business opportunity rather than a spiritual home. Living at once lavishly and hand to mouth, he posed variously as a member of the aristocracy, a naval officer, an army officer, and even as a former Governor of a British territory. He was described in an SIS report – probably written by Morton – as:

> very neatly dressed, usually wears an eyeglass, and of excellent address
> and good education; small to medium height, clean shaven, dark hair
> usually worn brushed right back from his forehead . . . WFR Macartney
> is completely unscrupulous, can never tell the truth about any matter, is
> very clever but not quite so clever as he thinks.

The final phrase (which has a Mortonesque flavour) appears to have some substance. Macartney certainly fostered the impression of a master criminal, well-connected, successful and charismatic. In a telegram to Dunderdale, Morton referred to Macartney's reputation as 'King of the Underworld': 'many first class cat burglars, safe breakers and confidence tricksters come to him for advice.' It is likely, however, that Morton was being facetious: in reality, Macartney seems to have been a somewhat inept and unlucky criminal, long on ideas but short on execution, with extravagant appetites but always short of cash. Nevertheless, his connections with the intelligence underworld, while probably less prestigious than he pretended, should not be undervalued: Morton, well aware of Macartney's history, did not do so.

In February 1926 Macartney was convicted of burglary – a somewhat mysterious incident[58] – and sentenced to nine months' imprisonment. On emerging from prison in October, desperate for money, he approached two newspapers, the *Sunday Worker* and the *Daily Herald*, offering to provide them with inside stories of his life as a Secret Service agent. These activities brought him to the renewed attention of both SIS and Scotland Yard. On 13 October Morton wrote to Ball at MI5, advising that an eye be kept on Macartney; and on 19 October, Inspector Liddell of Special Branch informed Vivian that the *Sunday Worker* had:

> made arrangements with Macartney to supply it with any information that he can obtain of impending attacks on the Reds, as he claims that he can secure this from past acquaintances in the Service. He is also to warn the paper of any plans against Russia. Further, he is supplying it with about a dozen articles on his experiences in the Service, together with inside information . . . He is joining the Communist Party of Great Britain.

SIS were unperturbed about Macartney's prospective 'revelations', considering them 'quite harmless and utterly untrue'. Section V were, however, interested in his attempts, through his approach to the *Sunday Worker* and *Daily Herald*, to get in touch with Soviet circles. From other sources they knew that members of staff on those newspapers had carried out certain information-gathering activities for the OGPU, both at home and through foreign correspondents. It was later discovered that during the winter of 1925–26, before his period of imprisonment, Macartney had been put in contact by the *Sunday Worker* with a shop steward named Messer, who had kept Macartney under close observation for some time before putting him in touch with the Soviet Secret Service. Despite SIS's suspicions, however, in the autumn of 1926 no concrete evidence was discovered of these connections, or of any illegal activities on Macartney's part, and no action was taken against him.

In late March 1927, however, an acquaintance of Macartney's, a young insurance broker named George Monkland, made contact with Admiral 'Blinker' Hall, saying that he had 'come across something curious which he thought would be of interest to the British Government': a lunch was arranged on 29 March with Hall and the former Deputy Chief of SIS, Freddie Browning, who still maintained an active interest in Intelligence matters.[59] Monkland handed over a document – described by Morton in his statement as 'a most intricate and exhaustive questionnaire on the Air Force of Great Britain'; Hall, on Browning's recommendation, passed it not to MI5, but to Sinclair, who gave it to Morton. The latter, according to his own account, immediately recognised the document to be 'the work of an expert' and considered that it 'could only have had origin in the Government Offices of a foreign power', probably Soviet Russia; an assessment that was confirmed by the Air Ministry, though they thought it was 'so complete that [it] must have been compiled by the united efforts of several experts'.

Morton lost no time in making contact with Monkland according to the procedures suggested by Browning, using 'emerald' as a code word and introducing himself as 'Peter Hamilton'. Morton said he adopted an assumed name because he 'could not discover any mutual acquaintance' with Monkland,[60] providing confirmation that it was his practice only to use an alias when dealing with contacts outside the Establishment 'circle', or (as in the case of Makgill) when any meetings or correspondence were likely to extend to 'outsiders'. Morton and Monkland met for the first time the next day, 30 March 1927. Their encounter was the first of many contacts in the next eight months, during which period Monkland acted as an intermediary between 'Peter Hamilton' (who also used the codename 'Sunfish') and Macartney, in an attempt to get the latter to incriminate himself, and in the process lead SIS to further Soviet agents and operations.

The route by which Morton became involved with the Macartney case is of some interest both in respect of the workings of British Intelligence and of Morton's own role. When first put in touch with Monkland through a mutual acquaintance, Admiral Hall's first reaction was to bring him together with Browning, rather than with Kell or someone else from MI5, the Agency that might have seemed the obvious choice to deal with the matter. Browning's instincts, too, were to refer the matter to SIS, not to MI5: although he himself had left SIS in 1919, his contacts there remained close, and he and Sinclair in particular were in regular contact. It may, of course, have been the two men's close relationship with Sinclair (in Hall's case, through a shared background in naval intelligence) that made them act as they did. Probably, however, they were also influenced by the document handed over by Monkland, with its implications of Soviet espionage: reflecting the perception not just that 'foreign' matters were SIS's responsibility, but also that MI5 did not have the expertise nor executive capability to deal with such matters. This was certainly Sinclair's view: his immediate reaction was to pass the questionnaire to Morton, not to Vivian and Section V, though they became involved; nor back to MI5, soon brought into the loop through Morton's communicating with Ball. The involvement of Macartney, who was known to SIS and had some previous, if tenuous connection with the organisation, only confirmed Sinclair in his view of how the matter should be handled. Soviet espionage was involved, and this was directly in his, and Morton's, line of business.

As for George Monkland, he seemed, as Morton admitted, a dubious character. Like Macartney, whom Monkland had known since 1919, he had a taste for the high life without the means to support it, and it was likely that he had been involved in some of Macartney's earlier financial escapades. From the start Morton was on his guard lest Monkland's approach were nothing more than an attempt to extract money, or, more seriously, might be inspired by Soviet Intelligence. He made extensive enquiries and arranged to have Monkland kept under close observation, his telephone tapped and his post intercepted. This involved close contact with MI5 and Scotland Yard, who had to secure the necessary warrants and undertake the tapping of phones and opening of mail. Morton shared the information received from Monkland with both these bodies, and also, at an early stage, involved the French *Sûreté*, whose help he needed in keeping track of Macartney during the latter's frequent trips to France.

Despite Monkland's equivocal history and dubious connections, however, Morton came to trust him, at least for the purposes of the operation (unlike Macartney, whom he considered an 'inveterate liar and crook'). He became convinced that Monkland was acting from patriotic motives, particularly in view of the fact that he never sought or received any payment for his services, despite being put to some trouble and anxiety in his intermediary role. When cross-examined in court by Mr St John Hutchinson as to whether he still trusted Monkland after the contents of the latter's correspondence suggested criminal activity, Morton replied: 'Certainly'; his reasoning clearly struck a chord with the Lord Chief Justice, presiding over the case, who remarked to St John Hutchinson that:

> when Long John Silver sent Hawkins to draw some rum he said 'I trust you' but he did not, he had got a measure on the barrel.[61]

Morton kept 'a measure on the barrel' throughout his dealings with Monkland, and at times was very suspicious of his actions, but remained 'perfectly convinced' nevertheless:

> that from whatever moment MONKLAND really did make up his mind that he would confide in the authorities, he did so quite honestly, at any rate in so far as anything is concerned which in his opinion related to the matter of alleged espionage. This fact appears to me to be all that really matters in view of present developments of this case.[62]

Monkland told Morton on 30 March that Macartney had admitted to being in the pay of the Comintern, whose 'chiefs' wanted information about the insurance of cargoes of munitions being sent to any of the States bordering the Soviet Union – information that Monkland, as a member of Lloyds, should be able to procure.

Indeed, he had done so on more than one occasion, passing on, for example, information about a cargo of rifles for Lithuania and receiving £25 for it. Now Macartney had asked Monkland whether he would like to procure 'still bigger money', and produced the questionnaire on the Air Force. Monkland had, he said, only cooperated with Macartney thus far in order to ascertain what he was up to, and had always intended to inform the authorities about it. Morton was sceptical of this explanation of the delay in coming forward, suspecting rather that Monkland's original purpose had been to extract cash from Macartney and his employers 'so long as he was not committing a serious offence in so doing': the questionnaire, however, was clearly a more difficult and dangerous project, and in Morton's view 'Monkland was both frightened off and also honestly unwilling to assist to betray his country'.[63] He showed Morton a copy of a letter given to him by Macartney, signed by one 'K.J. Johnson' and mentioning other agents apparently employed by Macartney. 'Johnson', Monkland told Morton, was:

> the pseudonym by which intermediary agents between the active agents and the directing authority on behalf of the Bolshevik secret service were always known. It was not strictly an alias, in that any person doing such work was referred to as 'a Mr Johnson'.[64]

If Morton were not already interested in Monkland's information, this last detail would have alerted him to the potential importance of Macartney and his contacts. SIS were already aware that ARCOS used 'Mr Johnson' as a generic name for people who did undercover work for them: Morton's own informant had confirmed this. Though Macartney himself might be a small time crook rather than an important agent, it seemed possible that he could provide information useful to ongoing investigation of undercover activities directed through ARCOS. Morton agreed to bring Monkland some information on British aircraft that could be passed on to Macartney in order to 'try and trace the channel of communication between Macartney and his chiefs', as well as to establish Monkland's own *bona fides*. Morton did this on 4 April 1927, as specified in his sworn statement: the two men met for a third time on 2 May; by the time they met again, on 30 May, the ARCOS raid had made the Macartney operation even more significant.

Meanwhile, however, further information on Macartney had been coming in, both from Monkland and from SIS stations overseas. He was known to make frequent trips to France, Germany and Holland. On 2 May 1927 Paris provided a copy of a GPU report indicating that Macartney, under the name of W.F. Hudson, was acting as an agent for Soviet Intelligence. On the following day Morton asked for a message to be sent to Dunderdale:

> For the past six months [Macartney] has been acting in this country as a Soviet SS agent, being particularly engaged in obtaining information about the British Air Force. He has certain sub agents here who get the

information for him. It is known for certain that he has given to one of these sub-agents an address for communications with himself in Paris . . . Macartney@*Hudson has further informed his subagent that he expects to be in Paris for several weeks, having gone there to be introduced to a certain person whom he has not met before . . . anything that can be ascertained about Macartney's activities in Paris are urgently required, including the name he is going by and the address he is living at; the person he is to be introduced to, his connections and the object for which he is going to Moscow, if he does go.

A similar request was also made of the French authorities, who sent a series of reports concerning Macartney's movements, indicating that he was more involved with an expatriate group of 'high class financial crooks' than with Soviet Intelligence. The person to whom he had hoped to be introduced was apparently Prince Carol of Roumania, who refused to receive him. While he was in Paris, Macartney had asked Monkland to act as post box in the UK for 'reports on British aircraft from certain undisclosed secret agents': for this, 'Mr Johnson' would pay Monkland £50 per month, though plans for Monkland to meet Johnson came to nothing at this stage.[65]

At this point arises a puzzling connection between Macartney and the ARCOS raid. In his statement to the Court, Morton reported that he had received a letter from Monkland dated 19 May, stating that on the evening of the raid, 12 May:

> Macartney had rung him up . . . in a great state, with instructions to burn or hide everything he had. Monkland further wrote that Macartney had said that he had fortunately heard at 10 a.m. on the morning of the day in question that the raid was to take place, and that he had given the people of ARCOS warning of it.[66] Being present myself at the raid on ARCOS I am personally convinced that the Soviet Authorities had not received any warning of it in the manner described by Macartney. Nevertheless, at a subsequent interview between Monkland and myself the former told me that Macartney had informed him that he had received the warning of the raid from a clerk in the Special Branch at Scotland Yard . . .[67]

Despite Morton's avowed 'personal conviction' that ARCOS had not been warned of the raid, and his dismissal of Macartney as a 'first class liar', he had to admit that most of his statements contained at least 'a substratum of truth usually as regards the essential features'. If, however, Macartney did receive information on the morning of 12 May from Special Branch – where it is known there were Soviet informants – then the accounts of the chronology leading up to the

---

* Symbol denoting 'alias'.

raid, given by Morton and others, must be challenged. They indicate that Special Branch were not informed of the impending raid until 12 p.m., and even the Chief Commissioner of Police and Assistant Commissioner, CID had only been told at 10 a.m.; before that, only Childs knew. If someone at Scotland Yard alerted Macartney on the morning of the 12th, they must have acted swiftly; swiftly enough, in any case, to allow ARCOS some hours to move or destroy material before the raid. This, of course, also conflicts with other reports suggesting that ARCOS had been warned of an impending raid some time before 12 May.

As Morton suggested in his Court statement on the Macartney case, there is little profit to be gained from such speculation. No documentation has been found to confirm or deny Macartney's story, though there would seem to be little point in his making it up for Monkland's benefit. If true, however, presumably Macartney feared that some papers might be found during the raid leading to him, and even to Monkland. What had Macartney told the Russians about Monkland? Or, indeed, about 'Peter Hamilton', whom Monkland was supposed to have represented to Macartney as a disaffected Air Force Staff Officer seeking money in return for information? The whole situation seemed both confusing and fraught with danger. However, Morton and Section V clearly decided that the potential 'prize' – a lead to those directing Soviet espionage activities in the UK – was worth the risk. After the ARCOS raid, the value of the prize was enhanced, since ARCOS was known to have shifted its centre of operations to Europe, opening up the possibility of still more extensive networks.

Morton continued to meet and correspond with Monkland throughout the summer of 1927, supplying information manufactured by the Air Force to satisfy Macartney's requests for performance reports on British aircraft and other details – including, in keeping with Soviet paranoia, a draft of the non-existent 'secret treaty between Stresemann, Briand and Chamberlain aimed against the USSR'.[68] The hoped-for 'prize', however, showed no signs of materialising. Macartney was observed travelling to Antwerp and Hamburg (from where ARCOS were now thought to be operating their espionage networks), as well as to Rotterdam, Berlin and Paris, but no conclusive evidence emerged. By September, as Morton later wrote to Commandant Lainey of the *Sûrêté*, it appeared that:

> the whole thing was going to be a misfire. No 'Mr Johnson' appeared; Macartney was out of funds, and on his own showing to Mr George Monkland . . . was not satisfied with his relations with the Soviet authorities.

At last, in November 1927, came a breakthrough. Monkland received a letter signed 'Johnson' arranging a meeting at 7 p.m. on 16 November in the teashop of the Marble Arch cinema. At that meeting Johnson, later identified as Georg Hansen,[69] gave Monkland (as he later admitted in Court) detailed instructions on how to undertake secret service work. He claimed to have been told to do this by a mysterious 'Dr Offenbach' (the Lord Chief Justice suggested 'this name had a certain connection with light opera'), but the terms of instruction were not unfamiliar to Morton, as he told Lainey:

> The young man introduced himself as Johnson and spent some 20 minutes cross-questioning George Monkland as to what he knew about Macartney. You will recognise that this is a regular GPU practice. He gave a concise but most admirable lecture to George Monkland on the care to be exercised when dealing with secret documents; that he was never to carry them with him but if he got any information was to communicate with Johnson who would arrange a meeting place. George Monkland was not to bring this information with him, but at the meeting place Johnson would give him an address to which he was to post it. Johnson, however, explained that this address would not be his own, which he refused to give to George Monkland, but that the material would be forwarded from that address to another, which was not given, where Johnson would examine it. If the information was important enough, Johnson himself would act as courier and take it straight back to Germany; if not, he would make arrangements to post it by a roundabout route to arrive in Berlin. From this and other facts it was quite clear that Johnson, though perhaps not an important member of the organisation, was definitely a paid, trained agent.

Although neither Morton's sworn statement nor supporting documentation is clear on this point, Monkland probably telephoned Morton after his meeting with 'Johnson' – and certainly before his next meeting with Morton on 18 November – to tell him what had happened (though Morton also had Monkland followed to his meeting with Johnson). Morton learned that a further meeting, between Macartney and Johnson, had been arranged for the following day, 17 November 1927. In the light of Monkland's account, and after discussion with the police, it was decided to risk making an arrest at that meeting, in case Johnson planned to leave the country immediately afterwards. Macartney and Hansen were arrested on 17 November and their quarters searched. As Morton recounted to Lainey, nothing incriminating was found at Hansen's lodgings, but Macartney was found to have a large book full of 'facts regarding British tanks and aeroplanes which could not have been obtained by any legal means and were definitely breaches of our Official Secrets Act'. The police also found letters and documents in Monkland's handwriting, and at their next meeting, on 18 November at the Ritz, Morton told Monkland that he had disclosed to the police the part played by the latter, assuring them that Monkland was 'entirely innocent of espionage' and would volunteer a statement.[70]

Macartney and Hansen were duly charged under the Official Secrets Acts of 1911 and 1920, and brought to trial. Their defence was 'total denial'; the incriminating documents had, they said, been forged. Against the advice of their Counsel they insisted on testifying themselves, giving the Attorney General

further opportunity to seal their fate. The documents found at Macartney's lodgings were incriminating in themselves, and Monkland's testimony survived
attempts by the Defence to discredit him as a witness. Morton's own account of
Macartney's repeated attempts, through Monkland, to secure military secrets were
both specific and detailed. In addition, witnesses were called to attest to the
genuineness of the documents and to confirm Macartney's movements: two
typists employed in a typing bureau in the Edgware Road, for example, swore that
Macartney had asked for certain letters to be typed under the name of Hudson.
All this, as Morton later stated in a report on the case sent to Dunderdale on 1
March 1928, 'settled the matter'. On 18 January 1928 Macartney and Hansen
were sentenced to ten years' imprisonment, the first two with hard labour. Their
appeal was dismissed on 27 February.

As far as Morton and SIS were concerned, a long operation had been brought
to a successful conclusion, even though many questions remained unanswered
and Macartney had been shown to be a rather less than effective spy. Indeed, it
would not seem unreasonable to conclude that the whole operation opened
up more lines of enquiry into organised crime than into Soviet espionage: the false
passports Macartney procured, for example, were thought to be used by 'crooks,
card sharpers and confidence tricksters who frequent the ocean liners, Monte
Carlo and sometimes Paris'. The trail to Soviet paymasters and agent handlers
proved a dead end, though some paths could be discerned in the undergrowth
of the case that might be worth exploring. Morton was clear, however, that there
had been a real and sinister connection between Macartney and Moscow, as he
told Dunderdale in a summary of the case:

> There is no doubt in the minds of the authorities that Macartney had,
> in England at least, two genuine sub-agents who were giving him
> information about British tanks. Work of attempting to discover these is
> continuing. It has since been ascertained beyond any doubt that Hansen
> was specially sent over by the remains of the Intelligence Service run
> by the Bolsheviks from ARCOS, which is now situated in Antwerp
> and Hamburg. It is suggested that the French authorities might pay
> great attention to the reconstituted ARCOS in these two cities, as we
> have information that the same persons as before are still controlling
> information work from there, certainly against England, and possibly
> against France, though on this last, we have admittedly only presumption
> to go on . . . Enquiry has been conducted into the means whereby
> Macartney obtained his false 'Hudson' passport, which has never
> yet come to light and which has almost undoubtedly been destroyed by
> now. It has been discovered that 14 British passports were obtained
> in the same manner, the means and individuals employed having no
> connection with the case which the French authorities were kind enough
> to bring to our notice and work up on our behalf . . . Effective measures
> have been taken to prevent a recurrence of this business . . . The severe

sentences imposed on Macartney and Hansen have caused a wave of apprehension to pass round the limited circle here, and it is quite certain that for a time at least they will lie very low.

This last was, perhaps, sufficient justification in itself for the long wooing of Monkland and the pursuit of Macartney. The case provides a rare example of an operation where Morton's role is documented in detail, and so of particular interest in considering his professional life.

As noted earlier, evidence of Morton's personal life between 1926 and 1928 is virtually non-existent. Apparently he spent the working week (usually including Saturday) in London, and weekends and holidays, if he took any, at Earlylands, where he tended his garden, planting vines (later making wine), and visited Chartwell if Churchill were in residence. In 1928, when Churchill began work on *The World Crisis*, his six-volume history of the First World War, Morton helped him with the collection of material and submitted detailed comments on those chapters dealing with Russia.[71] There is no record of their conversation on other matters during this period, but they continued to meet, and presumably discussed Soviet Russia, and indeed the full range of British foreign policy, when they did so.

Churchill's own preoccupations, as Chancellor of the Exchequer, were with the economy, and with cutting back Service estimates, based upon a presumption of long-term peace in Europe. Though the signs of illegal German rearmament were already clearly visible, neither he nor the rest of the Government wished to challenge them at this point, tending towards the view expressed by Churchill himself in *The Gathering Storm*; it was 'natural that a proud people vanquished in war should strike to rearm themselves as soon as possible'.[72] Germany had, after all, been brought into the concert of Europe as an equal with the other Powers at Locarno,[73] and had a permanent seat on the Council of the League of Nations. British and European statesmen sought stability and prosperity, not confrontation;[74] and, as J.V. Perowne of the Foreign Office noted on 25 September 1927, even if reports of German military preparations and disarmament defaults could be substantiated, 'what then?'[75] Morton's professional dealings led him to take a more jaundiced view of German intentions than either the FO or Churchill at this point. During the next few years, his career was to diversify in a way that brought both the Soviet and the German threat even more sharply into focus.

6

LOOSE ENDS: 1929–31

The years 1929 to 1931 saw the end of Morton's career in 'pure' Intelligence, in the sense that they were the last years in which he worked entirely within the Intelligence establishment. After 1931 the professional pursuit of Bolsheviks and their paymasters was superseded by an equally professional pursuit of evidence of the industrial and military preparations for a future war by Britain's potential enemies, principally Soviet Russia and Germany. The story of Morton's increasing preoccupation with economic and industrial intelligence, beginning with the formation in 1927–8 of Section VI of SIS (the Economic Section), falls to the next Chapter. It seems logical, however, first to carry the story of his Bolshevik-hunting activities through to their formal conclusion.

Between 1929 and 1931 Morton continued, as Head of Production, to search out and collect intelligence on hostile foreign espionage activities, both from SIS's overseas representatives and, working closely with Section V, from sources within the UK, passed on by a network of agents built up during the Makgill days[1] but now generally known as 'Casuals'. The use of domestic agents, though defended by Sinclair to the Secret Service Committee in 1925,[2] became a source of increasing trouble between SIS, MI5 and Scotland Yard and culminated in their transfer to MI5 in 1931 following a first-class row, with Morton at the centre.

Though Morton always enjoyed a good row, there are signs that the 1931 fracas may have been the final straw in a series of cumulative frustrations persuading him to seek a new career direction. Morton's apparent disenchantment with his role, and with that of SIS, at the turn of the decade might be attributed to a number of factors: the continued underfunding and neglect of the Intelligence services by central government, a trend only exacerbated with the advent of the second Labour Government in June 1929; the resumption four months later of diplomatic relations with the Soviet Union, whose pledges to forswear hostile propaganda were mocked by increasing Comintern subversive activity; the knowledge, acquired from both diplomatic and covert sources, that Germany was engaged in a businesslike rearmament programme and embracing political extremism; all these, combined with a certain staleness after ten years in the job, may well have played a part. He was almost forty, a man of naturally quick and impatient intellect and judgement, whose opinion of both politicians and civil servants had not improved with maturity and experience; he had lived through one devastating military conflict, and could imagine another; the death on 23 June 1929 of his father, who suffered cardiac failure at the age of eighty-five, must also have affected him. Perhaps he felt that it was time to perform before a bigger audience, and attempt to exert influence in a wider arena.

If such were indeed his impulses, they could only have been confirmed by the professional problems that he encountered between 1929 and 1931: a resurgence of the Zinoviev Letter controversy, raising the spectre of renewed 'enquiries' that might expose further the weaknesses of British Intelligence; the ongoing suspicion, hardening to knowledge, that the Soviet authorities had managed to place informants in a number of British official bodies – including Special Branch, two of whose officers were arrested in London in April 1929, thereby uncovering the fact that SIS activities at home and abroad had been vulnerable to Soviet penetration since 1922 at least; and finally the clash with Special Branch and MI5 over the use of the Casuals, and in particular over Maxwell Knight, whom Morton had 'presented' to SIS as a new contact in November 1929.

The story of Morton, and of SIS during 1929 to 1931 is in many ways messy, unsatisfactory and inconclusive. Perhaps that was how he himself felt. The events of those years were symptomatic not only of the *malaise* of the British Intelligence establishment, but also of an uncomfortable period in British politics, and a period of collapse and chaos in the wider world, heralded by the collapse of the New York Stock Exchange in October 1929. It was a period of transition to a more uncertain and dangerous world rather than, as many had hoped, the end of postwar readjustment and the dawn of a new stability. Similarly, the problems tackled by Morton during these years and described in the present chapter represent in many ways the end of his old life; a hangover from the past, co-existing with the beginning of the future.

The Zinoviev Letter again

The Zinoviev Letter had never really gone away. In April 1927 a Communist publisher in the Grays Inn Road in London had produced a book entitled *Anti-Soviet Forgeries*, giving details of a large number of allegedly forged documents including the Letter, and ascribing responsibility generally to 'Russian White Guards – counter-revolutionary *émigrés*', mentioning both Orlov and his (now estranged) deputy, Harald Sievert. Then in February 1928, following the court case that had exposed irregular foreign currency dealings by members of the Foreign Office's Northern Department, Baldwin ordered a Special Board of Enquiry,[3] in the course of which statements were made implying that the FO Under Secretary and former head of the Northern Department, J.D. Gregory, might have engineered the despatch of the Prime Minister's note to the Soviet Chargé on 25 October 1924 to serve his own financial ends. Although the Board concluded that there was 'not the slightest foundation' for such rumours and exonerated Gregory from any wrongdoing in connection with the Zinoviev Letter (he was sacked for the currency speculation), the Enquiry resurrected a number of unanswered questions, and prompted Ramsay MacDonald to request a Parliamentary debate on the Report, warning that the Labour Party might demand a further enquiry into the Zinoviev affair.

Sinclair, for one, was most unhappy at this proposal and wrote to Tyrrell expressing the hope that any further enquiry into the Letter would be 'sternly resisted'. He also sent to the FO copies of documents received from SIS sources in Russia, including a circular apparently issued by the Agitprop department of the CPGB and attacking MacDonald for not admitting that he had always thought the Letter a forgery. Although in the event MacDonald's motion for an enquiry was defeated in the House on 19 March 1928 by 326 to 132, the Francs Enquiry and the debate proved the trigger for a fresh spate of rumours concerning the authenticity of the letter and the possible identity of its authors if it were a forgery.

At this point Morton's old *bête noire* Vladimir Orlov enters the story again, and where Orlov was involved trouble was never far behind. His arrest in early March 1929 was no exception. The background to it lay in allegations made in 1928 that the US Senator William Borah had accepted substantial bribes from Moscow in return for advocating the recognition of the Soviet Government by Washington. The evidence lay in a number of documents discovered in Paris, later pronounced forgeries; Senator Borah was cleared by a committee of enquiry. An American journalist, H.R. Knickerbocker, working for the *New York Evening Post* in Berlin, decided to investigate the provenance of the forged documents, and went to the acknowledged expert on such matters, Orlov. The latter attempted to implicate his former colleague and now rival, Sievert, who seems to have retaliated by reporting Orlov and his co-forger Sumarakov to the police.[4] The waters were further muddied by the *Daily Herald*'s foreign editor, W.N. Ewer, who was told by an American journalist in Berlin that 'the German Government had the inside story of the Zinoviev Letter', and that the Labour Party might be able to extract political capital from the situation.

Though Ewer's subsequent article in the *Sunday Worker* on 24 March 1929 ('Forgery as a business – how "Red Letter" makers trade their goods') promised further revelations, they were not forthcoming, and it was not in the interests of the German authorities, who were funding both Orlov's and Sievert's operations, to prosecute them with any level of determination. Charges against Sievert, who suffered a nervous breakdown during the trial in July, were dropped: Orlov and Sumarakov were sentenced to four months' imprisonment but released immediately since they had been in detention since March. As the *Morning Post* reported, the evidence in the trial skirted over a good deal of thin ice in regard to the ways and means of international underground operations, and the trial concluded leaving many relevant details far from clear.

In the view of Sinclair and Morton, that lack of clarity was a source of considerable relief. Sinclair had greeted the news that Orlov had been arrested, and his headquarters raided, not just with interest, but with concern. He sent a personal message to Frank Foley, SIS's Head of Station in Berlin, on 4 March

1929, asking for a full report on the arrests of Orlov and Sumarakov, with copies of any documents concerned, as soon as possible; he also asked Morton for a comprehensive note on Orlov and his activities, which was supplied the following day. This note, which related Orlov's and his principal associates' personal history and that of his past relationship with SIS, concluded that:

> From various contradictory reports on Orlov, several indisputable facts stand out. Firstly he is no Bolshevik. He has always been an intriguer and politician, working his Intelligence Organisation for his own benefit firstly, for the benefit of the Russian Monarchist cause a bad second, while such European powers who have paid him money have been hardly anywhere. Orlov had a great belief that England and America would one day put Russia straight. The severance of personal relations with the British Intelligence in 1923 had a great effect on him. From that moment there is no doubt that he commenced forging documents and selling them to anyone ready to buy them, with the united objects of making money to keep himself going, and at the same time doing harm to the Bolsheviks.

The note did not mention the Zinoviev Letter, but it was clear that Sinclair was worried about what the German authorities' investigation might reveal on that subject. On 6 March he telegraphed again to Berlin, stating that 'any information regarding the alleged forgery of the ZINOVIEV letter is to be sent to me personally'. Foley replied on 11 March:

> Berlin police endeavouring to establish by microscopic examination of type whether ORLOFF forged ZINOVIEV letter. You must be prepared for official public statement shortly.

No such statement issued, however. Later, in July 1929, Harold Nicolson, Counsellor in HM Embassy in Berlin, told Sir R. Lindsay (who had left the Berlin Embassy on 1 July 1928 to succeed Tyrrell as FO Permanent Under Secretary) that he had been informed privately that the Russian Ambassador had suggested that the Orlov case might be a good opportunity to review the Zinoviev Letter affair, but that the German Foreign Office had no interest in reviving the controversy. As Sinclair commented to Lindsay on 5 July, the German authorities were already satisfied that Orlov had not written the letter.

Between March and July 1929, however, interposes an intriguing interlude. At some point in March, Morton made a trip to Czechoslovakia. The occasion for his visit was to investigate, as part of a War Office mission (though he himself travelled as an FO representative), a new kind of explosive.[5] While in Prague, Morton took the opportunity to gather further information on the case against Orlov, then in prison awaiting trial. A telegram of 7 May to SIS HQ from the head of station in Prague forwarded 'some particulars of ORLOV collected at the request of CO, made during his visit here'; Morton wrote on the telegram 'This is the Czech information regarding this man and it appears to be a good sound story.' No specific trace has been found of the information to which he was referring, but it presumably contributed to several detailed accounts of Orlov and his activities compiled by Morton around this time at Sinclair's behest. If Sinclair were anxious to find out urgently what the German investigation into Orlov was uncovering, it would have made sense to take advantage of this visit by Morton, Orlov's long-term contact, and intimately familiar with all the details of the Zinoviev affair. Prague was not so very far from Berlin: and to make enquiries from an adjacent capital, rather than one where Morton's presence might attract unwelcome attention, would also have been in keeping with Sinclair's, and indeed SIS's practice.

There are practically no references in SIS archives to overseas travel by senior officers, or by C himself: rumours of their presence in other countries can only be countered by evidence of their presence in London. This does not mean that they never travelled, indeed it would be odd if they did not. By the nature of their profession, however, they neither advertised their plans nor imparted details of their arrivals and departures. References to Morton's having visited other countries during the period 1919–31 are rare, but the evidence shows that he travelled to Czechoslovakia at least twice in 1929. Sinclair, and Morton himself, were clearly anxious about what Orlov's investigation and trial might reveal of SIS activities past and present, and Sinclair's desire to get as full a picture of the situation as possible is well documented. Whether what Morton learned on his visit set his, or Sinclair's mind at rest, we do not know. In any case, two months later the trial fizzled out and Orlov was freed to return to his former life, although the German authorities were now less accommodating. In 1931 they asked him to leave the country, and he moved his centre of operations to Brussels under an old alias, Orest Borovoi; one of Dunderdale's agents met him there shortly afterwards, and passed on to him a fake report on the Soviet Baltic Fleet which Orlov tried to sell to the Admiralty. SIS continued to keep an eye on his activities, though there was little direct contact.[6]

As far as the Zinoviev Letter was concerned, none of the threatened 'revelations' materialised and no one was much wiser in 1931 than they had been in 1924. If Morton and Sinclair knew more than they said or wrote, it was not and has not been revealed. In public (insofar as they ever went public), they stood by the authority of the supposed SIS Moscow source of the original report containing the Letter, FR3/K. The view expressed by Milicent Bagot, at the conclusion of her investigation in 1967–70,[7] is worth quoting:

> SIS always insisted on the authenticity of the Letter . . . it is possible that their attitude may have sprung partly from obstinacy and partly from a sense of insecurity as they felt under fire from such prominent Socialists as Parmoor, Trevelyan and Wedgewood, who were bent on the Service's destruction[8] . . . Nevertheless, the fact that the agent's reports continued

to be circulated until at least the spring of 1931 give the impression that SIS genuinely believed in his existence and reliability. On the other hand, Morton's reaction to criticism on several occasions was merely irritation, not the objective investigation of fresh leads.

Certainly, Sinclair's efforts to obtain information in 1929, aided and abetted by Morton, seemed geared to avoiding unwelcome revelations rather than to finding the truth. Perhaps Miss Bagot should be allowed to have the last word:

> There are too many *lacunae* for the truth about the Zinoviev Letter to be established beyond doubt. There is plenty of material with which conjectures could be justified but all the variations on the theme cannot be reconciled.

Though in the end nothing much new came out of the 1928–29 flurry of interest in the Zinoviev Letter, it is not hard to understand Sinclair's and Morton's concern, even if they had nothing to hide. The whole episode had been damaging to the Service's public reputation, at a time when other revelations – of damaging long-term Soviet penetration of Special Branch – were already rocking the British Intelligence establishment to its foundations and causing SIS, in particular, to wonder just how much of their organisation and operations had been laid bare to the Bolsheviks over the past ten years.

Mr Dale's diary

The events of April 1929, when two Special Branch officers were arrested and unmasked as Soviet agents who had for some years supplied information through a network run by the journalist W.N. Ewer,[9] confirmed SIS in many long-held suspicions about Special Branch in particular, and about Soviet penetration of official British bodies in general. In May 1925, for example, Morton had minuted to Sinclair suggesting that MI5 should be asked to interview the *Daily Telegraph* regarding an item entitled 'Spies in Britain', supposedly based on information from a former GPU official who claimed that his source was a British police report on Soviet spies in England ('Communists are busy penetrating into the Government offices and are able to arrange their own agents in these places'). Morton also sent the cutting to the SIS head of Station in Riga, asking him to supply copies of any recent reports indicating that the GPU had agents in Scotland Yard or in government offices. Sinclair agreed with Morton's proposal that if Riga produced any positive evidence of such agents, an attempt should be made to 'pass on dud material and see if it arrives in Moscow'. Further reports reached Morton in 1926 and 1927 indicating that Soviet agents were indeed in place in England, though no record survives of whether any attempt to entrap them by the use of bogus material was successful.

Meanwhile, SIS, like MI5, had been investigating the activities of W.N. Ewer: indeed, SIS's first recorded interest in his activities dated back to 1921.[10] Although it is not clear from what date or to what extent the two agencies shared their suspicions or their information, the evidence suggests a collaborative operation between 1925 and 1927 whereby MI5 maintained postal and telephone surveillance of Ewer and his group while SIS kept a watch on their movements abroad. According to a memorandum dated 30 April 1929 and sent to Lindsay at the Foreign Office by Sinclair on 7 May, this surveillance had proved conclusively:

> that the group, of which the head and financial controller was undoubtedly Ewer, were conducting Secret Service activities on behalf of, and with money supplied by, the Soviet Government and the Communist Party of Great Britain; that they were obtaining copies of documents and other S[ecret] S[ervice] information from the French Foreign Office through George Slocombe, Paris correspondent of the *Daily Herald*, who received 1,000 dollars a month for this work from Ewer; and that, through the same individual in Paris, they were acting as channels of communication between Indian Communists abroad and Communists in the UK. Their hostility to this Government was never in doubt.

Both Agencies continued their surveillance against Ewer and his group until the ARCOS raid in May 1927, after which they noted that the group appeared to go to ground and to be suffering from shortage of funds. In 1928, however, MI5 carried out a series of informative interviews with a former, disaffected associate of Ewer's, 'A. Allen', the name by which Arthur Lakey, a former Scotland Yard officer discharged from the force after the 1919 police strike,[11] was now known. Allen left the Ewer group in late 1927, and during the following year passed on a considerable amount of information to MI5, including the fact that two Special Branch officers had been in the pay of the group since 1922. According to Allen, these officers had passed on 'constant, detailed and accurate information', as the SIS memorandum described it:

> (i) of all enquiries carried out by the Special Branch, (ii) of all proposed action with regard to prosecutions and raids, (iii) of all Home Office decisions regarding aliens arriving in or wishing to enter this country, and (iv) of all Home Office Warrants for the secret postal interception and scrutiny of correspondence.

This information, together with further details obtained following the arrest on 11 April 1929 of the Special Branch officers concerned, Inspector Ginhoven and Sergeant Jane, together with a former police officer, Walter E. Dale, who had acted as a private detective for the group,[12] exposed a long catalogue of corruption and compromise that constituted, in Sinclair's view, 'a grave danger to the State'. His letter to Lindsay, drawing attention to the unsatisfactory nature of Special

Branch organisation and personnel, was expressed in his own very personal style: while the enclosed SIS memorandum bore Vivian's initials at foot, there are some distinctly Mortonesque passages, and in view of his position as 'C.O.' and his work with Section V he would certainly have been involved closely in its preparation. The revelations resulting from the Special Branch arrests must, indeed, have been particularly troubling for Section V, since the potential damage to SIS interests pertained most specifically to their area of work. As Sinclair told Lindsay, however, it was not impossible that the whole organisation could have been lain bare to Ewer's network through Special Branch corruption.

The most damning evidence to emerge from the case as far as SIS were concerned was contained in a diary kept by Dale from 1922 to 1927 and seized when he was arrested. This revealed, according to the SIS memorandum, that:

> throughout these five years unremitting surveillance was maintained by Dale and his friends upon the premises and personnel of SIS and of the Code and Cipher School, that the daily itinerary of the office cars was carefully watched, that the regular connection between SIS, Code and Cipher School, MI5, the Foreign Office and other Departments of Government, thus established, was carefully noted, that laborious efforts were made to identify and trace to their homes officers and members of the secretarial staff of both SIS and the Code and Cipher School, and that the move of both offices from their previous separate premises to joint premises at Broadway Buildings under a common style was accurately observed and recorded.

As the memorandum pointed out, despite the arrests and seizure of documents 'we have neither the beginning nor the end of this story': there was no way of knowing how widely the stream of information leakage from Special Branch might have flowed, or whether any SIS employees had in fact been suborned successfully in the same way as their police colleagues; it would be complacent to assume all the tributaries had been blocked. For Section V, the potential damage extended still further. Coupled with the watch kept on SIS activities in the UK, Ewer's group had also been able to make certain deductions from the information passed to them by Ginhoven and Jane. Dale's notes revealed the group's knowledge, for example, that two 'important Communist links' in foreign capitals were under observation by SIS:

> It seems hardly necessary to point out that, through such items of information and with the assistance of his foreign correspondents, it would be as simple for Ewer to trace the Representatives and agents of SIS abroad as it has been for him to trace the headquarters organisation in London, and with the information so gained he would be in a position to embarrass, or damage the credit of, the Government at home as seriously as to gull, betray and cripple SIS organisations abroad.

The revelations in Dale's diary, and the potential implications, were a severe shock to Sinclair and SIS, even though Special Branch had long been regarded as unreliable. In the light of Morton's own obsessive secrecy, and his professional preoccupation with Soviet espionage at home and abroad, it must be assumed that he, too was profoundly disturbed. Possibly it contributed to his feeling that the organisation to which he had devoted his life for the past ten years was losing its sense of direction; a sensation that could only have been enhanced by the political climate. At the time the SIS memorandum on the 'leakage' from Special Branch was prepared, Baldwin's Conservative Government was still, just, in power. The documentation makes it clear that SIS were suspicious not just of Ewer's Moscow connections but also of his links with the Labour Party. Though Ewer's network was controlled 'primarily in the interests of the Soviet Government and of the IIIrd International', his position on the *Daily Herald*, and his connections with the Party, enabled him to use the information he acquired in the interests of the Opposition under the guise of party politics; though Sinclair admitted that it was doubtful whether the Labour Party had any official cognisance of Ewer's underground operations.

There is no doubt that Morton's (and Sinclair's) sympathies lay in the Conservative camp, but the concerns they expressed about the Ewer revelations and the evidence of long-term leakage from Special Branch were directed much more to organisational than to political interests. Nevertheless, when he and his colleagues stressed that it was impossible to be sure that the Special Branch arrests had in fact stopped the rot, they drew attention in particular to the activities of other Ewer associates such as J.H. Hayes, another former police officer[13] who had been a Labour MP for the Edgehill division of Liverpool since 1923, and held a post as Parliamentary Private Secretary during the 1924 Labour Government, but who ran a detective bureau for Ewer and was responsible for putting him in touch with Ginhoven. Hayes attained Ministerial office as Vice Chamberlain in the Royal Household in the second Labour Government in June 1929. In these circumstances, mutual suspicion between the incoming Labour Government and the Intelligence services is hardly surprising. SIS also expressed unease at the Attorney General's decision not to prosecute Ewer or any of his associates,[14] though acknowledging the 'wisdom and correctness' of the desire to avoid a prosecution 'which would necessitate the publication in a Court of Law of many facts regarding the Secret Services and the Police'.[15] The question asked in the SIS memorandum, 'Are these persons and their organisations to be permitted to "carry on" undisturbed or not, and if not, by what methods are their activities to be curtailed?', remained unanswered.

In presenting SIS's arguments so fully to Lindsay, and urging him to put them to the Secretary of State, Sinclair did not miss the opportunity of reviving his longstanding campaign for the rationalisation of British Intelligence, coupling this with a demand for root and branch reform of Special Branch. One relevant passage in the May 1929 memorandum has a particular flavour of Morton, though it certainly expressed Sinclair's, and presumably Vivian's, view as well:

We must unflinchingly recognise as a result of this case what has long been apparent, namely, that the attitude of the responsible Special Branch officers towards political enquiries and the customary procedure of the Branch in respect of them, together with the internal organisation for handling papers, are completely out of keeping with the high standard, both of knowledge and of secrecy, not only demanded of a body working in conjunction with the Secret Services, but due also to the extreme intricacy and delicacy of the matters themselves with which the Special Branch is called upon to deal. Whereas it appears to be the practice to confide matters of the highest political delicacy *en bloc* to officers of the rank of Superintendent and under, these are spheres which, rightly considered, demand the attention of specialists of a standard of intellect, education and special qualifications far superior to that ordinarily possessed by officers of Superintendent's rank . . .

Although section SS1 of Special Branch, responsible for liaison with SIS, had in the past constituted a sort of 'buffer state' protecting the latter organisation from penetration, it was clear that something more would be required. Special Branch registry systems, and the workings of its Press Room, were also criticised. The memorandum concluded that:

While it is axiomatic that the Special Branch and the Secret Services are mutually dependent upon each other and complementary in their functions, and that an exact coordination of the latter is essential in the interests of efficiency no less than in those of public security, it seems hardly in conformity with the public interest that the connection should continue to exist under present conditions. It is suggested, therefore, that the radical reorganisation of the Special Branch on a basis allowing for a proper realisation of the intricacy, delicacy and secrecy of the subjects dealt with, should be undertaken forthwith.

These papers – ten pages of closely argued text – can have left Lindsay in no doubt of Sinclair's, and SIS's view of Special Branch. It seems doubtful, however, that the Permanent Under Secretary would have been inclined to heed Sinclair's urging to show them to the Foreign Secretary: in any case, within a month Chamberlain was no longer in office, and it is hard to imagine either that Arthur Henderson would have been inclined to read them, or that Lindsay would have wished him to do so. It soon became clear that the second Labour Government took a jaundiced view of the structure and orientation of the Intelligence establishment as a whole. Henderson, according to Sir Robert Vansittart, who succeeded Lindsay as PUS in January 1930, 'rated Secret Service like hard liquor, because he knew, and wanted to know, nothing of it'.[16] MacDonald and his colleagues also suspected, apparently with good reason, a 'dirty tricks' conspiracy by the Conservative Party, which had now enlisted the services of Sir

Joseph Ball, formerly of the Security Service.[17] Though no firm evidence has been found to link Morton, or Sinclair, with Ball's activities, the climate of mutual distrust could not have encouraged either SIS or FO officials to advertise the vulnerability of British Intelligence or launder its dirty linen under Ministers' gaze.

For the present, therefore, the situation remained unsatisfactorily static. There is no doubt, however, that the SIS opinion of Special Branch, never high, sank even lower, or that serious concerns had been raised about SIS internal security both at Headquarters and overseas. It was a worrying and uncertain time for the organisation as a whole, and threatened to undermine Morton's professional activities in particular. However, one aspect of these activities, involving the use of 'Casual' agents within the UK, was about to cause an even more severe organisational disturbance and to impel change in a way that the revelations about the Ewer group's activities – actually far more shocking – had failed to do. It is typical that it was to be jurisdictional rivalry, rather than concern about ongoing Soviet penetration of British institutions, that led to a reapportionment of anti-Bolshevik responsibilities between Special Branch, MI5 and SIS in 1931.

Colonel Carter and the Casuals

Morton, and Section V, used the Casuals, a number of whom had been inherited from Makgill's Industrial Intelligence Bureau, to infiltrate Communist or extreme left-wing organisations in the United Kingdom for two specific but linked purposes: to uncover channels of funding and instructions emanating from Moscow, and thereby to check and confirm SIS reports received from overseas. In the first of these endeavours SIS was, arguably, usurping the role of Special Branch, but as Sinclair had told the Secret Service Committee, he had been 'compelled' to make his own arrangements 'since neither MI5 nor Scotland Yard were prepared to do so'.[18] No definitive list of the Casuals has survived, but it is clear that in addition to the original network new contacts were constantly being sought. Especially prized were sources within the CPGB, preferably in the Executive Committee, or agents who were able to persuade or suborn members of the Committee to provide information.

One new Casual source acquired by Morton early in 1930 provides, despite the scanty nature of the documentation, an example of the problems faced by SIS in securing reliable information, of the need for independent confirmation, and also of the concomitant jurisdictional difficulties. In February 1930 Vivian noted to Sinclair that Morton had managed to secure a new source in the office of the *Daily Worker*, who was able to provide information regarding contacts between a British journalist and a member of the Soviet Trade Delegation in Berlin, known as Fischmann. Their correspondence, conducted through the Soviet diplomatic bag, served in turn to validate information received by SIS from a source in Germany codenamed KNICKERBOCKER, emanating from a network run by a German businessman. The KNICKERBOCKER material was shared with Special

Branch: Vivian noted with some scorn that Colonel Carter of Scotland Yard, who had been put in charge of all Special Branch sections in 1928, had forwarded one SIS report under his own signature as coming from one of his sources, and when it was returned to him, forgot where he had got it from and sent it back to Vivian, asking that it be kept confidential to protect his (Carter's) source. Morton commented: 'That is really very choice.' Meanwhile, despite the apparent corroboration from Morton's source, doubts began to be raised about the quality of information being received from KNICKERBOCKER. An SIS representative was detailed to look into it more closely in September 1931, and as a result of his scrutiny the reports were discredited as having been based entirely on overt material such as the German press. The whole network was, accordingly, dropped by SIS, but the episode shows how hard it was to find a reliable source and check its provenance.

One of the most well-known Casuals, however, and the one who was instrumental into pushing the tension between Special Branch and SIS over into outright warfare, was Maxwell Knight.[19] In his handling of Knight, Morton was at his most secretive and obfuscatory, and it is difficult to get at the truth. Much of the documentation regarding their relationship and Knight's work for SIS was prepared by Morton retrospectively when Colonel Carter was demanding a showdown, and consequently bears all the hallmarks of Morton's self-exculpatory style: distancing himself from the events, and certainly revealing far less than he knew. The following account of the episode must, therefore, come with a health warning. Morton's minute to Sinclair supposedly 'introducing' Knight, dated 16 November 1929, gives a good idea of what to expect:

> I have just heard of a man, Mr Maxwell Knight, now Proprietor of the Royal Oak Hotel, Withypool, Exmoor, Somerset. This man holds in his hand the threads of a small amateur detective or secret service in London, consisting of about 100 individuals in all walks of life, many of whom speak foreign languages . . . [he] has been wondering whether he could be of any use in view of the probable return of numbers of undesirable Russians to this country on the signing of the Dogvalevski Agreement.[20] I could see Maxwell Knight without disclosing my name or identity, only saying that I am in some way connected with non-political circles.

Sinclair responded: 'Yes, certainly, and let me know result.' It is, I suppose, just possible that Sinclair had not heard of Knight or encountered him before, but Knight and Morton had known each other for some years, even though they may have been out of contact while Knight had been living in Somerset for a short while.[21] Knight had been one of Makgill's most active lieutenants, and through him had been part of the network of informants run by Morton's Production Section; he knew other Casuals, and was in addition a friend of Kell and of Major Phillips of MI5, both close contacts of Morton himself.

The account of Morton's 'first' meeting with Knight, prepared subsequently for use with Special Branch, is similarly improbable. According to his 'Memorandum of the connection between M.K. and this office' (written, of course, in the third person):

> On or about 15th November 1929, Mrs Nesta Webster,[22] who is a private friend of Major Morton's and who has known him for a large number of years, told Major Morton that she was very anxious to try and get work of a certain kind for a young Mr Maxwell Knight, who was violently interested in communism, who apparently had a small organisation of agents working in the ranks of the Communist Party in this country (she did not know how this had come to pass), and who had friends and correspondents abroad as well as at home, so she thought.

The picture conjured up by this account of a kindly lady recommending a young and enthusiastic friend for somewhat unorthodox employment is irresistible, if incredible. In fact, it is clear from the surviving documentation that Morton's keenness to get Knight properly on to the payroll was based on his desire to secure for SIS Knight's connections and sources. He assured Sinclair that Knight:

> makes an excellent impression, is clearly perfectly honest, very discreet, and at need prepared to do anything, but is at the same time not wild. When required to for his previous masters, he and two friends burgled, three nights running, the premises of the local committee of the Communist Party in Scotland, the branch of the Labour Research Department there and the Y[oung] C[ommunist] L[eague] HQ.

Morton was well aware that MI5 were also interested in Knight, whose connection with SIS should, therefore, be kept from Kell and Phillips 'for reasons of policy'. Knight, he said, knew Carter, but avoided him 'like the plague', having come to his own opinion of the 'danger surrounding contact with the Special Branch'. No further pleading was required on Morton's part: following a meeting with Knight at the United Services Club in Pall Mall on 27 November 1929, the latter was taken on for a three months' trial at £35 per month plus expenses; Morton asked the SIS Paymaster to supply him with sixty used pound notes, out of series, to give to Knight as a first payment.

Morton and Knight now began a period of close collaboration. Knight proffered a number of further candidates for employment, including William Joyce, though he retracted Joyce's name shortly afterward on the grounds that he had 'made a fool of himself' over a girl and could not be trusted'.[23] Morton despatched Knight to various UK cities in search of information on Communist and other minority organisations. There are references to clandestine meetings in the concourse of St James's Park underground station (given the proximity of that building to Broadway, one wonders how 'clandestine' such meetings could be). At the end of Knight's three months' trial Sinclair agreed that the arrangement should be continued, and Morton later reported that 'with every passing month MK has got his agents nearer and nearer the centre of affairs'. He was, in fact, contemplating a 'new move' whereby it was hoped to 'obtain somebody right in the centre,' when a 'difficult situation' developed. The difficulty lay with Colonel Carter of Scotland Yard, who, despite Morton's assurance of Knight's discretion, was well aware of their association (Carter and Knight are recorded as having lunched together on more than one occasion) and of the activities of the Casuals generally, and was growing increasingly angry at what he regarded as an encroachment on his professional territory.

By the middle of 1930, Carter's patience with Morton and the Casuals was wearing very thin. Lunching with Knight at Hatchetts on 23 July, he demanded 'was Major Morton going to close down the whole of this business or was he not?' After the meal, Knight reported the ensuing conversation – or tirade – to Morton. Morton's account of Knight's encounter with Carter bears full quotation in the light of subsequent developments, though the likelihood of a certain over-dramatisation must be borne in mind:

(a) Colonel C. made use of such phrases as 'I want to get to the bottom of the whole of this business and I am going to'; 'He was out to smash the whole thing'; 'I can make things bloody unpleasant for you'; 'How would it be if I have the whole thing away to the Communist Party?' 'This is going to be a fight and I am going to fight until the last ditch'; 'I have my own position to consider to the exclusion of everything else'.

(b) Colonel C. states that he had had MK under observation. MK replied that he had noticed that. (Note: MK is under the impression that he was followed after having lunch with Colonel C, but the follower lost touch. MK is also under the impression that Colonel C has had enquiries made at the Overseas Club and possibly through Major Phillips at his home address in Withypool. Up to date no watching has occurred at MK's flat.)

(c) Colonel C is apparently labouring under the impression that Major Morton has 'exceeded his duties' and is doing the whole of this business without the knowledge of his chief. Major Morton is a 'worm' and Colonel C will make him 'go on his knees to him on the carpet at Scotland Yard before he has done'. Colonel C is also apparently under the impression that Major Morton's chief, in so far as he knows anything about this business, and probably Major Morton himself, is doing the whole of this thing for the Conservative Party, and presumably giving the latter official information when another Party is in Power. In this connection, Colonel C said 'we have a Government in power now whose policy is against this sort of work and I have to carry out their policy'. He made it clear that his own sympathies were with the Left Wing of the present Government, that he was dead against finding out anything about communists, and would hamper any such work as much as he could.

(d) Colonel C then attempted to frighten MK off doing this work for Major Morton or anybody else, by suggesting that he could make his life and that of his agents a misery to them and would not hesitate to do so. He closely cross-questioned MK regarding his motive for this work, and was totally unable to understand that the latter was (a) interested and (b) in his opinion loyally serving his King and Country.

After this outburst, Carter got down to business, discussing the possibility of Knight's working for him. According to Morton, however, the prospects were not promising:

If MK stopped working for Major Morton and then went to him and could show him honestly that he was not working for anybody else, and that he could tell him something he did not know already, which was very doubtful, he might offer him a job. At the same time he wished to make it clear that he was not offering him anything, had not offered him anything and [would] probably never offer him anything.

It is hard to estimate the degree of credence we should attach to this and other accounts of Knight's dealings both with Carter and with Morton. The latter certainly seemed concerned to portray Carter as a blustering fool with dangerous political views antithetic to the efficient operation of secret Intelligence. Without any counterbalancing account, it is impossible to judge the accuracy of this portrait, though a note prepared for the Secret Service Committee in June 1931 indicated that Carter's supervision of Special Branch, including both SS1 and SS2,[24] had not proved successful; and even if his language were less intemperate than Morton suggested, his attitude was certainly aggressive. It is, however, important to bear in mind Ball and his alleged 'dirty tricks' on behalf of the Conservative Party: it may be that Carter knew what was going on and was genuinely outraged. In support of this suggestion, a memorandum of 29 July 1930, apparently written by Morton, stated that Knight had been approached earlier that year by a clergyman friend who asked him to meet someone 'interested in communism'. This turned out to be a Conservative MP, who wished Knight to meet Ball. Morton apparently instructed Knight to agree to this suggestion and find out what Ball wanted:

if he found Mr [sic] Ball required the same information that he was giving to this office, MK could make his choice as to which he worked for, but could not work for both at the same time. On the other hand, if Mr Ball wanted any other sort of information, as actually turned out to be the case, MK could easily get out of the matter by saying it was not in his line.

What Ball wanted, apparently, was 'internal political information regarding the Liberal and Labour parties, which was totally outside MK's scope and a matter in which he was not interested'. Knight, on Morton's instructions, told Ball that he could have nothing to do with such matters, but that if at some future date the Conservative Party wanted to start an organisation for investigating Communism:

> MK would be very glad to hear what they had to put up. The whole matter was reported to CSS at the time. Since the date of this, MK has had no connection with Mr Ball or the Conservative Party in any way.

Though the above was probably written by Morton in the interests of justifying SIS's, and Knight's, actions, its excessive protestation makes uncomfortable reading. Were Sinclair and Morton sponsoring covert activities that were party political, rather than merely anti-Communist in nature? Or was the political climate engendered by the second Labour Government, hostile to the Intelligence establishment and tending, as in 1924, to the conspiratorial, encouraging inherently conservative institutions to veer dangerously near the political precipice? Was the whole affair the product of inter-Service rivalry and jockeying for position in competition for scarce resources? Or was Knight's 'violent' anti-Communism an incendiary factor? As far as Morton is concerned, at least, there is no firm evidence. The only certainty is that by the autumn of 1930 he had so thoroughly upset Carter that a meeting was arranged for 3 October between the latter, Vivian and Miss Saunders of Scotland Yard. The brief record of the meeting prepared by Vivian gave no indication that Morton attended, and indeed his presence might have been regarded as inflammatory. According to Vivian, agreement was reached that SIS would continue to collect information through their domestic sources, 'in consultation' with Scotland Yard, who conceded that the material they produced was useful. However, Vivian noted that following this agreement Carter had made a noise which 'implied distinct doubts whether the matter had yet been finally settled'.

Carter was certainly not satisfied. He continued to press for Morton to cease his activities, which he assumed wrongly were not known to Sinclair. Two weeks later, on 17 October, Morton prepared notes for Sinclair of his contacts with Knight, and of the latter's sources:

> As things seem to be hotting up a little . . . I have made out attached accounts of the . . . agents now employed regularly by this source, so that no misunderstandings may arise when the time comes to disclose the necessary information.

It proved impossible to settle the matter on an inter-Service basis, however, and in early 1931 the matter was referred to the dormant Secret Service Committee. Three meetings were held, on 27 April, 11 June and 22 June 1931 to 'discuss the difficulties which had arisen in the inter-relation between C's organisation and

Scotland Yard'.[25] Anderson, Fisher and Hankey were present on each occasion, as were Vansittart, Morton and Clifford Norton of the Foreign Office who acted as Secretary. Sinclair, Kell, Carter and Sir Trevor Bigham (Assistant Commissioner of the Metropolitan Police) attended the first meeting, and Liddell and Miller the second. It was soon clear that the differences between SIS and Scotland Yard were rooted in personalities – specifically, those of Carter and Morton – and would not be susceptible of easy reconciliation. Carter (rather in the forthright style normally adopted by Sinclair at such meetings) stated from the outset that SS1, comprising Liddell and Miller, was superfluous, and that their work, 'in so far as it was necessary', could be done by himself: he clearly regarded the section with suspicion as an outpost of SIS.

At the second meeting Liddell and Miller, in their turn, complained about Carter, declining, as the summary record put it, to 'respond to the appeal of Sir Warren Fisher for a different spirit'. They said he had reorganised the registry in such a way that 'they could not feel sure that they were seeing all the papers they considered necessary', and suggested that SS1 should be transferred to SIS (as had, indeed, been suggested at previous Secret Service Committee sessions). On this occasion, however, the Committee did not think that such a move would help to improve liaison between SIS and Scotland Yard. At the third meeting on 22 June 1931, Anderson put forward the suggestion that Kell should take over SS1 and all its duties, pointing out that:

> MI5 was already responsible for counter espionage not only for the fighting services but for all government departments, and that this was a logical extension of its duties. There would thus be only two organisations dealing with secret service work, C covering foreign countries, and MI5 the Empire.[26]

SS2, Anderson thought, could stay at Scotland Yard, but Fisher argued that it really belonged with the Home Office, as a 'central bureau of information about suspects for the whole of the country'. Anderson was charged with approaching Kell with a view to carrying out the proposed reorganisation.

This time, in contrast to what had happened after earlier Secret Service Committee enquiries, changes were implemented. Scotland Yard's anti-Communist functions, as embodied in SS1, were transferred to MI5, where Guy Liddell became deputy to Harker, head of B Branch, and went on to a distinguished career in the service;[27] as did Maxwell Knight, who with the rest of the Casuals also moved to MI5 where they became known as 'M section'.[28] From their new base, they continued to cooperate closely with Vivian and Section V of SIS, though their channels of communication were now more closely regulated. According to Curry's official history of the Security Service, the results were harmonious:

> These changes inaugurated a period of close and fruitful collaboration between the Security Service and SIS through the medium of Section V

133

which, under the direction of Major Vivian, became expert in the wide range of subjects covered by the activities of the Comintern . . . If due allowance is made for the shortage of funds and of staff, the degree of success obtained as a result of good collaboration can fairly be claimed as being on a high level.[29]

And what of Morton? Was he bruised by the battle with Special Branch? Did he regret the wholesale export of his contacts to the Security Service? No evidence has been found of his views on the Secret Service Committee's decisions, or what he felt about the row that was, the evidence suggests, at least in part a result of his methods and style. It is hard to imagine that he felt much regret: he had been supported throughout by Sinclair and by Vivian, whatever view they took of the part his somewhat high-handed approach may have played in the dispute. In any case, he had moved on. By 1931, he had already spent several years establishing a new area of expertise in industrial and economic intelligence, and was about to 'go public' by working for a sub-committee of the Committee of Imperial Defence. His days of hunting for 'Reds', whether under domestic or foreign beds, were numbered.

1. John Towlerton Leather
(1804–85)

2. Harriet Spencer Page
(1819–59)

3. Charles Falkiner Morton
(1843–1929)

4. Edith Harriet Leather (1856–1944)

5. Desmond Morton as Mandarin, c. 1900

6. Charlie, Edith and Desmond in the Brompton Rd, c. 1912

7. War Diary of 42nd Brigade, RFA, 1915

8. Ploegsteert Wood, 1919

HIS GREAT TASK DONE.—Earl Haig landing at Folkestone in 1919 after the German Armies had been finally defeated on the Western Front. The British Army was then occupying the Rhine. Lady Haig is seen following the Field-Marshal.

9. Haig returns from France, 1919
(DM top right)

10. Sir Mansfield Cumming, 'C'
1909–23

11. Sir Hugh Sinclair, 'C',
1923–39

12. Sir Stewart Menzies, 'C'
1939–51

13. Earlylands, Crockham Hill

14. 22 Kew Green

15. Winston Churchill

16. Desmond Morton, 1944

7

THE BEGINNINGS OF INDUSTRIAL INTELLIGENCE, 1927–31

'When Hitler came into power,' Morton told a panel of industrialists convened by the Prime Minister, Neville Chamberlain on 1 January 1939, 'he found ready a complete plan for the nation-wide mobilisation of Industry, worked out over the previous eleven years'. Soviet Russia, too, had begun scientific economic planning shortly after the First World War; so, indeed, had the United States, with the formation in 1922 by Bernard Baruch of the Industrial Council. By 1925, 'practically every foreign country had begun to do something'.[1] He forbore to add that despite his own best efforts, the British Government had been far slower to realise the necessity for industrial mobilisation. Nevertheless, Morton's was the driving spirit for the study of industrial intelligence in Britain and for its contribution to defence, rearmament and economic planning in the years leading up to the Second World War. The foundations of that contribution were laid between 1927 and 1931, firstly in Section VI of SIS, the Economic Section, and then in the Committee on Industrial Intelligence in Foreign Countries (FCI), a sub-committee of the CID, precursor of the Industrial Intelligence Centre (IIC) established in 1931, initially as a secret nucleus operating out of SIS.

During the 1920s Morton became convinced that both Soviet Russia and Germany posed an increasingly urgent threat to British interests that extended across the political, economic and military spheres, and that it was important to secure reliable and detailed information about industrial developments in those two countries and about their potential for conversion to military use in preparation for war. Morton was not the only person, and SIS not the only organisation, to be thinking along these lines, although in the creation of an Economic Section SIS was in the vanguard in taking concrete steps to collect economic intelligence and to assess its significance as a discrete body of information in the context of wider sources. Developments on the wider Whitehall front took longer to mature. The revival in 1929 by Ramsay MacDonald of an earlier initiative for a Committee of Economic Enquiry, that evolved into the Economic Advisory Council in 1930,[2] and Arthur Henderson's proposal to establish a 'politico-economic intelligence department in the Foreign Office'[3] are two examples of a growing realisation of the critical importance of economic factors in the formulation of policy, whether domestic or foreign. Similarly, at the official and military Staff level the study of the means of economic pressure on potential enemies, and of the economic foundations of those enemies' war potential, had been in hand since 1918, albeit at a low level of priority.[4] Before 1931, it would have been common ground that the enemy of first choice was Soviet Russia, with China and Japan in the second rank. Germany, though coming up fast on the rails, was still regarded as a lesser threat.

Section VI and SIS

Section VI was formed at some point in 1926–27, and possibly at Morton's instigation. The documentary evidence allows no greater precision. Sinclair must have been convinced of the utility of a more keenly focussed study of the industrial and military development of potential enemies, or he would not have authorised the creation of a new section, a decision he reserved exclusively to himself. There may have been some external impetus, from the Service Chiefs or even (as Morton later hinted) from Hankey; but evidence is sparse. Morton, however, was on record as emphasising the importance of economic intelligence, and it would have been in keeping with both his interest and his ambition to argue for the creation of a special section to collect it. Support for this view is given by a letter he wrote at the end of the Second World War to W.N. Medlicott (then writing the official history of the economic blockade), describing how he had been drawn into the study of 'a mysterious thing then called "industrial mobilisation"':

> In the SIS I had previously allocated to myself, apart from my official duties, the study of a number of reports which had been coming in, particularly from the French, about this new thing. The Germans already had a name for it, *Wehrwirtschaft*.[5]

All that can be said with any certainty is that by 1928 Section VI was in active operation, collating economic information from other SIS sections and elsewhere. Initially, at least, it consisted apparently of no more than Morton and a secretary, though he was able to call upon assistance from colleagues such as Plowden. In 1930, he was joined by F.F. 'Fred' Clively, who had worked for the British Mission in Baku in 1918, spoke 'perfect' Russian and had been recruited in 1924 after some years in business in Constantinople, beginning a partnership with Morton that was to last into the Second World War. During the first years of its existence, however, Section VI was very much a one man band and, as has been seen in the previous chapter, occupied only a part of Morton's professional life. Because it was so small, and because it worked closely with other sections of SIS (particularly the counter-espionage section, Section V), it is also very difficult to distinguish its activities from those of the rest of the organisation.

Morton's earlier contacts with Makgill, and his study of the workings of bodies like ARCOS and the *Uberseedienst*,[6] meant that he had a good professional appreciation of the link between economic factors and subversion, and of the potential for applying capitalist machinery to covert activities. More broadly than that, he had evidence attesting to the unceasing efforts of Germany and the Soviet Union (as well as other countries like Japan) to prepare both militarily and economically for future conflict, and to the high level of resource devoted by such countries to their own secret services, including economic intelligence. Some indication of this was given in a memorandum prepared by Vivian in December 1929 on 'Foreign Secret Service Finances'.[7] Although admitting the difficulty of assessing the true level of expenditure, since 'No Government, except that of Great Britain, would seem to be so ingenuous as openly to budget for, and accurately to publish, the amount annually intended for Secret Service expenditure', Vivian noted that the gross sum provided under 'Secret Funds' in the German budget for 1929 was over twenty million *Reichsmarks* (more than one million pounds), and that the German Foreign Office allocation included a minimum of 450,000 RM for 'economic intelligence' services. In addition:

A last point to bear in mind in regard to the German Secret Service is that much of its work is carried out by the various Nationalist Press and Publicity organisations, which are supported by Hugenberg and the 'Heavy' industrialists, so that the Secret Service does not have to depend on the Budget grants, large as they may seem to us . . .[8]

Business interests were also responsible for maintaining the secret services in the United States, although 'figures are not forthcoming'; the Japanese statistics were somewhat impenetrable, but it appeared that an earlier decrease in expenditure had in 1928–29 been followed by a new grant for 'combatting the spread of Communism and Dangerous Thoughts'. As far as the Soviet Union was concerned, it was thought that it must spend 'a colossal sum', though 'no guess can be made as to the figure'.

Vivian's discreetly worded memorandum was supported by a much larger body of intelligence collected by SIS, although very few examples of specific reports on the subject have survived. These, however, show good reasons for SIS's increasing emphasis on economic matters. One example was a series of reports received in the late 1920s on Soviet commercial espionage directed against Germany. These described a highly developed Soviet organisation known as the *Wirtschafts-Aussendienst* (WAD, Overseas Economic Service), run from Moscow. The WAD had offices in Berlin, Budapest, Paris, London and New York, but only in Germany had it the status of an independent organisation parallel with that maintained by Soviet Intelligence; the German Bureau also covered operations in Czechoslovakia, Holland, Luxembourg and Switzerland. Its duties included monitoring industrial development, trade relations and output, investigation of technical progress and illegal rearmament with particular emphasis on plans for the wartime mobilisation of peacetime production, and the enlistment of specialists in all branches of industry with practical knowledge of secret manufacturing methods. A report of December 1930 stated that the WAD employed four hundred and twenty 'instructors', two hundred of whom were controlled directly by Moscow, and that during 1930 nearly 30 engineers and chemists had been recruited to work in the Soviet Union.

Secret Intelligence on these Soviet activities was all the more alarming at a time when diplomatic information was hard to come by. The decision by the British Cabinet in May 1927 to break off diplomatic relations with the Soviet Union[9] had served merely to increase the siege mentality of the Bolshevik regime, a tendency enhanced by the inauguration of the Five Year Plan in October 1928 and its confirmation by the 16th Party Conference in April 1929. The decision to place heavy industry at the centre of the Soviet modernising effort, and the concomitant campaign of collectivisation and pressure on the rural peasantry, reinforced the impression that the Soviet Union was a country at war without and within, defending its future against hostile forces both external and internal.[10] When Henderson decided, soon after the Labour Government came into office on 5 June 1929, to open discussions with a view to the re-establishment of formal relations, he was well aware of the Soviet Government's neediness for a modicum of international recognition as well as of the potential dangers of such a move. He approached the matter more cautiously than had MacDonald in 1924, telling Hugh Dalton, in a reference to the Zinoviev Letter *débâcle*, that 'Russia has brought us down once, we can't afford to let it happen twice'.[11]

Predictably, negotiations were tortuous and tedious: the Soviet Ambassador in Paris, Dogvalevsky, sent over to deal with Henderson, insisted that his Government could accept no responsibility for Comintern activities; notes on propaganda were eventually agreed and Ambassadors were exchanged in December 1929. Six months later the British incumbent in Moscow, Sir Esmond Ovey,[12] reviewed the situation: bilateral relations were better, indeed referred to by some as a honeymoon, but this description, Sir Esmond thought, 'may appear more as having resulted from an unsuccessful marriage than from the commencement of a period of living happily ever after'. The tone of his review was, however, rather admiring of the Soviet diplomatic style. The organisation of the Soviet Government, he wrote, was:

> so skilful that hitherto they have succeeded in renewing relations with a large number of powers, none of whom can have from recent practice acquired any hope that the Government itself can seriously be brought to book. This problem will always be present, and it could be just as useless, to use a homely simile, to complain of the 'redness' of the Bolshevik Government as it would be to complain of the 'blackness' of the Government of Ethiopia, or the two-edgedness of Vatican diplomacy . . .[13]

Ovey's reporting contained ample evidence of aggressive Soviet paranoia. In one of his first despatches, on 15 December 1929, he reported Litvinov's emphasis on the 'circle of hostility which surrounds his country', even attributing the storm that delayed the Soviet mission's setting off for London to the machinations of Lord Birkenhead.[14] In February 1930 the Ambassador noted increased nervous tension in Moscow, 'partly due to strain accentuated by the industrial programme the success of which would be ruined by war'; and at the end of the year, accusations of an elaborate plot by engineers of the Union Cold Storage Company (supposedly supported by 'French and British capitalists') and a show trial led the Ambassador to ask 'What has the whole thing been about?'[15]

By this time, Henderson had already concluded gloomily that his efforts to normalise Anglo-Soviet relations had been poorly reciprocated:

> I can claim to have done more than any other to bring about resumption of relations with the Soviet Government in the teeth of strong formidable opposition, and my desire to develop and improve those relations continues; nevertheless my difficulties have been immensely increased by reason of the fact that far from campaign of propaganda and abuse undergoing some diminution as a result of action of His Majesty's Government in exchanging Ambassadors, campaign would seem to all appearance to have been increased in intensity since exchange has taken place.[16]

One can almost imagine Morton snorting 'I told you so'. Little in sympathy with a Labour administration, nor confident in the FO's judgement, he saw in the diplomatic reporting, as in the secret Intelligence he received, little to inspire optimism. Where Soviet industrialisation and modernisation elicited reluctant admiration from diplomats – even William Strang,[17] acting as Chargé in Moscow in the summer of 1930, remarked on the 'restrained and dignified' conduct of the Soviet workers and the emergence of a 'new kind of society'[18]– Morton saw an emerging economic and military threat. In this he was at one with the War Office, who were disturbed about Anglo-Soviet tension over Afghanistan, as well as about aggressive Russian intentions towards Poland, although he is unlikely to have concurred in their judgement that the current situation could lead to the downfall of the Soviet regime.[19] Secret Intelligence, on the contrary, indicated that although Stalin and his Party colleagues might be suffering the painful throes of their supercharged industrial revolution, their grip on power and determination to succeed were undiminished.

For Morton, reports received by Section VI of Soviet commercial espionage in Germany were as interesting and important in what they told him about Soviet industrial and military developments as about Germany. He took a special, and well-informed, interest in industrial and scientific developments and discoveries in other countries, a particular study of his since the First World War. In SIS during the early 1920s he had made it his business to collect reports of new industrial processes, inventions and the refinement of weapons technology, and following the establishment of Section VI continued to keep a professional eye out for developments that could be harnessed for British use. In 1929, for example, he made two trips to Czechoslovakia in pursuit of just such an invention: a new kind of explosive known as 'M/N' (or, according to the War Office file, 'Marmalade'), developed by a Czech chemist and said to be a chemical compound that passed through liquid, jelly and powder states during manufacture, and whose detonation caused an explosion with a force of more than one thousand times that of nitro glycerine.[20]

The owner of the rights to this explosive, Karel Bondy, president of the Avia Aeroplane Works in Czechoslovakia, was a friend of the British Minister at Prague, Sir Ronald Macleay, and through him let it be known that he would be willing to offer the invention to the British Government:

> According to M. Bondy, this explosive is so cheap, so easy to make and so powerful, that in wrong hands, such as the Bolsheviks or a country wishing to dominate the world by force of arms, it would be a world menace. He therefore, after considerable thought, has decided to offer full rights in this explosive to the British Government, as he considers the British Empire is the safest world institution to handle this invention. Though a rich man, he is quite frank that he will require a price, that his own country, Czecho-Slovakia, must have access to the explosive under certain conditions, and that if the explosive is manufactured for civil use, he will probably require some form of royalty.[21]

When Macleay reported this offer to the FO, they sent a representative over to question M. Bondy; and although the report does not give a name it seems clear that it was Morton, who was in Prague in March 1929 in connection with the Orlov trial.[22] It was certainly Morton who was nominated to represent the FO at the (abortive) trials of the explosive that took place at the Royal Arsenal at Woolwich on 15 August 1929; and who travelled with M. Bondy and a War Office mission to Czechoslovakia on 19 August, remaining there until 29 August in order to interview the scientists who had developed the explosive and observe further trials (which though still unsuccessful did provide evidence that an explosive of 'gigantic' power had been developed).[23] The reports on the explosive and its inconclusive trials provide a rare opportunity to observe Morton at work on behalf of Section VI, albeit under the Foreign Office umbrella; he may well have fulfilled such a role on other occasions that lie undetected in the official record.

If the theme of both open and secret reporting on the Soviet Union was threat and instability, the news from Germany was scarcely more encouraging. However, despite evidence of more or less blatant flouting by Germany of the military provisions of the Versailles treaty, there was little appetite in either the Baldwin or MacDonald governments for acting on it. The British Ambassador in Berlin, Lindsay, continued to discount or play down persistent rumours of illegal German rearmament until leaving in July 1928 to take up his post as PUS. Consequently, when in April 1929 he was given a photographic copy of a German War Office document obtained by SIS and giving 'the whole German scheme for mobilisation' that was supposed to have come into force on 1 May 1928, he remained sceptical, although the authenticity of the document was vouched for by Sinclair.[24] The British War Office, Lindsay told Chamberlain, were 'considerably excited' about the scheme which provided for the mobilisation of twenty-one divisions in thirty-six hours and sixty-three divisions in four weeks (the Treaty of Versailles permitted only seven infantry and three cavalry divisions). But, complained Sir Ronald, where was the evidence that the Germans had anything like the equipment they would need for these divisions?

> Hitherto the WO has held that Germany is practically without warlike equipment. I never heard it seriously maintained that any large caches existed (barring of course hoards of a few scores or hundreds of weapons hidden by lunatics). When there is serious evidence to the contrary, then there will be ground for very serious alarm . . . I should have thought that if we are clever enough to hear of this mobilization scheme, we should be clever enough to hear of the manufacture of 300 or 400 field guns & of 500,000 rifles. Before taking this too frightfully seriously, we must have it confirmed that the Treaty violations in the matter of equipment are far more serious than we have hitherto believed.

Chamberlain agreed:

> This is exactly what I anticipated. I am surprised that anyone should be surprised . . . It would be rash to assume that because the scheme requires more artillery than is authorised, that extra artillery is already in existence.[25]

The two men agreed to 'keep this paper absolutely secret & to communicate its existence to *no-one*'. The message of the secret memorandum, however, differed little except in detail from less confidential assessments of the military situation in Germany.

Within SIS, the convergence of secret Intelligence and open reporting must not only have looked pretty convincing, but also underlined the importance of obtaining further information on industrial mobilisation. Though it was to take time for Germany to supplant the Soviet Union as the principal potential enemy, the evidence suggests that Morton had made the mental shift to assess them as equally dangerous – with Germany moving into the lead – earlier than many in the British political, or indeed military establishments. In this his thinking may well have been in advance of that of his Chief.[26] In fact, British governments in power between 1927 and 1931 were more preoccupied with economic than with military developments in Germany. The prospect that Germany might be unable to maintain reparations payments, thus presenting Britain with an urgent budgetary problem, was matched by the understanding that until reparations ended German economic recovery was impossible.[27] These concerns were the spur for the intensive diplomacy of 1928–31 intended to ensure international cooperation both on reparations and on the related question of disarmament.[28] The efforts of Chamberlain, MacDonald and Henderson were overtaken by the European economic crisis precipitated by the collapse of the *Creditanstalt* in July 1931; by that point, however, the economic preconditions for the rise of political extremism in Germany had been in existence for some years.

During the late 1920s the FO received a series of ominous reports concerning political developments in Germany, and by early 1930 the British Ambassador in Berlin, now Sir Horace Rumbold, conceded that the growth of National Socialism was worrying. On 13 May he forwarded a note by his Military Attaché, Colonel J.H. Marshall-Cornwall, reporting a *Reichswehrministerium* contact as saying that the movement was 'far more of a menace to the present constitution than is Communism', and was attracting the attention of young officers as a means of escape from Germany's financial and political troubles:

> Another serious feature of the movement is the ascendancy which its leader, Adolf Hitler, has the power of exerting. He is a marvellous orator, and possesses an extraordinary gift for hypnotizing his audience and gaining adherents. Even though his policy is a negative one, his personal magnetism is such as to win over quite reasonable people to his standard, and it is this which constitutes the chief danger of the movement.[29]

In the elections held later that year, the National Socialists increased their *Reichstag* seats from twelve to one hundred and seven, polling nearly 6,500,000 votes.[30] Though Rumbold (in common with the other German parties contesting the election) was confident that the Nazi gains would be short-lived, the expression of discontent embodied in that election result was premonitory. By October 1930, Orme Sargent[31] was confessing to Rumbold that the FO had been struck by the renewed urgency of the demand in Germany for the abolition of demilitarisation restrictions imposed in the Rhineland; and by January 1931, even Rumbold admitted that in the current political and economic climate the Nazis were likely to win still more seats in future elections:

> in spite of the sporadic excesses of which its adherents have been guilty, of the fact that it is a party of negation rather than of construction and that its leaders are third or even fourth rate men.[32]

These reports confirmed publicly the information received secretly by SIS. Morton was also receiving regular information from his French colleagues in the *Deuxième Bureau*, who were themselves keeping a close eye on developments in Germany (and the Soviet Union).[33] He also obtained a considerable amount of information for Section VI from open sources, from which it was possible to learn quite a lot in the late 1920s about German economic planning and illegal rearmament, or indeed about Russian industrial developments. Writing to Liddell Hart about this period in 1967, Morton commented on how 'astoundingly easy' it had been to acquire information on manufacturing capacity, raw materials, manpower and other military information:

> Even the Germans and Russians published all sorts of Trade and Indus-trial returns, which could be checked against those of other importing and exporting countries; and many other technical publications of great value to our job.[34]

Everything he learned tended to support the conclusion that a study of German and Russian industrial development was an essential defensive tool. The mount-ing body of evidence, including letters from travelling British businessmen, reports from military attachés and press articles reporting the proud achievements of prominent industrial enterprises, was at the same time pushing British military and civil authorities, albeit reluctantly, towards the same conclusion.

FCI and IIC

Early indications of the way the wind was blowing emerged in the Advisory Committee on Trade Questions in Time of War (ATB Committee), established by the CID in 1924 to ensure – mindful of the importance of economic blockade during the earlier global conflict – that the necessary administrative machinery was prepared and kept in readiness for exerting economic pressure on an enemy in wartime.[35] This Committee, chaired first by Sir Victor Wellesley and then by Viscount Cecil, included Sir Edward Crowe, Controller of the Department of Overseas Trade, in its membership: its work on blockade machinery, how-ever, was interrupted constantly by demands from a range of departments to give detailed consideration to the means for exerting economic pressure on poten-tial enemies including, in 1927, Soviet Russia (the other candidates were China and Japan). During the same year, the War Office woke up to the fact that the withdrawal of the Allied Control Commission from Germany meant not just the release from responsibility, but the loss of inside information on German industrial mobilisation. Colonel Gosset, the British expert engaged on winding up the Commission, had produced a range of useful papers on German industrial organisation, raw materials, manufacturing output and manpower. These led the CIGS to realise that:

> great changes have taken, and are taking, place in German industry; it also leads one to the conclusion that it is essential to establish in this country some organization for the proper appreciation of the industrial intelligence of foreign countries in its military aspects ... A knowledge of a country's plans for industrial mobilization will therefore become as important as the knowledge of her plans for military mobilization.[36]

The Air Staff concurred: they, too, were interested in industrial intelligence that might supply information about potential bombing targets:

> vulnerable objectives of an industrial and economic character whose destruction or disorganisation would have a very direct and, in many cases, immediate effect on the military situation.[37]

The Service Chiefs realised, as they discussed the problem, that it might be useful to have some sort of joint sub-committee dealing with intelligence. In principle, they disapproved of such an idea, since although each considered his own intelligence staff both important and authoritative, each also held the somewhat contradictory view that intelligence branches constituted 'professional backwaters appropriate for eccentrics or those not fitted for command'.[38] In 1928, however, they were forced to admit that their own sources could not supply the necessary economic or industrial information, and that it would be helpful to be able to draw on a range of departments, such as the FO and Board of Trade; and even, perhaps, to consult trade organisations such as the Federation of British Industries or Lloyds of London. The CID admitted the need for coordination:

> The present organization, in which each Department has its own Intelligence Service, divided and sub-divided into a number of sections, makes such liaison very difficult, if not impossible.[39]

There was only one answer to the problem: a new sub-committee must be created. Nobody suggested making enquiries of any of the constituent bodies of the British secret Intelligence establishment, with whom each Service had its own liaison but which were regarded as necessarily peripheral to military – the only 'real' – intelligence. It did not occur to the CID in 1928, any more than it occurred initially to the Joint Intelligence Committee when it was established in 1936, that the Intelligence chiefs, Sinclair and Kell – or even the FO – should participate in such a sub-committee.[40]

A CID sub-committee on industrial intelligence in foreign countries (FCI Committee) was duly formed, although at the CID meeting held on 8 November 1928 some Ministers professed themselves unconvinced of the need to add another to the existing panoply of sub-committees merely to carry out what, in their view, amounted to nothing more than the collation and dissemination of information that was already available.[41] The matter was referred to a conference chaired by Hankey on 13 December 1928. Each representative pronounced his department already well supplied with intelligence, and more than willing to supply information to other departments – provided the latter made it clear precisely what information they wanted. However, Major-General Charles, the DMO&I, offered the startling admission at this meeting that 'conclusions that were come to by soldiers were not . . . necessarily correct'; he favoured a separate sub-committee. He was supported by Hankey, who felt that unless the work were carried out by a properly established CID sub-committee, it 'ran grave risks of dying':

> He knew of a number of examples where a subject had been taken up in one of the other Departments and had gone ahead well, under the influence possibly of an originator, but that when that driving influence had, owing to a change of appointments, disappeared, the subject had gradually been dropped.[42]

The conference decided that direct liaison should be established between the Service Departments and the Board of Trade, and that a sub-committee, consisting of representatives of the Service ministries, Board of Trade and Department of Overseas Trade, should be set up 'to deal with all matters arising out of this interchange which required joint discussion'. Recommending these decisions to the CID in a memorandum of 21 February 1929, the President of the Board of Trade, Sir Philip Cunliffe-Lister, made two provisos: British commercial representatives 'must take no action which could conceivably give rise to a charge of commercial espionage'; and the civil departments must be free to say when a suggested line of enquiry was beyond their resources. Nevertheless, he was confident that:

> the Intelligence Departments will, I think, find that the Civil Departments have already in their archives, or can obtain through their overseas officers, practically the whole of the industrial information required for defence purposes.[43]

The CID approved the proposal on 2 May 1929;[44] the first meeting of the new sub-committee did not, however, take place until March 1930, more than eighteen months after the CIGS and Chief of the Air Staff had submitted their memoranda stressing the need for information on industrial mobilisation (their apparent lack of any sense of urgency matched that of the ATB Committee, which met not at all in 1928 and 1930, and only once in 1929).

  This substantial hiatus between the establishment of the committee and its first meeting did, however, enable a certain amount of preliminary work to be undertaken within the departments involved. The results were not encouraging. At the first formal meeting of the FCI Committee on 20 March 1930, chaired by Crowe, it soon became clear that its members had become distinctly uneasy about their remit. Brigadier A.C. Temperley, Deputy DMO&I, summed up the general view when he stated that the General Staff had discovered the problem of studying industrial intelligence to be:

> considerably more complex than had at first been anticipated. The difficulty lay in the fact that no existing Department, and, indeed, no existing section of any Department, was responsible for studying this problem as a whole.[45]

The General Staff, he said, were not now sure that a new committee was the answer. Perhaps an officer should be appointed for a year to investigate the best methods of studying industrial mobilisation in foreign countries? This might be 'the germ out of which some permanent organisation might subsequently grow'. Crowe, understandably, was rather irritated by this attempt to go back on the decision reached by the CID. He discounted somewhat briskly the idea that any one officer could be found 'who had sufficiently expert knowledge of all the implications of the problem', and the Committee agreed to his suggestion that the best way to find out what was available and what was lacking might be to concentrate initially on the study of a particular country, using as a test case the Soviet Union, in regard to which 'impartial industrial information was scanty, but which nevertheless offered a number of different methods of obtaining information'.

Despite his dismissal of the idea of a single expert it seems likely that even at this stage Crowe had Morton, or more generally SIS, in mind when he referred to 'different methods of obtaining information'. Both men were later to say that Morton had begun supplying information on industrial mobilisation to the FCI in 1929–30. Crowe was certainly looking to sources outside the conventional medium of reports submitted by military attachés, or information derived from travelling businessmen. Whatever he may have had in mind, the FCI Committee's progress (or lack of it) during 1930 evidently confirmed his instincts. Proposals agreed at the Committee's second meeting on 16 June 1930 for departments to keep War Office branch MI3(c) informed of intelligence bearing on industrial, manufacturing and research matters, failed to achieve the desired results. Crowe's anxiety about the quality and quantity of economic intelligence available can also be detected in the proceedings of the ATB Committee, which agreed at its fifteenth meeting on 27 February 1931 that no further studies of individual countries should be undertaken without instructions from the Prime Minister.[46]

At the FCI Committee's third meeting in March 1931 the War Office, called to discuss their woefully inadequate paper on the trial scheme for the study of industrial intelligence in the USSR, confessed that they did not have the knowledge or the means to obtain the kind of detailed information required on industrial preparations in the Soviet Union. The obsessive secrecy of the Soviet authorities, combined with their readiness to interpret any Western initiatives as conspiracies to destabilise the Great Socialist Experiment, meant that the best that military intelligence could do was to deduce that:

> there was no doubt that a plan for industrial mobilisation existed in that
> country and was closely inter-locked with the five year plan.[47]

This unsurprising conclusion epitomised the failure of the FCI Committee to get to grips with the task its members had declared themselves ready and willing to tackle. Meanwhile, however, Crowe and Hankey had clearly come to the conclusion that for inside information it was necessary to turn to the professionals.

Contact had already been made with Sinclair, and they were aware that Section VI of SIS, under Morton, was making a study of industrial mobilisation in potential enemy countries, including the Soviet Union and Germany. Could that information be supplied to the FCI Committee, asked Crowe? Yes it could, responded Sinclair, pointing out hopefully that this would involve him in extra expense at a time when resources were already scarce. In response, Crowe (as Sinclair was to remind him a year later) 'expressed the hope that funds would be forthcoming to provide for this', but prudently made no firm commitment.[48] Nevertheless, Sinclair, without having extracted any firm reciprocal promise, agreed formally that Morton should supply information to the Committee.[49]

On 11 March 1931, Crowe informed his FCI colleagues that since they last met he had been having conversations 'with other interested and important people'. From this he had concluded that the Committee should focus on other countries as well as the Soviet Union, and that new methods of acquiring the necessary information must be devised, in addition to the departmental methods already in operation. He outlined a plan for a new central organisation, consisting of 'a nucleus staff working in close touch with the Department of Overseas Trade and other civilian and service Departments'. Though the minutes make no reference to where that staff might be located, Crowe presumably explained it to the Committee, as he warned them that 'the strictest secrecy on the question must be kept'.[50] In fact, Crowe's 'nucleus' was to be the Industrial Intelligence Centre, sited within SIS: and it was to be built on the knowledge and experience of Morton. In the words of the first FCI Report, dated 6 May 1932: 'The Sub-Committee were fortunate in obtaining the loan of the services of a suitable officer who had already studied the subject and was well-placed for gaining touch with sources of the desired information.'[51]

It did not take long for the new body to prove its worth to the FCI Committee, which met for the fourth time on 10 July 1931 to consider a secret memorandum prepared by the IIC – that is, Morton and Section VI of SIS – entitled 'Russia: industrial mobilisation for war',[52] based on 'information received from secret sources, supplemented and confirmed by extracts from publications'. Part I, 'Evidence that the theory of Industrial Mobilisation is known and understood in the USSR', stated that 'every step' of the Five Year Plan was assessed by the State Planning Commission, *Gosplan*, against both the domestic industrialisation objective and its value to the USSR's armed forces in the event of war. Part II, 'Evidence that the question of Industrial Mobilisation in the USSR is not confined to theory', reported that all Soviet industrial undertakings were divided into five categories, of which the first was armament and munition factories; and included information from 'reliable secret sources' who had visited Soviet Russia, such as a Swedish engineer who reported that a meat-mincing machine plant at Takhinsk had been 'so constructed as to permit of a quick switch over to shell production'. Part III, 'Preliminary description of the Soviet administrative machinery for studying and carrying out industrial organisation,' commented authoritatively on the organisation of the Soviet state, and on the existence and role of the Mobilisation Sections (*Mobotdel*) which existed in every important Soviet institution.

This report was entirely different from anything that could have been prepared by the Service intelligence branches. The level of detail, imparted with a peremptory authority and with a lavish sprinkling of acronyms and Russian designations, impressed the Committee, who deemed it 'very valuable' and sent it smartly to the CID. At one stroke the IIC, in the person of Morton, had established its credentials as the central source of official information on industrial mobilisation in foreign countries. The FCI Report of May 1932 assessed its impact more euphemistically:

> The institution of the Industrial Intelligence Centre resulted in a more rapid and copious flow of information regarding the country under study, viz. the USSR; while at the same time the increasing knowledge and the wider scope possessed by the Officer i/c Centre placed him in a position to originate enquiries and to collate the information.[53]

As ever, little documentation survives to attest to Morton's view of these developments, but it is likely that he viewed them with a mixture of satisfaction and exasperation. He and Sinclair would presumably have kept abreast of the administrative progress of the FCI Committee from the outset, if only from the circulation of CID papers, before Crowe appealed to them for help. What they felt about the complacence revealed in the CID's and FCI's deliberations is not recorded, but it is hard to imagine that they did not feel some sense of frustration when they read successive civil and military Departmental assertions that all the information required was of course already available to them; and that when those 'readily available' sources proved not to yield the information required, it was because it was simply 'too difficult' to obtain. Without Hankey's prompting and Crowe's chairmanship, it is unlikely that the Committee would ever have considered approaching SIS for access to the growing body of industrial intelligence held by Section VI. At a time when SIS was feeling particularly undervalued and under-resourced;[54] engaged in damaging turf wars with Special Branch;[55] swimming against a foreign policy tide of disarmament and defence cuts, while sitting on a mine of information about the warlike preparations of the Soviet Union and Germany; here, at last, was a chance to make use of some of that information, and to influence official minds and hearts.

For Morton personally, the establishment of the IIC provided the opportunity to break free of an organisational framework that had become restrictive and unrewarding. It is doubtful that he realised in the spring of 1931 that his appointment as Director of the IIC effectively meant the end of his mainstream SIS career, but he certainly saw immediately the scope for broadening his professional horizons. He let it be known more widely that he had a 'new job', and set about gathering information from a wider range of sources than hitherto. Churchill, for example, sent Morton a set of papers containing information on the industrial capacity of the USSR from Sir Thomas Holland, formerly president of the Indian Industrial Commission as well as of the Board of Munitions, that Morton pronounced to be 'most decidedly of significance to me in my new job'. He had also, he told Churchill, approached General Edmonds, official historian of the First World War working in the Historical Section of the CID, for similar information.[56] His secret sources enabled him to correct and supplement what he received from open source material, but he made it clear to Churchill that he was anxious to receive any material that might be relevant.[57]

It is not possible to do more than speculate whether Morton's 'new job' represented in some sense a relief to his senior SIS colleagues. Morton's approach to Intelligence, as has been seen, was neither collaborative nor emollient, albeit dynamic and effective. Perhaps his role, as 'C.O.' if not as 'Production', had come to sit less easily in the organisation SIS had become in 1929–31; an organisation in which Section V, for example, flourished under Vivian's more diplomatic leadership. This is mere conjecture: there is no solid evidence to suggest that Morton was being 'squeezed out' of SIS, however awkward a colleague he might be at times. Sinclair continued to support him, and clearly saw the work of the IIC as important. Nevertheless, although Morton continued to play a managerial role in SIS until at least 1933, and to take an active interest in the work of all its sections, 1931 was a watershed in his career. Henceforward his reputation, as a member of the secret world with connections in overt officialdom, was gradually to be superseded by that of a well-known and influential official whose 'shadowy' connections gave him access and authority that he would not hesitate to wield as a weapon over his more conventional colleagues.

8

A 'GENTLEMANLY FORM OF SPYING'[1]

The Industrial Intelligence Centre, 1931–37

If, despite his best efforts, Desmond Morton is remembered by historians and others intrigued by the labyrinthine workings of government, it is principally for his role in the half a dozen years leading up to the outbreak of the Second World War. Where his name is mentioned in accounts of the period, it is usually in one of two contexts: as Director of the Industrial Intelligence Centre (IIC), a shadowy but energetic figure with sinister connections, striving to present the hard facts of German rearmament to military and political authorities who paid too little attention, too late; or, still more intriguingly, as a man driven by impatience or conscience (or both) to pass secret information clandestinely to Winston Churchill, then 'in the wilderness', fuelling the latter's vigorous and heroic campaign to get a short-sighted government to wake up to incipient danger and rearm. Indeed, the dramatisation of Morton's character, in the BBC's successful 2002 drama *The Gathering Storm*, saw him immortalised by the distinguished actor Jim Broadbent as a trilby-hatted and trench-coated conspirator, a bluff spy facilitating the passing of surreptitious brown paper envelopes containing top secret assessments of German air power.

There is rather more truth in the first of these perceptions, concerning Morton's work with the IIC, than there is in the second, the attractive but unfortunately largely mythical idea of Morton acting as 'mole' for a Churchill excluded from the corridors of power. Both contain some elements of reality, but rest upon too narrow a foundation of fact to support the broader picture that has become accepted wisdom. However, these two, interlinked strands – the role of the IIC and the relationship with Churchill – provide a good basis on which to tell the story of Morton's life between 1931 and the end of 1937. The full history of the IIC's work and influence has yet to be written, although an early account (written while many of the papers were not yet available) remains both authoritative and illuminating.[2] This biography is not the place for such a detailed study, nor for a closely-argued contribution to enduring controversies concerning British Government policy in the 1930s, including that of 'appeasement'. The role of Churchill, too, has been the subject of innumerable studies in addition to Sir Martin Gilbert's magisterial biographical conspectus. In both areas, however, the career of Desmond Morton serves to cast a searching beam from an unexpected angle. Since the story of the IIC's development and impact is a complex one, it has been divided into two sections: the first describing the growth of the organisation and its sources of information, and the second its influence (or otherwise) on the development of government policy. A third section considers Morton's relationship with Churchill during the latter part of the period, including the allegation that he supplied him with secret information.

As ever, little record has been found of Morton's personal life during this period. It would not be unfair to say that the 1930s saw him at the peak of his professional powers: in his forties, with twenty years of military and Intelligence experience behind him, Whitehall-wise and Whitehall-wary, on terms of useful acquaintance if not close friendship with many of the political and military elite of the day. He knew whom to talk to and how to get things done. Presumably, particularly in these pre-war days, he had some social life; but apart from scattered references to Club lunches and Chartwell tennis parties, this aspect of his life remains a mystery. According to his own account, he spent his weeks in London, living with his mother in Beaufort Gardens, and his weekends at Earlylands. If he visited family, entertained guests, suffered illness or took holidays, no record has been found. The only way into his life is, as usual, through his work.

'Morton's new job': the development of the IIC, 1931–37

Until 1934, Morton and the IIC remained embedded firmly within SIS, where he continued to maintain a managerial role and some connection with the work of Section V. An increasing amount of his time was spent on Section VI/IIC work, however, though Sinclair had become progressively less willing to give the Centre house room or, more importantly, to pay for it. Only a year after the IIC's establishment, in May 1932, he wrote to Crowe at the Department of Overseas Trade, complaining of its cost to SIS: in the past twelve months, he said, this had amounted to £2,862 2s 3d:

> This includes Morton's salary, the rent of extra offices, typists, etc but does not include any extra charge in respect of our ordinary agents who have been employed upon collecting this information in addition to their other work. This added charge to my funds, which are already strained to breaking point owing to the difficulties in connection with the compensation that I have to pay to individuals abroad owing to the fall in the exchange due to our going off the Gold Standard, is really more than I can cope with, and I should be glad if you will give this matter your consideration with a view of either providing me with some extra money, or the taking over of the Industrial Mobilisation Section by some other Department.[3]

Sinclair got short shrift both from Crowe ('quite impossible for this Department to take over the Industrial Mobilisation Section') and from Hankey ('I think [SIS] ought to fit it in somehow, if necessary by letting something else go').[4] In fact, he was unable to shift the financial burden, at least in respect of Morton's salary, until 1935. But Sinclair's concerns may well have been broader. He wished to preserve (and retain control of) SIS operational and organisational methods, lest they become too entwined with those of the IIC; he may also have worried that the IIC opened a channel through which the Service departments, IIC customers as well as his own, learned more about SIS than he thought prudent. In any case, the secrecy of the IIC became increasingly unhelpful to its efficiency as its sphere of study expanded and its reputation grew. Commercial and industrial sources of information disliked the hole and corner aspect, preferring to deal more accountably with an official body, even if the material they supplied was highly confidential. From an SIS viewpoint, the IIC seemed an increasingly awkward cuckoo in the nest, hungry for information but making little contribution to the organisation.

SIS was, in fact, in a period of transition following the reorganisation of 1931 and had yet to find a purposeful operational direction in a deteriorating international situation. Sinclair felt that the IIC was a diversion from SIS's core business, yet did not seem entirely sure of what that core consisted. Short of resources as ever, the organisation was still concentrating on the Soviet foe and as yet paying scant operational attention to Germany or Japan (though, at the request of the Service departments, they were paying attention to US military and industrial developments, and to American Communism). Parallel liaison channels with French Intelligence were disappointingly unproductive, possibly because at this stage French secret Intelligence-gathering from within Germany was itself limited, and because of French problems in organisational communication equal to, if different from, those in Britain.[5] Later complaints about the shortcomings of British secret Intelligence in the immediate run-up to the Second World War had their roots in this uneasy period.[6]

For Morton, SIS formed an indispensable part of the IIC's information base, but he had also developed many other confidential sources, official, personal and commercial. A good example of the last is offered by his relationship with the Anglo-Persian Oil Company (APOC, the precursor of British Petroleum).[7] The initial contact was made through Vivian, head of Section V, who suggested to Morton in July 1931 that APOC, with its worldwide network of representatives, might be able to supply him with useful information on non-British oil producing concerns, particularly in Soviet Russia and Germany. When Morton expressed interest, Vivian discussed the matter with Colonel H.E. Medlicott, chief of the Security Branch at APOC, on 4 August, explaining about 'Morton's new job in Industrial Intelligence'. Medlicott agreed in principle that APOC might supply information to Morton, adding that 'it would make matters easier [if] this was divorced from great secrecy of Secret Service', and if a formal request were made by Crowe to Sir John Cadman, Chairman of APOC. The necessary arrangements were made.[8]

In preparation for what was to be a very fruitful relationship, Vivian sent to Medlicott in August 1931 a number of documents (apparently drafted by Morton) explaining the basis for and importance of the study of industrial intelligence. These included an SIS circular of 1 April 1931, issued immediately after the establishment of the IIC, explaining that it had been decided to carry out an intensive study, in respect of Soviet Russia and Germany, of the following subjects: industrial mobilisation; war materials (including explosives, gas and all calibre of guns); aircraft construction; research establishments; tractors and motors cars; the engineering, and iron and steel industries; fuels other than coal (including petrol and oils); minerals (including non-ferrous metals); rubber, cotton and flax. A further, undated, paper defined industrial intelligence as:

> any information regarding the industrial development of a country which may throw light upon the extent of its potential armed forces effort or plans

and explained that in modern warfare, a country's equipment and munitions were more important than its manpower:

> A country can only launch and maintain in the field that number of ships, military divisions or aircraft squadrons, which it can equip with machines and explosives. It is, therefore, now an accepted fact that an extensive study of a country's industry and industrial development must be carried out, in order to ascertain, not only how many armed force units it can maintain in war, but how long it can maintain them, and after what period of warfare a danger point can be expected at which the overtaxed resources of the country may crack.[9]

Vivian also sent Medlicott a copy of a document dated 4 July 1931, explaining the purpose of industrial intelligence:

> The objective to be attained is to discover which commodities, essential for the making of war, are lacking or restricted in the country under review. The greater the supply available within the selected country's frontiers, the less detailed study is necessary . . . It is the duty of the 'Industrial Mobilisation' expert to show in what manner and to what extent the requirements of the armed forces in explosives, weapons, equipment, supplies and transport, can be met and are likely to be met by Industry.[10]

Morton's lifelong interest in scientific matters in general, and the manufacture of armaments and munitions in particular, was an important component of his credentials as an 'Industrial Mobilisation expert'. Robert Young, who wrote a groundbreaking article on the IIC in 1976, reported the following opinion of Morton expressed by a former IIC official who wished to remain anonymous:

it was not only a matter of good looks, charm and fluent French, and naturally vast knowledge of the workings of the intelligence machine, he had an astonishing knowledge of industry, and the processes and problems of manufacture . . .[11]

It was just as important to know what to ask, and whom, for technical clarification. Again, his connection with APOC provides useful illustration. From late in 1931 Morton and Medlicott were in almost daily contact. Morton made a constant stream of requests for scientific details to be provided or checked. In July 1932, for example, he heard through diplomatic sources that the Soviet Government were extracting toluol (methyl benzene, capable of producing the explosive TNT) from crude petroleum found in the Baku district. APOC's chemical branch was able to confirm, confidentially, that this was possible and indeed likely. In the same month, Morton approached Medlicott for information concerning the specific gravity and general scientific data relating to petroleum extracted from oil wells at Gbely in Czechoslovakia: APOC supplied the answer. Though Morton certainly had more than the average layman's knowledge of scientific and industrial processes, he was also aware of the limits of that knowledge and was always ready to solicit expert help. It was this approach to the work of the IIC that enabled him to handle and present the kind of technical and industrial information that the Service intelligence branches seemed unable to manage or, at the very least, were unable to present to the FCI or CID in a comprehensible and relevant form.

As we have seen, Morton's first report for the IIC, on industrial mobilisation in Russia, had scored a decided success with the FCI Committee.[12] By November 1931, the IIC had produced twelve further reports, some in collaboration with the War Office. At the Committee's fifth meeting on 17 November, Crowe announced that the IIC had 'amply fulfilled expectations', and expressed warm thanks both to Morton and to Hector Leak of the Statistics Department of the Board of Trade (later its Director of Statistics), who had provided much help. The Committee agreed that in future G.S. Whitham, Assistant to the Director of Ordnance Factories in the War Office, should act as a technical consultant to the IIC.[13] This was a significant development, because Whitham was also Chairman of the CID's No. 1 Supply Committee, and his association with the IIC brought that body, and Morton himself, to the attention of the Principal Supply Officers' Committee responsible for British industrial mobilisation. It was always going to be difficult to get the military authorities (less so the civil) to accept that studies of foreign and domestic industrial capacity had any relevance to each other, but Whitham's association facilitated an interchange that helped the IIC to get closer to the core of British war planning than it might otherwise have done.

During the first three years of the IIC's work, its military customers pressed for information concerning Soviet Russia rather than Germany, since the former was perceived as a more immediate threat (after the Manchurian crisis, in September 1931, Japan was moved up the list).[14] Morton himself was increasingly preoccupied with German industrial mobilisation,[15] but accepted the War Office's request to make Russian information a priority, averring that 'knowledge of Industrial Mobilisation in one country greatly assisted the study of that subject in any other', although conditions in Germany and Russia were quite different.[16] The FCI was, indeed, fascinated by the information on the USSR Morton provided from secret sources. In late 1931, for example, an SIS representative reported the activities of one Victor Smirnov, a Soviet engineer who, under cover of a fact-finding visit to a number of German factories, including *Humboldt Deutschmotoren AG* in Cologne, had been engaged in industrial espionage. The IIC report based on this information was considered by the Committee on 19 February 1932 and caused a certain degree of alarm. Crowe said that he would not normally have attached much importance to it, since it seemed:

> of a somewhat sensational character and almost too good to be true. Other information had, however, come into his hands which indicated that similar enquiries were actually being conducted in this country [the UK]. He instanced the case of the recent letter published in the *Times* from Arcos asking firms to furnish certain information which might have a potential military value . . . MR WHITHAM said that the headings to the Questionnaire of the Arcos letter practically coincided with the headings under which investigations to firms in this country were conducted by the Director of Ordnance Factories. The information thus obtained would permit them to assess with some accuracy the capacity of a firm to produce munitions, provided they had access to the works and that the technical people of USSR had previous knowledge of the manufacture of armaments and munitions.[17]

Morton reinforced the perception of aggressive Soviet commercial espionage by reading out part of a further secret memorandum on (compulsory) counter-measures adopted in Germany, prompting the FCI to agree that Crowe should convey:

> informal but confidential warnings to certain business men, to be selected at his discretion, as to the extent and probable object of Russian enquiries to firms, together with an indication that such enquiries should be answered with extreme caution or disregarded.

A further IIC memorandum presented to the FCI in April 1932 was based on an SIS report of Soviet espionage carried out through the *Osoaviakhim*, a union of Soviet companies formed to further defence development in the USSR. Tactics included using aid agreements to entice German chemists to the USSR and then 'pump them dry' of information, and introducing Soviet personnel into foreign firms. The FCI took a grave view of such reports, and discussed at length the advisability of employing foreigners in British enterprises or of allowing British experts to give information to Soviet scientists. There was, however, no question of taking any formal action to protect British industrial secrets. Quite apart from the impropriety of disclosing confidential information to businessmen, the idea of any form of coercion was regarded as completely unacceptable. The FCI did, however, take one practical step, agreeing at their 6th meeting in February 1932 that (as suggested to Crowe by Morton) 'a representative of MI5 would add to the usefulness of the Committee'. Lt.-Col. Eric Holt-Wilson was co-opted as a member, and at the next meeting on 27 April 1932 presented a memorandum on protective measures against industrial espionage in the UK.[18]

The FCI held five further meetings between June 1932 and December 1933. Though the emphasis remained on Russia and Japan, industrial preparations by European countries, including Germany, took on a more menacing aspect following the appointment of Adolf Hitler as Chancellor of Germany on 30 January 1933.[19] By the end of 1933, the IIC – still comprising only the staff of Section VI, with occasional help from Leak and Whitham – had issued or were preparing memoranda on the industrial mobilisation of the USSR, Japan, Poland, Germany, France, Belgium, the Little Entente, Italy, Bulgaria, Hungary, Holland and Turkey,[20] as well as a number of technical papers on subjects such as munitions security and supply, and technical aid agreements. It is not surprising, therefore, that towards the end of the IIC's third year Morton and Clively, aided by the indefatigable Miss Gwynne, found their resources stretched to breaking point by demands from the Service departments and other customers. Morton, like any good departmental head, was skilled at pressing his claims for increased resource by advertising the scale and wide range of demands made upon him and his staff, but on this occasion he was not exaggerating. The IIC was fully occupied, collecting, collating and interpreting information, visiting commercial enterprises, quizzing scientific and military bodies on industrial processes, receiving visitors from the defence ministries, liaising with government departments and drafting reports, not to mention attending committee meetings.

In the second half of 1933, Morton was absent from IIC and related committees for several months, returning to work in January 1934. Though it is possible he was occupied with SIS business during that period, no trace of him has been found in the surviving documentation; and the possibility that he suffered a period of ill-health, possibly brought on by overwork, must at least be considered.[21] Throughout his career he pushed himself very hard, and at times the wound he suffered in 1917 could produce debilitating complications. There is no hard evidence on this occasion: but in any case, it had become clear that either the IIC must be reinforced or its workload reduced. On 1 December 1933 (Morton still absent), Hankey called an informal meeting, attended by Crowe and Service representatives, to discuss the problem. Faced with the alternatives of absorbing a considerable portion of the work themselves or agreeing a modest addition to the IIC staff, they had no difficulty in recommending the appointment of a deputy to Morton, in order to ensure the continuation of the IIC's 'very satisfactory' service. Sir James Rae, representing HM Treasury, accepted that 'in view of the arguments adduced he could not well stand out against this proposal'.[22]

Although the Service intelligence chiefs were quick to commend the work being done by the IIC, they remained uneasy about the implications of the Centre's growth in expertise and 'reach', and indeed about the scope of the FCI Committee itself. How far, they asked themselves (and each other), should the competence of the FCI, chaired by a civilian, extend? Was there not a danger that it might stray into areas that were not its responsibility? As for Morton, far from knowing his place, he thought nothing of talking to members of individual branches of the War Office, Admiralty and Air Ministry directly, without consulting their intelligence Chiefs! Links with the ATB and PSO Committees and other supply bodies only increased suspicion of the IIC's, and the FCI's activities.

The Service departments' feeling that things were not quite right did not, however, extend to agreement on how to improve them. At the 12th FCI meeting on 8 December 1933 Colonel L.R. Hill, the DMO&I, presented a note on industrial information regarding Germany, and proposed that a sub-committee should now be set up to evaluate that information for the benefit of the General Staff. Captain G.A. Scott, Deputy DNI, ventured the opinion that 'matters of high policy' were 'perhaps somewhat outside the scope of the Sub-Committee on Industrial Intelligence', and Crowe, 'speaking with great diffidence' was inclined to agree. It was the Deputy DMO&I who voiced Service uneasiness in more personal terms:

> BRIGADIER HAINING emphasised that responsibility for the work of the Study Centre should lie, not with Major Morton, but with the Service Departments mainly concerned. While Major Morton would be a permanent member, the Service Departments would provide members from their Geographical Sections according to the particular subject, the Chairman being nominated by the Chairman of the FCI Sub-Committee, according to the Defence Department primarily concerned in the particular question under discussion.[23]

In short, the arguments had moved on very little from those employed between 1929 and 1931. The military authorities resented the fact that they were forced to rely on civilian 'outsiders' (the respectability conferred by Morton's military record only extended so far), but could not agree a coordinated strategy for doing the job themselves. The IIC's terms of reference may have eliminated some duplication of effort, but 'did not at once succeed in reconciling the individual departments to the idea that the IIC should develop into a central organisation for the assessment of economic intelligence'.[24] In addition, Morton's habitual authoritative and even arrogant manner of conducting his business had clearly raised a number of hackles. But the Service departments had no sensible alternative to propose: at the very next FCI meeting, on 9 February 1934, Crowe's proposal for an Interdepartmental Study Group to examine each particular country or subject was agreed to be unworkable. Morton, after some delay, got his deputy: Martin Watson of the Consular Service. There was still occasional carping from both military and civilian authorities,[25] and the IIC's terms of reference and standing instructions were tweaked at regular intervals to define the Centre's scope and functions more precisely: adjustments welcomed, on the whole, by Morton, who was just as concerned as his customers that some limits should be set to the demands made on the IIC. Nevertheless, the IIC occupied an organisational space that no other body was in a position to fill, and in November 1934, at the 15th FCI meeting, Crowe tabled further congratulations on the work of Morton and his small team.[26]

If the IIC flourished, it now had to do so in the outdoor soil of Whitehall rather than in the hothouse of SIS. In October 1934, Sinclair finally took steps to separate the IIC from Section VI, giving the former some sort of independent existence (although it had its physical being in Broadway Buildings until it moved to 70 Victoria Street in the summer of 1936). An 'office order' from the SIS Chief announced that:

> As from October 9th 1934, the Section now composed of Major Morton, Mr Clively and their secretary will be known as the IIC and referred to in this office as ZS. The work of a circulating nature hitherto performed by Major Morton will be transferred to Major Plowden, who will become Head of Section VI (XS) while retaining his duties in charge of Section IVa (XM). Major Plowden, as head of Section VI, is to work with the IIC along the same lines as other circulating sections work with the government departments which they serve.

The IIC had become an external customer. Though Morton retained his close connections with SIS on a personal level, this seems to have marked the end (apart from his pay cheque) of his professional career in the service. Henceforth, though he continued to receive information from Section VI and other Sections, he was a consumer rather than a commissioner of secret information.

By mid-1935 the FCI members were again sympathetic to a plea for extra staff for the IIC. As Morton told the Committee on 14 June:

> The Industrial Intelligence Centre was no longer merely an enquiry centre nor a distributing agency, but was a small department which issued memoranda entailing a good deal of research work . . . In view of the varied nature and increased amount of work which had been necessitated by the international situation he had made certain recommendations with a view to increasing his staff, in order that the work could be carried out efficiently.[27]

Arrangements were made for a small addition to the IIC's clerical staff, though Morton's suggestion that the Services might wish to attach liaison officers to the Centre was dismissed as premature. Still, the IIC remained a small organisation. The nucleus of Morton, Clively and Miss Gwynne, now supplemented by Watson, expanded gradually to include a small number of female clerical and secretarial staff, with, on occasion, extra research assistance from other departments, including the FO's Economic Section. By May 1936, however, when Morton presented his report on the IIC's work during the past year, he was forced to admit that he was unable to keep up with demand. He made a further plea for extra staff, noting that the fact that the IIC was not an 'established' department in civil service terms was a disincentive to attracting the right calibre of candidate:

> a gentleman must possess the intellectual qualifications and experience which would make him a suitable candidate for admission as student to the Imperial Defence College. Such persons are rarely to be found in the open labour market, nor are they willing, if found, to accept the sort of salary, without accruing pension rights, which we are at present able to offer.[28]

The FCI, discussing this report on 11 May 1936, agreed that Morton needed extra resource. A small informal committee, comprising Edward Bridges of the Treasury, J.H. Jones of the Department of Overseas Trade and Morton himself, was appointed to look into the matter, and the CID agreed on 30 July to the strengthening of the IIC.[29] Arrangements were also made for it to be 'established' as part of the Department of Overseas Trade, thereby affording IIC staff access to civil service terms of employment and pensions, including the prospect of promotion; and opening the way for the recruitment of candidates capable, in Morton's words, of 'putting up a paper on the lines of a Cabinet paper'. He himself dropped his military rank and asked to be addressed henceforth as 'Mr Morton' (minute-takers in the various committees he attended followed this instruction faithfully, though he remained widely known as Major Morton).

Although he had pressed for the change in the IIC's status, Morton's own views on its translation were, predictably, scornful. Like most Intelligence men, he had hitherto rejected any implication that he was a civil servant, despite being paid from government funds. Writing to W.N. Medlicott at the end of the Second World War, he begged him not to use the phrase 'Industrial Intelligence Centre of the DoT' in the official history of the Blockade:

> I am no expert in the law but should I ever see any official statement that the IIC was 'of the DoT', I will try and pursue the author with all the brutality and venom of which the law permits. Please do not break my heart . . . It was necessary to attach the organisation as it then existed to some Department for rations, discipline and accounting purposes. Because Edward Crowe was the innocent channel through which we reported and was at the same time Head of the DoT, we were attached to the DoT. The views on this matter expressed by certain members of my staff would be recorded in a novel by a row of asterisks.[30]

Despite Morton's protestations, from 1 January 1937 the IIC was, indeed, part of the Department of Overseas Trade for all official purposes, and appeared as such in reference books. The incorporation of the IIC within the DoT during the last quarter of 1936 also marked the final break with SIS, which was henceforth relieved of any financial responsibility.

Meanwhile, parallel developments during the summer of 1936 had led to the further expansion of Morton's sphere of operation. Robert Young has written, with particular reference to Morton, that the IIC was 'composed of civilians, but civilians to whom the armed services are prepared to listen.'[31] Certainly they listened more intently between 1934 and 1936 than hitherto, as the IIC's message became increasingly topical and the Service Chiefs recognised that their overall intelligence base remained inadequate and poorly coordinated. Individually, they were collecting large amounts of information, and working closely (particularly in the case of the Air Ministry) with the IIC. There was, however, no effective mechanism for drawing all the available intelligence together and comparing it. In July 1935 the DMO&I, Major General Dill, wrote to Hankey about the increasing danger of 'uneconomical duplication' in the collation and recording of intelligence, and suggested that the remit of the FCI might be extended to cover 'all intelligence on which different departments depended', possibly changing its name to the 'Joint Intelligence Committee' or 'Intelligence Coordination Committee'. In particular, he noted a requirement for intelligence on air raid precautions and bombing targets. The Deputy Chiefs of Staff accepted that:

> the field of intelligence which it is now necessary to cover in time of peace in order to be properly prepared for the eventuality of war with any Great Power has been almost immeasurably extended and complicated by reason of (1) the extent to which modern war involves the whole of the resources of the nation; and (2) the vast extension of the zone of operations that has been brought about by the advance of aviation.[32]

One can almost imagine Morton grinding his teeth over this statement, obvious to anyone who had read IIC and FCI reports over the past four years. As usual, however, the Service representatives found it impossible to conceive that intelligence meant anything other than military intelligence. Though the scope of the FCI was to be enlarged to include air targets, the coordination problem was tackled by the creation of an Inter-Service Intelligence Committee, composed of the three Service Intelligence heads.[33] This 'abortive experiment'[34] led in June 1936 to the establishment of the Joint Intelligence Sub-Committee of the CID (JIC), on which Morton was co-opted from the outset, a measure of the degree to which his cross-cutting expertise and authority were now accepted. It held its first meeting on 7 July 1936 and he, or an IIC representative, attended nearly all JIC meetings between 1936 and 1939. In keeping with the 'we know best' attitude of the Service representatives,[35] there was initially no question of including the secret Intelligence agencies in the JIC's regular membership; nor was the FO represented until November 1938.[36]

In parallel, the decision was taken in May 1936 to establish an Air Targets Sub-Committee, comprising Service and IIC representatives, with targets divided into two categories, military and civil (ie relating to production and other non-military matters).[37] As Wing Commander C.E.H. Medhurst, head of Air Intelligence, explained to the FCI, the Air Ministry needed some 'clout' to ensure that businessmen, who were 'naturally anxious not to do anything which might imperil their trade relations with foreign countries,' should pass on useful and important information indicating possible targets.[38] The sub-committee held four meetings between December 1936 and April 1938: its minutes suggest that a considerable amount of time was spent discussing definitions and the division of responsibilities.[39]

There was considerable friction between Morton and the Secretary to the Air Targets Sub-Committee, Squadron-Leader Burge, who committed the cardinal sin of dismissing the IIC's reports as 'rather academic', preferring to rely on Air Intelligence.[40] Morton responded with predictable force, attempting unsuccessfully to insist on seeing Burge's memoranda in draft before they issued; when that failed, he resorted to producing alternative drafts. Morton enjoyed a fight like this, and intended to win:

> While I am willing, and even anxious to have my conclusions challenged since my desire, like yours, is to arrive at the truth, you will, I feel sure, agree that, failing a successful challenge, you must accept my conclusions on the facts for which I am responsible.[41]

It is possible that Burge and Morton found each other antipathetic: certainly, the latter's correspondence with other Air Ministry representatives, such as Medhurst and his successor Group Captain K.C. Buss, is more emollient, showing Morton very ready to defer to a well-argued case.[42] In return, Morton's inclusion on the committee ensured that the Air Ministry received valuable information on prospective targets from a wide range of other sources (including secret Intelligence), covering armaments and munitions factories, ammunition and petroleum stores (APOC were very useful here), transport links for the supply of raw materials and manufacturing plants.

In the event, the work of the Air Targets Committee was probably rather more useful than that of the pre-war JIC, which Morton found increasingly frustrating and which had virtually no impact on policy-making.[43] Nevertheless, his role in the creation of both new committees, as well as his presence on other bodies such as the ATB's Economic Pressure Committee, shows the extent to which the IIC was now regarded as an integral component of the bureaucratic defence machinery. On 5 July 1937, when the FCI considered the IIC's draft annual report, Crowe again congratulated Morton on his work, and observed, as the committee considered a recommendation from the Chiefs of Staff that the JIC and the FCI should review intelligence arrangements for the contingency of war with Germany, that 'the question appeared mainly to affect the Industrial Intelligence Centre which did practically the whole of the work for the Sub-Committee and also the Air Targets Sub-Committee'.[44]

The IIC was, indeed, drawn increasingly into wider discussions on defence and supply issues, though it continued to prepare its country memoranda and *ad hoc* reports and circulate them through the FCI (which did not meet between July 1937 and May 1938). The old problems of poor coordination between Service departments and other authorities persisted, however. At the end of 1937 the FCI Chairman, now T. St Quintin Hill, circulated, at Morton's request, a paper setting out the full terms of reference of the IIC and summarising its objectives. This paper (unsigned, but distinctly Mortonesque) explained that the IIC's first task, 'to assist in the collation, interpretation and distribution of foreign industrial intelligence', could also be carried out by other departments and committees, but the IIC alone had the authority to coordinate. Morton asked Hill to draw particular attention to the section on responsibilities:

> (i) . . . it is incumbent on Service Departments automatically to forward to the Industrial Intelligence Centre important industrial information received by them through their own channels; (ii) . . . the Industrial Intelligence Centre is entitled to circulate and comment upon important items of industrial intelligence received from any quarter [and] (iii) . . . to attempt to arrive at conclusions indicating what assistance a foreign country may expect to receive from its Industry in war; (iv) . . . all concerned are required to utilise memoranda on industrial intelligence, prepared by the Industrial Intelligence Centre and approved by other Departments concerned, as a common basis for further study of industrial intelligence.[45]

There followed a list of the committees attended by the Director of the IIC, and an extract from a CID memo (1139B) setting out in detail the mechanism for the collection, coordination, collation and interpretation of foreign industrial intelligence, plus liaison arrangements. This requirement for an unambiguous restatement of his and the IIC's authority is an example of the periodic need for endorsement and affirmation of his role that recurs throughout Morton's career, particularly at times when he felt that role either open to question, or receiving insufficient attention.[46]

While the official record makes it possible to trace the IIC's outward-facing activities, it is much harder to learn what went on within its office walls. Though now an 'open' organisation, much of the secrecy regarding IIC operations remained; after all, intelligence was its business, and confidentiality an ingrained habit in Morton, Clively and others who had begun their careers in the secret world. Those who worked for the IIC rarely discussed it, either then or later. Morton preferred to show his workings as little as possible, revealing only as much as was necessary to elicit extra resources when required. He fostered the impression to his customers of a busy and tightly-run organisation directed by himself with military precision: it was, apparently, his custom to wield his umbrella as a sword with appropriate flourish.[47] A unique and somewhat intriguing insight into the way his own staff saw him is offered by a former member of the IIC, reminiscing in 1984 about working there at the age of eighteen:

> All of the female staff except myself . . . came from St Godric's School. All of the male staff had been to Eton, Harrow or Rugby, later Sandhurst and Woolwich etc. Their office hours were 10am to 5pm plus TWO HOURS LUNCH . . . only myself and [the caretaker] worked normal hours 9 to 5pm an hour's lunch. The whole place was in a complete stupid shambles and as young as I was on my poor 37/6d a week wage I soon found two spies and received not a thanks but 2/6d pay rise! Churchill was a frequent visitor and presented me with a gift of a lovely lizard skin handbag addressed to 'Our dear little watchdog'. Major had a house near to Chartwell and a flat at Be[a]ufort Street . . . Miss Gwynne was in love with him but was ignored. She kissed Major's lung X Ray pictures every day . . .[48]

Even had Morton left any record of the Centre's work, he would hardly have included such tantalising (and intimate) detail, including the implication that all members of staff were constantly on the lookout for sources of information – 'spies'. Whatever her opinion of the IIC's working practices, the writer was clearly proud of her and her colleagues' achievements. As for poor Miss Gwynne, she remained devoted to Morton, who in turn relied on her as his personal assistant until his retirement in 1953. There is no indication that he was ever aware that her attentions were personal as well as professional.

By late 1937, Morton's position, and that of the IIC, seemed well-established in terms of authority and activity. Many of the IIC's initial operational difficulties had been overcome through his 'intimate knowledge of the intelligence machine and a knack for Whitehall empire-building [combined] with a forceful personality and considerable wit'.[49] Being active and in demand, however, was not the same thing as influencing policy, and the IIC's record must now be considered in the wider context.

Modern War:[50] the IIC and Whitehall

During the first three years of its existence the IIC had very little chance of making any meaningful contribution to defence or rearmament policy. If measured by the number and quality of the reports produced, or by the energy expended by its officers, its achievements were considerable. But in terms of influencing or even informing the formulation of foreign and defence policy, or of bringing important industrial developments in potential enemy countries to the attention of British policy-makers, its impact was negligible. This was not due to lack of effort on the part of Morton and his colleagues, nor because they exaggerated the nature of the threat. Though the message imparted by IIC memoranda was a serious one, its tone was minatory rather than alarmist, reporting the creation in certain countries of the economic and military preconditions for waging war, but not, at this stage, predicting any imminent conflict. At this stage, however, neither the military authorities, the Foreign Office nor the government as a whole were ready to hear what Morton and the IIC had to say. The National Government, formed in August 1931 under Ramsay MacDonald, with Neville Chamberlain as Chancellor of the Exchequer from November,[51] faced the twin problems of economic recovery and the financing of rearmament with unemployment running at seventeen percent of the labour force, and world trade badly disrupted by the suspension of the gold standard. They were more worried about the collapse of the German banking system than her military preparations, and in any case believed that Germany, an important trading partner, would be too preoccupied with her own economic recovery either to rearm or to embark on any foreign policy adventures.[52]

From 1934 onwards, however, as the economy began to emerge from depression, the tide of British policy began to turn, albeit reluctantly, in favour of preparation for an inevitable European conflict, though the Government continued to pursue the goal of general appeasement through the agreed mutual limitation of armaments. On 28 July 1934, Baldwin told the House of Commons that the development of air power meant that the British frontier was no longer 'the chalk cliffs of Dover', but the Rhine.[53] Three days later, the Defence Requirements Committee's programme for 'meeting the worst of our deficiencies' was approved by the Cabinet, albeit after four months of haggling and with its budgetary estimates reduced.[54] On 9 October the Chiefs of Staff agreed to plan on the basis of a war with Germany 'towards the end of 1939',[55] and in November the Cabinet agreed both to set up a German rearmament committee and to accelerate the RAF's air programme; Baldwin, in an even more noteworthy speech to the House on 28 November 1934, announced that HMG were 'determined, in no conditions, to accept any position of inferiority to what air force may be raised in Germany'.[56] The rhetoric, at any rate, had adopted a distinctly more belligerent tone. And although policy developed more cautiously, the British Government began to take some serious steps in the direction of rearmament and defensive planning.

The threat posed by the growth of German air power – or, as Churchill put it, 'the hideous curse of war from the air'[57] – was a particularly potent influence, inspiring apprehension among politicians and public alike. The Treaty of Versailles forbade Germany to have any aircraft industry at all; yet by 1934 the evidence of its growth and aggressive potential was inescapable. The prospect of a 'bombing war' aroused widespread revulsion (Baldwin would have banned the very concept of aerial warfare if he could). Nevertheless, since that seemed to be the kind of war for which Hitler was preparing, the Cabinet agreed on a series of measures to expand British air capacity, though agreement on the real extent of

German strength, and consequently the desirable British response, proved the subject of conflicting interpretation and bitter dissension.

In March 1934, a joint IIC/Air Intelligence memorandum on the German aircraft industry stated that its average monthly output had risen from forty airframes and sixty aero-engines at the end of 1932, to between sixty and seventy frames, and ninety and one hundred engines. The memorandum also noted that:

> a secret circular, reported to have been addressed by the German Air Ministry in September last to three of the largest aircraft firms, shows that the German Government is endeavouring to evolve types of sports and commercial aircraft which in time of war may be rapidly converted into efficient Fighters, Reconnaissance and Bombing aircraft. The expansion of the Industry, which is still continuing, is in no sense a natural industrial development. Its justification lies solely in orders placed on behalf of the Reich, or Nazi organisations, for aircraft of these types and for definite naval and military machines in direct defiance of the Treaty.[58]

When this report was considered by the CID on 31 May 1934, the Secretary of State for Air, Lord Londonderry, added that the Air Ministry had received further information showing that German preparations for aircraft production were 'now even more advanced';[59] and by November, Germany's monthly figures were one hundred and sixty to one hundred and eighty frames, and two hundred and fifty to three hundred engines, while the UK's monthly peacetime output was one hundred machines.[60]

Meanwhile, Morton and Medhurst, head of Air Intelligence, were exchanging information, although the latter regretted his inability to supply documentation on British manufacturing capacity:

> I am sorry to say we cannot give a figure for the capacity of the British industry today. We have nothing since the Charlton 1926 report, which is out of date. We have approached the matter on rather different lines compared to other countries. We have said what we should require under certain given conditions and have made plans to meet them.[61]

If Morton was surprised to learn that the Air Ministry could not say how many aircraft could be produced in 1934, he did not say so. Instead he persisted, writing to Medhurst on 26 September to ask whether it would be possible to supply 'the roughest of rough estimates' of the man-hours required to produce various sorts of airframes and engines;[62] after a short delay – 'the man who deals with this subject is away for a few days' – Medhurst provided estimates as requested, following them up with more detailed forecasts on 16 October. A month later, he sent the IIC a memorandum on the estimated expansion of the German aircraft industry to meet wartime wastage, asking for Morton's candid comments, 'because we are going to base our figures for aircraft production in this country very much on the lines of the ones we have produced for Germany, and I should be glad to know whether you think the latter a fair computation'.[63] Morton repaid Medhurst by sending him information on the production and secret storage of petroleum and gas in Germany, with maps (very useful for plotting bombing targets); some of this was gleaned from APOC, whom Morton was bombarding with technical requests relating to possible methods of manufacturing and storing aviation spirit.[64] The system of information exchange, built up with care by the IIC since 1931, was working well.

Meanwhile, the IIC's message was beginning to penetrate FO thinking. In February 1935, a study of updated statistics on the German Air force supplied by the Air Ministry and the IIC prompted Ralph Wigram, head of the FO's Central Department, to conclude that the current state of affairs was 'most alarming', meriting 'very careful reconsideration of our figures and the official comments of the Air Ministry', particularly at a time when the Government were considering the negotiation of an air pact with Germany.[65] A departmental memorandum commented that:

> the real criterion of strength in the air lies not so much in any of these figures as in the present manufacturing capacity of a country. This capacity will determine the output of aircraft in the vital period between the destruction of the original air fleet in the first few weeks of war, and the moment, possibly several months after the outbreak of war, when the factories, reorganised on a war footing, will be able to produce an emergency output. The German superiority over both France and our-selves in this respect is immeasurably great, as the German factories are already practically organised on an emergency war-time footing.[66]

Morton, who in general had little patience with the FO, was no doubt pleased that they seemed to be getting the point that industrial capacity was the crucial factor. The message appeared to have reached even the Prime Minister, who told the CID in April 1935 that he was 'prepared to consider any assistance necessary in order to get our aircraft industry organised on a sound basis':

> apart from the large numbers of aircraft Germany was actually pro-ducing, she was so organising her aircraft industry that she would be able to produce the numbers required without delay on the outbreak of war. We should ensure that our organisation was in a similar state and that our industry was able to produce what aircraft we required in an emergency. It was not a matter of actual production but of industrial organisation for production.[67]

In Morton's view, however, neither the FO, the CID nor the majority of the IIC's customers appreciated – or were willing to take on board – the full implications of his message. Germany was, indeed, expanding her industrial capacity at a furious rate, and producing aircraft and engines with increasing efficiency; but she was doing so, in his view, at considerable economic cost to herself. A further IIC/Air Ministry memorandum on the German aircraft industry, submitted to the CID in October 1935, pointed out that prominent German manufacturers such as Heinkel were now very concerned at the possibility of over-production; there was already a shortage of highly skilled labour. It was likely that in order to maintain the industry in a state of readiness capable of rapid expansion in case of war, large subsidies would be offered to manufacturers to enable them to export aircraft at prices with which the industries of other countries could not compete.[68] In Morton's view, this information should be put to constructive use, not just to frighten the Cabinet into agreeing greater resources for the RAF, but to feed into British defence supply planning, including the acquisition and conservation of vital raw materials, as well as into plans for mobilising British industry.

In the first objective he had some success: the twelfth annual report of the Principal Supply Officers' Committee, issued in December 1935 and drawn up on the basis that preparations should be completed in time for a possible conflict with Germany in 1939, incorporated as its Section V an IIC/FCI memorandum of July 1935 on Industrial Mobilisation in Foreign Countries.[69] But the idea of mobilising, or in any way directing British industry, remained controversial. The CID, in presenting to the Cabinet in March 1936 the DPRC's report on programmes of the defence services, acknowledged that it would take between three and five years to tackle 'the industrial problem'. Too little, too late, said the IIC, reviewing in a report of October 1936 the legislation adopted by a range of countries in order to plan for industrial mobilisation in peacetime:

> There is no longer any question as to whether planning in peace for national mobilisation in emergency is necessary or not, but merely as to the degree of intensity with which such planning is to be prosecuted.[70]

There is no doubt that the impact of Morton's message was inhibited by some institutional reluctance to accept (and therefore to act on) what were considered the IIC's more speculative reports. In November 1935, for example, Medhurst was unwilling to accept that the revival of the Italian aircraft industry might be linked with German plans for air expansion,[71] while the British Embassy in Berlin thought the IIC showed 'rather too much tendency to attribute to Germany in every respect the sort of Machiavellian super-intelligence which is easier to imagine than to create'.[72] Nor was this scepticism confined to reports on Germany. At the end of August 1936, Morton rang Ashton-Gwatkin at the FO with news that the Soviet Government had bought 20,000 tons of rice in Europe during the last ten days, bound ostensibly for Leningrad but, in Morton's view, intended as a Soviet contribution to the Communist cause in the Spanish Civil War. Members of the Economic Relations Department were sceptical, and took the view that nothing could, or should be done to stop the shipments. The general verdict, expressed by Laurence Collier, was that 'Major Morton is too suspicious!'[73]

The Chiefs of Staff might have been expected to have a keener awareness of the potential threat from Germany, but their response to it remained bedevilled by the same interdepartmental rivalry shown by their reaction to the IIC, as well as by competition for scarce resources. They continued to argue amongst themselves on the merits of naval limitation versus naval deterrence, of bombing as against anti-aircraft precautions, with little prospect of an agreed, let alone coordinated policy:

> What was missing in the deliberations of the Chiefs was a coherent vision, one that included economics, diplomacy and armed force, of how to deal with the manifold threats facing the Empire . . . Policy would have to come from the civilians.[74]

The civilians, however, failed signally to adopt the policies indicated by the available information on German rearmament, and on industrial mobilisation: a failure compounded, in Morton's view, by the fact that both Baldwin and Chamberlain were men with the right background to enable them to understand the situation, as he later wrote to Liddell Hart: 'Baldwin a steel man! Neville in close touch with Birmingham Industry etc!'[75]

In December 1936, Morton told the CID that the German aircraft industry had increased production considerably during the last quarter by reorganisation, although there was still a shortage of skilled labour.[76] Swinton, now Secretary of State for Air, acknowledged that the IIC's information 'disclosed a formidable situation', and that their figures on German air power had proved 'very near the mark'. Efforts would be made to convert more civil aircraft to military use in the UK. The idea that the British Government might be able to compete with Germany in her defensive precautions against air attack was, however, rejected, as Hoare told the CID in October 1937. The UK was not in a position to control essential industries:

> Nor must the Committee suppose that what had been done in Germany could be reproduced in this country in a short time. Germany had started on air raid precautions in 1927, and had naturally concentrated on the problem of passive defence during all those years when she was denied the means of active defence.[77]

Hoare's unchallenged statement, prompting the CID to recommend all departments to press forward with their preparations 'with the utmost urgency', might be seen, in one sense, as a measure of Morton's and the IIC's failure to get their message across. 1927 was the year when Morton had first started, from within SIS, passing on information on German economic mobilisation. Ten years later, the British Government was still unprepared for war. There were, of course, complex reasons for this, and one cannot lay the domestic and foreign policy decisions taken by British governments during the 1930s at Morton's door. It could equally be argued that without Morton and the IIC, interdepartmental awareness and coordination of economic intelligence would have been much less developed. The fact remains, however, that by 1937 the IIC had had no more than limited success in persuading the military and civil authorities of the importance of industrial intelligence, while their interest in it remained 'at best moderate'.[78]

In hindsight, it was easy for Morton, as for many other commentators, to criticise what he regarded as the failings of British defence planning in the 1930s. As Director of the IIC he had not been subject to the financial and political imperatives faced by successive governments; nor was his own information either comprehensive or infallible. Morton, and the IIC, have been criticised with some justification for the assumptions made in their reports about the efficiency of the German war machine, and for placing too much reliance on statistical calculation and extrapolation.[79] In recent years, scholarship has judged their efforts more kindly. But no matter how accurate and measured the IIC's intelligence, it was another matter to translate it into active defence preparations. In putting forward proposals for preventing Germany importing raw materials for armaments, or for prohibiting the export of much-needed aircraft to the British Empire, Morton was too far in advance of the political and economic situation; neither the will nor the machinery existed to take decisions that flew in the face of British foreign and trade policy. The idea of compromising 'normal' relations, even with Germany, was regarded as unacceptable, although the possibility of exerting economic pressure on Germany was discussed in the ATB Committee, and a sub-committee (on which the IIC was represented) was formed to consider the technical problems involved. Little progress was made until 1937, when plans for a future Ministry of Economic Warfare were being drawn up, and even then action was precluded until the outbreak of war.[80] The CID's conclusion, expressed in November 1933, that the exercise of economic pressure was impossible without recourse to war, remained largely unchallenged.[81]

The IIC's, and in particular Morton's principal achievement lay in the ability to make connections between sources that turned a disparate collection of interesting statistics into a damning set of facts. Through SIS, for example, Morton was able to supply Air Intelligence with a list of firms manufacturing Junker products in Germany, obtained from an informant who 'was able to take an exact copy of a short document kept in the manager's office of the Junker factory in Berlin'.[82] Information passed to the FO by the Air Attaché in Berlin, regarding the manufacture and storage of aviation fuel in Germany, was based in part on reports from APOC representatives in Germany that could be checked by Morton with Medlicott (despite the Air Ministry's insistence on the anonymity of their source). Morton was also receiving useful information through Churchill, who had a wide-ranging network of sources of his own, including close connections with French politicians who supplied him with information on German rearmament from their own intelligence departments – information that Morton was in a position to verify through SIS. In short, the IIC had established a sort of inbuilt cross-checking mechanism, that owed much to Morton's individual pedigree and connections. Checking the facts, however, was not enough. Morton possessed no locus for arguing his case other than through the IIC. In order to influence policy, a public voice was needed: a voice belonging to someone less constrained by official protocol and departmental control, willing to say in public and in Parliament what Morton could only say in private or in the committee room. Morton found such a voice in Churchill.

Morton and Churchill, 1934–37

Although Morton and Churchill had remained in contact since the First World War, as occasional correspondents, neighbours and friends with a common interest in military matters, from 1934 their relationship moved onto a plane at once more intimate and more professional. Their level of correspondence, previously intermittent and formal (Morton opened his letters 'Dear Mr Churchill' until March 1935) now became more frequent and less restrained. Each man realised and appreciated the other's potential for providing useful information that could add force to their separate, yet related efforts to ensure that the British Government was in full possession of the facts about what both men regarded as an imminent threat to European peace and to the British Empire.

Churchill, as a senior political figure and former Minister, out of office and free from the restraints of Cabinet responsibility, was ready and more than willing to publicise the rearmament of potential enemies and what he, and Morton, regarded as the inadequate British response. From 1934 onwards he embarked on an active campaign to provoke the government into an accelerated programme of defensive rearmament and the rapid expansion of the RAF. His was not a belligerent stance, nor, at this juncture, at odds with the main thrust of British foreign policy. Though bitterly opposed to government policy on India, he was sympathetic to the difficulties MacDonald and his colleagues faced in formulating a policy response to Hitler's increasingly provocative behaviour. A year earlier, in February 1933, he had criticised MacDonald and Chamberlain for the high level of unemployment in Britain, urging a comprehensive (and expensive) programme of public works.[83] In 1934, however, he took the view that with the worst of the economic crisis over, the main thrust of the government's effort and investment should be directed towards defence:

> A wise foreign policy should keep us free from war. But we must become once again a strong, well-defended resolute community able to protect ourselves and guard our rights and interests not only by moral, but if need be by physical force.[84]

Churchill's definition of a 'wise foreign policy' differed little in principle from that of the government he was to criticise so strongly during the next few years:

support for the League of Nations; helping to build up a confederation of nations 'so strong and sincere' that no aggressor would dare to challenge it; the use of diplomacy to persuade Hitler of the advisability of seeking a peaceful resolution of his grievances. Nor was there any basic disagreement on the need to rebuild British defences by investing in the development of all three Services, particularly the air force, although Churchill's views on the desirability and feasibility of rapid and extensive British rearmament were more far-reaching than MacDonald, Baldwin or Chamberlain could or would embrace at this stage. To Morton, however, they struck exactly the right note:

> I see clearly now that of course we must go on supporting the League so long as we are only called upon to pay a price we are prepared and able to afford. But in case the League prove in practice to be but a cardboard shield we must back it with our own steel.[85]

The frustration felt by Morton at the reluctance, and slowness of the government to act on what he considered hard fact made him even more willing to help Churchill, who could make potent political use of solid evidence of German rearmament to wrong-foot government ministers in public and Parliamentary debate. The two men's detailed correspondence, found in Churchill's own papers and reproduced at length in his official biography, reveals beyond doubt Morton's admiration and affection for Churchill, and his delight when the latter appeared to have 'scored a hit'. He regarded Churchill's exclusion from ministerial office as typical of the National Government's shortsighted attitude. Commiserating with Churchill's failure to be offered a post in Baldwin's Cabinet following the November 1935 general election, he wrote:

> Your position reminds me greatly and rather bitterly of the fighting services themselves, hailed as saviours in time of danger and, as the old tag has it, as brutal & licentious soldiery when the Public <u>believe</u> the danger to be far off. Before the last election it was on everyone's lips; 'We must have Winston in the Cabinet to act as a driving force.' Lulled by the false security of a 250 Conservative majority for four or five years, it is: 'Now everything is alright, we don't want a firebrand upsetting things. Nevertheless the Public do not realise the true strain of the situation and, unless I am very mistaken, they will not do so for a month or two. Then the word may again go round: 'Oh Lord! Make haste to help us!'[86]

It is hard to believe that Morton was not sufficiently aware of political realities to know that neither Baldwin nor the Conservative Party would willingly accept Churchill's inclusion in the government at this point. Even out of office, however, Churchill seemed a more effective conduit for the IIC's message than the official bodies it served.

During these years Churchill bombarded Morton with requests for an expert opinion on articles, books and confidential reports, seeking confirmation and correction, particularly on the subject of air power. Morton's response was forthcoming if cautious: while passing on freely the latest authoritative assessment of German (but not British) air strength, whether from IIC or Air Ministry sources, he remained careful to differentiate between current reports and future estimates, and between military and civil aircraft production, and to draw attention to the importance of Germany's acquiring or producing the requisite raw materials and fuel. By commenting from a position of inside knowledge on facts and figures supplied to Churchill from other sources, he sought to counterbalance the latter's tendency to hyperbole with a more sober assessment. At times he was irritated by Churchill's inattention to detail and what he considered to be a lack of understanding of the technical nuances of the information he supplied.[87] In the summer of 1934, for example, when Churchill (fuelled by statistics from Morton) engaged in a rather overheated correspondence with Lord Rothermere over the number of aeroplanes Germany was likely to have by the end of 1935, Morton thought both parties had got hold of the wrong end of the stick.[88] His letters to Churchill rarely betrayed his impatience, however. For while Morton's access to official statistics and technical expertise was of great value to Churchill, Morton received in return a double benefit: additional information from Churchill's varied network of sources, and the pleasure of seeing his dynamic oratorical and lobbying gifts employed in the fulfilment of what Churchill regarded as his duty: to 'arouse the Government and the country to the sense of the dangers by which we are being encompassed'.[89]

Morton supplied Churchill with information, corroboration and advice, telling him not just what he asked for but also what, in Morton's view, he needed to know. This raises the key question that has underpinned a central 'Morton myth': did he pass to Churchill information that the latter had no right to see? He had the opportunity to do so: the two men corresponded frequently, and contemporary observers have attested to their regular meetings at Chartwell, when Morton would stroll over after dinner for discussions late into the night, sometimes bringing with him useful documents – assumed by many to be secret Intelligence reports. According to one of Churchill's literary assistants, Morton pledged him to secrecy, professing 'high patriotic motives', while an innocent Churchill – who 'really had no guile' – was merely hungry for the information denied him by the authorities.[90] Stories like this have created an enduring impression that Morton deliberately supplied secret information to Churchill. In fairness, it must be said that this impression was fostered by the parties themselves, and in particular by Morton, who had his own reasons for perpetuating it.[91] There is, however, no hard documentary evidence to suggest that Morton supplied anything to Churchill that he would not have been entitled, and indeed in many cases welcome, to see. The evidence points, in fact, in the other direction.

There is, of course, no way of proving that Morton never showed Churchill a document whose circulation would have precluded his seeing it; but everything about his character and training argues against it. Morton was certainly a man to bend the rules where necessary: but the protection of secrecy had informed his entire professional career. He liked and admired Churchill and supported his efforts to alert government and country to the European threat; he believed that Churchill's energy and vision offered a chance to remedy the weakness of British defence policy; but he did not entirely trust him, nor the use he might make of the information that he put his way. Morton's chief value to Churchill was in checking and correcting information already supplied from other sources; indeed, on occasion Morton thanked Churchill for supplying *him* with information that might otherwise not have come his way, particularly from French sources.[92] Their correspondence makes it clear that although Morton may have drawn on secret sources to provide the information he supplied, he did not divulge those sources or show them to Churchill – who did not ask to see them. When Morton did pass papers to him, they were not, as has often been alleged, secret Intelligence reports, but copies of IIC papers and other documents circulated to the CID; the kind of reports for which Churchill was frequently on the circulation list, or which were sent to him for comment, sometimes at the Prime Minister's suggestion.

Churchill did not need to rely on Morton for secret information. Though out of office, he was by no means an outsider: as David Stafford puts it, if Churchill was in the wilderness, 'it was a brilliantly illuminated one in which he enjoyed impressive sources of information';[93] Sir Martin Gilbert, too, has revised his earlier views on the solitude of Churchill's 'inhabited wilderness'.[94] Churchill was, after all, a Privy Councillor, a former holder of senior Ministerial office, on close terms with all the key political and military figures of the day, familiar with the mechanics of defence estimates, requirements and planning both as suppli-cant (when at the Admiralty) and as budgetary arbiter (when Chancellor). He knew only too well the difficulties faced by the government, both politically and financially, in moving towards a policy of rearmament after a long period of defence cuts, with no public appetite for bellicosity. Out of office, he did not have to take such difficulties into consideration: always more attracted by initiative and action than by slow balance of judgement, he now saw a problem in need of a solution and wished fervently for an opportunity to propose one. He itched to be back in office (a desire that played a considerable part in his campaign for rearmament): MacDonald, Baldwin and Chamberlain, leading sometimes uneasy coalition Cabinets containing members implacably opposed to Churchill, shrank from the prospect of offering it to him. This did not mean, however, that they regarded him with hostility: exclusion from office did not mean exclusion from influence, although his behaviour sometimes provoked bitter political recrimination.

Churchill corresponded regularly with Baldwin, for example, even at times when the latter was fuming at the political difficulties caused by Churchill's interventions. He had friends and informants in all the major departments of state; further afield, foreign politicians like Flandin and Blum sent him regular budgets of information supplied by their own Intelligence services. From 1935 onwards he received a considerable amount of documentation through normal official channels, and although the use he made of their contents would, on more than one occasion, raise the question of how much he should be told, there was never any serious attempt to challenge his 'need to know'.[95] In November 1935, for example, his comments on an Air Ministry memorandum on the training organisation of the German air force were circulated to the CID. The Air Staff's response to these comments, though based (as Hankey pointed out) on secret information and a confidential statement from the French Government, was passed to Churchill, whose further riposte was again circulated to the CID.[96] The following year, Churchill was invited to give evidence before the Royal Commission on the Armament Industry (though he did not actually do so): in preparation for this, Morton forwarded to him, quite properly, two FCI memoranda, noting that the second, concerning the German attempt to capture the world armament trade, was based on secret information: 'Perhaps you could very kindly let me have these copies back in due course after you have made any notes that you require.'[97] There is little sign of the 'wilderness', or of cloak and dagger, in these dealings.

Some of Churchill's network of 'insiders', like Squadron Leader Anderson at the RAF, and Wigram at the Foreign Office, may have passed on to Churchill material of which their superiors did not approve.[98] In the case of Wigram, however, the documentary – as opposed to anecdotal – evidence suggests that much of the material he passed on was hardly 'secret', even if Churchill would not have seen it in the normal course of events; for example, extracts from despatches from Sir Eric Phipps in Berlin.[99] And after all, Wigram's superior, Vansittart, was aware of Wigram's communication with Churchill; if he suffered any pangs of conscience, these were occasioned more by the infringement of professional etiquette than by the level of sensitivity of the information imparted.[100]

There remains the matter of the famous 'piece of paper' that Morton later claimed had been signed by MacDonald, Baldwin or both, giving him permission to pass information to Churchill. According to R.W. Thompson, Morton told him and his wife, during their visit to his house at Kew Green in May 1960, that he had deliberately set out to brief Churchill on German rearmament, regarding him as 'the only man who had the qualities needed for the job'. To ease his conscience, however, he had gone to see MacDonald who had given him written permission – in a document now lodged in Morton's bank.[101] On the basis of this claim, Thompson, and others to whom he related the story, searched fruitlessly for the document, Thompson approaching Morton's executors after his death. A close study of Morton's way of doing business suggests that the existence of any such document is unlikely, if impossible to disprove. It is quite in character for Morton to have invented its existence after the event, in a typical exercise of self-exculpation and to deflect attention from his own role, and in accordance with the lifelong practice of the 'intelligence man' telling people what he wanted them to believe.

Baldwin and MacDonald may, of course, have given such permission orally; writing to Liddell Hart in 1963, Morton noted simply that 'Baldwin and Ramsay MacDonald gave permission for [Churchill] to receive certain papers about the military/economic strength of Germany, Russia, France, Italy etc.'[102] This seems plausible, though it is doubtful whether such permission were necessary: there are examples in the minutes of the CID, for example, when MacDonald said openly that it would be useful for Churchill to see a certain paper. No two accounts coincide exactly, some asserting with authority that Morton passed secret material to Churchill, others that Churchill's position as a Privy Councillor gave him sufficient access. On the basis of the available evidence, Morton's image as 'mole' does not stand up to scrutiny, though it was entirely in keeping with his character to enjoy the image while rejecting the reality. Since no papers have been found, in Morton's bank or anywhere else, to shed further light, there is no way of settling the question definitively at this distance. Perhaps the best answer is to emulate Churchill, who replied in response to a direct question on the point from Colville: 'Have another drop of brandy.'[103]

9

PLANNING FOR WAR WITH
GERMANY: 1938–39

Morton spent 1938 and 1939 preparing for a conflict he had long thought inevitable. British military authorities had, in theory at least, been planning since 1934 on the premise that 'our forces may have to be employed in five years from the present date, ie the end of 1939, and against a Germany in such a state of preparedness as she is likely to reach by that time'.[1] Even if the translation from planning to preparation had been imperfect and incomplete, the idea that war with Germany was a strong possibility by 1939 underlay the counsels of all the committees charged with the consideration of defensive and counter-offensive measures, committees on which Morton sat or to which he submitted the IIC's detailed economic intelligence reports.[2]

The question of whether and when Neville Chamberlain and his Cabinet believed that war with Germany was inevitable would require a book-length answer of its own. A case can be argued that Chamberlain's concern was to postpone the inevitable as long as possible, rather than to maintain an unrealistically optimistic hope of its avoidance. As far as Morton (or Churchill) was concerned, the result was the same: by the opening of 1938, Britain remained ill-prepared to face a conflict with a Germany grown strong and increasingly menacing to European peace, likely to command the active support of Italy and Japan; while Britain's own potential allies (principally France, the US remaining resolutely isolationist) inspired little confidence in the potency of their military assistance; and a Soviet Government seemingly intent on destroying its own military establishment through purge and execution could be relied on for neutrality at best.

As we have seen, Morton had become increasingly frustrated during 1931–37 by the slow pace of British rearmament and industrial mobilisation, as well as by the continued inability of the Service ministries to work together or to coordinate their intelligence activities effectively, despite the creation of the JIC. The energetic efforts of the Industrial Intelligence Centre, though achieving a much higher profile and impact in 1937 than in 1931, could not force the government into action. Only the 'pressure of facts', a phrase used on a number of occasions during 1938–39 by the Foreign Secretary, Lord Halifax, was to do that.[3] That pressure, though increasing steadily, did not become irresistible until September 1939.

From the beginning of 1938, however, Morton was able to sublimate his frustrations in a concrete plan of work. Though he continued, as Director of the IIC, to urge both his military and political masters to grasp the nettle of industrial mobilisation in Britain, and to encourage Churchill's advocacy of accelerated rearmament, he now had the opportunity to exercise his abilities in an enterprise to which they were ideally suited. At the 24th meeting of the ATB Committee on 11 June 1937, arrangements had been discussed for establishing what the Committee thought would be 'one of the most important departments in the next war': a 'Ministry of Blockade' or rather, as now suggested, a 'Ministry of Economic Warfare' (MEW): the latter term more appropriate since:

> It would be concerned with big economic questions and would be dealing, not only with enemy countries, but with neutrals and our Allies ... What was wanted was a good fighting machine which should be ready as quickly as possible after the outbreak of war so that as few weeks as possible were lost before bringing economic pressure to bear.[4]

The ATB decided that one sub-committee should be set up to work out proposals for such a ministry, and another to consider means of exerting economic pressure on Germany. In both of these Morton played an important part, and particularly in working out the structure, organisation and role of a Ministry of Economic Warfare, a project that was to occupy much of his time up to and after the outbreak of war in September 1939. Drawing up elaborate plans for a new government department whose business encapsulated his expertise and experience, and in which, as Director of the largest division in MEW, he was to play a dominant role in both policy and practice, fed his appetite for both organisational tidiness and personal power. The story of how MEW came into being is, therefore, a good way of telling Morton's story in 1938–39.

In parallel with the creation of MEW, during 1938–39 Morton can be seen to be steering an oblique but steady course back towards the secret world. In the past few years, while retaining certain links, he had put some distance between his professional activities and that of the three principal Intelligence Agencies, including the organisation where he had begun his career, SIS. Now, paradoxically, the establishment of a more conventional government department, together with the imminence of war, drew him back to them. This was partly a matter of temperament (one always senses in him an internal struggle between cloak and dagger, bowler hat and fountain pen). But it was also far-sightedness on his part. Morton saw economic warfare as a military operation 'comparable to the operations of the three Services in that its object is the defeat of the enemy, and complementary to them in that its function is to deprive the enemy of the material means of resistance'.[5] Disruption of the enemy's economy and supply mechanisms would require first-class intelligence and suggested clandestine methods, both technical (interception of communications, aerial reconnaissance) and human (espionage, sabotage and subversion). The path led squarely to Broadway

Buildings. In parallel with the story of MEW, therefore, we need to look at the story of British Intelligence, and SIS in particular, between 1938 and 1939. From the outbreak of war on 3 September 1939, the two strands of Morton's professional life, economic warfare and Intelligence, were to converge ever more closely.

The view of Brighton from the Pier:[6] building MEW, 1938–39

Following the approval by the CID on 4 March 1938 of the ATB's report on the organisation and constitution of a government department to conduct economic war against Germany,[7] J.W. Nicholls, of the FO's Western Department, was charged with coordinating detailed planning for what was to be a self-standing department under the direction of a Cabinet Minister, but with the FO as 'parent'. Contact between the two departments should, the Permanent Under Secretary insisted, be close, and information shared. In fact, Sargent went so far as to offer 'the three large reception rooms in the Foreign Office' as a home for MEW, though it soon became clear that this would be inadequate.[8] The planning process encompassed a number of bodies, including the Department of Overseas Trade (DoT), but from the beginning Morton was involved at every level, taking particular responsibility for designing what was to be the Intelligence Department, the largest in the Ministry.

Morton enjoyed himself immensely drawing up the blueprint for MEW. At last he had been presented with a virtually blank canvas for the kind of directive organisational design he had always relished, but which he had rarely been given the opportunity to indulge. Although FO officials had definite ideas about the shape and role of a Ministry that they intended to keep firmly under their control, Morton's long experience of economic intelligence, and extensive study of the economic and industrial preparations of potential enemies, put him in a very strong position to throw his weight about, something he always enjoyed doing. Both he and the IIC staff spent a great deal of time on the project, and the wording of some of the emerging documentation bears Morton's unmistakable stamp.

A detailed account of MEW's origins has been given in its official history,[9] and a brief summary is sufficient to indicate Morton's influence on the process. By June 1938 the Organisation Committee (headed by Sir Hughe Knatchbull-Hugessen)[10] was ready to submit an interim report. Its recommendations included the division of the Ministry into seven departments (Plans, Foreign Relations, Prize, Financial Pressure, Legal, Establishment and Intelligence), with more than one hundred and sixty administrative (ie non-clerical) staff. The functions of each department were set out in detailed annexes; much the largest, constituting more than half of the proposed staff complement of the Ministry, was the Intelligence Department, responsible for supplying the other departments with the information they needed to perform their functions, as well as for advising the Service ministries and other authorities on the output of armaments by the industries of enemy and neutral countries. The sixteen permanent staff of the IIC, including Morton, Clively, Watson and the inseparable Miss Gwynne, were to be absorbed wholesale in the Intelligence Department, which was to be divided into two main groups, A and B, the latter responsible for collating information received and the former for interpreting it. Both groups consisted of four sections, each headed by senior IIC officials: 'A' comprised Enemy Countries, Commodity Intelligence, Neutral Countries and Liaison and General sections; 'B' comprised Enemy Trade, Rationing, Black List and Prize Court sections.[11]

There was also an organogram giving the names of heads of department designate. Morton, of course, was to head the Intelligence Department: most of the others had long been familiar to him (some he had even been at school with). Ashton-Gwatkin, head of the FO's Economic Relations Department, was to head MEW's Plans and Coordination Department; Maurice Ingram, head of Southern Department, the Foreign Relations Department; Charles Baxter, head of Eastern Department, would lead the Prize Department; Sir William Robinson, FO Principal Establishment Officer, who had retired on 1 April 1938, was promptly written down to do the same job in MEW; Gerald Fitzmaurice, Third Legal Adviser in the FO, was to head MEW's Legal Department, while Sir George Mounsey, Under Secretary superintending the FO's Western Department, was to be overall Departmental Secretary responsible to the Minister. The calibre of those identified for immediate secondment to MEW on the outbreak of war was high, if traditionally-minded. MEW would start life directed by a group of senior, experienced officials already familiar with the issues: and familiar, too with Morton, though his views were to prove considerably in advance of theirs in respect of the role and authority to be accorded to the new department in wartime.

The Organising Committee's Final Report was ready in September.[12] In the intervening period the new Ministry had grown: the overall figure for the initial staff requirements of MEW was now six hundred and twelve, including one hundred and seventy-one administrative and two hundred and fifty-nine executive/clerical staff, together with one hundred and eleven typists and fifty messengers. The report was specific on the question of staffing for the Intelligence Department. Administrative staff were to be taken from the IIC, supplemented by principals from the DoT and Institute of Imperial Research; of the one hundred and eighty-seven executive and clerical staff required, some must have specific skills or experience, such as in statistical work, or the Railway Research Service. The report also raised a number of miscellaneous questions that were clearly of particular importance to the Intelligence Department, including the need for the interception and decoding of commercial wireless telephone messages, arrangements to be made with the Ministry of Information for a press reading service, and matters relating to overseas intelligence on foodstuffs and fodder.

Morton, and the Committee, had been thorough. They had also been driven by an awareness of the need for haste. In the months since the CID's commissioning of the work, the urgency of the requirement for an economic warfare Ministry that could be mobilised immediately in the event of war had increased sharply. In March 1938 Austria had been absorbed into the German Reich,[13] and Czechoslovakia, despite Hitler's protestations, looked to be next on the list. Chamberlain, now Prime Minister, who had pushed through an agreement with the Italian leader Mussolini in April, losing his Foreign Secretary in the process,[14] continued to pursue energetically the chimera of a European settlement through an understanding with Germany that might buy further time for British rearmament. The Cabinet, despite some internal disagreement of which Eden's resignation had been symbolic, were agreed that Britain was not ready to fight a war with Germany in 1938, but that becoming ready to do so was now a priority. The deteriorating European situation made the MEW planners' work even more urgent. Ashton-Gwatkin, who in August accompanied Lord Runciman to Prague on an ill-fated mission to reconcile the Czechoslovak Government with its Sudeten minority sufficiently to deflect Hitler's aggressive ambitions, wrote gloomily to his colleagues of 'a feeling of the imminence of the zero hour'.[15]

On 18 September 1938 the British Ambassador in Berlin, Sir Nevile Henderson, reported concentrations of troops near the Czech border.[16] The following day, Morton wrote to the Hon Cecil Farrer, head of the foreign division of DoT and designated head of 'A' Group in MEW's Intelligence Department, sending him what he called 'one or two documents which I think you might like to have by you in case we are suddenly called upon to found the Intelligence Department of MEW'. The letter enclosed a provisional diagram of the layout of the whole Ministry (the 'view of Brighton from the pier'), and a more detailed diagram of the Intelligence Department, together with what he called a 'preliminary explanatory note' – nine pages of instructions and rules of procedure. The latter document, referred to by Morton as 'Napoleon's address to his troops', certainly struck an imperious tone in places; all Sections, for example, were enjoined to:

> make full use of the <u>knowledge and views of other Departments of State</u>, especially when dealing with technical matters within the latters' province or questions likely to arouse controversy . . . At the same time, the exigencies of war, no less than the fact that the Ministry is an independent Department of State, demands [sic] that the Intelligence Department should put forward its own views when necessary, without previous consultation with other authorities.[17]

Morton also enclosed copies of papers describing the role of the Intelligence Department and proposals for the organisation of its overseas service; and a set of the papers prepared for an exercise carried out by the Imperial Defence College in September with which he had been closely involved. Organograms were included for each of the proposed eight sections of the Intelligence Department, with the numbers and grades of staff specified from the most senior (Principal) to the most junior temporary assistant.[18]

These plans were designed to allow MEW to come into being very quickly: how it would work thereafter was much less clear. Morton's own vision may have been of a dynamic department of state playing an equal part with other fighting Ministries, but he was far too old a hand to tie himself or his staff (present and future) to objectives and procedures that might not be deliverable or might be derailed by events. As he told Farrer, he was keen to avoid an over-bureaucratic approach:

> all officers are encouraged to use their own initiative, especially at the outset until experience has shown the extent to which preconceived notions will require modification in practice. They should bear in mind that both an over-rigid adherence to procedure and also too little regard for it defeat the object of wartime Intelligence. Their actions must in all cases primarily be governed by common sense, and they should recall above all things that, in a wartime Intelligence Service, rapidity of communication is as important as accuracy of statement . . .[19]

Morton was clearly anticipating early conflict, and indeed in late September 1938 the prospect of MEW's sudden creation seemed not unlikely. Nicholls, writing to Farrer on 23 September (just as Chamberlain, in Bad Godesberg, was delivering a strong protest against Hitler's demand that the Czech Government evacuate the Sudeten German territories by 26 September),[20] asked whether the DoT Comptroller General would allow those senior staff earmarked for MEW to transfer immediately.[21] Nicholls set out the procedure for activating MEW:

(1) When we think fit we shall summon the nucleus of the Ministry. This would consist of Morton and two or three only of his staff, the officers already designated in the Foreign Office, the officers to be provided by the Board of Trade, and, we hope, yourself and your personal assistant . . .

(2) Our next step would be to raise the question of establishing the Ministry at the Cabinet. As soon as the Cabinet had decided to do so, we should call in the rest of the officers designated for service in the Ministry from your own department, the IIC and the Board of Trade. As a temporary measure we should make accommodation for all these in the Foreign Office; thereafter we should be entirely responsible for their welfare, both from the point of view of A[ir] R[aid] P[recautions], evacuation and, as soon as agreement had been reached with the Treasury, their salaries. Whether in fact the salaries and other expenses would be borne on the Foreign Office vote or on a separate vote is not yet decided . . .[22]

Morton would have thought this order of priorities, with responsibility for paying MEW staff placed last, entirely typical of the civil service. As it turned out, there was no need to mobilise MEW quite yet. The Munich agreement of 30 September, reached during Chamberlain's third visit to Hitler within a month, blunted for a time the thrust of the Chancellor's aggression, even though the Czechoslovak President of the Council, General Sirovy, described its acceptance as 'the bitterest moment of his life'.[23] Morton's own view of the crisis is not recorded, though he certainly kept well abreast of its unfolding: on 25 September, together with Churchill and his son Randolph, he lunched with Jan Masaryk just before the Czech Minister delivered to the FO his government's initial verdict ('absolutely and unconditionally unacceptable') on Hitler's ultimatum to his country.[24] Churchill issued a statement calling for the return of Parliament, which Morton supported, but his overall view on the crisis and the British Government's policy is less easy to gauge. It seems likely that he would have argued in favour of accelerated military preparations, rather than for rejecting the deal secured by Chamberlain.

The Munich crisis and its aftermath provoked a wave of analysis, soul-searching, speculation and feverish planning throughout Whitehall, including the Intelligence Agencies and, albeit peripherally, the IIC.[25] Before considering Morton's role in this process, it is worth taking a brief look back at his other activities during the first nine months of 1938. Work on designing MEW had proceeded in parallel with his normal, full-time duties in the IIC, whose business had also increased in urgency in response to the menacing and sometimes dramatic international developments. Under his direction the IIC had produced a number of important reports, including a major study of 'The German Army – its present strength and possible rate of expansion in peace in war', first presented to the CID on 28 April 1938, updated in July and again in January 1939;[26] and another on German arms exports (Morton informed the CID on 15 May 1938 that British exports of armaments in 1937 amounted to £8.2 million, compared with the German figure of £18 million, sufficient to arm and equip about fifteen divisions annually).[27] Both these papers were referred to the Cabinet. Other studies included an examination of Germany's probable situation in the event of war in 1939 in regard to petroleum products, prepared for the ATB's Economic Pressure on Germany (EPG) Sub-Committee; and, for the JIC, a contribution to a study of the military implications of German aggression against Czechoslovakia and a paper on Italian industrial and military capacity.

His IIC work, therefore, kept Morton pretty busy. On 21 July 1938, for example, in addition to the JIC, he attended CID and ATB meetings as well. The pace of these bodies quickened as the European situation deteriorated, and even though he did not attend every meeting the commitment was not inconsiderable. As ever, he was conscientious and hard-working, though impatient when he felt the proceedings were a waste of time. His comments during somewhat circular discussions in the JIC, for example, on how best to acquire intelligence on Spain, or the need for departments to take measures to safeguard the secrecy of sensitive industrial information, reveal a degree of exasperation with a body that in 1938 showed little sign of being either joint or intelligent.[28] Meanwhile, he continued to correspond regularly with contacts in the Service Ministries, maintaining a particularly brisk exchange with the Air Ministry.

At the same time Morton continued to keep in close touch with Churchill, whose unremitting criticism of the government's failure to accelerate British rearmament programmes, or to work towards a defensive 'Grand Alliance' with France, kept him isolated politically, despite the fact that 'his wider, public popularity had never been so high, his speeches so in demand, nor his audiences so receptive'.[29] There is little written record of their contacts during 1938–39, though Morton continued to respond to requests for technical comment on documents received by Churchill from a range of sources, and to discuss the situation at Chartwell over or after dinner. Such correspondence as survives, on Morton's part at least, has an undertone of shared experience of the folly of governments: on 25 June 1938, for example, thanking Churchill for a copy of his recently published speeches on defence since 1928 (*Arms and the Covenant*), Morton wrote:

> It is a memory to me of years of struggle and not a little bitterness, as it must be in some ways to you. But you, and in an infinitely less degree I, are not the first to have told the truth to the people and become heartily unpopular for having done so. Modern Governments hate to be told uncomfortable truths . . . But whether they recognise the truth and mend their ways or reject it, both have the habit of crucifying the prophet of truth or, if this less virile epoch shrinks at such drastic action, they exterminate him with a gas cloud – of propaganda. However they have not silenced you yet, thank God, so there is some hope for the Empire still.[30]

He also wrote to Churchill on 3 July asking him to speak at the Imperial Defence College, an institution with which Morton was involved closely, acting as an instructor on some of its exercises and giving lectures there.[31] He helped to prepare the documentation for a major IDC exercise held in September 1938 (and closely linked to the MEW planning process), including twenty-four appendices containing trade, shipping and economic data on a wide range of countries, specifying the objectives to be achieved in putative negotiations with them, together with an assessment of the degree of pressure that could be applied on them both by Germany and by Britain and her allies.[32] Churchill agreed to speak to the IDC on 4 October, but withdrew in distress at the Czechoslovak situation, though speeches were made by a number of senior political and military figures. Morton himself delivered a lecture on 'Higher Command in War', concluding with a reference to the 'Fourth Arm of Defence, the Economic Arm, which covers the economic life of the nation'.[33]

Despite his pressing professional commitments during the summer of 1938, Morton found time to pay some attention to personal matters, of which family papers give us a very rare glimpse. On 23 August his cousin Claude Elles, elder daughter of the late Geraldine Morton by her second marriage to Sir Hugh Elles (and so grand-daughter of Morton's late uncle Gerald), was to marry Captain Evelyn Norie of the King's Own Royal Regiment at Holy Trinity Church, Brompton. Morton and his mother Edith were closely involved with the preparations – the reception was to be held at Beaufort Gardens – but Claude appears to have derived the impression that Morton's Roman Catholicism might prevent his attending a Church of England service unless in some official capacity, such as usher. The week before the wedding, on 16 August, he wrote to disabuse her, sending her a poem. The rarity of a personal letter from Morton unrelated to professional matters, enclosing a unique sample of his poetic style, makes their reproduction irresistible:

My dear Claude,

I see you did not know that I won the Newdigate at Oxford for English verse, or that I was seriously considered to fill the vacant post of Robert Bridges as Poet Laureate. Quite! No more did many other people.

But I am horrified to learn that Evelyn has not regurgitated whole stanzas and epics on your account. Hang it! I have written passionate poems to half the female population of Europe – and remain a batchelor [sic]. Perhaps that explains a lot of things. But away with poetry! I write of Law and Logic.

Mad am I, though method mar my madness. (Norwegian saga; like 'Bare is back without brother behind it'!) but not so utterly psychotic as ever to have said that I could not attend your heretical assemblies unless 'on duty'. Such is the snare of the English language. Well may I have contended, and with truth, that I cannot take part in ju-ju save in an official capacity, such as representing the Elder Brother of the Trinity at the feast of Yom Kippur, but the Church allows me any relaxation as an observer, *un assistant* (French, not English) or as audience – even without paying entertainment tax.

Moreover the Church is very human and knows how I should fret were I unable to wear my white top hat except at the Garden Party. Since the only other occasion, barring Ascot, to which I am too poor and too hard-worked to go, are heretical baptisms and weddings – well – there you are. Anyway, till next Tuesday and always.

Yours ever, Desmond

PS If Evelyn makes it worth my while I will pass him a weekly poem which he can initial and palm off on you as his own. I do the same thing daily in prose with various politicians.

PPS Do not reply. I will reply to myself for you: 'Idiot'. That's what you wanted to say, isn't it?

And the poem:

> Oh Lady! Hush!
> How can you ask that I so old and frail,
> With nearly fifty years experience
> As male
> Attendant
> At weddings, births and funerals
> Resplendent
> Sordid, wise or stupid and
> Transcendent,
> Should yet again bestir myself and
> Ush.
> Tush!
> Oh Lady, Say!
> Since you have no page to bear your train that day,
> Why
> Should not I,
> Arrayed in silken socks and sky-blue pants,
> Braving the high displeasure of my aunts,
> Perform this office for you?
> Or you
> Might prefer me dressed in purple
> Plush.
> 'ush!!
> No, Lady! No!!
> Dukes, dowagers and damsels, boys and men,
> When
> They grace your marriage
> Whether on foot, horse, bicycle or carriage
> Must
> Bust
> Themselves, the church, their stays (in several ways)
> To find themselves a seat
> Meet
> For each to sit upon
> Before I ush;
> No matter what the crowd, the rush, the
> Crush.
> So, Hush!

It is revealed in the Book of Revelations that there was in heaven silence for the space of half an hour. I now anticipate that blissful period. D.M.[34]

What Claude made of all this is not revealed, nor whether Morton did, in the end, 'ush'; possibly he did, since he is not listed by *The Times* as among the guests. The episode does, however, give some clues to his relationships with his family. For one, it reveals that he *did* have dealings with them; the letter to Claude is not that of an unfamiliar or rarely-seen cousin. Edith's position, as London-based matriarch, presumably ensured that he saw his family fairly regularly, despite the amount of time he spent either working or at Earlylands. It also suggests that if Morton, normally allergic to 'mixed' social engagements, had perforce to undertake them, he saw the need to adopt a certain persona in their execution. Claude's daughter, Mrs Angela Mynors, remembers him as a great wit and raconteur, always ready with a quip or funny story, but never letting down his defences to reveal any personal or professional detail. The impression is that he was fond, in his own way, of his family, and felt a strong sense of obligation towards them that would always bring him to do the 'right' thing if he could; but also that family relationships brought him into contact with emotions with which he felt awkward and ill-equipped to deal. As with all his personal affairs, however, the evidence is too slender to offer more than superficial psychological speculation.

Claude's wedding provided Morton with a rare opportunity for a day (or half day at least) away from the office. There were to be all too few such opportunities in the ensuing months. In the aftermath of Munich, the IIC was caught up in the fevered Whitehall-wide examination of future British policy following what Ashton-Gwatkin, in his contribution to the debate, called 'probably one of the decisive events of history'.[35] Sir Alexander Cadogan, in a series of summary memoranda drawing together FO contributions to the debate, deprecated the deficiencies in the British rearmament programme and discussed the possibility of reaching an agreement with Germany by colonial or other concessions. His references to economic issues, however, struck what must have seemed to Morton a depressingly complacent note, taking a somewhat fatalistic view of the respective strengths of Germany and the UK and making scant acknowledgement of the arguments and policies that Morton and his colleagues had been propounding for the past seven years. German economic dominance in central and eastern Europe was, Cadogan wrote, 'bound to develop, provided the German economic and financial structure can stand the strain'; it was, he considered, 'a fact to be reckoned with, like the rise of Japan', and 'very doubtful' whether the United Kingdom would be strong enough to withstand it. Although he added, modestly, that 'I confess I am not expert in economics and am ready to admit that I may misunderstand the problem', one can imagine Morton reading this and similar judgements, wondering gloomily whether Cadogan had ever read any IIC reports or heard the term 'economic warfare'.[36]

Morton's own contribution to the Munich post-mortem, dated 6 December 1938, confined itself carefully to the IIC's sphere of expertise, but pointed out yet again that to dismiss any possibility of using economic weapons against Germany was to miss an important trick. The object of 'Some Notes on the Economic Defence Results of the Cession of the Sudetenland' was, he said, to consider the broad effects of Czechoslovak frontier changes on Germany, although:

a complete picture of these effects would logically involve a review of
the defence position, as modified by the recent changes, of many other
European countries, since Germany's defence strength is ultimately not
an absolute but a relative quantity.

The paper summarised the effects on Germany of adding to her population 3–4
million people who would both produce, and consume, more food and other
goods, and calculated the balance of gain and loss to Germany as:

> a net loss in respect of raw material supply from domestic resources,
> which is one of Germany's pressing wartime problems; but a gain in so
> far as the new frontiers of the Reich improve German communications
> with those sources in Central and South-Eastern Europe capable of
> supplying the raw materials Germany needs . . . though the supplies
> of raw materials which may thus be placed more easily at Germany's
> disposal in war will be of value to her, they can by no means cover all
> her deficiencies, so that the statement sometimes made that, with the aid
> of the resources of South-Eastern Europe, the Reich is now blockade-
> proof, does not accord with the facts.[37]

There is no evidence that the IIC paper had any impact on the policy-making
process: by the time FO officials got round to commenting on it, its consideration
had been subsumed into an assessment of the economic consequences of
Germany's absorption of the rest of Czechoslovakia, in March 1939.

From late 1938 until the outbreak of war Morton and the IIC continued
to produce lengthy and detailed reports, based on a combination of secret
Intelligence, information from business sources and published material, on the
economic and industrial situation in Germany and other potentially hostile countries, and on the status of their armed forces; as well as to contribute to the major
appreciations and defence plans prepared by the Chiefs of Staff for the CID.
Such reports were received with polite and sometimes lively interest by civil and
military authorities and (when consulted) by Ministers, though their impact
cannot be said to have matched the effort that went into their production.
Morton's description of their reception, written to Liddell Hart many years later,
tended to the dramatic:

> I still have some of the reports somewhere which we put into the Chiefs
> of Staff, CID and Cabinet, but am probably liable to prosecution for
> possessing them. They raised a riot each time. But no-one could disprove
> them. Equally neither Baldwin nor Chamberlain wanted to believe them.
> In 1938, about November, we put in a report which turned out accurate
> to 99.5 percent, on the Army, Air Force and Fleet of Germany, if they
> went to war at the end of 1939, and, in addition, against instructions,
> showed why from the economic and industrial point of view they <u>would</u>

go to war in 1939 in August or September. I was cross-questioned for an hour in the CID by Neville and his Ministers, and roughly warned that if a spot of it leaked out, I would be hung. I boldly retorted that since Winston received copies at the PM's order, would he be hung too? Neville, much taken aback, suggested that he should not receive this one. I pointed out that he had already received it by his own order.[38]

It is, perhaps, unsurprising that in retrospect Morton should exaggerate the impact of the IIC's reports, in the light of his frustration at what he saw as the government's failure to act on their contents. Had he lived to see it, he might have been even more indignant to read the criticism of the IIC's work in some scholarly accounts of the period leading to the outbreak of the Second World War, in which a generally disparaging view of the performance of Chamberlain and his government has been extended to the IIC as well. While tribute has been paid to the depth and breadth of their reports, a consensus has emerged that Morton and his colleagues failed to understand the true nature of the Nazi regime and its policies, accepting national stereotypes too readily; drew too heavily on published sources instead of inside information; and reached over-optimistic conclusions on German economic weakness from inadequate data, insisting on measuring their estimates against a flawed concept of 'total war'.[39]

There is some truth in these strictures: as noted in Chapter 8, the IIC's estimates and statistics were not always reliable (though, as Medlicott points out, many of them turned out to be remarkably accurate); there was a tendency to emphasise the efficiency of German war preparations with insufficient attention paid to their shortcomings; it is true that the IIC made much use of what would now be called open source material; and its staff were certainly not immune from contemporary preconceptions regarding Teutonic efficiency. In short, the IIC was not infallible: its information was necessarily incomplete, and like all other public bodies of the period it suffered from certain prejudices. As an old Intelligence hand, Morton was the first to admit that much of the IIC's material must be treated with caution: it must be collated with other information from military, commercial and diplomatic sources so that an accurate picture could be built up. Morton's primary concern – and complaint – was that this process of collation was either non-existent or inadequate; and that even if synthesis were achieved, it made little impression on those in authority. It is likely that he would have agreed with the verdict of the official historian of British Intelligence:

the full weight of [the] civil departments was not brought to bear on economic intelligence assessments and that the interdepartmental system for economic intelligence which evolved under the CID remained somewhat isolated from the main stream of economic thought and discussion in Whitehall . . . in consequence of this limitation the general German economic system escaped regular and systematic discussion by the interdepartmental system.[40]

The IIC, Hinsley noted, was too small to cover all the ground, and was constantly in arrears with its programme: 'For this defect, to which the IIC did not fail to draw attention, the responsibility lay at the highest level.'

Whatever the IIC's weaknesses, it cannot be blamed for the fact that many of its recipients simply failed to read the reports or, if they did, to accept their implications. In the summer of 1939, when a series of false alarms, invasion scares and unwelcome surprises had forced Ministers and Service Chiefs to contemplate the real and present danger of war, many of the reports and surveys that were hurriedly commissioned, accompanied by the cry of 'intelligence failure', produced information almost identical to that included in earlier IIC productions. Though succumbing once more to hyperbole, Morton was not completely off-beam in writing to Liddell Hart, twenty-five years later that 'No-one loved us, since no politician in power likes to be given information, backed by facts and calculations, which entirely upsets his whole policy'.[41]

This is not to argue that Morton and the IIC were right while everyone else was wrong. It would be facile to dismiss Ministers, Service chiefs and officials as hidebound and incapable of imaginative policies, while Morton represented 'modern warfare'. Ministers were understandably reluctant, while accepting the necessity for rearmament, to contemplate the kind of 'war of national effort' that Morton described to a panel of industrialists gathered together by Chamberlain on 31 January 1939.[42] Even at that stage, despite all the planning papers predicated upon a conflict that year, war still seemed an unreal prospect. Opinions were divided as to whether Germany was, was not, or might soon be in economic difficulties; and in any case British domestic economic conditions left little room for manoeuvre, quite apart from industry's inbuilt resistance to the idea of government controls. As Morton realised only too well, 'On the one hand government in Britain was ideologically unsuited to persuade industry to cooperate and, on the other, the political control of industry in the Third Reich extended even further than British industrialists feared.'[43]

There was also a feeling – not entirely without foundation – that once British rearmament *really* got going, the Germans would soon be given an industrial run for their money. This confidence underlay the CID's unwillingness, for example, to accept the figures produced by the Air Staff and IIC for the output of the German aircraft industry, Kingsley Wood insisting in April 1939 that new British factories were 'in every way equal' to German ones, and that 'the great efficiency attributed to the Germans was exaggerated'.[44] Similarly, an IIC paper of May 1939 on the supply of armaments to Poland in time of war was criticised sharply by the JIC as 'inclined to exaggerate the position in respect of requirements of munitions', brushing aside Morton's explanations of transport and technical difficulties in supplying Poland from other countries, such as Russia.[45] A certain wilful over-confidence also underlay the British Government's approach to negotiations with the Soviet Government in the spring and summer of 1939.[46] Morton, asked in August 1939 to produce a paper on the defence economies of Germany and Italy for use by the UK Delegation in discussion with the Russian General

Staff, was horrified by the inaccuracy of the draft instructions for the Delegation who were, he protested, wholly unqualified to discuss 'the very difficult matters that might arise'. He clearly considered the whole enterprise fatally cavalier in approach,[47] a judgement with which it is hard to disagree, although the reasons for the failure of the negotiations were complex.

Though frustration at the obstinacy and inaction of both civilian and military planners was nothing new for Morton, it induced in him increasing bitterness and desperation as 1939 progressed, the likelihood of war increased and the possibilities of pre-emptive action diminished. This explains, perhaps, why he pinned such high hopes on the organisation of MEW, and on its scope and operational capability; and why he was to find its departmental actuality disappointing. Meanwhile, the same unpopularity suffered in 1938–39 by the IIC was being experienced in equal measure by the Intelligence agencies, and in particular by SIS, who had also contributed to the post-Munich navel-gazing exercise, and were warning of the imminent dangers of the European situation. Like Morton and the IIC, the agencies had to fight for adequate resources and found it difficult to make their views carry weight in the wider Whitehall balance. Both suffered from simultaneous neglect and suspicion on the part of the FO and the Service departments, who distrusted intrusion into their areas of responsibility. Each issued warnings that were ignored or misinterpreted and served only to damage their own reputations. In these circumstances Morton and his former Chief, Sinclair, found themselves with much in common.

'Always at war': SIS, 1938–39

Such a service as the SIS ought properly to regard itself as always at war. An actual state of war does not radically alter its functions, it only intensifies them.

This quotation from the SIS War Book, circulated to selected staff at the end of March 1937, exemplified both the strengths and weaknesses of SIS in the period leading up to the outbreak of the Second World War. Created in 1909 when conflict with Germany was anticipated, SIS had been working since 1919 in expectation of another, though the chief prospective opponent for much of the period was the Soviet Union. As seen in earlier chapters, it is hard to exaggerate the level of anxiety provoked after the 1917 Bolshevik Revolution by the subversive activities of the Comintern, with whom SIS was, indeed, 'always at war'. The all-consuming nature of that war led to some delay in the identification within SIS of Hitler's Nazi regime as the most urgent threat to peace: a delay that affected SIS's contribution to the process of planning for war with Germany, and indeed its effectiveness in the early months of the Second World War.

On reviewing the interwar history of SIS one might also be forgiven for concluding that the organisation was 'always at war' with Whitehall, as well:

whether fighting for independent existence, for increased resources, or to ensure that its special area of competence was recognised, the predominant impression is of an embattled organisation under siege. Though one might judge that the organisation brought at least some of its problems upon itself, it is hard not to conclude from the evidence that SIS, like the IIC, was actually performing pretty well, especially in some areas, and that its customers bore a significant share of the responsibility for the failure to appreciate its achievements.

Some areas of SIS activity in the 1930s had been notably successful. Section V, in charge of counter-espionage, had achieved under Vivian an impressive degree of penetration of communist organisations in Europe, with a high level of knowledge of Soviet-inspired subversion, particularly in Europe and the Far East. The Security Service, for example, relied heavily on Section V for overseas information to supplement its own intelligence obtained by intercepting correspondence and tapping telephones.[48] Since the early 1930s, the work of Vivian's overseas agents had been supplemented by the interception by GC&CS of the Comintern's clandestine communications from Moscow to Europe, known as MASK.[49] Other successes included the Noulens case, when the arrest in 1931 of the Comintern representative in Shanghai led to the seizure of the complete records of the Comintern's Far East Bureau;[50] and the recruitment in 1933 of a Comintern agent, Johann Heinrich deGraff (JONNY) by Frank Foley, head of the SIS station in Berlin. JONNY's information threw valuable light on Soviet subversion in the UK and, after he moved to the Far East, on the Soviet Communist Party's uneasy relationship with its Chinese counterpart.[51]

These welcome successes on the Comintern front, however, had the effect of taking the SIS eye partially off the Nazi ball; an oversight that extended to Italy and also to Japan, where penetration was rendered very difficult by a tight and professional security regime. In one sense, Morton's own departure from Broadway, when the IIC moved out into its own quarters in 1936,[52] had exacerbated the situation, since through his work in Section VI he had been one of the few senior officers paying dedicated attention to Germany. Although Section VI continued to operate in the realm of economic intelligence, its resources were very limited, and it found difficulty in coping with the demands made on it, not least by Morton and the IIC. As late as March 1939, Sinclair wrote to Morton that the head of Section VI was 'trying to develop an Intelligence system of his own for obtaining statistics of essential raw materials now being imported into, or purchased by, Germany, Italy and Japan, with the ultimate aim of expanding it to cover this matter during wartime'. Whether this was to replace or supplement the existing systems, established by Morton, is not revealed, though by the time that war broke out Section VI was ready to produce monthly reports, giving an SIS appreciation of the effects of economic warfare in Germany and neutral countries, that were sent directly to Morton at MEW.

In the late 1930s SIS remained a small organisation with a wide, and expanding remit. As the international situation worsened, demands for information increased sharply but no extra resources were allocated to enable it to meet them. Of all

SIS's customers, the armed forces were 'the most pressing and the least satisfied', with SIS acting, as one critical account put it:

> more as a postbox than as a filter between the customer departments and the field, with the result that the many Service demands were passed, often verbatim, to Representatives who had no possible chance of satisfying them and were, in fact, already drowning in a welter of previous requirements.

Germany was not the only urgent focus of requirements: events in the Mediterranean, with the Spanish Civil War on one side and a potentially hostile Italy on the other; the additional commitment imposed in 1937 of gathering information on Ireland;[53] requests from the Admiralty for ship-watching along the coasts of Norway, Sweden and the Low Countries; all these and other, more complex, demands, extended an already stretched Service to breaking point. The head of the SIS station in Brussels, for example, complained that he had been instructed to concentrate on acquiring intelligence about German air preparations: but then received an urgent request to produce naval information for the Admiralty. How, he asked, was he to reconcile these competing demands, with minimal resources (in July 1938 Brussels had two groups and four independent agents working into Germany, organising couriers through the Captain of a Rhine tugboat)? Similar pleas were received from other stations. Coverage of German affairs was often spasmodic and fragmented. In these circumstances the arrest and interrogation in August 1938 of Captain Thomas Kendrick, head of SIS's Vienna station, leading to the temporary withdrawal from Berlin of Foley and his staff, was a major setback.[54]

The Service Ministries were particularly critical of SIS's failure to produce sufficient detailed tactical and technical intelligence. The Air Ministry complained of 'an almost complete lack of factual intelligence on German aircraft production, armaments and reserves of raw material', although since both SIS and the IIC had supplied regular information in these areas it is possible that the problem was caused by a lack of communication between the complainants and the Intelligence Staffs. Nevertheless, Sinclair and his deputies, Menzies and Vivian, did not deny that SIS had a problem. Justly proud of their organisation's successes against Communism, they were not unaware that the SIS's European coverage had become unbalanced and badly overstretched.

Sinclair took a number of steps to try to ameliorate the situation and enable SIS to cope with the increasing demands placed upon it. In 1936 he had set up Z Section, a UK-based agent running organisation under Claude Dansey with the aim of gathering intelligence from Germany and Italy on political and military matters. Z was kept quite separate from Headquarters, operating out of Bush House in London under cover of the export department of Geoffrey Duveen and Company. Dansey ran his own small staff, including Jewish émigrés and other exiles, and supposedly communicated with SIS only through Sinclair, although the evidence suggests that Morton too received information directly from Dansey.

On the outbreak of war in September 1939 Z Section moved in its entirety to Switzerland, in order to expand its Axis contacts.[55]

In addition, Sinclair created in early 1938 a small section similar to Z but working out of the main SIS establishment, charged with the penetration of Germany and Italy. This section, which began with two officers, drew its agents from business, journalistic and academic circles and had some modest success on a range of topics including economic intelligence. On the latter it naturally came into contact with Morton, with whom (as with Dansey) it shared certain sources. One of these was a shadowy organisation known as the British Industrial Secret Service (BISS), run by the Canadian businessman W.S. Stephenson, a man whose exploits were later to become the stuff of legend.[56] Stephenson, peripherally involved in Intelligence during the First World War, had built up a highly successful career as a businessman, becoming a millionaire through enterprises such as the Pressed Steel Company, which apparently made ninety percent of car bodies for British automobile manufacturers. Although claims that he secretly furnished details of German rearmament to Churchill during the interwar period seem dubious, it is true that he built up an international network of contacts and informants concerned principally with obtaining secret industrial information to enable financial houses to judge the advisability of pursuing business propositions (the parallels between Stephenson and Makgill[57] in this respect are striking). It is not surprising, therefore, that he and Morton had come into contact, although it has not proved possible to date precisely the beginning of their association. Stephenson had established informal links with SIS on a number of levels, and Menzies, too, may well have come into contact with him personally during the mid-1930s.

In July 1939, however, Stephenson made his first formal contact with SIS through official channels, using the Conservative MP and businessman Sir Ralph Glyn as intermediary. Glyn claimed that he had for some time been passing on 'special items' of BISS information to the FO, but now realised that 'this was not the correct procedure': Stephenson's organisation, according to Glyn, was now 'entirely at the disposal of HMG'. Menzies directed that the head of SIS's UK-based German/Italian penetration section should interview Stephenson, and the resulting meeting on 12 July 1939 elicited more information concerning the scope and objectives of BISS, which Glyn and Stephenson alleged had 'extensive connections in business and financial circles in this country and abroad', including an émigré Russian businessman resident in Stockholm who had connections in the Baltic countries as well as sources of information within Russia.[58]

Stephenson made a good impression, and his interlocutor considered that the proposal for BISS to supply information to SIS had 'possibilities':

> He is a Canadian with a quiet manner, and evidently knows a great deal about Continental affairs and industrial matters. During a short discussion on the oil and non-ferrous metal questions he showed that he possesses a thorough grasp of the situation.

Nevertheless, SIS were firm in their refusal to contemplate any formal arrangement unless Stephenson divulged the identity of his sources, despite strong endorsement of BISS's value by the DNI, Admiral Godfrey, and by Morton, who said he considered its material 'invaluable'. The hurdle was not overcome until immediately after the outbreak of war, by which time it had emerged that a number of Stephenson's 'sources' were in fact local SIS representatives who had been supplying information to BISS to supplement their income. Though this revelation confirmed SIS's resolution not to offer any significant financial payments to Stephenson it also, ironically, increased their confidence in the product, and in early September 1939 agreement was reached on a scheme for BISS (now known as Industrial Secret Intelligence, ISI) to pass information to SIS through the latter's local representatives, with SIS controlling both agents and finances. Though there were further obstacles to be overcome, a mutually beneficial working relationship was established, although the information supplied by ISI was always valued more highly by Morton than by SIS.

Sinclair made other changes to the SIS organisation. During 1938 three new sections were added to Headquarters: VIII (Communications), IX (Special Operations) and X (Telephone Interception). None of these was well-staffed, and Headquarters remained very small. Apart from the seven circulating sections and three new specialist sections, three 'G' sections, each staffed by one officer, handled regional coverage, while another handled liaison. One of the G officers doubled up as Chief of Staff to Sinclair. Menzies had the title of 'Assistant' and Vivian of 'Deputy' Chief, and both supported Sinclair as second in command when required. By the spring of 1939, however, there were still less than forty-five people working in Broadway. Morton knew almost all of them very well.

Section VIII, under Major (later Sir) Richard Gambier-Parry,[59] had the difficult task of trying to introduce the use of radio to reluctant agents (an instruction issued in November 1938 that representatives should only recruit agents willing and able to use radio was very unpopular), and of ensuring that representatives could maintain communications in wartime. Section X dealt with the telephone interception of foreign embassies, and the protection of British telephone services overseas. It was, however, Section IX, also known as Section D, that was of most relevance to Morton and his work. Headed by Major Lawrence Grand, seconded to SIS from the Royal Engineers – a flamboyant, somewhat maverick figure with a wide circle of business contacts, and a friend of Morton's – D's business was sabotage. Together with the propaganda organisation based at Electra House (EH) and a War Office section known as MI(R), it was to form the nucleus of the Special Operations Executive (SOE) established in the summer of 1940.[60]

The idea for a SIS section devoted to sabotage had, in fact, first been mooted in 1935, apparently by Menzies (though Dansey later claimed it). Over the next couple of years the idea matured without developing, but in January 1938 the suggestion was put to Sinclair that 'planning in respect of sabotage is closely linked up with XS [the head of Section VI], in that plans for Sabotage in enemy countries would be with reference in the main to dockyards and factories.' However, the idea of absorbing sabotage within the Economic Section by the addition of extra staff was rejected not just by the head of that Section but by other senior SIS officers, who agreed that a separate section was required, working directly to C. This was evidently the trigger for Sinclair's recruitment of Grand. The proposed link with Section VI is interesting, however, and raises the possibility that Morton played some part in the planning of D from an early stage. The evidence is ambiguous. But his friendship with Grand; his frustration with official inaction; and his particular professional interest in Scandinavia and Romania, from an economic warfare perspective, are surely strong pointers to his involvement, with the knowledge and possibly encouragement of Sinclair.[61]

In any case, Section D's first directive (drafted by Grand himself), containing a list of possible sabotage objectives in Germany, made it clear that here was the potential muscle needed to wage the kind of economic warfare Morton had in mind when the blueprint for MEW was drawn up; and indeed for carrying out pre-emptive measures designed to deny the potential enemy sources of supply. Sinclair's verdict that 'the planning of [D's] operations should be concentrated in the first instance on the transport of iron ore from Sweden and of oil from Roumania'[62] also fitted in with Morton's own views about what might be attempted in peacetime. The importance of denying, or at least reducing the supply of Swedish iron ore to Germany was, in theory at least, widely accepted in Whitehall, though there was less agreement on practical steps to be taken. In the case of the FO, for example, fruitless attempts in early 1939 to exert diplomatic pressure on Sweden, followed by the negotiation of an (equally fruitless) war trade agreement later in the year, were hampered by the Board of Trade.[63] Military authorities, particularly the Admiralty, were also involved, although active planning for measures to impede the iron ore trade took no firm shape until the outbreak of war. D, on the other hand, began investigations into Swedish iron ore almost as soon as the Section was established, sending A.F. Rickman to Sweden in July 1938, ostensibly to write a book on the Swedish iron ore industry (indeed, he actually wrote one), but in fact to produce a secret report on the export of Swedish iron ore through Oxelösund.[64]

Similarly, there was a general consensus on the potential value of Romanian oil to Germany if she were to overrun that country, although Morton raised some practical questions about transport.[65] Information on the extent and potential of German oil stocks and petroleum manufacture remained unreliable, though the view expressed by Morton in May 1939, with the agreement of the Service Departments, that even with complete control of the Romanian oil wells 'we do not think Germany, and still less Germany together with Italy, could obtain enough petroleum to carry on for more than a year', proved to be optimistically wide of the mark.[66] Again, serious planning for pre-emptive operations for the control of Danube shipping did not begin until war broke out, but in February 1939 Grand sent Sinclair a memorandum reporting that an agent had been recruited in a Romanian oil company, examining possible lines of attack on Romanian oil fields and stressing the need to send sabotage materials to Bucharest. Further local information was obtained in the summer of 1939.[67]

Grand's plans, however, had begun to ring alarm bells in the FO. A note by Sinclair of 29 March 1939 recorded that following a meeting on 23 March between Halifax, the CIGS, Cadogan, Menzies and Grand, the Secretary of State had 'given orders that, pending further consideration in complete detail of what it is proposed to do, and how it is proposed to accomplish it, no further steps are to be taken' towards sabotage operations. Grand was told firmly to put everything but propaganda operations on hold. Neither the FO nor the Cabinet were ready to contemplate any aggressive action that might provoke early conflict. Though Grand put forward further schemes to Sinclair in the spring of 1939, such as sending an agitator to provoke a strike in the iron ore works at Luleå, and stressing that 'IIC state that cutting off the iron ore from Germany will . . . restrict the German powers of resistance to two months', Sinclair remained obdurate: D was to drop everything but information-gathering activities.

Sinclair's attempts to expand and refocus SIS's capability laid the foundation for a bigger, better and more effective organisation, but without a massive injection of resources – and a change in attitude on the part of SIS's customers – there was little chance for SIS to do more in 1938–39 than to plan, like Morton, for war with Germany. The fault lay on both sides. Certainly there were weaknesses in SIS: in personnel (over-populated by what Victor ('Bill') Cavendish-Bentinck, wartime chairman of the JIC, called 'old boys' who had been in SIS since the First World War and 'fancied themselves as spy-masters');[68] in capability (much better at long-term strategic than short-term tactical intelligence); and in method (poor communication and liaison with agents in the field, plus a tendency to sloppiness in checking facts before passing reports on to their customers).

In SIS's defence, however, it must be said that the perennial failure of those customers – particularly in the Service departments – to talk to each other, or to take seriously and handle properly the information that they did receive, let alone to share intelligence of mutual interest, was also a prime cause of the poor perception not just of SIS, but of all the Agencies. The official histories of British wartime Intelligence, and of the Security Service, describe at length similar obstacles faced not just by SIS but by its sister organisation, GC&CS, as well as by MI5 in their wartime preparations.[69] What is more, the Foreign Office, which had no dedicated intelligence analysis capability of its own but regarded itself as the authority on its interpretation nevertheless, compounded the problem. The FO did not sit on the JIC until November 1938, and a short-lived initiative in April 1939 for the fast-tracking of intelligence requiring quick decisions, by setting up a Situation Report Centre with FO representation, resulted only in the SRC's merger with the JIC.[70] To quote the official history of Intelligence again, these difficulties arose from 'defects that were arising at all levels in conditions of near-war in consequence of the autonomy of the Service intelligence branches and of the peace-time separation from them of the Foreign Office'.[71] The same attitudes faced by the Agencies since the First World War, and by Morton and the

IIC in the 1930s – that only military intelligence was 'real' intelligence, only officers with no future worked in the intelligence branches, and that secret Intelligence officers were dangerous if gifted amateurs best kept out of sight – continued to prevail.

A good example of this is offered by an exchange of minutes in early 1939, revealing the level of suspicion endemic among some FO officials regarding 'secret reporting'. As well as illustrating the credibility gap faced by SIS, it has some relevance to Morton and to MEW, since the main protagonists in the debate were Mounsey, Secretary designate to MEW, and Jebb, who as Private Secretary to the PUS performed a liaison role with the Agencies, and who was himself to move to MEW (to work with SOE) in August 1940. The exchange had its roots in the Government's decision to pass on to the United States and other allies warnings received early in 1939 from secret sources of an imminent German attack on Holland.[72] SIS had considered the threat credible, as part of a general pattern of information indicating that Hitler's aggressive intentions now lay west, rather than eastwards. It also conformed to reports of increasing enemy espionage on UK soil, indicating that Holland was the largest base for German activities: the *Deuxième Bureau* estimated that between fifty and eighty percent of agents entering France or the UK came from Holland.

When the information relating to an attack on Holland proved unfounded, however, Mounsey complained bitterly in minutes of 3 and 6 March 1939 that the episode had been both humiliating and damaging. If the totalitarian states were really planning to provoke a crisis, he said, a credible warning was much more likely to come from 'ordinary' than from secret sources, which were 'unsettling, liable to influence our own policy in an undesirable way, and may be both embarrassing to us and even actively mischievous'. The FO, he complained, had undermined their position and authority by taking action 'of a highly sensational and highly disturbing kind on information which they are unable to guarantee'. The result had been to revive an atmosphere of mutual distrust and recrimination between Britain and Germany just at a time when the Prime Minister was trying to carry out his policy of appeasement. Dismissive of the role of secret agents – 'they have a secret mission, and they must justify it . . . if nothing comes to hand for them to report, they must earn their pay by finding something' – Mounsey professed himself 'heretic enough to embrace all reports of a secret nature in my general dislike':

> This seems to me a very serious matter. Are we going to remain so attached to reliance on secret reports, which tie our hands in all directions, that we are going to continue acting on them in disregard of the clear warnings we now have of the effect which such action may have, firstly on the rest of the Empire, and secondly on the rest of the world?[73]

By the time Jebb responded to this onslaught at the end of March, Nazi troops had marched into Prague and, as Jebb put it, the policy of appeasement had 'receded rather into the background for the time being'. He protested that Mounsey's view of SIS reports as 'obtained by "hired assassins" who are sent out from this country to spy the land' was 'not at all how the system works in practice':

> The greatest possible caution is observed in regard to all alarmist reports and, under the new system, whenever a report conflicts in any way with what one of our Missions has been saying, a copy is either sent out to the Head of that Mission, or shown to him on the spot, and his observations invited. If the Head of the Mission says that he thinks that report is nonsense it does not, in practice go forward.[74]

While defending SIS, however, Jebb was critical of secret reports from other sources, such as 'K' (MI5), which 'has not got quite the same experience or background as is possessed by 'C'', and deprecated the 'enormous mass of rumour put about by more or less interested intermediaries' (including politicians), over which the FO had little control. Cadogan, asked to comment on this exchange, expressed himself much in sympathy with Mounsey, admitting that in his new role as PUS he found his exposure to secret reports 'distracting':

> But I cannot ignore that they did warn us of the September crisis, and they did not give any colour to the ridiculous optimism that prevailed up to the rape of Czechoslovakia, of which our official reports did not give us much warning . . . It is perhaps unfair – on March 31 – to challenge a minute written by Sir G. Mounsey on March 3. But when he complains that these reports operate 'to the exclusion of the contemporaneous pursuit of a policy of settlement', I can't help observing that they may not have been so wide of the mark.[75]

Cadogan's mildly charitable conclusion has not always been shared by historians, but it is possible to argue that, like the IIC, SIS's pre-war record has been judged over-harshly.[76] There were certainly mistakes in emphasis: the insistence until the end of 1938 that Hitler's next moves after Czechoslovakia would be to the east, not west; over-emphasis on the degree of dissent within the Nazi leadership and thus overestimation of the potential for removing the Chancellor. But it is only too easy to fall into the trap of hindsight. Despite the organisation's lack of resource and a certain imbalance of focus, the evidence and detail contained in the secret reports transmitted to the Foreign Office, the Service Ministries and indeed to the Cabinet were on the whole impressive and substantially correct; nor was their judgement (as expressed in December 1938) of Hitler's character and purpose so wide of the mark:

> Among his characteristics are fanaticism, mysticism, ruthlessness, cunning, vanity, moods of exaltation and depression, fits of bitter and self-righteous resentment, and what can only be termed a streak of mad-

ness; but with it all there is great tenacity of purpose, which has often been combined with extraordinary clarity of vision. He has gained the reputation of being always able to choose the right moment and right method for 'getting away with it'. In the eyes of his disciples, and increasingly in his own, 'the Führer is always right'. He has unbounded self-confidence, which has grown in proportion to the strength of the machine he has created; but it is a self-confidence which has latterly been tempered less than hitherto with patience and restraint.[77]

The full significance of SIS's reporting could only be appreciated – like that of the IIC – by placing it in the wider context of diplomatic reporting, military and economic information. SIS's responsibility, after all, was for the collection and dissemination, not the analysis of intelligence. This was a distinction well understood by Morton, who had made it on behalf of the IIC in countless committee meetings since the early 1930s: as he told the JIC on 18 May 1939, 'final appreciation was not his business'.[78] What he *did* regard as his business, however, was economic warfare: MEW could plan it, but SIS could, he thought, help him to wage it. The first few months of the war were to show him that neither MEW nor SIS was equal to the task without an injection of political will that would force a sea change in the organisational attitudes of those authorities traditionally responsible for the waging of war.

10

THE FIREPROOF CURTAIN:
3 SEPTEMBER 1939–15 MAY 1940

The Ministry of Economic Warfare came into being on 3 September 1939, springing fully-armed from the brow of the Foreign Office rather as the goddess Pallas Athene did from Zeus. To continue the metaphor, MEW was assumed to have been born with a good deal of knowledge and wisdom, bearing a powerful weapon that would shorten the war against Germany: an enemy that (to mix metaphors), even if it were 'no Achilles with a single vital spot . . . is vulnerable and can be bled to death if dealt sufficient wounds'.[1] Nevertheless, during the early stages of the war this particular goddess was generally ignored not only by her irascible parent, but by the whole panoply of Whitehall gods – from the Cabinet to the Service Ministries to the Joint Planning Staff – despite their peacetime acceptance of the importance of planning for economic warfare. It was, as Morton wrote to MEW's official historian in May 1945, as if a fireproof curtain had fallen on the outbreak of war.[2]

MEW's performance during the so-called 'Phoney' or 'Twilight' war,[3] the period of uneasy limbo underlain by feverish planning that lasted from 3 September 1939 until the German invasion of Denmark and Norway on 10 April 1940, proved an inevitable disappointment to those who had expected so much of it, and an irritant to those who were incapable of looking beyond the traditional channels of wartime command. No matter how hard it tried (and on a practical level it tried very hard), MEW could not win. The story of its early struggles, described somewhat unkindly as 'feverish administrative activity with a fallacious sense of achievement', has been told authoritatively in its official history.[4] What that account does not, and cannot convey is the extent of the disappointment and frustration felt by its Director of Intelligence.

As one of the principal architects of MEW, who had spent so much time planning for the establishment of the new Ministry and who had committed to it entirely the personnel and expertise of his earlier creation, the Industrial Intelligence Centre, Morton's disappointment was doubly bitter. Not only was he frustrated by institutional barriers, but his new post failed to afford him the weight of influence he had anticipated. Instead of playing a key role in the prosecution of the war, he found himself in the kind of role he had always derided, that of a senior civil servant running a division of a large ministry. His concept of economic warfare was active and aggressive, not legislative and defensive, and he felt both inhibited and impotent. MEW, he soon discovered, 'could never be so offensive as the economic offensive demanded'.[5]

This is not the place to examine MEW's record in detail, nor the merits of British military strategy. But it is relevant to consider Morton's personal performance at that Ministry, which was, if not inadequate, less effective than his previous history might have indicated. In the early months of the Second World War, despite his forceful personality and distinguished record, we hear his voice but do not feel his hand. In the mass of contemporary memoirs and diaries covering this period and published after the war, he scarcely appears, despite the fact that he was now a respectable civil servant whose wartime role could be referred to openly. Apart from rare references to his attendance at Churchill's 'Tuesday' dinners, or meals with senior civil servants, his name does not appear among those who lunched, dined or chatted in the corridors of power. Everyone knew him: professionally, he had many colleagues and contacts; but few friends in those Whitehall quarters where it mattered. His own character – solitary, formal, guarded – undoubtedly accounted for a great deal of this. He was not an easy man to know well. Nevertheless, the fact is that in September 1939 he was well-known: nearly fifty years old, an experienced Whitehall warrior with a formidable expertise in economic and scientific matters, let alone intelligence, highly regarded by Churchill and others, and respected if not always liked; why did he not make more impact?

To try to answer this question it is once more the twin tracks of economic warfare and Intelligence that must be followed. As a senior civil servant, Morton's official route to the corridors of power lay through his Minister; he was fortunate in having an alternative (and potentially more influential) route to the Cabinet through Churchill. Neither was to prove effective in turning government policy in favour of active economic warfare. As this became increasingly clear, the secret world – and, in particular, SIS, from whom as MEW's Director of Intelligence Morton sought and received a constant stream of information – offered what seemed to him the only opportunity for implementing the plans drawn up so carefully in anticipation of MEW's creation. For within SIS (and in particular within Section D), despite the moratorium imposed in March 1939 on all but propaganda activities,[6] a good deal of detailed planning relevant to economic warfare had been going on and continued in the early months of the war. Though most of these schemes, too, were to be vitiated by political indecision and military realities – in the words of the late Roy Jenkins, the Cabinet 'willed the end without willing the means'[7] – the comparatively active role that SIS was willing to play in waging economic warfare ensured that Morton's gravitation towards the old familiar byways of secret Intelligence, noted in the previous chapter, became more marked.

SIS was not, however, a firm stone in the wartime tide on which Morton could rest his foot. The period between the outbreak of war and Churchill's appointment as Prime Minister in May 1940 was one of anxiety and turbulence for the British Intelligence establishment in general, and for SIS in particular. All the agencies struggled to adapt to wartime demands and conditions; the uncertainties of the *drôle de guerre* served only to emphasise the failure to predict Hitler's next moves, and the major triumphs of code-breaking and double-agent running were yet to come. Their performance, regarded as substandard by their political masters and the Service Chiefs, was subjected to a wide-ranging investigation by Hankey, then Minister without Portfolio, between December 1939 and March 1940, giving the jigsaw of British Intelligence a brisk shake-up during which some pieces fell out. And if that were not enough, SIS suffered humiliation at Venlo, loss through death of a long-serving Chief and uneasy relations with political and military authorities caused by the egregious activities of Section D and its head.

For Morton, this period of difficulty and transition for the agencies, while causing some professional frustration, was to have its positive aspects. Working closely with the Intelligence world, where his knowledge and experience gave him some natural authority, offered him the opportunity to flex his organisational muscles in a less bureaucratic arena. In matters relating to Intelligence, his advice was sought, and valued – not by everyone, but certainly by Churchill, by Hankey, and widely enough to count. In a way, the difficulties faced by SIS and her sister agencies provided Morton with a window of opportunity: not to re-enter their world wholesale, but to take a critical look through the glass that enabled him to develop a liaison role for himself at the point of intersection between overt and covert spheres of decisions and action. It was a role on which Churchill, as Prime Minister, was to set high value in the early years of the War.

Great Expectations: Morton and MEW

It is difficult to avoid the conclusion that MEW made very little contribution to British Government policy during the first eight months of the war.[8] At first sight the sheer quantity – and, often, quality – of the papers produced, plans elaborated, controls instituted – belies this harsh verdict. But activity did not equate with impact. An elaborate system of contraband control was set in place, with naval patrols to detect and confiscate suspect cargoes; Black Lists were created to restrict illicit trade; war trade agreements were negotiated with neutral countries; numerous elaborate studies were produced (principally by the Intelligence Division) of the current and potential economic condition of the enemy; detailed schemes were developed for the interdiction or restriction of German imports and exports, particularly in key commodities such as iron ore and petroleum. But those responsible for the conduct of the war – the War Cabinet and Chiefs of Staff – paid lip service only to the concept or practice of economic warfare. Contraband control and war trade agreements, the only weapons MEW was allowed to use, could not be effective without political will and military muscle, both of which were lacking. It was a situation that neither the Ministry nor the 'forceful and persuasive'[9] Morton proved able to alter.

There were a number of reasons for MEW's impotence, many of which were outside its control: the political will of the Prime Minister, unwilling to imperil the uneasy stalemate that offered breathing space to strengthen the political and military position of Britain and her French ally; the reluctance of the Foreign Office to abandon the peacetime constraints of diplomacy or to infringe 'legitimate neutral rights and traditional standards of good conduct';[10] the strategic dynamics of the Anglo-French military relationship;[11] even, on a more local and mundane level, the practical difficulties of administering a complex blockade control system with inexperienced staff. The fledgling MEW was far too young to overcome such obstacles without the protection of a powerful sponsor. It did not, unfortunately, find this in its first Minister, Ronald Cross, described by his successor Hugh Dalton as:

> a well-mannered man, of good presence, in private life a merchant banker, after the war a successful Governor of Tasmania. But he was not a commanding figure, and I doubt whether he carried great weight in the Cabinet or with his colleagues individually.[12]

Cross was outgunned easily by the Service Chiefs, the Treasury and the FO; also by the Board of Trade and the Supply departments, who had the support of Chamberlain's powerful adviser, Sir Horace Wilson. Even for Churchill, an enthusiastic supporter of the idea of economic warfare and Cabinet champion of dynamic action, the interests of his own department, the Admiralty, and the wider policy concerns of the War Cabinet had to come before those of MEW.

What of MEW's senior civil servants, men with long practice of guiding (and outmaneouvring) junior or inexperienced Ministers? With the exception of Morton and a few IIC colleagues, they were seconded from the 'old' departments, FO, Treasury and Board of Trade, and seemed disinclined to forsake their first allegiance. Dalton, whose Shadow Cabinet responsibility included liaison with MEW, wrote in the *Daily Herald* that British diplomats were 'tired and elderly, too traditional and too gentlemanly to be a match for Hitler's gangsters'.[13] There is certainly little sign of their speaking up for a more active MEW role. The Director General, the distinguished Treasury mandarin, Sir Frederick Leith-Ross, began his time at MEW in September 1939 with a memorandum setting out 'the general objectives at which we should aim', which included trying to maintain or increase UK export levels in wartime, attempting to control neutral shipping by refusing insurance cover against War Risks, and 'exercising financial pressure through tightening up credits to any country which does not give us full cooperation'.[14] Even during a Phoney War, this surely seemed ridiculously optimistic (as Morton pointed out on other papers). It was certainly not a framework designed to accommodate schemes for direct action against Germany's economic base, by intercepting her imports on the high seas, bombing her stores of aviation fuel, placing mines to disrupt Rhine transport or using other means of sabotage.[15]

And what of Morton himself? If it is really true that he 'quickly emerged as [MEW's] leading figure, easily dominating his minister',[16] what difference did he make? To some extent there was little he could do to redress the balance of power. There was an unbridgeable credibility gap between MEW and those responsible for the political and military direction of the war. After twenty years' talking about the importance of active economic warfare, implementation of the schemes developed in such visionary detail before 1939 was to prove impossible until war 'really' began in the spring in 1940; until Hitler selected his next European victim (the Soviet invasion of Finland at the end of November 1939 almost did the trick, but not quite); until Italy and the Soviet Union made their minds up finally which side they were on; until the future of France was made uncompromisingly clear; and, crucially, until the Board of Trade and British industry accepted that 'business as usual' was no longer sustainable.[17]

Paradoxically, the depth of this credibility gap must be ascribed at least in part to Morton, whose increasingly successful promotion of the IIC message during the 1930s had created both a false sense of security and an uneasy sense of doubt in the minds of his political and military customers. Prewar reports of Germany's accelerated rearmament had been accompanied by estimates of her increased need for raw materials to keep up the pace; in particular, her requirements for petroleum-related products and for iron and steel, in order to support her fast-expanding air force and armaments industry, were considered to far outstrip her domestic supply. Though these reports had not been accepted without reserve, the information provided by the IIC, not only on Germany but on other potential enemies such as Italy, Japan and the Soviet Union, produced, by the time war broke out, a tendency to both over-confidence and excessive caution. Over-confidence, in that the political and military authorities dared to hope that German rearmament and the stocks she was forced to expend in the initial phases of the war might weaken her both economically and militarily, so that by the time con-flict began in earnest Britain and France would be in a stronger position not only to fight, but even to impose a negotiated peace. At the same time, they worried that aggressive economic measures against Germany, rather than shortening the war, might actually make matters worse by alienating neutrals and pushing currently 'uncommitted' countries such as Italy or the Soviet Union[18] into active war against the UK. In short, neither the Chiefs of Staff nor the government as a whole knew whether to believe that Germany was weak or strong; could sustain a long war or win a short one; whether her economic position was improving or deteriorating in relation to that of the Western Allies; and whether schemes designed to curtail or stop key German imports were sure to have the desired effect.

Morton's personal performance at MEW is also something of a paradox. On one level, he was in his element, confident and knowledgeable, producing reports and opinions that were masterly in their grasp of economic detail and its wider context. A good example is offered by the question of Swedish iron ore, a subject to which Morton devoted much personal attention, and which also occupied a good deal of War Cabinet time during the early months of the war.[19] The desirability of restricting the supply of this key commodity to Germany was agreed in principle at every level, diplomatic, political and military, and the argument was strengthened as it became increasingly clear, during negotiations for the War Trade agreement, that the Swedes would not only refuse to decrease the volume of their exports, but would accede to German demands to increase them. Morton's assessment of the situation, in a minute of 2 October 1939, shows him at his succinct (if somewhat condescending) best:

> in a year's time nearly the full normal quota of Swedish iron ore could be made to reach Germany from Swedish ports alone. The Swedes know this. The Germans know this; I think we may accept that we too now know this. Although the Swedish Delegation are honourable gentlemen, in sympathy with our cause, they, and the whole of their country, are terrified of the Germans and not in the least afraid of us. This is not because we are powerless to do hurt to Sweden, but because they believe we will not use that power, and, anyhow, because the pressure we can bring to bear is only in the economic field, the effect of which cannot rapidly be felt, while Germany is able to take immediate military action.[20]

This, despite Swedish protestations, was generally unarguable. He was on far less firm ground, however, in such confident predictions as that expressed in a report at the end of November 1939:

> a complete stoppage of Swedish exports of iron ore to Germany now would, barring unpredictable developments, end the war in a few months.[21]

Such a claim, if substantiated, looked to be an unanswerable argument in favour of pre-emptive UK measures, whether through naval action in the Baltic or through even bolder moves to take control of the iron ore fields. It would have been a tall order – indeed impossible – for Morton to provide the Cabinet or Chiefs of Staff with conclusive evidence that cutting off the Swedish iron ore supply to Germany would, in fact, bring the war to a rapid conclusion. But to convince, he needed to bridge the gap between cause and effect, to produce a reasoned analysis that would carry assertion through to practical implementation. He seemed unable to do this: while his presentation of the situation might be masterly, his arguments in favour of action were crude and showy, and hedged around with qualifications that negated their impact. He might persuade Churchill, and through him the War Cabinet or even the Military Coordination Committee, that cutting off Swedish iron ore supplies was vital: but he could not persuade them that he understood the political or military implications of the decision to take action that breached international conventions of neutrality and might, conceivably, provoke Germany into a Scandinavian invasion or the Soviet Union into conflict with the UK.

It would be unfair to ascribe to Morton responsibility for the failure of the British Government to implement plans to effect the 'complete stoppage' of the Swedish iron ore trade, any more than for their failure to take other aggressive economic measures to deny oil and other key imports to Germany. All these schemes did receive serious consideration by the Cabinet on the basis of facts, figures and intelligence supplied by Morton; the reasons for their non-implementation are complex and have their roots in political and military uncertainty on the part of both the British and French Governments.[22] But it is hard to avoid the conclusion that Morton, when put to the test in MEW, was to some extent found wanting. Being Director of Intelligence in MEW was a step change from the IIC: somehow, he seemed unable or unwilling to take advantage of the greater power and authority that his position offered, a reluctance that may have been rooted in his customary desire to avoid any personal blame by keeping his head below the parapet.

On a day to day level, too, Morton's personal contribution to the MEW record seems curiously muted. The majority of Ministerial or Service requests (except those from Churchill, to which he always attended personally), were passed on, quite properly, to his section heads: but his covering minutes display little of his usual firm direction or what he himself referred to as 'a certain cheerfulness of style',[23] and his comments on his colleagues' productions were, on the whole, oddly uncritical and lacking a sense of urgency. It was almost as if his absorption into a large government department had inculcated a new spirit of humility and abnegation ('we feel it to be for Higher Authority to decide whether the Naval difficulties inherent in establishing [shipping] control are so great as to outweigh the importance of the functions it would perform').[24] Humility and deference were not characteristics that would previously have been claimed by or attributed to Desmond Morton.

His papers were hedged with qualifications and disclaimers, far exceeding his customary caution in presenting reports and statistics. He referred constantly to the inadequate numbers and inferior quality of his staff, showing a lack of spirit that persisted until his departure from MEW in May 1940, despite the occasional reversion to type ('The Ministry of Economic Warfare in its various Departments reserve the fullest right to ignore instructions received from any other quarter!!!!').[25] It was not that there was a dramatic loss of performance on Morton's part: somehow, this makes his poor form more noticeable. Although he continued to work extremely hard and his authoritative reports were usually well-received, his change of approach and style, even if superficial, not only bored and alienated his interlocutors, but also tended to diminish the value and impact of his contribution to the policy debate.

Why was Morton's tenure as Director of Intelligence at MEW so uneasy? He has left some clues to the external factors, including the 'fireproof curtain' that seemed to fall between MEW and other Departments on the outbreak of war. In particular, he noted that he and his colleagues lost touch with the Chiefs of Staff. As he later pointed out to Medlicott, 'This was ridiculous, since the IIC had been associated with them in drawing up the very plans which presumably were being put into execution.' But the problem was not just a temporary failure of communication:

> The trouble was that the military men of those days really dealt with us on a personal basis. They knew Watson or Owen or Clively or Morton as people. They accepted that we were types unlikely to discuss secret war planning with the *Daily Mirror*, but they could not bring themselves to admit that war was really the concern of men in plain clothes.[26]

Morton was exaggerating to some extent. The Chiefs of Staff may have been unwilling to give due weight to MEW's views in questions of high policy, but on a working level Morton retained close contacts such as Burge at the Air Ministry, and Lieutenant Ian Fleming in Naval Intelligence.[27] Nevertheless, he was concerned that the 'fireproof curtain' meant that MEW was not receiving all the information it needed to operate effectively. When Fleming wrote to him on 16 November asking whether Morton saw 'Consular Y' reports – intercepted merchant shipping signals received by the Admiralty – Morton replied that he did not, but would 'very much like to do so, as it appears that they might be of considerable value to us'. Fleming arranged for Morton to receive the messages daily, stipulating that they must be handled 'in every way as Most Secret documents'.[28]

Morton was not alone in feeling marginalised. Hugh Gaitskell, head of the Enemy Countries section of the Economic Warfare Intelligence Department (EWI), complained to Jebb in December 1939 that Intelligence Division was being denied access to foreign official publications containing useful statistics.[29] Morton himself, although in receipt of regular reports from SIS and GC&CS, felt that neither he nor his superiors were receiving all they required. As he wrote to Professor Noel Hall, head of EWI, on 13 January 1940:

> The point is the old one that for a variety of reasons the people at the top are apt to get starved of information and only to see formal papers called for or prepared for particular purposes. You probably see more than I do and I see more than the Director-General . . . At present he, like all of us, hears scraps from prominent people, which scraps may not be sufficient to give him a sketch of the whole position.[30]

Morton also complained, like many others, about the heavy hand of the Treasury. He shared Keynes's opinion that one reason for the 'chaotic' state of British wartime administration was the lack of any consistent and intelligible coordination of economic policy.[31] Morton wrote to Churchill in this vein on 14 October 1939:

The Treasury may be full of brilliant men, but they cannot know the technical detail of everything. If, as at present, through their octopus-like grip, they prevent the spending of 6d until they have had the reason fully explained to their satisfaction, we may keep our money until we have lost the war. To my mind, there is no question but that the Treasury, as part of the economic organisation of the country, ought to be co-ordinated, together with any other economic Ministries, and not itself to be in control. If we live to see written a sober history of the last few years, and particularly of the last few weeks, it will, I am sure, be shown that why you have not got your neutral shipping; why we are in danger of a rationing scheme for foodstuffs nearly as severe as in Germany; why the Contraband control is full of leaks; why we cannot seemingly push our export trade; is due primarily to the Treasury stranglehold, caused, if I may go further, by an unconscious worship of money for money's sake.[32]

Unlike Morton, Keynes had no official position at the beginning of the war, nor did he wish for one. In the words of his biographer, he was 'too eminent to be made an ordinary civil servant, and too stimulating to be let loose in Whitehall'.[33] Morton, though certainly not equal in stature, knowledge or ability to Keynes, shared in some measure his unsuitability to be either an ordinary civil servant or let loose in Whitehall.

The root of the problem may simply have been that Morton disliked his job. Both in SIS and the IIC he had worked in small organisations where it was possible to know everyone and everything that went on. This was not feasible in a Division of over five hundred people, and although there were ample senior staff to absolve him of the necessity for small decisions, he either could not or would not avoid getting involved in the red tape and sealing wax side of Ministry work.[34] Nor was it possible to just *do* things: he had to follow the established channels, respect hierarchies, deal with staff who simply did not understand what he wanted – working practices that he found deeply uncongenial. The sheer size of the Division, and the complexity of its structure so carefully devised by Morton and others, brought its own difficulties. Apart from those he had brought over from IIC, and a few senior officials hand-picked for the job, most staff had little or no experience in what was rather a specialised area of work and were, in Morton's view, quite unsuited to it. On 10 November 1939 Morton set down on paper for Sir W. Robinson what he regarded as the necessary qualifications for an officer working in the intelligence field. He tried to approach the matter tactfully:

An Officer of the very highest qualifications and calibre in certain directions may have no 'flair' for Intelligence work. In the 22 years in which I have been doing this work myself I have proved this contention over and over again. The converse naturally holds. An Officer who is really first-class at Intelligence work may be no use whatever in other directions where other qualifications are needed.

The first essential, he explained, was 'to have an intensely enquiring mind, a keen but nevertheless controlled imagination and other qualities that go to make up a first-class detective'. This 'detective flair' could be found among all classes of society. His final paragraph makes it clear that it was the 'civil service' aspect that struck to the very heart of the problem:

> officers to do Intelligence work in every grade must be picked not because they have already proved themselves good at the normal work of their grade but because they have the detective sense and the Intelligence flair. It is against their own interests as well as that of the Intelligence organisation to which they are attached for them to attempt this work unless they possess that flair.[35]

With a few exceptions, Morton discerned little 'flair' among the members of his Division. And if he found the staff unsatisfactory, the organisation, so carefully designed, seemed oddly opaque. On Christmas Day 1939, working as usual in his office at the London School of Economics,[36] he wrote to H.W. Rowbottom of Shell Oil, regarding a ship held up by the Prize Department. Acknowledging Rowbottom's seasonal good wishes, Morton expressed the view that in his present job, he needed 'prayers and supplications as well!'

> My great difficulty at present is to try and discover who is in charge of what. Having been brought up first of all in the Army for many years, and then under the Committee of Imperial Defence where such issues were always clear, there are elements of nightmare in the present position. However, the great thing is to retain one's balance and, if possible, a sense of humour . . .[37]

As Morton was writing this letter Churchill was hard at work in the Admiralty, writing to Chamberlain that as Naval Intelligence reports pointed to the Germans becoming 'increasingly interested' in Scandinavia, the seizure of the Swedish iron ore fields 'may be the shortest and surest road to the end',[38] a view long propagated by Morton. It is not hard to imagine that the latter would much rather have been discussing this with Churchill than puzzling over 'who is in charge of what' at MEW.

It would have been out of character if Morton had not tried to improve his job, and the record makes it clear that he did so within the limits of his authority. Nevertheless, it is hard to view his time at MEW as a success. Whether by ability, circumstance, frustration or sheer dislike of his situation, he felt constrained and his performance suffered. This sense of constraint was shared in some measure by

SIS, in whose activities Morton took an increasing interest as his disillusionment with MEW grew.

The vicious circle: Morton and SIS

If MEW found it frustrating not to be taken seriously by the Chiefs of Staff, SIS, as a long-established agency dedicated to the collection and distribution of foreign intelligence, found it doubly so. As we have seen, Sinclair and his colleagues had made considerable efforts during 1938–39 to 'modernise' SIS and improve the range and quality of the information they provided to Whitehall, as well as their technical capability; they felt they were – or should be – an important part of the military intelligence machine (even adopting the alternative designation 'MI6' to underline this). Nevertheless, during the early part of the war SIS, in common with its sister agencies, found itself caught in what the official history of British Intelligence calls a vicious circle:

> Until the intelligence sent to them increased and their evaluation of it improved, the intelligence branches could not establish a reputation for reliability with the political and operational 'use' authorities. But until those authorities came to place greater reliance on the intelligence branches there could not be much movement towards the effective application of intelligence to the conduct of the war, either within each Service or at the inter-departmental level where the JIC had been set up to serve the Chiefs of Staff and the War Cabinet.[39]

It was in an attempt to break this circle that a major review of the British Secret Services was commissioned by Chamberlain, Halifax and the Service Ministers, and undertaken by Hankey, in his capacity as Minister without Portfolio, between December 1939 and May 1940. Morton gave evidence to Hankey in preparation of his report on SIS, as an important customer and former member of the organisation; indeed, he took a keen interest in the whole Review, which was to inform his future career in 10 Downing Street. He understood only too well the 'vicious circle' in which the agencies were caught. On the one hand, he knew the difficulties of operating an Intelligence service with inadequate resources, of reaching any reliable conclusions in the face of conflicting evidence obtained under hostile conditions, and of interpreting the information received. He knew, from his endeavours on multiple Whitehall committees, how hard it was to get the armed Services to take proper account of the intelligence received (particularly if it emanated from non-military sources), and to coordinate effectively with other relevant authorities. But he was also aware, from his connections with Churchill and other Ministers, and from preparing memoranda for the War Cabinet, of the difficulties involved in taking decisions to commit British military or strategic resources in the face of uncertain or inadequate intelligence. He may have found it difficult to translate this knowledge and understanding into an effective performance at MEW: he was much more confident in the exercise of his judgement in the Intelligence sphere. It is not surprising, therefore, that we can detect his influence – and, possibly, ambition – in the fortunes of British Intelligence, and particularly of SIS, during the first winter of the war.

Two episodes serve to illustrate this. The first concerns the debate over who should succeed Sinclair as Chief of SIS. On the outbreak of war Sinclair was already ill with cancer, and his condition deteriorated rapidly during September and October 1939. Cadogan noted in his diary on 30 October that 'poor C' had been operated on the day before: 'I'm afraid it's hopeless, though he may go on for some time';[40] he died on 4 November. Cadogan noted on 5 November that Menzies had brought him a 'sealed letter from 'C' recommending him (M) as successor', but clearly did not regard the question of who should be the next Chief of SIS as a foregone conclusion. Cadogan himself was 'not satisfied that Menzies is the man', and reported in his diary a series of discussions on the issue during the days following Sinclair's death, with Hankey, Horace Wilson and Halifax among others; he describes a struggle between Halifax (who wanted Menzies) and Churchill, who had a candidate of his own to put forward, until at a meeting held by the Prime Minister on 28 November 'H[alifax] played his hand well & won the trick.' Menzies was informed of his appointment on the following day.[41]

Cadogan is circumspect in his diary on the matter of possible alternative candidates, and similar reticence on the part of others involved, combined with a lack of official documentation, means that the question of who else might have been in the running to succeed Sinclair remains somewhat mysterious.[42] Two names that have been mentioned are those of the DNI, Admiral Godfrey, and the head of SIS's Z organisation, Claude Dansey. Godfrey's biographer, however, casts reasonable doubt on the idea of his candidature, as does David Stafford's account of Churchill's exasperation with Godfrey, leading him to prefer a former naval attaché in Berlin, Captain Gerald Muirhead-Gould.[43] As for Dansey, the confident account by his biographers is more convincing of his ambition than of the fact that he was a credible candidate.[44] Though a successful and even brilliant Intelligence officer, he was an unpopular figure within SIS: one officer who worked with him described him as a trouble-maker, dishonest, and 'a man of irrational dislikes', whom Sinclair had decreed should never be given a job at Head Office. Nevertheless, the fact that Dansey travelled to London from Section Z's Zurich headquarters immediately after Sinclair's death would seem to indicate an interest in the job.[45] According to one account, however, he returned to Zurich and informed a colleague that it was 'Definitely not the job for me, my boy. Nothing but poodle-faking to the Prime Minister.' There is, in fact, no conclusive evidence that either Godfrey or Dansey was considered seriously: though the latter, despite the late Admiral's strictures, was to return to London as Menzies' Deputy in 1940.

Evidence of Morton's interest in the succession to the post of 'C' is equally unsatisfactory. He left no record of his reaction to Sinclair's death, but they had had a long association and their ties had remained close in professional, if not personal terms. He would certainly have had a view on the succession question, knowing all the supposed potential candidates well, though regrettably no record of this view has been found. A more intriguing question is whether he considered himself as a potential successor to Sinclair. In the light of his background and character, it is hard to imagine that he did not, particularly given his dissatisfaction with MEW even at that stage. All his training and long Intelligence career, and past evidence of his ambition when serving in SIS, point in that direction: his position as Director of Intelligence in MEW, and his perceived closeness to Churchill and to the Intelligence establishment, must have put him in the frame; indeed, it was thought in SIS that Dansey's remarks about 'poodle-faking' referred to Morton, whom he considered too deferential to Ministerial command.

The question of whether Morton's name might have received serious consideration is more difficult. A senior Whitehall figure, familiar with SIS yet conversant with the wider Intelligence context, ambitious, able, with plenty of ideas on how things should be done: all these factors could be adduced in support of his candidature. They could also weigh against it: Morton had made himself fairly unpopular in some senior military and political circles. Of those involved, Hankey was most familiar with Morton: Halifax, Cadogan and Horace Wilson would certainly have known him, but not perhaps well enough to consider him seriously. Relations with the FO generally – an important part of the power base for any future 'C' – were professional but not cordial; and Morton certainly lacked Menzies' impressive social connections. Churchill might have supported his old friend and ally, but there is no evidence that he did so. It is possible that even at this stage Churchill preferred Morton as a more mobile conduit to the Intelligence community, rather than tied to a single agency. Surviving evidence of Morton's potential candidature is tantalising and insubstantial: but sufficient to make it impossible to ignore.

Whatever may have gone on behind the Whitehall scenes, Menzies, who had long been groomed for authority by his late Chief, acting as his deputy for some years, won the day. He and Morton were almost exact contemporaries, and their careers had followed similar paths since schooldays. Though quite different in style and character, their shared military background and professional training, including a deeply-ingrained habit of secrecy, was a bond, and their correspondence during the winter of 1939–40 indicates a close, professional and confidential, if not warm, relationship. It is possible to discern other common traits too, including ambition and pride in their position and influence; after Morton's move to 10 Downing Street, an underlying element of rivalry grew more marked. Meanwhile, however, whether or not Morton had aspired to be Chief of SIS, he remained an important figure in Whitehall with a good deal of influence in Intelligence matters, and enjoying a much closer relationship with Churchill – a central figure in the War Cabinet – than did Menzies. The extent to which he made use of this position is illustrated by his involvement with the investigation into the Secret Services conducted by Hankey.

Morton's contribution to the Hankey review was not limited to his role as Director of MEW, although it was in that capacity that he gave formal evidence. He and Hankey had a long association dating back to the early days of industrial intelligence, when Hankey had been instrumental in the choice of Morton to set up the IIC. As Minister without Portfolio, Hankey retained the watching brief on Intelligence matters that he had held since the First World War as a member of the Prime Minister's Secret Service Committee. He was a natural choice to conduct the investigation, which was restricted initially to foreign intelligence, including both SIS and GC&CS, then extended to home security (MI5) as well.[46] His report on SIS listed Morton as one of the people who had collaborated closely in its preparation, and it seems that he consulted Morton on the review as a whole.[47] This process was to prove an important preparation for the role Morton assumed in May 1940.

The decision in December 1939 to launch, during wartime, an investigation into the Secret Services indicates the depth of dissatisfaction felt within the War Cabinet at the performance of the agencies during the first few months of the conflict. Menzies, as the new SIS Chief, found himself faced with complaints from the Service Ministries at the quality and quantity of intelligence received, and with general disquiet at the activities of Section D. The humiliating incident at Venlo in November 1939, when two British agents were arrested after being lured to a small Dutch town near the German border to meet alleged German conspirators willing to discuss peace terms, damaged the reputation of both SIS and its new Chief badly.[48] As far as MI5 was concerned, dissatisfaction was rooted in the perception that its head, Kell, who had held the post since 1909, was not up to the job of a wartime Director: it was already clear that the heavy responsibilities of both domestic and Imperial security (including the threat of Fifth Column activities), were straining the organisation to breaking point.[49] The only part of the Intelligence establishment given a completely clean bill of health was GC&CS, whose cryptographic activities were so secret that Hankey thought it 'inadvisable to put anything at all on paper about its present work', recommending that 'the utmost care should be exercised by all those who have knowledge of the existence of this work, not even to mention it except in conditions where secrecy is certain to be inviolable'.[50]

The recommendations set out in Hankey's report on SIS, sent to the Prime Minister on 11 March 1940, make it clear that the problems identified were not new: poorly-targeted intelligence with inadequate technical detail, failure in communication and coordination, misunderstandings as to the degree of interpretation required, distribution difficulties. The report reflected in particular the unease felt by the War Cabinet at the activities of Section D: Hankey prefaced his remarks in this section by the statement that 'At first sight the natural instinct of any humane person is to recoil from this undesirable business as something he would rather know nothing about.'[51] His recommendations in this area were confined to the need for better liaison with the other authorities involved, such as the DMI and Sir Campbell Stuart's propaganda organisation,[52] and betray

Hankey's self-confessed failure to get to the bottom of what was going on. As far as Section D was concerned, the Hankey review did nothing to ameliorate the general suspicion of its activities, and contributed to the centrifugal momentum that was already carrying Grand's operation to the edge of SIS and towards what would become SOE.[53]

As far as SIS as an organisation was concerned, however, the report was generally encouraging. Hankey pointed out that many of his recommendations had already been implemented or set in train by the new Chief, including the reorganisation of SIS HQ and the decentralisation of control to allow for more efficient management of the 'War Station' (Bletchley Park, where GC&CS and a number of SIS sections had moved before the outbreak the war).[54] Hankey's conclusions came as a relief to Menzies, who had displayed some alarm at the prospect that all the work done over the past two years to fit SIS for war might be undone as a result of the Review. As he wrote to Jebb on 14 February 1940:

> The machine can be destroyed by a stroke of the pen, lessons can be forgotten overnight, but I can personally conceive no greater catastrophe from a national point of view. It might be well said of us in that case, as was said of other purblind citizens years ago – 'Virtutem videant intabescantque relicta'.[55]

Hankey did not recommend the 'abandonment' or amalgamation of SIS, nor did he contest Menzies' arguments in response to Service complaints of inadequate detailed Intelligence on such subjects as the movement of enemy ships, details of the output of German factories or the numbers of aircraft at German aerodromes:

> S[ecret] S[ervice] point out that a certain amount of information of a detailed character is already supplied but that it takes years to develop regular and dependable sources for the above classes of intelligence. The funds available before the war were not sufficient for this and it is extremely difficult to build up the necessary contacts in time of war. It must be recognised also that a long time is required before the machine can be built up afresh in Poland and Czecho-Slovakia and even in Holland, where the Venloo [sic] incident has badly dislocated the organisation. Similarly, a fresh machine for Finland could not be provided at a moment's notice.[56]

Hankey was sympathetic to these arguments and to their financial implications. He did not question the proposed increase of the Secret Service vote by Supplementary Estimate to £1,100,000 for 1939–40, noting that 'special schemes' were 'often very expensive', and expressed himself as confident that Menzies would exercise close control of SIS expenditure. The report concluded with a tribute to the 'healthy spirit of loyalty, *esprit de corps* and devotion to duty which animates all ranks of SS'.

In his formal evidence to Hankey, given on 17 January 1940, Morton stuck closely to his brief as MEW's Director of Intelligence. His criticisms of SIS were expressed carefully in the context of his current role, and betrayed little of his detailed understanding of how SIS actually worked. The result is typically disingenuous, scattered with references to 'improvements' intended to serve his own purposes. Thus, for example, in analysing what was wrong with SIS Intelligence:

> Mr Morton found it difficult to say why exactly the system was not working well, but he thought that it was largely because 'C''s representatives abroad did not know precisely what sort of information was required. The SIS had, he thought, essentially a military character, with a 'strong political adjunct' in the shape of the Economic Section, which ... was not perhaps very strong and ought to be reinforced. But the real question was how to graft the secret economic work on to the official wartime governmental machine. In other words, the problem was largely one of <u>liaison</u>, and he must admit that there had lately been signs of improvement in this direction.[57]

Morton even suggested that it might be 'desirable to resuscitate the old FCI Committee of the CID to enable the economic factor to be duly assessed in its relation to strategical and political questions'. This proposal was unlikely to be considered seriously in the context of the already complex wartime committee structure, but it is indicative of the extent to which Morton looked back longingly to a forum in which his voice had carried powerful weight. He also seems to have had his eye on Section VI of SIS: referring to MI10, a branch of the War Office set up 'owing to its dissatisfaction with the information supplied by the MEW', he expressed the view that 'when the MEW had succeeded in getting its branch of the SIS organised properly', the branch might disappear. Morton clearly hoped Hankey's recommendations for SIS would strengthen his influence over at least part of that organisation, with which he regarded himself as having an intimate connection.

The main thrust of Morton's evidence, however, was directed towards the areas in which SIS was most closely involved with MEW, as a source of intelligence, and as a potential vehicle for the implementation of offensive economic warfare. Though not uncritical of the organisation on a professional level, he relied heavily on what SIS could provide, and kept up a constant stream of correspondence with Sinclair, Menzies and Section VI in particular between September 1939 and May 1940. In his evidence to Hankey, Morton categorised what MEW received from SIS as '(1) SIS intelligence, strictly speaking, (2) commercial intercepts, (3) Facilities for conducting economic warfare of a subterranean nature ('D''s organisation), (4) Telephone intercepts.'[58] Typically, he was not content to assume the role of customer, but had views on the design of the product as well.

Morton was most critical of category (1), what he called SIS Intelligence 'proper', which in the broader sense of intelligence received from overseas was of central importance to MEW. CX reports and intelligence summaries compiled at SIS HQ provided Intelligence Division with valuable and detailed information on German industry, troop movements or transport arrangements; on Nazi activities in neutral countries that might affect economic relations; on the situation in the Balkans or the Baltic; on the effectiveness of the contraband control system and the principal points of 'leakage'; and on the effect that the economic measures implemented by the British Government were having both on Germany and on neutral countries. Section VI prepared a monthly report on economic warfare that was valued by the FO as well as the MEW for its intelligence on the direct consequences of the war for the economic position of the enemy.[59]

As an experienced SIS customer – he had, after all, written such reports as well as receiving them at the IIC throughout the 1930s – Morton was both discriminating and demanding. Quick to complain if he considered the intelligence received to be substandard, he encouraged MEW staff to make detailed criticisms of SIS reports. While this might prove irritating to the circulating Section in question, his opinion was, nevertheless, valued at a time when SIS was anxious to improve its profile and image in Whitehall. An exchange of correspondence in January 1940 gives the flavour of this. Menzies had asked Morton over lunch for his opinion on the reports received by MEW from SIS sources, and for suggestions as to what else he would like to see. In a letter of 18 January 1940 Morton reported that he had reviewed all SIS reports received by MEW and comments on them for a specific period, and now conceded that MEW was in fact receiving 'rather more material than I supposed to be the case', though he also considered the criticisms of it 'too favourable'; 'I cannot get people here to be nasty and crude about things as we used to be in IIC.' He then set out other intelligence that MEW wanted 'very badly', such as hard evidence that Consular officers could use to prosecute companies trading with the enemy, the 'bribery of a statistical officer in the Headquarters of the Customs of each of the countries surrounding Germany', and more information on frontier traffic, 'particularly across the Danish and Italian frontiers'.

Morton's letter was passed to Section VI, whose head, in a minute of 21 January 1940, was inclined to disagree that MEW comments were too lenient: 'I can assure you that we have had some very rude criticisms'; he also considered that Morton's letter showed him to be 'still not cognisant of all the material that we have sent'. Consular officers were, the Section head insisted, kept fully informed by SIS representatives. He accepted, however, the desirability of further statistical and frontier information, and had 'no real complaint' at Morton's letter:

> it is respectfully suggested that he be thanked for it and for the suggestions and comment therein and given the assurance that every effort will be made to make good the deficiencies to which he calls our attention.

Whether this conclusion was offered to Menzies humbly or between gritted teeth is not revealed; it does, however, give some indication of SIS anxiety that its intelligence should be both relevant and valued.

The second of Morton's 'categories' of intelligence – and the one to which he attached the highest importance – was commercial intercepts. These were passed to MEW through SIS, but were issued by GC&CS's Commercial Section, established in 1938, which scanned and selected from foreign traffic, mainly in plain language or commercial codes, and whose prime customer was the IIC.[60] In wartime the Intelligence Division of MEW received commercial intercepts not just on Germany's economic position, but on Italy, Japan and the Soviet Union; as the war progressed, the interception of neutral traffic with countries suspected of trading with Germany, such as Spain and Portugal, acquired increasing significance. Morton told Hankey that '60% of the evidence required for seizures of cargoes was derived from the C[ommercial] S[ection] series'.[61]

Intercepted messages between Berlin and Moscow were, Morton wrote to Menzies on 30 November 1939:

> of the utmost importance, since they disclose for the first time what is really going on between Russia and Germany in the way of trade and the supply to the latter of vital foodstuffs and raw materials. You will see that at present there is little doubt that the Russo-German Trade Agreement has hitherto proved an almost complete frost in practice.

The commercial traffic could also provide intelligence on German industrial production: an intercepted telegram of 14 October 1939, regarding shipments of Saar coal and coke to Italy, was used by Intelligence Division to prepare a report (shared with the French Government's economic mission in London) on the effect of military operations in the Saar on German industrial production.[62] Diplomatic traffic supplemented the commercial sources: on 8 December 1939 Morton and Hall were informed of the contents of a telegram from the Japanese Foreign Minister to his Ambassador in Berlin, stating that the Germans should be told 'not to torpedo Japanese ships'; they were also to be reminded that:

> Japan is already helping Germany by exporting goods via the Trans-Siberian Railway, and that Germany has only to get Russia to allow shipments to be made in her name for Tin, Rubber and Wolfram from the Far East to be sent to Russia for re-export to Germany. The Ambassador is particularly requested to put forward this as one of his own bright ideas.[63]

Commercial intercepts, supplemented by diplomatic traffic where relevant, were an important source for all Intelligence Division's major reports. Similarly, Category (4), in the form of telephone intercepts provided by SIS, was of value in providing information concerning enemy or neutral economic arrangements, or relating specifically to commercial activities that contravened Trading with the Enemy regulations. To supplement MEW's coverage, Morton wrote to Menzies on 5 December 1939 asking that he might receive copies of MI5's telephone intercepts under the same conditions as those from SIS.

Morton's remarks to Hankey on the subject of his third category, 'facilities for conducting economic warfare of a subterranean nature', were brief and bland:

> D did not of course provide information, but elaborated plans which were put into effect by agreement with the Ministry, the Service Departments and the Foreign Office. This system . . . worked well and he had no complaints to make, though the dynamic personality of Major Grand was in some respects a difficulty.[64]

His economy of expression in referring to Section D extends, unfortunately for the historian, into the files of both MEW and SIS. It is extremely difficult to find any traces of Morton at this period in the context of 'subterranean' economic warfare, although we know that he continued to press for both overt (military) and covert (sabotage) action. The story of Section D's activities during the winter of 1939–40 has been told in some detail in SOE's official history.[65] They were concentrated on the targets Morton had long advocated, Scandinavia and the Danube, together with a certain amount of propaganda activity and attempts to establish connections with potentially subversive groups in Germany and occupied territories. But few of their plans came to fruition, and some enterprises caused a great deal of trouble to little effect; the ensuing impression was, as Mackenzie put it, 'one of great energy spread thinly over an immense field', though he points out, justly, that it was almost impossible for Section D (like MEW) to produce 'visible results' at this stage of the war.[66] Morton's own involvement in D's abortive schemes remains largely undocumented, and it is difficult to say more than that he undoubtedly was well-informed about, if not actively involved in Section D's plans and projects, most of which were directly linked to MEW objectives. In keeping with both official convention and personal habit, however, he rarely referred to them directly.[67]

As so often, it is necessary to approach Morton's connection with Section D obliquely: in this case, through his close interest during this period in the Industrial Secret Intelligence (ISI) organisation run by Stephenson.[68] The plan agreed at the beginning of September 1939 for the ISI network to pass information to London through SIS channels was implemented initially in Sweden, a country in which Stephenson, Morton and SIS shared a keen interest. Stephenson, whose business concerns gave him a strong interest in Sweden's iron ore industry, travelled there regularly during the 1930s: he may well have been supplying Morton and the IIC with information on the value of iron ore imports to the German war effort, and had contact with members of Section D before the formal ISI/SIS arrangement was set up.[69] MEW's Intelligence Division was, of course, very anxious to receive information on Swedish trade. Morton already had some important contacts, such as the Wallenberg brothers[70] and the prominent industrialist Axel Johnsson, and was keen to open up more channels. From an SIS viewpoint, Sweden's importance was not confined to the iron ore trade: Stockholm was a focus of espionage activity in the Baltic area with many German, Polish and Soviet agents based there.[71]

The setting up of a working arrangement in Sweden between SIS and ISI in September 1939 proved problematic. Disagreements over money – SIS insisted on 'complete control of agents and all financial matters' – meant that it took some time for final arrangements to be negotiated, and both Morton and Glyn, who had promoted ISI's value to SIS,[72] became impatient. On 11 September 1939 Glyn presented the following note to SIS entitled 'MEW and ISI', drafted by Morton and intended to clarify the situation:

Intelligence Division of MEW have repeatedly stated that the ISI service is of the highest value if the peace-time standard can be retained. They recognise its special 'make-up'. ISI must, in the nature of things, be considered Secret Service and, therefore, under the War Organisation must look to the S[ecret] S[ervice] for necessary facilities for communication, priority of messages, freedom from censorship etc. This must involve some control by the SS. The value of ISI is to remain what it is and not to be absorbed into any Department. Its non-official characteristics are essential for its success. This indicates that its centre and clearing house must remain under WSS [Stephenson].

Liaison with MEW will be maintained by R[alph] G[lyn]. All commercial and industrial intelligence, either received or required will be dealt with under Morton's direction in the Intelligence Division of MEW and distribution of reports will be arranged by him. Political and general Reports received at ISI Centre will be collected by SS and dealt with by them through their own distribution system. Any special information required by SS will be passed by them direct to WSS who will deal with it in the most appropriate way. This side of the work is outside the scope of MEW, though Morton would desire to see such 'political' reports as may be thought to have bearings on the field of work covered by MEW. The machinery to enable ISI to function with the greatest efficiency must be outlined by WSS and it is for the SS to make the proper arrangements. Members of the War Cabinet who know from Morton what is his opinion as to the value of ISI have all stated that the service should be made available. This can only be done by the prompt good will of the SS. On no account should ISI be absorbed into the SS organisation, for the reasons given. Much valuable time has already been wasted and time presses, and there are today lying idle the means of obtaining news of first-rate importance. If the delay is allowed to continue existing personnel will drift away and the organisation must suffer.

Morton followed up this document with a letter to Menzies, who complained that Stephenson had 'ludicrous ideas on finance and I have – even in war time – to consider the unfortunate taxpayer'. In the event, Stephenson agreed to proceed initially on a voluntary basis, and on 29 September left for Stockholm to establish the link between his own agent there and a 'reliable Englishman' nominated by the local SIS representative to act as intermediary (and who turned out to have been a paid informant of Stephenson's for some time).

ISI's activities in Stockholm, carried on under the label of the International Mining Trust Ltd (IMT), produced a modest amount of intelligence, but sufficient for SIS to agree to pay IMT a subsidy of £100 per month from March 1940. Section VI, like Morton, found its information particularly useful, noting on 24 March 1940 that 'we cannot afford to lose any source of information on USSR'. Stephenson's agent, however, proved both capricious and unreliable (MI5 had him down on a list of Nazi sympathisers in Sweden), and had to be bailed out by Marcus Wallenberg after being arrested by the Swedish authorities at the beginning of May. Thereafter the value of the operation diminished, particularly after Stephenson went to the United States as 'C''s personal representative;[73] by that time Morton, too, had wider interests to pursue.

Both ISI and Section D communicated with London through the SIS station in Stockholm – but Menzies, echoing Morton and Glyn, was insistent that ISI should remain separate from, even if run and financed by, SIS. Nevertheless, Stephenson's activities looked suspiciously similar to what Section D was up to, although a note by Section I of 23 September 1939 had warned that 'We must make it clear to Stephenson that we are primarily and exclusively an information service and cannot actively participate in any schemes for economic warfare that he may put up, though we should be ready to give him introduction to the proper quarters.' There seems little doubt that he already had access to the 'proper quarters'; he appears, for example, to have been involved in Rickman's schemes, and with plans for an attack on Oxelösund, one of the main ports for the export of iron ore (Operation 'Lumps'), although his role was almost certainly less prominent than he (or his biographers) later claimed.[74]

From Menzies' point of view, it was by no means clear that the modest value of ISI's intelligence outweighed the potential problems with the FO that might be caused by yet another set of 'secret' agents operating within Sweden. The British Minister in Stockholm, Sir Victor Mallet, addressed a series of complaints to SIS through Jebb throughout the winter of 1939–40 concerning the 'embarrassments' caused to the Legation by the use of diplomatic or consular cover for intelligence activities: the arrest of Rickman on 20 April 1940 brought matters to a head:

> I do not want you to think that I am blind to the fact that it may sometimes be necessary to employ methods of this kind when we are waging a war against an enemy who hits persistently below the belt. But my complaints are, firstly, that our sleuths seem to be to be thoroughly bad at their job: so far they have achieved little in Sweden beyond

putting me and themselves in an awkward position. Secondly, I am inclined to doubt whether the game is worth the candle in a country where not only are the police and the military very much on the alert and counter-espionage highly developed, but where a policy of mutual confidence has shown itself repeatedly to be the one which pays best.[75]

No record has been found of Mallet's reaction to the arrest of Stephenson's agent two weeks later, though the latter's speedy release on the personal intervention of Marcus Wallenberg and the Swedish Foreign Minister, in contrast to Rickman's eight year prison sentence, would seem to indicate that ISI was more sure-footed than Section D in its Scandinavian dealings. At least Stephenson's agent was not operating under British diplomatic cover, though it appears that his role, and that of the 'International Mining Trust', was as irritating to the SIS representative in Stockholm as Rickman's was to Mallet. In response to a request from SIS HQ in June 1940 as to whether the information provided by IMT merited continued funding, the head of Station responded that he was unable to answer the question without knowing more about what was going on:

> I have no idea who IMT is or where he, she or it lives. To deal with this matter properly it would appear that I must get into closer touch with him, her or it . . . I should be glad to receive your assistance, therefore, as to whether in your view it is desirable for me to have closer contact with IMT or whether to continue to treat the concern rather as a disembodied spirit.

It is hard not to have some sympathy with this rather irritable response: even Peter Tennant, who as Press Attaché at the British Legation observed matters at first hand, confessed that 'the whole affair had bewildered me with names of organisations and people of whom I had never heard'.[76] How much Morton knew is unclear: as ever, he was adept at covering his tracks or, more accurately, in leaving none in the first place.

In public, Morton was content to concur with the official line that Section D, and in particular its 'dynamic' head, Grand, were unpredictable and worrying. In private, D's schemes for 'subterranean' activities seemed to offer the only opportunity for any form of active economic warfare to be prosecuted. The War Cabinet and Chiefs of Staff continued to discuss the possibilities of action in Romania, on the Rhine and most particularly in Norway, but it was not until April 1940 that they came to any point of decision.[77] French vacillation, as well as military considerations, bore a considerable part of the blame for this. But by the time naval forces were despatched to Norway, Germany had itself invaded Norway and Denmark and the whole enterprise seemed increasingly irrelevant; it was not even found possible to cut off the iron ore supplies, a move that Morton, and indeed Churchill, had advocated since 1938. The Norwegian campaign did, indeed, have far-reaching consequences as 'a medium-grade military catastrophe and a major political catalyst at home'.[78] In economic warfare terms, however, it was too little, too late.

This account of Morton's activities during the Phoney War has so far made very little reference to his relationship with Churchill. There is scant documentary evidence of their contacts during this period, but sufficient to indicate that the two men were in touch regularly. Churchill continued to value Morton's facts and figures about German rearmament: on 14 January 1940, for example, recommending to Admirals Pound and Phillips an analysis of the U Boat position as 'a very interesting paper from Major Morton, whose knowledge I believe to be very accurate.'[79] He also urged his military and Cabinet colleagues to pay greater attention to the work done by Morton and MEW on assessing the military capacity of enemy, or potentially enemy countries. Churchill's insistence on the importance of such work underlay his suggestion to Ismay[80] in April 1940 that Morton, together with Oliver Lyttelton and Frederick Lindemann,[81] should be taken on as a kind of central liaison staff to provide information to the War Cabinet, a proposal that foreshadowed the arrangements Churchill, as Prime Minister was to put in place two weeks later.[82]

The first week of May 1940, however, changed the futures of both Churchill and Morton for good. Both men, by this point in the war, had reached in their own fashion a point of near-desperation at the limitations of their respective roles. Each chafed against the constraints of his position and yearned for greater freedom to act, while at the same time apprehensive at the prospect of greater power and responsibility.[83] Although as First Lord Churchill played an important role in the War Cabinet, and was given increasingly heavy responsibilities by Chamberlain in relation to defence, the reins of power remained firmly in the Prime Minister's hands, though both Parliamentary and public opinion was turning against him. Morton, confined within MEW, shared Churchill's frustrations at the Cabinet's failure to take action in Scandinavia and elsewhere, as well as a growing alarm at the defeatist attitude of the French (gleaned in Morton's case from his dealings with their Economic Blockade authorities), and at increasingly strong intelligence of an imminent aggressive move by Hitler against the Low Countries and France. No evidence survives of exchanges between Churchill and Morton during the political and military crisis that led on 10 May to Chamberlain's resignation and Churchill's appointment as Prime Minister and as Minister of Defence,[84] nor during the ensuing somewhat confused period of Administration-building. Nevertheless it is clear that Churchill intended from the outset to keep Morton by him in his new role, and to draw on both his knowledge and experience, particularly in Intelligence matters. Even as the War Cabinet met at 4.30 pm on 10 May – the meeting at which Chamberlain announced his intention to resign – Morton was noting that he had, on Churchill's instructions, given a message to the Chiefs of Staff and Ismay concerning bringing battalions from abroad to the UK, and the internment of aliens.[85]

Churchill was summoned to Buckingham Palace on the evening of 10 May, and returned to the Admiralty to begin forming his Government. Whatever his apprehensions at the enormity of the task in front of him, he was both delighted and relieved at his new appointment. 'At last', he wrote in his memoirs, 'I had the authority to give directions over the whole scene. I felt as if I were walking with destiny, and that all my past life had been but a preparation for this hour and for this trial.'[86] He arrived in Downing Street, as Colville later wrote, 'like a jet-propelled rocket', ready to reorganise not only the Government but the whole of his official machinery, setting up a Private Office (an expression 'foreign to 10 Downing Street') that comprised not only Private Secretaries but 'alarming unknown quantities' in the form of Bracken, Morton and Lindemann, his tried and trusted peacetime advisers.[87] Morton, translated rapidly from MEW to Downing Street, doubtless shared Churchill's delight and relief – but he was also triumphant, as the following letter to Menzies dated 15 May 1940 makes clear:

Secret

My dear C,

This is to let you know that the Prime Minister has done me the honour of appointing me to his personal staff to keep personal liaison with certain civil departments, including yours. This will in no way cut across any existing arrangements, but I should be so glad if you could from now on send to me by name copies of any reports of yours which you think are of sufficient importance of which you think I ought to be informed.

For the time being I am keeping my office at MEW and moving to the Prime Minister's office as soon as he takes over No. 10, Downing Street, a matter which will depend on events. Meanwhile, my address for communications of the kind I refer to is simply; Major Morton, (Personal), c/o Ministry of Economic Warfare as hitherto.

Naturally it is intended that I should be at your service at any time should you wish to speak about any matter which you would like considered rapidly in the highest quarters.

I am also directed to keep in close touch with Lord Hankey, especially in regard to the activities in which Mr D plays a part. Would you therefore please let Mr D know whatever you see fit and instruct him accordingly.

Yours ever,
Desmond

Two days later Morton moved into his office in Downing Street. For him, as for the new Prime Minister, the Phoney War was over in more senses than one.

11

THE MORTON MYTH

Downing Street, May 1940–July 1945

Of all the periods in Morton's highly secretive life, his time in Downing Street poses the greatest difficulties to the biographer. This seems perverse: it was a time when he was at his most 'visible' both in Whitehall and internationally, installed at the heart of government as Churchill's confidential adviser with special responsibility for liaison with the Intelligence community and with Allied governments in exile, and consulted by the Prime Minister on a wide range of issues. Diligent and tireless in committee work, ubiquitous in the incestuous social life of Europe's London-based exiles and overseas visitors, thorn in the flesh of the Chiefs of Staff, the Foreign Office's bad fairy – his name can be found more frequently in official documentation between May 1940 and July1945 than at any other period of his life. Yet in many ways he is at his most elusive during the war years, and the massive and still expanding bibliography of the period serves only to obscure his role further.

The reasons for this are complex. Firstly, Morton had no official position other than as a member of the Prime Minister's personal staff. Unlike the other 'extra-mural myrmidons'[1] whom Churchill gathered to him in 10 Downing Street in May 1940 and later, Morton did not move into any substantive job: Brendan Bracken, already acting as Churchill's PPS, became Minister of Information in July 1941; 'Prof' Lindemann, as Churchill's scientific and economic adviser, had an official title as head of the 'Prime Minister's Statistical Department'.[2] Other senior figures trusted by Churchill, such as Beaverbrook, Swinton and Lyttelton, were given specific Ministerial or official tasks. By contrast, Morton's role as Churchill's personal adviser on Intelligence and Allied liaison was never formalised and came to be duplicated and to some extent supplanted by more authoritative competitors. This did not in itself diminish his activity nor negate his usefulness: but no amount of redefinition of his duties (a favourite pastime at all stages of his career) could make them official, in either civil, military or administrative terms. The consequent lack of status has affected both the perception and the documentation of his role.

Secondly, the absence of any memoir or personal letter by Morton is a particular disadvantage during the war years. Even the busiest and most reticent officials, Ministers and military men could be drawn to keep some note of their experiences during the fast-moving, troubling and difficult wartime period, or to write them down afterwards, imparting a valuable impression of what it was like to be in a position of responsibility, to work with Churchill, to face adversity, triumph and day to day problems. Whether it be Dalton or Eden, Ismay or Brooke, Hankey or Cadogan, Moran or Colville (to name only a few), they give some idea of what it felt like to be in senior positions of responsibility during a world war, and of the impact on their personal and family lives. We have almost no idea what Morton's life was like, what he thought of his job or his colleagues, what his reaction was to ongoing events: the only substantial source of reference to his experiences, the series of letters to R.W. Thompson written twenty and more years later, were too retrospective, and too (deliberately) fit for purpose to have any real value as a wartime testament; and in any case they were about Churchill, not himself. They reveal nothing of Morton's personal wartime existence – where he spent his leisure time and with whom, how he, friends or relations were affected by the conflict; only a few details can be gleaned from family recollection and chance references in the official record.

A third difficulty is that Morton's anomalous and amorphous position was largely deliberate, both on the part of Churchill and of Morton himself. Morton's value to Churchill lay to a large extent in his lack of military, departmental or Ministerial affiliation: his career, contacts and experience gave him the ability to approach, at any level, any branch of the Services or government department, and to enter their most secret recesses; with the authority of the Prime Minister behind him, he could pass on directives, make suggestions, demands and criticisms freely without consideration for upsetting superior officers or subverting the chain of command – he answered to Churchill alone. Similarly, in his liaison duties with governments in exile, he acted in parallel with and often independently of established channels of communication. While this could cause intense annoyance to those – like Eden[3] – who bore formal responsibility for relations with these often awkward Allies, it also enabled Morton to do what he did best. Getting things done, upsetting complacency and cutting through red tape was a feature of Churchill's premiership style: he did not care what eggs were broken if the resulting omelette helped to win the war; and Morton was an organisational egg-scrambler of long pedigree.[4]

At the root of the problem, however, is the power of the Morton myth, planted in the fog of war, nourished by Morton himself, and cultivated in retrospect by the reminiscences of contemporary observers and wartime historiography. Even those who see him as a marginal (and marginalised) figure, with an exaggerated sense of his own importance, have been wary of dismissing him altogether; there is a sense that he is too mysterious a figure to be underestimated. He gave – or created – the impression of omnipresence; the late Sir William Deakin remembered him as 'sitting quietly in the corner' at every important meeting,[5] a recollection that is as powerful as it is impossible to substantiate or disprove. He had no hesitation in invoking superior authority to open any official door that might be closed against him. His position at No 10 afforded him access not just to Churchill but also, in consequence, to the War Cabinet, to the Chiefs of Staff, to government departments such as MEW and the FO, to the JIC and to the individual Agencies. As a result, each of these constituencies and many more suspected him of knowing and doing far more than he knew or did. This was the foundation of the Morton myth.

It is a myth that has been augmented, rather than diminished, as the wartime period grows more distant and memories fade. The essential secrecy of the Intelligence world has lent added credence to stories of Morton's influence in that arena, creating an air of mystery that spilled over into other areas. This secrecy, combined with his apparent ubiquity and a somewhat abrasive style, provoked a number of his wartime colleagues and contacts to blame him for scuppering their various schemes, by design or what they saw as blundering. Spears's description of him as 'the fifth wheel on any coach'[6] would have been endorsed heartily by many that Morton did business with, such as Oliver Harvey, Eden's Private Secretary, who thought Morton had 'enthusiasm without wisdom' and could not 'keep his mouth shut'.[7] Others more intimately involved with Churchill's affairs, such as Colville, had a better informed understanding of his activities even if they tended to be dismissive of his power and influence.[8]

What then, did Morton do, or not do, during the war? Thirty years ago, Stephen Roskill wrote in his biography of Hankey – another 'Man of Secrets' – that since the bibliography of the Second World War was already so vast he intended to confine himself to the main subjects on which Hankey was consulted, or pursued on his own initiative.[9] Even such a constrained approach to Morton's wartime career is unsatisfactory. Neither his voluminous official correspondence, nor the records of the committees he attended, explain satisfactorily the assertions and assumptions about his activities that persist in the (now even vaster) wartime literature. An entire volume could be written on his wartime activities without getting to the heart of the Morton myth, and without altering in any material sense the conclusions already set out in many existing scholarly and authoritative accounts of the period. Faced with a whole forest's worth of documentation collected for this biography, a radical approach has been chosen: not to attempt to give any detailed account of what Morton did in the Second World War, save in one aspect, that of his Intelligence activities; and, further, to concentrate principally on SIS and its related bodies, for this purpose defined as the Government Code & Cypher School (GC&CS), the Special Operations Executive (SOE) and British Security Coordination (BSC).

This approach will, undeniably, leave out a good deal, but it has a dual justification. The first is archival in nature: most of Morton's wartime activities, such as his role as chairman of the Committee on Foreign (Allied) Resistance, as a member of the Security Executive or as Churchill's informal intermediary with the Free French and other Allied authorities, are amply documented in The National Archives and other collections open to public scrutiny, whereas the evidence of his Intelligence work is less obvious, less available and more complex of interpretation. The second justification is Morton himself: throughout his career, it is through the prism of the 'Intelligence man' that his character, career and achievements are revealed most clearly. The secret world offers the best opportunity to test the basis and validity of the Morton myth. This chapter will, therefore, give an illustrative and roughly chronological account of what Morton did during his service in Downing Street, indicating the range of his activities, his movements and the dynamics of his relationship with Churchill and other colleagues. The next chapter will examine, in greater detail, his liaison work with SIS and related bodies and his involvement in the organisational side of Intelligence.

When Churchill became Prime Minister and Minister of Defence in May 1940 he faced the challenge of re-inventing the British war effort, civil and military, with few friends and no allies, in the near certainty of French collapse and the possibility of an invasion of British soil. If this prospect were grim, it soon became blacker with the enforced withdrawal of the British Expeditionary Force from France, the disastrous end to the Norwegian campaign and Italy's entry into the war on Hitler's side. And while Britain stood alone against Hitler, Churchill's personal position was scarcely less isolated: a Prime Minister appointed in crisis, with some old and stalwart supporters but few political allies, initially the object of official distrust, bearing the weight of enormous public expectation.[10] Little wonder that in the early months of his premiership he relied heavily on those trusted friends and advisers he had brought with him to No. 10 – in particular, Bracken, Lindemann and Morton, the trio described by Hugh Dalton, the new Minister of Economic Warfare, as the 'Brains Trust';[11] while Colville, who had been working in Chamberlain's Private Office since October 1939, compared their arrival in Downing Street with that of the Horsemen of the Apocalypse.[12]

These men were a vital resource when what Churchill needed was a quick, flexible response to his urgent enquiries on everything from enemy aliens to air raid shelters, at a time when he had not yet assembled the kind of support network later provided by the War Cabinet machinery and by senior advisers such as Bridges, Ismay and Brooke.[13] He called on Bracken, Lindemann and Morton for information and action on whatever was uppermost in his mind at the time, bombarding them with minutes and scribbled notes, summoning them to his presence at all hours of the day or night and inviting them to dine with him or spend the weekend at Chequers.[14] It was a period of intense pressure and responsibility for the Prime Minister to which, as most accounts agree, he rose magnificently. Colville, whose diary had contained many disparaging remarks about Churchill since the outbreak of war, had changed his mind by 19 May 1940:

> whatever Winston's shortcomings, he seems to be the man for the occasion. His spirit is indomitable and even if France and England should be lost, I feel he would carry on the crusade himself with a band of privateers. Perhaps my judgements of him have been harsh, but the situation was very different a few weeks ago.[15]

For Morton and others close to the dynamic force that was Churchill, it was a heady period. There seems little doubt that Morton enjoyed it: indeed, in many ways it is likely that the second half of 1940 and first half of 1941 were the most fulfilling, even happiest months of his long professional life, despite the grimness of the international scene. He was at the centre of power and of events, inspired and needed by a leader he respected, with plenty of work to do and ample opportunity for employing his talents and exerting his influence. The situation also brought out the best in him socially, as Colville described:

> he endeared himself to all at No. 10. In the office 'mess' established by Brendan Bracken when the air raids began, Morton was the life and soul of the party. Only Bracken could out-talk him and, like Bracken, he provided a genial antidote to the gloomiest news and the noisiest bombs.[16]

This type of (male) camaraderie, born of hard work in a good cause, suited Morton's personality, just as his role as Churchill's Intelligence adviser suited him far better than that of Director of Intelligence in MEW. Both he and Churchill had, in a sense, found their niche.

During 1940 and 1941 Churchill kept Morton close by him and on call.[17] Although Morton's principal brief was Intelligence liaison, neither he nor Churchill regarded this as a disqualification for his getting involved in other areas, and Morton was quick to offer advice and suggestions on almost every aspect of the direction of the war.[18] Churchill was selective in his acceptance of such offers, though always liable to fire miscellaneous queries in Morton's direction. In particular, he used Morton as informal intermediary with de Gaulle and the Free French,[19] and later with the exiled governments of other occupied territories such as Poland, the Netherlands and Yugoslavia. There was an Intelligence dimension to this liaison work that made it a good fit with Morton's portfolio, but his remit was interpreted widely. Churchill used Morton as a multi-channel source of information – 'Thief and Policeman in one kitchen', to borrow an apt description from another context:[20] his eyes and ears in those quarters he did not have time to inspect personally; the personal embodiment of the Prime Minister's own will and determination to make things happen, a crude but effective method of driving forward progress while waiting for more formalised mechanisms to catch up. It was a role that suited Morton's temperament and talents far better than any more conventional appointment, as Churchill clearly recognised.

In personal terms, too, Churchill liked to have Morton around, as an old and familiar companion as well as an adviser, though never on terms as intimate as Lindemann or Bracken. A good illustration of their relationship is given in Colville's description of a trip to Chartwell in June 1941, when Churchill, 'ruminating deeply about the fate of Tobruk', inspected his goldfish, 'conversing the while with the Yellow Cat and with Desmond about his garden'.[21] Towards the end of 1941, however, a change can be detected both in their relationship and in Morton's position, which became less central, moving gradually towards the periphery of the circles of wartime power and influence, while the ties of personal association with Churchill also loosened. Their correspondence, a crude but indicative method of assessing the activity and importance of Morton's role, decreased considerably in frequency from late 1941 onwards, though never ceasing entirely. There was no rapid transition, nor any specific action or event that precipitated it: rather, it was the result of Churchill's growing confidence in his position, the development of the War Cabinet machinery and the course of the war itself.

A year into his premiership, Churchill had learned to rely on Cabinet colleagues, military advisers and senior officials, who themselves had grown in confidence, as well as on the expanding War Cabinet machinery, and had become more discriminating about targeting his demands and requests (though always liable to task the nearest person to hand). Of course the Prime Minister was, famously, resistant to counsel, as described by Colville:

> The list of Churchill's advisers is a short one, for he was little responsive to advice. However, when he did have confidence in a man, it was wholeheartedly given and seldom withdrawn. He was prepared to listen to colleagues or military chiefs or his friends. Sometimes what they said would lead him to modify his immediate thoughts and change his mind. Not even Ismay or Bridges or Brooke could prevail on him to alter course once a decision had been maturely considered and firmly made. His will was his own and in the last resort it was adamant. This did not mean he was impervious to argument, but because he was so strong, indeed sometimes so fierce, in his method of declaring his intention, it needed resolution and preferably wiliness to modify it. His official advisers were all resolute men and with experience they learned to be wily.[22]

Doubtless Churchill's official advisers would have said that resolution and wiliness were also required to circumvent and counteract the influence of personal advisers such as Morton. As they became more skilled at doing so, and the Prime Minister placed greater trust in them, he needed Morton less. Although always determined to follow his own instincts, Churchill naturally consulted Eden on foreign affairs, Ismay or Brooke on administrative and military questions and Menzies on Intelligence matters, rather than an old friend with good contacts but no official position. That lack of position was, in itself, noteworthy. As Colville later wrote, Morton's 'zeal was boundless, he took endless pains to serve . . . and the kindness of his nature was matched by deep religious faith and fervent patriotism'.[23] His diplomatic skills and political sense were, however, less reliable: this, combined with a tendency to antagonise his interlocutors, seems to have deprived him of the senior responsibilities that might have been anticipated. He was never considered – even by Churchill – as a serious contender for any of the appointments for which his knowledge and experience might seem to have fitted him. In the whirling centrifuge that was wartime government, he was bound to drift to the perimeter.

The course of the war must also be taken into account. By the end of 1941, Churchill's priorities had been altered by the Battle of the Atlantic, war in the Middle and Near East, and the need to consider Britain's new allies, the Soviet Union and United States of America.[24] Following the US entry into the war in December 1941 his relationship with Roosevelt, always important, became even more intense. After 1942, when the tide finally seemed to be turning in favour of the Allies, it was his relationship with Roosevelt and Stalin, discussions on the launching of a second front in Europe, and the fortunes of war in the Far East that dominated Churchill's attention. The affairs of the occupied powers, including the Free French, became a less urgent preoccupation and remained so, apart from brief periods, until the end of the war, a trend accelerated by Roosevelt's lack of regard for de Gaulle. Although Morton remained intensely active in those areas where he had, on Churchill's behalf, established some authority, he was rarely employed in matters relating to the 'Big Three'. Thus he stepped backwards, albeit inadvertently, to the edge of the beam cast by the spotlight that illuminated Churchill; and their relationship, both professional and personal, never regained the degree of intimacy and confidence that had existed in 1940–41.

That Morton was aware of what was happening can be inferred from a curious episode in October 1941, when he issued for the benefit of Churchill's secretariat an 'office notice' setting out his own duties and responsibilities; the kind of re-statement that he had initiated at other points in his career when feeling uncertain or undervalued. Apparently prompted by his not being included in the distribution of some paper, on 13 October he sent a draft to John Martin, Churchill's Principal Private Secretary, commenting that 'if there is still some misunderstanding in the Private Office about my duties for the Prime Minister I am not surprised!' He then set out a list of 'regular duties' with which he had been charged by the Prime Minister, 'apart from any special work he may require':

> These regular duties are concerned mainly with Foreign Office, MEW, M of I[nformation], Secret Services, Foreign Governments in this country, the Free French Movement, Select Committee of the House on National Expenditure. They may be summarised as
>
> a. To be Chairman of the War Cabinet Committee on Foreign (Allied) Resistance.
> b. To be Chairman of the War Cabinet Committee on Foreign (Allied) Resistance Committee (Syria).
> c. To maintain a personal liaison on behalf of the Prime Minister with Allied Governments in this country and with the Free French Movement.
> d. To represent the Prime Minister on the Security Executive (Lord Swinton).
> e. To advise the Prime Minister on demand or as necessary about the Secret Organisations of HMG (SIS, Security Service, SOE).

f. To advise the Prime Minister on demand or as necessary upon economic warfare matters.

g. At the request of Mr Bracken to maintain touch with the Political Warfare Executive and the Ministerial Committee controlling it.

h. To maintain touch on behalf of the Prime Minister with the Chairman of the Select Committee of the House of Commons on National Expenditure.[25]

This formidable catalogue does not conceal the fact that most of Morton's duties were 'on demand' rather than officially codified. From late 1941 onwards the summons came less and less frequently, though never ceasing entirely.

There were, however, two fixed points in Morton's wartime schedule: membership of the Home Defence Security Executive (HDSE, shortened to SE) and the Committee on French (later Foreign Allied) Resistance (CFR), both of which were established in the first six weeks of Churchill's premiership and reflected the latter's preoccupation at that time with the twin threats of internal subversion and external invasion. The War Cabinet approved on 28 May 1940 the establishment of the SE to 'consider questions relating to defence against the Fifth Column and to initiate action',[26] chaired by Viscount Swinton with a core membership representing the Home Office, MI5, SIS and GHQ Home Forces, plus Morton on Churchill's behalf. Morton took a zealous approach to the threat from 'aliens' and a potential Fifth Column, and had urged the Prime Minister to act.[27] He almost certainly added alarmist detail, derived from his old colleague Maxwell Knight, now in MI5,[28] to reports surrounding the arrest on 20 May of Tyler Kent.[29] Churchill himself, though certainly concerned by the potential for a double invasion from without and within, took a generally balanced view of the need to root out subversive tendencies while avoiding 'an excess of spy-mania'.[30] He welcomed the idea of tackling the danger through a committee under a sound man like Swinton, who might also be trusted to sort out underlying problems in MI5,[31] but did not concern himself with the details, even requiring from Morton a detailed reminder, in mid-July 1940, of what the Security Executive was all about.[32]

The SE, described by Swinton's biographer as 'a curious phenomenon, even among the mass of *ad hoc* organizations spawned by the exigencies of war',[33] held twenty meetings altogether in 1940, and one hundred and nine in total, holding its final session on 26 July 1945.[34] Morton attended nearly all of them, as well as meetings of the Security Intelligence Centre (SIC), which supported the Executive by collating information, coordinating the activities of the security services and 'providing investigators with intelligent guidance on the lines their investigations should take'.[35] He also participated in a number of other SE sub-committees and *ad hoc* conferences.[36] Though the supposed German subversive organisation in Britain proved illusory, the Executive's functions enlarged to include the coordination of domestic security measures generally, including censorship, monitoring of Fascist and Communist activity and Irish security; and later to undertake the direction of certain overseas security organisations.[37]

Meanwhile the SIC, on which the Service Directors of Intelligence sat and which was headed by Morton's old friend, the sinister Sir Joseph Ball,[38] extended its enquiries into more technical (and secret) matters such as the hostile use of broadcasting services, control of radiology equipment, explosives and wireless receivers.

The SE evolved both in scope and volume during the course of the war, while retaining its core responsibility for ensuring the effective operation of war prepa-rations in the field of security. In June 1942, Swinton, whose direction of the SE had impressed Morton favourably,[39] was succeeded as Chairman by Duff Cooper, then Chancellor of the Duchy of Lancaster.[40] At the end of 1943, when Duff Cooper was himself due to move on, Churchill, in one of those fits of random but short-lived inspiration that his officials had to contend with, seems to have asked Morton to take over the chair of the SE. This was scotched politely but firmly by Bridges, and Sir Herbert Creedy assumed the chair in January 1944, without ministerial rank, while Morton retained his place as the Prime Minister's representative. It was an odd episode, notable chiefly for the fact that none of those consulted, including Bracken, considered Morton's chairmanship a viable proposition.[41]

Morton remained a conscientious participant in the SE throughout the war, proffering his views, on Churchill's behalf, on any issue that arose, from the vet-ting of Allied volunteers and Irish security to the prevention of the theft of firearms from military stores. In return he received a good deal of useful inside information, particularly in regard to the activities of the Security Service, for which Swinton had been given Ministerial responsibility in June 1940.[42] Where the SE's agenda fell within his professional experience, such as considering how to prevent the Communist Party of Great Britain from exploiting public sympathies when the German invasion of the Soviet Union on 22 June 1941 turned the latter country into an ally, his interventions were especially authoritative.[43] However, the major-ity of Morton's contributions to SE proceedings were concerned with the treatment of Frenchmen in the UK, Gaullist and otherwise, for here there was a clear overlap with his work on the Committee on French Resistance.

This Committee held its first meeting on 21 June 1940, the day after Morton had suggested to Cadogan that there should be 'an individual or a small com-mittee set up within the FO to coordinate policy towards France and to consider, more widely, the attitude we may have to adopt towards Allied or ex-Allied citizens in this country'.[44] Though Churchill was not keen on the idea, comment-ing that 'We are getting into waters where consultation is v[er]y difficult',[45] he was reluctant to unravel an arrangement endorsed by the FO, and the CFR, chaired by Vansittart, began to meet almost daily. Initially, its work included the drafting of agreements with de Gaulle, dealing with the various French missions in the UK and considering how to prevent the French Navy falling into German hands and ensure the Allied affiliation of French colonies. In August 1940 Vansittart resigned and was replaced as Chairman by Morton,[46] who immediately sought to expand the committee's remit. Despite what appears to have been an attempt by the FO to resist this,[47] the CFR's terms of reference were redrawn to include all Allies whose countries were occupied and their governments exiled. Now known as the Committee on Foreign (Allied) Resistance (its acronym remained CFR), its purpose was:

(a) to make recommendations on the means calculated to stimulate the resistance to the common enemy of those allied countries and their overseas possessions as may from time to time be designated by the Secretary of State for Foreign Affairs

(b) to ensure co-ordination of action between the Departments concerned in giving effect to the policy laid down by the War Cabinet.[48]

This seemed a promisingly broad remit, but with no executive function the CFR could do little more than get in the way of the FO, although it served a useful purpose in imposing some consistency on dealings with the disparate and often difficult governments in exile, and in collating interdepartmental views and coordinating policy on practical issues such as the welfare of refugees. Morton, who clearly appreciated the status afforded by his role as chairman (permitting himself a certain grandiosity of style and referring in correspondence to 'my Committee'), did his best to raise the CFR's profile, spending the first six months of 1941, for example, on a major exercise to coordinate interdepartmental views into a memorandum for the Chiefs of Staff on 'Plans if France Resumes the Fight'.[49] In fact, any success the CFR had in interdepartmental liaison was due more to Morton's personal connections than to the committee's authority. It was he who bridged the gap between SE and CFR, frequently explaining the views of one to the other, as well as liaising with MI5 and coping with representations from de Gaulle (who held strong views on Frenchmen of any persuasion) and with the remonstrations of the FO, who wished to keep control over policy towards both the Free French and Vichy. Morton also had an eye to the interests of both SIS and SOE in the intelligence (and potential recruits) that might be gleaned from Frenchmen or other Allied nationals arriving in the UK. Straddling the divide between Intelligence, domestic security and political relations with governments in exile, Morton performed what was at times a delicate balancing act with skill and ingenuity.

The volume and importance of business handled in the CFR diminished gradually as the Allied authorities developed direct channels of communication with the British Government, and the committee petered out early in 1943.[50] Though Morton had relished his position as chairman, he had long abandoned any illusion that the CFR could make any significant contribution to policy-making. His role as intermediary with the Allied authorities remained, however: and Churchill had always been far more interested in this than in the proceedings of the CFR, however important the agenda. His use of Morton as a cut-out with awkward customers, entrusting him with messages he preferred not to send through official channels, irritated the FO, though their antagonism was generally kept within the bounds of courtesy since Morton was known to have Churchill's ear, authority and confidence. To some extent, official resentment was tempered by the knowledge that his access and information could be valuable. Morton had mutually beneficial working relations with senior officials like Strang and Sargent, and others, like 'Hal' Mack, Frank Roberts and Richard Speaight,[51] discovered that if properly handled Morton could be a mine of information as well as a good means of fast-tracking to the Prime Minister. They also had to admit that he knew how to engage with de Gaulle: as René Pleven[52] told Charles Peake[53] on 31 October 1942, a visit from Morton, at a time when 'the General was both depressed and doubtful', had 'lifted Anglo-French relations on to that sentimental and emotional plane which always drew a response from the General, and this was the moment when we might expect to find him anxious to cooperate'.[54] It is clear from Cadogan's diaries, however, that he regarded Morton as a nuisance, a view held even more strongly by Eden, who replaced Halifax as Foreign Secretary on 22 December 1940. Eden's comment in November 1942, 'I wish Morton at the bottom of the sea',[55] represented his opinion throughout the war. Apart from any personal antipathy,[56] Morton's interventions, particularly in relation to de Gaulle, served to highlight – and, in Eden's view, exacerbate – differences of view with Churchill on French policy.[57]

Morton's value to Churchill as an interlocutor with the Free French and authorities representing other occupied powers rested on several factors. Firstly, he was good at dealing with their leaders personally. He spoke fluent French, had decent formal manners and a military bearing, all assets in what was a painful, and sometimes humiliating situation for men who had seen their countries overrun and felt powerless. He had the merit of representing the Prime Minister directly, offering an opportunity to play off various parts of the British Government against each other: de Gaulle certainly appreciated the potential advantage afforded by giving a slightly different message to Eden, Spears and (through Morton) Churchill. But Morton did not only talk to heads of government or those at ministerial level: he also developed a useful network of contacts at other levels, particularly in the area of secret Intelligence. Here his liaison activities were useful not just to Churchill but also to SIS and other Agencies. By 1942, however, those British authorities who had ongoing business with the 'Allied resistance' had established their own, more reliable and authoritative channels of communication, and were inclined to view Morton as muddying the waters.

Morton's role was not for the fainthearted, involving frequent clashes with the FO and other departments and agencies, but it suited his talents and temperament and he showed a considerable degree of tenacity and patience in fulfilling it. There is, however, little evidence that his activities had any real impact on the direction of policy. This was not due to lack of effort on his part, for he was always on the look-out for opportunities to make a contribution (or, as some would say, to interfere). In August 1942, for example, he sought authority to prepare 'a cold-blooded study . . . of the evidence which we possess from all sources on the extent of the support for de Gaulle in France and Vichy Colonies', a task which would necessitate the collation of information from SIS, SOE, the FO and the Directorates of Naval, Military and Air Intelligence.[58] Churchill agreed, but Morton's 'magnum opus', dated 17 September 1942 and referring to de Gaulle as 'Charles of Arc', was received with little more than polite attention;[59] those consulted preferring to research and produce their own reports. As far as the FO were concerned, it was a time-consuming if harmless exercise that did little to reduce their suspicions of Morton.

It has to be acknowledged that these suspicions were based on doubts about Morton's judgement as well as dislike of his (and Churchill's) disregard for orthodox channels. Morton's involvement in the planning of the ill-fated Dakar expedition in the summer of 1940,[60] and the embarrassing Muselier affair in January 1941,[61] undermined confidence in both his discretion and his political sense. Later episodes, such as when his hand was detected in de Gaulle's removal in October 1942 of Dejean from the foreign affairs portfolio on the French National Committee, in favour of Pleven, made matters worse. Eden, already annoyed that Morton had been present at his and Churchill's meeting with de Gaulle on 30 September, commented on 18 October that 'we should get on better if there were fewer fingers in the pie – English fingers', and Harvey noted in his diary that Morton had 'had his head washed for interfering'.[62] Though Morton was included in subsequent meetings at Churchill's request, and was present at planning discussions for the TORCH landings,[63] both the FO and the military authorities excluded him from their counsels as much as it lay in their power to do so.

Although the evidence might suggest that Morton owed any influence he had to Churchill, rather than to his own knowledge or experience, it would be wrong to discount the latter. People approached him because of his secret connections and his supposed influence with Churchill, and the more they did so, the more his reputation for intrigue increased. In May 1943, for example, Dr Gerbrandy, Prime Minister of the Netherlands Government, approached Morton – who had acted as intermediary in the autumn of 1941 in the establishment of relations between British and Dutch secret services[64] – to ask what could be done to help Dutch military personnel who were being threatened with imprisonment by the Germans because they had been in the Army in 1940. Morton thought that Gerbrandy's scheme for bombing German lines of communication to prevent Dutch forces being moved was impractical – 'Holland is a small country and the Germans can perfectly well make the unfortunate Dutch walk' – as well as likely to provoke reprisals. He passed the problem on to Lord Selborne[65] for SOE consideration, meanwhile offering some practical suggestions:

> measures might be taken to muddle all correspondence and records necessary for the proposed enregistration and . . . instructions might be given to the certain key men to try to conceal their identity, while forms and returns might be filled up wrongly on a large scale as was done

successfully in Czechoslovakia some months ago. I understand that our
Secret people could provide money and possibly other facilities . . .[66]

This was, presumably, the kind of episode on which Anthony Powell based certain
aspects of Sir Magnus Donners in *The Military Philosophers*.[67]

A further example is offered by confidential contacts between June and
September 1943 with Marcus Wallenberg, who with his brother Jacob ran the
Stockholms Enskilda Bank, and acted throughout the war as intermediaries
for Carl Goerdeler, one of the leaders of German resistance to Hitler.[68] The
suggestion that peace feelers from Germany were treated more seriously by the
British Government than the official documentation indicates has been raised in
a number of studies, and because of his position and contacts Morton is one of
the figures suspected of involvement. Although no new evidence has been found
to suggest that Morton, any more than Churchill, was involved in discussions for
a separate peace, or gave countenance to any 'deal' with the German opposition,
documentation concerning Morton's contacts with Wallenberg in 1943, discovered in the vaults of the *Stockholms Enskilda Bank* as recently as 1997, provides
an interesting window into his activities on Churchill's behalf.

Following a visit to Stockholm by Goerdeler in May 1943 to discuss plans
for the overthrow of Hitler by dissident German generals, Jacob Wallenberg wrote
to his brother Marcus, then in London, asking him to contact Churchill, either
directly or through Morton, to ask on Goerdeler's behalf whether Churchill would
agree to the cessation of military attacks 'while the liberation action in Germany
is under way', and whether a peace settlement without unconditional surrender
would be acceptable to the Western Allies.[69] Marcus contacted Morton, whom
he knew both from pre-war negotiations for an Anglo-Swedish trade agreement,
and through mutual friendship with the banker Sir Charles Hambro, now the
operational director of SOE; they met on 4 June. According to Wallenberg's notes
of the meeting, Morton described Churchill's war objectives as clear:

> To W.C., the goal was to uproot the Nazi gangster rule that had led the
> world into this war and brought destruction, oppression and lawlessness
> over large parts of Europe and rocked the whole world. As long as the
> Nazi system prevailed and as long as there was a chance that it would be
> restored there was no future security in the relations between nations and
> thus no basis for the reconstruction of the world and for the economic
> and social security of the nations. It was therefore not possible to adopt
> an attitude towards questions from German revolutionary candidates
> about the Allies' reaction to a Germany cleansed from Hitler and his
> gang by a movement led by generals, public officials, industrialists and
> unionists. One would have to 'wait and see' . . .[70]

Morton went on to describe the kind of German regime that would find favour
with the Allies, suggesting that a period of reconstruction and reform would be

needed before any peace settlement could be reached. Much of this would have raised few eyebrows in Whitehall, although Morton's references to Russia – 'the intentions and policy of which were observed with great, but concealed, distrust' – were perhaps more personal than politic. At the end of the interview, he offered Wallenberg some encouragement for Goerdeler:

> In reply to my final question, whether D.M. considered a peace agreement without 'unconditional surrender' impossible, he answered categorically no. W.C. did not wish to prolong the war unnecessarily, for the sake of war. The most important thing was to exterminate Nazism and to create guarantees for a lasting peace in the future . . . D.M. also declared emphatically that all bombing of revolting [*sic*] places would be stopped, if they only were provided with proper and credible information about the situation. D.M. said that he did not need to consult W.C. further as regards these points. They were for certain.[71]

Wallenberg thought Morton appeared inclined to pursue contact with Goerdeler, suggesting that he might 'himself go to St[ockho]lm for a meeting with the relevant German person', but further approaches were passed on to Hambro, who wrote to Marcus on 29 September:

> You will recollect that when you were last here you spoke to someone in high circles about certain plans of some of the professional warriors in a neighbouring country unfriendly to mine . . . Action will be construed as an act of good faith and proof that they are serious people with standing and influence in their country. *No undertaking* of any kind can be given or expected. *No one* must know that you and I are in touch on this matter and above all *no one* at HM Legation. From now on you will send all communications in regard to this matter to me by the same route as you receive this letter.[72]

Whether Morton withdrew voluntarily from further contact on grounds of prudence, or whether he was told to do so, is not revealed. As an example of his style, however, the exchange with Wallenberg is instructive.

These episodes show how the unofficial and confidential nature of Morton's liaison duties created the ideal preconditions for the myth that he was both ubiquitous and powerful, an impression he did little to discourage. A natural corollary of this was that when affairs turned out badly, it was Morton, rather than Churchill, who took the blame. Failure to secure an interview with the Prime Minister, an unfavourable decision or the disappointing reception of a message, was ascribed to the malign influence of his gatekeeper. It was a role Morton was more than willing to assume, but it has led to further enduring 'Morton myths'. Two brief examples must suffice. The first is in relation to policy towards the Yugoslav revolt, and in particular to the transfer in 1943–44 of British support from Mihailovic and his Cetnik forces to Tito and the Partisans, a decision that was to lead ultimately to Mihailovic's capture and execution and to Tito's becoming Communist dictator of Yugoslavia until his death in 1980.[73] The issue aroused strong feelings at the time and in retrospect, partly because British agents were involved on both sides. Morton was thought by some to have influenced Churchill's views by arguing for continued support of Mihailovic: Bill (later Sir William) Deakin, parachuted by SOE into Montenegro at the end of May 1943 to make contact with the Partisans, believed that Morton deliberately suppressed a pro-Partisan report from SOE in Cairo on the grounds that it was not in accordance with FO policy, and that as a Roman Catholic Morton was 'very much against Tito'. Although in later years Sir William's recollection of the detail was imperfect, he remained convinced that Morton had misrepresented his and SOE's views, just as he believed that Morton's position as 'a very confidential adviser' to Churchill owed its influence to 'the approval and probably the pressure of MI5 and MI6'.[74]

This a good example of how Morton's liaison role could by its very nature foster a misleading impression that both Morton and Churchill were happy to perpetuate, the former because he wished to be seen as privy to secret information, and the latter because he wished to conceal the nature of his own sources. Whatever Morton's views, as far as Churchill was concerned the decisive information on the question of British support for Yugoslav resistance – a key factor in the context of Allied planning for a Second Front in Europe[75] – came from what he termed 'Boniface', the material obtained from Enigma decrypts that has become known as Ultra.[76] The 'suppressed' report was enclosed in an 'envelope of secret information' sent to Churchill by R.G. Casey, Minister of State in Cairo,[77] and passed to Morton for comment before Churchill saw it. It seemed to Morton, on the basis of his information, that this document, which included the stark comment that it was 'no longer possible to support Mihailovic as the leader of all Serbian lands and the Partisan movement must be regarded as a whole', was 'wrong in fact, misleading in conclusion and recommends a course of policy opposed to that agreed upon by the Foreign Office, the Yugoslav Government, SOE and the Chiefs of Staff'. After consulting Sargent at the FO and Churchill's Private Secretaries, it was agreed that an alternative report should be prepared in London.[78]

Morton's reaction shows not that he wished to distort the information reaching the Prime Minister, but that he – like the Private Secretaries and his FO contacts – was not in possession of all the facts.[79] What Churchill wanted was a report based on information gathered on the ground, to supplement his Ultra decrypts, as a note of 12 June 1943 made clear:

> The Prime Minister has asked . . . for a two-page report on what is happening in Yugoslavia. He wishes to know how much is being done by the Partisans and how much by General Mihailovitch, and how many supporters each has, and he would like a map to illustrate the areas in

which they both operate. The Prime Minister asked for this after reading a yellow box, and asked that the Report should be obtained 'from the Intelligence services'.[80]

Morton's intervention meant that the report Churchill received, an SOE appreciation prepared in London and dated 18 June 1943,[81] was not what he had asked for, though it contributed to the ongoing policy debate. It did not affect the decision taken at the end of June that both the Communist Partisans and the Croat guerrillas should henceforth receive British military support; presaging Churchill's determination, announced to Roosevelt and Stalin at Teheran in November 1943, to abandon support for Mihailovic altogether. Those decisions, despite the existence of conspiracy theories involving Morton, SOE in Cairo and other parties, were based squarely on Churchill's favourite, and most reliable source: Ultra.

The second illustration of the 'Morton myth' shows how his position as Churchill's gatekeeper could bring down odium upon himself – and also how his manner of dealing with interlocutors who did not impress him could serve to make a basic misunderstanding worse. Just as Deakin believed all his life that Morton had deliberately suppressed the report on Tito, so the late Jan Nowak-Jezioranski, who acted as wartime courier between the Polish Home (Secret) Army and his government in exile in London, believed until his death that Morton deliberately made a false report to Churchill of an interview on 10 February 1944.[82] Nowak had expected to see Churchill personally, and was not pleased at being fobbed off with Morton, who on his side found Nowak unimpressive.[83] The result of the interview was confusion and considerable Polish outrage: according to Nowak's account, Jozef Zaranski, adviser to the Polish Prime Minister Stanislaw Mikolajczyk, 'threw up his hands' and declared that in his whole career he had 'never heard anything like this'.[84] Nowak also claimed that Sir Owen O'Malley, HM Ambassador to the Polish Government in exile, told him that Morton belonged to a group 'which, where Polish affairs were concerned, had had a negative influence on the prime minister'.[85] (It is interesting to speculate whether O'Malley, who had been forced to resign from the FO in 1928 over the Francs scandal, retained any unpleasant recollection of Morton's role in that and the related Zinoviev Letter episode.[86])

Although the evidence in British archives does not support the somewhat dramatic claims made by Nowak, it is clear that the way Morton handled their interview was at the root of the problem. Churchill, who at the Defence Committee meeting on 3 February 1944 had instructed that every effort should be made to increase the help sent to the Polish Resistance, asked Morton to see Nowak. This was also the recommendation of Selborne, who provided Morton beforehand with a map of the approximate disposition of the Polish Secret Army in Poland that appeared to show that the Poles were 'holding down a pretty substantial [German] force'.[87] After the interview on 10 February, Morton wrote to Selborne that Nowak, while 'obviously a good, sincere man', seemed 'to lack confident knowledge of the sort of things one wants to know about the Polish Resistance movement'. When questioned, Nowak had admitted that the figures on the map represented not German battalions, but 'the number of battalions which, in the opinion of the Poles, the Germans could make out of the German personnel employed on various duties in the areas of Poland concerned if they ceased to perform their present duties'. Morton continued:

> Nowak also told me that in his private opinion, the Polish Secret Army was not in a position to undertake any sort of operations which could be called military. He said that on the one hand the Polish countryside was not suitable for guerrillas, still less for anything approaching Tito's army. He added, moreover, that the Poles as a whole were not prepared to undertake activities which would lead to reprisals upon Polish villages, civilians, women and children. I naturally forebore to rub in Tito's reaction to the risk of reprisals, which seems to differ so greatly from that of the Poles, though I did mention it.[88]

This was Morton at his most dismissive, and it is easy to see how the unfavourable comparison between Tito's Partisans and the Polish Resistance would have been deeply wounding to Nowak. It is equally clear that Morton, who was familiar with the somewhat complex structures of Polish Intelligence,[89] found what he described as Nowak's 'semi-conscious revelations', which seemed rather different to the upbeat impression given by the Polish General Staff in London, 'a little disturbing'. Selborne agreed, though pointing out that Nowak was 'a propaganda agent and his impressions on military matters may not, therefore, be correct'. He undertook to have the information on the map checked with the Order of Battle of German Forces in Poland as known to the War Office.[90] Meanwhile, as far as Morton was concerned, the incident was closed, and although Nowak and his government may have taken it more seriously, it must be set against the wider context. Morton's concern, as he had told Selborne, was 'to avoid giving the Prime Minister a false impression'. A week after his interview with Morton, Nowak was filled with rage on hearing Churchill, in the House of Commons, declare that it was 'reasonable and just' for Russia to annex Polish territory up to the Curzon Line;[91] and on 29 February 1944, Churchill sent a personal telegram to General Wilson at AFHQ, stressing that supplies for the French Maquis and Poland must not be 'at the expense of those to partisans and others in the Balkans', in order to prevent the Germans withdrawing troops from the area.[92] In the run-up to OVERLORD, the Allied landings in France planned for the summer of 1944, broader strategic concerns were at stake than support for the beleaguered Polish Resistance, however sympathetic Churchill – or Morton – may have been.

This review of Morton's wartime activities ends with a brief account of the three occasions on which it is known that he travelled overseas: to North Africa with Churchill in late 1943; on Churchill's behalf to France in September 1944;

and to the Middle East in June 1945. It was not usual for Morton to accompany Churchill on his wartime travels: as he later told R.W. Thompson, his role was to read incoming papers in the Prime Minister's absence, and discuss them with him on his return: 'This was one of his customs, to use me as a stooge on his return from abroad, and we spoke freely.'[93] The three trips are interesting less for their content than as further indications of the way in which Morton's function changed in the later years of the war. In 1943, the sphere of his activities had shifted from the central policy direction of the war (represented by Churchill) to more practical economic issues; his visit to North Africa had a concrete purpose. In 1944, he was increasingly drawn into civil affairs issues, particularly in regard to supply, that were raised by Allied advances in Europe.[94] Discussion of such matters occupied part of his trip to France, though it was essentially a reconnaissance for a visit by Churchill. The origins of his tour of Greece and the Middle East, in June 1945, are more obscure, but it can only have been a source of irritation both to the FO and the military authorities.

During 1943, the focus of Free French affairs had shifted to North Africa, where Generals de Gaulle and Giraud vied for control of Free French forces; the formation on 3 June of a Committee of National Liberation based in Algiers and run jointly by de Gaulle and Giraud, and the winding up of the Free French movement in London,[95] confirmed this trend. Morton's work on French matters had shifted to questions of supply: in November 1942, soon after the Allied landings, he had been appointed chairman of the War Cabinet Committee on Allied African Economic Affairs (AEA), set up to deal with matters arising from the adherence to the Allied cause of colonial territories in Africa, including coordination with the North Africa Economic Board (NAEB), a supply organisation set up the Americans.[96] It was on AEA and NAEB business that Morton set sail on the *Renown* on 14 November 1943 with Churchill and the Chiefs of Staff, who were *en route* via Gibraltar for the Teheran Conference and talks in Cairo with Roosevelt and the American COS.[97]

Since this seems to have been the only occasion when Morton was present during Churchill's extensive wartime travels, it is unfortunate that apart from a few letters to Mack at the FO he left no record of his trip. Some details can be found in entries in the diary of Harold Macmillan,[98] who had been appointed Minister Resident at AFHQ Algiers in January 1943, and with whom Morton stayed for much of his visit, travelling with him to Cairo and later to Tunis to see Churchill, who had been ill for much of December.[99] This was the first prolonged contact between Morton and Macmillan, who got on well and found each other useful. Macmillan thought Morton a 'most agreeable guest' and a 'pleasant and intelligent man', and treated him well, giving lunches and dinners to which he invited the principal players in French North African affairs, including Macmillan's US opposite number, Robert Murphy,[100] as well as the British and American heads of the NAEB. When Churchill left Cairo for Teheran Morton and Macmillan stayed behind and, back in Algiers, the two men walked in the mountains with Roger Makins[101] (who had been assigned to Macmillan's staff).

On Christmas Day they flew up to Tunis to join Churchill for lunch, then Macmillan returned to Algiers leaving Morton in Tunis from where he returned to London.[102]

At the end of August 1944, the liberation of Paris and the formation of de Gaulle's Provisional Government turned Churchill's thoughts towards a possible visit to France, although there was no immediate prospect of this at a time when his health was not good, he was worried by the progress of the Italian and Burma campaigns and about to leave (on 5 September) for a meeting in Quebec with Roosevelt that seemed likely to be bedevilled by strategic disagreements.[103] It is possible that the idea of a future visit, however nebulous, together with the desire for news about his beloved France, lay behind his agreement to Morton's trip. Morton was away from 9–22 September, also visiting Brussels ('at the request of SHAEF'), and wrote up his impressions for Churchill on his return. On 15 September he had told the newly-appointed British Ambassador in Paris, Duff Cooper, that 'the Prime Minister would want to come here as soon as possible after the opening of Parliament, which would be in a fortnight to three weeks'. The Ambassador's response was discouraging:

> I said that he could not possibly come until he had recognized the Government, and that we must arrange for him to receive a proper invitation from de Gaulle. Nothing could do more harm than if he came as a part of SHAEF and lived outside Paris with them at Versailles.[104]

Morton's account imparted a similar message with more subtlety. If Churchill were to visit either Versailles or Paris, several weeks' notice would be required to make arrangements and ensure security: if these precautions were taken, the risk would be 'no greater than in peace time', and he assured Churchill that the people of Paris longed to see him, and he would 'get a rapturous welcome'. However, he felt bound to warn Churchill:

> that the people of Paris and of France generally have no idea that you and General de Gaulle are not the best of friends. It would come to them as a great shock if you did not meet the French Administration and General de Gaulle when in Paris, and generally treat the Administration as if it were a Provisional Government, even though it might not have been officially recognised.[105]

De Gaulle, Morton reported, was 'venerated as the standard-bearer of French liberation', although should he 'wish to descend from his unique pedestal to become a political leader when times are more normal, even de Gaulle's closest friends say that he will have to prove his ability in this role before the French accept him at his own valuation'. By the time Churchill had read Morton's report, events and his own plans had moved on, and the visit was eventually timed to coincide with the armistice celebrations in November. Nevertheless, he probably enjoyed reading – as Morton presumably enjoyed seeing – that 'Apart from the gravest deficiencies in communications and transport, Paris is normal. I could not find a pane of glass broken in the whole city, which is as beautiful as ever'.[106]

The tortuous (and tortured) story of British policy in Greece during the Second World War, of Churchill's near-obsessional interest in Greek affairs and support for King George II, and of the conflicting aims of the FO and the British military authorities, has been told elsewhere.[107] During the summer of 1945, the implementation of the Varkiza Agreement of 12 February 1945 between the Greek Government and delegates of the Greek National Liberation Front, providing for a plebiscite and elections, was the subject of international discussion.[108] The situation certainly needed no help from Morton, and his visit to Athens, Cairo and Caserta during the second half of June may have had its origins in a temporary whim of Churchill's, or even in Morton's own desire to get out of the country and do something useful. Morton's interview on 14 June with the Regent, who assured him that 'Mr Churchill was the saviour of European civilisation if it could be attributed to the act under God of one man', may have been heartwarming, but as Morton himself commented, it 'added little to my knowledge of affairs in Greece'.[109]

It was not clear from the surviving documentation what Morton set out to achieve. The evidence does suggest, however, that British authorities in the area, from Field-Marshal Alexander[110] downwards, took the opportunity of his visit to raise a number of local jurisdictional and personnel difficulties, knowing that he would report back to Churchill. He was also asked to represent certain more serious concerns, such as those raised by the activities of the Russian Mission in Greece who, on the excuse of repatriating Soviet citizens and POWs, were 'making a nuisance of themselves in the usual heavy Soviet fashion'.[111] Morton did his best to be helpful: but it is hard to avoid the impression that the trip was a welcome diversion from inaction in Whitehall and uncertainty about his own future, rather than serving any useful purpose.

1945 had begun on a high note for Morton, who was created Knight Commander of the British Empire on 1 January. One can only assume that he regretted that his mother, Edith, did not live to see him receive this honour: she died in 1944. The knighthood was a reward for his long career as well as for his wartime efforts in Churchill's service.[112] In terms of the future, however, the honour seemed to presage the beginning of a downward slope rather than the start of a new stage. He was fifty-four years of age: not young, but not yet old – Churchill was, after all, seventy-one. At the end of May, the war in Europe at an end, Churchill asked one of his Private Secretaries to elicit from Morton a note of his duties. The resulting schedule is of interest, in comparison with that prepared in 1941 (see pp. 230–31 above):

    1. To act as personal liaison between the Prime Minister, and the Prime Minister or Governments of European Allies and Liberated Territories.

He acts as such when specifically instructed or at the demand of the Foreign Governments when, through a knowledge of Whitehall, he is frequently able to assist them to place their demands and difficulties before the British authorities concerned through the proper channels.

2. Through inspection of the Prime Minister's private minutes and a knowledge of his policy, to advise and warn on demand, or as necessary, Permanent Officials of all Civilian Government Departments.

3. As instructed by the Prime Minister from time to time to represent the Prime Minister's point of view, or to act as an observer in his interests on Government Committees. At the present time the chief are:

a. The London Coordinating Committee on Supply (Anglo-American)
b. The organisation known as The Supply Committee on Liberated and Occupied Areas (SLAO)
c. The Foreign Office Committee on 'International Problems of the Transitional Period'
d. The Security Executive
e. The Home Office Committee on 'Overseas Travel'
f. Various *ad hoc* Committees

4. To act at need as a special Liaison Office between the Prime Minister and the Governmental Secret Services, i.e., SIS, SOE, MI5, PWE.[113]

While this statement is couched in Morton's customary somewhat self-important style, his covering minute to Churchill – sad, and rather disillusioned in tone – reflected uncertainty about his position and his future, as well, perhaps, as the extent to which, like everyone else, he was thoroughly tired of the war. He had been told, he said, that his post was a Civil Service appointment independent of any change of government, but that did not 'prevent any Prime Minister abolishing the post or appointing to it whom he pleases'. Its title was unsatisfactory, conveying 'little or nothing to the Civil Service, and in the Armed Forces is one applied to an officer of low rank and powers' – a heartfelt statement, based on his personal experience since May 1940. In fact, he recommended the abolition of the post, and the absorption of its remaining duties in those of the Principal Private Secretary: they were, he said:

not easy to describe in greater detail. Much of the work has been built up as a result of personal connection and must lapse with the present incumbent. With the end of the war in Europe and the departure of the Allied Governments to their own countries, other duties I have performed are moribund.[114]

Though Morton continued in Churchill's service until the latter ceased to be Prime Minister on 26 July 1945, and remained on good terms with him – attending a 'stag party' at Chequers on the final weekend[115] – everything was, in fact, at an end: his position, his closeness to Churchill, and so, despite his network of connections, any real influence he had ever possessed. It was the end of the most exciting, and – at least in the early wartime years – fulfilling period in his life.

12

INTELLIGENCE LIAISON, MAY 1940–JULY 1945

Morton's central brief as Intelligence adviser to the Prime Minister, as described in his letter to Menzies of 15 May 1940,[1] was 'to keep personal liaison with certain civil Departments', including SIS. It was his Intelligence experience and connections that formed the basis of his reputation, and constituted his principal value to Churchill. This area of his wartime activities merits, therefore, more detailed consideration. Yet even in this sphere, the 'Morton myth' is pervasive. His long period of service as an SIS officer, his close personal connections with the heads and senior officials of all the Agencies, his familiarity with the methods and minutiae of the secret world, are all undeniable facts. Together with Churchill's *imprimatur*, they conferred an authority that he invoked when exercising his right to be kept informed, to be consulted, to intervene if he saw fit. That authority did not, however, lead to the status and responsibility in the Intelligence field that he sought. The evidence shows that much of the influence Morton is thought to have exerted during the Second World War was transitory, and that in this sphere, as in his non-Intelligence activities, his role diminished as the war progressed.

Nevertheless, his contribution was significant. His liaison activities were carried out both skilfully and conscientiously, producing valuable information for Churchill (particularly in the early part of the war) and oiling the perennially squeaky wheels of inter-Agency communication. It is likely, even probable, that he was involved in more clandestine plans and operations than will ever be known, since the evidence is lacking. But as the Intelligence establishment evolved and multiplied, creating opportunities for senior management and leadership posts, Morton found himself passed over and left behind. In this, his fate was in contrast to that of his contemporary, Stewart Menzies. Menzies is, in a sense, the surprise beneficiary of an examination of Morton's wartime Intelligence activities: the evidence shows that while Morton's role and influence were less than has been supposed, Menzies was far more dynamic and successful, in professional terms, than has often been thought.

Nevertheless, Menzies represented merely one part, though a large and important one, of the Intelligence landscape. He developed a close relationship with Churchill that gained him considerable influence, edging out that of Morton. As Chief of SIS, however, he could not claim to be an impartial actor in wider organisational issues, as Morton could. Though Morton may have failed to secure a position of power or responsibility commensurate with his ambitions, he never relinquished the authority that his role as Churchill's Intelligence adviser conferred, and in that capacity was still intervening in – and being consulted on – organisational matters until the end of the war. As so often in Morton's career, this means that his activities afford a unique vantage point for the study of areas of the Intelligence landscape that would otherwise remain in shadow.

Though focussed on SIS, Morton's liaison brief ranged widely over the entire wartime Intelligence landscape, including the Radio Security Service (RSS) and the 'Aspidistra' project, the Twenty Committee and the Double Cross system, the Political Warfare Executive, the deception work of London Controlling Section and an almost obsessive interest in German covert activities in Ireland.[2] This chapter, however, will focus principally on his activities in relation to SIS and GC&CS, and to the SIS 'offshoots', British Security Coordination (BSC) and the Special Operations Executive (SOE). In each of these there is a Morton myth to explore; and their wartime fortunes, jointly and severally, illustrate the range and nature of his activities. There is a natural chronological division, in that after the end of 1941 Morton's attempts to influence the affairs of these bodies were being deflected with greater success by those in charge of them who, where they could not work with him, worked round him. In this situation he turned his attention increasingly to organisational intervention.

SIS and GC&CS: Morton and Menzies

As an ex-SIS officer, Morton's inclinations and sympathies lay with that organisation. His background gave him a natural solidarity with Menzies and SIS's senior staff, all of whom he knew well. Though he could be, and was, critical of SIS's organisation and performance, and was quite capable of working behind the scenes to undermine its autonomy and to influence Churchill towards his own schemes for reform, he defended the organisation, on the whole, from the challenge of other Agencies and in particular against the Service Intelligence directors (who saw no reason to let war influence their views on what constituted 'real', i.e. military intelligence). For their part, Menzies and his colleagues must surely have hoped that Morton's position in the Prime Minister's office would prove advantageous to SIS, both in respect of Whitehall competition for scarce resources, and to ensure that SIS's product was recognised and valued by those responsible for the direction of the war.

On his arrival in Downing Street in May 1940 Morton lost no time, as we have seen, in contacting Menzies, who reciprocated promptly, taking personal responsibility for sending him daily batches of CX reports, scientific data, intelligence summaries and other information for the Prime Minister's benefit.[3] It was in Menzies' interest to do so, since Morton's liaison role provided a valuable opportunity to advertise SIS's work at a time when organisationally and operationally that Service was at a low ebb. Resources, always tight, became even tighter as

SIS found itself competing with parts of the military machine on whom it had hitherto relied for its logistical support. The Services, themselves preoccupied with practical questions of supply and production as well as intelligence, were disinclined to involve themselves in SIS's problems, partly from a desire to respect its autonomy and partly because of a perceived decline in the value to them of its product.[4]

In the second half of 1940 SIS's administrative and accommodation arrangements were chaotic: there was an awkward division of responsibilities between Dansey, who as ACSS remained in London as Menzies' deputy, and Vivian (VCSS) who was in charge of the War Station at Bletchley Park and presided over the allocation of resources between SIS and GC&CS. Menzies himself fretted that his rank of Colonel put him at a disadvantage with his Agency and Service counterparts.[5] Meanwhile, SIS HQ was in a state of upheaval as some of those sections sent to Bletchley Park on the outbreak of war drifted back to London when the War Station bulged at the seams. The move of Section V to St Albans, and the expansion of counter-espionage work in cooperation with MI5,[6] complicated the split both administratively and geographically, as well as proving a source of friction between Dansey and Vivian. Most importantly, of course, the fall of France had led to the loss of all SIS posts in Northern and North-Western Europe, with further losses as Hitler swept across Europe. It was not a situation to inspire Whitehall's confidence in SIS's capacity either to meet an invasion threat or to engage in counter-espionage.

Menzies was anxious to demonstrate to his Whitehall colleagues, and to Churchill, that he still had plenty to offer in terms of both intelligence and action. But as he found when he addressed a meeting of the Secret Service Committee on 3 June 1940, convened by Cadogan to consider the reorganisation of SIS necessitated by the German occupation of the French coast, the assembled officials and Directors of Intelligence (plus Morton) were more interested in details of the communication and coordination of secret reports from overseas, and the use made of intercepts, than in SIS's efforts to re-establish communications and organisations behind the German lines. In particular, they wanted to know about 'the part which the SIS might play in the event of an invasion of Great Britain': a very real and present danger in the summer of 1940.[7]

Though its networks were lost, SIS could still provide Intelligence from human sources,[8] and throughout the summer of 1940 Menzies passed on regular reports to Morton, including information from a highly-placed SIS source in Berlin and corroborative reports from Scandinavian, Baltic and Polish sources; from 17 July he also provided a 'Weekly Summary of Intelligence' for Churchill's personal perusal. Human Intelligence reports ranged from predictions of imminent invasion – the Weekly Summary for 5 August stated that all leave for German troops in Northern France and Holland had been cancelled, with infantry and Panzer divisions embarking at Memel and Stettin – to indications of a postponement until mid-September, a view supported by French Intelligence, via Colonel Bertrand.[9] Morton and Menzies also held regular discussions on what was known of German invasion plans and the likelihood of their being disrupted by the RAF's bombing raids. It was not until the end of October 1940, after SIS's Berlin source had reported that invasion had now been put back until 'early 1941', that Churchill and the Defence Committee felt able to conclude that the danger was now 'relatively remote'.[10] Throughout this period Menzies and Morton were in close contact, the latter enjoying a high degree of access to SIS reporting and to its officials.[11] With the decline of the threat of invasion, however, came a corresponding decline in their regular secret correspondence, and the evidence indicates that from mid-1941 onwards Menzies tended to report directly to Churchill, rather than through Morton.

Human Intelligence reports from SIS were only one strand, though an important one, of the overall picture. Menzies also supplied Morton with copies of intercepts by GC&CS of diplomatic telegraphic traffic, known as 'BJs'.[12] Churchill had always been interested in such Intelligence, and characteristically wanted to see everything, not just what SIS thought he should see. He gave instructions in early August 1940 that in future SIS should not pre-select the intercepts, but send 'authentic documents in their original form' to Downing Street, where Morton would 'inspect them for me and submit what he considers of major importance'.[13] In these early months of the premiership, Morton's role in sifting through voluminous amounts of 'flimsies', selecting those of greatest import and annotating them on the basis of his (and SIS's) knowledge and experience, kept him abreast of developments while preventing Churchill from being overwhelmed by a wealth of indigestible intelligence. However, even Morton could not have kept up with the huge amount of diplomatic decrypts – 8,600 in 1940, rising to 13,000 in 1941 – and by late 1941 they were being handled with other material from GC&CS, though Morton still took a close interest.[14]

Menzies showed no signs of resenting the necessity of sending Morton SIS reports or diplomatic intercepts: rather, he welcomed the opportunity to ensure that Churchill got what he wanted.[15] He was much less willing, however, to relinquish any control over his prime asset: the Enigma material supplied by the GC&CS codebreakers at Bletchley Park – Ultra, as it would later be called.[16] Though still in its infancy in the summer of 1940, this source of intelligence, and in particular German Air Force (GAF) Enigma, played a valuable role both in giving warning of forthcoming air raids on Britain, and in providing details of GAF strengths and dispositions.[17] Ultra was SIS's trump card, the goose that laid the golden eggs as Churchill would have it, and conferred on Menzies, as GC&CS's proud parent, a degree of control that gave him an edge over his Army, Naval and Air colleagues and allowed him to spin a web with himself at the centre, 'like a rather elegant and ineffective spider commanding every point of growth'.[18] It also laid the foundation for the closer relationship between the SIS Chief and the Prime Minister that would diminish Morton's liaison role, even if this took some time to develop.

Morton's supposed role in the handling of Ultra is an integral part of the Morton myth. Most accounts of Ultra, and of its undoubted fascination for

Churchill, assume that Morton was not only in on the secret but exercised the same role that he did with other SIS Intelligence, pre-selecting messages for the Prime Minister and commenting on them. The evidence for this, however, is at best ambiguous. Morton certainly knew *about* Ultra: as Churchill's personal adviser on Intelligence, and a close associate of Menzies he was well aware of what went on at Bletchley Park, and indeed he knew of the work of the Polish Enigma codebreakers whom Colonel Bertrand, with SIS cooperation, helped to escape first from Poland and then, in June 1940, from France;[19] nor could he have failed to be aware of the arrangements made for delivering Enigma decrypts to Downing Street.[20] He took a hand on practical issues such as GC&CS's staffing difficulties, and was instrumental in September 1940 in ensuring, through Hankey, that a number of skilled signalling officers were assigned to Bletchley Park rather than to other interception stations.[21] But Morton's name never appeared on the Ultra circulation lists – even later in the war, when the circle of knowledge had widened considerably – and none of the documentary sources adduced in support of his membership of the 'charmed circle' can be proven to refer to Ultra, rather than to other sources of intelligence. In fact, they tend to suggest the contrary.

In *Ultra Goes to War*, Ronald Lewin gave a detailed account (on which most subsequent accounts have been based) of Morton's supposed Ultra access based on information from Sir Arthur Benson, who had worked with Morton at No. 10. Lewin considered it a 'curious and touching sign of the meticulous security with which these secret matters were conducted' that it was not until long after the war that Benson realised 'he had been handling Ultra for Churchill'; but the details quoted in Benson's letter of how the material arrived in double-locked boxes that were 'opened always in the presence of Miss Gwynne' (who supposedly counted and listed the 'flimsies')[22] refer to the way in which Morton dealt with diplomatic intercepts, not to Ultra handling protocols. This is plain from the evidence detailing Morton's BJ arrangements with Menzies, and the extent to which knowledge of Ultra was restricted so that even Churchill's Private Secretaries were not aware of what was in the 'buff boxes'. A letter from Morton to Menzies dated 27 September 1940, much quoted as evidence of his access, actually indicates that he did *not* see the material:

Most Secret

Dear C,

In confirmation of my telephone message, I have been personally directed by the Prime Minister to inform you that he wishes you to send him daily all the ENIGMA messages.

These are to be sent in a locked box with a clear notice stuck to it "THIS BOX IS ONLY TO BE OPENED BY THE PRIME MINISTER IN PERSON".

After seeing the messages he will return them to you.

Yours ever,
Desmond Morton

P.S. As there will be no check possible here, would you please institute a check on receipt of returned documents to see that you have got them all back.[23]

The postscript, in particular, does not square with Benson's account, nor with Morton's acting as intermediary. Yet surely in a personal letter to Menzies, which Morton would have no reason to think would ever see the light of day, there would have been no reason not to refer to his own role, if he had one? It would, indeed, have been typical for him to do so, just as it was in character for him to let Whitehall associates assume that he was party to all Churchill's most confidential counsels. On the following day, however, as if to reinforce Morton's note, Eric Seal, Churchill's Principal Private Secretary, gave the following instructions to Private Office staff:

> Will everybody please take note that from now on boxes will come regularly every day from 'C' marked 'only to be opened by the Prime Minister in person'. This marking is not mere camouflage and is to be taken seriously. The boxes are to be put on the Prime Minister's desk and left for him to re-lock. They will be returned to 'C'. In any case of doubt as to whether a particular box comes within this category, it should be brought immediately to me.[24]

There are other, similar examples supporting the conclusion that awareness of the Ultra product was restricted severely on the orders of Churchill (who continued to refer to it by the codename 'Boniface'),[25] and that Morton was not party to it. Similarly, a number of sources confirm Colville's account that 'Brigadier Menzies used to deliver [the messages] personally to No 10 in ancient buff coloured boxes marked VRI and the Prime Minister himself kept the only key'.[26] Churchill insisted on the application of a 'need to know' rule: and Morton's position, involving liaison rather than planning or executive decision, conferred no such need. If he did *not* see Ultra, a number of otherwise puzzling episodes – such as that recounted in the previous chapter in connection of the 'suppressed' report on Tito and the Partisans[27] – make better sense. It is impossible, of course, to state beyond doubt that Morton was not 'on the list' either formally or informally. As the volume of material sent daily to Churchill by Menzies increased, it becomes less easy to distinguish in the official record how it was handled and what Morton saw. He died before the Ultra secret was first revealed in print, and in any case would never have divulged the truth. But within this framework of uncertainty, it is hard to avoid the conclusion from the available evidence that one of the wartime roles for which Morton is best known was one that he did not fulfil.

While Morton may not have been on the Ultra list, during 1940 and 1941 he was an effective conduit for other SIS/GC&CS intelligence intended for the Prime Minister; and thereby instrumental, whether intentionally or not, in raising SIS's, and in particular Menzies' stock. Not only did Menzies advertise SIS's efforts by sending information through Morton, but by insisting on retaining personal control over Ultra and delivering its product personally to Churchill whenever possible, he ensured that the Prime Minister got to know him personally. By April 1941 Dalton, who had a good nose for where power lay, noted in his diary that Churchill now thought Menzies 'a wonderful fellow and was always sending for him'; characteristically, he added 'then we must not have quarrels with C, who has become so invulnerable'.[28] Though Menzies' movements remain, for obvious reasons, sparsely documented, there is sufficient evidence to show that during the winter of 1940–41 he became a regular visitor to Downing Street.[29]

By the spring of 1941, SIS's operational fortunes had begun to improve, though progress was slow. Both as a result of SIS's own efforts, and through the assistance received from Allied secret services (particularly the Free French and Polish) directed from London, some improvised European networks had begun to be built up, based mainly on local *réseaux*. The expansion of liaison functions to deal with Allied services drew Morton, as chairman of the CFR and Churchill's informal channel of communication with the governments in exile, even further into SIS business.[30] He did not, however, attend the next meeting of the Secret Service Committee in March 1941, at which Menzies felt able to give a better account of SIS's performance than in the previous June. But the Service Intelligence Directors, while acknowledging that 'information from aerial reconnaissance and from interception was improving', remained critical of 'a lack of up-to-date information from agents' and the 'impossibility of obtaining exact information' in regard to the threat of invasion.[31] Menzies defended himself on the grounds of problems with transport and communications – areas where he felt the Air Ministry and Admiralty had been less than helpful, though Morton had offered to intervene on SIS's behalf with Churchill.[32] The Committee was not unsympathetic, but the fact remained that SIS was unable to deliver the information the Services needed on the massing of German troops or Order of Battle, and the situation was soon to deteriorate still further following the overrunning of Yugoslavia and Greece in April 1941.

In defending his organisation's performance, Menzies identified for the Committee two particular problem areas: lack of reliable information from American contacts, and the difficulties posed by the creation and expansion of SO2, the operational arm of the Special Operations Executive (SOE), whose interests, as Menzies put it, 'in many respects ran counter to his own'.[33] In fact, Menzies was less than frank with the Committee about the extent of his US contacts and the problems caused by SOE, both of which were considerably greater than he implied. Before taking SIS's story forward from the spring of 1941, we must turn aside to examine these 'problem areas', since each offers an insight into Morton's influence and activities. In both cases, too, the evidence indicates that the myth was somewhat different to the reality; and that the role of Menzies was more prominent than has often been supposed.

BSC: British Security Coordination and the 'two Bills'

The story of the development of the Anglo-American Intelligence relationship, and in particular of British influence on the establishment in July 1941 of the US Coordinator of Information (COI), precursor of the Office of Strategic Services (OSS) established in June 1942 and of the post-war Central Intelligence Agency (CIA), remains the subject of research and some speculation.[34] At the centre of the story and of the literature are two men who in the view of many (especially themselves) came to symbolise the Anglo-American Intelligence relationship, W.S. ('Little Bill', later Sir William) Stephenson, and Major-General William ('Wild Bill') Donovan.[35] Each is a figure about whom much myth has been woven, by themselves and others, and the full extent of their activities and contacts retains an element of mystery. Both were influential: Stephenson as head of British Security Coordination (BSC), the organisation he created in New York at Menzies' request;[36] and Donovan, working with Stephenson as intermediary between Roosevelt and Churchill, persuading the former to supply clandestine military supplies to the UK before the USA entered the war, and from June 1941 head of the COI and thus one of the architects of the US Intelligence establishment.

Morton's part in the story was largely that of intermediary. Contemporary American observers, such as US Ambassador in London Joseph Kennedy, his Military Attaché General Raymond E. Lee, and Ernest Cuneo, a US lawyer with close intelligence and political connections, saw him as a 'top level operator', a 'discreet and shadowy figure' with a 'through wire' to Churchill.[37] By this they meant that he was the man to approach with an urgent message for the Prime Minister. In respect of Stephenson and Donovan he was seen principally as a facilitator of what were assumed to be close personal relationships with Churchill enjoyed by both men. However, the evidence suggests that Churchill met Donovan on no more than one or two occasions, and may never have met Stephenson at all.[38] Any dealings with the Prime Minister were conducted almost exclusively through Morton, a central point of contact. Churchill was uninterested in the detail of clandestine liaison arrangements, being concerned principally with his own relationship with Roosevelt, and with senior US representatives such as Harry Hopkins. He was also reluctant, in the summer of 1940 at least, 'to give our secrets until the United States is much nearer to the war than she is now'.[39] He was content to leave intelligence liaison with Stephenson, Donovan and others to Morton on a personal, and Menzies on an operational, level.

It was, in fact, Menzies who was most effective in building the practical working relationship between British and American intelligence (and thereby laying the foundations for US post-war Intelligence institutions). When Morton boasted to Colonel Ian Jacob in September 1941 that 'to all intents and purposes

US security is being run for them at the President's request by the British',[40] he was referring to Stephenson and BSC: both reporting to Menzies. Stephenson, as we have seen, had approached SIS in 1939, with Morton's support, to secure Menzies' sponsorship for his industrial intelligence network.[41] No sooner had the arrangement been established satisfactorily in the spring of 1940, however, than Stephenson turned his attention, at Menzies' request, to exploring closer links with the US authorities; in particular, to establishing a closer relationship between SIS and the Federal Bureau of Investigation (FBI).[42] Stephenson had spent much time in the US, where Menzies wished to increase the scope of SIS operations, and to cooperate more closely with both official and less formal authorities, establishing his own channels rather than, for example, going through MI5 to the FBI. At this stage there was no central coordination of 'US Intelligence' in any institutional form, only disconnected and rival bodies that sought to draw on the experience of their British analogues: Menzies wanted it to be he, and SIS, that provided it.

Stephenson travelled to New York early in April 1940, reporting to Menzies on 17 April that he had established successfully a channel of communication between 'C' and J. Edgar Hoover, head of the FBI; their contacts were to be conducted under the names of 'Scott' (Menzies) and 'Jones' (Hoover). According to Stephenson, Hoover wished him to remain in the US as the SIS Chief's personal representative – an idea that undoubtedly appealed to (and may have been inspired by) Stephenson's ambition and desire for personal aggrandisement. Menzies was attracted by the proposal, responding on 11 May: 'I like the suggestion of you being my personal contact with Jones at Washington, but it is considered you should return to London first of all for consultation and instruction.' Their discussions persuaded Menzies that the proposed arrangement would be of value not only to SIS but to the FO too, as he wrote to Jebb on 3 June 1940:

I have appointed Mr W.S. Stephenson to take charge of my organisation in the USA and Mexico. As I have explained to you, he has a good contact with an official who sees the President *daily*. I believe this may prove of great value to the Foreign Office in the future outside and beyond the matters on which that official will give assistance to Stephenson. Stephenson leaves this week. Officially he will go as Principal Passport Control Officer for the USA. I feel that he should have contact with the Ambassador, and should like him to have a personal letter from Cadogan to the effect that it may at times be desirable for the Ambassador to have personal contact with Mr Stephenson.[43]

Cadogan supplied the letter as requested, describing Stephenson to the British Ambassador, Lord Lothian, on 10 June as 'an exceptional person who has extremely good contacts in the United States'. Meanwhile, however, Lothian was engaged in trying to persuade Halifax and the FO to accept a parallel offer from William Wiseman, SIS's First World War intermediary, who promised that for

£100,000 he could set up 'the best possible intelligence service in the United States' for the British.[44] But Wiseman, who like Stephenson had spent the inter-war years dabbling on the fringes of Intelligence while pursuing a lucrative commercial career, was regarded with considerable suspicion by the US Embassy in London, as well as by Menzies, who told a Foreign Office meeting on 5 June that 'both his predecessors had had very strong views about Sir William Wiseman and had recommended that he should on no account be employed by His Majesty's Government'.[45] In the end Lothian and Halifax, though reluctant to reject Wiseman's offer out of hand, deferred to Menzies' strongly expressed view that 'any scheme he wishes to initiate shall be placed before Stephenson in detail before any steps are taken or any financial liability is incurred', in order to 'avoid overlapping, confusion and irritation being caused to the United States authorities by a multitude of people claiming to be a channel of communication for confidential matters'.[46]

Morton supported Stephenson's appointment: he had no doubts about pre-ferring him to Wiseman, about whose activities he had expressed doubts in the past. Having Stephenson in place as a confidential channel of communication between SIS and the FBI, with a direct line to the President through Hoover and the potential for wider ranging connections, offered a useful opportunity for feeding the Americans with information Churchill thought they should have, as well as receiving it. But Menzies took care to retain control of the channel of communication with Stephenson as far as possible: it was from Menzies that Stephenson received his instructions, and it was Menzies who passed on reports and messages to Morton and others.[47] It is true that Stephenson proved by no means easy to control: through his organisation based in New York, known as British Security Coordination (BSC) from January 1941, he sought a monopoly on all secret British activities in the US, and was certainly capable of going behind Menzies' back to achieve this. But the record shows that he operated far less independently than he wished others to think.

Some of Stephenson's initiatives cut across work already being done by the FO and other ministries. In August 1940, for example, he put forward an elaborate proposal for the organisation of propaganda in the US, while in October 1940 he demanded from the FO, through Menzies, guidance on 'general policy and requirements in relation to America', on the grounds that 'his "behind the scenes" machine is constantly gaining in power and can be used most effectively if given some long-range direction in addition to immediate specific requirements'.[48] Menzies had to make some attempt to rein Stephenson in when other authorities objected. Nevertheless, he appreciated the 'vast volume of intelligence' that Stephenson was providing, and agreed with the conclusion of a secret report of October 1941 that:

> [Stephenson] has at the moment an almost unassailable personal position in the USA; apart from being controller of all British secret activities, he is in a sense the backdoor contact with the White House – a not

unimportant role when the rather quixotic character of its present proprietor is taken into consideration.[49]

Menzies was prepared to cope with the fallout from Stephenson's activities because of the advantage they brought to SIS, both in terms of information and of SIS's position within the Intelligence community. BSC was also important to SIS as a point of contact for the various bodies involved in US Intelligence who, though not prepared to work together, were 'willing to show all their results to 'C''s representatives in New York'.[50]

Conflicts of interest and jurisdictional difficulties were inevitable when BSC came to represent SOE and its propaganda arm, the Political Warfare Executive, and the Security Executive/Security Service in the US, as well as SIS, and extended its activities to Latin America and the Caribbean. There were complaints from the FBI and Canadian Intelligence as well as from Swinton in the UK. Some attempts were made to restrict Stephenson's range: in April 1942, for example, control of BSC's Security Division was transferred to the Security Executive. In April 1943 a meeting of the Secret Service Committee, attended by Morton, considered whether Stephenson should cease to represent MI5 in the USA, Canada and the West Indies; the possibility was even discussed that he should cease to work for SIS. When the Committee met again on 30 July 1943, however, Vivian, who had been sent to the US to review SIS arrangements there, reported that BSC conducted its operations with 'great efficiency', and the Committee agreed that Stephenson should be 'given an immediate assurance that he had the complete confidence of all the British Services which he represents in the Western Hemisphere'.

Although Stephenson was certainly a maverick figure, disinclined to respect the chain of command and capable of using his very good connections with the White House and elsewhere to further his own schemes, he nevertheless continued to represent SIS (despite giving the impression, according to one commentator, that 'he would no more have been station chief under Menzies than Donovan would have run the New York FBI office for J. Edgar Hoover').[51] Similarly, SIS remained in overall control of BSC, though working with other bodies, despite Stephenson's claims, in the official history of BSC and elsewhere, that he alone was responsible for BSC and its achievements. The official record suggests that Morton's channel of communication to BSC ran through Menzies: if Morton was in parallel contact on Churchill's behalf with Stephenson, the evidence has not survived.

Menzies' dealings with another back-door entrant to the White House – Donovan, like Stephenson a First World War flying ace, involved on the periphery of Intelligence in the interwar years – are less well-documented and have been obscured by Stephenson's claims,[52] but were nevertheless important. When Donovan, apparently at the request of Colonel Frank Knox, US Navy Secretary, visited the UK in July 1940, ostensibly to make a survey of 'Fifth Column methods',[53] he evidently had discussions with Menzies and SIS as well as with

Swinton and the Security Service. It seems that Menzies and Donovan remained in close touch from then on, and Donovan's second visit in December 1940 and subsequent tour of Europe and the Middle East were arranged and funded through SIS, with the knowledge and support of the FO.[54] Though Menzies was concerned to encourage, through Donovan, the provision of US war supplies to the UK,[55] he was equally concerned to influence the emerging organisation of American Intelligence, and this was at the core of his ongoing relationship with Donovan and of the work of BSC. Donovan's appointment by Roosevelt as Coordinator of Intelligence in June 1941 was seen as an achievement by Menzies as well as by Stephenson, who telegraphed to his Chief on 18 June:

> Bill [Donovan] accuses me of having 'intrigued and driven' him into appointment. You can imagine how relieved I am after three months of battle and jockeying for position at Washington that 'our man' is in a position of such importance to our efforts.[56]

Once Donovan was in place, Menzies used every channel to cultivate the relationship, including that offered by the visit to New York of the Director of Naval Intelligence, Admiral Godfrey, and his assistant Ian Fleming in July 1941. An early report from Fleming to Menzies, dated 19 July, is revealing:

> Organization as at present shaping is clearly not one which will produce concrete items of serviceable intelligence though its effect on US intelligence departments should be stimulating . . . Guidance into more fruitful channels will have to be vigorously exercised by Mr Stephenson with whom Donovan intends to work in closest collaboration . . . President is very enthusiastic and Donovan has his full support but rumour that Donovan is British nominee and hireling of British SIS is spreading and should be carefully watched . . . Value of this organization to British intelligence will depend entirely on Mr Stephenson.

It would be interesting to know whether Menzies passed this report on to Morton – also a close contact of Fleming's. The fact that the DNI's mission reported to SIS, however, shows the extent to which Menzies had established himself as the central point of contact. His relationship with Donovan gave Menzies a direct back-channel to Roosevelt, and was fundamental to the increasing closeness of the Anglo-US Intelligence relationship following the US entry into the war in December 1941 after Pearl Harbour, and to the development of what was later to become the CIA.

What part, if any, did Morton play in all this? As far as Stephenson is concerned, there is little sign of their continuing contact after he became SIS's representative in New York, though Morton kept Churchill informed of Menzies' reports on contacts with Hoover.[57] Morton's prewar relationship with Stephenson makes it more likely they kept in touch. In contrast, it is unclear whether Morton had met Donovan before an interview with him in London on 21 July 1940, and his report to Churchill of their meeting betrayed no sign of prior acquaintance.[58] Similarly, when Donovan visited the UK again in December 1940, heralded by an enthusiastic recommendation from Stephenson passed on by Menzies ('Donovan is presently the *strongest* friend whom we have here'), Morton's less than fulsome response gives no indication that the two men had been in touch in the interim:

Dear C,

The Prime Minister knows well the value of Donovan to us, though rightly or wrongly he considers Donovan to be over optimistic. I did not know he was coming here in the next few days. I should very much like to see him if he will see me and would be more than ready to offer him a lunch if he will honour me. I will remind the Prime Minister of Donovan's propinquity.

Yours ever,

Desmond Morton

It is, of course, possible that Morton and Donovan were closely in touch despite this formality, but again, if so, the evidence has not survived. The documentation suggests that it was Menzies who was at the heart of the Anglo-US intelligence relationship, directing covert liaison channels, while Morton maintained confidential, but more overt links on Churchill's behalf with Americans, civil or military, who sought access to the Prime Minister. This conclusion is supported by the range of Menzies' other liaison initiatives, including arranging through Stephenson for two FBI officers, Clegg and Hince, to visit the UK from December 1940 to January 1941 to study the organisation and methods of both SIS and GC&CS,[59] as well as his involvement in liaison between the two countries' naval intelligence authorities. In a letter written to Henry Hopkinson at the FO on 2 April 1941, giving 'a few examples of the work which I have personally been able to organise', Menzies also claimed credit for the decision – 'thought inadvisable in some quarters' – to bring over US signals experts to consult with GC&CS, leading to the latter's acquisition of important Japanese material, and the establishment 'under my direction' of a fruitful Anglo-American collaboration in procuring enemy and neutral cyphers.[60] Though Menzies was naturally keen to promote his own achievements, there is nothing to suggest that he was wrong to stress his own key role. In fact, his letter was defensive rather than boastful: he was aware, as he told Hopkinson, that 'there was still a feeling of restlessness regarding the SIS in certain high quarters', despite the value of the 'special Boniface material'. By this time, however, his relationship with Churchill was sufficiently secure for him to promote SIS's interests directly, rather than through Morton.

The decline in the Morton-Menzies correspondence after mid-1941 extends to American affairs, so that it is difficult to be sure of Morton's later involvement in US liaison. From other sources it is clear that he continued to work closely on Churchill's behalf with the US Embassy in London, and to see important American visitors on his behalf. Nothing has been found, however, to indicate that he played any more influential role. Menzies, on the other hand, continued to work closely with both Stephenson and Donovan, his professional relationship with the latter deepening after the US entry into the war and the establishment of the OSS in June 1942 (in which Menzies played some part). Relations between SIS, SOE and OSS in connection with the Torch landings, subsequent cooperation in North Africa and elsewhere, and later in preparation for Overlord, were complex and often difficult. Morton was certainly aware of this, and had an interest in respect of his dealings with the Free French and French North Africa. Nothing has been found, however, to indicate any significant role in the developing Anglo-American Intelligence relationship in the latter part of the war, while the close connections between Churchill and Roosevelt, and between the UK and US Chiefs of Staff – as well as Ultra, which Morton did not see – diminished his significance.

SOE: the Special Operations Executive

If Menzies was pleased with his achievements in establishing liaison with US Intelligence, he was far less sanguine about the situation in regard to the threat posed to SIS by the Special Operations Executive, formed in July 1940 from an obscure research section of the War Office (MI(R)), an equally obscure propaganda section of the FO (Electra House) and Section IX or D of SIS; its object to 'set Europe ablaze' through sabotage, subversion and propaganda.[61] Menzies had struggled, but failed, to keep control over the operational part of SOE (the former Section D), which used his facilities and communications, and which he rightly foresaw would compete with SIS for resources while engaged in provocative activities that posed a direct threat to SIS's covert Intelligence-gathering overseas. If he had hoped that Morton's influence or interventions on SIS's behalf would weight the scales against SOE, he was to be disappointed.

SOE was a body in whose formation Morton had both a personal and a professional interest, through his own SIS background, his relationship with the head of Section D, Major Lawrence Grand, and his attempts, when Director of Intelligence at MEW, to secure the implementation of aggressive economic warfare and sabotage operations against Germany.[62] It was also a project dear to Churchill's heart. Hitler's rapid advances in Europe and Scandinavia in April and May 1940, and in particular the imminent collapse of France, increased his determination in the first weeks of his premiership – in tandem with defence against external invasion or internal subversion – to take the offensive against Hitler's forces through 'subterranean' warfare in all its guises, military, economic and propaganda: he dreamed, according to David Stafford, 'of a democratic Fifth Column that would pay the Germans back in their own subversive coin'.[63] The

Security Executive would tackle the Fifth Column at home: a new organisation was required to create a Fifth Column overseas.

Morton clearly regarded the creation of a 'subterranean' organisation as part of his brief, as he wrote to Churchill on 27 June 1940:

> When I first came on to your staff you instructed me to keep in touch on your behalf with Fifth Column activities in this country and sabotage. I interpret the latter as embracing all offensive underground activities in enemy and enemy-occupied countries.
>
> You have made a great step forward in appointing Lord Swinton to centralise the necessary information and activity against enemy Fifth Column activities in this country. On the other hand offensive underground activities against the enemy do not appear either to be sufficiently centralized or to be carried out with the necessary vigour.
>
> I firmly believe that strong underground action against the enemy abroad through Sabotage, secret propaganda, passive resistance and revolutionary activity, if carefully thought out and coordinated, can play an important part in helping to defeat the enemy. In fact, 'Secret Service' of this type is now in my opinion even more necessary than gathering information from behind the enemy lines . . . Subject to your approval I propose to go further into this question with all concerned and to put up a report, if possible with recommendations, for the centralization and proper control of these important offensive measures, which in my opinion are hanging fire.[64]

This minute reflects the urgent desire of both the new Prime Minister and his Intelligence adviser, at a time of crisis, for action as well as – or even more than – information; and implies that Morton shared, to some extent at least, Churchill's and the Chiefs of Staff's doubts about the competence and capacity of SIS. It also shows that Morton envisaged a central role for himself in the fashioning of what was to become SOE. Unfortunately, by the time it was written he had already missed the boat: the initiative had been seized by Hugh Dalton who, although not given formal responsibility for what he termed the 'Ministry of Ungentlemanly Warfare' (MUW) until 16 July 1940, had begun to plot its scope, organisation and personnel as soon as he was appointed Minister of Economic Warfare on 15 May. Impatient of the cautious plans of the Chiefs of Staff ('always apt to be girlish'[65]), Dalton had earmarked not Morton but Jebb, Cadogan's Private Secretary, as the man to take forward what was to be SOE, telling him on 9 June that 'he should be given an instruction to investigate everything and question everyone in this field, and to report'.[66]

Jebb, a tough and ambitious young diplomat, was unwilling, as he told Cadogan, to take the post of 'Head Saboteur',[67] but he was willing to help Dalton set up the new organisation. He quickly identified the need to get rid of Grand, a 'dangerous charlatan': a view shared, he told Cadogan, by 'everyone who possesses both sense & any long acquaintance with D', though not, he admitted, by Morton, Hankey or 'new Ministers who have no experience of him':

> His judgement is almost always wrong, his knowledge wide but alarmingly superficial, his organisation in many respects a laughing stock, & he is a consistent, fluent & unmitigated liar. The only good point about him that I have been able to discover is that he is generous & liked by his staff, which includes one or two able persons. But to pit such a man against the German General Staff & the German Military Intelligence Service is like arranging an attack on a Panzer division by an actor mounted on a donkey.[68]

Whatever Morton may have had in mind for the coordination of underground activity, it is unlikely to have included the dismissal of his old friend 'Mr D' who, as he assured Churchill on 27 June, had 'an organisation and considerable funds', and was 'more or less' controlled by C.[69] Though accepting the need for proper approval of Section D projects, Morton envisaged rather, as he wrote to the DMI, 'Paddy' Beaumont-Nesbitt, on 28 June, that this authority would be exercised by someone with similar powers in relation to sabotage and overseas subversion to those given to Swinton in respect of internal subversion.[70] Possibly he saw himself in this role; or at least in a key position on any project board.

The new Minister for Economic Warfare, however, had his own ideas, and in Dalton – chosen by Churchill to head up SOE not least because he was one of Attlee's 'tough guys'[71] – Morton met his match. Dalton had originally been impressed by Morton, describing him as 'the live wire whom PM has stolen from my Ministry'.[72] At a meeting held at the FO on 1 July to discuss the proposed sabotage and subversion organisation he agreed broadly with Morton's suggestion that there should be a Swinton-like figure in charge, though Dalton saw himself, together with Attlee, as fulfilling that role.[73] By mid-July, however, Dalton felt much less charitably towards Morton, whom he suspected, with Bracken and Lindemann (labelled collectively as 'the parasites'), of influencing Churchill against him. He was not alone in his suspicions: Cadogan noted in his diary on 11 July that 'PM (put up to it by Morton) is against Dalton taking over and wants to lump the whole thing under Swinton',[74] and two days later Attlee warned Dalton that Morton 'worked on the PM', 'takes too much upon himself' and 'wants watching'.[75] Morton himself told Dalton on 13 July that 'it was the PM himself who . . . wondered whether the whole thing shouldn't be under one head, linking up with what S[winton] is doing now'.[76] Morton was also dismissive of the idea that Vansittart should be appointed to assist Dalton with SOE, saying that 'Van was now too old and had lost the power of taking decisions'. Dalton was unimpressed by this, noting that Morton 'spoke ill of many and well of no-one, except the Colonel [Grand] who, he says, has a mind rather like the PM's.'[77]

This meeting set the tone for a battle of wills between Morton and Dalton that the latter never intended to lose. Morton's attempts to influence Churchill against

Dalton, or to impose his own views on the organisation and operation of SOE with the Prime Minister's authority behind him, were parried skilfully by Dalton (supported by Attlee), as well as by Jebb and Sir Frank Nelson, SOE's Operatinal Director (CD). Menzies, who argued strongly against the executive control of Section D passing to MEW while SIS remained responsible to the FO, warning Jebb on 4 September of the 'grave disadvantages of running two sections of the Secret Service, with intimately interlocking interests, under two masters', was equally unsuccessful in his representations. A note of 15 September 1940, attached to a memorandum by Jebb on subversion, set out the position in stark terms:

> D is a separate, secret organisation, forming part of a larger organisation under the control of Mr Dalton. The function of this organisation is the promotion of Subversion. For general purposes of administration and disciplines, therefore, the D organisation comes under Mr Dalton and not under the Foreign Secretary. The function of C, who operates under the control of the Foreign Secretary, is the collection, collation and distribution of secret information and intelligence. At the same time D is intimately associated with C, both on historical and on practical grounds, and if he is to function efficiently, it must be with the friendly cooperation of C.[78]

'C's friendly cooperation was required, not requested; and to reinforce the fact that control of Section D had passed comprehensively away from SIS to SOE, Dalton dismissed Grand, informing him by letter on 18 September 1940 that 'under the re-organisation on which I have now decided, there will be no further opportunity for the use of your services'.[79] Grand found it hard to believe that Dalton either would or could dismiss him so summarily, and a number of his influential supporters, including Morton, shared his scepticism. Within three months, however, Grand found himself posted to India with the Royal Engineers.[80] Although relations with Morton improved after this – Jebb reported that 'King Bomba [Dalton's name for Grand] having lost the game,' Morton was 'much more disposed to play with us'[81] – Dalton remained wary, and was unsurprised when Nelson told him on 22 November that he had evidence that Morton was 'no friend of his or G's [Jebb's] or mine, and would much like to discredit our whole show'.[82]

The relationship between Morton, Dalton and SOE was soured further in the second half of 1940 by another matter altogether, and one that offers an insight into Morton's private affairs so rare as to merit a detailed account. A chance find in the archives has revealed that between May and the end of October 1940 Morton spent the better part of each week in occupation of a serviced flat, No 150 Whitehall Court, the rent for which was paid from the budget of Section D of SIS, from whom SO2, the operational arm of SOE, inherited the charge. This came to light in the autumn of 1940 when Squadron Leader J.F. Venner, a professional accountant asked to look into SOE's confused early funding arrangements,[83] discovered that the flat had been rented on 26 May 1940 at the request of the Prime Minister's office in the name of a 'Colonel L. Graham' who, on investigation, proved to be Morton. The weekly rent of £6 6s 0d (the equivalent of around £220 today), inflated to an average of £16 (£560) by meals – and, in particular, by drinks and cigarettes – was borne by SIS out of Section D's budget. Grand had been the beneficiary of a similar arrangement, inhabiting a suite (under the name of Mr Douglas) in St Ermin's Hotel. Grand was more extravagant than Morton, frequently running up weekly bills of £40 (nearly £1500) that included such items as laundry, fruit, taxis and biscuits.

The original arrangements to rent these apartments as a charge to Section D had, presumably, been approved by Menzies; and while those in charge of SOE finances (including Dalton) took steps to terminate them by the end of 1940, there was no implication of real impropriety. Morton's prewar routine of spending the working week in London and weekends at Earlylands was clearly hard to sustain in wartime when such distinctions (or even the distinction between day and night) disappeared; and frequent meetings at odd hours, combined with Churchill's nocturnal working habits, also made it less practicable for Morton to use his mother's house in Chelsea as a London base. He needed to be within close call of Downing Street and the rest of Whitehall, and a serviced flat, where he could order meals and have laundry done, avoided the inconvenience (and expense) of maintaining a separate establishment or servants.

The surviving weekly accounts for 150 Whitehall Court from June–October 1940 offer a rare insight into Morton's habits. They show that he spent an average of three nights a week there and sometimes more, as well as calling regularly in for meals during a busy working day, and was usually back at the flat on Sunday nights in order to be ready for early meetings on Monday. In the week beginning 23 June, for example, he lunched there on Monday, Tuesday, Friday and Saturday, and dined on Monday, Saturday and Sunday, when he also ordered wine at a cost of £3 7s 8d. His bill for spirits was £4 7s 10d, with 13s 8d for cigarettes and cigars. The pattern of expenditure suggests that he entertained at Whitehall Court, which would have provided a useful, and private, meeting place away from the bustle of the War Cabinet offices. Indeed, it appears that Dalton himself may have lunched there on 21 June 1940 with Morton and Rex Fletcher.[84] There is, however, no record of the names of other visitors to Whitehall Court. Morton rarely spent Saturday nights in London, possibly in order to attend church on Sunday, but no clue has been found as to whether he did this in London or the country.

Venner's investigations into SOE finances in October 1940 led him to challenge Morton about the Whitehall Court apartment, and by the end of the year the tenancy had been terminated.[85] The last reference to the matter appears in Dalton's diary for 16 December 1940, when he noted:

Commander Fletcher calls at my request to discuss Whitehall Court. He is oliaginous [*sic*] and ill at ease. I make it clear that I have no wish to be awkward and will authorise the necessary action to clear the accounts and end the lease. I say that the DM [Morton] has not been either candid or helpful.[86]

It would be interesting to know whether the original suggestion for the rental of the Whitehall Court flat came from Grand, from Menzies or from Morton himself. Whatever the truth, Morton certainly took advantage of SIS's somewhat opaque funding arrangements to secure free lodgings and make his own professional life easier at a time of considerable pressure. From the biographer's standpoint one can only be grateful that he did. It is easy to understand, however, why SOE declined to continue the arrangement. Nothing has been found to indicate that any alternative was sought, or how Morton managed for the balance of the war. He certainly lived for part of the time at his mother's house, but also slept in the No 10 Annexe (now the Cabinet War Rooms, where a small room in the present museum is designated as 'Desmond Morton's room'). It could not, however, match the privacy – or, presumably, level of service – afforded by Whitehall Court.

Discussions over terminating the Whitehall Court arrangement did not improve Morton's relations with Dalton, who could not, however, ignore Morton's message that Churchill would like to hear more about what SOE was up to, sending to No 10 a pile of reports on 8 January 1941. As Dalton suspected, Morton got hold of these first, forwarding them to the Prime Minister with a short, condescending summary minute that began 'Dr Dalton's covering letter hardly expresses what I have tried to urge, namely, that he should (a) inform you briefly when he has succeeded in doing anything of importance; (b) apply to you for aid if he needs it'.[87] Morton's tone was scarcely less patronising in his dealings with Jebb and Nelson, who generally succeeded nevertheless in maintaining a workable balance between resisting Morton's interference and exploiting his access to the Prime Minister.

In February 1941, however, matters came to a head when Jebb, on Dalton's instructions, wrote to Morton:

> As you know, both he [Dalton] and indeed all of us much appreciate the efforts you are making to help the SOE to take its proper place in the picture and I need hardly say that I, myself, would welcome any ideas or suggestions that may occur to you, to say nothing of constructive criticisms of our work. It would, however, be a help if, on matters of business connected with SO2, you would normally address yourself either to me or CD [Nelson] . . . If, however, you take up matters direct with other members of the organisation there is a certain danger of wires being crossed, particularly owing to the fact that only CD and myself are in a position to see the whole picture, that nearly all our activities are as delicate as they are dubious, and that not all our staff have been very long on the job.[88]

This courteous, if firm rebuke produced an outburst from Morton, who telephoned Nelson in a fury, asking him whether he was 'aware that he had power from the Prime Minister to call for persons and papers, which meant that if he chose to write to any of my subordinates or any of Jebb's subordinates he could do so without being indicted thereto'. Though Nelson tactfully suggested it was 'much ado about nothing', Morton 'branched off into a diatribe on organisation and persons, the sense of which was that the Prime Minister hated Dalton, hated Jebb, hated me, hated the entire Organisation and everybody in it, and that it was only through the efforts of Major Desmond Morton (who felt that the Organisation was an important one and was serving an important purpose) that it had been allowed to continue as long as it had'. Threatening to 'wash his hands' of SOE, he put down the receiver.[89]

By this stage neither Jebb, Nelson nor Dalton ('This sort of thing is a most frightful bore') was inclined to take Morton's displays of temperament too seriously. Attlee, informed of the row, assured Dalton that Churchill was perfectly happy with SOE's progress and had denied angrily that either Morton or Bracken had any right to criticise it in his name: 'he considered that I was doing a good job of work'.[90] Meanwhile, Morton regained his equilibrium sufficiently to pay a visit to SOE's country HQ on 22 February, sending Dalton an almost obsequious letter of thanks: 'I hope that when the war is ended and it is allowed us to lift a little the veil of secrecy, some brilliant brain may sympathetically, but humorously, describe the complicated labour undertaken so ably by that devoted band of people whom I have had the great honour to visit.'[91] The damage was done, however. For the rest of 1941 day to day business between Morton and SOE proceeded in an atmosphere of somewhat chilly courtesy, while Dalton, Jebb and Nelson were too preoccupied both with SOE's growing operational activities in Europe, as well as organisational difficulties, to take much notice of his interventions. On 19 December 1941, in the context of a row between Dalton and Bracken over responsibility for overseas propaganda, Morton suggested to Dalton that 'he might help by trying his hand at a first rough re-draft' of the SOE Charter, which was now out of date. Dalton did not rise to this: 'I said that I did not think he need attempt this, as I intended to consider the whole question over Christmas. He said that he was going away tomorrow for a week's leave, the first he had had since the war. I said that I hoped he would enjoy himself.'[92] On that note of stalemate they parted: two months later Dalton had handed over responsibility for SOE to the new Minister, Selborne.

Morton attempted to exploit the change by suggesting to Churchill on 23 February 1942 that he should assist with a 'dispassionate enquiry' into the overlap between SOE and the work done by Bracken and Menzies, and into 'whether SOE is properly carrying out the functions of sabotage and other subversive action'. For once, Eden was in agreement with Morton, telling Churchill that SOE needed 'a thorough overhaul and probably a severe pruning'; there was mention of dividing SOE in two under the COS and FO. Dalton's valedictory report, however, came down firmly on the side of the *status quo* and Churchill's decision to appoint Selborne was, he told Eden and Bracken, intended to quell any further argument:

> I offered the post of MEW to Lord Wolmer and he accepted it on the clear basis that he would be responsible for the MUW organization in all its branches subject to coming to amicable arrangements with you and the MOI about certain overlaps. I think you will find the difficulties which previously existed will be removed by the change in personalities.[93]

There was to be an enquiry into SOE's activities and relations with other departments, but after discussion with Eden and Bracken, Selborne asked Oliver Stanley to take it on.[94] Morton's name was not mentioned.

Selborne was a very different ministerial head of SOE from Dalton; less brilliant and dynamic, perhaps, but quietly competent, anxious to make things work and not to upset Eden, to whom (unlike Dalton) he was inclined to defer. Selborne also got on well with Morton, valuing his advice and knowledge on economic warfare as well as Intelligence, and understood the importance of his access to Churchill. Their voluminous correspondence is friendly as well as professional. Other changes in personnel, with Hambro replacing Nelson as CD, and Colonel Harry Sporborg taking over Jebb's role, also helped to improve Morton's relations with SOE. But while Selborne, Hambro and others were grateful for Morton's help and happy to oblige him with information that would reach Churchill, any attempts at interference with the running of the organisation were deflected politely but firmly. This may in part have been due to Eden's influence on Selborne; but it was also because in the ongoing struggle for strategic priority and resources between SOE and SIS, it was suspected that Morton was inclined to take SIS's part. It was not as simple as that: Morton was quite capable of proposing a scheme detrimental to SIS if he thought it a good idea, or (better still) one that offered an opportunity for his own participation. Nevertheless, most of his interventions were a direct result of an instruction from Churchill – though it is true Morton sometimes used the Prime Minister's more random impulses to stir things up, with the result that his initiatives tended to cause trouble rather than solve problems. This was certainly true in the sphere of Intelligence organisation from 1942 onwards.

Organisational reform: the SIS-SOE struggle, and Intelligence coordination

The same dissatisfaction with the performance and coordination of British Intelligence that had led to Hankey's review in the winter of 1939–40 persisted throughout the war, despite periodic attempts to tackle the problem. In the autumn of 1940 Attlee, as Lord Privy Seal, argued for some single authority to 'co-ordinate and improve' Intelligence, both 'secret' and military, and was unimpressed by the complacence of a Chiefs of Staff report produced at Churchill's request:

The argument that this is not the time to make a change only amounts to this, that because we are fighting for our lives we should continue to use an inefficient instrument. It is precisely because we are engaged in a critical war that we ought to do now, late though it is, what should have been done years ago. There should be one directing mind at the head of the Intelligence Service. The three Departments of the fighting Services and the SIS should be co-ordinated.[95]

Though Churchill agreed with the War Cabinet that better coordination was important, no action was taken: neither Attlee's ideas nor a follow-up minute by Morton in January 1941, proposing the establishment of an 'Intelligence Executive' responsible for 'appreciating information available on events in foreign countries',[96] held much attraction at a time when a German invasion remained a possibility; in any case, Ismay was already taking steps, on Churchill's orders, to develop the War Cabinet machinery and the JIC so as to improve the coordination and use of Intelligence. The problem remained, however, and was compounded by growing tensions between SIS and SOE as the latter organisation expanded. SIS feared, as Hinsley put it, that 'sporadic sabotage would endanger long-term intelligence plans' and that 'SOE's methods were insecure'.[97] SOE, meanwhile, was growing increasingly frustrated at what it regarded as persistent SIS obstruction, including a refusal in April 1941 to allow SOE to handle its own codes and signals.

By the time Selborne took over, tension with SIS had reached boiling point. On 27 March 1942 Jebb sent a long minute to his new Minister forwarding a memorandum by the outgoing CD, Nelson, complaining bitterly of SIS. Though both men were careful to stress their good personal relations with Menzies and his staff, they were highly critical of the organisation, in which, Jebb wrote, there was:

> too much of what I would call the 'false beard' mentality . . . more especially among those who have been in the show for a very long time. Times have changed, and 'secret' activities are now the rule rather than the exception . . . It does not now really matter in the least if the enemy knows who is responsible for any particular secret service or, indeed, how it is run, provided he does not know what it is doing. The idea of a deeply mysterious 'Master Spy', sitting in some unknown office and directing an army of anonymous agents is as out of date as it is romantic . . . I would not want to suggest that SOE themselves are entirely free from the 'false beard' mentality; still less that they have not, as CD himself admits, probably, on occasions, done things which have earned the legitimate displeasure of 'C'. What I do maintain is that SOE has consistently put all its cards on the table in its dealings with 'C', while 'C' has kept nearly all his in his hand – I will not say up his sleeve![98]

Nelson, in his memorandum (which annexed notes on a number of specific instances of SIS 'obstruction'), was even more direct:

When we began to get into our stride as a new organisation towards the end of 1940 the SIS attitude was that we were a rather ineffective and ridiculous collection of amateurs who might endanger SIS and all their works if we were not kept quiet somehow. Now their attitude appears to be that we are dangerous rivals and that if we are not squashed quickly we shall eventually squash them. The changed attitude is in my view due to the fact that we have outstripped them in many directions and have proved ourselves in many directions to be a more efficient organisation.[99]

Battle lines had been drawn. It was just the sort of situation Morton enjoyed, offering an opportunity to intercede and put forward ideas of his own. The first sign of his intervention did not appear until the middle of May 1942, but he was clearly involved before this. Indeed, in a minute to Ismay's deputy, General Sir Leslie (Jo) Hollis of 19 May, he stated that 'some weeks ago I was formally directed by the Prime Minister to see the Ministers and principal officers concerned with SIS and SOE'.[100] Although it has not proved possible to pinpoint Churchill's instruction more exactly, he must surely have been provoked into action by documents crossing his desk in March and April 1942 – some no doubt passed to him by Morton – revealing a state of affairs so fraught with drama that it deserves description in some detail.

Selborne, worried by the 'deplorable state of affairs' revealed by Nelson's memorandum, suggested to Eden on 31 March that there should be regular SOE/SIS meetings, presided over by a 'Conciliator'.[101] He then presented a paper to the War Cabinet, described as 'odd' by Cadogan and 'extraordinary' by Menzies, rebutting what he called 'baseless calumnies' about SOE's personnel, operations and financial situation, and claiming that 'very fine results' had been achieved by 'men of high distinction' in SOE who were 'naturally indignant' at rumours 'which have originated from interested parties, and at the levity with which they have been given currency by responsible persons who appear to have little idea of the difficulties inherent in their task'.[102] Menzies, commenting on this document to the FO, pointed out that many of SOE's successes mentioned in the paper could not have taken place without SIS's help, and rejected altogether the idea of a 'Conciliator':

What is required is a final act of priority, which must be accepted by both Services. If it is decided that SOE has priority, then it must be realised, without any equivocation, that information will suffer. If I have operational priority, I do not think it will necessarily interfere much with SOE . . . We shall never be able to settle any question satisfactorily until His Majesty's Government have made up their minds on the question of priority. To-day, just as twelve months ago, when SOE began to get active, that is the problem.[103]

No doubt Menzies knew he would get no straight decision on priorities, but he was successful in opposing the idea of a Conciliator. Instead, it was agreed that in future 'C' should be represented on the Joint Planning Committee, and should attend a fortnightly meeting with SOE at the FO. There seemed to be a truce: but the calm was shattered two weeks later by a Joint Planning Staff paper that outraged both SIS and the Foreign Office. The paper (which the JPS were told smartly to withdraw before it reached the JIC, let alone the COS), included the following conclusions:

(a) Unified control of the activities of SOE and SIS is essential.
(b) Their activities must be governed primarily by strategic considerations, and coordinated with those of the regular Military forces.
(c) Where the interests of Allied and neutral countries are affected, the system of control must allow for consultation with the Foreign Office, the interests of which must be safeguarded, but direct Foreign Office control is undesirable.[104]

On this basis, the JPS proposed that 'SOE and SIS should form parts of a single organisation' under the direction of the COS, 'provision being made for consultation with the Foreign Office'.

Both SIS and the FO rejected conclusions and recommendations alike. The FO pointed out that the JPS proposals would involve 'first, a reversal of the decision which the Prime Minister has recently confirmed that SOE shall be under the control of the Minister of Economic Warfare, and secondly, a change in the British Constitution to wrest SIS from the control of the Foreign Secretary'. Menzies took the opportunity to stress SOE's dependence on SIS, as well as SIS's integral connection with the FO:

The individuals who drew up this paper without consulting me, do not appreciate that the Foreign Office *must* remain the parent, and that the removal of control from the Foreign Secretary to another Minister would complicate matters, and might well endanger SIS becoming involved in political questions which, since its inception, it has studiously avoided. If an Executive Head is necessary, this individual should clearly be the Head of the Secret Service, as it should be borne in mind that SOE have always meticulously followed the methods used by the SIS, and without the latter's assistance from the earliest stages, could not have conducted its business . . . I am confident that if the control of SOE reverted to the Foreign Office, many difficulties would automatically disappear, and if it is not improper to take a German analogy, the subversive organisation would be under the Head of the Secret Service.[105]

Menzies reinforced his arguments by attaching a 'memo by an officer in SIS', clearly Dansey, who claimed to have been the originator in 1937 of the idea for a small sabotage unit which would make use of the sort of agents – 'dissatisfied engineers and Communist organisations' – who were more fitted for sabotage than for obtaining information. He was now dismayed by SOE's competition with SIS and regarded efforts at cooperation as 'rather useless'. Echoing Menzies, he concluded that 'the real point, which has been lost sight of', was: 'Does the War Cabinet consider information should precede action, or that action should precede information?'[106]

The Chiefs of Staff were both astonished and exasperated by the amount of time and energy devoted to this inter-Agency strife. To Hollis, therefore, a minute from Morton of 19 May seemed to represent the voice of calm reason:

> Past difficulties between the two organisations owe their origin to two main causes. The first is a conflict of personalities, which may well have been removed as a result of certain recent changes in the direction of SOE. I understand, at any rate, that both parties are now ready to forget the past and to do their best to cooperate.
>
> The second cause, though less delicate, is more difficult. It arises from a legitimate and inevitable conflict of interests. The aim of SIS is only to obtain information. To do this they require their agents to fade into the background and to avoid disturbances in their area. SOE are required to create disturbance. I have suggested to Lord Selborne, Sir Charles Hambro and Brigadier Menzies that this natural divergence of aim should not be taken as a personal matter and is capable of resolution. The Heads of both organisations should disclose to one another their secret plans and arrangements. If SOE propose or are instructed to take action which SIS claim will seriously risk any important flow of information, Sir C. Hambro and Brigadier Menzies should compile a very brief joint memorandum, setting out facts which can hardly be disputed. This memorandum should then be submitted either to the Chiefs or to the Foreign Secretary according to the nature of the information risked. If these high Authorities, having been made aware of the risk run and choose to take it, Brigadier Menzies cannot be held to blame if the particular flow of information ceases as a result of SOE activity.

Then came the sting in the tail: as ever, Morton could not resist putting forward a proposal that seemed to offer an opening for 'an officer of sufficient experience', i.e. himself:

> Neither the personnel of SOE nor of SIS includes an officer or official of sufficient experience at the HQ of Government to know 'how the machine works'. This leads frequently to failure to consult the proper authorities at the right time, and what is sometimes more important, in the right way. SOE now consists exclusively of temporary Government Servants. Although Brigadier Menzies and several of his immediate subordinates have served the Government for many years, they have

270

inevitably done so in a special atmosphere of secrecy, which has denied them the experience and contacts of an officer or official serving in an equivalent position in one of the ordinary Departments of State . . . By the Prime Minister's direction I have told Selborne, Sir C. Hambro and Brigadier Menzies that, should they care to make use of my services to advise them at any time on matters of this kind. I shall be entirely at their disposal. I do not yet know what will come of this.[107]

Hollis thought Morton's minute very helpful and was, he told Ismay, in favour of taking him up on his offer. The Chiefs of Staff were less enthusiastic: one member (it is not revealed which) still thought 'some fundamental change in the higher direction of SOE and SIS was required', while the other two realised 'that any fundamental change in the ministerial control of these respective bodies was impracticable at the present time'. Morton was asked to explain the position to the COS in person; he did so on 29 May, and was followed at subsequent meetings by Hambro and Menzies. As a result of this consultation the COS agreed on 8 June that there should be regular meetings, and an exchange of secret information between SOE and SIS. There was no further mention of help from Morton, who set out the new position in a minute to Hollis of 20 July 1942:

1. In order to reduce causes of friction between SOE and SIS, the former has agreed to circulate no information to Government Departments but to pass to SIS all information received. Responsibility for circulation to Government Departments then falls upon SIS.

2. This is the only sound procedure when the information concerned is of a general Intelligence character without special urgency by its connection with current or impending operations.[108]

The documentation does not reveal whether Morton's offer to help was considered seriously, or why it was rejected. It seems likely that despite the reasonableness of his proposals, neither the COS, SOE or SIS welcomed the idea of his having any general authority in mediating what Ismay referred to as 'the SOE versus C barging match'.[109] Meanwhile, Selborne had commissioned a report on SOE by J.C. (later Sir John) Hanbury-Williams, a director of the Bank of England (who subsequently joined SOE), and Eddie Playfair[110] of the Treasury. He sent a copy to Morton on 1 July, telling him that the report was 'immensely satisfactory' because it came 'to precisely the same conclusions which I had myself reached' in his earlier memorandum for the War Cabinet. The Report, while acquitting SOE of charges of nepotism, corruption or incompetence, made a number of recommendations for organisational reform. Morton's comments on it were somewhat critical: he did not, he said, consider that the Report did enough to meet criticisms of overstaffing or financial waste, and thought that it said either 'too much or too little' about relations with SIS; on the organisational points, he commented that 'as an outsider' he 'found it difficult to understand without some chart of the organisation', a remark whose disingenuousness might be attributed to his pique at not being involved in the review. Hambro had, however, 'urged strongly his desire to let the matter rest', and Morton had promised 'to do nothing further about it unless you or he asked me to do so'.[111]

After these exchanges Morton seems to have withdrawn from the SOE-SIS arena for some months. His next intervention, however, incensed Eden. The occasion was the 'Clamorgan affair' in October 1942: an aircraft carrying Lt Clamorgan of the Free French Forces to Gibraltar on SOE business to liaise with the US Army crashed on Spanish territory, and the documents he had been carrying, including identity cards, secret letters and a report containing names and details of secret Allied organisations in North Africa, were passed to the Germans. Morton sent a dramatic minute to Churchill on 22 October, beginning 'Owing to incredible acts of folly, if not worse, on the part of the Fighting French Headquarters, the British, American and Polish Secret Services have been given away to the Germans.'[112] The minute wrong-footed Eden, who had heard nothing of the affair and asked Cadogan what it was all about, commenting that he 'deprecated Morton's usually extravagant language'. Cadogan reassured him that Menzies had told him about the incident as soon as it occurred, and had 'warned his own people implicated': 'Major Morton has taken the matter up rather excitedly with the PM. But I don't know that this last action is quite as useful as the others.' Eden thanked him, and asked for a draft reply to Churchill, 'who has been wrought by Major Morton into indignation'. To him, it was one more example of unhelpful interference by Morton.[113]

A few days later, however, another intervention by Morton provoked Churchill into action, this time to the wrath of Ismay. An incident where a report from Berne on the bombing of Genoa appeared to have been held up by the Air Ministry led Morton to suggest to Churchill, in a minute of 30 October 1942, that it was time to revisit 'whether the present organisation of Intelligence in general cannot be improved'; he took the opportunity to re-present his minute of January 1941,[114] and to suggest, once more, that he be authorised to act:

> I no longer have that close personal touch with Intelligence affairs which I enjoyed before May 1940 when Director of Intelligence at MEW, and would therefore need your authority and a little time before reaching a firm opinion on present arrangements. I nevertheless believe that more juice could be squeezed from the lemon were it found possible to pursue the ideas raised by you in Cabinet in January 1941. Alternatively, should this be too difficult, I believe that further improvements in our organisation could be effected if someone were given power and time to examine the present arrangements on a wide basis.[115]

Churchill's response was to ask Morton 'Is there no arrangement by which all Intelligence of the Departments is brought together?' Further discussion produced authority for Morton to address a long and somewhat pompous letter to Ismay, saying that Churchill had directed him to arrange that in future the Service Intelligence Directors should keep 'C' informed of any activities relevant to SIS, and that 'the Admiralty, War Office and Air Ministry should be instructed to send to me any reports on foreign countries or affairs received by them direct . . . which contain information bearing upon policy'.[116]

Ismay was more than irritated by Morton's minute to Churchill which, as he told him on 3 November 1942, was 'full of inaccuracies'; he hoped Morton would withdraw it 'and thus save me the necessity of pointing out its inaccuracies', while he was 'looking into' how Churchill's wishes might be met. Morton was not one to be abashed by such admonishment, and doubtless enjoyed the difficulties his minute provoked. Colonel Denis Capel Dunn, Secretary to the JIC, was given the task of explaining to the Services the necessity of providing Morton with 'all general intelligence telegrams and also messages and letters from Service Attachés abroad': a demand Capel Dunn described as 'embarrassing and irritating'. He reported to Ismay on 6 November 1942 that he had 'had to make myself rather unpopular with the Sections of the Intelligence Directorates in the Service Ministries by involving them in this research at this particular juncture' (two days before the North African landings). Ismay's minute to Morton explaining the system that would be put in place to meet Churchill's wishes was chilly and formal, and asked that if Morton had any similar matters to raise he should do so with Capel Dunn.[117] Morton was unrepentant: in his view a serious point had been made. The Prime Minister wanted to see, or be told about *any* report of note; he did not want departments deciding what he should see. Though it was clearly impossible for Churchill to see everything, there is no doubt that he was behind Morton in this, using him to stir up the Intelligence authorities. As Churchill minuted to Ismay on 5 November, 'You should see I get a better service': Morton's tactics, however annoying, achieved that.

The agreements reached in the summer of 1942 between SOE and SIS did not end their friction, which was increased by incidents such as the Clamorgan case, and more seriously by German penetration of SOE in the Low Countries, and by severe problems with SOE organisation in the Middle East.[118] The necessity to reorganise SOE's Cairo HQ in the autumn of 1943 led Morton to propose, yet again, an examination by 'a small Committee of suitable officers and officials' of the potential for reforming SOE as an organisation.[119] He received a polite response, but by this time he no longer had either the authority or the position to drive such a proposal forward. Churchill ruled that the question should be dealt with by Ministers, and Eden was equally firm that any investigation must come under the auspices of the FO. Morton found himself excluded not just from the discussions, but from his regular sources of information. Neither Menzies, nor Selborne, nor any other Intelligence authorities needed his intervention, or intercession, any longer.

During 1944 Morton was more closely involved with SOE on operational matters, in relation to plans for dropping arms to the French Resistance

Movement; but in November 1944, when he was tempted to comment more generally on organisational issues, Selborne made it clear that 'there can be no material alteration in the size or shape of SOE until after the defeat of Germany except for such changes as may be necessary to meet any alterations in the war situation', although 'the whole of our set up is automatically under review'. He suggested that Morton familiarise himself with SOE organisation so that he could 'explain to the Foreign Office how all this works', but Morton replied on 27 November that 'unless I am invited to do something, I ought not to get in touch'.[120] He was not invited to 'do something', nor was he involved in a committee set up by Cadogan to consider the future organisation of SIS. His role as Intelligence adviser had run its course. For the balance of the war he was occupied almost exclusively with French and other Allied affairs.[121] Though it was perhaps inevitable, it was not surprising if he felt his Intelligence role – the core of his career for so many years – had been allowed to evaporate, and with it his own influence. It is a pity that Churchill's letter of 15 October 1947 regarding the form of words he proposed to use in his memoirs referred exclusively to Morton's prewar contribution, for it remained true throughout the Second World War as well:

> When I read all these letters and papers you wrote for me and think of our prolonged conversations I feel how very great is my debt to you, and I know that no thought ever crossed your mind but that of the public interest.[122]

To the best of his considerable abilities, Morton had fulfilled the charge laid on him in May 1940. The myth may have been more powerful than the reality: but without both, we would know much less about the workings of British wartime Intelligence.

13

TREASURY TROUBLESHOOTER: 1946–53

There are few clues as to how Morton spent his time in the last quarter of 1945. Clearly there was no longer any place for him in Downing Street, but neither did he wish to retire.[1] If no one offered him a job, he must remain in the Civil Service (however much he disclaimed membership of that professional cadre). He made it clear that at the age of fifty-four he regarded retirement, or even a period of inactivity, as financially impossible. In any case, Morton was not cut out for leisure. By nature both active and energetic, he wanted, as well as feeling he needed, to work. There was, however, no immediate or obvious call for his services in the autumn of 1945. He had no particular academic, military, political or business allegiance to provide opportunities for employment; no close friends or allies seeking his cooperation in a new venture. Lack of any defined role or future prospects must have made the adjustment to peacetime conditions after five years of strenuous effort difficult.

After a few months in the Cabinet Offices, however, he was called to arms by his paymasters, the Treasury. As a well-known (if not always well-loved) Whitehall figure with long experience of government and expertise in economic, financial, industrial and intelligence matters, his skills were in demand. Between January 1946 and his retirement in April 1953 he undertook three major representational tasks for the Treasury on the British Government's behalf: from 1946 to 1949 as the UK's representative on the Inter-Allied Reparation Agency and on the Tripartite Gold Commission in Brussels; during the second half of 1949 as UK member of the United Nations' Economic Survey Group in the Middle East (the Clapp Mission); and from 1950 to 1951 investigating civil aviation in the Middle East and bringing to a conclusion the negotiation of an agreement between Britain and Iraq. Each of these three missions, carried out with his usual vigour and style, tested his abilities, patience and health: each was carried out successfully, though his methods and approach were apt to raise eyebrows and voices in the Treasury and elsewhere. Each little-known episode is also interesting in its own right.

Reparations and restitution: Brussels, 1946–49

For His Majesty's Treasury, 1945 was a dreadful year, despite the ending of six years of war. Against a background of virtual national bankruptcy, struggling to move from a war to a peacetime economy, dealing with new Ministers in a Labour Government, at the mercy of a dominant American benefactor determined to cut off the Lend-Lease lifeline as soon as possible,[2] Treasury staff were tested to the utmost by the demands of a series of international conferences and discussions that could hardly have been more important to Britain's future, including the negotiation of the agreement for a US loan to Britain signed on 6 December 1945.[3] At the same time, they had to make a key contribution to complex and stormy international negotiations on the fate of Germany and her assets.[4] Though this responsibility was shared by other departments, such as the Control Office for Germany and Austria (COGA) and the FO, it was the Treasury who supplied the expert negotiating teams. Not enough senior, experienced officials were available to meet all these demands.[5]

In particular, the Treasury felt unable to meet the resource requirements resulting from the Paris Conference on Reparation, which met between 9 November and 21 December 1945, its Final Act embodying an international reparations agreement, the establishment of an Inter-Allied Reparation Agency (IARA) in Brussels, and an agreement for the restitution of monetary and non-monetary gold.[6] Though Sir David Waley, head of the UK Delegation to the Allied Reparation Commission,[7] had been at Paris, neither he nor any of his team could be spared to represent Britain on the IARA or associated bodies. It was judged, rightly, that quadripartite negotiations on German reparation and industrial disarmament taking place within the Allied Control Machinery in Berlin were more important;[8] the IARA's job, broadly defined by the Paris Agreement as dealing with the nuts and bolts of restitution and reparation delivery, would be to follow instructions from the British Element of the Control Commission for Germany (CCG(BE)), and to consider issues such as the liquidation of German assets in Allied and neutral countries and the distribution of German shipping. The Treasury (and the government as a whole) underestimated both the significance and the complexities of what IARA would have to deal with, and cast about for a figure of suitable stature to undertake what they thought would be a narrowly defined representative role. Morton, experienced in the ways of government, familiar with international policy and with some degree of economic expertise, seemed an ideal candidate; and he was available.

Not everyone welcomed his appointment, agreed in early January 1946 and announced by the Treasury on the 17th. The Foreign Office, who had not been consulted, were less than pleased. Edmund Hall-Patch, a Treasury official now superintending the FO's Economic Relations Department, commented that if consulted 'we might have expressed some reserves as to the person who has been selected', and reported that the Minister of State, Philip Noel-Baker, considered the appointment 'most unfortunate', though unwilling to raise formal objection. Cadogan agreed:

We know Sir D. Morton's failings and propensities but I shd hope that in this particular job there wd not be so much occasion for them to obtrude themselves. In the circumstances I think we shd let the appointment stand. In all other respects Sir D. Morton is very well-qualified.[9]

It was agreed that Hall-Patch should have a 'straight talk' to Morton, while writing formally to warn the Treasury that:

the Foreign Office feel that every possible care should be taken to ensure that the Reparation Agency remains scrupulously within its terms of reference. The possibilities of friction with the Control Commission and the various interested Governments are very real, and may become embarrassing if the terms of reference agreed upon are not respected.[10]

Since the reservations about Morton's suitability were obviously based on previous knowledge of his style and methods, it is perhaps surprising that anyone considered a 'straight talk' from Hall-Patch would have any effect on him. He pre-empted the lecture in any case by producing on 6 January a three page note on the 'organisation of the Office and duties of the UK delegate to IARA',[11] indicating no great enthusiasm for his new post: it seemed to him, he said, that the Delegate's duties would largely be reduced to saying '"d'accord", "agreed", "OK" or the opposite', although he was concerned at the potential difficulties of coordinating the views of a wide range of Whitehall departments into his instructions. Perhaps by way of compensation, he went on to make detailed (if unrealistic) stipulations regarding the staffing, accommodation and communications arrangements that would be required both in Brussels and in London. Well aware that the important decisions on reparation would be taken in Berlin and London, he stressed that the UK Delegate must have access to both CCG(BE) and COGA, and play a real part in their work. Despite Hall-Patch's talking-to on 8 January, Morton lost no time in writing to General Sir Brian Robertson, Chief of Staff of the British Zone of Germany, suggesting that the latter should attach a liaison officer to 'my Brussels office', which he envisaged as 'something like a second Embassy';[12] an indication that even if his role were to be formulaic he intended it to have some stature.

In the event neither Morton nor the Treasury were correct in their presumptions regarding the scope and importance of the IARA job. Though the important decisions on reparations were indeed made in Berlin, critical discussions on the discovery, division and disposal of German external assets took place in Brussels, while the vexed question of Nazi gold soon expanded in importance so as to constitute almost a job on its own. The Brussels negotiations were in some ways a microcosm of those in Berlin, and suffered the same strains and stresses.[13] They also involved a large number of countries, some of whom (such as Greece and Yugoslavia) had a direct and urgent interest in restitution and reparation, but whose knowledge and experience of the issues, and politics, involved were limited: Morton complained, in a letter of 26 February 1946 circulated to the Cabinet's GEN 72 Committee, that 'at least half of the Delegates together with their Governments at home seem to have only the foggiest idea of the meaning of the Paris Agreement'.[14] Some were already under the influence of the Soviet Union who, though not a signatory of the Paris Agreement, took a keen interest in the IARA's work and made regular bids for observer status.

The first session of the IARA Assembly met from 28 February to 7 March 1946, and Morton soon found himself fully occupied in meetings that might last for eight or nine hours, required to become an immediate expert on every subject from shipping to budgetary procedures to coal. Despite his earlier requests, he had been allocated only a skeleton staff and usually found himself the sole competent UK representative on all committees. The wartime routine of long days and seven-day weeks seemed to have returned. Moreover, Morton's apprehensions about the potential for logistical difficulties proved justified. Although the issues he was dealing with concerned a wide range of departments in London in addition to the Treasury, the latter proved hopelessly slow and disorganised about collating and transmitting instructions to their frustrated representative in Brussels; the fact that all telegraphic communication was conducted through the FO did not help.[15]

Time and again Morton telegraphed for urgent instructions before attending a meeting at which he would be required to present the authorised UK view on a technical, but nevertheless significant issue, pointing out that if he did not do this the US view would always prevail by default.[16] On 9 March 1946, for example, following a meeting of the Committee on Industrial Property Rights, he requested urgent instructions on how to respond to a letter from the Assembly to the Occupation Powers regarding information on German industrial processes, and:

> any other information which I ought to have in my own mind when dealing with this matter over which there are prospects of considerable trouble from the non-Occupying Powers who are filled with rumours and fears that the 'Big Three' intend to exploit their advantages unfairly.[17]

The Treasury's reaction was to ask the FO what they thought; tentatively, they replied that the Board of Trade, Patent Office and COGA might have a view, but no-one addressed Morton's wider political concerns.[18] This instance was typical: instructions, when they arrived at all, reached Morton too late for him to give them proper weight, contained poorly coordinated and sometimes contradictory messages, and rarely addressed the wider considerations raised by discussions at Brussels. In these circumstances, he used his discretion, rather as the Treasury, and the FO, had hoped he would not. His attitude was encapsulated in a letter of September 1947 to Jack Abbott of the Treasury: 'Failing a comment from you, I shall merrily go on making decisions here according to that light which God has given me.'[19]

While Morton might be difficult to control, he was both conscientious and competent, and although both Treasury and FO might groan faintly at some of his more bullish interventions in the Assembly or committees and at the facetious tone of his reports, they had little choice but to trust to his judgement. Reluctant to send any additional experts to Brussels, they had to defer to the man on the spot. In fact, Morton had in some respects a better understanding, based on his wartime experience, of the power politics underlying the IARA, and of their relationship to the quadripartite negotiations in Berlin, than his Treasury handlers did, though they dismissed somewhat defensively his perceptive analysis of Soviet tactics, and of the influence of the personality of General Clay, saying they were 'his own opinions and not those of the Treasury'.[20] The extensive IARA correspondence preserved in FO and Treasury files contains many illustrations of the acuity of his judgement. In May 1946, for example, Foreign Secretary Ernest Bevin endorsed personally Morton's refusal to concede Soviet-inspired Yugoslav demands for extra reparations, since, as Morton put it, to agree 'would be to cheat not only ourselves but our other Allies and to put a premium upon dishonesty'.[21]

As the IARA Assembly got into its stride, holding three major sessions between February and July 1946, both Treasury and FO began to take a somewhat more relaxed attitude to Morton's activities, recognising his value as an old hand at dealing with awkward customers of all nationalities, in particular the French and Americans. While he may not always have 'respected' his terms of reference, he was generally surefooted and more than capable of dealing with technical subjects, though on some issues expert reinforcement from London was needed.[22] They saw little occasion to reproach him – and were, in any case, chary of doing so, in view of his quick temper when challenged. When John Coulson wrote to him from the FO on 14 March 1946, suggesting that the tone of his telegrams indicated 'a certain lack of sympathy with the attitude of your Greek colleague'[23] and reminding him that 'it remains our policy to give the maximum support to the Greeks and to ensure that they derive as much benefit as is possible out of the reparation settlement', Morton's response was predictably indignant:

> I can assure you wholeheartedly that I am not lacking in sympathy for the Greeks and have in no way changed my mind since June last year when under instructions from the Cabinet I visited their country as well as Italy and made certain recommendations by telegram which must be on file at the Foreign Office.

He went on to explain that his tactics had, in fact, earned the gratitude of the Greek delegate. The letter concluded with a more general comment on his new job:

> In one sense I am, but in another, I am not enjoying Brussels. I like plenty of work and have certainly got it here. The pressure reminds me of Dunkirk days. On the other hand the failure of whoever is to blame to provide me with the promised housing and office accommodation is the most serious handicap. We are trying to carry out the work of a large Embassy in a hotel – or for what it is worth two separate hotels. When I

refer to the work of a large Embassy, I have in mind its volume and do not intend to magnify its importance.[24]

In May 1946 Morton was asked by the Treasury whether he would agree, in addition to his IARA duties, to represent the UK on an informal tripartite committee of experts (American, British and French) set up in Brussels to implement the provisions of Part III of the Paris Agreement concerning the restitution of monetary gold.[25] The request was made in some desperation: neither Treasury, Bank of England nor FO had been able to identify anyone who could be spared. Morton had little choice but to agree, though he could hardly have anticipated the extent to which the Tripartite Commission for the Restitution of Monetary Gold (TGC), as the committee became in September 1946, was to dominate his professional life for the next two and a half years. As with the IARA, the Treasury underestimated initially the significance of the issue. Waley (presumably on the grounds that the UK had no claim to restituted gold, and that the bulk of gold found in Germany was in the US Zone) wrote to Morton on 26 June 1946 that 'in general we were little interested and could leave the initiative to the country which holds the gold and the country which wants it'.[26] This proved to be a hopelessly simplistic view of the UK's responsibilities, and both Morton and the Treasury were plunged rapidly into the technical complexities and the political implications of dealing with looted gold: 'Of all the reparations and restitution issues discussed before and during the post-war settlement . . . one of the most intractable'.[27]

The discovery, identification, control and allocation of looted gold were issues of both symbolic and monetary importance to the three TGC powers, to all those countries whose gold reserves had been raided by the Nazis, and to those former neutrals who had, whether intentionally or not, handled Nazi gold and still held it. By the time the TGC came formally into existence on 27 September 1946, Morton had already been involved for several months in difficult tripartite discussions, exposing the fact that the three governments held quite different views as to the definition of monetary gold and whether it was to extend to private, as well as central bank holdings.[28] These were issues on which the views of the Bank of England, as well as the FO, were crucial, but the Treasury's performance in coordinating instructions to send to Morton in Brussels remained inconsistent.

The strain imposed not just by the demands of his job, but also by the hand-to-mouth physical circumstances in which he and his office operated, soon began to tell on Morton. By November 1946 he was complaining of being overworked and underpaid,[29] and his health had begun to suffer. He took two weeks off at Christmas, remaining in the UK until 14 January 1947 (though still attending Whitehall meetings), but on his return seems to have been overwhelmed by the pressure of his duties. His judgement came into question – William Beckett, FO Legal Adviser, expressed the opinion on 24 January that Morton had 'gone rather off the rails' over the negotiation of an IARA inter-custodial arrangement[30] – and his reporting acquired an almost hysterical tinge. His habitual conscientiousness, combined with frustration at the slowness of Whitehall response and impatience with what he regarded as the deliberate obtuseness of his US counterpart, all contributed to the problem. The documentation makes it clear that the Treasury thought he was both overwrought and demanding. However, Douglas Carter of TWED, conducting complex negotiations in Brussels on German external assets, found himself facing the same difficulties, struggling single-handed with multiple committees and inadequate instructions. He, like Morton, complained, begging the department for help: 'Your take it or leave it attitude is not universally popular and there is a danger that the United States will get too much of its own way'; but the response – 'Please do your best alone . . . cheer up' was equally unsatisfactory.[31]

Towards the end of February 1947, after much discussion, the Treasury agreed to appoint Colonel Sir Ronald Wingate, Morton's old friend,[32] as his Alternate on the IARA and the TGC. While the assistance was undoubtedly welcome, the terms on which it was offered served to inflame, rather than soothe his agitation. The Treasury's letter of 21 February 1947, with Morton's marginal comments in square brackets, is worth quotation in full:

My dear Desmond,

You will be glad to hear that after certain doubts and difficulties, an agreement has now been reached with Wingate as your Alternate, and that we are hoping that he will join the Treasury staff on the 3rd March. Briefly, the arrangements with him are that the Treasury will pay for furnished accommodation, and give him an allowance of £800 in addition while he is in Brussels. (The rate of allowance is of course the same as yours, but we are not providing him with food and various other services, and he is, moreover, married.) *[Is this an excuse in case I should be jealous!!!]*

As I have said, it was not without some difficulty that we decided on making an appointment on these terms, which represent a considerable addition to the already heavy expenses of our representation in Brussels. *[What appalling rot.]* We feel that we ought to make a serious effort to recoup at least a substantial part of this extra expenditure on assistance by saving on other parts of the establishment, and we look forward with confidence to your co-operation in securing such savings. *[Impertinent young oaf!]* It might be at a later stage that someone from here could go out and see whether economies could be suggested on the spot, but in the meantime, it would perhaps be best if you could manage one day soon (before midnight, I trust) to see whether any proposals can be put forward. (Off hand, for instance, I am wondering what the present position is as regards Miss Dowdey).

Yours ever,

Peter Humphreys-Davies[33]

It might be argued that such a letter would be enough to send anyone into hysterics. Morton battled on throughout February and early March, when the TGC finally agreed, after tortuous discussions, to send a letter to Austria, Poland and Italy inviting them to put forward their claims for the restitution of monetary gold; meanwhile he and Carter worked through the night on drafts of an international agreement on German external assets.[34] But Morton was not merely overworked: he was seriously ill, and on 1 April 1947 returned to the UK to undergo an operation for the removal of a kidney; he was not to return to Brussels until September.

Other than brief references in official documentation to Morton's absence from Brussels, little detail can be discovered about his illness and hospitalisation. On 12 June 1947, he wrote to Eddie Playfair, an old friend, asking for 'a plain "yes" or "no" without any frills' as to whether the Treasury wished him to resume his appointment in Brussels after his recuperation (they did). He made it quite clear that he regarded his job as having played an important part in his collapse:

> Until my recent illness I was as strong as a horse. My doctors assure me, with obvious sincerity, that upon complete recovery I shall be just as strong again. But, with the difference that I cannot again risk a similar illness. Heaven has provided man with only two kidneys, and I have now lost one of these apparently essential organs. There is no moral doubt that general conditions of work, to which I freely consented during the last year, have at least hastened the end of Kidney No. 1. The conclusion is inescapable . . .
>
> In January 1946 it was assumed that, as Delegate, I should need to be in Brussels only during Sessions, when it was recognised I should have a lot of hard work for seven days a week. At other times I would be free to return to England to work to the same end in the Treasury. During stays in England I should be able to take reasonable leave, including one day in seven off, which in addition to keeping me fit, would enable me to look after my private affairs in this country . . . What is required is to make the conditions of the Delegate's work correspond more nearly with what was anticipated when existing arrangements were first made.[35]

While making allowances for Morton's natural tendency to hyperbole, there is no doubt that he had borne a heavy burden in Brussels during the past year, increased by his own propensity for hard work and attention to detail. His protests, however, fell on deaf ears. No doubt the Treasury, overstretched and distracted by multiple demands, felt impatient with his regular requests for more staff and better accommodation. But it is also without doubt that they relied on him to an extent that threatened to break his spirit, as well as his health.

During his recuperation from surgery Morton continued to keep abreast of events, attending meetings and engaging in voluminous correspondence. The record shows that he took a broader view of the IARA's and TGC's activities than some of his Whitehall mentors. At a meeting with the FO's German Section on 10 July 1947 he gave a masterly summary of the TGC's work and the problems that had arisen;[36] and on 14 July provided Mr Raven, of Rothschilds (who had been appointed as expert adviser to the UK Delegation to the TGC) with a comprehensive seven-page analysis of the situation, appending a copy of the relevant section of the Paris Agreement.[37] On 11 August he wrote to Playfair, advising that greater attention be paid to the restitution of monetary gold, both in Brussels and London:

Both the French and US Governments seem to regard the Gold Commission more seriously than do we. For them it is a tool for use at need in developing their respective foreign policies. As in the case of IARA, the French Commissioner regularly receives instructions direct from M. Bidault. The US Commissioner is instructed by the State Department and also, in particular, directly by General Clay. The actions of both these Commissioners are not confined to working out technical problems . . .

The time at which and the manner whereby the gold is eventually made available to successful claimants will be of high importance in relation to the national economies concerned: hence to their foreign policies. Both will affect European reconstruction, the Marshall plan[38] and relevant first class issues. Claimants are aware of this. They include our mutual friends and countries at present under Soviet influence . . .

I have insufficient information to dilate with certainty on the policy underlying an attack by claimant countries upon the Gold Commission or the three Powers which set it up. I suggest however that the policy of countries under Soviet influence is to cause dissension so as to slow down the rehabilitation of Western democratic Europe . . . If it can be shown that the USA is one of the Powers which, through lack of skill or legal right, has failed to create a maximum [gold] pool, the USA as the wealthiest country in the world shall, if possible, be made to pay forfeit. It is just too bad if the UK is in the dock too.[39]

There is no indication that Morton's analysis had any effect on the Treasury. On his return to Brussels on 2 September 1947, he found himself plunged into arrangements for a proposed interim distribution of gold, during which the US Delegate was forced to admit that much of the gold stored in the depository at Frankfurt had been looked after in a very slapdash fashion. The resulting decision to move the gold to the Bank of England caused even more problems.[40] Morton had to handle long and difficult discussions with little guidance: by 24 September he was complaining to Denis Rickett at the Treasury that 'there has been something most frightfully wrong ever since the start of my Mission in February 1946 in so far as concerns instructions and help given me from London . . . hardly a week has passed in which your Delegate, whether he be myself or Wingate, has not been placed in a position of grave anxiety, personal or official embarrassment and humiliation, or other discomfort'.[41] Playfair offered sympathy – 'This gold business is enough to drive one to suicide'[42] – but no action. The rest of the year was occupied by arrangements to move the Frankfurt gold to London: the only good news, according to Morton, being that the US Commissioner, Russell Dorr, had returned home 'suffering from a nervous breakdown which I have done a great deal to foster'; though Morton thought little better of Dorr's deputy, confessing to R.W. Thompson on 24 November 1947 that 'You and I are the sort of people who find it very hard really to like America and Americans en masse'.[43]

On 19 December 1947 Morton announced that as he had 'not had one day's holiday, not even a Sunday' since September, he proposed to spend Christmas at Earlylands, though prepared to 'answer the telephone or go to London as necessary'. He also predicted that during 1948 IARA work would gradually decrease in importance if not in magnitude, and that by the spring of 1949 there would be no further need for a permanent Delegate in Brussels. He expressed himself willing to serve for 'something like the next 6 or 8 months', though making no secret that 'other jobs would be preferable'.[44] While his work with the IARA and TGC had undoubtedly both exhausted and depressed him, his low spirits had a deeper origin, as shown by an unusually expansive letter he wrote to Thompson on 6 December. Referring to 'that deep disappointment which has come to all good men in that the dread winter of war . . . has not yet been succeeded by the newbirth of spring', he went on to castigate in bitter terms what he called Pride ('"*Orgueil*", not "*fierté*"'), to be found both in Moscow and Washington:

> This foul old crone in new clothes and with her face lifted by men, utterly consumed with a desire for their own personal power, is fast corrupting the lovely innocence of youth in all the countries where she claims to reign as Queen. All their right, spontaneous and natural enthusiasms to live, to die, to work and to suffer for the sake of others, their fellow men and women, is being exploited and turned to evil ends, the ends of their secret masters, by lies and lies and yet more lies . . .
>
> In my opinion you are terribly right to divide the present world into Europe, Moscow and the USA . . . Of the two the European must choose to range himself rather with Washington rather than Moscow. There can be no doubt about that, but it is not altogether a palatable business. Whatever the difference in result and implication between Moscow Imperialism and American Imperialism, and those differences are very great, the cause of both is our old enemy Pride, who has been given a new lease of life in the USA as well as in OGPU, OSNA & NKVD-ridden countries. Perhaps we would do well to remember that even after all her fortunes, Europe is not wholly free from that damnable disability.[45]

Christmas always produced dark thoughts in Morton, but his mood at the turn of 1947, as the Cold War deepened, seems to have been particularly black.

1948 brought little relief. The problems caused by the collection, allocation and distribution of the looted gold seemed both insuperable and interminable, and the files reveal a deep disillusionment, as well as anxiety about the delays in the TGC, caused largely by the US Delegate, whom Morton considered 'incredibly slow in thought in deed'.[46] He did not feel that anyone in London was listening to him, beginning one minute to Playfair 'I would like to put the following on record even if no one wishes to comment on the matter or give me specific instructions.'[47] Nor did he consider that anyone in London really understood the issues involved. Invited to attend a series of meetings in April 1948 in the FO to discuss the German level of industry and the Economic Recovery Programme in the context of reparations, he professed himself horrified by the 'appalling piffle that has been talked by various departmental representatives', none of whom knew 'the first practical thing about economics, industry or organisation . . . we are wandering in a country of fantasy surrounded by the shapes of Bedlam, and deafened by the howling of mad dogs. The canine ululations have a marked Pittsburg accent . . . Where we go from here, assuming that Bedlam is full, I do not know.'[48]

Although Morton was right in foreseeing the stabilisation of IARA business during 1948, the TGC continued to keep him busy. Gradually progress was made: between June and August 1948 the Frankfurt gold was at last moved to the Bank of England, though arguments continued as to whether gold collected in the British Zone under Military Government Law 53 should be included in the pool.[49] Meanwhile, in May the first payment of gold was made to Czechoslovakia, a decision taken at a long meeting of the TGC which left Morton 'fainting with frustration, wrecked with weariness and boiling with bile'.[50] Though the gold story had a long way to run – the TGC was not finally wound up until 1998 – Morton's part in it was coming to an end. By the summer of 1948 he was spending most of his time at the Treasury in London and actively casting around for another job, leaving Wingate to undertake the representational duties in Brussels.[51]

Morton returned to Brussels for a final stint at the end of November 1948, confessing that he was 'bored stiff with Brussels, reparations, and a great many other things as well', though he had to admit 'that life in London in winter with daily fogs, and the monotony of the food and existence generally' was little better.[52] A letter written to Denis Wheatley on 1 January 1949 shows him as rather sorry for himself, describing his exile to Brussels as a form of punishment:

> We exiles (Ronald Wingate & self) condemned to live outside our own land, because our names have been 'connected with that accursed one of W.S. Churchill', are very greatly cheered when anyone remembers us. Ronald & I refer to ourselves as the Legion of the Lost and sympathise correspondingly with the poor political prisoners of the NKVD. It is but a question of degree. H.M.'s present 'Government' (note quotation marks!) has intimated to us both that because of our disgraceful past and the part we played, however, small, in an ancient victory, we must be

tortured slowly to suicide or madness (see your own Toby Jugg![53])
Ronald & I do not like it. No sir! Not at all![54]

The complaint that he was being somehow punished for his former association
with Churchill was one that Morton made on a number of occasions. It is undoubtedly true that he was unpopular with some Labour ministers, partly because
he represented what they saw as the reactionary old guard. However, nothing has
been found to indicate that this had any influence on his deployment by the
Treasury, who, as the current Chapter shows, valued his experience rather than
otherwise.

By February 1949 Morton was arguing that responsibility for IARA should be
transferred to the Embassy in Brussels, with Wingate serving as UK Delegate
under the Ambassador's authority: 'both Colonel Wingate and myself frankly
want some more work to do than IARA can possibly provide'.[55] Neither Treasury
nor FO were disposed to persuade him to stay on. Wingate was informed formally
on 31 March 1949 that while Morton would, nominally, remain Delegate for
the time being, Wingate should henceforth 'assume full and direct responsibility'
as head of the UK Missions to IARA and the TGC.[56] Morton received little thanks
for what had been an extremely demanding and arduous assignment, but he was
now looking forward, not back. He was ready, both physically and mentally, for a
new challenge.

Refugees and resettlement: the Clapp Mission, 1949

No sooner had Morton emerged from the technical complexities and political
frustrations of reparations and restitution than he found himself plunged into one
of the most intractable issues in British foreign policy in the immediate post-
war period: Palestine. In July 1949 he was nominated as UK member and Deputy
Chairman of the UN's Economic Survey Mission to the Middle East, charged
with finding a solution to the problem of the enormous number of Arab refugees
– nearly one million – who had fled or been driven from their homes in Palestine
by the Jewish authorities and who now gathered miserably in camps in the Arab
areas of Palestine, in Syria, Transjordan, the Lebanon and Egypt.[57]

The provision of emergency relief to these refugees posed a humanitarian
challenge to the international community, but the issue of their long-term resettlement struck to the very heart of the Arab-Israeli conflict, and its wider, Cold War
context of Great Power hegemony in the Middle East, as well as being entwined
inextricably with US foreign policy and the Anglo-American relationship. The
Survey Mission, which toured the region between September and December
1949, trod a political minefield. Its members required toughness and ingenuity
as well as strategic awareness and diplomatic skills. Though it could not be
claimed that Morton possessed all of these in equal measure, even his critics had
to admit that he did a good job in extremely difficult circumstances; doing, once
more, a job that no one else wanted or was available to do.

By the end of the war in Europe in May 1945, the Holocaust had imparted a desperate and determined impetus to the Zionist campaign for the creation of a Jewish National Home, as well as inspiring a wave of sympathy and support for that aspiration, particularly in the United States where half of the world's surviving Jews lived.[58] The British Government, to whom the Mandate for Palestine had been entrusted in 1920, came under extreme pressure to increase Jewish immigration beyond the limits set in the 1939 White Paper on Palestine,[59] while faced with implacable opposition from the Arab states whose goodwill was essential to the British position (and oil supplies) in the region. These mutually contradictory imperatives, set against a wider context of Soviet expansionism, presented the Labour Government, and in particular Ernest Bevin, with a problem that was to 'cause him more angry frustration and bring down more bitter criticism on his head than any other issue in his whole career'.[60] During his first three years as Foreign Secretary, despite the pressing demands of the European situation, he expended considerable time and effort on a settlement of the Palestine issue, to little avail.

By the end of 1948 the British Mandate had been surrendered to the United Nations Organisation (UN), President Truman had recognised the Jewish state, and hopes of a compromise settlement that would be acceptable to both Zionists and Arabs, based on the partition of Palestine, had foundered on the rocks of Israeli's military triumph over the Arabs and on US refusal, rooted in domestic electoral considerations, to endorse any plan unacceptable to the Jews. Though exasperated by Truman's attitude, Bevin and his colleagues could not allow differences over Palestine to endanger the Anglo-American relationship at a time when the Marshall Plan, the Berlin crisis and plans for a security alliance all made transatlantic solidarity vital. At the turn of the year, a political solution to the Palestine problem seemed little nearer – the UN's Mediator, Count Bernadotte, had been assassinated by Jewish terrorists on 17 September 1948 – while the US Government, though supportive of the Zionist cause, was unwilling to enforce any settlement that threatened regional stability by alienating the Arabs. The refugee problem offered an opportunity to set the political issue on one side for a while. Though the British Government disagreed with this approach, arguing that the refugee problem was linked inextricably to a political settlement, US policy (and financing) were decisive.

In March 1949 George McGhee, who had been appointed Special Assistant for Arab Refugees to the US Secretary of State, Dean Acheson, pressed the British Government to agree to the appointment under UN auspices of an Economic Survey Group or Mission, which would visit the region, accompanied by technical experts, to advise on plans for the resettlement of the refugees and make recommendations for financing and implementation.[61] Despite British reservations that this would only serve to delay the urgent provision of relief ('All these poor people will die, while we argue ourselves round and round', Bevin protested[62]), there was little choice but to agree to the American plan. As the FO put it: 'The most important single factor in the situation is to ensure American participation and provision of American funds. For this purpose we must show willingness to cooperate to the best of our ability.'[63]

The British Government was asked to nominate a UK member of the Group, who would act as Deputy to the (as yet unidentified) US chairman. The FO thought this should be 'someone of international standing in the field of finance', such as Lord Brand, or even a well-known figure such as Earl Mountbatten, arguing that 'a man of high ability in negotiation and of world-wide reputation would be far more effective in achieving resettlement than, say a leading businessman or financial expert'.[64] The Treasury, however, recommended Morton, partly on the practical grounds that his work with the IARA was coming to an end, and that since he was already drawing a salary 'expenditure on his appointment to the Survey Group would be limited to his travelling expenses, subsistence and incidental expense'. The FO response was unenthusiastic, but when all the other candidates fell away for one reason or another they acquiesced somewhat reluctantly, rather as they had agreed his nomination to the IARA in 1946. In another echo of Morton's earlier appointment, Strang, now PUS, noted on 4 July 1949 Bevin's view on the nomination: 'He does not think him a good choice, but does not wish to object'.[65]

The FO were anxious that the UK representative should be of sufficient stature to be influential:

> The Americans are making the running at the moment in regard to the Survey Group. We have had to accept a number of proposals from them (especially in connection with the 'United Nations façade') with which we are not in sympathy. But we have always hoped that once the Survey Group started work we would be able to keep it on the right lines. In order to ensure that this happens our representation should be as strong as possible.[66]

They raised with the Treasury the question of Morton's alleged 'pro-Zionist' views, but this objection was rejected on the grounds that, 'as a Civil Servant, Sir D. Morton could not in any case be regarded as having expressed personal views'.[67] It is not clear what prompted this concern, though it may have arisen because of Churchill's support for the idea of a Jewish state. In his work for the Economic Survey Mission, however, Morton, certainly betrayed no such prejudice, and indeed was criticised by Israeli authorities for being too pro-Arab. In fact he was sympathetic to the concerns of both sides, while displaying an even-handed exasperation with their tactics.

Morton seems to have been moderately enthusiastic about his new task, writing to the Treasury on 28 June asking for a selection of papers to read and 'a brief list of personalities and bodies involved'. He also, characteristically, made a number of detailed stipulations regarding his status and about the proposed organisation of the Mission, stressing in particular that the national representatives should be responsible to their governments, rather than to the UN. Though both

Treasury and FO clearly regarded his comments as over-pedantic, his concerns were to prove well-grounded, the Mission dogged by tensions between UN and national interests. McGhee welcomed Morton's nomination, having met him in London, but expressed the hope that he 'would not be too much of a *prima donna*', and made it clear that any suggestion that the members of the Mission were functioning as official representatives of their governments would be unacceptable to the State Department.[68] On this point, as indeed on every other, the US view prevailed, and Morton surrendered gracefully, acknowledging to John Beith of Eastern Department that '[he] who pays the piper calls the tune':

> I want to make it clear, that in so far as I am concerned, I remain your humble servant, and subject to dictates of conscience or my own very marked private interests which I could not forego, I remain prepared to do exactly what you want, even though I might have to admit a degree of 'no enthusiasm' for the administrative arrangements'.[69]

During July and August 1949, while preparations for the establishment of the Mission continued – an American Chairman had yet to be found – Morton, with his usual thoroughness, did his homework, sending to the FO on 11 August a memorandum on Palestine Arab Refugees, and commenting on 24 August on the appointment of experts in the areas suggested by the State Department, such as irrigation, agriculture and public works (though he could not resist facetious comment on the category 'Community Services': 'I presume that Community Singing is not the intention, nor any other heart-lifting exercises, of which Mr Butlin is the recognised expert?').[70] The terms of reference were set out formally in a letter to the British Delegation at the UN from the Secretary General, Trygve Lie, received on 25 August. The Mission, to consist of a US Chairman with three Deputy Chairmen nominated by the British, French and Turkish Governments, was charged with 'examining the economic situation in the countries affected by recent hostilities in Palestine', and with recommending an integrated programme to 'enable the Governments concerned to further such measures and development programmes as are required to overcome economic dislocations created by hostilities', to 'facilitate the repatriation, resettlement and economic and social rehabilitation of the refugees' and to 'promote economic conditions conducive to maintenance of peace and stability in the area'. This ambitious programme was to be accomplished in six to eight weeks. On matters of detail, Deputy Chairmen would be paid a salary by the UN of $15,000 p.a., plus a representational allowance of $1500 p.a. and a subsistence allowance of $12 per day for those without dependants. The UN would also pay all travel expenses and for insurance up to $60,000.[71] (The financial provisions were significant, as difficulties over payment, currency conversion and tax deductions dogged Morton throughout the Mission.)

On the following day, 26 August 1949, Truman issued a statement announcing that Gordon R. Clapp, Chairman of the Board of Directors of the Tennessee

Valley Authority,[72] would lead the Mission. From the British point of view the appointment of Clapp was more acceptable than the rest of the President's statement, which staked a firm claim to US interests in an area considered to be a British sphere of influence, and contained not-so-subtle hints about the evils of imperialism.[73] There was, however, little to be done. The Economic Survey Mission set sail into uncharted and stormy waters with an American wind in its sails. Strang, briefing Morton on 6 September, the day before he left London, could only stress that HM Government would object strongly if the Mission's wide terms of reference were 'made the means whereby the United Nations assumed responsibility for Middle Eastern development in general', and that he hoped Morton would keep in close touch with British representatives in the region who would 'give him the latest information on the rapidly fluctuating political situation'.[74]

After a preliminary meeting in Lausanne with the Palestine Conciliation Commission, the Clapp Mission made its headquarters in Beirut, where Morton arrived on 11 September. The Lebanese Government were better disposed than most of their Arab neighbours towards the Mission, though sharing their suspicion that its purpose, as the Beirut press put it, was 'to enable the Jews to obtain access to the resources of the Arab world and to try to bring about economic cooperation between Israel and the Arabs'.[75] Clapp, Morton and their colleagues found themselves in an atmosphere that was cool, though not openly hostile. Morton's first impressions were contained in a letter of 13 September to Michael Wright, the FO Under-Secretary superintending Eastern Department, describing what he called the 'violent but diffuse' activities in which the Mission had been engaged so far.

Morton had, perhaps surprisingly, taken to Clapp at once, disarmed on learning that he had never before travelled outside the southern United States and welcomed Morton's help with diplomatic and political matters. (As Morton found Clapp 'though ignorant, very quick-witted', the latter's plea for help may have owed as much to a shrewd appreciation of the best way to handle Morton as to a genuine need for advice.) Morton's verdict on his French and Turkish colleagues was also favourable: the first 'old for his years but a very pleasant personality and a completely trained diplomat', the second, though 'officially only an electrical engineer', had 'very strong views of considered and intelligent character' and spoke excellent French and English 'but will only refer to Jews in his own tongue which none of us can follow'.[76] Following this initial report, neither the French nor the Turkish representative was mentioned other than in passing in any of the documentation relating to the Mission.

The letter ended with a complaint, to be repeated in many subsequent communications, that Morton had as yet received no pay, forcing him to secure an advance of $5,000 from a 'guileless Establishment Officer'. While it is true that Morton tended to make a fuss over his personal arrangements, expecting the Treasury or FO to sort it out for him rather than doing it himself, it is also undoubtedly true that he, and other members of the Mission, suffered from the endemic inefficiency of UN bureaucracy. British exchange regulations precluded his drawing any of his normal salary while overseas, and his needs, living in hotels, were not inconsiderable. Clapp, like other senior American envoys, was a rich man in his own right. Morton was not, and found it embarrassing if not humiliating to have to borrow from British Embassy funds in the countries he visited, and to engage in a constant stream of correspondence to secure his entitlements. His tendency to dramatise his situation – a manuscript letter to Burrows of 20 September bewailed that he was 'considered too unimportant to have a typist', had 'no car and no pay' and 'not enough money to buy a newspaper' – devalued a genuine grievance. It is worth making this point, though the details of his complaints and responses to them are too tedious to rehearse further. Suffice it say he was probably more sinned against than sinning.

Morton's letter to Wright also contained the first of many disobliging references to Trygve Lie, of whom he clearly retained unfavourable memories from wartime days. He had, he said, contemplated sending Lie 'one of my famous telegrams which would have read, "Having known you well as Foreign Secretary of Norway during the war, I fully understand your reluctance to continue in that sphere or even to return to your country. I should, however, be glad to learn on what assumption you consider yourself fit to administer a corporal's guard let alone the somewhat more complicated affairs of UNO". I assure you that I shall not do anything so rash.'[77] Maybe not; but Morton made no secret of his low opinion of Lie, or indeed of most of the UN establishment, and his voice carried loud and far. Such language struck a jarring note, and while the FO or Treasury were not unsympathetic to his complaints of UN inefficiency and even corruption, they considered that they should either be made formally, or not at all.[78]

By 16 September, when it was clear that invitations for the Mission to visit other Arab countries were unlikely to be forthcoming, Clapp and his colleagues decided to propose themselves, on the basis that the 'problem of permanent resettlement of Arab refugees will be set aside for the present in favour of attempting to find, in collaboration with governments, temporary employment for refugees in place of direct relief "pending their eventual repatriation or resettlement in whatever measure future political development may show to be necessary and practical"'. The feasibility of financing approved relief works externally would be discussed, and Clapp and Morton would try to prepare the way for informal talks between experts.[79] This initiative produced immediate results from their hosts, the Lebanese Government (though the Foreign Minister, after a cordial meeting with Morton, asked the British Minister to keep secret the fact that it had taken place).[80] A few days later, the Iraqi Government also agreed to have 'a general discussion with members of the Mission', and plans were laid to visit Egypt, Jordan and Syria before the end of September, though Saudi Arabia still held out.

However, Arab distrust of the Mission was undiminished. According to J.M. Troutbeck, summarising the situation from BMEO on 20 September, this suspicion was due to four principal causes:

(a) the Group is a large formidable body manned solely by foreigners who come, with the exception of the Turks, from 'partition' countries. It is therefore a possible threat to Arab independence.

(b) It derives its origin from the United Nations which, in the Arabs' view has consistently [favoured] Israel against themselves.

(c) They suspect therefore that it may be an indirect means of getting them to accept a political settlement with Israel even more unfavourable than what they have already rejected.

(d) Above all, they fear one of the principal objects of the group will be to integrate Middle East economy . . . which they think will be the first step towards Israeli economic domination.

The result was, as Troutbeck put it, that 'all the Arab bristles are well out, and I think it will depend largely on Mr Clapp and his colleagues whether they can break down these suspicions'.[81] Morton found this telegram 'very helpful': the Mission, he said, was 'tainted at birth with some of the odium acquired by its parentage'; it was for this reason that the decision had been taken to interpret their terms of reference so as to emphasise the economic development of the Middle East, while assuring the Arab states that 'the Mission will in no way demand as a condition of financial aid that the Arab Governments must resume commercial relations with Israel'.[82]

The FO were uneasy about this change of emphasis, fearing that 'complete avoidance of political issues and concentration on temporary relief works will defeat the purpose for which [the Mission] was set up', but Morton, while agreeing to put these reservations to Clapp, stressed the importance of the Mission's taking a flexible approach which would, he said, be liable to alteration as a result of the discussions in Egypt, Syria and Jordan on which they had just embarked. Both he and Clapp took the view that there was little point in the Mission's sitting in Beirut because no-one would talk to them: better to engage in technical discussions that might lead to broader agreement. Unless the FO or State Department had a better idea, that was what they would do. When the Mission returned to Beirut at the beginning of October, Morton wrote that 'We do not feel we have been unsuccessful': the Lebanese Government had agreed to set up a Ministerial Committee to work out practical details of relief schemes; the Egyptian Government, which had initially refused all cooperation, ended by producing a plan to reduce the numbers of refugees in the Gaza area; in Jordan, talks were already taking place with Mission experts for relief projects; while the Syrian Government, unwilling to be arraigned as 'the only non-cooperative Arab state', had agreed to further talks though maintaining a hostile public stance. This represented real if modest progress, and the FO, though in disagreement with some of Morton's interpretative comment, had no alternative strategy to offer.[83]

In early October 1949 reports appeared in the Arab and Israeli press attributing various comments about the Mission to Morton, though he assured the FO that he had 'refused to give any interview or make any statement or even talk unofficially to the press since joining this mission'. In the light of this categorical statement the FO decided to consult him regarding a report that had appeared in the *Sunday Observer* as early as 11 September, claiming that Morton's appointment heralded a new direction in British policy in the Middle East, but Morton repeated his denial, adding that 'Curiously enough these and other astonishing statements attributed sometimes to Clapp and sometimes to me have rather assisted this mission than otherwise but that is an act of God'.[84] This was neither the first nor the last time that Morton was forced to deny that he had been the source for press reports concerning the Mission. It would certainly have been out of character for him to brief the press, but equally he was in the habit of holding forth to members of the Mission in local hotels, and his voice, as Colville memorably put it, was loud enough to 'penetrate the ramparts of a medieval castle'.[85] It is noteworthy that few of the press reports attributed their remarks to Clapp, or to the French and Turkish Deputy Chairmen. Morton was secretive, but not always discreet.

Now the Mission prepared to visit Israel. Amidst wrangling over dates, the Israeli security authorities warned that they could not guarantee Morton's safety, as there were 'certain ex-terrorist groups who resented the United Kingdom's return into the Palestine picture through the Survey Mission and who may be tempted to demonstrate their disapproval'. Although Sir Alexander Knox Helm, the British Minister, thought that the Israelis were merely being 'over-cautious', the FO reacted sharply, instructing him to state that all the British members of the Mission would be visiting in their capacity as officials of the UN, and that 'Israel's inability to guarantee their safety should therefore be communicated to the Secretary-General'. The Israelis, realising that they had made a blunder, tried to backtrack, but Clapp, taking the threat equally seriously, said the Mission would not go to Israel unless the government have 'fullest and clearest assurances for the safety of all members of the mission'.

The storm blew over, and in the view of Eastern Department the fuss did the Israelis good. 'They are still too apt to try to wriggle out of the normal obligations of a Government when it suits them'.[86] It is not clear from the documentation whether the Israelis were making a point about Morton in particular or the British in general, but in any case he had no intention of letting threats stop him from visiting Israel. Later, after the Mission was over, he referred to the episode in typically forthright terms in a letter to Dennis Wheatley:

> The Jews threatened to shoot me, but have so far failed to carry out their threat, or even to throw a brickbat in my direction. I am still not anti-Jew but I am violently anti that thing which has been set up and called itself 'Israel'. That thing is about as much Jewry as I am, being in no sense a cross section of world Jewry, but mainly composed of the scrapings of the East European and Russian Ghettoes.[87]

The Mission's visit to Israel was short (9–11 October 1949) and dominated by long speeches from ministers 'attempting to prove Israel was the only honest state in the world and had been treated disgracefully'. Even allowing for Morton's tendency to exaggeration, it is clear that both he and Clapp were taken aback by the frankness of the Israeli position, as set out by Moshe Sharrett and David Horowitz[88] and described in Morton's report to the FO: the UN, 'having allowed Israel to get away with so much was now forced to support Israel politically'; Israel would not pay compensation to dispossessed Arabs 'whether refugees or not'; 'everything depended on Israel becoming industrial and financial masters of the Middle East'; 'even if the enthusiasm of world Jewry for Israel was waning financially he [Horowitz] could always whip it up politically by various devices'.[89] As there was no formal record of the meetings, it is impossible to say how close Morton's report was to what was actually said. His account was not challenged in the FO, where the Israeli statements were described as 'typical', though Knox Helm (who clearly did not like Morton), commented to Burrows:

> I hold no brief for the Israelis, but I think that a certain objectivity is desirable. And I confess that I was bit shattered at the interpretation which Morton gave to Clapp at the Sharon Hotel of something I had told him in this Legation two hours before. I hardly recognised it.[90]

On 25 October Horowitz, too, complained in a letter to Morton about 'untrue and unreasonable' statements attributed to him, but received a dismissive response.[91] The likelihood is that Morton's reports exaggerated in degree, rather than in substance.

From Israel the Mission moved on to Bagdad, where they were received cordially by Nuri Pasha, who announced his intention to cooperate fully with the Mission in respect of finding employment for Palestinian refugees, though he 'politely but firmly gave it as his personal view that the United States was to blame for the whole mess'.[92] The Mission then returned to Beirut to draft its interim report, which both State Department and FO wished to 'steer'. The process was complicated by plans which had meanwhile been drawn up by the UN to set up a new organisation which would take over the distribution of relief to the Palestine refugees, and be responsible for selecting development projects that would attract loans from international sources. The State Department wanted these plans to be reflected in the Mission's interim report, but the FO considered they were likely to create new difficulties without solving 'the difficult practical problems of how a political settlement is to be made acceptable to both sides and how money is to be found to maintain and rehabilitate the refugees'.[93] The Mission, in Beirut, was caught between a rock and a hard place, indeed several hard places, represented by the UN on one side and a variety of governments, including their own, on the other.

At this point Bevin began to take a closer interest. To him, the UN's proposals for the future treatment of the refugee question invoked yet again the unwelcome spectre of UN control over development in the Middle East. He set out his views in a telegram to Middle East posts on 1 November 1949:

I realise that the Americans are naturally preoccupied with the framing of proposals in such as way as to secure Congressional approval and that for this purpose they have to emphasise the United Nations aspect of the solutions proposed. Nevertheless this tendency may lead us into danger. The last thing we want is for the United Nations as such to have any control over general development in the Middle East (eg Nile Waters). Once this was established we should in the end find ourselves faced with Russian intervention. Even United States intervention must be carefully handled. We have done almost all the preparatory work through British Middle East Office and British firms and we believe that our experience and our special relations with most of the governments are essential for the effective execution of development and relief works. American finance is equally necessary but this must be applied without the ill-effects of American inexperience in dealing with this area and of the existing prejudice against America in the Middle East.[94]

Bevin's view was that unless the US Government would produce practical suggestions as to how the money for relief and relief works could be raised, any UN Resolution should do no more than express the opinion that the time had come for a serious attempt to solve the refugee problem by a combination of resettlement and repatriation.

Against this backdrop, the Clapp Mission's interim report was inevitably constrained. Its recommendations, summarised by the FO for their Middle East representatives on 10 November, were based on the principle of substituting public works for relief, with a new agency set up to administer both schemes after April 1950, and a drastic reduction in the number of rations to be issued from 1 January 1950.[95] Troutbeck, in Cairo, felt that the report represented 'a policy of despair':

We seem to have lost hope of obtaining even funds required for keeping refugees alive for more than a strictly limited period ... I feel we are unduly optimistic if we believe that this would induce either Arab States, or still more, Israel to take a more realistic attitude to resettlement and repatriation. I do not believe any Middle East country has any great humanitarian interest in fate of refugees ... The constructive work which one hopes will follow from Clapp Mission would be hopelessly prejudiced. If first fruit of Mission's work were mass starvation of very people it was designed to succour nobody would feel any confidence in its ability to take effective action in any other respect.[96]

Troutbeck was not the only British representative in the Middle East to point out the 'frightening' implications of a set of recommendations that relied on regional governments to assume, voluntarily, responsibility for the refugees. Both FO and State Department, however, mindful of the political and financial implications of greater commitment, considered the Mission's recommendations satisfactory. An FO telegram to Middle Eastern posts, giving a 'line to take' on the report, trod a fine line between realism and complacence:

> In our view the Mission's recommendations are constructive and almost entirely acceptable. In particular, we welcome the proposal that the refugees should be given the opportunity to work, as their continued idleness is harmful both to the individual and the community. Since it is proposed that much of the refugee labour shall be employed on public works from which the Middle East countries will derive benefit, the closer association of the Middle East Governments with the administration of relief is clearly desirable. Moreover, it is unlikely that the United Nations will agree to continue to contribute large sums of money if they cannot be assured of the cooperation of the Arab Governments in the most effective method of spending it. It may be, therefore, that the alternative to accepting the present report is to have no United Nations scheme for continued relief, in which case the refugees would be left a burden to the local Governments immediately and not, as the report suggests, in 1951. Finally it is the hope of His Majesty's Government that the constructive economic approach which the present proposals show, will pave the way for a solution of the political deadlock.[97]

This telegram encapsulated the realities of the situation at the end of 1949, and the impossibility of the Clapp Mission's fulfilling its remit. Despite the Mission's insistence that any new agency should not come under UN auspices, only a UN-sponsored agency had any chance of support from the Americans, and therefore of attracting serious finance. The only alternative, to transfer responsibility to the International Refugee Organisation, was rejected by both British and American Governments, the former fearing the implications of an open-ended financial commitment for IRO contributors, and the latter adamant in opposition to a committee whose contributors included 'some in South America who may object to the United States continuing to spend money in under-developed areas outside the American continent'. Both governments also knew that the IRO, regarded as a 'Jewish' organisation, was unacceptable to the Arab world.[98]

On 29 November Morton was informed that the British and US Governments were likely to sponsor a UN resolution endorsing the Clapp Mission's interim report, and setting up a Near East Relief and Works Agency (NERWA) to administer relief and organise relief works, with an Advisory Commission consisting of representatives of the UK, US, France and Turkey to 'advise and assist the Director'. It would not contain any reference to long-term development, other than that NERWA should advise Middle East governments about steps to be taken when relief ceased. This resolution did not, it was stressed, mean that the British Government were any less anxious to bring about long-term development, or that they ignored the need for external 'assistance and stimulation'; but they believed that 'this assistance can best be given by strengthening BMEO as necessary and arranging for *ad hoc* consultation between BMEO and American experts and in some cases also French experts'.

To fit in with this policy, the Clapp Mission's final report should recommend that the Arab governments set up national development boards, preferably in regional cooperation, and should urge outside governments to provide them with all possible technical and financial assistance.[99] On the following day, in the UN Ad Hoc Political Committee, representatives of all four governments involved in the Survey Mission expressed their support for the interim report and for the resolution based on it. Cadogan, for the UK,[100] 'appealed to Israel to take the positive steps required of it to comply with the elementary principles of justice and to the Arab States to seek a settlement of all outstanding issues since it was only within the framework of such a settlement that a final solution to the refugee problem could be found'.[101] The resolution was adopted by the General Assembly on 8 December without discussion by forty-seven votes to none with six abstentions. Both the Arab states and the Israelis, though expressing disappointment that more money was not on offer, clearly considered that the outcome could have been much less favourable to them.

The wheel had therefore come full circle on the refugee issue: no decisions were taken on long-term relief and resettlement, for which responsibility was to be transferred to the local governments, and discussion was now focussed on the establishment of a new organisation, just as earlier in 1949 it had focussed on the Survey Mission. The Clapp Mission had little left to do but draw up its final report, which urged Middle East governments, the UN and 'member Governments which desire to proffer friendly assistance' to recognise that 'peace and stability can only come when the people enjoy a higher standard of life which can only be achieved through their own efforts. There is no short cut to prosperity which must come through the development of resources by the Governments and the peoples' own pride'.[102] Morton, with Clapp, returned to London, where the two men gave an account of the Mission's activities to an interdepartmental meeting on 20 December.[103] All concerned realised, as E.B. Boothby of the FO's Eastern Department commented on 3 January 1950, that 'the policy of putting responsibility squarely on the shoulders of local governments involves the risk of much suffering for the refugees'. Nevertheless, according to Trefor Evans of the Middle East Secretariat, the 'inevitable inefficiency and corruption' was 'the price we will have to pay for putting responsibility for the refugees squarely on the shoulders of the local governments'.[104] The general mood seems to have been one of resignation rather than disappointment.

Morton's personal views on the outcome of the Mission are harder to gauge. He expressed himself in highly coloured terms in a letter of 4 January 1950 to Dennis Wheatley:

It was like living in a dime novel. It was a wonderful Mission of four men – American, French, Turkish and self, all of whom absolutely clicked from the word 'go'. But we found ourselves surrounded by emissaries of that fat slob, Trygvie [sic] Lie, all of whom were mad, Bolsheviks, Jews or incapable. They were sent to spy upon us in the interests of Trygvie Lie or in the interests of Tel Aviv. We had to adopt measures which would find a worthy place in some of your books in order to defeat these gentlemen. We did however.[105]

Despite its defiant tone, this letter suggests that Morton found the whole experience of the Mission rather bruising as well as challenging. The difficulties of the political situation in the Middle East, and the ultimate reliance on American finance, made it very hard for the Mission to make any meaningful recommendations except on a detailed local level, or to make any creative suggestions that did not involve direct UN intervention in a way that the British Government, at least, rejected. Neither Clapp, Morton nor any of their colleagues had the political or financial authority to fulfil the grandiose aims set out by the Secretary-General in August 1949: and it is hard to believe that any group, however high-powered, could have done so; indeed, more eminent and authoritative representatives might have been even less successful in getting the Arab and Israeli governments to engage with the Mission.

It would, however, be wrong to suggest that the Mission achieved nothing. Although it secured no long-term solution, the rather callous terminology of the final Report does not reflect the Mission's considerable efforts to try and ameliorate the refugees' plight. Its members worked hard to engage with governments whose hostility they had to overcome, entering into difficult and circuitous negotiations to set up a relief project, or to provide food and shelter for a small number of refugees. In this Morton played a full part, and his direct and practical approach was valued by Clapp and appreciated by the Mission's interlocutors. The Middle East was (and is) a complex and subtle arena in which to operate, with cultural and religious factors to consider as well as political and economic. Morton, despite the impression given by his reporting, showed considerable sensitivity to these factors and, as always, was prepared to work for twelve hours a day, seven days a week, however unfavourable the conditions. The fact that some of his judgements were regarded by the FO as off-beam or plain wrong, and his incurable tendency to facetiousness, does not obscure the solidity of his contribution, for which Bevin wrote to thank him on 28 February 1950.[106] His outspoken criticism of the UN in general and the Secretary General in particular ruled out his candidature as UK member of the Advisory Commission to NERWA;[107] but in the light of his views on the UN it is hard to imagine that he would have wished for such an appointment. As far as he was concerned, the receipt of a cheque for $3,699.32 from the UN, acknowledged in a letter of 23 March 1950 to the FO,[108] marked the overdue terminus to an episode that had brought some personal embarrassment as well as a measure of professional satisfaction.

Civil aviation in the Middle East, 1950–51

Morton emerged from the Clapp Mission with an undisguised contempt for the UN Secretariat and a profound interest in the Middle East. He appears to have set himself to develop the latter with his usual thoroughness, since during the first half of 1950 the only documentary record of his activities consists of articles written and talks delivered on the region, such as an article on 'The Development of the Middle East', sent to Michael Wright on 3 March, and a speech on 'The Middle East in World Politics', delivered to a course at Ashridge between 17 and 20 March.[109] Meanwhile, he continued to work in the Treasury, and presumably, since he was still nominally UK Delegate to the IARA, paid some regard to reparations matters. In the autumn, however, he was called upon to employ his Middle Eastern experience again, this time in the service of the Ministry of Civil Aviation (MCA). It is not clear whether the commission originated with the Treasury or from a personal connection, but someone – who knew both him and his reputation – evidently recommended him as the right man for the job. That job was to ensure that Britain continued to control civil aviation in the Middle East.

Since the end of the Second World War, the British Government had struggled to defend UK airlines and routes against the aggressive expansion of US companies across the globe.[110] The Americans, using leverage gained during the negotiations for the loan agreement signed on 6 December 1945, had struck a tough bargain at the Bermuda Conference in February 1946 in regard to the so-called 'Five Freedoms of the Air';[111] nevertheless, as far as the Middle East was concerned it had generally proved possible to reach a *modus vivendi*, the US taking a greater interest in the oil producing countries of Saudi Arabia and Iran, while British interests were centred in Egypt, Iraq, Syria and Lebanon and the Gulf States.[112] Between 1946 and 1950 the British Government pursued a policy of reaching civil aviation agreements with the states concerned in order to prevent foreign companies from establishing themselves in the region, as well as to guard against the threat of expanding Russian influence. Their general objective was for the national carrier, the British Overseas Airways Corporation (BOAC) to dominate the long-haul routes, while local companies, owned or licensed by the British, carried short-haul regional traffic.

By 1950, protracted negotiations with Iraq, Syria and Lebanon were hanging fire, while British influence in the region was being tested by a combination of nationalist aspiration and foreign competition. Strained relations between the Arab states and the British Government over Palestine and Israel had introduced a political element into the civil aviation issues: Iraq's declaration of a state of emergency in May 1948 during Arab-Israeli hostilities, including a ban on overflying, had not been lifted, partly in order to prevent Jews in Iraq from travelling to Israel; and since the Arab League had voted unanimously to expel any member negotiating a separate peace with Israel, any relaxation of the ban might be considered to breach the Arab blockade. In this situation, Iraq, Syria and the Lebanon were inclined to delay negotiations and to extract a high price for agreement, while the Gulf States were also flexing their nationalist muscles.

Although a civil aviation agreement had been signed with Kuwait in 1949, two Lebanese companies had been flouting its terms by carrying passengers and freight in and out of the Sheikhdom, while refusing to allow Cyprus Airways (a British financed company) reciprocal rights. Similar challenges were anticipated from Iranian and Iraqi companies. There had been much discussion between the MCA and the FO as to how British rights might be enforced in the face of the MCA's reluctance to maintain expensive equipment and staff at airports rarely used by UK aircraft, and the FO's reluctance to employ empty threats that might worsen Anglo-Arab relations. In June 1950, an interdepartmental meeting agreed that a working group should be set up responsible for 'the solution of the major issues in Gulf aviation', but by August no action had been taken. The impending visit to London of Sir Rupert Hay, Minister Resident in the Gulf States, who had demanded to know what was going on, finally provoked the MCA into action.

It is unclear whether the Treasury or the FO instigated Morton's involvement, but in mid-August 1950 his name was being mentioned as a 'high-level negotiator' who might be sent out to the Middle East to force to a conclusion negotiations for a civil aviation agreement with Iraq and to progress those with Syria and the Lebanon. By 28 August he had, as was his custom, drawn up a comprehensive and cogent summary of the situation; it concluded that what HM Representatives at Bagdad, Damascus and Beirut needed was not a negotiator to supplant their authority, but proper, detailed instructions from the Ministry on which they themselves could reopen or conclude existing negotiations. If a special negotiator were required, it was essential that before his arrival the outline text of an agreement should have been reached by both parties, and for each to make clear to the other their full demands for specific routes and other details. 'Failing this', said Morton, 'the special negotiator will be kicking his heels abroad while the other party "consider[s] the proposal" *in camera*, whereby he will cease to have any value as a special negotiator and possibly go mad.'[113]

At an interdepartmental meeting on 11 September, Morton proposed that a full brief be sent to HM Ambassador at Bagdad to enable him to conclude negotiations with the Iraqi Government on the basis of a pre-existing draft: he himself, as a 'special representative of the Minister', would pay a visit to the Persian Gulf and on his way back 'call in at Baghdad and assist the Ambassador in the completion of negotiations if required'.[114] John Slater, of the FO's General Department, noted after the meeting that in his view there would be no point in Morton's visit: he had no expert knowledge of the subject, and the Ambassador already had an experienced Civil Air Attaché, B.G. Barnard, on whom to call. Sir William Hayter, Superintending Under Secretary, agreed, having discussed the matter with L.C. Dunnett, Under Secretary superintending the Air Division at MCA:

He told me that the MCA's particular anxiety was to conclude the agreements with Iraq, Syria and Lebanon as quickly as possible. Their idea had been that Sir Desmond shd. do the whole thing & go to the three capitals to negotiate agreements but he was being difficult, saying that it wd. be wrong for him to go out & negotiate over the heads of the Ambassadors. Mr. D. described Sir Desmond's project for a visit to the Gulf as a 'tortuous' approach: neither Sir G. Cribbett nor he wished Sir D.M. to go off at a tangent. The main objective shd. be to negotiate the agreements with Iraq, Syria & the Lebanon: the question of a visit to the Gulf cd. be pursued later.[115]

Despite this apparent lack of enthusiasm in both FO and MCA, plans proceeded for Morton to visit the Gulf. On 27 September the FO sent the following somewhat disingenuous telegram to Bagdad, copied to Beirut, Bahrain, Damascus and Alexandria:

> Sir Desmond Morton will be visiting the Persian Gulf as special representative of the Minister of Civil Aviation and intends to leave London by British Overseas Airways Corporation on Saturday October 14. We should be grateful to know whether it would be convenient if he spent two to three days in Bagdad on the way to discuss certain relevant questions with you and your Civil Air Attaché. Sir Desmond is familiar with our proposal to negotiate an air agreement with the Iraqi Government.[116]

A follow-up telegram to Beirut and Damascus informed the Ambassadors that Morton would be returning via their capitals, so that they would 'have the opportunity, should you desire, of discussing with him any question concerning civil aviation'.

It is evident that departmental objections had been overridden to ensure that Morton's tour of the Gulf should proceed. The question is, by whom? In the absence of any satisfactory documentary evidence, the finger of suspicion would seem to point either to the Minister for Civil Aviation himself, Lord Pakenham,[117] or to his Permanent Secretary, Sir Arnold Overton. The former was a prominent member of the Catholic laity who knew Morton well; the latter appears to have given Morton confidential instructions for the trip. It is also possible that pressure was exerted at a senior level by the FO, perhaps by Strang, who saw Morton as a 'fixer', if sometimes a troublesome one. Morton himself had neither the power nor the influence to press the scheme, even if he had so wished, and in any case his scruples about going over the head of diplomatic representatives were both genuine and well-founded. The key Ambassadors in the region were known to him personally, from the wartime period if not from his recent work with the Clapp Mission: Sir Henry Mack in Bagdad, W.H. Montagu-Pollock in Damascus, Sir W. Houston-Boswall in Beirut. He was well aware that nothing could be achieved unless these men approved and welcomed his intervention. In any event, by late September 1950 it was decided that Morton should tour the Middle East on Pakenham's behalf, and report on the prospect of successful negotiations.

During the next fortnight Morton attended a number of meetings on aspects of civil aviation problems in the Middle East. His recent travels with the Clapp Mission had given him a good appreciation of the political situation in the region, its international context and the potential difficulties of his task. He was under no illusion that either the Sheikhs or the Iraqi, Lebanese and Syrian Governments would capitulate easily to British demands, and was inclined to scoff at the MCA's somewhat legalistic proposals for dealing with such problems as how to prevent aircraft from landing at aerodromes without permission. A letter he wrote to the MCA on 3 October in this connection is worth quoting as a representative example of his 'troubleshooting' style:

I think I am in the best traditions of diplomacy in claiming that it is fatal to employ anything like threats unless, in the ultimate event, one not only intends, but is able to implement them . . . There are still places in the world where a threat of legal procedures in a court of law merely causes the person threatened to laugh like a horse. Moreover, when the local chief spiv is the Prime Minister's son, the laughter may be even more derisive.

However, let us take heart! I see that I may refuse the operator petrol. This won't help in the case in question, since he will have enough on board to get back with. I may also instruct the Air Traffic Control Officer to refuse the aircraft permission to take off. I am glad it is the Air Traffic Control Officer who does this and not me. I suppose he will stand in front of the airplane with his hand up. From what I have seen of Lebanese pilots, who usually move around with a sub-machine gun, a couple of Mills bombs and a set of carving knives distributed about their person, I propose to inform Mr. Champness [MCA representative at Kuwait] that he is an authorised person to serve a formal notice on the Commander of the Aircraft . . .

However, we are getting warmer. Obstructions may be placed in the way of the aircraft on the taxi-way. There are not many trees in Bahrein, and in spite of much local unemployment, the inhabitants would require considerable pay before acting as an obstruction. There is of course always Rupert Hay's car, or even – dare I suggest it? – a large pile of MCA *paperasserie* which I am sure could be spared for building a wall across the runway.

I think we have the solution however in removing some essential parts of the aircraft's engines . . . a couple of bursts of machine gun fire aimed roughly at where the engine of the said aircraft is understood to be attached to the fuselage, should succeed in removing quite a number of essential small parts. A similar method would undoubtedly be the safest to be employed for puncturing the tyres . . .

Of course if after all this the FO find themselves with a local war on their hands, it will be no good blaming me, since I have made arrangements with the Kuwait Oil Company to place at my disposal free of charge to HM Government, one of the aircraft which they hire from Skyways, with a pilot and enough petrol aboard to enable me to reach Lhassa, where I am sure that the Dalai Lama has need of a skilled European adviser to assist him in maintaining his present incarnation against the objections to it manifested by the Chinese Communists.[118]

This letter, which Morton signed off '*Moriturus te salute*'*, is a good example of why middle-ranking civil servants of all departments tended to dislike him heartily, while their superiors, particularly those with earlier experience of his ways, tended to display a more tolerant humour and ignore his more egregious efforts. As usual, behind the facetious badinage lay a serious point. There was little prospect of enforcing British authority over aircraft and airfields if the states concerned were determined to flout it: the only way forward was to reach agreement through face to face talks conducted by a tough negotiator with the facts at his fingertips. Morton, however flippant his approach seemed from the outside, was well suited to such a role.

Morton left London on 14 October and spent more than six weeks touring the Middle East, visiting Bagdad, Bahrain, Dhahran, Kuwait, Sharjah, Damascus and Beirut, returning on 3 December. On his return he submitted a comprehensive general report, together with separate reports on civil aviation issues in the Persian Gulf, Iraq, Syria, the Lebanon, Cyprus and Kuwait, all (relatively) sober documents whose general conclusion reinforced the points made in his original memorandum of 28 August: before effective local action could be taken by HM Representatives to conclude civil aviation agreements or to enforce British legal rights, the MCA and indeed the British Government needed to take firm decisions on what routes and facilities they required and what measures they were prepared to take to secure them. Without such decisions, communicated clearly to local representatives frustrated by dealing with multiple sections of the MCA, no progress could be made.[119]

Morton's tour proved a useful catalyst in crystallising MCA and FO views on the way ahead. It also reassured British diplomatic representatives in the states concerned that someone in London was taking their concerns seriously, and appreciated, as Morton's report put it, that 'civil aviation questions are, more often than not, bound up with diplomatic and political issues, even to a greater degree than other forms of trade and commerce'. They had welcomed Morton's visit and appreciated his willingness to interrogate recalcitrant Middle Eastern officials and airline representatives about the practice, rather than the theory governing civil aviation operations. If his opinions of some of the players involved – such as Colonel Mostert, a South African lent by BOAC to Iraqi Airways as an adviser, whom Morton described as 'doing his best to do down the UK in the

---

* About to die, I salute you.

interest of Iraq[120] – tended to raise a diplomatic eyebrow, his hosts did not protest; Morton was only voicing what they thought privately but were too discreet to say publicly. In a stalemate situation, a somewhat outrageous third party sent from London, with the Minister's backing, could be a very useful agent for change.

In any case, Morton's visit appeared to clear a log jam. The FO focussed its attention on the Kuwait problem, and in December 1950 Bevin agreed to the issue of a King's Regulation that would permit an 'authorised person' (the local MCA representative) to take disciplinary action against the companies operating between Beirut and Kuwait without permission.[121] On 18 January 1951, Mack reported from Bagdad that negotiations for a civil air agreement were about to be resumed.[122] Although these proceeded both satisfactorily and swiftly (in Iraqi terms), it soon became apparent that a final push would be needed to iron out remaining difficulties and bring the talks to a conclusion. While the Iraqis indicated that they would withdraw their opposition to the carriage of traffic by British airlines between Bagdad and the Levant States, the MCA were not happy with the proposed concessions demanded in return, intended to limit long-haul traffic in the interests of Iraqi Airways. They proposed that Morton should return to Bagdad in March for the final stages of the discussions. As Slater noted on 20 February, the MCA had 'no confidence in the Civil Air Attaché's ability to conclude these negotiations', adding 'I sympathise with this attitude . . . Whether Sir D. is the right person to put things right is another matter, but if Sir George Cribbett & Sir Arnold Overton think so, then we can hardly say them nay. Personally, I remain sceptical.'[123]

Morton did his homework before setting out, attending meetings and annoying the MCA by tabulating the routes sought by UK airlines and assigning numbers to them. They could not, however, argue with his succinct summary of the situation:

> The only bargaining counter we have resides in the question of British cabotage* in the Gulf. This is actually a weak point, since overriding policy prevents us from ultimately denying this to the Iraqis. Whereas I shall not exchange this British cabotage for Cyprus Airways requirements, I should make what play I can with it in order to meet BOAC requirements . . . The UK standard attitude is to treat each country separately and to measure what we give to each country by what each country is ready to give to us in return. If the UK gives cabotage rights to any one country, it must be in return for some demonstrable favour from that country.[124]

In his first session with the Iraqi negotiating committee on 13 March, Morton set out the British Government's position, warning the Iraqis that the UK required adequate compensation for Gulf cabotage before any agreement could be reached, and assuring that they were not obliged to give the US or any other country the

---

* i.e. the right to control air traffic originating and terminating within a given country.

same rights as those given to the UK. The Americans, reported Morton, were 'alarmed lest we should take this independent attitude but I have professed myself unable to understand complicated American argument in view of my newness at this game. Idiot boy is useful gambit.'[125]

A crisis was reached at the end of March, based on what Morton called the 'sensitivity' of the Iraqis regarding fifth freedom rights between the Levant and Bagdad, and traffic between Iraq and the Gulf. The activities of the local Cyprus Airways representative, who appeared to be trying to secure advantages for his company by a backstairs route at the expense of BOAC, also caused some trouble until the MCA (who had evidently got used to Morton by now) suggested 'that in your own inimitable way you might advise him to watch his step'.[126] There were to be many setbacks, accompanied by a flurry of telegraphic traffic between Bagdad and London, before the Air Services agreement was finally signed by the Iraqi Minister of Communications and Works on 19 April – 'Thank goodness!' exclaimed Slater when the news arrived.[127] No account of the negotiations, however, can possibly match that prepared by Morton himself, dated 1 May 1951. It is such a perfect – or, to some horrified official readers, most imperfect – example of his style that it has been reproduced in full as an Annex at the end of this book. Couched in the form of an official despatch, it is irreverent, hilarious and undoubtedly embellished by an element of fantasy.[128] Certain passages, such as the descriptions of how Barnard – 'a tower of strength in these difficulties' – acquired supplies of the requisite paper and ribbon with which to print and bind the text of the agreement, literally bring tears to the eyes. The report's reception in London, however, was mixed.

Morton's despatch tested the humour of the MCA considerably: Cribbett was inclined to indignation, demanding to know from Barnard whether Morton's accounts of bribery and sleight-of-hand were accurate; if so, he would be 'hesitant about sending Sir Desmond Morton abroad to negotiate again'. In Bagdad, however, Troubeck took a more relaxed attitude about 'Sir Desmond Morton's *jeu d'esprit*':

> Morton cannot have intended this document to be taken literally. I am sure he would not seriously attempt to defend such statements as that in the second paragraph, to the effect that there is a conscious arrangement between Nuri Pasha and his son to divide between them the functions of Government and private gain. It would be a pity if the Ministry of Civil Aviation were to read too much into Morton's witticisms, and to draw the conclusion that he was an irresponsible negotiator. In fact the gaiety of spirit to which he has given perhaps unfortunate expression in this despatch was an enormous asset during the negotiations which he conducted here . . .[129]

The FO, too, were inclined to be indulgent. Slater confessed that he had prompted Morton to write the report 'after he had entertained us enormously on the subject for a couple of hours', and Harpham noted, pertinently, that 'the agreement reached is a good one'. Both Makins and Strang agreed that the whole business was being taken too seriously: as Strang commented, he and Makins 'had much to do with Desmond Morton in our time and neither of us would underestimate his skill as a negotiator'. The last word should, perhaps, be given to Makins, writing a soothing letter to Cribbett on 15 June:

> I confess that I read the copy of this document which was sent to us with keen enjoyment, perhaps because I have a disposition to levity and think that the role of 'farceur' is one which should occasionally be allowed even in official life. However, it was no doubt a pity that Desmond Morton clothed his humour in such an official guise, and I can quite understand your desire to check on what he said . . . As Troutbeck suggests, there is no doubt that, with Desmond Morton's tendencies towards the telling of tall stories and the pulling of legs, go also many qualities which make him a good negotiator, especially in the wilder and woollier countries.[130]

On receipt of this letter, Cribbett agreed the incident should be regarded as closed: 'We should certainly not allow it to influence us in any views we might form about Morton's ability as a negotiator of Air Agreements. On that, we shall naturally judge him solely by results.[131]

Morton returned from Bagdad at the end of April 1951, and retired from the Treasury on 1 April 1953, at the age of sixty-one. There is almost no evidence as to what he did between those two dates. No doubt he continued to work hard in the Treasury, but he was clearly preparing for retirement, as he wrote to R.W. Thompson on 9 November 1951:

> The Treasury still finds me for the moment, but I am hoping to move my private abode at the end of January next from 3 Beaufort Gardens to 22 Kew Green, of which I have been lucky enough to be able to buy the freehold at a very reasonable price, so I am told. It is an original early Georgian mansion, tiny, but full of character and in a lovely part which in some ways, especially at night, might be in the middle of the country, but is only 20 minutes by underground to Westminster.[132]

The move to Kew Green in 1952, when he gave up his house at Crockham Hill, marked in effect the end of his long service in central government. Without further evidence, one must conclude that he spent the next year preparing for a life outside Whitehall. Over the last two years of his official career, however, Morton has (not for the first time) succeeded in drawing a veil.

14

ENERGETICALLY AWAITING
DEATH:[1] 1953–71

Throughout his long life Morton was never happier than when extremely busy, even if he complained about his schedule: 'I like plenty of work', as he wrote to John Coulson in the FO in March 1946.[2] He worked scarcely less hard in retirement, slowing down somewhat only in the last few years before his death on 31 July 1971 at the age of seventy-nine. He worked rigorously long hours for the NHS until March 1966, undertook other voluntary work and was extremely active in the affairs of the Catholic Laity, maintaining all the while an extensive correspondence with those who sought the (non-attributable) benefit of his knowledge and experience on a wide range of political, economic and theological matters. As well as satisfying his personal ethical, and perhaps psychological imperative to be occupied usefully at all times, these activities provided him with the professional and social contacts that prevented life after Whitehall from seeming barren and isolated.

During these years he lived at 22 Kew Green, in the Georgian terraced house he had bought in 1952. Also in residence were 'West', his late mother's elderly maid, plus Mrs Helen Pither, a housekeeper whose services he had inherited when he bought the house. Both these women (who, apparently, lived on terms of some mutual antagonism) seemed to require almost as much care from him as he received from them. Though he spent many of his days in central London, travelling there by underground and by bus, lunching at his club as in the past, he also involved himself in the local community, attending St Winifred's church at Kew, and becoming a governor of a boy's school in Surrey. He took a great deal of pride in his garden, and enjoyed the wild life that it attracted, as well as the company of his cat Jezebel (who had, he alleged, a taste for Italian vermouth).[3] His busy schedule, both domestic and public, seems only to have slackened in pace during the summer months when the various bodies he served took a break. No sign has been found that Morton himself took holidays in the sense of going away from home.[4] Another regular feature were bouts of illness during the winter months, sometimes life-threatening and usually serious enough to lay him low for a number of weeks.

Nearly all the surviving evidence of Morton's life in retirement comes from his correspondence, and principally from the long series of letters he exchanged with

R.W. Thompson; other correspondents included Sir Basil Liddell Hart and Dennis Wheatley.[5] Thompson, a journalist and writer, first met Morton in 1943 when serving in the Intelligence Corps.[6] The two men began to correspond in 1944, when Thompson sought Morton's advice about future employment, and exchanged regular letters after 1951 when Thompson had retired to Suffolk as a full-time author, writing principally on military subjects. During the later 1950s and early 1960s he sought actively to draw on Morton's knowledge and experience for his book *The Price of Victory*, and most especially for his study of Churchill, *The Yankee Marlborough*, published in 1963.[7] Morton, who encouraged and helped Thompson a great deal but was inclined to be critical of his approach and judgements, always insisted that no reference to him must be made in any of Thompson's books; there is little doubt that he would have vetoed the publication of a selection of their correspondence concerning Churchill, which appeared in 1976.[8] This interesting but highly selective collection, including forthright and negative expressions of view from Morton on Churchill's character and record, was greeted with dismay and disappointment by those who had known both men well, including Churchill's daughter Mary (Lady Soames) and Sir William Deakin.[9]

The impression of Morton given by the extracts printed in Thompson's book is of an embittered and disillusioned man, venting his disappointment at his exclusion from Churchill's inner circle at the end of the war by destructive criticism. This is a pity, since the full correspondence preserved in the Liddell Hart Centre for Military Archives (covering the period from 1944 until March 1971) is far more positive, revealing a generous as well as keenly analytical spirit in Morton, and contains many examples of his correcting Thompson's over-critical (as he saw it) view of Churchill. These letters are a treasure trove of Morton's opinions on a wide range of subjects, ranging from politics to philosophy and psychology, and especially religion. They also provide the greatest amount of detail on Morton's domestic situation and daily routine available at any period of his life, and so are an invaluable resource to the biographer of a man whose individual existence has proved so elusive. There must, of course, be a health warning, as always with Morton: while his letters to Thompson are often frank, he remained rigidly discreet about his professional activities both before and during the war, and told Thompson only what he thought he should know – and what he wanted him to think. Despite this qualification, however, the correspondence is the most revealing source of information on Morton's later years, and forms the backbone of this chapter.

On retirement Morton seems to have severed all connection with Whitehall and the Intelligence community, save for one curious episode immediately after leaving the Treasury when his name was mentioned in connection with a project sponsored by the FO's Information Research Department (IRD).[10] This began as an attempt to set up a British equivalent to the French organisation *Paix et Liberté*,[11] but evolved into an IRD plan to set up an 'open' organisation to manage covertly controlled research, publicity and publishing in the UK. IRD initially saw advantages in creating a anti-Communist organisation that would ensure the British point of view was represented in like-minded international bodies, filling what was perceived as a 'gap in the organisation of the fight against Soviet political warfare in the United Kingdom'. When approached as a possible head of such a body, Morton responded with some enthusiasm, drawing up an elaborate plan for 'Operation Cut-Out' that envisaged a committee, 'posing as a voluntary anti-communist body, subsidised by certain powerful industrial and commercial interests, who do not desire to appear', which would coordinate anti-Communist activities, commission 'research into the broad political problems of the world including particularly the nature and the basis of Soviet Communist policy and the theory and practice of defence of a free society,' and direct a publications programme.[12]

Morton's detailed plan, firmly rooted in the clandestine world and based on his Intelligence expertise, alarmed IRD, who were now turning their attention to a simpler and less ambitious idea: the creation of a covertly controlled agency in the UK to issue IRD material over an unofficial imprint. They had no wish for the sponsorship of powerful interests (a suggestion reminiscent of Sir George Makgill's activities in the 1920s[13]), as one official commented:

the more city magnates, big business and large employers of labour keep away from the Committee, except as buyers of pamphlets which the Committee may produce, the better. Nor do we want to preserve 'an aura of mystery'; I admit that mystery sometimes is an advantage as a bait to people whose assistance you want, but in this case I do not think it is necessary and the disadvantages certainly outweigh this advantage.[14]

The idea was eventually scotched by the Cabinet's Official Committee on Communism (Home), who ruled that the provision of government money to such an organisation, even from secret funds, was too risky a business, and asked IRD to submit a plan that did not depend on subsidy. Though IRD continued to discuss the feasibility of a much-scaled down scheme during the latter part of 1953, Morton's candidature as chairman of the proposed committee was dropped, at least in part because of his association with the 'Sword of the Spirit', an ecumenical organisation founded in the late 1940s by lay Catholics to educate church and society about the international agenda, with the aim of uniting Christians against a common threat (Communism).[15] The interest of the episode as far as Morton was concerned lies in what it revealed about the strength of his anti-Communist sentiments, and about how he was viewed by IRD and more widely in Whitehall. One official argued that while Morton was an ideal representative to liaise with *Paix et Liberté*, 'with his name and title, his Old Etonian aura, his excellent French, and even his religion, which is the right kind', he was far less suitable for 'the only kind of work that really needs doing in this country – among trade unionists etc'. Others disagreed, pointing out that Morton's 'lifelong experience in these matters' made him ideal for the job, while his 'old Etonian aura' was not necessarily a disadvantage in labour and trade union circles – both Dalton and Gaitskell, after all, had a similar background. In the end, however, Morton was 'much too deeply identified as a member of the Mandarin class' for IRD purposes: in fact, the documentation suggests they were rather scared of him, both personally and by reputation. The Morton myth remained powerful.

This seems to have been the only occasion when the official world (in the guise of Whitehall or Intelligence) beckoned Morton from retirement. Though he had been intrigued by the IRD scheme, which fell squarely within his professional experience as well as his political inclinations, the documentation suggests he was not unhappy when it failed to materialise, suspecting that it would involve considerable effort for little reward. Meanwhile, he found himself much in demand throughout the United Kingdom as a lecturer and after-dinner speaker on international affairs and on military matters. His experience, and long years of reading and research, made him a compelling lecturer on a wide range of topics including Western Union, the Middle East and, particularly, the Soviet Union and Communism. His correspondence reveals similar preoccupations. The death of Stalin on 5 May 1953 provoked him to comment, in correspondence with Liddell Hart, on the 'extraordinary' degree of control that had been exercised by the Soviet leader, and its implications for military strategy: 'It is less difficult to decide action if you are possessed of relatively unlimited cannon fodder and complete ruthlessness'.[16] Liddell Hart was much impressed by Morton's 'perspicacity and balanced judgement', and in October 1953 sought in vain to persuade him to contribute an article on strategy and policy to a symposium on the Soviet army. Morton refused to write anything for publication – 'I feel an invincible reluctance to doing what you suggest' – but expanded at some length on the importance of paying due attention to the influence of Communist philosophy, and methods of thought and action:

I am positive that unless every step continues to be taken by the Party leaders . . . in strict accord with the very detailed principles of 'the Philosophy', the collapse of Communism as such will soon occur – and don't the leaders know it . . . all leaders must ever watch their colleagues for deviationism, and will themselves be deviationist should they fail to take every advantage of error on the part of the Colleagues, be they never so highly respected in the Party, and be their unmasking as traitors to the personal advantage of the Party member who brings to light their betrayal of the People. A party leader has no friends in the bourgeois sense of that word. He has no morals in the bourgeois sense of the word. By remembering this unalterable precept, it is assured that the worthiest Party Members become the leaders of the Party. (Or, in bourgeois language, wait till your boss has an off-day and then cut the sod's throat and take his job.) Jolly regime, isn't it?[17]

Morton enjoyed 'opining' to interested audiences, particularly of students: he took an evangelical view of educating British youth in world affairs. Meanwhile, he plunged into a demanding role as the chairman from 1956 of the board of governors of the Postgraduate General Teaching Hospitals of London University, also serving as a governor of St Luke's Woodside (a psychiatric hospital) and of both Hammersmith and Middlesex Hospitals, as well as being active on a number of related committees and in the affairs of the Catholic church. He remained Grand Master of the Civil Service Catholic Guild until November 1954, and was increasingly involved in a number of projects initiated by the Roman Catholic laity in both theological and social matters. In October 1956, on his return from giving a lecture at the University of Nottingham, he wrote to Thompson about his schedule:

> I am a perfect fool, and know it. But since my retirement I have con-
> tinually added to the number of things I undertake to do, with the result
> that several days a week I almost have to be carried to bed when I get
> in . . . What knocks me now is the travelling about in Undergrounds
> and Busses. By these means, the only ones open to me, it is practically
> an hour's journey from this house to most of the spots I have to visit in
> London. In the evenings, one can never get a seat; and standing for the
> best part of an hour, after having done a day's work, puts the tin lid on
> it . . . However I am still able to start the day at 6.30 a.m. and do about
> a 70 hour working week. I must cut that down soon though . . .[18]

Even allowing for an element of exaggeration, this was a demanding routine for a man in his mid-sixties with a bullet lodged near his heart. A later passage in the same letter shows that Morton approached his voluntary duties in rather the same spirit as he had his official ones – an effective approach, if irritating to those on the receiving end:

> I now have to go and spend the morning trying to calm several of 32
> Professors and Professorinnens, who are as jealous and temperamental
> as *prime ballerine assolute*, independent of sex. The lady who runs the
> 24 million volt cyclotron is always trying to direct a neutron stream
> through the Professor of medicine of whom she harbours unjust sus-
> picions. Whether his hair is coming out by reason of the neutrons, post-
> graduate students or age, is a moot point. Later I must attend a meeting
> of excitable Roman Catholics who seem to want to emulate Guido
> Fawkes. Not that a successful coup of this kind, directed at the Commons
> this time, instead of the Lords, might not have its advantages; but if
> anyone is to try such extreme methods, surely it had better be the
> Communists. Tomorrow, Friday, I have a Board meeting of a Medical
> School which has gone bust and then must buy food for the weekend; my
> cook being able only to walk as far as to buy trout and liver for the cat.[19]

This letter is one of a large number in similar vein, interspersing political comment or military reminiscence with details of his voluntary work and long anecdotes about the servants, the cat or the family of robins who had taken up residence in his hedge. These domestic details, as well providing an insight into the tender-hearted side of his character, reveal the extent to which both his faith and a strong sense of duty informed the way he ordered his life in retirement. While he clearly still enjoyed using his sharp intellect to outwit officialdom in the pursuit of important goals (such as securing funding to build the new Hammersmith Hospital), he also took seriously the responsibility of his position as head of the small household at Kew, providing creature comforts such as central heating or new plumbing not just for himself, but for the benefit of his dependants. As he wrote to Thompson in September 1963:

> I believe that it was always in the tradition of both my father and my mother's families to regard [servants] as friends, and in the late Victorian feudalism into which I was born, the 'good' squire and his lady looked after all persons 'dwelling within the manor' with great human and beneficent care.[20]

It was the same sense of duty that underlay the care, and time he took in giving his advice to Thompson, for which he refused any thanks:

> I can hope to avoid pride of a serious nature, since I fully recognise – as do you – that any good thing whatsoever, in thought word or deed, is done or effected by God alone, and the only slight credit that any of us can take in such a matter is that we did not resist being the unworthy instruments of God's will and act.[21]

This humility did not, however, mean that he minced his words, as witnessed by a letter of August 1958 to Thompson, who was writing a book about his own life:

> The gist of vesting the ordinary in the robes of God is a very rare one. It has nothing whatever to do with exaggeration . . . Psychologically your book gives me the impression of a man in blinkers, looking only ahead at an unknown future; seeking for an object in life, without any knowledge whatever of what that object might be or where it is to be found. That unconscious attitude is fatal to the writing of a psychological type of autobiography . . . [you should] go on doing war books or others which are formally commissioned and look on the writing of your ultimate biography as a hobby for the time being.[22]

Early in 1958 Morton had been very ill: a scrawled note of 15 February informed Thompson that he 'had a temperature of 104.7 and, seriously, a priest standing by to give me the last Sacrament'. There is no indication whether this was a recurrence of the bronchial trouble, linked to his First World War wound, that usually plagued him in the New Year, or whether it was in connection with the operation to which he referred in a letter a few months later, commenting: 'I am 67, with a bullet through the heart, one kidney removed, also the prostate gland and two half lungs. This is not conducive to very violent exercise, such as all-in wrestling or climbing Goat Fell.'[23] Shortly after this, however, he had recovered sufficiently to send detailed comments to Thompson, explaining why 'compared with the British Armies the Americans were amateurs'. (This was, he said, due to the longer British tradition of quality generalship: 'Neither the British nor the Americans feel that a successful General is likely to be a good Prime Minister, but the Americans feel that any successful politician can become a good General.')[24]

This pattern was repeated in subsequent years: periods of intensive activity, working long hours on behalf of the Teaching Hospitals or other voluntary bodies in the autumn, followed by the collapse of his health in January and February, then a period of convalescence followed by more intensive activity, from he which endeavoured to recover during the summer months. Regular correspondence, particularly with Thompson, was maintained throughout. Though complaining frequently of exhaustion, he obviously enjoyed himself, boasting to Thompson of his skill in 'oppressing architects', and describing how he welcomed the return of warmer weather when 'I slowly renew my youth and regain certain powers of invective, useful for correspondence with the Minister of Health and his officials, particularly the latter'.[25] As always, he was invigorated by a challenge:

> I am always very glad to get to bed by 10.30 p.m. and go to sleep without any trouble, while I wake up about 6.30 a.m. equally peaceful, until I recall that it is another day and that I must get up in about a quarter of an hour; whereupon I meditate like Macbeth, 'Tomorrow and tomorrow and tomorrow'. I am glad to add that soon after I have resumed an erect stance, thought of battle with various irritating persons revives me for 'Once more into the breach'.[26]

According to a letter he wrote to Dennis Wheatley, Morton was known in the Ministry of Health as 'The Minister's Bane': this may have been one of his inventions, but was probably not far from the truth.[27] On the other hand, there is no doubt that his administrative ability, toughness and intellectual rigour made him a formidable force in the world of health service planning.

Morton's letters to Thompson allow some glimpses into the details of his personal life at Kew Green. Throughout his career he had complained of his (comparative) poverty, by which he meant lack of a private income or capital assets, and having to live on his salary. Now, in retirement, his pension and the death of his mother had provided some financial security, though he was very aware of his household responsibilities, and still inclined to complain. The following extract from a letter in November 1962 is worth quotation, both as a representative sample and as an unusually detailed account of his personal affairs:

Although I have (now) no financial worries, a fact which many people would envy – and rightly, it is a very odd thought that an old bachelor with £50,000 invested in sound stock, no mortgage on a house he owns, and a pension of £1,500 per annum in addition, as well as the Old Age pension of £2.17.6 a week, cannot afford to own a motor car in London, unless he draw about £1,000 a year out of his capital. And since I hold the view that in London, no one over 70 should drive his own car – a chauffeur would mean drawing yet a further £800 or more out of his capital. I am not complaining in the very least, but it is odd to think that the above figures in gross sums, when the income Tax, Surtax and other Government *direct* taxes have done their work, there is left about £2,500 a year, out of which three aged people subsist – admittedly in reasonable comfort and a small house maintained, not to mention two cats. When I first came here ten years ago, having, thank goodness, decided to cut all losses, sell everything else saleable and keep expenses down, I used to draw a weekly cheque for food and wages of £15, which included spending pocket money. We have lived all along in exactly the same style, but I now draw a weekly cheque of £35. My annual bills for lighting and heating ten years ago were c. £45 and are now £200. For a season ticket on the Underground to London was £2.15.0 a quarter and is now £8.15.0 a quarter and so it goes on.[28]

It is difficult to tell how much of Morton's expenditure went towards his own personal enjoyment, or to hospitality. Certainly he enjoyed good food and drink, both at home and when lunching with friends and acquaintances at London clubs. There are no references to attendance at concerts, or the ballet, which he is said to have enjoyed, and his schedule hardly seems to have allowed for such indulgence. He appears to have remained reluctant either to visit friends' houses, whether in London or the country, and to have entertained rarely, though it is impossible to be sure of this. Certainly he resisted any attempts by Thompson, Liddell Hart or others to entice him to gatherings where he suspected the press might be present, claiming 'an intense and almost pathological abhorrence of personal publicity'.[29] Though he corresponded frequently with Thompson and took an interest in his family, they rarely met.

Some of Morton's family, in particular his cousin Gillian (Gil) Elles, grand-daughter of his uncle Gerald and daughter of Sir Hugh Elles by his first wife Geraldine Morton, are known to have visited him at Kew Green. Gil (now Mrs Parker), who was to play an important part in Morton's life in his last years, remembers first meeting him at Beaufort Gardens when she was 'about 11', when she became intoxicated on Pimms' offered by him. When nursing during the Second World War, she often stayed the night with his mother, 'Aunt Edith', cycling back to Beaufort Gardens during the Blitz, and sometimes saw Morton there: she remembers that Edith always refused to use a shelter, but remained in an upstairs room, 'chandeliers and portraits swinging around', during air raids.[30]

In the latter part of the war Gil was nursing in Abyssinia, and after returning to the UK became a psychoanalyst, with a number of her early patients Holocaust survivors and refugees. She often visited Morton at Kew Green, and he wrote to Thompson in 1966 that he had 'regarded her for many years as though she were my own daughter'.[31] He also entertained friends on occasion, including R.H. (Richard) Parker, who was widowed in 1958 and was to marry Gil in 1963.[32] John Parker, Richard's son by his first wife, remembers going to Sunday lunch at Kew Green after his mother's death, and describes Morton as very hospitable, as well as 'very aware of the level of hospitality he considered appropriate to his position'.[33]

Morton's correspondence indicates some scaling down of his activities from about 1964. Part of this was due, he said, to the election of a Labour Government, which meant that 'all and every kind of development has been suspended' in respect of his NHS Board, though he had become involved in sitting on Whitley Councils for the Health Service.[34] But his increasingly frequent bouts of bronchial trouble had begun to take their toll, forcing him to spend more time in Kew rather than travelling into central London. At the beginning of 1965 both the elderly ladies who 'looked after' him were also ill, raising for him the spectre of living alone, something he clearly dreaded: 'absolute alone-ness produces in me the most appalling psychopathic reactions of loneliness, which are quite unendurable save for very short periods'.[35] A further period of ill-health a few months later increased his depression, and the feeling that all his efforts were to no avail: 'it is all a waste of time and certainly a weariness of the flesh. However much they are warned that they are working on the wrong lines for the wrong objective, men obstinately go on doing so, until the resultant nothingness forces them to scrap everything and start again.'[36] The death of Richard Parker in the autumn of 1965 upset him greatly; he had become a member of the family as well as an old friend, and Gil's distress compounded his own. In all the circumstances, although he claimed to dread his retirement from the health service in March 1966 – 'What on earth I shall do with myself from then on, I have no idea, seeing that I am physically not yet a wreck and believe myself mentally to be remaining sound'[37] – it is hard to believe that he did not also welcome the cessation of what had become a punishing physical routine. At the time of his second 'retirement' he was seventy-five years old.

During 1966 his health became more precarious. Apart from the usual bronchial troubles, he had a fall in his garden in August, hitting his head and bruising his ribs: he noted with gratitude that Gil had 'given up her evenings, after curing lunatics all day', to come and help look after him; though, characteristically, he added that he had been very helpful to her by 'rewriting' her book on the medical treatment of neurosis.[38] Nor did he sink into inactivity. Apart from writing to Thompson, he noted in February 1967 that he had been advising Robert Sencourt[39] on a book he was writing, and giving 'advice to the RC hierarchy in this country' on organisational matters. As usual, he found his interlocutors wanting:

I find myself astonished at the apparent lack of knowledge on the part of these Bishops, of the first principles of 'organisation and 'administration'. No amount of charity and good will can make up for that . . . It looks as if I may be drawn into a highly confidential Committee, composed of Clerics and lay persons, with latter in a majority, which the Bishops are contemplating setting up. I should find this interesting in my declining years, but most probably equally frustrating and arduous.[40]

This seems to have been a reference to the Laity Commission for England and Wales which, he thought, would keep him 'pleasantly busy' in a way he enjoyed: 'Our job, in plain language, is to be rude about Bishops and Priests – not individually, but *en masse* – when they deserve it, and to push them into obeying the decisions of the Council for modernising the Church'.[41] This was surely a task after his heart, calling for the same skills he had employed when Director of the Industrial Intelligence Centre: though later correspondence suggests that differences between the Catholic Union, on whose Council Morton sat, and other Catholic bodies caused his participation to be short-lived.[42]

Meanwhile, he had grown increasingly anxious about his personal situation, as he told Thompson in February 1967: 'One of the nightmares of the aged, who feel themselves growing physically less able to fend for themselves alone, as every month passes, is that of what is to happen if they get left absolutely alone in the real sense.'[43] His anxiety was removed when Gil Parker – 'my cousin and heiress' – moved into Kew Green in August 1967, living with him but retaining her own consulting rooms: 'She says there is extraordinarily little difference between decrepit and decaying old gentlemen like me, and her "unbalanced" children.'[44] His delight in this solution is clear from his correspondence: apart from relieving his solitude, Gil's presence in his household gave him a new enthusiasm for his own interests and displaced his anxieties about his own health. His letters recovered some of their joviality, and occasional facetiousness, and domestic disasters weighed less heavily on him. When Gil herself suffered health problems in 1968 and 1969, he was consumed with anxiety:

What I should do, were she to die, I cannot imagine. At my age and only relatively good health, I could not live alone in this house. I have no other available relative or even friend who could – or would – come and 'look after the old man' . . . without Gillian Parker . . . to organise this and above all to sleep in, in case of accidents during the night either to old West or me, life would be highly precarious, and unbearably lonely, as I think you can see.[45]

Gil, who treated her cousin with an admirable mixture of briskness and sympathy, was an indispensable support to him in the last few years of his life. Although he was still able to 'argue with Bishops', to grant an interview to Arthur Marder on naval strategy, or upbraid Thompson for his views of Churchill ('Frankly and bluntly, you have not got Winston right at all in a number of very important ways'[46]), his formidable energy and determination finally began to ebb. In April 1969 he consented to be interviewed by Miss Milicent Bagot, a recently-retired member of MI5, who was conducting an investigation into the Zinoviev Letter of 1924.[47] However, she found the interview, conducted on 28 April, disappointing. Morton claimed to have very little recollection of the events in question, though volunteering the information that Menzies had posted a copy of the Letter to the *Daily Mail*, asking Morton to go with him to the letterbox as a witness; a story that was greeted in SIS with 'amazement and disbelief'. The recording of the interview provokes two conflicting impressions: one of an elderly man, with failing faculties and memory, who found it understandably difficult to recall the detail of events that took place more than forty years before. The other (and stronger) impression is of someone who had no intention of breaking the habit of a lifetime by revealing the details of Intelligence matters, even to an 'insider'; at times it sounds as if he were toying with Bagot. Apart from the Letter, he denied any recollection of Makgill or any of his informants, and even of Sidney Reilly and Paul Dukes. Bagot had hoped that Morton, a central figure in the Zinoviev affair, would be able to cast some light on its many mysteries: but this was something that he either could not, or would not do.

At the beginning of 1971, Morton was laid low by 'a germ hitherto unknown to science' and apologised to Thompson for being unable to answer a letter. He did manage to write on 14 January to Lord Craigmyle, secretary of the Catholic Union, a letter signed in a weak and wavering hand, although the text retained some of his old spark.[48] In May, much against his wishes, Morton had to spend time in Hammersmith Hospital with a heart complaint; and on 6 July Gil wrote on his behalf to Thompson, explaining that he had had a slight stroke and could not write. Although described as 'progressing reasonably well', he never returned home, taking great comfort from a visit by Cardinal Heenan, who was 'a great spiritual support for him'. He died in Hammersmith Hospital on 31 July 1971 at the age of seventy-nine, the cause of death given as bronchopneumonia and cerebrovascular disease. He had, Gil wrote to Thompson on 8 August, been 'gallant and independent to the end & it was wonderful that he was so active about the things that mattered to him until the very last few weeks'.[49] A Requiem Mass, celebrated by Cardinal Heenan in Westminster Cathedral on 15 September 1971, was attended by many of those who had known him in all his guises: as Intelligence officer, as senior government official, and as tireless worker for the Health Service and for the Roman Catholic Church. It was a fitting celebration of a varied life in which faith had been the central pillar.

Morton was a man who always liked to have the last word, and it is only fair to allow him to end this chapter. His correspondence contains many examples of self-examination, which became more frequent and searching as he grew older: there was always a tension between his firm belief that 'whatever happens to you is what God wants', and the equally firm conviction that 'God gave Freedom to Man, and Man constantly uses that freedom wrongly and with evil intent'.[50] In terms of his own life, this translated into a combination of humility, tinged by the realisation that his career had perhaps not been as successful as he would have wished; and pride, based on what he had been a part of, and had achieved. Many of his later letters reflected these conflicting feelings (often couched in a somewhat didactic form for Thompson, whom Morton considered insufficiently inclined to count his blessings). As a postscript to his life, however, a letter written in October 1962 seems to capture both his style and his spirit:

> I have no sort of message for the world. I have always been interested in other people – of any kind or class, but chiefly those I have actually met with. In my time I have been a rather good mathematician and with the makings of a musician of some parts. I ought to have been a lawyer, being fascinated by the extremely pedantic accuracy and inaccuracies of the law; while always fully recognising that Law is not justice by a long chalk. I should have preferred the criminal law, for the occasional delight in getting my client off quite legally by processes of law, when I strongly suspect he is as guilty as Hell . . . However, I am equally content as things are at having been a back-room boy in the mansions of the great, where I was probably of little use . . . Whenever occasionally an ancient crony whom I have not seen for years, asks me what I am doing now, I always say, Energetically awaiting death.[51]

EPILOGUE

Morton and Churchill

The relationship between Morton and Churchill, a long friendship and professional association, requires some final comment. It has been suggested by some contemporaries and later commentators that Morton, his usefulness to Churchill exhausted, was, if not cast, set aside in 1945, leading to the bitterness expressed in his published letters to R.W. Thompson, where he described Churchill as 'the most ego-centric man I have ever known', whose 'ruthless use of power horrified me'.[1] This impression has served to exaggerate and dramatise the inevitable weakening of the ties between Morton and Churchill in their diverging postwar lives, as well as to diminish somewhat unfairly both men's reputation.

Through two world wars and the intervening 'wilderness years', Churchill set a high value on the character, talents, knowledge and experience of the 'brilliant and gallant officer' he had first met in Ploegsteert in 1916. While he may never have been on the same terms of intimacy with Morton as with Bracken or Lindemann, there is no doubt that he liked, trusted and relied on him, and recognised the contribution Morton had made to his own fortunes. This outweighed any disappointment or annoyance he felt at Morton's failures or indiscretions, and he remained loyal to his friend, while recognising his limitations. Though their close connection ended in 1945 when Churchill left office, he retained affection and respect for Morton long after they ceased to have regular contact.

For his part, Morton recognised that, as he wrote to Thompson in August 1960:

> Winston was unquestionably a Great Man, as the world counts greatness, and however much later historians than any now alive discover and disclose his terrific weaknesses or worse, they will still be bound to write his name in Valhalla, even though it may be more difficult to find it in Heaven.[2]

He never altered this opinion, however harsh his criticism of Churchill's character and actions might be. Some of his letters to Thompson do indeed reveal a deep bitterness, and a distaste amounting at times to revulsion, for certain of Churchill's habits and actions during and after the Second World War. But these feelings were inspired less by the perception that he, Morton, had been treated badly, than by disappointment that his old friend was capable of what Morton considered to be actions unworthy of a great man. Stephen Roskill, who knew Morton in his later years, saw no sign that he was 'embittered' about his treatment by Churchill, describing his retirement as 'full and contented'.[3] This did not preclude critical analysis expressed, in typical Mortonesque fashion, both fiercely and forcefully, and with the inestimable benefit conferred on those in retirement by hindsight.

Morton's judgements, always informed by his religious conviction and a somewhat fastidious personal reticence, grew harsher in retrospect, when no longer tempered by the day to day experience of political and military necessity. While working with and for Churchill, Morton, like many others, understood and forgave much: though he left no contemporary record, other accounts, such as that given by Alanbrooke in his diaries, show that Morton was not alone in detecting a growing impatience, even brutality in Churchill's manner during the Second World War, alienating many who worked with and for him. Churchill's own wife had reproved him for his 'rough sarcastic & overbearing manner' with colleagues and subordinates as early as July 1940,[4] and in August 1941 Colville noted a conversation with Jack Churchill and Morton about:

> the rising annoyance in the House of Commons at the PM's personal resentment of criticism – which is meant to be helpful – and the offence which has been given to many people, including Ministers, by his treatment of them. Desmond goes so far as to say that PM is losing many people's friendship.[5]

Much can, of course, be ascribed to the enormous stress and strain of the wartime premiership, itself the subject of many studies. There is no doubt that many of those who worked closely with Churchill found him overbearing and difficult at times, though their belief in his leadership generally carried them through. They were tough men, Morton included; occasional exasperation or wounded feelings were tempered by admiration and affection. The contemporary evidence certainly does not suggest any deliberate withdrawal by Morton on grounds of distaste or hurt feelings. Events, and time, brought a gradual end to a friendship that was always based more on shared interests than on shared psychology. Although he displayed an external persona that could be deliberately brash and even crude, Morton was a private and deeply religious man who set high store on the qualities of a 'self-controlled gentleman, thinking of the feelings of others and prepared to accept as his duty whatever state of life he seemed to have been called into'.[6] These were qualities that no war leader, let alone Churchill, could afford to embrace, as Morton himself recognised.

Churchill and Morton were complex characters, sharing certain characteristics: desire for action, impatience, a taste for showmanship; perhaps, also, as suggested by Sir Martin Gilbert, a certain reluctance towards personal intimacy.[7] They understood one another better than either was willing to acknowledge to the other. Their differences, however, in background, beliefs and aspirations as well as in experience and capability, were more marked than the similarities, and this contributed to the gradual weakening of their long friendship more than any event or any action on Churchill's part. Perhaps the best illustration lies in how the two men hoped to be remembered. Morton wrote in 1960:

> I cannot imagine an epitaph I would desire more than that when I die, someone might say, really believing it, that Desmond Morton might have been a greater figure in the affairs of his country, had he been less of a gentleman.[8]

For Churchill, to be a great figure in the affairs of his country was precisely how he wished to be remembered; to be thought 'a gentleman' was not only of less consequence, it was irrelevant. If Morton really believed what he wrote, it holds the key to much of his character and career; but it may have been no more than what he wanted others to believe about him. As always with the 'man of mystery', there is no way of telling what was true.

ANNEX

Despatch from Sir Desmond Morton to the Ministry of
Civil Aviation, describing the events leading up to the
signature of an Air Services Agreement between
H.M. Government and the Royal Iraqi Government
[*GA 93/49*]

Confidential   London, May 1 1951

Sir:

It has been suggested to me that, although the main events culminating in
the recent signature in Bagdad of an Air Services Agreement between H.M.
Government and the Royal Iraqi Government are covered by telegrams exchanged
during the negotiations, a somewhat fuller account of certain incidents might
prove of interest, as presenting features believed to be unusual in the making of
international Treaties.

2. Accompanied by Mr. John Brancker, a Director of the British Overseas
Airways Corporation, I arrived in Bagdad on Sunday, March 11 last, having previously been assured that the Iraqi Government was ready to embark upon
immediate, intensive negotiations. This proved to be a slight exaggeration, since
Monday, March 12, was spent in assisting the Iraqis to determine who, if anyone,
had power to negotiate with us. However, as soon as it was realised that the Iraqi
constitution only allowed the full Council of Ministers in corporate session
to decide anything, a negotiating Committee was quickly formed. By way of
compromise this Committee included no Cabinet Minister, but consisted of one
ex-Cabinet Minister, H.E. Abdul Jabbar Chelabi, now Director General of
Communications and Works, together with Sayed Akram Mushtaq, Director
of Civil Aviation, later replaced by Sayed Theodore Lawrence, the Deputy
Director, an Arab despite his name, but a Christian and therefore debarred in
practice from holding higher rank in the hierarchy. To these were added Colonel
Sabah es Said, son of the Prime Minister and officially General Manager of Iraqi
Airways, but actually more concerned in amassing a large fortune by dubious
means, so that his father, while appearing presently incorruptible, may nevertheless count upon a reasonable pension upon retiring by taking half of his son's
illicit gains. There were also present the Chief and Deputy Chief Legal Advisers

from the Ministry of Foreign Affairs; the first being of the Saleh family. I failed to obtain the name of the second, who never uttered during the five weeks of negotiations. Nor did the chief lawyer intervene much, after being informed publicly by Chelabi at an early session that he appeared to be equally ignorant of English and Arabic, and that if he had ever read any Air Agreement in either language, he must have done so in his sleep, which state he was advised to re-enter permanently with the utmost speed. The Iraqi negotiators were completed by Colonel Mostert, the British Adviser on Civil Aviation, lent to Iraqi Airways by BOAC.

3. The British party consisted of the Civil Air Attaché, Mr. Barnard, Mr. Brancker and myself, though we were later joined by Mr. Platt, Commercial Manager of Cyprus Airways. The first meeting began very early in the morning of Tuesday, March 13.

4. Subsequent negotiations may be likened to a symphony in three movements: the Overture, conducted at a 'tempo rubato' owing to the incidence of Easter, which was observed in Whitehall but is not mentioned in the Koran, and to the fact that Thursday and Friday, being the Moslem Saturday and Sunday, it was difficult to make the combined machine work save on Mondays, Tuesdays and Wednesdays. The second movement was pure 'scherzo', owing to the curious interventions of Mr. Platt. The Finale was certainly 'Allegro con brio', with every instrument keeping to its own tune, measure and key.

5. The first meeting lasted all day without a pause for solid refreshment. Beginning in the Ministry of Communications, it was adjourned at about 1 o'clock to the offices of Iraqi Airways and later to the Iraqi Club, where drinks were provided in quantity, and the Iraqi Delegation was unexpectedly joined by a famous Arabian architect, who described himself as a Communist detesting Russians, the Chief Electrical Engineer of Iraqi Railways, who was most interesting on the subject of blowing up trains with electrical detonators, the Governor of the National Bank, who used to be the Prime Minister's dentist, and by the Barman. At about 6 o'clock in the evening, it was calculated by the engineer that the Negotiators had consumed 1.37 bottles of gin apiece. Thereafter the Barman, seeing my incipient distress and presumably taking me for a slightly eccentric Moslem, thrust a plateful of sandwiches into my lap, with the remark, 'This no pig, you eat safe'. We subsequently adjourned.

6. By then it had become clear that nothing could be achieved save through the piecemeal elimination of obstacles, of which the first was Colonel Mostert, whose enthusiasm for Iraqi interests appeared to outweigh all discretion in favour of his permanent masters, B.O.A.C. However Mr. Brancker kindly took certain steps, whereafter Colonel Mostert left for Ceylon. Unfortunately the gallant Colonel's pernicious ideas had by that time been warmly espoused by Akram Mushtaq. He, like all the Iraqis with whom we had to deal, has great charm and no mean intelligence. He is however an advanced psychoneurotic and exists largely on morphine. He has spent some time in Switzerland undergoing a cure for this, but having abandoned the struggle at half-way stage, is now rather worse than

before. He attempts suicide every three months with monotonous regularity. Ably assisted by my colleagues, I apparently caused him so many brain storms that after a fortnight he collapsed and retired on permanent leave of absence.

7. Colonel Sabah was the last mountain to be levelled. One evening he elected to discover how much whiskey he could consume at one session, determining that his limit was 3¼ bottles, after which he fell down some stone steps and broke two ribs. This left only Abdul Jabbar Chelabi and Sayed Lawrence – both were reasonable people – apart from our two silent pillars of legal wisdom. Progress might then have been rapid had it not been for the unexpected appearance of Mr. Platt, followed three days later by an 'Immediate' telegram from Cyprus announcing his impending arrival.

8. Mr. Platt said he had been sent to Bagdad because we were 'selling Cyprus Airways down the drain for the benefit of B.O.A.C.'. I do not wish to infer that Mr. Platt was ever anything but courteous towards myself and members of the British Delegation. He did however insist that he had plenipotentiary powers from Cyprus Airways to make whatever commercial arrangements he chose with Iraqi Airways. In any case it is perhaps permissible to suggest that he may not have been quite the right person even for that task, which he began by visiting Colonel Sabah es Said alone. I do not know exactly what passed, but the result was temporarily prejudicial to subsequent good relations between the two air lines concerned. It is true that Colonel Sabah, in an endeavour to doctor his broken ribs had strapped himself up with strips of sheet covered in fish glue, and on trying to renew the dressing had removed a large area of skin. This alone, however, would hardly account for the complete disappearance of his normal charm. On talking to me later about Mr. Platt, he made statements highly critical of the latter's presumed ancestry.

9. The subsequent efforts of Mr. Brancker and myself to persuade Mr. Platt that, whatever his manner of approach to Iraqi Airways had been, some other manner – almost any other manner – might be more desirable, were disastrous. Unknown to the rest of us, Mr. Platt wrote a 16-page letter in his own hand-writing, apparently intending to send it in draft as a peace offering to the offended Colonel. In practice, however, he did not send this letter in draft form, which would have been bad enough, but signed and dated it before despatch. He then found he had kept no copy and could only remember roughly that it included a number of solemn promises on behalf of Cyprus Airways. His attempted reconstruction of the letter revealed so many dreadful possibilities of embarrass-ment to our negotiations, that the only thing to do was somehow to engender its disappearance. Fortunately Colonel Sabah regarded this letter as affording such valuable material for blackmail that, instead of consigning it to his secret safe, of which most of his staff had provided themselves with duplicate keys, he carried it about on his person, Consequently, by means into which I have not dared enquire, Mr. Brancker gained possession of the unfortunate letter and burned it; thereafter persuading Mr. Platt to entrust the commercial affairs of Cyprus Airways to him and to return himself to Nicosia. Before leaving Bagdad, however, Mr. Platt

signed a number of different letters calculated to meet varying future possibilities. These, together with a few sheets signed in blank by Mr. Platt in case of accidents, were locked up in the Embassy.

10. The Easter Festival and certain quite different holidays appertaining to the Shia and Sunni Sects of Islam now being things of the past, negotiations proceeded apace, provisional agreement being reached on April 15. Since the main text of the Agreement was not in dispute, Mr. Barnard had previously obtained the consent of the Ministry of Foreign Affairs to translate it from English into Arabic, so as to avoid unnecessary delay in the concluding stages. This should have proved no difficult task since the greater part of the text had been adequately translated six months earlier.

11. Our minds had already been exercised as to the form in which our provisional agreement might be recorded. Abdul Jabbar Chelabi and his Minister, H.E. Dhai Jafar, were as anxious as ourselves to record something meaningful, but the peculiarities of the Iraqi Constitution already mentioned, rendered impossible an agreed Minute, the provisional initialling of the Agreement or any other customary device to the same end. In these doubts H.E. Nuri Pasha es Said, the Prime Minister, intervened by instructing Dhai Jafar to propose the full Agreement unexpectedly before the Council of Ministers. It later became clear that the Prime Minister's motives were not unconnected with the internal politics of Iraq, where the Acting Foreign Minister is an opponent of and a potential successor to Nuri himself, and whose power had been waxing to an uncomfortable degree; whereas Dhai Jafar had been one of the Prime Minister's staunch supporters.

12. At 11 am on Sunday, April 15, I was informed personally by the Minister of Communications that with Nuri's support he had just rushed the Agreement through the Council on the unusual plea that if negotiations with the British were to be further prolonged, he would soon have no staff left in his Ministry. The Council however had only authorised the Minister to initial the Agreement, fully realising that at any future date it could thus be declared invalid. However, before the ink was dry on the Council's decision, the Prime Minister betook himself to the Prince Regent and persuaded H.R.H. to issue an A'lan in the most full and final terms, authorising the Minister of Communications to complete and sign the Agreement, from which act there could be no retrograde step.

13. This was a great blow to the prestige of the Acting Foreign Minister, as was intended by Nuri Said. It was a greater blow to him still when, on the following day he received an urgent letter from the Lebanon enclosing a handsome cheque with a promise of more to come should he succeed in preventing the signature of the Agreement, since the latter acknowledged British Suzerainty over Civil Aviation in Kuwait, Bahrain and along the Trucial Coast.

14. These events really put the Acting Foreign Minister on his mettle. He wrote at once forbidding the Minister of Communications to sign, A'lan or no A'lan. In some perturbation Dhai Jafar asked our advice. We felt impelled to recommend that he should not receive the Acting Foreign Minister's letter until after he had signed the Agreement, pointing out that in well conducted Administrations

official letters from other Government Departments were never delivered straight on the desks of their addressees but were passed through a registry for numbering. We observed that in England this process might be completed in a few minutes, but felt sure that it could be arranged to take somewhat longer in Bagdad. In parenthesis I may add that although the Minister of Communications read the alarming instruction on April 16, he had not officially received the letter before my departure from Bagdad on April 20.

15. These delaying tactics were clearly insufficient. Speedy action was essential. Mr. Barnard at once enquired at the Ministry of Foreign Affairs regarding the translation only to be informed that nothing had been done, though it was of course possible that the Acting Minister of Foreign Affairs had given certain instructions. At the same time it was found that the Ministry of Foreign Affairs alone kept stocks of the beautiful paper upon which Treaties have to be inscribed. No responsible official in the Ministry would part with any. This proved no baffle, since for a relatively small expenditure a farash handed Mr. Barnard several quires out of a window.

16. It was then discovered that the Minister of Communications had no typist or typewriter capable of handling English. Here H.M. Ambassador came to the rescue, and although the only elegant typewriter in possession of the Embassy also showed distressing signs of a spirit independent of that of the kind lady who pressed its keys, the necessary two fair copies of the Agreement in English were ready within 24 hours.

17. There still remained the Arabic version. Chelabi overcame the absence of typists in his Ministry by demanding a roll call of all paid officials, whereby it was discovered that some two or three hundred persons, happily including half a dozen typists, had been drawing Government pay for the past few years but had never attended for duty. All were summoned, including a Deputy Secretary General, whom the Secretary General himself had never previously encountered.

18. Thus on Wednesday morning all was nearly ready. The last lack was ribbon for binding the Agreement and two appropriate seals. Mr. Barnard, who was a tower of strength in these difficulties, visited the bazaar and returned with many yards of ribbon of different colour and width, sold normally for tying up boxes of mixed sweets. I rejected a three-inch ribbon of red, white and blue, and a bright red one inscribed 'Nestlé's' in gold letters, for one of more convenient width in the plain green of the Prophet. There was also some difficulty about the Iraqi seal; the one kept by the Ministry of Foreign Affairs was inaccessible, since that Department, learning of our fevered activities, had put itself into a state of siege. I understand that the official seal of the Prince Regent was obtained by one person holding H.R.H. in conversation while another removed the seal from the royal desk. I trust it has found its way back.

19. The above details, including a check of the Arabic by the Oriental Councillor and Secretary of H.M. Embassy, to both of whom I am most grateful for their intensive efforts in this regard, occupied the British Delegation, H.M.

Embassy and the whole of the Iraqi Ministry of Communications until 12.45 p.m. on Wednesday, April 18, the act of signature being fixed for 1 p.m. that day. This could hardly be delayed in view of the increasingly pointed efforts of the Ministry of Foreign Affairs to intervene.

20. Punctually however at 1 o'clock, a cortège, headed by the car of H.M. Ambassador, drew up at the Ministry. A small crowd milling in the courtyard was explained as the farashes of the Ministry of Communications specially mobilised for the purpose, keeping at bay most of the employees of the Ministry of Foreign Affairs, whose ill-natured intentions could only be surmised. With a speed hitherto unknown in Iraq, and uncommon elsewhere, signatures were appended in the right places and at three minutes past one, H.E. Dhai Jafar sank back in his chair exclaiming in Arabic, 'in the name of God I need coffee'. He afterwards added in English, 'By some means, I know not how, you have made the Ministry of Communications do three months' work in two days'.

21. In conclusion I must express my deep appreciation of the assistance accorded me by the Staff of H.M. Embassy, nearly all of whom were drawn into the negotiations in one capacity or another, especially in the final stage. My warm thanks are also due to my colleagues Mr. Brancker and Mr. Barnard, whose ingenuity in overcoming unexpected difficulties bears testimony to their previous experience in many trades other than diplomacy.

> I have the honour to be, Sir
> With great truth and regard,
>> Your humble and obedient servant,
>> [Desmond Morton]

NOTES

INTRODUCTION

1 See Anthony Powell, *The Military Philosophers* (London: Heinemann, 1968, pp. 191–95), ninth in his twelve-volume novel, *A Dance to the Music of Time*. Powell explained in his own memoirs, *To Keep the Ball Rolling* (London: Penguin edn, 1983, pp. 303–04) that the episode in question, featuring the influential industrialist Sir Magnus Donners, was based on Morton; in view of Donners's voyeuristic tendencies, Morton would have been unlikely to appreciate the identification.

2 R. Makins to Sir G. Cribbett, Ministry of Civil Aviation, 15 June 1951: GA 93/53, FO 371/93182, TNA.

1 ANCESTRAL VOICES

1 *Winds of Change 1914–1939* (London: Macmillan, 1966). It was the first of six volumes of Macmillan memoirs covering the period 1914–63.

2 Morton to Thompson, 15 August 1966, Thompson papers 1/3, Liddell Hart Centre for Military Archives, Kings College, London (hereafter LHCMA).

3 Interview with Mrs Gil Parker, 25 June 2002.

4 Thomas Morton (1802–79) wrote a large number of predominantly one-act plays, mostly on historical themes. It is not clear how many of these were performed, but *Sink or Swim* opened at the Royal Olympic Theatre on 2 August 1852, while *A Pretty Piece of Business* was first performed at the Royal Haymarket Theatre on 18 November 1853. He also wrote extensive textual analysis of Shakespeare. John Maddison Morton (1811–91) specialised in farce: his most famous work was *Box and Cox*. This play, first performed in 1847, provided the inspiration for Cox and Box, a short comic operetta by F.C. Burnard and Arthur Sullivan, which was first performed in 1867 and is still performed today.

5 Thomas Morton (1764–1838). His other works included *Columbus, or a world discovered* (1792), *The School of Reform, or How to Rule a Husband* (1805) and *A Roland for an Oliver* (1819).

6 Henry Boylan (ed), *A Dictionary of Irish Biography* (Dublin: Gill & Macmillan, 1988).

7 Lieut-Gen. Sir Gerald de Courcy Morton, KCIE, CVO, CB, 1845–1906. 6th Foot (Royal Warwickshire) Regiment 1863, Adjutant 1867–71, ADC then Private Secretary to Lieut. Governor of the Punjab 1871–77, Assistant Adjutant General during Afghan campaign, later Adjutant General of India 1895–98, Major General in Command of Lahore District 1898–1901, in Command of Dublin district then of 7th Division at the Curragh, 1902–06.

8 Edith's scrapbook contains a cutting from *The Bystander*, dated 11 April 1906, on the official enquiry into this famous 'ragging' case. A member of the Scots Guards, said

to be 'dirty' and 'smelly', had been 'courtmartialled' by his fellow officers, which entailed being forced to strip and get into a bath where water, oil, feathers and jam were poured over him; he later escaped by jumping out of a window. The Commander told the Court of Enquiry that he had told his men to 'deal with' their supposedly offensive fellow subaltern themselves, but had intended them to use moral persuasion.

9 *Irish Times*, 21 April 1906; Boer War story from anonymous newspaper cutting in Edith's scrapbook.

10 Though very little documentary evidence of Edith's earlier life has been found, there are tantalising snippets of information on her movements. For example, her father wrote to his grandson Gerard on 19 September 1882: 'Aunt Edith is in Italy with some friends, but we expect her home again in a few days.'

11 A biography of John Towlerton Leather, *Contractor Leather*, by Dr David Leather, was published by the Leather Family History Society in 2005. I am grateful to Dr Leather for allowing me to consult the work in draft.

12 JTL built the Dale Dyke Dam whose failure in March 1864 caused the great Flood of Sheffield, the worst Victorian disaster: 250 dead and over 4000 homes flooded. Although he assumed the failure of the dam was due to a landslide, and the subsequent enquiry exonerated him from responsibility, JTL was deeply affected by the event, giving considerable sums of money to the victims' fund and paying pensions out of his own pocket to the dependants of those who died. More than a century later, further investigations established that the way the dam had been built, with vertical steps cut in the clay, had in fact caused the collapse: *Contractor Leather*, 'The Great Sheffield Flood', pp. 89–108.

13 *Contractor Leather*, p. 61.

14 This letter, from a collection made available by Mr George Franks, was enclosed in a tiny black-edged envelope.

15 Extract from the minutes of the Berwickshire Naturalists Club 1885–6, courtesy of the Leather Family History Society.

16 JTL to Edith Leather, 29 August 1883.

17 JTL's will is discussed in an interesting article in the journal of the Leather Family History Society, *Leather Lines*, August 2002.

18 Morton to Thompson, 30 November 1967, Thompson papers 1/3, LHCMA.

19 R.F. Wigram (1890–1936), Counsellor in the FO at the time of his death; F.T.A. Ashton-Gwatkin (1889–1976), FO 1921–47, seconded to MEW 1939; S.G. (later Sir Stewart) Menzies (1890–1968), Chief of the Secret Intelligence Service 1939–51.

20 The Hon Edward Lyttelton, 1855–1942, son of the 4th Baron Lyttelton, took over from the Reverend Edward Warre at the end of the summer half, 1905. Lyttelton moved to Eton from being Headmaster at Haileybury, and had already written extensively on educational matters, including a notable treatise on *The Causes and Prevention of Immorality in Schools* (1887).

21 In a letter to R.W. Thompson of 4 August 1963, Morton wrote that the date brought 'memories of helping the Adjutant of the Sheffield "garrison" . . . affix to every possible place in Sheffield the Proclamation of General Mobilisation.' (Thompson papers 1/2, LHCMA)

22 Morton to Thompson, 25 September 1961, printed in part in R.W. Thompson, *Churchill and Morton* (London: Hodder & Stoughton, 1976), pp. 185–88.

23 Hew Strachan, *The First World War*, Volume I, *To Arms* (Oxford: Oxford University Press, 2001), Chapter 2, *Willingly to War*, pp. 136–38. Although he is here describing the attraction of war for writers and intellectuals, rather than for soldiers, in view of what is known of Morton's character and interests the following judgement may be apposite: 'for men whose inclinations and callings tended to render them solitary, not the least of war's attractions was its effect in integrating their individual aspirations with those of society as a whole.'

24 General Sir Martin Farndale, *History of the Royal Regiment of Artillery: Western Front 1914–18* (Royal Artillery Institution, 1986), p. 7. For an interesting account of the diversity of views on the probable length of the war and their basis see Strachan, *First World War*, pp. 1005–14, 'The Short-War Illusion'.

2 PROPHESYING WAR

1 General, later Field-Marshal Sir Douglas Haig, 1st Earl Haig (1861–1928) had served in the Sudan and the Boer War, and led I Corps, BEF and then the 1st Army before succeeding Sir John French as C-in-C in December 1915. Lt. Gen Sir Horace Smith-Dorrien (1858–1930) commanded II Corps at the beginning of WWI but did not get on with French and was sacked after the German gas attack at Ypres in 1915.

2 The Commander-in-Chief's difficulties in communicating with the French, and the events that led up to Le Cateau, were well described by Edward Spears in *Liaison 1914* (London: Eyre & Spottiswode, 1930), Chapter 4.

3 Major A.F. Becke, *The Royal Regiment of Artillery at Le Cateau, 26 August 1914* (London: HMSO, 1919), p. 19.

4 Strachan, *The First World War*, p. 223. In his official despatch of 7 September 1914 to the Secretary of State for War, French paid tribute to Smith-Dorrien, asserting that 'the saving of the left wing of the army under my command on the morning of the 26th August could never have been accomplished unless a commander of rare and unusual coolness, intrepidity and determination had been present to personally conduct the operations' (*The World War I Collection, British Battles of World War I* (London: TSO, 2001), p. 285).

5 Becke, *Le Cateau*, p. 73.

6 Becke, *Le Cateau*, p. 37.

7 3rd Division lost only 3 Other Ranks and 4 horses, in contrast to 5th Division who lost at least 14 officers, 124 Other Ranks and 230 horses: Becke, *Le Cateau*, p. 84.

8 Becke, *Le Cateau*, p. 71.

9 Despatch of 7 September 1914 (see note 4 above), p. 285.

10 Michael Howard, *The First World War* (OUP), 2002, p. 43.

11 Farndale, *History of the Royal Regiment of Artillery*, p. 335.

12 Cf. Strachan, *First World War*, pp. 199–201.

13 *Ibid*, p. 6.

14 Farndale, *History of the Royal Regiment of Artillery*, p. 349.

15 Diary of 2nd Lt A.E. Robinson, 29th battery, 42nd Brigade RFA, Royal Artillery Historical Trust collection MD/89, Firepower Museum, Woolwich Arsenal.

16 W.S. (later Sir Winston) Churchill (1874–1965), journalist, soldier, author, politician: served in a wide range of Ministerial posts including Home Secretary, 1st Lord of the Admiralty, Secretary of State for War and Secretary of State for the Colonies; Prime Minister 1940–45 and 1951–55.

17 When told of his new command, Churchill, anxious to get into the right spirit, asked his wife to send him a one-volume edition of the poetry of Robert Burns (Martin Gilbert, *Winston S. Churchill*, Volume III (London: Heinemann,1971, hereafter MGIII), p. 629.

18 MGIII, p. 661.

19 Maj. Gen Sir Edward Louis Spears (born Spiers), 1887–1974, liaison officer between British and French Commanders in Chief, 1914; head of British Military Mission, Paris, 1917–20; Conservative MP 1922–45; head of British Mission to General de Gaulle, June 1940, head of Mission to Syria and Lebanon, 1942–44; a founder of the Institute of Directors and chairman of its Council until 1965.

20 Max Egremont, *Under Two Flags* (Phoenix edn, 1997), p. 9.

21 Martin Gilbert, *In Search of Churchill* (Harpercollins edn, 1993), p. 97.

22 MGIII, pp. 738ff.

23 War Diary of the 42nd Brigade, RFA, WO 95/1401, TNA

24 Morton to Thompson, 26 September 1964, Thompson papers 1/3, LHCMA. Morton's recollection on this point accords with that of Stewart Menzies, who is said to have described the curriculum at Eton as 'a queer blend of God, Greek and guns': Anthony Cave Brown, *The Secret Servant: The Life of Sir Stewart Menzies, Churchill's Spymaster* (London: Michael Joseph, 1988), p. 32.

25 Morton to Thompson, 11 October 1959, Thompson papers 1/1, LHCMA.

26 Michael Moynihan, *God on our side, the British Padre in World War One* (London: Secker & Warburg,1983), quoted in Stephen H. Louden, *Chaplains in Conflict: the role of Army Chaplains since 1914* (London: Avon Books, 1996), p. 51.

27 T. Johnstone and J. Hagerty, *The Cross on the Sword: Catholic Chaplains in the Forces* (London: Geoffrey Chapman, 1996), p. 106.

28 Robert Graves, *Goodbye to All That* (Penguin revised edn, 1957), pp. 197–99.

29 War Diary of 2nd Lt Robinson, Royal Artillery Museum, p. 40.

30 Johnstone and Hagerty, *Cross on the Sword*, p. 106.

31 *Ibid.*, p. 109.

32 Quoted in Egremont, *Under Two Flags*, p. 40.

33 Cf. Howard, *First World War*, p. 66; the military historian Sir Basil Liddell Hart later wrote of the Chantilly Conference: 'The military cupboard was abundantly stocked with men and munitions, but its shelves were bare of constructive ideas' (B.H. Liddell Hart, *History of the First World War* (London: Papermac edn 1997, p. 298); French was succeeded as C-in-C of the BEF by Haig on 19 December 1915.

34 Howard, *First World War*, pp. 76–7.

35 Morton to Thompson, 14 July 1958, Thompson papers 1/1, LHCMA.

36 Liddell Hart, *History of the First World War*, p. 233.

37 *Ibid.*, p. 247.

38 The United States formally declared war on Germany on 6 April 1917. The publication on 1 March of a telegram (decoded by British Naval Intelligence) sent in January 1917 by the German Foreign Minister, Zimmerman, to the Mexican Government proposing an alliance against the USA and the Mexican (re)conquest of Texas, New Mexico and Arizona, was instrumental in influencing the American decision to enter the war: see Christopher Andrew, *Secret Service: the Making of the British Intelligence Community* (London: Sceptre edn, 1986), pp. 169–76.

39 42nd Brigade War Diary, WO 95/1401, PRO.

40 *Ibid.*

41 A relative of the Count was later implicated in the Zinoviev Letter affair (see Chapter IV). It is an intriguing notion, though unverifiable, that Morton formed his earliest links with the dissident White Russian community during his month's stay at the hospital.

42 Medical Report, MoD records.

43 From a collection of family papers made available by Mrs Angela Mynors, Morton's cousin.

44 Morton to Liddell Hart, 17 July 1961, LH 1/531, LHCMA.

45 Liddell Hart, *History of the First World War*, p. 327.

46 Howard, *First World War*, p. 108.

47 *Ibid.*, pp. 109–10. A detailed analysis by Robert Blake of what he called Lloyd George's 'alarming' pursuit of unity of command, and of Haig's reactions, is given in his Introduction to *The Private Papers of Douglas Haig 1914–1919*, ed. Robert Blake (London: Eyre & Spottiswode, 1952).

48 Haig's diary and personal papers betray little self-doubt at this period. In a letter to Sir William Robertson on 9 December 1917, he responded robustly to the CIGS's account of Cabinet criticism of Haig's handling of the campaign: if the Prime Minister

had lost confidence, he should replace him at once; if not, 'then all carping criticism should cease, and I should be both supported and trusted . . . We must be prepared in war-time for ups and downs and should do our best to go on an even keel' (*The Private Papers of Douglas Haig*, p. 271). The most recent edition of Haig's papers adds detail to the earlier publication but supports its general thrust: Gary Sheffield and John Bourne (eds), *Douglas Haig: War Diaries 1914–18* (London: Weidenfeld & Nicolson, 2005), pp. 345–69.

49 Morton to Liddell Hart, 17 July 1961, LH 1/531, LHCMA. Denis Winter, in an uncompromisingly critical assessment of Haig, describes the latter's hatred and distrust of politicians, quoting a letter written by Haig to his wife on 12 March 1918: 'There are depths of insincerity and almost dishonesty in politics to which no soldier could stoop.' Denis Winter, *Haig's Command: a Reassessment* (London: Penguin edn, 1991), p. 25.

50 Neither the 1952 nor the 2005 editions of Haig's diaries and private papers mention his ADCs, including Morton, by name.

51 Liddell Hart to Morton, 24 July 1961, LH 1/531, LHCMA.

52 Morton to Liddell Hart, 17 July 1961, LH 1/531, LHCMA.

53 Morton to Thompson, 19 September 1962, Thompson papers 1/2, LHCMA.

54 During WW1 Sir John (later Viscount) Simon (1873–1954) served as Attorney General (1914–15) and Home Secretary (1915–16); later Ministerial roles included Foreign Secretary (1931–35) and Chancellor of the Exchequer (1937–40). He wrote to Morton on 13 October 1917, thanking him for the trouble he had taken to prepare for his visit to Intelligence HQ, and regretting that alternative plans by General Charteris (Director of Military Intelligence) had made him 'lose my cicerone' (letter from private collection made available by George Franks).

55 Morton to Thompson, 25 September 1961, quoted in Thompson, *Churchill and Morton*, p. 184.

56 Egremont, *Under Two Flags*, pp. 54–5.

57 The best and most vivid account, though nearly twenty years old, of the swift and somewhat chaotic development of the Intelligence Corps on the Western Front since 1914, remains that of Professor Christopher Andrew in *Secret Service*, Chapter 4, 'Secret Intelligence on the Western Front'. One of Andrew's sources for this period, *The History of Military Intelligence during the Great War 1914–1919*, compiled in 1920 by the then Director of Military Intelligence, Maj-Gen Sir William Thwaites (WO 32/10776, TNA), is especially useful.

58 Morton to Liddell Hart, 17 July 1961, quoted in Andrew, *Secret Service*, p. 250. Even Haig, despite his support for Charteris, acknowledged his faults and admitted that 'it was a mistake for him to specialise entirely in Intelligence work': diary entry for 9 December 1917, *War Diaries*, p. 359.

59 Commander, later Sir Mansfield Cumming, 1859–1923. Born Mansfield George Smith, he took the name Cumming after his second marriage in 1889. Retired from the Royal Navy in 1885, and was in charge of boom defence at Southampton when the Director of Naval Intelligence approached him in August 1909 with a proposal for a 'new billet' in the Secret Service Bureau. He was knighted in 1919. Details of his life and career are elusive, but the fullest account is that by Alan Judd, *The Quest for C: Mansfield Cumming and the Founding of the Secret Service* (London: HarperCollins, 1999). *V. ibid.*, Chapter 14, for an account of wartime networks, such as the *Dame Blanche*, run by Cumming.

60 The Secret Service Bureau was formed in October 1909 on the recommendation of the Haldane Committee, set up by the Committee of Imperial Defence to examine the related problems of acquiring intelligence about Germany and counter-intelligence directed against German espionage. The Bureau comprised originally two branches, one dealing with counter-espionage (MI5, under Colonel, later Sir Vernon Kell), and

one with foreign intelligence (SIS, under Cumming). The two men soon agreed to work independently. For an account of the work of the Haldane Committee and the origins of the Secret Service Bureau see Judd, *The Quest for C*, Chapter 3–5, also the official history of MI5 by J.C. Curry, *The Security Service 1908–45* (London: Public Record Office, 1999), Chapter II, Part I.

61 Cave Brown, *Secret Servant*, p. 91. Chapters 11 and 12 give an account of Menzies' experiences in the Ypres Salient, where he and his brother were said to have been the only two officers to survive from their Regiment.

62 Sir A.H.M. Sinclair (later Viscount Thurso), 1890–1970: after serving under Churchill in the Royal Scots Fusiliers, served as Squadron-Commander in the Life Guards 1916–17 and Major in the Guards Machine Gun Regiment, 1918. later served as Churchill's Private Secretary at the War Office and Colonial Office; Liberal MP 1922–45, Secretary of State for Air 1940–45.

63 Winston Churchill, *The Second World War*, Vol. I, *The Gathering Storm* (London: Cassell, 1948), p. 63.

64 See Trevor Wilson and Robin Prior, 'Conflict, Technology and the Impact of Industrialisation: the Great War, 1914–18' in *The Journal of Strategic Studies*, vol. 24, No. 3 (September 2001), pp. 128–57.

65 See MGIII, pp. 679–80. Morton recalled his first experience of the tank in a letter to Liddell Hart on 30 July 1961: 'I remember being mightily surprised at the size of old Granny, expecting something smaller.' Haig, he noted, had concluded that the tank was impractical and lost interest in it just as its potential was beginning to emerge (LH 1/531, LHCMA).

66 Memorandum for Lloyd George, 10 September 1918: see Martin Gilbert, *Winston S. Churchill*, Volume IV (London: Heinemann, 1975, hereafter MGIV), pp. 144–45.

67 Lt. Col., later General Sir Hugh Elles (1880–1946): Commandant of Tank Corps Training Centre 1919–23, Director of Military Training at the War Office, 1930–33; Master-General of Ordnance 1934–37; Regional Commissioner for South-West England, 1939–45.

68 Letter of 12 May 1918 from a private collection made available by George Franks.

69 Letter of 22 July 1918, *ibid.*

70 Morton to Liddell Hart, 17 July 1961, LH 1/531, LHCMA.

71 Hardinge was not enjoying himself. He wrote to Sir Ronald Wingate on 24 January 1919: 'You can imagine the constant annoyances that occur and the friction that arises when so many bigwigs congregate under one roof and expect to have the very best of everything and nothing to pay . . . Sometimes I feel almost a Bolshevik' (Hardinge papers, Cambridge University Library, vols. 40–41).

72 Sir M.P.A. (later Baron) Hankey (1877–1963): Secretary to the Cabinet War Committee 1915–16, to the War Cabinet 1916–18 and to the Cabinet 1919–38; Secretary to the Committee of Imperial Defence 1912–38; Minister without Portfolio 1939–40, Chancellor of the Duchy of Lancaster 1940–41, Paymaster General 1941–42.

73 Letter from FO to DMO&I, MoD records.

3 MAJOR MORTON OF SIS: 1919–22

1 M.R.D. Foot, *SOE: The Special Operations Executive 1940–46* (London: Pimlico edn, 1999), p. 8.

2 Interview with the Lady Soames, DBE, 7 April 2000. Lady Soames explained that she and her friends did not wish Morton any ill, but were inspired more by a macabre fascination with his medical condition.

3 Judd, *The Quest for C*, pp. 321–22.

4 Judd, *The Quest for C*, p. 72.

5 The details of the background and early history of Kell's organisation are set out in Kirke's 'History of Military Intelligence Directorate during the Great War 1914–1919', WO 32/10776, TNA. See also Curry, *Security Service*. In April 1910, six months after the creation of the Secret Service Bureau, Cumming and Kell agreed that their respective sections were 'totally different' and that it would be 'better for both that we should work separately': Judd, *The Quest for C*, p. 168. Kell (1873–1942), like Cumming, was knighted in 1919.

6 See Judd, *The Quest for C*, p. 73, and Chapters 3–5 *passim*; see also Andrew, *Secret Service*, Chapter II. A brief but useful explanation of official attitudes towards Intelligence in the early years of the 20th century can also be found in the opening pages of Volume I of F.H. Hinsley *et al.*, *British Intelligence in the Second World War* Volumes I–V (HMSO, 1979–90).

7 Cf. Judd, *The Quest for C*, pp. 262–64.

8 Quoted in full *ibid.*, pp. 154–59.

9 *Ibid.*, p. 136.

10 *Ibid.*, p. 331.

11 See in particular *The Intimate Papers of Colonel House* (1926) and Sir A. Willert, *The Road to Safety* (London: Verschoyle, 1952); also W.B. Fowler, *British-American Relations 1917–19: the role of Sir William Wiseman* (Princeton University Press, 1969).

12 See below, pp. 193–94 and 253–56.

13 Judd, *The Quest for C*, pp. 313 and 349.

14 Sir S.J.G. Hoare (later Viscount Templewood), 1880–1959: after working for SIS during the First World War, served as Secretary of State for Air (1922–24, 1924–29 and 1940), Secretary of State for India, 1931–35, Foreign Secretary 1935, 1st Lord of the Admiralty 1936–37, Home Secretary 1937–39, Lord Privy Seal 1939–40 and HM Ambassador to Spain, 1940–44.

15 Templewood Papers, part II, Box 2, file 4a, Cambridge University Library.

16 Cf. W.N. Medlicott, *The Economic Blockade* (revised edn, HMSO, 1978), Introduction to Volume I.

17 Judd, *The Quest for C*, pp. 426–27.

18 Report of Secret Service Committee, February 1919, CAB 127/356, TNA.

19 See MGIV, pp. 181–93; Paul Addison, *Churchill on the Home Front 1900–1955* (London: Jonathan Cape, 1992), pp. 201–10.

20 Memoranda GT 6665 and 6690 by the First Lord of the Admiralty and Home Secretary respectively, 16 and 23 January 1919, CAB 127/356, TNA.

21 Report of Secret Service Committee, 1919, CAB 127/356, TNA.

22 For an account based upon Security Service records of the Committee's deliberations and the Directorate of Intelligence see Victor Madeira, 'No wishful thinking allowed: Secret Service Committee and intelligence reform in Great Britain, 1919–22', *Intelligence and National Security*, vol. 18, No. 1, Spring 2003, pp. 1–20.

23 In this context 'overseas' excludes Imperial Intelligence, which came within the purview of MI5, not SIS.

24 Judd, *The Quest for C*, Chapter 19.

25 In his diary for 25 August 1919, Hankey noted that Churchill 'obviously does not care to be a War Minister without a war in prospect and finds the task of curtailing expenditure distasteful'. Hankey added that he had urged the Prime Minister to abolish the Air Ministry and the Ministries of Munitions, Shipping and Food as soon as possible: 'otherwise bankruptcy stares us in the face' (HNKY 1/5, Churchill College Archive Centre, Cambridge, hereafter CCAC).

26 Judd, *The Quest for C*, pp. 318 and 354.

27 Minutes of Secret Service Committee, KV 4/151, TNA; see also Madeira, 'No wishful thinking' (note 22).

28 See Judd, *The Quest for C*, pp. 389–93.

29 Report on Naval Intelligence, 1919, by Captain Somerville RN, cited in Judd, *The Quest for C*, pp. 382 and 388.

30 Judd, *The Quest for C*, p. 392.

31 Churchill, *The Gathering Storm*, p. 63.

32 Extract from the diary of the wife of R.W. Thompson, dated 1 May 1960, recording a (rare) visit by the Thompsons that day to Morton's house at Kew Green: Thompson papers 1/7, LHCMA.

33 Cumming's diary makes no mention of Morton until September 1920, over a year after he joined, but the sparseness of the diary entries at this point (cf. Judd, p. 443) suggests this is of little significance.

34 Judd, *The Quest for C*, pp. 283–92, including an account of how Cumming lost his leg in the car accident in which his son died in October 1914. See also the colourful description of Cumming's sanctum by one of his agents, Sir Paul Dukes, in *Red Dusk and the Morrow* (London: 1923), quoted alongside a contemporary picture of Whitehall Court in Andrew Cook, *On His Majesty's Secret Service: Sidney Reilly Codename ST1* (London: Tempus, 2002), pp. 129–31.

35 Judd, *The Quest for C*, pp. 453–54.

36 Col. C.R. Maude, based in Berlin in 1919 and later working for SIS there, wrote a memorandum on 31 December 1919 on Russo-German relations, transmitted to London for the DMI. He noted of the Intelligence Department of the German War Office: 'Their business apart from collecting information appears to be to foment disorder. They are in communication with the Bolsheviks by air, and via Stockholm and Finland' (*Documents on British Foreign Policy 1919–1939* (hereafter *DBFP*), First Series, Vol. III (London: HMSO, 1949), No. 294 (170992/4232/18).

37 The most active of these organisations, in which Morton took a close interest, was run by Freiherr Hanshuber von Durant, but was financed by private funds from Germany and sponsored by a number of prominent German figures including General von Ludendorff. Its supporters, interestingly, included prominent Communist revolutionaries such as Karl Radek.

38 See Chapter IV below.

39 Details of Tinsley's wartime exploits are given by Judd, *The Quest for C*. Tinsley's deputy in Rotterdam, however, Captain Henry Landau of *Dame Blanche* fame, fared less well in opening the Berlin office in October 1919 and later left the Service, coming in for severe criticism for publishing his wartime experiences in *All's Fair*, 1934.

40 See, for example, Henry Landau's account of his briefing by Cumming, quoted in Judd, *The Quest for C*, pp. 360–61. There are other similar examples, including that of Sidney Reilly.

41 Speech by Lloyd George, 16 April 1919, quoted in Introductory note to Chapter II of *DBFP*, First Series, Vol. III, p. 308.

42 Despatch 5556 to Paris, 21 August 1919, printed *ibid.*, No. 399 (118716/91/38).

43 Memo on Allied Policy in Russia, 28 July 1919, printed *ibid.*, No. 342 (108847/ 91/38). Harvey (First Lord Harvey of Tasburgh, 1893–1968) later served as Private Secretary to Anthony Eden as Foreign Secretary, 1936–38 and 1941–45; and as HM Ambassador in Paris, 1939–41 and 1948–54.

44 Cf. Roy Jenkins, *Churchill* (London: Macmillan, 2001), p. 350, describing Churchill's failure to understand the extent of British war-weariness at this time: 'His pulsating energy made him rarely weary, and almost never of war.'

45 Five months later, back in London, Hoare was arguing in favour of negotiations with the Bolsheviks, since 'once the Bolsheviks have won the civil war, Bolshevism will die of inanition'; *DBFP, First Series*, Vol. III, No. 619.

46 A wide range of these reports, from diplomatic, military and commercial sources, are printed in *DBFP*, First Series, especially Vols. III, XI and XII.

47 See Christopher Andrew and Vasili Mitrokhin, *The Mitrokhin Archive; the KGB in Europe and the West* (London, 1999), pp. 36–40.

48 This controversial episode, centred on the activities of British agent Robert Bruce Lockhart and which has been dealt with at length in many accounts, falls outside the scope of this book. For details, including SIS involvement, see, for example, Gordon Brook Shepherd, *Iron Maze* (London, 1998), Chapters 5 and 6, and Cook (who calls it the 'Reilly plot'), *Sidney Reilly*, Chapter 9. Bruce Lockhart's own account was given in *Memoirs of a British Agent* (London: 1932).

49 Judd, *The Quest for C*, p. 434.

50 A brief account of these 'Russian adventures' is given by Judd, *The Quest for C*, Chapter 18. For greater detail see Brook-Shepherd, *Iron Maze*, which also gives extensive reference to many autobiographical and biographical accounts.

51 Judd, *The Quest for C*, p. 434.

52 Minute from Morton to Menzies, asking him to put forward Reilly, currently a temporary Lieutenant in the RAF, for an honorary commission as an Army Major. This minute (which received a negative response) has been quoted in several accounts of Reilly's life and activities, including Brook-Shepherd, *Iron Maze*, and Andrew Cook, *Sidney Reilly*. The recent biographies of Reilly by Cook (see note 34 above) and by Richard B. Spence (*Trust No One; the Secret World of Sidney Reilly* (Los Angeles: Feral House, 2003)) are based on extensive archival research and give, from contrasting perspectives, as full an account of his career as can be constructed from the evidence available to their authors. See also Robin Bruce Lockhart *Reilly: Ace of Spies* (London: Hodder & Stoughton, 1967), an account influenced strongly by Reilly himself.

53 Memorandum of 5 December 1919 by Sidney Reilly, Templewood papers, Cambridge University library.

54 See Cook, *Sidney Reilly*, pp. 156–64, and Brook-Shepherd, *Iron Maze*, Chapter 9.

55 Boris Savinkov (1877–1925): Russian nihilist condemned to death for the assassination of Archduke Serge, 1905, escaped to Switzerland, returned to serve in Provisional Government, 1917, then joined White Russian forces and represented them in Paris. Engaged continuously in anti-Bolshevik activities, he was condemned to death when he returned to the Soviet Union in 1924 and died in prison there.

56 Cf. Gill Bennett, *A most extraordinary and mysterious business: the Zinoviev Letter of 1924* (London: FCO, 1999), pp. 54–5.

57 Spence, *Trust No one*, p. 284 quotes part of this letter.

58 Cf. Spence, *Trust No One*, p. 283: 'By the forepart of 1920, so far as SIS was concerned Reilly had given excellent value as a British agent.' The memorandum of 5 December 1919, cited in note 53 above, provides solid evidence of Reilly's activities.

59 Judd, *The Quest for C*, pp. 457–58.

60 Although Bruce Lockhart (*Ace of Spies*) refers to him as A. Maclaren (as does Andrew, *Secret Service*, p. 412), calling him Commander Andrew Maclaren), it is clearly the same man. Presumably Maclaren used this name on occasion.

61 Vladimir, or Grigorievitch Orlov, also known as K.W. Orbanski, 1882–1940: sometime Greek missionary in the US, General Criminal Investigator for the Tsarist regime and then head of the Bolshevik Criminal Investigation Department; escaped from Russia 1918, worked for both Wrangel and Denikin; met Reilly through Savinkov. From 1921, in Berlin ran an intelligence and forgery bureau and was reputed to be in the pay of the British, Germans, Poles and Russians (Red and White). See further Chapter 6 below.

62 Judd, *The Quest for C*, pp. 445 and 447, quotes Cumming's diary entry for 19 August 1920, recording his agreement to pay £500 to Orlov and £80 a month to Dukes. The exact sums paid to Reilly and Maclaren are not recorded.

63 This episode has been described in various accounts of Reilly's doings; see, for example, Cook, *Sidney Reilly*, pp. 176–77.

64 Reilly did indeed go on to cause trouble in Poland, including upsetting the Foreign Office by using the Embassy cypher to send telegrams under his own name, and becoming embroiled in Savinkov's plans for a foray over the Russian border: see Cook, *Sidney Reilly*, pp. 177–78.

65 It is not clear how close a relationship Morton had with Paul Dukes during this period, as no documentation has survived. There are indications, however, that they were in contact.

66 See Chapter IV below.

67 Cf. Cook, *Sidney Reilly*, pp. 178.

68 *Ibid.*, pp. 180–81.

69 Diary entry for 1 April 1921, SPRS 2/4, CCAC.

70 Diary entry for 2 August 1922, SPRS 2/5, CCAC. Interestingly, on 6 July 1922 Spears noted that he lunched with 'the Orloffs'.

71 Sir N.F.W. Fisher (1879–1948), Permanent Secretary to the Treasury and head of the Civil Service, 1919–39; Defence Commissioner, north-western region, 1939–40, Special Commissioner organising services and clearance in London, 1940–42.

72 Sir Eyre Crowe (1864–1925) joined the FO in 1885 and served with the British Delegation at many international conferences and conventions, 1887–1911; Assistant Under Secretary 1912, and PUS from 1920 until his death.

73 Note by Niemeyer and minute by from Fisher to Chamberlain, 13 March 1921, CAB 127/357; minutes of meetings of Secret Service Committee on 27 and 31 May, 2, 23 and 30 June 1921, CAB 127/355; report of Committee, 27 July 1921, CAB 127/357, TNA.

74 See Judd, *The Quest for C*, p. 459.

75 This entry is quoted in part in Judd, *The Quest for C*, p. 459.

76 Judd, *the Quest for C*, p. 461. My interpretation of the abbreviations in Cumming's diary differs from that of Alan Judd on this point.

77 During the early 1920s, however, it appears that Archibald Sinclair, rather than Morton acted as Churchill's conduit on Intelligence matters: see David Stafford, *Churchill and Secret Service* (London: John Murray, 1997), pp. 116.

4 THE OCCULT OCTOPUS, 1923–26

1 Andrew, *Secret Service*, pp. 420–21. See also Judd, *The Quest for C*, Chapter 20.

2 The extensive renovation of Chartwell brought the cost up to at least £20,000, and the property was always to prove a drain on the Churchill family finances. Nevertheless, Chartwell is, as Roy Jenkins put it, 'one of the two most evocative political shrines in the Western world' (Jenkins, *Churchill*, pp. 357–59). (The other 'shrine' was, appropriately, Roosevelt's Hyde Park in the Hudson Valley.)

3 Lady Soames has no recollection of such visits by her father and thinks this 'legend' improbable.

4 Lt.-Col. B.M.F. Franks, DSO, MC (1910–1982). Joined No. 8 Commando in 1940, fought in Crete, later Chief of Staff of Special Air Service Brigade HQ, Middle East.

5 Franks to Thompson, 11 August 1976, Thompson papers 1/7, LHCMA.

6 Sir George Makgill, Bt., 1868–1926. Succeeded to the title as 11th Baronet in 1906.

7 *DBFP*, First Series, Vol. XXV, No. 46, Mr Hodgson's telegram No. 67 of 13 April 1923 (N 3334/3198/38).

8 *V. ibid.*, No. 53, for the memorandum communicated to the Soviet Government; the Cabinet Conclusions of 2 May 1923 are quoted extensively in note 1. The Cabinet admitted that the 'secret source' was 'actually known to the Russian Soviet Government'.

9 See Chapter 3, pp. 57–8.

10 These reports were published as Cmd. 1581, 1582 and 1589 of 14 December 1921, 28 January 1922 and 21 February 1922 respectively.

11 Treasury memorandum on Secret Service 1922/23, January 1922, CAB 127/358, TNA.

12 Note on the Secret Service by the Secretary of State for War, January 1922, CAB 127/360, TNA.

13 This figure included £25,000 to allow for the absorption in SIS in 1922–23 of work done by the Intelligence Branch of the General Staff in Constantinople, Egypt and the Rhine.

14 CAB 127/356, TNA. The desirability of obtaining 'economic, financial and industrial' intelligence is worth noting, in the light of Morton's work in SIS later in the 1920s.

15 Judd, *The Quest for C*, pp. 469–70.

16 A note by the Secretary at the foot of the Conclusions stated that Churchill wished to record his dissent: in his view, the Secret Service Committee was to report to the Conference on the allocation of the £200,000, while 'the final decision as to the aggregate amount to be inserted in the 1922–23 estimates for Secret Service was reserved until the Conference could see what essential services would have to be abandoned' (CAB 127/356, TNA). The Committee's work proceeded, however, on the basis that £200,000 was agreed.

17 The draft minutes of the Committee on Secret Service, 1922 and its report of 4 April are in CAB 127/356, TNA.

18 Report of the Committee on Secret Service, *ibid*.

19 Second meeting of the Committee on Secret Service, 24 March 1922, CAB 127/356, TNA.

20 Major, later Colonel Valentine Vivian, CMG, CBE (1886–1969), formerly Assistant Director of Central Intelligence in the Indian Police. Head of counter-espionage in SIS for many years, he rose to be VCSS.

21 On the transition from the wartime Military Control to the peacetime Passport Control system and its role in British Intelligence see Andrew, *Secret Service*, pp. 346–50.

22 See Chapter 3.

23 See Andrew, *Secret Service*, pp. 421–22 for a colourful description of 'Quex' and his habits, including that of driving round London in a large open Lancia.

24 Cf. Andrew, *Secret Service*, pp. 419–21. In 1919 GC&CS had been established within the Admiralty, though Curzon had argued that its natural home was the FO (see discussions in HW 3/34, TNA). Two years later he returned to the charge successfully when it was clear that virtually all the agency's work was against the diplomatic communications of other countries. GC&CS was transferred operationally to the FO in August 1921, though the formal financial transfer did not take place until 1 April 1922. As a result of this initiative by Curzon and of his own selection to succeed Cumming, Sinclair found himself, less than a year later, as 'C' and thus within the FO ambit, in a position to resume supervision of GC&CS.

25 Sinclair to Crowe, 3 November 1923, FO 1093/66, TNA.

26 Morton to Thompson, 9 December 1960, Thompson papers 1/1, LHCMA.

27 Morton to Thompson, 16 August 1958, Thompson papers 1/1, LHCMA.

28 See pp. 81–2 below.

29 See Chapter 6 below, pp. 128–32. Charles Henry Maxwell Knight (1898–1968): RNVR, 1914–18; sometime journalist and hotelier, employed by MI5 from 1931; later well-known as 'Uncle Max' for presenting nature programmes on the BBC. For an account of his life see Anthony Masters, *The Man who was M: The Life of Maxwell Knight* Oxford: Basil Blackwell, 1984), a book that should be treated with caution on Intelligence matters but gives some interesting details of Knight's extraordinary

career. See also the biography of William Joyce, one of Knight's contacts: Peter Martland, *Lord Haw Haw; The English voice of Nazi Germany* (The National Archives, 2003).

30 Classic examples are the Richard Hannay novels of John Buchan, in which Jews, 'Levantines', Bolsheviks and devotees of the esoteric were often bracketed together in infamy: see, for example, *Mr Standfast* (1919) and *The Three Hostages* (1924). See also Dorothy L. Sayers, *Murder Must Advertise* (1933), and Ngaio Marsh, *Spinsters in Jeopardy* (1954).

31 Edward Alexander Crowley (1875–1947), took the name of Aleister; sometimes called the 'Great Beast'. Renowned occult practitioner, traveller, drug addict, hypnotist, seducer, mountaineer and novelist. For an account of his confused and mysterious life see Martin Booth, *A Magick Life: A Biography of Aleister Crowley* (London: Hodder & Stoughton, 2000).

32 Booth, *A Magick Life*, pp. 327–29.

33 See the Vicomte Leon de Poncins, *Freemasonry and the Vatican* (London, 1968; pb edn), pp. 155–56. This somewhat intemperate tracts bears study, if only for the extensive quotations from Papal pronouncements and from pro-Freemasonry writers.

34 De Poncins, *Freemasonry and the Vatican*, p. 18.

35 For an indication of White Russian activities in the UK see Bennett, *Zinoviev Letter*, pp. 28–32.

36 Vigilance committees were formed by local shop stewards, sometimes in defiance of national union policy, in an attempt to force concessions from employers: they were particularly active in the North East of England.

37 The Nuntia Bureau, closely connected with (and also funded by) the German Ministry for Internal Affairs and the Prussian Government, was later to form the nucleus of the *Abwehrabteiling I*, the German Secret Intelligence Service: see Curry, *Security Service*, p. 81.

38 General Alexander Kutepov, described by Christopher Andrew as 'brave, upright, teetotal, politically naïve and an easy target for the OGPU' (Andrew & Mitrokhin, *Mitrokhin Archive* I, p. 53). Nevertheless, unlike Savinkov and Reilly, he refused to be lured back to Russia and had to be kidnapped, dying on the journey; see Christopher Andrew and Oleg Gordievsky, *KGB: the Inside Story of its Foreign Operations from Lenin to Gorbachev* (London: Sceptre edn, 1991), pp. 165–66.

39 Orlov's description, in his memoirs, of the life of a spy applied exactly to his own situation: 'The pay is good, as every chief knows that at the end of six months his spy will be working for the other side as well, and that he will only serve that party honourably which rewards him more generously'; *The Secret Dossier: My Memoirs of Russia's Political Underworld* (1932), quoted in Bennett, *Zinoviev Letter*, p. 30.

40 Major (later Sir) G. Joseph Ball (1885–1961), employed in MI5 from 1918 and head of B Branch, responsible for counter-espionage; moved to Conservative Central Office in 1926, and was Director of Research there 1930–39. Generally considered responsible for a variety of political 'dirty tricks'.

41 Cf. Curry, *Security Service*, pp. 92–3.

42 Childs became Assistant Commissioner, Special Branch on 5 December 1921, taking on the additional role of Assistant Commissioner, Criminal Investigation Department on 1 April 1922. In June 1925 he told Sir Russell Scott, Controller of Establishments in HM Treasury, that when he took over his duties in Scotland Yard from Sir Basil Thomson he received nothing but 'an empty safe, a desk full of empty drawers and a sheet of clean blotting paper' (note of 30 June 1925, CAB 127/366, TNA).

43 See Chapter 5 below.

44 See Chapter 6 below. See also Nigel West and Oleg Tsarev, *Crown Jewels: The British Secrets at the Heart of the KGB Archives* (London: HarperCollins, 1998),

p. 32, where the two detectives in question had already been identified prior to the release of the Security Service files to the TNA.

45 See Stafford, *Churchill and Secret Service*, p. 144, and Chapter 8 *passim*.

46 Bennett, *Zinoviev Letter*, p. 28.

47 James Ramsay MacDonald (1866–1937), leader of the Labour Party 1922–31 and first Labour Prime Minister (and Foreign Secretary) 1924, Prime Minister 1929–31 and as head of National Government 1931–35, Lord President of the Council 1935–37.

48 Quoted in David Marquand, *Ramsay MacDonald* (London: Jonathan Cape, 1977), p. 297.

49 *DBFP*, First Series, Vol. XXV, Nos. 207–8.

50 Bennett, *Zinoviev Letter*, pp. 6–8.

51 *Ibid.*, pp. 10–11.

52 *V. ibid.*, pp. 91–2 and *passim*.

53 *Ibid.*, pp. 47–55.

54 *Ibid.*, p. 35: a facsimile of the first page of the copy of the report from Riga is reproduced facing p. 34.

55 *V. ibid.*, p. 31, showing that Morton was in regular communication with Ball at MI5 regarding such documents.

56 *Ibid.*, p. 37.

57 Miss Milicent Bagot CBE (1907–2006), who conducted an investigation into the Zinoviev Letter on behalf of the Intelligence Agencies in 1967–70, agreed with this judgement, suggesting that the most likely explanation was that Morton had asked Finney 'loaded' questions: Bennett, *Zinoviev Letter*, p. 37.

58 On this point see Bennett, *Zinoviev Letter*, p. 31.

59 That does not preclude a proliferation of books based on such theories: see, for example, West and Tsarev, *Crown Jewels*, Chapter II.

60 Cabinet Conclusions (58)24, 4 November 1924, CAB 23/48, TNA.

61 Cabinet Conclusions (60)24, 19 November 1924, CAB 23/49: Bennett, *Zinoviev Letter*, pp. 80–1.

62 A more detailed exposition of the five reasons is given in Bennett, *Zinoviev Letter*, pp. 81–82.

63 See Bennett, *Zinoviev Letter*, Chapter I.

64 Lewis Chester, Stephen Fay and Hugo Young, *The Zinoviev Letter: A Political Intrigue* (London: Heinemann, 1967), pp. 44–7 and 56–60.

65 Cf. Bennett, *Zinoviev Letter*, pp. 79 and 89–90.

66 *Ibid.*, pp. 56–65 and Annex F.

67 *Ibid.*, pp. 40–47. See also Chester, Fay and Young, *Zinoviev Letter*.

68 Bennett, *Zinoviev Letter*, p. 92.

69 Reports received from Riga in August and September 1924 stated that Dzerzhinski had told the *Sovnarkom* he was worried about foreign secret service agents penetrating Soviet missions overseas, and that a special commission had been set up to investigate the leakage of secret documents. Morton had noted on the latter report that it was 'confirmation of genuineness' of the Riga material, '& also a warning as to how careful we must be at this time'.

70 Sir Wyndham Childs told MacDonald's committee of enquiry on 4 November that he was in no position to question the authenticity of the Letter as he 'had no means whatever to go upon as I knew nothing about the sources from which it was obtained and cared less': Bennett, *Zinoviev Letter*, p. 79.

71 See pp. 55–6 above.

72 Ernest Bramah, *Kai Lung's Golden Hours* (Penguin edn, 1938; first published 1922), p. 30.

5 'GOD SAVE THE KING AND HIS AGENTS PROVOCATEURS!':1926–28

1 Letter from Chamberlain to Sir W. Joynson-Hicks, 5 May 1925, printed in *DBFP*, First Series, Vol. XXV, No. 312.
2 For documentation in 1925 on Soviet penetration in India, Afghanistan and Persia, see *DBFP*, First Series, Vol. XXV, Nos. 300, 303, 327, 333 and 335.
3 Letter of 26 April 1924, FO 1093/67, TNA.
4 Note by Baldwin, 10 February 1925, CAB 127/365, TNA.
5 Sinclair to Crowe, 25 February 1925, FO 1093/67, TNA.
6 Minutes of Secret Service Committee 1925, FO 1093/68, TNA.
7 A copy of this document, sent to the Committee's Secretary, Nevile Bland, on 18 March 1925, is in CAB 127/364, as well as in FO 1093/67, TNA.
8 Note by Hankey, 27 March 1925, FO 1093/67, TNA.
9 Following the death of Crowe in April 1925, Sir William Tyrrell, the new PUS at the Foreign Office, was appointed to take his place on the Secret Service Committee, while Sir John Anderson, who had attended all the meetings in an advisory capacity, became a full member.
10 Note from Fisher to Baldwin, 19 June 1925, CAB 127/361; the Scott report is in CAB 127/366.
11 Report of Secret Service Committee 1925, FO 1093/69, TNA. The full text is printed as Annex E in Bennett, *Zinoviev Letter*.
12 *Ibid.*
13 Minutes of 10th meeting of Secret Service Committee, 15 June 1925, FO 1093/68, TNA.
14 Report of Secret Service Committee 1925, FO 1093/69, TNA.
15 Vivian later claimed in a memorandum dated 30 April 1929 that the move to Broadway had been necessitated by the realisation that the previous HQ was under surveillance from W.N. Ewer and 'his gang', who, however, succeeded in tracking down the new premises within a few months. This claim was, however, made in a document intended to underline the risks of leakage from Special Branch, and may have been exaggerated: cf. Chapter VI below.
16 See Andrew, *Secret Service*, pp. 449–50.
17 Section V was not, as stated by Curry (*Security Service*, pp. 55, 85 and 101–2), created after the 1931 reorganisation when certain 'Casual' SIS agents were transferred to the Security Service. Nor, at this stage, was its only function liaison with the Security Service.
18 Minutes of Second meeting of Secret Service Committee, 2 March 1925, FO 1093/68, TNA.
19 *Ibid.*
20 See Chapter 6 below.
21 Lack of any documentary reference to the creation of the role of 'CO' – a new one in SIS – encourages the suspicion that it was thought up by Morton himself. From the middle of 1926 onwards many SIS documents bear a distinctive printed stamp, 'C.O.' in red capitals. The designation bore no connotation of lieutenancy: Sinclair appointed no formal deputy or Vice Chief until shortly before the outbreak of the Second World War, though Menzies, head of Section IV, answered for him during absences. The designation was retained after Morton left SIS, evolving into 'COS', Chief of Staff, at the beginning of the Second World War.
22 Although referring to the period after 1931, the descriptions given by Curry of SIS's functional relations with the Security Service, and of their respective response to the pre-WWII Communist threat, are useful here: *Security Service*, pp. 52–58 and 82–99.
23 *DBFP*, Series Ia, Vol. II, No. 422.

24 Letter from Chamberlain to Sir R. Lindsay, 1 March 1927, *DBFP*, Series Ia, Vol. III, No. 32.

25 Cmd 2874 of 1927, *Documents illustrating the Hostile Activities of the Soviet Government and Third International against Great Britain.*

26 Andrew, *Secret Service*, pp. 470–71. The importance of the material (generally known as BRIDE and VENONA) derived by British and American cryptanalysts from the tiny proportion of messages that were read as a result of mistakes made by Soviet communicators under the stress of the Second World War is some indication of what was lost by these revelations.

27 Security Service files on the ARCOS raid are now in The National Archives: *Recovery of British official documents by raids on ARCOS Ltd, May 1927*, KV 3/15 and 3/16; other files relevant to ARCOS can be found in classes KV 2 and 3. The Security Service accounts of the raid portray the operation as on the whole more straightforward, and successful, than equivalent SIS records. The latter provide useful and indeed intriguing detail, though they must be treated with caution.

28 1,083 police officers had been dismissed by the Metropolitan Police following strike action in 1919. In a letter of 7 May 1929 to Sir R. Lindsay, then PUS at the Foreign Office, Sinclair noted that 'Soviet connections' had been established by a number of police strikers immediately after their dismissal in August 1919, forming a 'pernicious group' ripe for 'corruption' by the Communist agent and *Daily Herald* foreign editor W.N. Ewer.

29 For interesting detail on these suspicions see the Security Service file on Kirchenstein, KV 3/17, TNA.

30 See Security Service file KV 2/1020 on Percy Glading *et. al.*, TNA. I am grateful to David Burke for this reference.

31 KV 3/15, TNA.

32 See Chapter 6 below.

33 Designated thus in Security Service files KV 3/15 and 3/16, TNA, similarly informant 'Y'.

34 Unsigned note of 31 March 1927, KV 3/15, TNA.

35 Memorandum by Sinclair on the ARCOS case, sent to the FO on 28 June 1925, FO 1093/73, TNA.

36 See Andrew, *Secret Service*, pp. 469–70.

37 KV 3/315, TNA.

38 In a despatch of 21 April 1927, Mr Peters of the British Embassy in Moscow commented that he had 'spent almost six years in Moscow, and it would be true to say that almost every non-communist Russian I have met during that time and most foreigners have proclaimed the inevitability of a financial crash in the near future' (*DBFP*, Series Ia, Vol. III, No. 158).

39 Memo. by Gregory, 10 December 1926, printed in *DBFP*, Series Ia, Vol. II, No. 350.

40 Cf. *DBFP*, Series Ia, Vol. III, No. 212 for a memo. of 27 May 1927 by Mr. C.F.A. (later Sir Christopher) Warner of the Foreign Office on the STD's privileges.

41 Third meeting of Secret Service Committee, 24 June 1927, FO 1093/71, TNA.

42 Fourth meeting of Secret Service Committee, 30 June 1927, FO 1093/71, TNA.

43 Michael Smith, 'The Government Code and Cypher School and the First Cold War', in Michael Smith & Rakph Erskine (eds), *Action This Day: Bletchley Park from the breaking of the Enigma Code to the birth of the modern computer* (London: Bantam Press, 2001) pp. 15–40.

44 *DBFP*, Series Ia, Vol. III, No. 191.

45 Morton's account was substantiated in many factual respects by that of Inspector Clanchy, who took part in the raid. His description of entering a room in which a quantity of paper was being burned by Anton Miller, who when challenged replied in

broken English that he was 'burning decoded telegrams', rivals Morton's for deadpan understatement.

46 Moscow despatch No. 204, 19 May 1927: *DBFP*, Series Ia, Vol. III, No. 204.

47 *V. ibid.*, Nos. 208 and 215; Cabinet Conclusions 23(27), CAB 23/55, TNA.

48 The document in question, which had been translated from the Russian and only just brought to Sinclair's attention, contained the minutes of a meeting on 21 April 1927 of the 'Agitation Propaganda Commission of the London Cell of the V.K.P.' (i.e. the All-Union Communist Party). As Sinclair emphasised to Tyrrell, the minutes showed three members of the Soviet Legation (Maisky, Lidin and Gladun) 'making reports to, and *receiving instructions from* the Agitation Propaganda Commission'.

49 Memorandum by Sinclair on the ARCOS case, FO 1093/73, TNA.

50 First meeting of Secret Service Committee, 11 March 1927, FO 1093/71. A report from the Director of Public Prosecutions of 30 December 1926 on the 'leakage' that had caused the Prime Minister to convene the Committee can be found in FO 1093/73, TNA.

51 Tyrrell to Fisher, 14 March 1927, FO 1093/73, TNA.

52 Memorandum by Sinclair on the ARCOS case, FO 1093/73, TNA.

53 Statement by Anderson at Third meeting of the Secret Service Committee, 24 June 1927, FO 1093/71, TNA.

54 A highly coloured account of their association was given in Compton Mackenzie, *Greek Memories* (London: Cassell, 2nd edn, 1939). See also Mackenzie, *My Life and Times: Octave Five 1915–1923* (London: Chatto & Windus, 1966).

55 Letter from Mackenzie to Christopher Stone, 13 December 1933. I am grateful to Dr Peter Martland for making a copy of this letter available.

56 DPP 1/84, 'Wilfred Francis Remington Macartney and George Hansen', TNA.

57 Cf. Mackenzie, *My Life and Times*, and Andrew, *Secret Service*, pp. 469–70. In his sworn statement Morton was scathing about Macartney's claim, asserting that the work he had done as Military Control Officer entitled him to call himself a member of the Secret Service 'about as much as the work of a Solicitor's office boy would entitle the latter to call himself a lawyer'. It is true that he was never employed formally by SIS, and his work was a very minor 'secret' offshoot; this does not, however, diminish the value of his wartime service which was agreed to have been creditable.

58 Morton later noted that it was probable that there was 'a great deal behind that story which has never come out', but no further details of the incident have been found.

59 Information regarding Monkland's first contact with Hall and Browning was given in Morton's sworn statement, DPP 1/84, TNA.

60 Morton's sworn statement, DPP 1/84, TNA.

61 Transcript of shorthand notes of court proceedings, DPP 1/84, TNA.

62 Morton's sworn statement, p. 8, DPP 1/84, TNA.

63 *Ibid.*, pp. 8–9.

64 *Ibid.*

65 Morton's statement, pp. 13–14, DPP 1/84, TNA.

66 *Ibid.*, p. 15 and Document 3.

67 *Ibid.*, p. 15.

68 Morton's sworn statement, p. 23, DPP 1/84, TNA.

69 Hansen, who claimed to be a language student, was a former editor of the German Communist paper *Ruhrecho*, and though expelled from the KPD in 1925 had continued to work in Germany for the Communists, this time Soviet. He was suspected of close connections with ARCOS.

70 Morton's statement, p. 27, DPP 1/84, TNA.

71 See correspondence in CHAR 8/218–19, CCAC; also MGV, pp. 298 and 309.

72 Churchill, *Gathering Storm*, p. 34.

73 For details of the treaties signed following the Locarno Conference, 5–16 October

1925, amounting to a general political reconciliation in Western Europe and recognition of the rehabilitation of Germany, see *DBFP*, First Series, Vol. XVII.

74 Every year the FO prepared a memorandum on the foreign policy of HMG, with a list of British commitments in their relative order of importance. The version issued on 1 April 1927 provides a useful conspectus of official British policy at this point: see *DBFP*, Series Ia, Vol. III, Appendix.

75 *Ibid.*, No. 308.

6 LOOSE ENDS: 1929–31

1 See Chapter 4 above.

2 See pp. 91–2 above.

3 See Bennett, *Zinoviev Letter*, pp. 56–65. Part III of the Report of the enquiry dated 25 February 1928, relating to the Letter, is printed *ibid.*, Annex F.

4 There are several versions of what happened; *The Times* reports on 4 and 5 July 1929 conflict with that given to SIS by the *Polizeiprásdium*, reporting that it was Knickerbocker who reported Sumarakov to the police. There seems little doubt, however, that Sievert and Orlov incriminated each other.

5 See Chapter 7 below.

6 In March 1936, for example, Orlov was writing to Scotland Yard on notepaper styling himself *Conseiller d'Etat de la Russie Impériale*. Vivian commented that the correspondence showed that 'our old friend Vladimir Orlov is still at his old games'.

7 For Miss Bagot's investigation of 1967–70 see Bennett, *Zinoviev Letter*, Introduction.

8 According to Thomas Jones's *Whitehall Diary*, vol. I (London: Oxford University Press, 1969), at a Cabinet meeting on 31 October 1924 Lord Parmoor (Lord President of the Council), Sir Charles Trevelyan (President of the Board of Education) and Josiah Wedgewood (Chancellor of the Duchy of Lancaster) had been among those clamouring for a full public enquiry into the Zinoviev Letter Affair, opposing MacDonald's suggestion that it was important to distinguish between the conduct of civil servants and the authenticity of the Letter. According to Jones, J.H. Thomas, Secretary of State for the Colonies, had suggested that they were 'sitting on a volcano', but Parmoor and Trevelyan were 'quite prepared to blow up the FO if they could get rid of the spy system' (pp. 298–301).

9 A detailed account of the Ewer network and the case of Inspector Ginhoven and Sergeant Jane, based on Security Service files released at The National Archives, can be found in Victor Madeira, 'Moscow's interwar infiltration of British Intelligence, 1919–1929', *Historical Journal*, vol. 4, December 2003, pp. 915–33. I am grateful to Mr Madeira for allowing me to consult this article before publication. See also Curry, *Security Service* pp. 96–8.

10 Security Service records indicate that Ewer began working for Moscow as early as 1919: see Madeira, 'Moscow's interwar Infiltration'.

11 Madeira, 'Moscow's interwar infiltration'. Cf. also p. 96 above.

12 Dale had also been discharged from the Police force following the 1919 strike.

13 Described in the SIS memo. as 'the secretary and prime mover of the illegal National Union of Police and Prison Officials'.

14 Ginhoven and Jane were dismissed from the force by a Disciplinary Board on 2 May 1929.

15 Cf. on this point Curry, *Security Service* p. 97: 'This case is important because it illustrates both the potentialities and the limitations of the Security Service in peacetime. It shows how it could obtain great success in penetrating an espionage organisation and also how it was difficult to take action to bring such an organisation to an end.'

16 R.G. Vansittart, *The Mist Procession: The Autobiography of Lord Vansittart* (London: Hutchinson, 1958), p. 397.

17 Andrew, *Secret Service*, p. 481–84.

18 See p. 92 above.

19 See p. 72 above.

20 i.e. the Anglo-Soviet agreements signed on the resumption of diplomatic relations in October 1929; M. Dogvalevski, Soviet Ambassador in Paris, had conducted the negotiations in London on behalf of the Soviet Government. See *DBFP*, Second Series, Vol. VII, Nos. 10–39, *passim*.

21 Some account of Knight's attempt at the country life is given in Masters, *The Man who was M*, pp. 22–26. The details given by Masters of Knight's supposed employment by MI5 prior to 1931 are not corroborated by SIS documentation, which indicates that he was working for Morton until all the Casuals were transferred to MI5 in 1931. However, many details of Knight's activities and contacts remain unclear.

22 Nesta Webster, *née* Bevan, was a prominent right wing conspiracy theorist and writer active during the 1920s, and involved with the British fascist movement. Anti-semitic, she wrote a number of increasingly strident works including *Boche and Bolshevik*, 1923. It is likely that Morton got to know her through Sir George Makgill, and that he used her and her connections for professional purposes.

23 On Joyce's activities at this time, see Martland, *Lord Haw Haw*, pp. 14–15.

24 See p. 77 above.

25 Documentation regarding the 1931 meetings of the Secret Service Committee can be found in FO 1093/74, TNA.

26 *Ibid*. Details of the 1931 meetings of the Secret Service Committee are given in a summary note by Norton dated 24 June, rather than in separate minutes.

27 For details of Liddell's career see Nigel West (ed), *The Guy Liddell Diaries, Vol. I: 1939–42* and *Vol II: 1942–45* (London: Routledge, 2005).

28 See Curry, *Security Service*, pp. 101–07.

29 Curry, *Security Service*, pp. 103 and 107.

7 THE BEGINNINGS OF INDUSTRIAL INTELLIGENCE, 1927–31

1 A copy of Morton's 'Statement to the Prime Minister's Panel of Industrialists on January 31st 1939' was communicated to the Foreign Office by the Department of Overseas Trade (W 3221/617/50, FO 371/23994, TNA).

2 On the birth of the EAC see Keith Middlemas and John Barnes, *Baldwin* (London: Weidenfeld & Nicolson, 1969), pp. 313–16, and Stephen Roskill, *Hankey, Man of Secrets* (3 vols, London: Collins, 1970–74), vol. iii, pp. 391–92. Cf. also G.C. Peden, *The Treasury and British Public Policy* (Oxford: Oxford University Press, 2000), p. 196: 'The Treasury showed no enthusiasm for bringing economists into Whitehall on a permanent basis.'

3 Henderson was Foreign Secretary in the second Labour government, 1929–31. See memo by Sir V. Wellesley, FO Deputy Under Secretary, 1 December 1930, 'A proposal for the establishment of a politico-economic intelligence department in the Foreign Office', W 12855/12855/50, FO 371/14939, TNA. The department was not established until 1932. See also David Carlton, *MacDonald versus Henderson: the foreign policy of the second Labour Government* (London: Macmillan, 1970), pp. 24–25, quoting a letter from Henderson to MacDonald in March 1931: 'unless our foreign policy is so equipped as to take the fullest account of the movements in the economic sphere we cannot expect to derive all the advantage to which the country is entitled from the activities of its foreign service.'

4   See Medlicott, *Economic Blockade*, Introduction to Vol. I, pp. 1–12.

5   Morton to Medlicott, 3 May 1945, private collection. On the role of *Wehrwirtschaft* (literally 'defence economy') and the German Army's economic planning see Alan Milward, *The German Economy at War* (London: The Athlone Press, 1965), Chapter 1.

6   See Chapter 4 above.

7   Memo. dated 6 December 1929 and forwarded that day to HM Treasury by Nevile Bland (CAB 127/367, TNA).

8   *Ibid.*

9   See Chapter 5, p. 104.

10   See Geoffrey Hosking, *A History of the Soviet Union* (London: Final edn, Fontana, 1992), pp. 151–68: 'Collectivization renewed the psychosis of wartime, only now in conditions of peace, and accustomed party officials to regarding themselves as an occupying force in a hostile country.' See also the 1928 analysis by Soviet economists, summarised by P. Gent of the Foreign Office in a memo. of 21 May: 'Industrialisation gives independence from foreign countries and secures national defence!' (N 2773/31/38, FO 371/13312, TNA).

11   Hugh Dalton, *Call Back Yesterday: Memoirs, 1887–1931* (London: Muller, 1953), p. 231. E.H.J.N. (later Lord) Dalton, 1887–1962, lawyer, academic and Labour MP since 1924, served as FO Under-Secretary 1929–31, Minister of Economic Warfare 1940–42, President of the Board of Trade 1942–45, and in other Ministerial posts including Chancellor of the Exchequer (1945–47) until 1951.

12   Ovey (1879–1963) was a somewhat unexpected choice for the job, since he had not served in or around Russia before, although apparently speaking some Russian.

13   Moscow despatch No. 327 of 3 June 1930, *DBFP*, Series II, Vol. VII, No. 88.

14   The Earl of Birkenhead (formerly Sir F.E. Smith) was virulently opposed to the Bolshevik regime and had, as Secretary of State for India from November 1924 to October 1928, urged strongly that the British Government should use force against the perceived Soviet threat to Afghanistan: see Keith Neilson, 'Pursued by a Bear': British estimates of Soviet military strength and Anglo-Soviet relations 1922–1939', *Canadian Journal of History/Annales canadiennes d'histoire*, XXVIII, August 1993, pp. 189–221; cf. also the biography of Birkenhead by his son, the second Earl: '*F.E.*' (London: Eyre & Spottiswode, 1965), Chapter XXXI.

15   *DBFP*, Series II, Vol. VII, Nos. 41, 62, 88 and 104–31.

16   FO telegram No. 77 to Moscow, 26 February 1930, printed *ibid.*, No. 69.

17   William (later Lord) Strang (1893–1978), FO 1919, Counsellor 1932, AUS 1939, PUS 1949–53.

18   *DBFP*, Series II, Vol. VII, No. 95. Cf. also J. Haslam, *Soviet Foreign Policy 1930–33: the impact of the Depression* (London: Palgrave Macmillan, 1983), on the way in which the Five Year Plan raised the Soviet regime's prestige: 'Disbelief that an economy could be planned – and in Russia – was rapidly ebbing' (p. 6).

19   See Neilson, 'Pursued by a bear', citing for example a memorandum by the CIGS, Sir George Milne, in October 1928 on 'The Military Situation in Russia', printed in *DBFP*, Series IA, Vol. V, No. 194.

20   See the WO report of 22 October 1929 on explosive 'M/N' in the file 'Explosive M/N: papers with M Karel Bondy on tests; negotiations on rights to M/N (aka MARMALADE) involving MI 1 and the Foreign Office', AIR 2/19212, TNA.

21   Appendix B to War Office report of 22 October 1929, AIR 2/19212, TNA.

22   See pp. 120–21.

23   See documentation in AIR 2/19212, TNA.

24   Documentation concerning this mobilisation scheme and its assessment can be found in FO 1093/78, TNA.

25   FO 1093/78, TNA.

26 Cf. Andrew, *Secret Service*, p. 495.

27 Cf. Peden, *Treasury and British Public Policy*, pp. 233–37 and 275–76.

28 Documentation on the international negotiations on European and security issues during 1928–31 is printed in *DBFP*, Series IA, Vols V and VI, and Second Series, Vol. II, *passim*.

29 *DBFP*, Second Series, Vol. I, No. 305.

30 *Ibid.*, No. 321.

31 O.G. (late Sir Orme) 'Moley' Sargent (1884–1962), FO 1906, Counsellor 1926, AUS 1933, DUS 1939, PUS 1946–49.

32 *DBFP*, Second Series, Vol. I, Nos. 327 and 344.

33 For detailed information on French Intelligence at this period see the first three chapters of Peter Jackson, *France and the Nazi Menace: Intelligence and Policy-Making 1933–1939* (Oxford: Oxford University Press, 2000).

34 Morton to Liddell Hart, 20 March 1967, LH 1/531, LHCMA.

35 Terms of reference of the ATB Committee, CAB 47/1, TNA.

36 Memo. CID 906B by the Secretary of State for War, Sir L. Worthington-Evans, circulating a memo by the CIGS, 9 August 1928, 'The Need for an organization to study industrial intelligence (including industrial mobilization) in foreign countries', CAB 48/1, TNA. See also Wesley Wark, *The Ultimate Enemy: British Intelligence and Nazi Germany 1933–1939* (Ithaca, NY: Cornell University Press, 1985).

37 Memo. CID 909B by the Secretary of State for Air (Sir S. Hoare), circulating a note by the Chief of the Air Staff, 31 August 1928, CAB 48/1, TNA.

38 See Percy Cradock, *Know Your Enemy: How the Joint Intelligence Committee Saw the World* (London: John Murray, 2002). Though referring to the formation of the JIC in 1936, it is just as applicable to the inception of the sub-committee on Industrial Intelligence in Foreign Countries (FCI) of the CID.

39 CID 906B, CAB 48/1, TNA.

40 Colonel Eric Holt-Wilson of MI5 was co-opted onto the FCI Committee in 1932, but FO and Treasury representatives were not included in the membership until 1935: cf. Hinsley, *British Intelligence in the Second World War*, vol. 1, p. 33.

41 Minutes of the 238th meeting of the CID, 8 November 1928, CAB 2/5.

42 Minutes of a Conference on industrial intelligence in foreign countries, 13 December 1928, CAB 48/1, TNA.

43 CID 932B of 21 February 1929, CAB 48/1, TNA.

44 CID 242nd meeting, 2 May 1929, CAB 2/5, TNA.

45 Minutes of FCI 1st meeting, 20 March 1930, CAB 48/2, TNA.

46 Minutes of 15th ATB Committee, 27 February 1931, CAB 47/1, TNA.

47 Minutes of FCI 3rd meeting, 11 March 1931, CAB 48/2, TNA.

48 Sinclair to Crowe, 17 May 1932, CAB 127/371.

49 No firm date can be put upon Crowe's approach to Sinclair; in a letter of 3 May 1945 to W.N. Medlicott, Morton wrote that it was 'just before New Year 1930'. He described being sent by Sinclair to see Crowe, 'who broke into mysterious paeans of joy that I was going to "undertake the work"'. Crowe sent him in turn to see Hankey ('whom I already knew well'), who directed him to see the Prime Minister, Ramsay MacDonald: 'The outcome was that I was told to create an office for the study of industrial mobilisation in foreign countries.'

50 Minutes of 3rd FCI meeting, CAB 48/2.

51 FCI 19, Report of Sub-Committee on Industrial Intelligence in Foreign Countries, CAB 48/3, TNA.

52 ICF/9, 6 July 1931, CAB 48/3, TNA.

53 FCI 19, CAB 48/3, TNA.

54 Cf. Andrew, *Secret Service*, pp. 494–95; Vansittart, *The Mist Procession*, pp. 397–98.

55 See Chapter 6 above.

56 Morton to Churchill, 16 April 1931, printed in MGV, CV2, p. 316.
57 Morton to Churchill, 18 April 1931, printed *ibid.*, p. 317.

8 A 'GENTLEMANLY FORM OF SPYING': THE INDUSTRIAL INTELLIGENCE CENTRE, 1931–37

1 Sir John Colville's description of economic intelligence: see *The Churchillians* (London: Weidenfeld & Nicolson, 1981), p. 204. Sir John 'Jock' Colville (1915–87) served as a Private Secretary to Chamberlain and then to Churchill, 1939–41, and again to Churchill in 1943–45. His memoirs *Footprints in Time* (London: Collins, 1976), *The Churchillians* and his published diaries *The Fringes of Power: Downing Street Diaries 1939–1955* (London: Hodder & Stoughton, 1985) form an important source on Churchill's inner circle, including Morton.
2 Wark, *The Ultimate Enemy.* I am grateful to Professor Wark for the opportunity to discuss with him the work of the IIC.
3 Sinclair to Crowe (Department of Overseas Trade), 17 May 1932, CAB 127/371, TNA.
4 Crowe to Hankey, 18 May 1932 and minute by Hankey, 21 May 1932, CAB 127/371, TNA.
5 See Jackson, *France and the Nazi Menace*, Chapter I.
6 Cf. on this point Hinsley, Vol. 1, pp. 47–8, where he points out that there is no simple explanation for deficiency of the SIS espionage system and SIGINT in the approach to war.
7 The APOC, renamed the Anglo-Iranian Oil Company (AIOC) from 1935, became the British Petroleum Company Ltd in 1954. I am indebted to Mr Peter Housego, Manager, Global Archive Management, BP, for access to archival material relating to Morton and the IIC.
8 Correspondence in the file 'Industrial Information re Various Countries', Arc ref 129910, BP Archive.
9 Undated note attached to a letter from Vivian to Medlicott (APOC), 13 August 1931: Industrial Information re Various Countries, Arc Ref 129910, BP Archive.
10 Industrial Information re Various Countries, Arc Ref 129910, BP Archive.
11 Robert Young, 'Spokesmen for Economic Warfare: the Industrial Intelligence Centre in the 1930s', *European Studies Review*, 6, 1976, n. 40.
12 See pp. 147–48 above.
13 FCI 5th meeting, 17 November 1931, CAB 48/2, TNA.
14 Documentation on the Far Eastern crisis precipitated by the occupation by Japan of the Chinese state of Manchuria in September 1931 is printed in *DBFP*, Second Series, Vols. IX–XI.
15 In February 1933 he instructed that an agent of Clively's supplying information from within ARCOS should be paid off since detailed reports on the USSR were 'no longer necessary as a regular course'.
16 FCI 5th meeting, 17 November 1931, CAB 48/2, TNA.
17 FCI 6th meeting, 19 February 1932, CAB 48/2, TNA.
18 FCI 7th meeting, 27 April 1932, CAB 48/2, TNA. The Committee later agreed on a confidential pamphlet to be issued to the heads of selected firms whose activities might render them likely objects of foreign espionage: by early 1934 130 copies had been issued (CID 1139B of 22 February 1934, CAB 4/22, TNA).
19 See *DBFP*, Second Series, Vol. IV, Nos. 230–33. A memo. dated 15 February 1933 by the commercial counsellor to the British Embassy in Berlin noted that despite the severe economic difficulties faced by the new German Government, debt cancellation and investment had contributed to an industrial boom: 'While it is impossible to commend the financial methods by which German firms obtained the means to equip

themselves, it must be remembered that the Americans pressed money upon them . . . By the end of 1929 German industry was undoubtedly over-equipped beyond any possible demand that even the continuance of the most wonderful boom could have caused'; *ibid.*, No. 241.

20 List given in Appendix to minutes of 13th FCI meeting on 9 February 1934, a draft note and standing instructions relating to the IIC up to 1 January 1934: CAB 48/2, TNA.

21 Morton's absence is confirmed by the minutes of the 12th FCI meeting on 8 December, at which it was agreed to convene a special 'interdepartmental study group', to meet 'as soon as possible after Major Morton's return' (CAB 48/2, TNA).

22 Record of conference held on 1 December 1933, CAB 48/4, TNA.

23 FCI 12th meeting, 8 December 1933, CAB 48/2, TNA.

24 Hinsley, Vol. 1, p. 31.

25 See, for example, FCI 52, remarks by Whitham, 5 February 1934, CAB 48/4, TNA.

26 FCI 15th meeting, 28 November 1934, CAB 48/2, TNA.

27 FCI 16th meeting, 16 June 1935, CAB 48/2, TNA.

28 FCI 87 of 7 May 1936, CAB 48/4, TNA.

29 FCI 20th meeting, 11 May 1936, CAB 48/2, TNA.

30 Morton to Medlicott, 3 May 1945, private collection.

31 Young, 'Spokesmen for Economic Warfare', p. 438.

32 Dill's letter to Hankey was submitted to the Deputy Chiefs of Staff as DCOS 3 of 9 October 1935, CAB 54/3. Details of the ensuing discussions and negotiations, which were to lead to the formation of the Joint Intelligence Sub-Committee, can be followed in the records of the various committees, and are helpfully summarised in a confidential memorandum of 1974, drawn up for use by Sir H. Hinsley in preparing the official history of British intelligence during the Second World War (CAB 56/7, TNA).

33 DCOS 4, 1 January 1936, CAB 54/3, approved by the CID at its 273rd meeting on 30 January, CAB 2/6, TNA.

34 Hinsley, vol. 1, pp. 34–5.

35 A neat description taken from the 1974 account of JIC's prewar work, CAB 56/7, TNA.

36 *V. ibid.* The 1974 memo commented that the FO did 'not appear to have appreciated the advantages of bringing together in peacetime all the various agencies involved in intelligence so as to present a broader background than would otherwise be possible against which to judge a single-service view of the war plans of potential enemies'. Ashton-Gwatkin had, however, commented in February 1936 that while the enlargement of the FCI to include air targets did not immediately concern the FO, they were 'considerably interested' in the enlargement of the scope of the IIC into 'a general clearing house of intelligence' (W 1382/80/50, FO 371/20454, TNA).

37 FCI 20th meeting, 11 May 1936, CAB 48/2, TNA.

38 FCI 19th meeting, 26 March 1936, CAB 48/2, TNA.

39 The minutes of the Air Targets Sub-Committee are preserved in CAB 48/8, TNA.

40 Minute by Burge (Air Ministry), 13 May 1937, AIR 5/1154, TNA.

41 Morton to Burge (Air Ministry), 28 July 1937, AIR 5/1154, TNA.

42 See, for example, correspondence between Morton and Buss in October 1937 regarding FCI memo ICF/47 on estimated German fuel requirements (FO 837/425, TNA).

43 Cf. Cradock, *Know Your Enemy*, Chapter I.

44 FCI 22nd meeting, 5 July 1937, CAB 48/2, TNA.

45 FCI 108, 29 November 1937, CAB 48/5, TNA.

46 See, for example, Chapter 11 below for similar exercises in 1941 and 1945.

47 I am indebted to Professor Wesley Wark for this detail, supplied to him by a (now deceased) former member of the IIC.

48 Letter from the Ian Sayer Collection.
49 Wark, *Ultimate Enemy*, p. 160.
50 Writing to W.N. Medlicott in 1948, Morton stated that it had been recognised in the 1930s, in 'what was then called "modern war" . . . that the ultimate ability of a nation to wage war resided in factors which were civilian, industrial and economic. Obviously, therefore, the destruction of these elements at the disposal of the enemy and the protection of similar elements at the disposal of ourselves and our Allies, were matters of the utmost importance.' Although one of Morton's chief complaints was the failure of the relevant British authorities to recognise these 'obvious' truths, his formulation serves as what might now be called the 'mission statement' of the IIC.
51 Neville Chamberlain (1869–1940), younger brother of Sir Austen, had served in a variety of ministerial posts since 1922. Chancellor of the Exchequer between 1923–24 and from 1931–37, he was Prime Minister and leader of the Conservative Party from 1937 until May 1940.
52 In 1932–33 British exports to Germany were worth £25.4, while she imported £30.5m in German goods. See Neil Forbes, *Doing business with the Nazis: Britain's Economic and Financial Relations with Germany 1931–39* (London: Frank Cass, 2000), pp. 123–24 and 137–38. On the National Government's economic policy at this period see Peden, *Treasury and Public Policy*, pp. 247–49 and 275–80.
53 292 *H.C. Debs., 5th ser.*, col. 2339: see *DBFP*, Second Series, Vol. VI, No. 547.
54 CAB(31)34 of 31 July 1934, CAB 23/79, TNA. A useful account of the DRC's work at this time is given in Roskill, *Hankey*, vol. iii, Chapter 2, *The Fight for Rearmament January 1933–August 1934*.
55 COS 133rd meeting, 9 October 1934, CAB 53/5, TNA.
56 295 *H.C. Debs, 5th ser.*, col. 883: see *DBFP*, Second Series, Vol. II, No. 387.
57 Phrase taken from notes made by Churchill for a broadcast, 16 January 1934: CHAR 9/109, printed in MGV/CV2, pp. 701–13.
58 FCI 58, CAB 48/4, TNA.
59 CID 264th meeting, 31 May 1934, CAB 2/6, TNA.
60 CID 266th meeting, 22 November 1934, CAB 2/6, TNA.
61 Medhurst to Morton, 21 March 1934, AIR 5/1154, TNA. This file of correspondence between the IIC and Air Intelligence between 1934 and 1939 is a treasure trove of detail on Morton's and the IIC's working methods, and on his interaction with the Service Ministries.
62 Morton to Medhurst, 26 September 1934, AIR 5/1154, TNA.
63 Correspondence between Medhurst and Morton, September–November 1934, all in AIR 5/1154, TNA.
64 Correspondence between Morton and Medlicott (APOC), Industrial Information re Various Countries, Arc Ref 129910, BP Archive.
65 See *DBFP*, Second Series, Vol. XII, Chapter IV *passim*, especially Nos. 400, 446, 448, 479, 483.
66 Memo. on German Air Force, 28 February 1935, with FO minuting, C 1866/55/18, FO 371/18828, TNA.
67 269th CID meeting, 16 April 1935, CAB 2/6, TNA.
68 FCI 78 (Revised), 25 October 1935, CAB 48/4, TNA.
69 PSO 521, circulated to the CID as paper 1200-B of 9 December 1935, incorporating FCI 74 of 30 July 1935; CAB 4/24, TNA.
70 FCI 94 of 28 October 1936, CAB 48/4, TNA.
71 Correspondence between Medhurst and Clively, 14 and 19 June 1935, and between Medhurst and Morton, 5–20 November 1935, all in AIR 5/1154, TNA.
72 Berlin Chancery to Central Department, 31 December 1935, C 61/4/18, FO 371/19883, TNA.
73 Minutes of 29 August–10 September 1936, W 10229/9549/41, FO 371/20574, TNA.

74 See Charles Ramsay and M.A. Ramsay, 'Giving a lead in the right direction: Sir Robert Vansittart and the Defence Requirements Sub-Committee', in *Diplomacy and Statecraft*, vol. 6, March 1995, No. 1, pp. 39–60.

75 Morton to Liddell Hart, 28 February 1967, LH 1/531, LHCMA. Chamberlain succeeded Baldwin as PM on 28 May 1937.

76 286th CID meeting, 17 December 1936, CAB 2/6, TNA.

77 299th CID meeting, 14 October 1937, CAB 2/6, TNA.

78 Hinsley, vol. 1, pp. 33–4.

79 See, for example, Wark, *Ultimate Enemy*, pp. 164–67 and 172–74.

80 See Chapter 9 below.

81 On 9 November 1933 the CID took at its 261st meeting a report by the ATB Committee on the possibility of 'exerting economic pressure on Germany by the Powers particularly interested in preventing Germany's rearmament', but concluded that they were 'powerless' as there was no such thing as 'pacific blockade' (CAB 2/6, TNA).

82 Morton to Medhurst, 19 July 1934, AIR 5/1154, TNA.

83 MGV/CV2, p. 450.

84 Notes for a broadcast, 16 January 1934, CHAR 9/109, printed in MGV/CV2, pp. 701–13.

85 Morton to Churchill, 26 October 1935, CHAR 2/237, CCAC.

86 Morton to Churchill, 26 November 1935, CHAR 2/237, printed in MGV/CV2, pp. 1301–2.

87 See Morton to Liddell Hart, 20 March 1967, complaining that Churchill had 'let the side down on the matter of British rearmament': 'He [Churchill] accepted my papers – though he usually exaggerated the figures about foreign countries when speaking or writing in public; but was unable to see that this defeated his own ends, since any industrialist would know that his figures were impossible. Also he seemed to think that when you wanted guns, shells, rifles, clothing, warships or aircraft, you merely telephoned a manufacturer and the good would be delivered "off the peg".' (LH 1/531, LHMCA).

88 See correspondence between Churchill, Rothermere and Morton, printed in MGV/CV2, pp. 836–51.

89 Churchill to Sir T. Inskip (Minister for the Coordination of Defence), 25 May 1936, CHAR 2/269, CCAC.

90 See Gilbert, *In Search of Churchill*, p. 142 for this account of information from John Wheldon.

91 See on this point Gilbert, *In search of Churchill*, pp. 117–18: 'Morton was a man who believed in mystery.' As Gilbert shows, Churchill perpetuated the mystery in his own writings.

92 See, for example, Morton to Churchill, 24 April 1936, CHAR 2/266A, CCAC.

93 Stafford, *Churchill and Secret Service*, p. 146.

94 Gilbert, *In Search of Churchill*, Chapter VII.

95 An abortive attempt in October 1937 by Hankey to reprimand Churchill, for passing on information received clandestinely from serving officers, can be followed in HNKY 5/1, CCAC.

96 CID 1198B and 1205B, 13 November and 17 December 1935, CAB 4/24, TNA.

97 Morton to Churchill, 10 February 1936, CHAR 2/281, printed in MGV/CV3, p. 40.

98 An account of Churchill's dealings with both Anderson and Wigram can be found in Gilbert, *In Search of Churchill*.

99 See, for example, MGV, CV/2, p. 1304.

100 This does not, of course, diminish the dramatic effect of the film, *The Gathering Storm*, though its depiction of an older Morton corrupting a young, idealistic Wigram is somewhat wide of the mark: Wigram was a year older than Morton and they had been contemporaries at Eton.

101 Diary notes of Mel Thompson, 1 May 1960, Thompson papers 1/7, LHCMA.
102 Morton to Liddell Hart, 9 May 1963, LH 1/531, LHCMA.
103 Colville, *Footprints in Time*, p. 95.

9 PLANNING FOR WAR WITH GERMANY: 1938–39

1 See conclusions of 133rd COS meeting, 9 October 1934, CAB 53/5, TNA.
2 'Planning for War with Germany', the paper drafted on the basis of the COS's 1934 terms of reference, passed in successive versions through a number of committees, including the Joint Planning Sub-Committee, Deputy Chiefs of Staff Committee and the Defence Plans (Policy) Sub-Committee, set up by the CID in February 1937. Its iterations can be followed in the proceedings of these bodies: at their 189th meeting on 26 January 1938 the JPSC commissioned a memorandum on revised terms of reference for an appreciation of the situation in the event of war against Germany; a date of April 1939 was now postulated.
3 Halifax became Foreign Secretary on the resignation of Eden in February 1938. The first occasion on which he appears to have used the phrase is in conversation with von Ribbentrop (appointed German Foreign Minister on 4 February 1938), reported to Berlin in telegram No. 70 of 10 March: 'the experience of all history went to show that the pressure of facts was sometimes more powerful than the wills of men: and if once war should start in Central Europe, it was quite impossible to say where it might not end, or who might not become involved' (*DBFP*, Third Series, Vol. I, No. 8).
4 ATB 24th meeting, CAB 47/1, TNA.
5 *Handbook of Economic Warfare*, 24 July 1939, FO 837/3, TNA: see Medlicott, *Economic Blockade*, vol. I, p. 17.
6 A phrase used by Morton in a letter of 19 September 1938 to the Hon Cecil Farrer at the Department of Overseas Trade, referring to the provisional organisational layout of MEW (ICF/968, FO 837/2, TNA).
7 ATB 26th meeting, 11 February 1938, CAB 47/1, and CID 312th meeting of 4 March, CAB 2/7, TNA.
8 These three rooms are now known as the Locarno Suite, the grandest of the FCO's 'fine rooms'. At that time, however, they were anything but grand, and during the Second World War were divided up into temporary partitioned offices that hid the glories of the gilded ceiling until the much later refurbishment.
9 Medlicott, *Economic Blockade*, Introduction to Part I.
10 Sir Hughe Montgomery Knatchbull-Hugessen, 1886–1971. Diplomatic posts included British Minister in the Baltic States (1930–34), Teheran (1934–36) and Peking (1936–37); in 1939 he was appointed HM Ambassador in Ankara.
11 ATB 173/MEWOC 13 of 20 June 1938, FO 837/2, TNA.
12 MEWOC 15 of 14 September 1938, FO 837/2, TNA.
13 For an account of the Austrian crisis see *DBFP*, Third Series, Chapter I.
14 Eden resigned on 20 February 1938 over Chamberlain's determination to negotiate an Anglo-Italian agreement, though their disagreement was as much one of method and style as of policy: cf. *DBFP*, Second Series, Vol. XIX, Nos. 561 and 568.
15 Runciman's mission is documented in *DBFP*, Third Series, Vol. II. Ashton-Gwatkin's bulletins to the FO from Prague were not encouraging. On 9 August he wrote to Strang: 'There is the utmost mistrust, a feeling of the imminence of the zero hour, and a fatalistic carelessness about its consequences when it does strike. People are much less squeamish here about war and its terrors than they are in more civilised lands' (No. 598). By the end of August Runciman was referring to Czechoslovakia as 'this accursed country' (letter to Halifax, 30 August 1938, *ibid.*, No. 723).
16 He qualified this two days later by stating that he had 'no reasons to believe that Herr Hitler seeks to achieve more than incorporation of Sudeten areas into Germany',

though the situation was clearly volatile: see *DBFP*, Third Series, Vol. II, Nos. 923 and 980.

17 DI/1, 23 September 1938, FO 837/2, TNA.

18 Morton to Farrer, 19 September 1938, with attachments DI/1, OC/7, OC/8 plus diagrams, FO 837/2, TNA.

19 DI/1, 23 September 1938, FO 837/2, TNA. Morton's wording here was close to that of the SIS War Book, which stated, for example, that 'the foundation of successful espionage rests paradoxically on the absence of constricting rules'.

20 *DBFP*, Third Series, Vol. II, Nos. 1033–1087, *passim*.

21 Hill replied that he could not 'agree to breaking up the Department piecemeal unless instructed to do so by an authority qualified to give such instructions', but Farrer, and an assistant, appear to have been given permission to move over to the embryonic organisation immediately: FO 837/2, TNA.

22 Nicholls to Farrer, 23 September 1938, FO 837/2, TNA.

23 See *DBFP*, Third Series, Vol. II, Nos. 1224–29, *passim*.

24 See MGV, p. 982

25 Cf. on this point Wark, *Ultimate Enemy*, p. 180.

26 CID 320th meeting, 28 April 1938, CAB 2/7, TNA. The memo., CID 1421B, was updated in July and taken by the CID at their 331st meeting on 27 July as CID 1449B; and as CID 1507B taken at the 345th CID meeting on 26 January 1939.

27 CID 322nd meeting, 15 May 1938, CAB 2/7, TNA, taking CID 1426B.

28 See, for example, JIC 15th and 17th meetings, 25 April and 15 June 1938, CAB 56/1, TNA. Cf. Hinsley, Vol. 1, p. 37.

29 MGV, p. 1031.

30 Morton to Churchill, 25 June 1938, printed in MGV/CV3, pp. 1077–78.

31 See Medlicott, *Economic Blockade*, Part I, p. 16. Medlicott's information on this point was taken almost verbatim from a letter written to him by Morton on 3 May 1945 (private collection). Morton's correspondence with Churchill concerning the proposal for the latter to speak to the IDC is in CHAR 2/336, CCAC.

32 Documentation relating to IDC exercise No. 8 can be found in FO 837/1B, TNA.

33 Morton sent the printed text of his lecture to Churchill in a letter of 11 November 1938, CHAR 2/337, CCAC. The phrase 'fourth arm of defence' had been used by Inskip in a slightly different way in his report to the Cabinet in December 1937, 'Defence Expenditure in Future Years', with reference to economic stability. See also G.C. Peden, 'A Matter of Timing: the economic background to British Foreign policy 1937–1939', *History*, vol. 69 (1984), p. 16.

34 Letter and poem reproduced with the kind permission of Mrs Angela Mynors.

35 See the papers collected by Cadogan for the Secretary of State in November 1938, under the general title 'Possible future course of British policy', C 14471/42/18, FO 371/21659, TNA. On this collection see also David Dilks, 'Flashes of Intelligence: the Foreign Office, the SIS and Security before the Second World War', in Christopher Andrew and David Dilks (eds), *The Missing Dimension: Governments and Intelligence Communities in the Twentieth Century* (London: Palgrave Macmillan, 1984).

36 Minute by Cadogan (PUS), 14 October 1938, C 14471/42/18, FO 371/21659, TNA; printed in part in David Dilks (ed), *The Diaries of Sir Alexander Cadogan 1938–1945* (London: Cassell, 1971), pp. 116–20.

37 ICF/1143 of 6 December 1938, C 14471/42/18, FO 371/21659, TNA.

38 Morton to Liddell Hart, 9 July 1961, LH 1/531, LHCMA.

39 See, for example, Wark, *Ultimate Enemy*, p. 233; Andrew, *Secret Service*, p. 599; and J.R. Ferris, 'Indulged in all too little? Vansittart, intelligence and appeasement', reproduced in J.R. Ferris, *Intelligence and Strategy: Selected Essays* (London: Routledge, 2005), where he refers to intelligence on German military and industrial

capacity as 'often striking in accuracy and detail but, equally it was often misleading or misguided' (p. 61).

40 Hinsley, *British Intelligence*, vol. 1, p. 33.

41 Morton to Liddell Hart, 9 July 1961, LH 1/531, LHCMA.

42 Statement by Morton to PM's panel of industrialists, W 3221/617/50, FO 371/23994, TNA. See the opening of Chapter 7 above.

43 Forbes, *Doing business with the Nazis*, p. 228.

44 CID 353rd meeting, 20 April 1939, CAB 2/8, TNA.

45 JIC 26th meeting, 18 May 1939, CAB 56/1, TNA.

46 The course of these ultimately abortive negotiations can be followed in *DBFP*, Third Series, Vols. VI and VII.

47 For Morton's intervention on the instructions to the UK Delegation to Moscow, see DCOS meetings in August 1939 in CAB 54/2, and DCOS 178 of 16 August 1939, CAB 54/11, TNA. His former Chief, Sinclair, was equally unenthusiastic, considering allied negotiations with the Russians as 'a new and dangerous form of appeasement' (minute by Oliphant reporting a conversation with Sinclair, 20 March 1939, C 3968/3356/18, quoted in Andrew, *Secret Service*, pp. 592–93).

48 Curry, *Security Service*, pp. 142–43.

49 MASK material has been transferred to TNA in class HW 17. See also Nigel West, *MASK: MI5's penetration of the Communist Party of Great Britain* (London: Routledge, 2005).

50 Newly-released papers relating to the Noulens case were transferred to TNA in 2005 (FO 1093/92–103). See also Frederick S Litten, 'The Noulens Affair', in *The China Quarterly*, 138 (June 1994), pp. 492–512.

51 Some details of the JONNY case are given in Michael Smith, *Foley: The Spy who saved 10,000 Jews* (London: Hodder & Stoughton, 1999).

52 See Chapter 8 above.

53 The remit of SIS's Irish section increased considerably in 1937 when the post of Governor General was abolished under the new Irish constitution, and the Irish Government became less amenable to information-sharing. See Eunan O'Halpin, *Defending Ireland: the Irish State and its Enemies since 1922* (Oxford: Oxford University Press, 1999), pp. 129–42, and O'Halpin (ed), *MI5 and Ireland 1939–1945: The Official History* (Dublin, Irish Academic Press, 2003), pp. 20–24 and *passim*.

54 Smith, *Foley*, pp. 115–17.

55 For an account of Z's prewar activities see Anthony Read and David Fisher, *Colonel Z: The life and Times of a Master of Spies* (London: Hodder & Stoughton, 1984), Chapters Sixteen and Seventeen.

56 Much has been written on Stephenson, but none of the accounts is reliable. According to British Intelligence records, the code name 'Intrepid' was never used in relation to Stephenson, despite William Stevenson's *A Man Called Intrepid: the Secret War 1939–1945* (London: Macmillan, 1976), and Thomas F. Troy's *Wild Bill and Intrepid: Donovan, Stephenson and the Origin of CIA* (New Haven: Yale University Press, 1996). Nor do the archives support Stevenson's assertion that Stephenson played a central role in British intelligence throughout the interwar period. H. Montgomery Hyde's *The Quiet Canadian; the Secret Service Story of Sir William Stephenson* (London: Hamish Hamilton, 1962) should also be treated with caution, but does contain a reasonably accurate account of Stephenson's interwar business career and introduction to SIS. None of the books mentions Stephenson's industrial intelligence work, the only element of his interwar career that is documented satisfactorily in British Intelligence archives.

57 See Chapter 4 above.

58 This source, a former NKID employee who had refused to return to the Soviet Union in 1931 after a diplomatic posting in Stockholm, had also for some time been a source

of the SIS representative in Stockholm, although he was suspected of receiving money from the Soviet and (later) German intelligence services.

59 For an accounts of Gambier-Parry's career, including his appointment as Director of Communications for the FO and SIS jointly, see his entry in the *Oxford Dictionary of National Biography* (Oxford University Press).

60 See Chapter 12 below. On SOE's origins see the official history by William Mackenzie, *The Secret History of SOE: the Special Operations Executive 1940–1945* (written 1945–47; published London: St Ermin's Press, 2000), pp. 5–11 and Chapter V.

61 This view is shared by Wark: *Ultimate Enemy*, p. 178.

62 Mackenzie, *SOE*, pp. 4–5.

63 See, for example, minuting on a DoT letter of 1 March 1939 to the FO, N 1189/1189/42, FO 371/23706, TNA.

64 Mackenzie, *SOE*, pp. 16–18. See also Thomas Munch-Petersen, 'Confessions of a British Agent: Section D in Sweden, 1938–40', in *Utrikespolitik och historia, Studier tillagnade Wilhelm M. Carlgren* (1987), pp. 175–88, which usefully draws together the historiographical sources. See also Chapter 10 below.

65 Minute from Jebb to Cadogan based on a conversation with Morton, 13 April 1939, C 5296/454/18, FO 371/23048, TNA.

66 Morton to Jebb, 1 May 1939, C 6467/454/18, FO 371/23048, TNA.

67 Mackenzie, *SOE*, pp. 23–25.

68 See Patrick Howarth, *Intelligence Chief Extraordinary: The Life of the Ninth Duke of Portland* (Oxford: Bodley Head, 1986), pp. 174–75.

69 Hinsley, Vol. 1, Chapter I, and Curry, *Security Service*, Chapter III.

70 Hinsley, Vol. 1, pp. 41–42. See also the useful summary account of the JIC's early history, prepared as a basis for Hinsley by the Cabinet Historical Section (undated, but preserved in a 1974 file, CAB 56/7, TNA).

71 Hinsley, Vol. 1, p. 42.

72 For an account of this episode see the *Cadogan Diaries*, pp. 139–54. Andrew, *Secret Service*, p. 581 points out that there were twenty warnings from secret sources of impending Axis aggression between mid-December 1938 and mid-April 1939. Cadogan's *Diaries* are a good source generally on these warnings and give the flavour of their reception in Whitehall.

73 Minutes by Mounsey, 3 and 6 March 1939, FO 1093/84, TNA.

74 Minute by Jebb, 31 March 1939, FO 1093/84, TNA

75 Minute by Cadogan, 31 March 1939, FO 1093/84, TNA. An SIS memo of 18 September 1938 was included in the collection put together by Cadogan after Munich, C 14471/42/18, FO 371/21659, TNA. See also Dilks, 'Flashes of Intelligence', pp. 118–22.

76 Andrew's verdict that the intelligence supplied from secret sources during the nine months before the outbreak of war 'varied from excellent to dreadful' is perhaps a little too sweeping, though his rider that 'Whitehall found the greatest difficulty in distinguishing between the two' finds a mark (*Secret Service*, p. 580).

77 Most Secret memo on 'Germany: Factors, Aims, Methods, etc', 20 December 1938, sent to Jebb at the FO by Sinclair on 2 January 1939, FO 1093/84, TNA.

78 JIC 26th meeting, 18 May 1939, CAB 56/1, TNA.

10 THE FIREPROOF CURTAIN:
3 SEPTEMBER 1939–15 MAY 1940

1 Medlicott, *Economic Blockade*, Vol. I, p. 47.

2 Morton to Medlicott, 3 May 1945, private collection.

3 Churchill used the latter term, which he had borrowed from Neville Chamberlain, in Part II of the first volume of his history of *The Second World War*.

4 Medlicott, *Economic Blockade*, Vol. I, Part I.
5 *Ibid.*, p. 44.
6 See Chapter 9, p. 196.
7 Jenkins, *Churchill*, p. 566.
8 In this assessment I am less charitable than MEW's official historian, to whose more authoritative account I defer on all matters of detail. Even Medlicott, however, describes the early part of the war as the phase of 'great expectations', and sees the fact that the reputation of economic weapons declined even as their effectiveness increased as 'one of the broad paradoxes' of the story of the Economic Blockade.
9 A phrase used to describe Morton by Professor Patrick Salmon in 'British plans for Economic Warfare against Germany 1937–1939: the problem of Swedish iron ore', in Walter Laquer (ed), *The Second World War: Essays in Military and Political History* (London, 1982). More recently, Talbot Imlay has written of Morton's 'energy and ambition' as a significant factor in ensuring that 'MEW quickly carved out an independent and influential position for itself within Whitehall' (Talbot Charles Imlay, 'A reassessment of Anglo-French strategy during the Phony War, 1939–40', *English Historical Review*, vol. cxix, 481, April 2004. I would argue that however energetic and ambitious Morton might have been, MEW was sidelined and ineffective during the Phoney War.
10 Medlicott, *Economic Blockade*, Vol. I, p. 46.
11 See Imlay, 'A reassessment of Anglo-French Strategy'.
12 Hugh Dalton, *The Fateful Years: Memoirs 1931–1945* (London: Muller, 1957), p. 280.
13 See Ben Pimlott, *Hugh Dalton* (London: Papermac edn, 1986), p. 270.
14 Memo by Leith-Ross, 14 September 1939, FO 837/5, TNA.
15 There is an extensive literature on all these (abortive) schemes, including Medlicott's *Economic Blockade* and Churchill's own highly-coloured account in his memoirs, and the records are available at The National Archives. It would be impossible to describe them all in this biography, although certain schemes (such as those relating to Swedish iron ore) come into the story in the Intelligence context.
16 Imlay, 'A reassessment of Anglo-French Strategy'.
17 An interesting exchange of correspondence in December 1939 between Morton and the City Editor of the *Sunday Times* on the attitude of British business interests to economic warfare is preserved in PREM 7/1, TNA.
18 Despite the Anti-Comintern and Nazi-Soviet Pacts, the British Government hoped that Italy and Russia might behave as neutrals, albeit 'equivocal' or 'unfriendly' neutrals (Medlicott's description). From the beginning of the war, however, MEW's Intelligence Division supplied regular information on Russian and Italian trade with Germany, disguised or channelled through third parties.
19 For a full account see Salmon, 'British economic warfare against Germany'.
20 Minute of 2 October 1939, FO 837/24, TNA.
21 I/81/1 of 27 November 1939, FO 837/802 part I, TNA.
22 A good account of these schemes and Churchill's role is given in Gilbert, *Finest Hour: Winston Churchill 1939–41* (London: Heinemann, 1983). On the Anglo-French aspect see Imlay, 'A reassessment of Anglo-French Strategy'.
23 Morton to Coulson (FO), 14 October 1939, FO 837/146, TNA.
24 Memo I/2300/7 for the JPSC on Contraband Control in the Aegean, 1 November 1939, FO 837/146, TNA.
25 Minute by Morton, 15 April 1940, FO 837/23, TNA.
26 Morton to Medlicott, 3 May 1945, private collection.
27 Ian Fleming (1908–46) had been a journalist and stockbroker before the war, when he became a Naval Lieutenant and personal assistant to the Director of Naval Intelligence. A close associate of Morton's during the war, he later became famous as the author of the James Bond books, as well as *Chitty Chitty Bang Bang*.

28 Correspondence between Morton and Fleming, 16–23 November 1939, PREM 7/1, TNA.

29 Gaitskell to Jebb, 21 December 1939, C 20907/32/18, FO 371/23004, TNA. According to his biographer Gaitskell leaked information to Dalton 'to be used as ammunition in his campaign against Chamberlain and for a new National Government', with the approval of Ronald Cross (Brian Brivati, *Hugh Gaitskell* (London: Hodder & Stoughton, 1997), p. 47. Gaitskell (1906–63) joined MEW from his academic job at University College London. In 1945 he became a Labour MP and served in a number of Ministerial posts including as Chancellor of the Exchequer, 1950–51. He was Leader of the Labour Party from 1955 until his death.

30 Morton to Hall, 13 January 1940, FO 837/23, TNA.

31 See Robert Skidelsky, *John Maynard Keynes*, Vol. 3: *Fighting for Britain, 1937–1946* (London: Macmillan, 2000), pp. 48–9. Lord Keynes (1883–1946), distinguished economist, philanthropist and patron of the arts, served as a member of the EAC from 1930–39 and as economic adviser to the Chancellor of the Exchequer, 1940–46.

32 Morton to Churchill, 14 October 1939, CHAR 23/1, CCAC.

33 Skidelsky, *Keynes*, Vol. 3, p. 47.

34 For an example of Morton's attention to the minutiae of bureaucratic obstruction, see his formal complaint to Mounsey regarding the operations of the Registry (minute of 1 April 1940, FO 837/23, TNA).

35 Minute of 10 November 1939, FO 837/23, TNA.

36 MEW remained at the LSE building in Houghton Street, London WC2 until March 1940, when it moved into Berkeley Square House, SW1.

37 Morton to Rowbottom, 25 December 1939, FO 837/146, TNA.

38 Gilbert, *Finest Hour*, p. 111.

39 Hinsley, Vol. 1, p. 92.

40 Cadogan diary, entry for 30 October 1939, ACAD 1/8, CCAC.

41 Cadogan diary, entries 4–29 November 1939, ACAD 1/8, CCAC.

42 A useful summary of the literature on this point is given in Philip H.J. Davies, *MI6 and the Machinery of Spying* (London: Frank Cass Publishers, 2004), pp. 100–01. See also Andrew, *Secret Service*, pp. 612–14.

43 See Patrick Beesley, *Very Special Admiral: the Life of Admiral J.H. Godfrey C.B.* (London: Hamish Hamilton, 1980), pp. 139–40, and Stafford, *Churchill and Secret Service*, pp. 164–65.

44 Read and Fisher, *Colonel Z*, pp. 195–200.

45 Cadogan noted in his diary a visit from Dansey on 16 November, although not the subject of their conversation: 'I'm sure he's very clever & very subtle, but I have no proof of it because I can't hear 10% of what he says.' (ACAD 1/8, CCAC)

46 Hankey's report of 11 March 1940 on SIS and supporting papers can be found in CAB 63/192, TNA. His subsequent report into the Security Service (MI5), completed on his last day in office (10 May 1940), is in CAB 63/193.

47 Some examples of Hankey's reliance on Morton for information and advice are preserved in correspondence in PREM 7/1, TNA.

48 For an account of the Venlo incident see Andrew, *Secret Service*, pp. 609–16.

49 See Curry, *Security Service*, pp. 145–46.

50 Hankey report on SIS, paras. 8–9, CAB 63/192, TNA.

51 Hankey report on SIS, para. 45, CAB 63/192, TNA.

52 For a brief account of the work of 'EH' (Electra House) in the field of propaganda in enemy countries, see Mackenzie, *SOE*, pp. 5–7.

53 See Chapter 12 below.

54 For interesting background to Bletchley's development as a war station see Marion Hill, *Bletchley Park People: Churchill's Geese that never Cackled* (Sutton Publishing, 2004), Chapter I.

55 Jebb supplied the translation of Menzies' phrase: 'Let them regard virtue & pine in despair at her abandonment (Persius).' (Menzies to Jebb, 14 February 1940, CAB 63/192, TNA.)

56 Hankey report on SIS, paras. 29–30, CAB 63/192, TNA.

57 'Summary of evidence supplied to Lord Hankey in his investigation of the Secret Intelligence Service', CAB 63/192, TNA.

58 'Summary of evidence supplied to Lord Hankey in his investigation of the Secret Intelligence Service', CAB 63/192, TNA.

59 Some examples of these monthly reports can be found in TNA, eg that for October 1939 (C 18336/32/18, FO 371/23004).

60 See Hinsley, Vol. 1, pp. 25–6. The Commercial Section's reports which were sent to the IIC and to MEW can be found in HW 29, TNA.

61 'Summary of evidence supplied to Lord Hankey in his investigation of the Secret Intelligence Service', CAB 63/192, TNA.

62 Minutes by Morton and Hall, November 1939, FO 837/429, TNA.

63 Note by Brand, 8 December 1939, FO 837/429, TNA.

64 'Summary of evidence supplied to Lord Hankey in his investigation of the Secret Intelligence Service', CAB 63/192, TNA.

65 See Mackenzie, *SOE*, Chapter II, 'The work of D Section'.

66 Mackenzie, *SOE*, pp. 36–37.

67 A useful exception, which shows both that Morton was well-informed on D's plans and was consulted as being so, is a letter written to Hankey on 18 October 1939, clearly in response to an urgent request for information on plans for 'violent action in regard to Roumanian oil supplies': PREM 7/1, TNA.

68 See pp. 193–94.

69 Peter Tennant, *Touchlines of War* (The University of Hull Press, 1992), p. 128.

70 Marcus and Jakob Wallenberg, prominent Swedish industrialists who ran the *Stockholms Enskilda Bank*. Both Marcus and Jakob were used by the Swedish Government as semi-official representatives. Marcus travelled frequently to the UK, playing a key role in the negotiation of the Anglo-Swedish War Trade Agreement, and was related by marriage to the British banker Charles Hambro, involved with MEW and later SOE. Jakob was closely involved with German Resistance groups, and Marcus also played a part in abortive peace negotiations. The full history of the Wallenbergs remains somewhat mysterious, but some useful studies have been published by the Swedish Foundation for Economic History Research within Banking and Enterprise, which manages the archives of the *Stockholms Enskilda Bank*. For an account of the intelligence context to the Wallenbergs' activities see Tennant, *Touchlines of War*.

71 See Tennant, *Touchlines of War*.

72 See p. 193.

73 See Chapter 12 below.

74 On Operation Lumps, see Mackenzie, SOE, pp. 17–20. A misleading account of Stephenson's Scandinavian role is given in Hyde, *The Quiet Canadian*, and followed by Munch-Petersen, 'Confessions of a British Agent'. The account in Mackenzie of Section D's Scandinavian projects, including the Rickman affair, follows the documentation more closely but is circumspect on Stephenson's role (*SOE*, pp. 16–22). ISI is not mentioned in any of the accounts.

75 Mallet to Jebb, 12 May 1940, PUSD records, FCO.

76 Tennant, *Touchlines of War*, p. 129.

77 A detailed account of the difficulties attendant on the decision to send naval forces to Norway is given in Gilbert, *Finest Hour*, Chapter 10, the title of which is 'Scandinavia: the failure to decide'.

78 Jenkins, *Churchill*, p. 575.

79 Churchill minute, 14 January 1940, CHAR 19/6, reproduced in Martin Gilbert, *The Churchill War Papers: At the Admiralty* (London: Heinemann, 1993), p. 641 (hereafter *War Papers* I).

80 Major General (later Lord) Hastings ('Pug') Ismay, secretary to the CID since 1938; he became Chief of Staff to Churchill as Minister of Defence from May 1940, and sat on the COS Committee.

81 Oliver Lyttelton, later Lord Chandos (1893–1972), industrialist and a strong advocate in the 1930s of the Government's taking early steps to secure raw materials against a future war. Much admired by Churchill, he was part of the small group the latter gathered round him when appointed Prime Minister, though Lyttelton only became an MP and entered the War Cabinet (as President of the Board of Trade) in October 1940: see Simon Ball, *The Guardsmen: Harold Macmillan, Three Friends and the World They Made* (London: HarperCollins, 2004). For an account of the life and career of Churchill's staunch friend and scientific adviser, Frederick Lindemann (later Lord Cherwell, 1886–1957) see Adrian Fort, *'Prof': the Life of Frederick Lindemann* (London: Jonathan Cape, 2003).

82 On this proposal see *The Memoirs of General the Lord Ismay* (London: Heinemann, 1960), pp. 112–14; extract quoted in Gilbert, *War Papers* I, p. 1171.

83 Gilbert, *Finest Hour*, Chapters 14 and 15, gives a revealing account of Churchill's simultaneous impatience with and awareness of Chamberlain's handling of his increasingly heavy responsibilities, showing that Churchill both relished and feared the prospect of the Premiership. Morton's ambiguity over the prospect of assuming a more prominent role has been indicated earlier in this chapter.

84 The account in *Finest Hour*, Chapter 16, refers to most other versions of the events in question, including Churchill's own memoirs. For a detailed analysis see Robert Blake, 'How Churchill became Prime Minister', in Robert Blake and Wm Roger Louis (eds), *Churchill* (Oxford: Oxford University Press, 1993), pp. 257–74.

85 Note of 10 May 1940, PREM 7/2, TNA.

86 Churchill, *Gathering Storm*, p. 527.

87 Colville, *Footprints in Time*, p. 75.

11 THE MORTON MYTH: DOWNING STREET, MAY 1940–JULY 1945

 1 Colville's phrase, applied to Bracken, Morton and Lindemann: *Footprints in Time*, p. 75.

 2 See C.J. Hamilton, 'The Decline of Churchill's "Garden Suburb" and Rise of his Private Office': the Prime Minister's Department, 1940–45', *Twentieth Century British History*, vol. 12, No. 2, 2001, p. 141: 'Morton's wartime career differed from those of his two colleagues in that he managed neither to concentrate his efforts nor remain in the centre of power.' On a practical point, Morton was transferred on to the establishment of HM Treasury, and paid at the level of an Assistant Under Secretary.

 3 Eden succeeded Halifax as Foreign Secretary on 22 December 1940.

 4 Morton himself made use of the omelette analogy in a letter to R.W. Thompson dated 29 August 1960, and published in Thompson, *Churchill and Morton* (p. 87): '[Churchill] was always supremely confident that after his object had been gained, he would be able to mend the eggs he had broken in cooking his omelette. That is of course opportunism, but rather an unusual and "magnificent" variety.'

 5 Interview with the late Sir William Deakin, 29 July 1999. F.W.D. Deakin (1913–2005), historian and soldier, helped Churchill to research and write his war histories both in the 1930s and after World War II. Attached to SOE from 1941, he led the first British Military Mission to Tito in the summer of 1943 and later served in the British Embassy in Belgrade. In 1950 he became the first Warden of St Antony's

College, Oxford and was president of the British Committee for the History of the Second World War.

6 Egremont, *Under Two Flags*, p. 236.

7 John Harvey (ed), *The War Diaries of Oliver Harvey 1941–45* (London: Collins, 1978), pp. 166 and 257.

8 See, for example, Colville, *Footprints in Time*, p. 95.

9 Roskill, *Hankey, Man of Secrets*, vol. iii, p. 421.

10 Churchill's political isolation and the suspicion with which he was regarded on assuming the Premiership is represented in all major accounts of this period. A recent analysis, by Simon Ball, in *The Guardsmen*, summed it up thus: 'No serious pre-war politician was a Churchillian. Churchill's praetorian guard was therefore a rag-tag and bobtail of outsiders and amateurs' (p. 216). On the other hand, as Robert Blake put it, 'One should not forget his assets: a small but devoted group of supporters; galvanic energy; an unrivalled power of oratory when words really mattered; a simple British patriotism; a real sense of destiny, that he was the chosen man to save the nation; above all an extraordinary optimism and confidence against all the odds' ('How Churchill became Prime Minister', in Blake & Louis, *Churchill*).

11 Dalton diary for 16 June 1940, quoted in Ben Pimlott (ed), *The Second World War Diary of Hugh Dalton 1940–45* (London: Jonathan Cape, 1986), p. 41: 'It is put to me that Winston is surrounded by stimulants – his "Brains Trust", Morton, "the Prof" (Lindemann), Brendan Bracken etc. What he really needs, some think, are sedatives.'

12 Colville, *Churchillians*, p. 205. A less respectful term used by John (later Sir John) Martin (PS and, from 1941–45, PPS to Churchill) was the 'crazy gang': see Hamilton, 'The Decline of Churchill's Garden Suburb', p. 134.

13 Sir Edward (later Lord) Bridges had been Cabinet Secretary since 1938, and was head of the War Cabinet machinery. General Sir Alan Brooke (later Field Marshal Viscount Alanbrooke) served as CIGS from December 1941 until 1946: see Alex Danchev and Daniel Todman (eds), *Field Marshal Lord Alanbrooke, War Diaries 1939–1945* (London: Phoenix Press, 2002). For a useful description of the Defence Secretariat machinery see *The Memoirs of General the Lord Ismay*, Chapter VI.

14 An apt description of the position of Bracken, Lindemann and Morton is given in Hamilton, 'The Decline of Churchill's "Garden Suburb"': 'an active and personal means of liaison between him and whatsoever element in society, within government or outside, that would benefit from such a link' (p. 136).

15 Colville, *Fringes of Power*, p. 136.

16 Colville, *Churchillians*, p. 205.

17 Initially Morton was accommodated in 10 Downing Street in the room that had been used by Sir Horace Wilson, moving across the road to the No 10 Annexe, above the War Rooms, when it was ready for occupation in September 1940 (cf Gilbert, *Finest Hour*, pp. 782–83).

18 A collection of Morton's minutes to Churchill can be found in PREM 7/3–6, TNA. Churchill's minutes to Morton can be traced in PREM 3 and PREM 4, and in a useful collection in CHAR 20, CCAC.

19 General Charles de Gaulle had just been appointed Under Secretary for National Defence when Reynaud's government fell. On 17 June 1940, the day that Pétain sued for armistice, de Gaulle flew to Britain with Spears, who described him as 'all that was now left of the spirit of France': Major-General Sir Edward L Spears, *Assignment to Catastrophe*, Vol. II, *The Fall of France, June 1940* (London: Heinemann 1954), p. 323.

20 A phrase used in the context of the Radio Security Service or Section (RSS), formed early in 1939 to monitor clandestine and illicit radio communications from the UK. Originally run by the War Office with the help of the GPO, it was transferred to SIS in 1941 on the basis that the greatest efficiency would be gained by entrusting it to the

same authority responsible for operating clandestine communications officially (see Hinsley, vol. 4, pp. 72–3).

21 Colville, *Fringes of Power*, p. 403.

22 Colville, *Churchillians*, p. 134.

23 Colville, *Footprints in Time*, p. 95.

24 The Grand Alliance, a term coined by Churchill to describe all nations fighting against the Axis powers, but usually taken to refer to the UK, USA and USSR, came into being in 1941 when the German attack on the Soviet Union on 22 June, and the Japanese attack on the US Fleet at Pearl Harbor on 7 December, brought those two countries into the war against Hitler.

25 Morton to Martin, 13 October 1941, enclosing draft Notice, PREM 4/80/3, TNA. Thanking Morton on 14 October, Martin stated that he would circulate an office notice; 'but, as it is human to err, there will no doubt continue to be sins of omission from time to time and it would help if you could always let me know of any which come to your notice' (*ibid*).

26 J.A. Cross, *Lord Swinton* (Oxford: Clarendon Press, 1982), pp. 223–24. For the establishment of the Security Executive see Chamberlain's memo for the War Cabinet, WP(40)172 of 27 May 1940, CAB 66/8, TNA. The title HDSE was changed to SE in October 1941 to avoid confusion with other Home Office bodies, but for simplicity the contraction SE is used throughout.

27 Morton made a number of suggestions to Churchill in favour of a restrictive policy, such as a curfew for aliens between 9pm and 7am, to which the latter responded 'Discrimination is needed' (Morton to Churchill, 27 May 1940, with note by Churchill, PREM 7/2, TNA).

28 Cf. p. 133. Anthony Masters, in *The Man who was M*, alleged that Morton maintained a close relationship with Knight during the war, consulting him 'over all counter-subversion and counter-intelligence matters', and 'going direct to Knight for situation reports rather than speaking to Kell himself'. In return, he says that Morton provided a 'hot line' to Churchill that gave Knight 'substantial power' and support for his somewhat idiosyncratic and independent methods of operation (pp. 115–20). No evidence of such contacts between Knight and Morton have been found either in Security Service or in SIS archives. It is likely that the two men were in contact, and that Morton used Knight as a source of information on MI5, but less plausible that this afforded Knight any particular advantage. Morton was not popular in MI5, and Churchill is unlikely to have taken much interest in Knight.

29 Tyler Kent, a cipher clerk in the US Embassy in London, was found with a suitcase containing stolen documents and keys to the Embassy's code and file rooms: for a brief account of his arrest and that of his accomplice, Anna Wolkoff, see Stafford, *Churchill and Secret Service*, pp. 177–79. Full details of the Kent and Wolkoff cases, and those of possible associates, can be found in Security Service files released in class KV 2, e.g. pieces 543–5 and 839–43; see also the account by Knight in KV 4/227, TNA.

30 Minute by Churchill with WP(40)172 of 27 May 1940, PREM 3/418/1, TNA. Although Churchill was certainly prepared to authorise the widespread detention of enemy aliens and other strong measures to combat a potential Fifth Column threat (cf. Stafford, *Churchill and Secret Service*, pp. 176–78), he was also quick to recognise the importance of avoiding over-reaction and accepted more willingly than some of his advisers that the threat was illusory.

31 Hankey's report on the Security Service, dated 11 May 1940 and prepared as part of his wider investigation into British Intelligence (see Chapter 10) had criticised both the leadership and the organisation of that organisation (CAB 63/193, TNA).

32 Morton to Churchill, 16 July 1940, PREM 3/418/1, TNA.

33 Cross, *Swinton*, p. 226.

34 Minutes of SE meetings and papers are in CAB 93/2–3, TNA.

35 First meeting of Security Intelligence Centre, 15 June 1940, CAB 93/5, TNA. By mid-1941, when the existence of any substantial Fifth Column in Britain had been discounted, the SIC was re-absorbed into the SE, and in March 1942 Swinton announced that the name SIC should no longer be used, as Security Executive (SE) would cover all relevant activities (SE memo, 13 March 1942, CAB 21/3498, TNA).

36 The principal standing committees were the Liaison Officers' conference, the Committee on Control at Ports, the Committee on Communism and the Conference on Control of Missions. A brief account of their work is given in a useful official survey of the SE's work prepared in February 1946 and preserved in CAB 21/3498, TNA.

37 The SE's overseas responsibilities included the Security Division of BSC (see p. 256 below) and other overseas security matters that were, technically, outside the remit of either MI5 or SIS. A brief account is given in the memo of February 1946 (see note 36 above), but the picture was a complex one. Some of these activities, such as the security of British-controlled undertakings overseas of importance to the war effort, and contraband control, were of interest to Morton, but he does not seem to have been involved in any detail with this side of the SE's work.

38 Churchill questioned Swinton's choice of Ball to head the SIC, but both Swinton and Morton defended him as the best man for the job: see Swinton to Churchill, 10 June 1940, and Morton to Churchill, 11 June, PREM 3/418/1, TNA. Ball's involvement with the SE ended in 1941.

39 See Morton to Churchill, 16 July and 14 August 1940, PREM 3/418/1, TNA.

40 Alfred Duff Cooper, later 1st Viscount Norwich (1890–1954) began his career in the FO; Conservative MP from 1924, resigned as First Lord of the Admiralty in 1938 in protest at the Munich agreement, returned in 1940 as Minister of Information. Served in Singapore, 1941–42, succeeded Swinton as head of the SE June 1942, representative to the French Committee for National Liberation in Algiers from October 1942; HM Ambassador in Paris, 1944–47.

41 See correspondence between Bridges and Morton, November–December 1943, in CAB 21/3499, TNA. In a note of 8 December Bridges recorded his views on the 'undesirability of the Prime Minister's Personal Assistant becoming Chairman of the Security Executive while continuing to serve the Prime Minister in that capacity'. T.L. Rowan, Churchill's Private Secretary, also spoke of the matter with Bracken, who 'strongly agreed that this was politically undesirable'. No more was heard of this proposal from Churchill, which may or may not have been prompted by Morton.

42 As foreshadowed in Hankey's report on the Security Service, both Kell and his deputy Holt-Wilson were dismissed in June 1940. Swinton became Executive Head of MI5 with a remit to help the new Director General, Morton's old adversary Harker, to 'reorganise the Service'. A first hand account of the effect of Swinton's 'reforms' on the Security Service can be followed in West (ed), *The Guy Liddell Diaries*.

43 See, for example, the 41st, 46th, 53rd and 54th SE meetings, 9 July, 27 August, 12 and 26 November 1941, CAB 93/2, TNA.

44 Morton to Cadogan, 20 June 1940, PREM 7/9, TNA.

45 Comment by Churchill on minute from Morton, 24 June 1940, PREM 7/2. TNA.

46 Morton may have sought the chairmanship from the start, since he apparently set out systematically to undermine Vansittart's position, hinting that the latter was 'past it'. Since others also complained of Van's inconsistency and forgetfulness it may be that Morton's complaints were justified, but his professed surprise at Vansittart's decision seems somewhat disingenuous.

47 Cadogan noted in his diary on 15 August 1940: 'Discussion with H[alifax] & Morton about latter's ambitious scheme to extend scope of his Cttee. I think we scotched it kindly' (ACAD 1/9, CCAC).

48 Terms of reference and composition of the Committee on Foreign (Allied) Resistance, circulated as CFR(40)1 on 16 August 1940, FO 892/5, TNA.

49 Documentation on the preparation of this paper can be followed in FO files in Z 92/17, as well as in CAB 85/25, TNA.

50 Its last recorded meeting seems to have taken place in January 1943. Records of the CFR can be found in CAB 85/22–26; 1940 minutes and related correspondence are also in PREM 7/8–9 and in FO 892/5, TNA.

51 W.H.B. (later Sir Henry) Mack (1894–1974), FO 1921, later Ambassador in Vienna, Bagdad and Buenos Aires; F.K. (later Sir Frank) Roberts (1907–98), FO 1930, later Ambassador in Moscow and Bonn; R.L. Speaight (1906–76), FO 1929, later Ambassador in Rangoon and Sofia.

52 René Pleven (1901–93) held various posts in the Free French administration, later serving in de Gaulle's government as Finance Minister 1944–46; Prime Minister twice during 1951–52; various ministerial posts, 1969–73.

53 In June 1940 Spears was appointed head of the official British mission to what became the French National Committee. On his appointment as Minister to Syria and Lebanon in February 1942 he was succeeded as British Representative to the French National Committee in London by C.B.P. Peake, formerly Counsellor in HM Embassy in Washington.

54 Minute by Peake, 31 October 1942, Z 8501/90/17, FO 371/31950, TNA.

55 Eden's comment was prompted by Morton's interview with de Gaulle on 30 October 1942, which the FO considered had cut across the line they were trying to take: see correspondence in Z 8501/90/17, FO 371/31950, TNA.

56 On 9 July 1960, Morton wrote to Thompson: 'I don't like Eden as a man, and I have never liked his foreign policy' (quoted in Thompson, *Churchill and Morton*, p. 49). Eden himself omitted any mention of Morton from his wartime memoirs.

57 Both Churchill and Eden, like Spears, had a strong emotional attachment to France that affected their views of policy. Their differences were of emphasis rather than substance, though Eden's support for de Gaulle annoyed Churchill at periods when he was considering a strategic approach to Vichy or, in the face of Roosevelt's dislike of de Gaulle, favoured an alternative French champion.

58 Morton to Churchill, 28 August 1942, PREM 7/6, TNA.

59 Correspondence concerning the preparation of Morton's memo, sent to Hambro (SOE) and others on 17 September 1942, can be found in HS 6/316, TNA.

60 Of this Anglo-French expedition in August–September 1940 (Operation *Menace*) for the occupation of Dakar in order to rally French forces in Africa to the Allied cause, Hinsley wrote that it was difficult to know whether it was 'a tale of avoidable errors' or 'a list of unavoidable misfortunes' (vol. 1, p. 158). Though the expedition was planned by de Gaulle and Spears, and agreed (mostly) by Churchill, the documentation suggests a strong supporting role by Morton. For Spears's view of the expedition see Egremont, *Under Two Flags*, pp. 200–12.

61 Churchill ordered the arrest of Admiral Emile Muselier, de Gaulle's deputy, in London on 1 January 1941, on the basis of documents alleging that Muselier had betrayed the Dakar expedition to Vichy forces. These had been shown to Morton on 28 December 1940 by Guy Liddell, who made it clear that MI5 'could give no guarantee whatsoever about the source of the information'. The documents turned out to be forgeries, and Churchill had to apologise to de Gaulle. See West (ed), *The Guy Liddell Diaries*, vol. I, pp. 117–24. Although Morton clearly played a part in the affair, the decision was Churchill's: Cadogan noted in his diary for 3 January 1941: 'It was that baby Dictator who ordered immediate (and premature) action.' (ACAD 1/10, CCAC)

62 Record of meeting with de Gaulle, 30 September 1942, with minute by Eden, 18 October 1942, Z 7530/90/17, FO 371/31950, TNA; *War Diaries of Oliver Harvey*, entry for 18 October 1942, p. 169.

63 Operation Torch began on 8 November 1942 when three Allied task forces, comprising some 65,000 (principally US) troops, landed in Morocco and Algeria. This move, together with the ceasefire ordered on 10 November by Admiral Darlan, C-in-C Vichy armed forces, led to the German invasion of unoccupied France on 11 November and to an escalation of the North African campaign.

64 See correspondence in PREM 3/221/13B, TNA.

65 Selborne, formerly Viscount Wolmer (1877–1971), succeeded Dalton as Minister of Economic Warfare in February 1942. His extensive correspondence with Morton can be found in HS 8/924, TNA.

66 Morton to Gerbrandy, 3 May 1943, also correspondence between Morton and Selborne, 3–15 May 1943, HS 8/924, TNA.

67 See Introduction above, note 1.

68 See Chapter 10, note 70. A new and interesting light on the activities of Goerdeler and the Wallenbergs, and on Marcus's contacts with Morton, is given in Gert Nylander, 'German Resistance Movement and England', published in 1999 as *Banking and Enterprise*, No 2 by The Foundation for Economic History Research within Banking and Enterprise, Stockholm. The Foundation manages the historical archives of the *Stockholms Enskilda Bank*, and Nylander's publication draws on documentation discovered by the Bank in 1997.

69 Letter from Jacob to Marcus Wallenberg, 21 May 1943, printed (in original and translation) in Nylander, *German Resistance Movement*, pp. 55–61.

70 Translated transcription of Marcus Wallenberg's handwritten notes of a meeting with Morton, June 1943, printed in Nylander, *German Resistance Movement*, pp. 63–69.

71 Nylander, *German Resistance Movement*, p. 67.

72 Transcription of handwritten letter from Hambro to Marcus Wallenberg, 29 September 1943, printed in Nylander, *German Resistance Movement*, pp. 78–79.

73 General Dragolub ('Draza') Mihailovic (1893–1946), leader of the revolt against the Germans in Yugoslavia and Minister of War in the post-coup Yugoslav government, was captured by the Partisans in March 1946 and executed after a show trial. Josip Broz (1892–1980), known as Tito, secretary of the Yugoslav Communist party and Partisan leader, fought against both the Germans and Mihailovic and later, as Marshal Tito, ruled Yugoslavia as Dictator until his death. A useful account of the background to the Yugoslav situation from an SOE viewpoint can be found in Mackenzie, *SOE*, Chapter VI.

74 Interview with the late Sir William Deakin, 29 July 1999.

75 An Allied decision to launch a second front in Europe was taken at the Trident conference in Washington in May 1943. Thereafter, as Ismay put it in a minute to Churchill on 4 October 1943, the key factor was that 'on military grounds we should not relax our efforts to contain as many German divisions as possible in Greece and Yugoslavia' (PREM 3/66/2, TNA).

76 See pp. 249–51 below.

77 Casey to Admiral Sir Andrew Cunningham, CinC Mediterranean, 1 June 1943, PREM 3/510/7, TNA. The information did not reach Algiers in time for Churchill to see it before he left, and was sent on to London.

78 See correspondence between Peck, Morton, Martin and Sargent, 7–10 June 1943, PREM 3/510/7, TNA.

79 See pp. 249–51 below for evidence supporting the argument that Morton was not privy to Ultra.

80 F.D.L. Brown to T.L. Rowan, 12 June 1943, sent on to Morton on 13 June with a request that he 'put in hand the production of the two page report for which the Prime Minister asks' (PREM 3/510/7, TNA).

81 COS(43)336(0) of 23 June 1943 circulated to the War Cabinet a letter from Lord Selborne, Minister of Economic Warfare, covering an SOE appreciation of the

situation in Yugoslavia 'approved by the Foreign Office, the War Office and "C"' (PREM 3/510/7, TNA).

82 Jan Nowak-Jezioranski (1914–2005) recounted this episode in his memoir *Courier from Warsaw* (London: Collins/Harvill, 1982), pp. 260–64; his note of his meeting with Morton is reproduced *ibid.*, Appendix VII. In an interview with the author in 2001, M. Nowak speculated that Morton's motive for falsifying the report was that he was working secretly for the Soviet Union.

83 Correspondence regarding the arrangements for Morton, rather than Churchill, to see Nowak can be found in PREM 3/352/14A, TNA. Nowak had been recommended warmly to Churchill by Eden in a minute of 25 January, but Morton was sceptical even before his meeting with Nowak.

84 Nowak, *Courier from Warsaw*, p. 262.

85 Nowak, *Courier from Warsaw*, p. 264.

86 See Bennett, *Zinoviev Letter*, pp. 56–65 and Annex F. O'Malley was reinstated in April 1929.

87 Selborne to Morton, 9 February 1944, HS 8/924,TNA.

88 Morton to Selborne, 10 February 1944, HS 8/924, TNA.

89 See Gill Bennett, 'Polish-British Intelligence Cooperation', in the Report of the Anglo-Polish Historical Committee, *Intelligence Cooperation between Poland and Great Britain during World War II* (London: Valentine Mitchell, 2005), Chapter 15.

90 Selborne to Morton, 14 February 1944, HS 8/924, TNA.

91 See Gilbert, *Road to Victory: Winston S. Churchill 1941–1945* (London: Heinemann, 1986), p. 691, also pp. 681–88. Cf. Nowak, *Courier from Warsaw*, pp. 266–69.

92 Morton sent a copy of this signal, T 415/4, to Selborne on 29 February 1944: the latter replied on 2 March that he 'need hardly say' how glad he was to see it (HS 8/924, TNA).

93 Morton to Thompson, 30 March 1962, Thompson papers 1/2, LHCMA.

94 Morton set out his activities in regard to economic liaison, supply issues and other aspects of civil affairs in a minute to Martin of 24 May 1944 (PREM 4/80/3, TNA). Minutes to Churchill dated 15 June and 24 July 1944, asking whether he could sit on committees dealing with French civil affairs, and the promotion of British exports, show that he did not feel fully employed, however (PREM 7/5, TNA).

95 For Morton's involvement see, for example, the record of a meeting on the winding up of the Free French on 5 July 1943: Z 7269/68/17, FO 371/36032, TNA.

96 Correspondence relating to Morton's work on the AEA Committee can be found in PREM 7/10, TNA. It was wound up in October 1944 following the liberation of France and Belgium.

97 The Teheran Conference, which opened on 28 November 1942, was the first at which Marshal Stalin participated in top-level Allied strategic discussions. For an account from Churchill's perspective of the conference, and of the succeeding talks in Cairo see Gilbert, *Road to Victory*, Chapters 34 and 35.

98 Maurice Harold Macmillan (1894–1986), 1st Earl of Stockton, Conservative MP 1923–29 and from 1931. Later served as Minister of Defence, Foreign Secretary, Chancellor of the Exchequer and Prime Minister (1957–63).

99 See Gilbert, *Road to Victory*, pp. 602–13.

100 Robert D. Murphy (1894–1978), US diplomat, charged with preparing the ground for Operation Torch, and subsequently appointed as Roosevelt's personal representative with the rank of Minister to French North Africa. He later served as an adviser to US Presidents Kennedy, Johnson and Nixon.

101 R.M.M. (later Sir Roger) Makins, later Lord Sherfield (1904–96), served at AFHQ as Macmillan's assistant 1943–44. Later posts included AUS, then DUS, FO, 1947–52, HM Ambassador in Washington 1953–56, Joint Permanent Secretary to the Treasury 1956–59, Chairman of the UK Atomic Energy Authority 1960–64.

102 For references to Morton's North African trip see Harold Macmillan, *War Diaries: The Mediterranean 1943–45* (London: Macmillan, 1984), pp. 293–339.
103 See Gilbert, *Road to Victory*, Chapter 50.
104 Entry for 15 September 1944, printed in John Julius Norwich (ed), *The Duff Cooper Diaries* (London: Weidenfeld & Nicolson, 2005), p. 321.
105 Morton to Churchill, 25 September 1944, PREM 7/5, TNA.
106 Morton to Churchill, *ibid*.
107 See, for example, the *Alanbrooke War Diaries*, *passim*, and the account by C.M. Woodhouse, former Commander of the Allied Military Mission to the Greek Guerrillas, *Apple of Discord* (London, 1948).
108 For a summary of the situation in August 1945, see *DBPO*, Series I, Volume VI (London: HMSO, 1991), No. 3.
109 Morton to HM Minister in Athens, 14 June 1945, PREM 7/11, TNA.
110 Supreme Allied Commander, Mediterranean Forces (SACMED).
111 Morton to Chief of Staff, AFHQ, 25 June 1945, PREM 7/11, TNA.
112 Writing to Thompson on 14 July 1958, Morton was less than gracious about his knighthood: 'The KCB I got, presumably, for standing Winston for four years and it wasn't worth it. Take this last in any way you like' (Thompson papers 1/1, LHCMA). I am disinclined to take this disclaimer too seriously.
113 'Activities of Sir D. Morton as PA to the PM, May 1945', sent to Churchill on 1 June 1945, PREM 4/80/3, TNA.
114 Morton to Churchill, 1 June 1945, PREM 4/80/3, TNA. A marginal note, undated, by Martin read: 'P.M. I should like to have discussed this with Sir D. Morton, but had no opportunity before his departure' (for Athens, presumably).
115 Colville, *Fringes of Power*, p. 702.

12 INTELLIGENCE LIAISON, MAY 1940–JULY 1945

1 See p. 223 above.
2 See Bibliography for studies of these aspects of wartime Intelligence.
3 Menzies appears to have sent the first batch of reports almost on receipt of Morton's 15 May letter, and Morton began to send appreciative notes of thanks, both on his own and on Churchill's behalf – 'I told the Prime Minister your latest news yesterday . . . He was very grateful for the information' (Morton to Menzies, 18 May).
4 See Hinsley, vol. 1, pp. 274–78.
5 FO officials sympathised with Menzies' concerns, Jebb minuting to Cadogan on 12 July 1940 that it was 'a scandal that Harker [now DG of MI5] should have been promoted to be a Brigadier, while Menzies remains a Colonel'. Cadogan appealed to the CIGS, Dill, to make Menzies a Major General, but the War Office refused to do more than make him a Brigadier, backdated to give him seniority to Harker. Correspondence on this matter, revealing a somewhat obsessive anxiety on the part of Menzies, is preserved in PUSD files, FCO.
6 No attempt is made here to go into the details of SIS/MI5 counter-espionage activities, the Double Cross system etc. Although Morton kept himself abreast of developments, no evidence has been found to indicate that he played any role in these areas other than as a conduit of information to Churchill, or to keep an eye on the treatment of Frenchmen. Curry, *Security Service*, and the *Liddell Diaries* are good sources on MI5's wartime work.
7 Note of meeting held at FO, 3 June 1940, PUSD files. The note does not record what actions, if any, flowed directly from the meeting, though two new SIS sections were set up, one under Frank Foley to rebuild SIS networks in Occupied Europe, and one to deal with providing SIS with air and sea communications
8 Hinsley, vol. 1, Chapter 5 reviews a range of sources of intelligence received in

relation to a potential German invasion of Britain, but is naturally discreet on the details of human sources.

9 Colonel, later General Gustave Bertrand, head of the *Sections des Examens* (cryptographic section) of the *Deuxième Bureau*, an outstanding figure in wartime intelligence who carried on his activities in support of British, and, in particular, Polish Intelligence while ostensibly working for the Vichy authorities. For further details of his activities see the Report of the Anglo-Polish Historical Committee.

10 DO(40)39th meeting, 31 October 1940, CAB 69/1, TNA.

11 A good example of their cooperative working was in relation to the interrogation of Hitler's deputy, Rudolf Hess, whose plane landed unexpectedly in Scotland on 11 May 1941. At Churchill's request, Menzies submitted copies of all the interrogation reports and related papers to Morton, who commented on them for the Prime Minister's benefit, though nothing has been found to support the theory that he saw Hess or knew anything about his flight until he arrived. On this and other 'Morton myths' connected with Hess see John Costello, *Ten Days that saved the West* (London: Bantam Press, 1991), David Stafford (ed), *Flight from Reality: Rudolf Hess and his Mission to Scotland 1941* (London: Pimlico, 2002) and James R. Leutze (ed), *The London Journals of General Raymond E. Lee* (Boston: Little Brown, 1971), pp. 441 and 464–65. The official record does not suggest Morton's role was in any way sinister.

12 ie 'Blue Jackets' (sometimes called 'Blue Jumbos'), a name apparently conferred by the FO after the colour of the folders in which they were circulated. However, the designation never appeared on any GC&CS reports, whose serial numbers run continuously from November 1919 to the end of the Second World War.

13 Churchill to Ismay, 5 August 1940: see Hinsley, vol. 1, p. 295. This instruction proved quite burdensome to SIS, since Churchill's habit of referring to information that had not yet filtered through to his Ministerial colleagues led them to demand personal copies of BJs for Cadogan and to the Service Directors of Intelligence as well, so that their Ministers and Chiefs could keep up to date.

14 GC&CS's diplomatic decrypts ('BJs') are in HW 12, TNA. Over 61,000 were issued between 1940 and 1944.

15 The Morton-Menzies correspondence preserved in SIS archives, confidential and friendly in tone, does not support the dismissive judgement of Menzies' biographer that the SIS Chief did 'not concern himself too much about Morton, whom 'C' regarded as a buffoon who would trip himself sooner rather than later': Cave Brown, *The Secret Servant*, p. 272.

16 The designation 'Ultra', originally indicating a very high security classification ('ultra secret'), was not used in the Enigma context at this stage in the war. The codename 'Boniface' was used for decrypted material from Bletchley Park, conforming to the official cover story that the material was received from an agent, and Churchill continued to use Boniface when he referred to it. Accounts differ as to the exact date when Ultra (abbreviated on documents to U) came into general use, but since Ultra has become the commonly accepted term to cover all decrypted material, whatever its source, I have followed the convention of using it in a generic sense. A good account is given in Stephen Budiansky, *Battle of Wits; The Complete Story of Codebreaking in World War II* (London: Viking, 2000).

17 See Hinsley, vol. 1, Chapter 5 for the part GAF Enigma played in assessing the likelihood of invasion. Technical details of the breaking of the Air key are given in Budiansky, *Battle of Wits*, Chapter 6; see also Ralph Erskine, 'Breaking Air Force and Army Enigma', in Smith & Erskine (eds), *Action This Day*.

18 Ronald Lewin, *Ultra Goes to War* (London: Penguin edn, 2001), p. 67. Lewin is rather unkind about Menzies, though conceding that 'the whisperers charged him with incompetence rather than corruption' (p. 660); one of the whisperers was Denis

Wheatley, good friend of Morton and wartime member of the London Controlling Section engaged in strategic deception, who later wrote of Menzies' 'extraordinary good fortune' in controlling Ultra, thus avoiding being 'kicked out as hopelessly incompetent' (Denis Wheatley, 'Deception in World War II', *RUSI Journal*, vol. 121, No 3, September 1976). The official record, however, shows Menzies in a better and more proactive light.

19 Report of the Anglo-Polish Historical Committee, pp. 225–27.

20 On the mechanics of Ultra's progress from Bletchley to Downing Street via Broadway Buildings see Hinsley, vol. 1, pp. 143–48 and 161–62; see also the official history of Special Liaison Units in HW 49/5, TNA. Lewin, *Ultra Goes to War*, Chapter 7, and F.W. Winterbotham, *The Ultra Secret* (London: Weidenfeld & Nicolson, 1974), Chapters 3–5, have provided, with some variation, the basis for a number of later accounts, but the latter, in particular, should be treated with caution in the light of what is known of Menzies' determination to keep Ultra under his own control.

21 See correspondence in CAB 163/11, TNA.

22 Lewin, *Ultra Goes to War*, pp. 187–88.

23 Morton to Menzies, 27 September 1940, HW 1/1, TNA. HW 1 also contains the wartime correspondence between Menzies and Churchill concerning Sigint (the 'Dir/C Archive').

24 Minute by Seal, 28 September 1940, PREM 4/80/3, TNA.

25 Although, as David Reynolds has pointed out, Churchill had always been 'something of a loose cannon in intelligence matters', contemporary observers confirm his concern to protect the existence Ultra during the war, and he agreed to extensive 'censorship' of his memoirs to keep the secret: David Reynolds, 'The Ultra Secret and Churchill's war memoirs' in *Intelligence and National Security*, vol. 20, No. 2, June 2005, pp. 209–24.

26 Colville, *Fringes of Power*, pp. 294–95.

27 See pp. 238–39.

28 Dalton diary entry, 29 April 1941, LSE/DALTON/1/24.

29 One indicator of the frequency of the meetings between Menzies and Churchill is the sparseness of their secret correspondence as preserved in SIS records: they did not need to commit much to paper.

30 SIS liaison with Polish Intelligence and non-Gaullist French Intelligence was handled by section A4, while A5 handled Free French Intelligence. Morton was in close contact with both of these, while also maintaining his own channels of communication with the Polish and French *Deuxième Bureaux*.

31 Record of second meeting of Secret Service Committee, 19 March 1941, PUSD records, FCO.

32 On 22 January 1941, for example, Morton wrote to Menzies asking if he had 'serious trouble with the physical transport of your men between this country and foreign countries', offering to speak to Churchill on SIS's behalf 'in collaboration with Ismay'. In a further letter of 28 January, he told Menzies that the shortage of air transport was affecting a range of departments, so that 'to avoid a big bang being reduced to a loud pop, someone in the chain between the JIC and the Minister of Defence ought to intervene to swell the Intelligence arguments with those of other equally important interests. The opposition is sufficiently formidable to warrant the best possible case being made.'

33 Record of second meeting of Secret Service Committee, 19 March 1941, PUSD records, FCO.

34 For a useful survey see Christopher Andrew, *For the President's eyes only: Secret Intelligence and the American Presidency from Washington to Bush* (London: HarperCollins, 1995), Chapters 3 and 4.

35 On Stephenson, see Chapter 9 above, note 56. A colourful description of Donovan's

early career is given in Joseph E Persico, *Roosevelt's Secret War* (New York, 2001); see also Anthony Cave Brown, *Wild Bill Donovan: the Last Hero* (New York: Times Books, 1982), and Thomas F. Troy, *Donovan and the CIA* (Washington DC: CIA Center for the Study of Intelligence, 1981). Troy's *Will Bill and Intrepid* usefully links the two men.

36 The official history of BSC, *British Security Coordination: the secret history of British Intelligence in the Americas 1940–45*, commissioned by Stephenson and completed in 1945, was long kept secret but is now in TNA and was published in 1998 by St Ermin's Press with a foreword by Nigel West. It is a fascinating document containing a great deal of detailed information about BSC, but was influenced strongly by Stephenson and as such must be treated with great caution except where independent evidence is available.

37 See for example Troy, *Wild Bill and Intrepid*, p. 185; Leutze, *The London Journal of General Raymond E Lee 1940–41*, pp. 464–65. Leutze had interviewed Morton in 1967, as the latter described in a letter to Thompson (Morton to Thompson, 24 June 1967, Thompson papers 1/3, LHCMA.

38 No evidence has been found to substantiate Stephenson's claims that he was Churchill's personal representative, nor indeed that he ever met the Prime Minister. It is telling, as Troy has pointed out, that Stephenson rates no more than a passing mention from Gilbert and no mention at all in the published Roosevelt-Churchill correspondence. Colville, too, denied that Stephenson and Churchill ever met. For a discussion of the evidence on both sides see Troy, *Wild Bill and Intrepid*, Chapter 13. Stephenson also told Troy that 'in the interwar years he had secretly furnished vital intelligence on German steel production'; but as Troy says, such information was furnished via Morton and the IIC, not to Churchill directly.

39 Churchill to Ismay, 17 July 1940, quoted in Gilbert, *Finest Hour*, p. 672.

40 Morton to Jacob, 18 September 1941, PREM 3/463/2, TNA, quoted in Troy, *Wild Bill and Intrepid*, pp. 132–33.

41 See p. 193 above.

42 For an informative recent account that acknowledges the centrality of Menzies' role see Douglas Charles, 'The origins of American central intelligence', in *Intelligence and National Security*, vol. 20, June 2005, No. 2, pp. 225–37.

43 Menzies to Jebb, 3 June 1940, PUSD files, FCO. According to US immigration records Stephenson and his wife arrived in New York harbour on 21 June 1940 on the SS *Britannic*: see Troy, *Wild Bill and Intrepid*, pp. 34–5.

44 Memo by Wiseman of 3 June 1940, preserved with other correspondence about Wiseman in PUSD files, FCO.

45 Record of meeting on 5 June 1940, PUSD files, FCO. Wiseman's lack of success in persuading senior officials of his *bona fides* was due at least in part to his association with the Jewish law firm of Kuhn Loeb: in a note of 3 June, Menzies stated that a friend of his in the City felt that 'any association of HMG with such a person would present the German propaganda machine with a first class opportunity of rubbing in what has constantly been reiterated, ie that we are in the hands of the Jews'.

46 Menzies to Jebb, 21 June 1940. FO telegram No. 1272 to Lothian of 26 June 1940 stated that following interviews with both Jebb and Menzies, Wiseman was now reconciled to working only through Stephenson. The wisdom of Menzies' and others' reservations about Wiseman was confirmed by later reports of his association with prominent pro-Nazis in the US (PUSD files, FCO).

47 Menzies always described Stephenson, in accordance with SIS convention, as 'my representative', even if Stephenson later claimed to have felt 'considerable contempt for Menzies and the SIS as he found it in 1940' (Troy, *Wild Bill and Intrepid*, p. 41). No evidence has been found to support Stephenson's assertion that he insisted on sending his reports directly to Churchill: if he sent copies to Morton none has been found.

48 Menzies to Henry Hopkinson (FO), 3 October 1940, PUSD records, FCO.
49 Unsigned report on visit to USA, PUSD files, FCO. The purpose of the visit had been to report on the progress of SOE in North America, so it is possible that the report was written by someone from that organisation.
50 Minute by P. Loxley (FO), 10 April 1942, PUSD files, FCO.
51 Troy, *Wild Bill and Intrepid*, p. 184.
52 Stephenson's proprietary attitude to Donovan, and the claims made by him and by Cave Brown in *Last Hero* that Donovan was in fact a British agent, are discussed in detail in Troy, *Wild Bill and Intrepid*. Nothing has been found in SIS archives to substantiate these assertions.
53 Washington telegram No 1311 of 11 July 1940, A 3542/90/45, quoted in Troy, *Wild Bill and Intrepid*, p. 45. *V. ibid.* for evidence concerning the origins and details of this visit, which remain unclear.
54 The origins and details of Donovan's second trip, on which he was accompanied by Stephenson, are also uncertain, but FO involvement in the arrangements can be followed in file A 183/45 of 1941, FO 371/26194, TNA. Variant accounts can also be found in the secondary literature. Nothing has been found to indicate any involvement by Morton in these arrangements.
55 In a letter to Hopkinson at the FO of 2 April 1941, Menzies wrote: 'Although I do not wish to emphasise unduly the role which I played in connection with Bill Donovan's visit to this country and elsewhere, I know he has no illusions regarding the extent to which I have been able to help him. You will recollect that when the decision to hand over the destroyers was made known, he wired "Give yourself fifty pats on the back"' (PUSD records, FCO). On the arrangement made in August 1940 for the supply of US destroyers see Gilbert, *Finest Hour*, pp. 732–33. Morton, in a letter of 5 July 1959 to R.W. Thompson, described the deal as 'sheer blackmail on the part of Roosevelt' (Thompson papers 1/1, LHCMA).
56 Stephenson to Menzies, transmitted to Hopkinson (FO) on 19 June 1941 (PUSD records, FCO). The same message is quoted in Troy, *Wild Bill and Intrepid*, p. 130.
57 See, for example, Morton to Churchill, 22 July 1940, PREM 7/7, TNA.
58 Morton to Churchill, 21 July 1940, PREM 7/1, TNA.
59 On Clegg and Hince's visit see Charles, 'The origins of American central intelligence'.
60 Menzies to Hopkinson, 2 April 1941, PUSD records, FCO. For an account of the first visit to GC&CS of American cryptographers in January–February 1941 see Budiansky, *Battle of Wits*, pp. 172–79. On its significance see also Michael Smith, 'An undervalued effort: how the British broke Japan's codes', and David Alvarez, 'Most helpful and cooperative: GC&CS and the development of American diplomatic cryptanalysis', both in Smith & Erskine (eds), *Action This Day*.
61 For a detailed account of the component parts and formation of SOE see Mackenzie, *SOE*, Part I. See also MRD Foot, *SOE: An Outline History of the Special Operations Executive 1940–46* (London: Pimlico edn, 1999), Chapter I. A memorandum for the War Cabinet by Chamberlain, WP(40)271 of 19 July 1940, on SE and SOE, made it clear how much SIS's authority had been eroded: Lord Swinton was given operational control over 'all the activities of MI6 in Great Britain and in Eire', and he and Dalton were to 'arrange for any consultation that may be mutually helpful or may be necessary' to prevent an overlap between the SE and SOE (CAB 121/305A, TNA).
62 See Chapter 10.
63 Stafford, *Churchill and Secret Service*, p. 186.
64 Morton to Churchill, 27 June 1940, PREM 7/7, TNA.
65 Dalton diary entry of 10 July 1940, quoted in Pimlott, *Dalton War Diaries*, pp. 56–7.
66 Dalton diary entries of 5 and 6 June 1940, quoted in Pimlott, *Dalton War Diaries*, pp. 35, 37.

67 Jebb to Cadogan, 13 June 1940: 'what you want is a tough & intelligent soldier with a knowledge of Europe & a good eye for men' (PUSD files, FCO). The eventual design of SOE provided for a Chief Executive Officer (Jebb), with Sir Frank Nelson as operational head of SO2 ('CD'), and R.A. Leeper, head of the FO's Political Intelligence Department, as head of SOE's propaganda arm, SO1; see Mackenzie, *SOE*, pp. 75–84.

68 Jebb to Cadogan, 13 June 1940, PUSD files, FCO.

69 Morton to Churchill, 27 June 1940, PREM 7/7, TNA.

70 Morton to Beaumont-Nesbitt, 28 June 1940, copy found in SOE records.

71 According to Dalton's diary for 10 May 1940, Clement Attlee, who entered Churchill's Government as Lord Privy Seal, assured him that he would get a Department of his own and told him: 'A member of the Government said to me the other day "We shall want all your tough guys"; and, said the little man, "you are one of those".' (Dalton diary, 10 May 1940, LSE/DALTON/1/22)

72 Dalton diary entries of 16 and 18 May 1940, quoted in Pimlott, *Dalton War Diary*, pp. 9 and 12. In his own memoirs Dalton described Morton as 'a fighting man and a fount of energy and bright ideas' (Dalton, *The Fateful Years*, p. 327).

73 Dalton diary entry for 1 July 1940, quoted in Pimlott, *Dalton War Diary*, p. 52. A record of the meeting held at the FO, where the attendance included the Foreign Secretary, DMI, Menzies and Hankey, is in the Dalton papers, LSE/DALTON/7/3.

74 Cadogan *Diaries*, p. 312. Cadogan commented that the idea of Swinton's taking over SOE was 'sloppy: we want to get someone to take a grip on Sabotage &c and pull it into shape. *I* think Dalton the best man.'

75 Dalton diary entry, 13 July 1940, LSE/DALTON/1/23. Part of this entry is quoted in Pimlott, *Dalton War Diary*, pp. 58–9.

76 Whether influenced by Morton or not, Churchill did hang on to the idea of Swinton's taking on SOE as well as the SE. On 9 July 1940, in response to a memo from Halifax on underground warfare, Churchill asked for Morton's views, commenting: 'I still think the Department could be under Swinton as a second branch of his work' (Churchill to Morton, 9 July 1940, CHAR 20/13, CCAC).

77 Dalton diary entry, 13 July 1940, LSE/DALTON/1/23. Presumably Morton meant this as a compliment to Grand.

78 Annex II to memo of October 5 1940 by Jebb, 'Subversion: a description of the special operations machine, and some suggestions as to future policy' (PUSD files, FCO).

79 Dalton to Grand, 18 September 1940, Dalton papers LSE/DALTON/7/3.

80 Dalton's campaign to get rid of Grand, whom he called 'King Bomba', overcame a spirited rearguard action by the latter who tried to claim that he was medically unfit for an overseas posting because of insomnia and arranged for his passage to be cancelled on the authority of 'someone from the so-called "Ministry of Defence" [i.e. No. 10]'. By October 1940, however, both the DMO&I and Menzies shared Dalton's determination that Grand should take a long sea voyage on a ship that was 'going a bloody long way'. Dalton recorded in his diary on 20 November that Grand had finally been seen boarding a ship at Liverpool: 'This seems conclusive at last.' The saga can be followed in the unpublished Dalton diaries in the LSE archives.

81 Dalton diary entry, 2 October 1940, LSE/DALTON/1/23.

82 Dalton diary entry, 22 November 1940, quote in Pimlott, *Dalton War Diary*, p. 106.

83 See Mackenzie, *SOE*, p. 80, where Venner, who became SOE's Director of Finance, is described as 'an accountant of genius'.

84 Dalton diary entry, 21 June 1940, quoted in Pimlott, *Dalton War Diary*, p. 44. The implication that this lunch took place at Whitehall Court is contained in a later entry, 30 October 1940 (LSE/DALTON/1/23). Lt Commander R.T.H. (Rex) Fletcher, later 1st Baron Winser, was a Labour MP 1935–42 and Private Secretary to the First Lord

of the Admiralty, Sir A.V. Alexander, 1940–41. He was a friend of Morton's, and Dalton's diary reveals that he passed on a good deal of information (and gossip).

85 Dalton noted in his diary on 30 October 1940 that Jebb had showed him a letter from Morton about 150 Whitehall Court (LSE/DALTON/1/23).

86 Dalton diary entry, 16 December 1940, LSE/DALTON/1/23.

87 Morton to Churchill, 11 January 1941, PREM 7/7, TNA.

88 Jebb to Morton, 15 February 1941, HS 6/309, TNA.

89 Note by Nelson, 17 February 1941, HS 6/309, TNA.

90 Dalton diary entries, 17 and 24 February 1941, quoted in Pimlott, *Dalton War Diary*, pp. 160 and 168.

91 Morton to Dalton, 24 February 1941, Dalton papers, LSE/DALTON/7/3. In his diary Dalton described this letter as a 'most oliaginous and excessively effusive roofer' (Pimlott, *Dalton War Diary*, p. 164).

92 'Most secret and strictly confidential' note of interview by Dalton, 19 December 1941, LSE/DALTON/18/2.

93 Minutes by Morton and Eden, 23 February 1942, letter from Dalton to Churchill with final report on SOE, 23 February, minute from Churchill to Eden and Bracken, 25 February 1942, PREM 3/365/8, TNA.

94 Selborne to Churchill, PREM 3/365/8, TNA.

95 Minute from Attlee to Churchill, 28 November 1940; COS(40)932 Final, 14 November, and correspondence July–December 1940 on the coordination of Intelligence, PREM 4/97/11.

96 Morton to Churchill, 20 January 1941, PREM 4/97/11, TNA.

97 Hinsley, vol. 1, p. 278.

98 Jebb to Selborne, 27 March 1942, PUSD files, FCO.

99 Memo. by Nelson, 'SOE's relationship with SIS', 4 March 1942, PUSD files, FCO.

100 Morton to Hollis, 19 May 1942, CAB 121/305A, TNA.

101 Selborne to Eden, 31 March 1942, PUSD files, FCO.

102 Selborne to Churchill, 10 April 1942, circulated as WP(42)170, PUSD files, FCO.

103 Menzies to Loxley (FO), 27 April 1942, PUSD files, FCO.

104 JP(42)502, 15 May 1942, 'SOE and SIS coordination', CAB 121/305A, TNA.

105 Comments by Menzies on JPS paper, 12 May 1942, PUSD files, FCO.

106 'Memo by an Officer in SIS', 11 May 1942, PUSD files, FCO.

107 Morton to Hollis, 19 May 1942, CAB 121/305A, TNA.

108 Morton to Hollis, 20 July 1942, CAB 121/305A.

109 Note by Ismay, 15 July 1942, CAB 121/305A.

110 E.W. (later Sir Edward) Playfair, 1909–99, served in HMT 1934–46 and 1947–56, and in COGA 1946–47. Permanent Under Secretary of State for War, 1956–59 and Permanent Secretary, Ministry of Defence 1960–61.

111 Correspondence between Selborne and Morton, 1–10 July 1942, PUSD files, FCO; on the 'Playfair Report' see Mackenzie, *SOE*, pp. 342–43.

112 Morton to Churchill, 22 October 1942, PUSD files, FCO.

113 Minutes between Eden and Cadogan, 25–26 October 1942, PUSD files, FCO.

114 See p. 267 above.

115 Morton to Churchill, 30 October 1942, PUSD files, FCO.

116 Minutes between Churchill and Morton, 1–3 November 1942, Morton to Ismay, 2 and 3 November 1942, CAB 163/3, TNA.

117 Correspondence between Capel Dunn and the Service Intelligence Directorates, Ismay to Morton, 6 November 1942, CAB 163/3, TNA.

118 Documentation on these issues can be followed in CAB 121/305A, TNA. See also M.R.D. Foot, *SOE in the Low Countries* (London: St Ermins Press, 2001), and Mackenzie, *SOE*, Chapters VIII and XXI.

119 Morton to Hollis, 16 September 1943, CAB 121/305A, TNA.

120 Correspondence between Selborne and Morton, November 1944, HS 8/924, TNA.
121 There are a number of stories alleging Morton's continuing involvement in clandestine operations, including that related by John Ainsworth Davies (writing as Christopher Creighton) in *Op JB: The Last Great Secret of the Second World War* (London: Simon and Schuster, 1996). See also the comments by Milton Shulman in his memoirs, *Marilyn, Hitler and Me* (London: Andre Deutsch, 1998). Nothing has been found in British Intelligence archives to support the idea of an elaborate scheme, in which both Morton and Fleming are said to have taken part, to exfiltrate Martin Bormann in 1945: and at the operative dates both men can be proved to have been elsewhere.
122 Churchill to Morton, 15 October 1947, PREM 7/16, TNA.

13 TREASURY TROUBLESHOOTER: 1946–1953

1 In a letter to Sir Basil Liddell Hart of 9 May 1963, Morton wrote that he had been 'technically personal assistant to Clem Attlee for a few months and did indeed do some things for him; but I persuaded him without much difficulty that there was no job for such a post on the official staff of No. 10' (LH1/531, LHCMA). The 'persuasion' is presumably a reference to his minutes written in May 1945 (see pp. 243–44 above), but no trace has been found of any particular 'jobs' he did for Attlee, who had succeeded Churchill as Prime Minister on 26 July 1945.
2 On the sudden cessation of Lend-Lease in August 1945 see documentation in *DBPO*, Series I, Vol. III, Chapter I.
3 Negotiations included the implementation of the 1944 Bretton Woods Agreements setting up the World Bank and International Bank for Reconstruction and Development, the establishment of the United Nations Organisation at the San Francisco Conference held April–June 1945 and the complex financial and industrial arrangements attached to the Protocol signed at the conclusion of the Potsdam Conference on 2 July. For detailed documentation of Bretton Woods and San Francisco see volumes in the series *Foreign Relations of the United States* (hereafter FRUS); for Potsdam see *DBPO*, Series I, Vol. I, and for the negotiation of the US loan, Vol. III. See also L.S. Pressnell, *External Economic Policy since the War*, vol. I (London: HMSO, 1986), and Peden, *Treasury and British Public Policy*.
4 For the background to Allied negotiations on reparations and German assets see *DBPO*, Series I, Vol. V.
5 See Peden, *Treasury and British Public Policy*, pp. 358 and 366–75.
6 The Final Act of the Reparations Conference, which came into operation on 24 January 1946, was published as Cmd 6721 of 1946. For an account of the Conference and its implications see *Nazi Gold: Information from the British Archives, Parts I and II* (FCO Historians, History Notes Nos 11 and 12, 1996 and 1997, Foreign & Commonwealth Office), hereafter cited as *Nazi Gold I and II*.
7 The ARC had been established by the Protocol of German Reparation drawn up at the Yalta Conference in February 1945. A useful background note by Waley is printed in *DBPO*, Series I, Vol. V, No. 10.
8 Detailed documentation of these negotiations can be found in *DBPO*, Series I, Vol. V.
9 Minutes by Hall-Patch and Cadogan, 7 and 8 January 1946, UE 168/22/77, FO 371/53134, TNA.
10 Hall-Patch to Waley, 10 January 1946, UE 168/22/77, FO 371/35134, TNA.
11 Note by Morton, 6 January 1946, sent to Hall-Patch on 7 January, UE 182/22/77, FO 371/53134, TNA. A Cabinet Committee, GEN 72, had been set up to deal with reparations issues, and Morton had studied GEN 72/68 and 72/69 of 28 and 31 December 1945.
12 Morton to Robertson, 8 January 1946, FO 1030/299, TNA. In the event, political

wrangling in IARA led to the setting up of a liaison office in Berlin rather than the other way round.

13 Detailed documentation of discussions in the Control Council in Berlin and other bodies can be found in *DBPO*, Series I, Vol. V. The difficulties posed by French objections to any form of centralised German administration, and by US determination to force through implementation of the Potsdam decisions, if necessary by supporting exigent Soviet demands, were reflected in IARA discussions in Brussels.

14 Letter from Morton dated 26 February 1946, circulated as GEN 72/77 of 5 March, UE 976/22/77, FO 371/53135, TNA. The signatories of the Paris Agreement were Albania, Australia, Belgium, Canada, Denmark, Egypt, France, Greece, India, Luxembourg, Norway, New Zealand, the Netherlands, Czechoslovakia, South Africa, the UK, the United States and Yugoslavia.

15 Morton's telegraphic correspondence with the Treasury was sent via the Brussels Embassy and the FO, though letters were sometimes sent direct. The FO files contain ongoing correspondence on the practical difficulties caused by this arrangement, though the general view, as expressed by J.G. Ward of the FO's Reconstruction Department on 25 July 1946, was that 'FO may be making a mistake if for reasons of convenience it allows Treasury or any other outside Dept to canalise corresp[ondence] with the British Rep^tve at an international conference with a big political slant' (UE 2977/22/77, FO 371/53138, TNA).

16 Summing up the problem in a letter of 2 May 1947 to David Pitblado, Morton complained that 'the Board of Trade, Ministry of Supply and TWED and others write direct and independently to Brussels sending formal instructions, which have on occasions been incompatible with the policy pursued by other Departments, though doubtless consistent with the policy of the single Department concerned. The point is that any action by the UK Delegate in Brussels in any field of Reparations has a repercussion on the whole field' (PREM 7/15, TNA). (D.B. (later Sir David) Pitblado, 1912–97, served in the Dominions Office before the war, then (1942) in the War Cabinet Offices, from where he transferred to HMT. PPS to Attlee, Churchill and Eden as Prime Ministers, 1951–56.)

17 Brussels telegram VICTIM 126 from Morton to the Foreign Office for HMT, 9 March 1946, UE 1032/22/77, FO 371/53135, TNA.

18 Lincoln (FO) to Jennings (HMT), 15 March 1946, UE 1032/22/77, FO 371/53135, TNA.

19 Morton to Abbott (HMT), 15 September 1947, T 236/932, TNA.

20 Jennings (HMT) to Turner (COGA), 28 March 1946, commenting on Morton to Jennings, 22 March, UE 1320/22/77, FO 371/53136, TNA. Lt-Gen Lucius D. Clay was Commanding General of the US Group of the Control Commission for Germany. Despite the Treasury's dismissive comments, Morton's view that Clay was 'playing politics all the time', and that his attitude was rooted in a 'markedly authoritarian' personality, was undoubtedly shared by Clay's British interlocutors in Berlin.

21 Brussels telegram 338 VICTIM, 22 May 1946, UE 2187/22/77, FO 371/53137, TNA. Morton commented that Yugoslav threats to withdraw from IARA were connected with 'the situation on wider Soviet front' and should be resisted. Bevin wrote at the foot of this telegram: 'This attitude to Yugoslavia is correct remain firm. EB.'

22 The IARA Committee on German External Assets proved particularly demanding, and Douglas Carter, of Trading with the Enemy Department, spent a good deal of time in Brussels in 1946–47 participating in its proceedings. His detailed reports to the Economic Warfare Department of the FO can be found in UE files in the FO archive at TNA.

23 Coulson to Morton, 14 March 1946, UE 891/22/77; as a member of Economic Relations Department Coulson was very familiar with Morton and his ways. Morton had described a meeting at which the Greek delegate 'came armed with many pages

of script which I have good reason to believe contained many bitter phrases' that he later did not use, commenting: 'I hope that the line I took not only made a good point for the United Kingdom but helped to accelerate my Greek colleague's rate of discard which it was intended to do' (Brussels telegram VICTIM 94, 1 March 1946, UE 891/22/77, FO 371/53135, TNA).

24 Morton to Coulson (FO), 22 March 1946, UE 1274/22/66, FO 371/53136, TNA.

25 Part III of the Final Act stated that all monetary gold found in Germany by the Allied forces, except for coins of numismatic or historical value, should be pooled for delivery as restitution to the formerly occupied countries in proportion to their respective losses through looting or wrongful removal to Germany. Non-monetary gold, defined in May 1947 after much tricky negotiation as 'all unidentifiable articles of intrinsic value looted from persons confined by Nazis in concentration camps', came under Part I, Article 8 of the Final Act, which stated that all non-monetary gold found in Germany should be made available to the Inter-Governmental Committee on Refugees for the rehabilitation of non-repatriable persons who had suffered at the hands of the Nazis. For full details see *Nazi Gold II*.

26 Waley to Morton, 26 June 1946, T 236/986, TNA, quoted in *Nazi Gold II*, p. 11.

27 *Nazi Gold I*, p. 9.

28 See *Nazi Gold II*, pp. 11ff. Both the French and American Governments were inclined to the wider definition, while the British view, as expressed by Morton, was that to allow claims for private holdings would mean that 'no-one will get any gold at all for a very long time' (*ibid.*).

29 Morton to Humphreys-Davies (HMT), 15 September 1946, PREM 7/15, TNA.

30 Minute by Beckett, 24 January 1947, UE 594/6/77, FO 371/62838, TNA.

31 Brussels tel. VICTIM 58 from Carter, 20 February 1947, and FO tel. 96 VICTIM to Brussels, 22 February 1947, UE 1087/6/77, FO 371/62840, TNA.

32 Sir R.E.L. Wingate, Bart (1889–1978), who had a distinguished career in the Middle East and India between the wars, served in MEW, accompanied the Dakar expedition in 1940 as Political Agent and worked with SOE in West Africa. From 1942 he was in LCS, becoming Deputy Controlling Officer in March 1943 and later writing the 'Historical Record of Deception in the War against Germany and Italy', preserved in CAB 154/100–101, TNA. He and Morton had close professional connections throughout the Second World War but may well have known each other long before.

33 Humphreys-Davies (HMT) to Morton, 21 February 1947, PREM 7/15, TNA.

34 For an account of TGC discussions at this time see *Nazi Gold II*. Negotiations for an agreement on German assets can be followed in file UE 6/77 in the FO archives at TNA.

35 Morton to Playfair (HMT), 12 June 1947, PREM 7/15, TNA.

36 Record of meeting at Norfolk House, 10 July 1947, T 236/988, TNA.

37 Morton to Raven, 14 July 1947, T 236/931, TNA.

38 The Marshall Plan or Economic Recovery Programme was drawn up in the summer of 1947 following the US Secretary of State's announcement on 5 June that the US would provide economic help for the restoration of European prosperity. See Alan Milward, *The Reconstruction of Western Europe* (London: Routledge, 1984).

39 Memo from Morton to Playfair (HMT), 11 August 1947, T 236/932, TNA.

40 See *Nazi Gold II*, pp. 17ff.

41 Morton to Rickett (HMT), 24 September 1947, PREM 7/15, TNA.

42 Morton to Playfair (HMT), 27 September 1947, and Playfair to Morton, 4 October, T 236/983, TNA.

43 Morton to Thompson, 24 November 1947, Thompson papers 1/1, LHCMA.

44 Morton to Rickett (HMT), 19 December 1947, PREM 7/15, TNA.

45 Morton to Thompson, 6 December 1947, Thompson papers 1/1, LHCMA.

46 Morton to D.H. Maitland (HMT), 21 January 1948, T 236/985, TNA.

47 Morton to Playfair (HMT), 25 March 1948, T 236/1019.

48 Morton to Wingate, 5 April 1948, PREM 7/15, TNA.

49 See *Nazi Gold II*, pp. 22–24.

50 Morton to Abbott (HMT), 4 May 1948, T 236/1020, TNA.

51 Morton wrote to Wingate on 10 August 1948 regarding proposals for cutting down the UK Delegation's establishment in Brussels: 'I wonder how long it would take Stalin to settle a trifle of this sort if it was a question of Soviet representation' (PREM 7/15, TNA).

52 Morton to Witham (RDR Division, CCG(BE)), 26 November 1948, PREM 7/15, TNA.

53 Wheatley's novel of the supernatural, *The Haunting of Toby Jugg*, had been published in 1948.

54 Morton to Wheatley, 1 January 1949, Wheatley papers, Ian Sayer Collection.

55 Note by Morton of meeting with Roger Stevens (FO), 3 February 1949, PREM 7/15, TNA.

56 Robertson (HMT) to Wingate (Brussels), 31 March 1949, PREM 7/15, TNA.

57 In September 1948 Sir Raphael Cilento, head of the UN's Disaster Relief Organisation, estimated the total number of refugees as 400,000, with roughly half still in Palestine and half in neighbouring states. By December, when Cilento had been succeeded by an American, Stanton Griffis, it was 750,000, comprising roughly 500,000 in Palestine, 50,000 within Israel and the rest in neighbouring Arab states; numbers rose to 950,000 by the spring of 1949 (details of UN estimates of Arab refugees can be found in correspondence in file E 10748/31, FO 371/68677-83, TNA).

58 According to a memo of 30 April 1949 by the FO Permanent Under-Secretary's Committee (PUSC), 5m out of the world's 10m Jews resided in the US (PUSC(19), E 13989/1052/65, FO 371/75067, TNA).

59 The 1939 White Paper setting out the British Government's policy in regard to Palestine envisaged the creation of an independent Palestinian state within ten years, with power shared by Arabs and Jews. Meanwhile, Jewish immigration to Palestine was restricted to 75,000 over the next five years.

60 Alan Bullock, *Ernest Bevin, Foreign Secretary* (London: Heinemann, 1983), p. 164. Bullock is a useful source for a succinct account of the Palestine issue, 1945–50.

61 A UNGA Resolution of 19 November 1948, which had established the UN Relief for Palestine Refugees programme (UNRPR), provided for the appointment of a technical committee of enquiry into possible schemes for the employment and resettlement of refugees. The British authorities had hoped, however, that this work could be carried out instead by existing bodies such as the British Middle East Office (BMEO) where the requisite technical expertise already lay.

62 Minute on Beirut tel. No 129 to FO, 9 March 1949, E 3165/1821/31, FO 371/75421, TNA.

63 Minute by J.G.S. Beith, FO Eastern Department, 14 May 1949, E 5970/1821/31, FO 371/75426, TNA.

64 FO Eastern Department minuting, 25 May and 3 June 1949, E 7344, 7442/1821/31, FO 371/75429, TNA.

65 FO minuting on the Survey Group, 14 June–4 July 1949, E 7558, 7817, 7957, 8166/1821/31, FO 371/75430-31, TNA.

66 Minute by Maitland, 13 June 1949, E 7625/1821/31, FO 371/75430, TNA.

67 Minute by Maitland, 14 June 1949, E 7558/1821/31, FO 371/75430, TNA.

68 F.R. Hoyer Millar (HM Embassy, Washington) to Michael Wright, Under-Secretary superintending Eastern Department, 22 July 1949, E 9401/1821/31, FO 371/75435, TNA.

69 Morton to Beith (Eastern Department), 29 July 1949, E 9603/1821/31, FO 371/75435, TNA.

70 Morton to Sheringham (FO), 12 and 24 August 1949, E 9884, 10323/1821/31, FO 371/75436, TNA.

71 UKDel New York tel 1720 to FO, 25 August 1949, E 10315/1821/31, FO 371/75436, TNA.

72 The Tennessee Valley Authority scheme (TVA), an extensive flood control and irrigation development in the south-eastern US, was established in 1933 as part of President Roosevelt's New Deal programme of major public works to provide employment and stimulate economic prosperity. Clapp was general manager of the project from 1939–46, when Truman appointed him to head the board of directors.

73 Statement by the President, 26 August 1949, copy in E 10797/1821/31, FO 371/75437, TNA.

74 Brief by Burrows (FO), with minute by Strang, 6 September 1949, E 11182/1821/31, FO 371/75438, TNA.

75 Beirut tel 551 to FO, 10 September 1949, E 11003/1821/31, FO 371/75438, TNA.

76 Morton to Wright, 13 September 1949, E 11897/1821/31, FO 371/75440, TNA.

77 Morton to Wright, *ibid.*

78 In mid-November, Morton submitted to the Middle East Secretariat of the FO a full list of the personnel of the Mission, which ran to some sixty persons, marking against their names those who had been 'given to us by the Secretary-General of the United Nations unasked'. Although the FO considered many of Morton's comments 'somewhat lurid', they agreed that the Mission was 'grossly over-staffed', though it was agreed that it would be better for Clapp to raise the matter himself with the UN (E 14231/1821/31, FO 371/75449, TNA).

79 Beirut tel 564 to FO, 16 September 1949, E 11297/1821/31, FO 371/75439, TNA.

80 Beirut tel 565 to FO, 17 September 1949, E 11320/1821/31, FO 371/75439, TNA.

81 BMEO Cairo tel 414 to FO, 20 September 1949, E 11425/1821/31, FO 371/75439, TNA.

82 Beirut tel 582 to FO, 23 September 1949, E 11580/1821/31, FO 371/75439, TNA.

83 For Morton's comments on the Mission's visits see Beirut tels 609 and 613, 1 and 2 October 1949, with Eastern Department minuting, E 11917, 11933/1821/31, FO 371/75441, TNA.

84 Beirut tels 619 and 643, 3 and 13 October 1949, with FO minuting and press cuttings, E 11938 and 12415/1821/31, FO 371/75441, 75443, TNA.

85 Colville, *Fringes of Power*, p. 211.

86 Telegrams dated 27 September–1 October 1949 relating to the threat to Morton's safety can be found in E 11678–11916/1821/31, FO 371/75440, TNA.

87 Morton to Wheatley, 4 January 1950, Wheatley papers, Ian Sayer Collection.

88 Respectively Israeli Foreign Minister and Director General of the Ministry of Finance.

89 Beirut tel 642 to FO, 13 October 1949, E 12411/1821/31, FO 371/75443, TNA.

90 Knox Helm (Tel Aviv) to Burrows (Eastern Department), 17 October 1949, E 12745/1821/31, FO 371/75444. TNA.

91 Correspondence between Horowitz and Morton, 25 October and 4 November 1949, PREM 7/13, TNA.

92 Beirut tel 662 to FO, 18 October 1949, E 12637/1821/31, FO 371/75444, TNA.

93 Minute by Sheringham (Eastern Department), 28 October 1949, E 13351/1821/31, FO 371/75445, TNA.

94 FO tels 10356 and 10447 to Washington, repeated to Middle East posts plus Paris and Angora [Ankara], 1 November 1949, E 13239, 13351/1821/31, FO 371/75445, TNA.

95 Summary of the interim report in FO tel 1934 to Cairo, 10 November 1949, and full text, E 13588/1821/31, FO 371/75446.

96 BMEO tel 484 from Cairo to FO, 12 November 1949, E 13701/1821/31, FO 371/75446, TNA.

97 FO tel to Cairo and Middle East posts, 19 November 1949, E 13588/1821/31, FO 371/75446, TNA.

98 UKDel New York tel 2692 to FO, 25 November 1949, E 14154/1821/31, FO 371/75448, TNA.

99 FO tel 974 to Beirut, 29 November 1949, E 14439/1821/31, FO 371/75449, TNA.

100 Sir A. Cadogan had been UK Permanent Representative to the United Nations since January 1946.

101 UKDel New York tel 2765, 30 November 1949, E 14442/1821/31, FO 371/75449, TNA

102 Outline of draft findings sent to the FO by Morton on 5 December 1949 in Beirut tel 800, E 14582/1821/31, FO 371/75450, TNA.

103 Record of meeting on 20 December 1949, E 15407/1821/31, FO 371/75452, TNA.

104 See minuting on EE 1825/2 of 1950, FO 371/82242, TNA.

105 Morton to Wheatley, 4 January 1950, Wheatley papers, Ian Sayer Collection.

106 Bevin to Morton, 28 February 1950; Morton's reply of 1 March noted that the job had been 'a queer one', but that Bevin's letter 'more than makes up for all its queerness' (EE 1824/21, FO 371/82241, TNA).

107 The Treasury had assumed that Morton would be the obvious candidate to serve on the Advisory Commission of NERWA, but Lie soon made it clear that such an appointment would be resented bitterly. Sir Henry Knight, former adviser to the Secretary of State for India, was nominated instead.

108 Morton to Sheringham (FO), 23 March 1950, EE 18124/24, FO 371/82241, TNA.

109 Morton to Wright, 3 March 1950, enclosing text of article, E 1102/4, FO 371/81941, TNA. His presence at Ashridge was noted in *The Times*, 7 March 1950.

110 Documentation on this struggle during 1945–46 can be found in *DBPO*, Series I, Vols. III and IV.

111 See *DBPO*, Series I, Vol. IV. For the Air Transport Agreement signed on 11 February *v. ibid.*, No. 28. The 'five freedoms', which had been defined in the International Air Transport Agreement negotiated at the Chicago Conference in 1944, conferred the right (1) to fly across a territory without landing, (2) to land for non-traffic purposes, (3) to put down passengers, mail and cargo taken on in the territory of the state whose nationality the aircraft possessed, (4) to take on passengers, mail and cargo destined for the state whose nationality the aircraft possessed, and (5) to take on passengers, mail and cargo destined for the territory of any other contracting state and to put down passengers, mail and cargo coming from any such territory. The British government did not wish to grant Fifth Freedom rights in any territory under its protection.

112 The British Protected States in the Persian Gulf, Kuwait, Bahrain, Sharjah and Qatar, were independent sovereign Sheikhdoms which had granted to HMG by treaty jurisdiction over all British subjects and most foreigners. In practice this gave the British Government considerable influence over the operation of foreign companies in the region, partly because the Sheikhdoms had little company law of their own. The constitutional and legal position was, however, complex and open to challenge.

113 Memo by Morton DM/01, 28 August 1950, sent to W. Harpham at the FO's General Department on 5 September, GA 4/44, FO 371/84710, TNA.

114 Note of meeting on negotiation of the proposed UK-Iraq agreement, 11 September 1950, GA 4/45, FO 371/84710, TNA.

115 Minutes by Slater and Hayter, 11 and 12 September 1950, GA 4/45, FO 371/84710, TNA.

116 FO tel 549 to Bagdad, 27 September 1950, GA 4/47, FO 371/84710, TNA.

117 Lord (Frank) Pakenham, later the 7th Earl of Longford (1902–2001), prominent Catholic and legal reformer; served as Lord Privy Seal in Harold Wilson's Labour Government, 1964–70.

118 Morton (Treasury) to Mills (MCA), 3 October 1950, GA 35/99, FO 371/84747, TNA.

119 Morton's reports on his tour of the Persian Gulf and Middle East, October–December 1950, are in PREM 7/12, TNA.

120 In a note of 14 November 1950 Morton described Mostert as having 'all the short-sighted obstinacy of the primitive Boer farmer' and an 'innate dislike of the English' (GA 4/55, FO 371/84710, TNA). BOAC defended their employee's integrity some-what indignantly, though admitting that he tended to take an obstructionist and negative attitude.

121 On 16 December Sir Rupert Hay informed the Political Agent at Kuwait that Bevin had agreed to allow the King's Regulation which should now be discussed with the Ruler: Bahrain telegram 48 Saving to Kuwait, 16 December 1950, GA 35/130, FO 371/84749, TNA.

122 Bagdad tel 44 to FO, 18 January 1951, GA 93/1, FO 371/93181, TNA.

123 Minute by Slater, 20 February 1951; FO tel 182 to Bagdad of 23 February informed Mack that it was proposed that Morton should visit Bagdad about the middle of March (GA 93/5, FO 371/93181, TNA).

124 Minute by Morton, 8 March 1951, GA 93/11, FO 371/93181, TNA.

125 Bagdad tel 185 from Morton to Cribbett, 14 March 1951, GA 93/22, FO 371/93181, TNA.

126 FO tel 277 to Bagdad, 29 March 1951, GA 93/22, FO 371/93181, TNA, in which file the negotiations can be tracked.

127 Minute by Slater (General Dept, FO) on Bagdad tel 332, 20 April 1951, GA 93/43, FO 371/93182, TNA. The Agreement was published as Cmd. 8393 of 1951, 'Agreement between the Government of the United Kingdom and the Government of Iraq for Air Services between and beyond their respective territories'.

128 Report by Morton on the negotiation of an Air Services agreement between HM Government and the Royal Iraqi Government, 1 May 1951, GA 93/49, FO 371/93182, TNA.

129 Minute by Harpham (General Dept, FO) reporting Cribbett's views, 10 May 1951, GA 93/49. Letter from Troutbeck to E.A. Berthoud (FO), 6 June, GA 93/53, FO 371/93182, TNA.

130 Makins (FO) to Cribbett (MCA), 15 June 1951, GA 93/53, FO 371/93182, TNA.

131 Cribbett (MCA) to Makins (FO), 19 June 1951, GA 93/56, FO 371/93182, TNA.

132 Morton to Thompson, 9 November 1951, Thompson papers 1/1, LHCMA. 22 Kew Green has a Blue Plaque, commemorating not Morton but Arthur Hughes (1832–1915), the pre-Raphaelite painter who lived (and died) there.

14 ENERGETICALLY AWAITING DEATH: 1953–71

1 A phrase used by Morton in a letter to R.W. Thompson, dated 11 October 1962: see p. 318 below

2 See p. 279 above.

3 Morton wrote to Thompson on 18 October 1956 that he had refused to allow his cook to have a cat: 'However, the patron saint of cats has resolved the potential difficulty, by providing a Persian, coal black and suitably appealing, which does not belong to us here. It refuses to live in a house, but comes and knocks on the front door when it wants food, comfort or to be dried (by the cook) with one of my best bath towels. Happily it cannot reach the electric bell.' (Thompson papers 1/1, LHCMA). Jezebel seems to have moved in, since she is a regular feature of Morton's letters and produced several litters of kittens in the folds of his drawing room curtains.

4 Morton wrote to Thompson on 4 July 1958: 'I do not go away, partly because I am much happier at home, and partly because where in hades would I go to? All my rich friends and relations are dead, and to stay in a hotel with nothing to do and only the

usual type of hotel dweller to talk to, would be purgatory (Thompson papers 1/1, LHCMA).

5 Morton's correspondence with both Thompson and Liddell Hart is preserved in the Liddell Hart Centre for Military Archives at King's College London. I am indebted to Mr Ian Sayer for making available to me copies of Morton's correspondence with Wheatley (concerned principally with books both had read, or arrangements to meet).

6 Thompson to Sir W. Deakin, 2 December 1974, Thompson papers 1/7, LHCMA.

7 R.W. Thompson, *The Price of Victory* (London: Constable, 1960); *The Yankee Marlborough* (London: George Allen & Unwin, 1963).

8 Thompson, *Churchill and Morton*. In a letter of 9 December 1961 Morton wrote to Thompson: 'if you every refer to me publicly in your book or anywhere else, I shall never forgive you' (printed in part *ibid.*, pp. 203–4).

9 Lady Soames told the author in 2000 that she had been 'shocked and upset' by the book, though sympathetic to Morton's feelings at being excluded from Churchill's friendship, as he saw it, after 1945. Sir W. Deakin wrote to Thompson on 3 August 1976 describing himself as 'shocked and bewildered' by the book (Thompson papers 1/7, LHCMA).

10 IRD was set up in 1948 as part of the British Government's effort to combat Soviet propaganda and Communist influence worldwide. It was funded from the Secret Vote, but made use of the overt tools of public diplomacy, such as the BBC World Service, the press and exchange and visitor programmes. It was wound up in 1977. For an account of its origins and early work see FCO History Note No. 9, *IRD: Origins and Establishment of the Foreign Office Information Research Department, 1946–48* (FCO, 1995). A selection of IRD files is being released to The National Archives in a rolling programme, and can be found in FO 1110.

11 An anti-Communist group set up in July 1948 by the Radical Socialist Deputy Jean-Paul David, who wished to establish links with a similar organisation in the UK. An IRD note on *Paix et Liberté* dated 18 February 1953 is preserved at PR 143/9, FO 1110/547, TNA.

12 IRD papers, FCO.

13 See Chapter 4 above.

14 IRD papers, FCO.

15 The focus of the Sword of the Spirit, which was supported by Cardinal Hinsley, was 'a just social order'. Apart from the reference in IRD papers, no evidence has been found linking Morton to the organisation, but its aims were in accordance with his views, and his prominence in Catholic laity matters makes it likely that he was associated with it in some way.

16 Morton to Liddell Hart, 3 April 1953, LH 1/531, LHCMA.

17 Morton to Liddell Hart, 12 November 1953, LH 1/531,LHCMA. See also correspondence 23 October–5 November 1953, *ibid.*

18 Morton to Thompson, 18 October 1956, Thompson papers 1/1, LHCMA.

19 *Ibid.*

20 Morton to Thompson, 22 August 1963, Thompson papers 1/2, LHCMA.

21 Morton to Thompson, 22 May 1957, Thompson 1/1, LHCMA.

22 Morton to Thompson, 25 August 1958, Thompson 1/1, LHCMA. Morton's words had some effect in that Thompson entitled his next book *Boy in Blinkers* (1958).

23 Morton to Thompson, 15 February and 4 July 1958, Thompson papers 1/1, LHCMA.

24 Morton to Thompson, 26 July 1958, Thompson papers 1/1, LHCMA.

25 Morton to Thompson, 5 June 1962, Thompson papers1/2, LHCMA.

26 Morton to Thompson, 3 July 1962, Thompson papers 1/2, LHCMA.

27 Morton to Wheatley, 19 November 1959, Ian Sayer collection. The letter continued: 'Not your line, but if my recruitment of an irregular but determined force to march to

the Ministry of Health and hang the Minister and many of his deplorable staff gets nearer realisation, I feel sure you will join up as "Chief Mystifier of the Enemy".'

28 Morton to Thompson, 12 November 1962, Thompson papers 1/2, LHCMA.
29 Morton to Liddell Hart, 25 March 1967, LH 1/53, LHCMA.
30 Interview with the author, 25 June 2002.
31 Morton to Thompson, 17 January 1966, Thompson papers 1/3, LHCMA.
32 It is not clear when Morton and Parker first met, though Morton told Thompson that they had 'worked together, officially and unofficially, in various jobs and interests for nearly 30 years continuously'. Parker had served in the Indian Civil Service until returning to the UK in 1936. During the Second World War he was in the Ministry of Information, and subsequently worked in CCG(BE) on the re-establishment of German Trades Unions. In 1955 Morton proposed him to serve on the Board of the Hammersmith Hospitals. Parker's first wife, the artist Olivia Lucas, died in 1958; she did not get on with Morton, and did not visit him with her husband. Parker had met Gil Elles at Beaufort Gardens during the war, then again at Kew Green in 1959. However, Parker was already a sick man when they married and died two years later. (Information from John Parker, Richard Parker's son by his first wife).
33 Interview with John and Mrs Gil Parker, June 2002.
34 Whitley Councils were joint employer-employee industrial councils, set up to decide matters of pay and conditions.
35 Morton to Thompson, 18 January 1965, Thompson papers 1/3, LHCMA.
36 Morton to Thompson, 23 June 1965, Thompson papers 1/3, LHCMA.
37 Morton to Thompson, 17 January 1966, Thompson papers 1/3, LHCMA.
38 Morton to Thompson, letters of 15 and 27 August 1966, Thompson papers 1/3, LHCMA.
39 Literary critic, and author of a number of books on themes related to religion and the Catholic church.
40 Morton to Thompson, 28 February 1967, Thompson papers 1/3, LHCMA.
41 Morton to Thompson, 18 September 1967, Thompson papers 1/3, LHCMA.
42 In a letter of 23 December 1970 to Mr Philip Daniel, Vice-Chairman of the National Council for the Lay Apostolate, Morton wrote that only he and the Duke of Norfolk 'remain alive and aware of the uproar which took place when I myself was mistakenly appointed a member of the Laity Commission. An uneasy compromise was reached, with the agreed proviso of "Never again must the mistake be made". The fact is that the Catholic Union is and remains absolutely *sui generis*, and has no relations with any other Catholic Body in the world'. I am grateful to Mr Daniel for making copies of this correspondence available.
43 Morton to Thompson, 23 April 1967, Thompson papers 1/3, LHCMA.
44 Morton to Thompson, 29 July 1967, Thompson papers 1/3, LHCMA.
45 Morton to Thompson, 28 July 1969, Thompson papers 1/3, LHCMA.
46 Morton to Thompson, 26 October 1970, Thompson papers 1/3, LHCMA.
47 See Bennett, *Zinoviev Letter of 1924*, p. 2. Miss Bagot's memorandum of 1970 commented extensively on the part played by Morton in the affair.
48 Morton to Craigmyle, 14 January 1971, copy made available by Mr Philip Daniel. Rejecting a suggestion by J.W. Partridge, chairman of the National Council for the Lay Apostolate, concerning liaison between that body and the Catholic Union, Morton's letter concluded: 'I hope however we can avoid discussing that with Partridge, pheasants, hares and other rare and unseemly beasts of the forest.'
49 Mrs Gil Parker to Thompson, 6 July and 8 August 1971, Thompson papers 1/7, LHCMA.
50 Morton to Thompson, 9 December 1961, Thompson papers 1/2, LHCMA.
51 Morton to Thompson, 11 October 1962, Thompson papers 1/2, LHCMA.

EPILOGUE

1 Morton to Thompson, 11 October 1959, Thompson papers 1/1, LHCMA.
2 Morton to Thompson, 20 August 1960, quoted in Thompson, *Churchill and Morton*, p. 78.
3 Roskill to Joan Bright Astley, 11 September 1976. I am grateful to Mrs Bright Astley for permission to cite this letter.
4 Mary Soames (ed), *Speaking for Themselves: the Personal Letters of Winston and Clementine Churchill* (London: Black Swan edn, 1999), p. 454.
5 Colville, *Fringes of Power*, p. 428.
6 Morton to Thompson, 1 July 1960, quoted in *Churchill and Morton*, p. 45.
7 Interview with Sir Martin Gilbert, 26 November 2003. In Sir Martin's view, Churchill's only close friendships were with Beaverbrook and Lindemann; and, like Morton, he was never wholly at ease on intimate terms with women.
8 Morton to Thompson, 26 July 1960, quoted in *Churchill and Morton*, p. 61.

SOURCE NOTE AND
BIBLIOGRAPHY

Note on Sources

The records of the Secret Intelligence Service are not released into the public domain, in line with the organisation's commitment never to reveal the identities of individuals or organisations cooperating with them. No file references or file titles are given in the text or notes for records that are not available to public inspection. This applies also to files of the FCO's Permanent Under-Secretary's Department (PUSD), except for the pre-Second World War papers that have already been transferred into the public domain.

Unpublished documents

BP Archive, University of Warwick

Cambridge University Library (CUL)
    Hardinge, Lord
    Templewood, Lord

Churchill College Archives Centre, Cambridge (CCAC)
    Cadogan, Sir Alexander (ACAD)
    Churchill, Sir Winston (CHUR)
    Chartwell Trust Papers (CHAR)
    Hankey, Lord (HNKY)
    Spears, Sir Edward (SPRS)
    Vansittart, Lord (VNST)
    Wilkinson, Gerald (WILK)

Imperial War Museum, London (IWM)
    Kell, Sir Vernon

Liddell Hart Centre for Military Archives, King's College, London (LHCMA)
    Liddell Hart, Sir Basil
    Thompson, R.W.

London School of Economics Archives (LSE)
    Dalton, Hugh

Royal Artillery Historical Trust, Firepower Museum, Royal Arsenal, Woolwich (RAHT)
War Diary of 2nd Lt A.E. Robinson, MD/89
42nd Brigade War Diary

The National Archives, Kew, Surrey (TNA)
Admiralty (ADM)
Air Ministry (AIR)
Cabinet Office (CAB)
Foreign Office (FO)
Government Code & Cypher School (HW)
Prime Minister's Office (PREM)
Security Service (KV)
Special Operations Executive (HS)
Treasury (T)
War Office (WO)

Published Documents and Official Histories

British Security Coordination: The Secret History of British Intelligence in the Americas 1940–45 (completed 1945; published London: St Ermin's Press, 1998)
Curry, J.C.: *The Security Service 1908–45* (London: Public Record Office, 1999)
Documents on British Foreign Policy 1919–1939 (DBFP)(London: HMSO, 1946–86)
First Series (1919–25, 27 vols)
Series Ia (1925–29, 7 vols)
Second Series (1931–38, 21 vols)
Third Series (1938–39, 9 vols plus Index))
Documents on British Policy Overseas (DBPO) (London: HMSO/TSO/Frank Cass, 1984–)
Series I (1945–50, 8 vols)
Series II (1950–60, 4 vols)
Series III (1960–, 3 vols)
Foot, M.R.D.: *SOE in France* (London: HMSO, 1966; revised edn Frank Cass, 2004)
SOE in the Low Countries (London: St Ermins Press, 2001)
FCO History Notes (London: Foreign & Commonwealth Office)
No. 7: *My Purdah Lady: the Foreign Office and the Secret Vote, 1782–1909* (1994)
No. 9: *IRD: Origins and Establishment of the Foreign Office Information Research Department, 1946–48* (1995)
Nos. 11 & 12: *Nazi Gold: Information from the British Archives, Parts I and II* (1996, 1997)
No. 14: *A most extraordinary and mysterious business: the Zinoviev Letter of 1924* (1999)
Garnett, David: *The Secret History of PWE: the Political Warfare Executive 1939–45* (completed 1947; published London: St Ermin's Press, 2002).
Hinsley, F.H. *et al*, *British Intelligence in the Second World War*, vols. 1–5 (London: HMSO, 1979–90)
Mackenzie, William: *The Secret History of SOE: the Special Operations Executive 1940–1945* (completed 1947; published London: St Ermin's Press, 2000)

Medlicott, W.N.: *The Economic Blockade*, Vols. I and II (London: HMSO, revised edn 1978; first published 1952)

O'Halpin, Eunan (ed): *MI5 and Ireland 1939–1945: The Official History* (Dublin: Irish Academic Press, 2003)

Pressnell, L.S.: *External Economic Policy since the War*, vol. I (London: HMSO, 1986)

Report of the Anglo-Polish Historical Committee, *Intelligence Cooperation between Poland and Great Britain during World War II* (Vol I: London: Valentine Mitchell, 2005; Vol II (Documents): Warsaw, 2006)

Richards, Brooks: *Secret Flotillas: Vol. I: Clandestine Sea Operations to Brittany, 1940–1944; Vol. II: Clandestine Sea Operations in the Mediterranean, North Africa and the Adriatic 1940–1944* (London: Frank Cass, 2004; one-volume edn published HMSO, 1996)

The World War I Collection: *British Battles of World War I, 1914–15* (London: The Stationery Office, 2001)

Biography, Diary and Memoir

Avon, The Earl of: *The Eden Memoirs* (London: Cassell, 1960–65): *Full Circle* (1960), *Facing the Dictators* (1962), *The Reckoning* (1965)

Ball, Simon: *The Guardsmen: Harold Macmillan, Three Friends and the World They Made* (London: HarperCollins, 2004)

Beesly, Patrick: *Very Special Admiral: The Life of Admiral J.H. Godfrey C.B.* (London: Hamish Hamilton, 1980)

Birkenhead, The Second Earl of: *F.E.: The Life of F.E. Smith, the First Earl of Birkenhead, by his son* (London, Eyre & Spottiswode, 1965)

Blake, Robert (ed), *The Private Papers of Douglas Haig 1914–1919* (London: Eyre & Spottiswode, 1952)

Booth, Martin: *A Magick Life: A Biography of Aleister Crowley* (London: Hodder & Stoughton, 2000)

Brendon, Piers: *Winston Churchill: A Biography* (New York: Harper & Row, 1984)

Bright Astley, Joan: *The Inner Circle: A View of War at the Top* (London: Hutchinson, 1971)

Brivati, Brian: *Hugh Gaitskell* (London: Hodder & Stoughton, 1997)

Bruce Lockhart, Robert: *Memoirs of a British Agent* (London: 1932)

Bruce Lockhart, Robin: *Reilly: Ace of Spies* (London: Hodder & Stoughton, 1967)

Bullock, Alan: *Ernest Bevin, Foreign Secretary* (London: Heinemann, 1983)
    Hitler and Stalin: Parallel Lives (London: revised edn, Fontana Press, 1998)

Cave Brown, Anthony: *Wild Bill Donovan: the Last Hero* (New York: Times Books, 1982)
    The Secret Servant: The Life of Sir Stewart Menzies, Churchill's Spymaster (London: Michael Joseph, 1988)

Charmley, John: *Duff Cooper: The Authorized Biography* (London: Weidenfeld & Nicolson, 1986)
    Churchill: the End of Glory (London: Hodder & Stoughton, 1993)

Churchill, Randolph S.: *Winston Churchill, Vols. I–II and Companion Volumes* (London: Heinemann, 1966–69)
    Vol. I. Youth 1874–1900 (1966) (with two Companion Volumes, 1967)
    Vol. II. Young Statesman 1900–14 (1967) (with three Companion Volumes, 1969)

Churchill, W.S.: *The Second World War, Vols. I–VI* (London: Cassell, 1948–54):
　Vol. I: The Gathering Storm (1948)
　Vol. II: Their Finest Hour (1949)
　Vol. III: The Grand Alliance (1950)
　Vol. IV: The Hinge of Fate (1951)
　Vol. V: Closing the Ring (1952)
　Vol. VI: Triumph and Tragedy (1954)
Colville, John: *Footprints in Time: Memories* (London: Collins, 1976)
　The Churchillians (London: Weidenfeld & Nicolson, 1981)
　The Fringes of Power: Downing Street Diaries 1939–1955 (London: Hodder & Stoughton, 1985)
Cook, Andrew: *On His Majesty's Secret Service: Sidney Reilly Codename ST1* (London: Tempus, 2002; revised edn published 2004 as *Ace of Spies: the True Story of Sidney Reilly*)
　To Kill Rasputin: the Life and Death of Grigori Rasputin (London: Tempus, 2005)
Cross, J.A.: *Lord Swinton* (Oxford: Clarendon Press, 1982)
Dalton, Hugh: *Call Back Yesterday: Memoirs, 1887–1931* (London: Muller, 1953)
　The Fateful Years: Memoirs 1931–1945 (London: Muller, 1957)
Danchev, Alex: *Alchemist of War: The Life of Basil Liddell Hart* (London: Weidenfeld & Nicolson, 1998)
　with Todman, Daniel (eds), *Field Marshal Lord Alanbrooke, War Diaries 1939–1945* (London: Phoenix Press, 2002)
De Gaulle, Charles: *Mémoires de Guerre, Vols. I–III* (Librairie Plon edn, 1952–59):
　L'Appel, 1940–1942 (1952)
　L'Unité, 1942–1944 (1956)
　Le Salut, 1944–1946 (1959)
Dilks, David (ed), *The Diaries of Sir Alexander Cadogan 1938–1945* (London: Cassell, 1971)
Dukes, Paul: *Red Dusk and the Morrow* (London: 1923)
Egremont, Max: *Under Two Flags: The Life of Major General Sir Edward Spears* (London: Phoenix edn, 1997)
Fort, Adrian: *'Prof': the life of Frederick Lindemann* (London: Jonathan Cape, 2003)
Gilbert, Martin: *Winston Churchill*, Vols. III–VIII and Companion Volumes (London: Heinemann, 1971–88)
　Vol. III. 1914–16 (1971) (with two Companion Volumes, 1972)
　Vol. IV. 1917–22 (1975) (with three Companion Volumes, 1977)
　Vol. V. 1922–39 (1976) (with three Companion Volumes, 1979–82)
　Vol. VI. Finest Hour, 1939–41 (1983)
　Vol. VII. Road to Victory 1941–1945 (1986)
　Vol. VIII. Never Despair, 1945–65 (1988)
　The Churchill War Papers: Vol. I: At the Admiralty, 1939–1940; Vol. II, Never Surrender, May–December 1940; Vol. III, The Ever-Widening war, 1941 (London: Heinemann, 1993–2000)
　In Search of Churchill (London: HarperCollins pb edn, 1995)
House, Edward Mandell: *The Intimate Papers of Colonel House* (Scholarly Press edn, 1971; first published 1926)
Graves, Robert: *Goodbye to All That* (London: Penguin revised edn, 1957)
Harvey, John (ed), *The War Diaries of Oliver Harvey 1941–45* (London: Collins, 1978)

Hill, Marion: *Bletchley Park People: Churchill's Geese that Never Cackled* (Sutton Publishing, 2004)

Howarth, Patrick: *Intelligence Chief Extraordinary: The Life of the Ninth Duke of Portland* (Oxford: Bodley Head, 1986)

Irving, David: *Churchill's War: Vol. II, Triumph in Adversity* (London: Focal Point Publications, 2001)

Ismay, Lord: *Memoirs of General the Lord Ismay* (London: Heinemann, 1960)

Jenkins, Roy: *Churchill* (London: Macmillan, 2001)

Jones, Thomas: *A Diary with Letters, 1931–1950* (London: Oxford University Press, 1954)

Whitehall Diary Volume I, 1916–25 (London: Oxford University Press, 1969)

Judd, Alan: *The Quest for C: Mansfield Cumming and the Founding of the Secret Service* (London: HarperCollins, 1999)

Kimball, Warren F. (ed): *Churchill & Roosevelt: The Complete Correspondence* (3 vols. Princeton, NJ: Princeton University Press, 1984)
I. *Alliance Emerging*
II. *Alliance Forged*
III. *Alliance Declining*

Landau, Henry: *All's Fair* (London: 1934)

Leather, David: *Contractor Leather: John Towlerton Leather (1804–1885), Hydraulic Engineer and Contractor of Railways and Sea Defences* (Bradford: Leather Family History Society, 2005)

Leutze, James R. (ed): *The London Journals of General Raymond E. Lee* (Boston: Little Brown, 1971)

Lycett, Andrew: *Ian Fleming* (London: Weidenfeld & Nicolson, 1995)

Mackenzie, Compton: *Greek Memories* (London: Cassell, 1933)

My Life and Times: Octave Five, 1915–1923 (London: Chatto & Windus, 1966)

Maclean, Fitzroy: *Eastern Approaches* (London: Jonathan Cape, 1949)

Macmillan, Harold: *Winds of Change: 1914–1939* (London: Macmillan, 1966)

The Blast of War: 1939–1945 (London: Macmillan, 1967)

War Diaries: The Mediterranean 1943–45 (London: Macmillan, 1984)

Marks, Leo: *Between Silk and Cyanide: A Codemaker's war, 1941–1945* (London: HarperCollins, 1998)

Marquand, David: *Ramsay MacDonald* (London: Jonathan Cape, 1977)

Martland, Peter: *Lord Haw Haw: The English Voice of Nazi Germany* (London: The National Archives, 2003)

Masters, Anthony: *The Man who was M: The Life of Maxwell Knight* (Oxford: Basil Blackwell, 1984)

Middlemas, Keith & Barnes, John: *Baldwin: a biography* (London: Weidenfeld & Nicolson, 1969)

Montgomery Hyde, H.: *The Quiet Canadian: the Secret Service Story of Sir William Stephenson* (London: Hamish Hamilton, 1962)

Moran, Lord: *Winston Churchill: The Struggle for Survival 1940–65* (London: Constable, 1966; abridged and revised edn published as *Churchill at War 1940–45*, Constable & Robinson Ltd, 2002)

Murphy, Robert D.: *Diplomat among Warriors* (London: Collins, 1964)

Norwich, John Julius (ed): *The Duff Cooper Diaries* (London: Weidenfeld & Nicolson, 2005)

Nowak-Jezioranski, Jan: *Courier from Warsaw* (London: Collins/Harvill, 1982)

Orlov, Vladimir: *The Secret Dossier: My Memoirs of Russia's Political Underworld* (1932)

Pimlott, Ben: *Hugh Dalton* (London: Papermac edn, 1986)

(ed) *The Second World War Diary of Hugh Dalton 1940–45* (London: Jonathan Cape, 1986)

(ed) *The Political Diary of Hugh Dalton 1918–40, 1945–60* (London: Jonathan Cape, 1986)

Powell, Anthony: *To Keep the Ball Rolling: The Memoirs of Anthony Powell* (London: Penguin edn, 1983)

Read, Anthony & Fisher, David: *Colonel Z: the Life and Times of a Master of Spies* (London: Hodder & Stoughton, 1984)

Rose, Kenneth: *Elusive Rothschild: The Life of Victor, Third Baron* (London: Weidenfeld & Nicolson, 2003)

Roskill, Stephen: *Hankey, Man of Secrets*, vols. I–III (London: Collins, 1970–74)

Sheffield, Gary & Bourne, John (eds), *Douglas Haig: War Diaries 1914–18* (London: Weidenfeld & Nicolson, 2005)

Shulman, Milton: *Marilyn, Hitler and Me: The Memoirs of Milton Shulman* (London: André Deutsch, 1998)

Skidelsky, Robert: *John Maynard Keynes* (London: Macmillan, 1983–2000), 3 vols
John Maynard Keynes: Hopes Betrayed 1883–1920 (1983)
John Maynard Keynes: The Economist as Saviour 1920–1937 (1992)
John Maynard Keynes: Fighting for Britain 1937–1946 (2000)

Smith, Michael: *Foley: The Spy who saved 10,000 Jews* (London: Hodder & Stoughton, 1999)

Soames, Mary: *Clementine Churchill, by her daughter* (London: Cassell, 1979)

(ed) *Speaking for themselves: the personal letters of Winston and Clementine Churchill* (London: Doubleday, 1998)

Spears, Edward: *Liaison 1914* (London: Eyre & Spottiswode, 1930)
Assignment to Catastrophe: Vol. I: Prelude to Dunkirk; Vol. II, The Fall of France (London: Heinemann, 1954)

Spence, Richard B.: *Trust No One: the Secret World of Sidney Reilly* (Los Angeles: Feral House, 2002)

Stevenson, William: *A Man called Intrepid: the Secret War 1939–1945* (London: Macmillan, 1976)

Tennant, Peter: *Touchlines of War* (The University of Hull Press, 1992)

Thompson, R.W.: *The Yankee Marlborough* (London: George Allen & Unwin, 1963
Churchill and Morton: Correspondence between Major Sir Desmond Morton and R.W. Thompson (London: Hodder & Stoughton, 1976)

Vansittart, Robert G.: *The Mist Procession: The Autobiography of Lord Vansittart* (London: Hutchinson, 1958)

West, Nigel (ed), *The Guy Liddell Diaries, Volume I: 1939–42* and *Volume II: 1942–45* (London: Routledge, 2005)

Wheatley, Dennis: *Stranger than Fiction (War Papers for the Joint Planning Staff* (London: Hutchinson, 1959)

Wilkinson, Peter & Bright Astley, Joan: *Gubbins and SOE* (London: Leo Cooper, 1993)

Willert, Sir Arthur: *The Road to Safety* (London: Verschoyle, 1952)

Williams, Charles: *The Last Great Frenchman: A life of General de Gaulle* (New York: John Wiley & Sons, 1993)

Woodhouse, C.M.: *Apple of Discord* (London, 1948)

Secondary works

Addison, Paul: *Churchill on the Home Front 1900–1955* (London: Jonathan Cape, 1992)

Andrew, Christopher: *Secret Service: the Making of the British Intelligence Community* (London: Sceptre edn 1986, first published 1985)

    For the President's eyes only: Secret Intelligence and the American Presidency from Washington to Bush (London: HarperCollins, 1995)

    with **Dilks, David** (eds): *The Missing Dimension: Governments and Intelligence Communities in the Twentieth Century* (London: Palgrave Macmillan, 1984)

    with **Noakes, Jeremy** (eds): *Intelligence and International Relations 1900–1945* (University of Exeter Press, 1987)

    with **Gordievsky, Oleg:** *KGB: The Inside Story of its Foreign Operations from Lenin to Gorbachev* (London: Hodder & Stoughton, 1990)

    with **Mitrokhin, Vasili:** *The Mitrokhin Archive: the KGB in Europe and the West* (London: Penguin, 1999)

    with **Mitrokhin, Vasili:** the Mitrokhin Archive II: the KGB and the World (London: Penguin, 2005)

Alvarez, David: 'Most helpful and cooperative: GC&CS and the development of American diplomatic cryptanalysis', in Smith & Erskine (eds), *Action This day*

Becke, Major A.F.: *The Royal Artillery Regiment of Artillery at Le Cateau, 26 August 1914* (London: HMSO, 1919)

Bell, P.M.H.: *A Certain Eventuality: Britain and the Fall of France* (Farnborough, Hampshire: Saxon House, 1974)

Bennett, Gill: *A most extraordinary and mysterious business: the Zinoviev Letter of 1924* (London: FCO, 1999)

Blake, Robert, 'How Churchill became Prime Minister', in Blake & Louis, *Churchill*

Blake, Robert & Louis, Wm Roger (eds): *Churchill* (Oxford: Oxford University Press, 1993)

Bramah, Ernest: *Kai Lung's Golden Hours* (Penguin edn, 1938; first published 1922)

Brook Shepherd, Gordon: *The Storm Petrels: The first Soviet defectors, 1928–1938* (London: Collins, 1977)

    Iron Maze: the Western Secret Services and the Bolsheviks (London: Macmillan, 1998)

Budiansky, Stephen: *Battle of Wits: the Complete Story of Codebreaking in World War II* (London: Viking, 2000)

Carlton, David: *MacDonald versus Henderson: the foreign policy of the second Labour Government* (London: Macmillan, 1970)

    'Churchill and the two "Evil Empires"', *Transactions of the Royal Historical Society*, 6th series, vol.11, 2001

Cave Brown, Anthony: *Bodyguard of Lies: The Extraordinary True Story behind D-Day* (London: HarperCollins edn, 2002; first published 1975)

Charles, Douglas: 'The origins of American central intelligence', *Intelligence and National Security*, vol. 20, June 2005, No. 2

Chester, Lewis, Fay, Stephen & Young, Hugo: The Zinoviev Letter: A Political Intrigue (London: Heinemann, 1967)

Conwell-Evans, T.P.: *None So Blind: a study of the crisis years, 1930–1939, based on the private papers of Group Captain M.G. Christie* (London: Harrison & Sons, 1947)

Costello, John: *Ten Days that Saved the West* (London: Bantam Press, 1991)

Cradock, Percy: *Know Your Enemy: How the Joint Intelligence Committee Saw the World* (London: John Murray, 2002)

Creighton, Christopher: *Op JB: The Last Great Secret of the Second World War* (London: Simon and Schuster, 1996).

Davies, Philip H.J.: *MI6 and the Machinery of Spying* (London: Frank Cass, 2004)

Deacon, Richard: *A History of the British Secret Service* (London: Frederick Muller, 1969)

Dear, I.C.B. & Foot, M.R.D.: *The Oxford Companion to the Second World War* (Oxford: Oxford University Press, 1995)

Denniston, Robin: 'Diplomatic Eavesdropping 1922–44: A new source discovered', *Intelligence and National Security*, vol. 10, No. 3, July 1995

De Poncins, Vicomte Leon: *Freemasonry and the Vatican* (London: 1968 edn)

Dilks, David: 'Flashes of intelligence: the Foreign Office, the SIS and security before the Second World War', Andrew & Dilks (eds), *Missing Dimension*

Farndale, General Sir Martin: *History of the Royal Regiment of Artillery: Western Front 1914–18* (Royal Artillery Institution, 1986)

Ferris, John Robert: *Intelligence and Strategy: Selected Essays* (London: Routledge, 2005)

Foot, M.R.D.: *SOE: The Special Operations Executive 1940–46* (London: Pimlico edn, 1999; first published 1984)

Forbes, Neil: *Doing business with the Nazis: Britain's Economic and Financial Relations with Germany 1931–39* (London: Frank Cass, 2000)

Fowler, W.B.: *British-American Relations 1917–19: the role of Sir William Wiseman* (Princeton: Princeton University Press, 1969)

Hamilton, C.J.: 'The Decline of Churchill's "Garden Suburb" and Rise of his Private Office': the Prime Minister's Department, 1940–45', *Twentieth Century British History*, vol. 12, No. 2, 2001

Haslam, Jonathan: *Soviet Foreign Policy 1930–33: the impact of the Depression* (London, Palgrave Macmillan, 1983)

Hinsley, F.H. & Stripp, Alan: *Code Breakers: The Inside Story of Bletchley Park* (Oxford: Oxford University Press, 1993)

Holt, Thaddeus: *The Deceivers: Allied Military Deception in the Second World War* (London: Weidenfeld & Nicolson, 2004)

Hosking, Geoffrey: *A History of the Soviet Union* (London: Final edn, Fontana, 1992)

Howard, Michael: *The First World War* (Oxford: Oxford University Press, 2002)

Imlay, Talbot Charles: 'A reassessment of Anglo-French strategy during the Phony War, 1939–40', *English Historical Review*, vol. cxix, 481, April 2004

Jackson, Peter: *France and the Nazi menace: Intelligence and policy-making, 1933–1939* (Oxford: Oxford University Press, 2000)

Jeffrey, Keith and Sharp, Alan: 'Lord Curzon and Secret Intelligence', in Andrew & Noakes (eds), *Intelligence and International Relations 1900–1945* (University of Exeter, 1987)

Johnstone, T. and Hagerty, J.: *The Cross on the Sword: Catholic Chaplains in the Forces* (London: Geoffrey Chapman, 1996)

Jones, R.V.: *Most Secret War* (London: Hamish Hamilton, 1978)

Lewin, Ronald: *Ultra goes to War* (London: Penguin edn, 2001; first published 1978)

Liddell Hart, B.H.: *History of the First World War* (London, Papermac edn, 1997; first published 1930)

Litten, Frederick: 'The Noulens Affair', *The China Quarterly*, 138 (June 1994)

Louden, Stephen H.: *Chaplains in Conflict: the Role of Army Chaplains since 1914* (London: Avon Books, 1996)

Madeira, Victor: 'No wishful thinking allowed: Secret Service Committee and Intelligence Reform in Great Britain, 1919–22', *Intelligence and National Security*, vol. 18, No. 1, Spring 2003)

'Moscow's interwar infiltration of British Intelligence 1919–1929', *Historical Journal*, vol. 4, December 2003

Masterman, J.C.: *The Double Cross System* (London: History Book Club, 1972; reprinted with introduction by Nigel West, Pimlico, 1995)

Milward, Alan: *The German Economy at War* (London: The Athlone Press, 1965)
The Reconstruction of Western Europe, 1945–51 (London: Routledge, 1984)

Moynihan, Michael: *God on our side: the British Padre in World War One* (London: Secker & Warburg, 1983)

Munch-Petersen, Thomas: 'Confessions of a British Agent: Section D in Sweden, 1938–40', *Utrikespolitik och historia, Studier tillagnade Wilhelm M. Carlgren* (Stockholm, 1987)

Neilson, Keith: '"Pursued by a bear": British estimates of Soviet military strength and Anglo-Soviet relations 1922–1939', *Canadian Journal of History/Annales canadiennes d'histore*, XXVIII, August 1993

Nylander, Gert: 'German Resistance Movement and England', *Banking and Enterprise* No 2 (Stockholm: The Foundation for Economic History Research within Banking and Enterprise, 1999)

O'Halpin, Eunan: *Defending Ireland: the Irish State and its Enemies since 1922* (Oxford: Oxford University Press, 1999)

'British Intelligence, the Republican Movement and the IRA's German Links 1935–45', in Hearghal McGarry (ed), *Republicanism in Modern Ireland* (Dublin, 2003)

Peden, G.C.: *The Treasury and British Public Policy 1906–1959* (Oxford: Oxford University Press, 2000)

'A matter of timing: the economic background to British foreign policy, 1937–1939', *History*, vol. 69 (1984)

Persico, Joseph E.: *Roosevelt's Secret War* (New York, 2001);

Pidgeon, Geoffrey: *The Secret Wireless War: the Story of MI6 Communications 1939–45* (London: UPSO, 2003).

Ramsay, Charles & Ramsay, M.A.: 'Giving a lead in the right direction: Sir Robert Vansittart and the Defence Requirements Sub-Committee', *Diplomacy and Statecraft*, vol. 6, March 1995, No. 1

Reynolds, David: I*n Command of History: Churchill Fighting and Writing the Second World War* (London: Allen Lane, 2004)

'The Ultra Secret and Churchill's war memoirs', *Intelligence and National Security*, vol. 20, No. 2, June 2005

World War to Cold War: Churchill, Roosevelt and the International History of the 1940s (Oxford: Oxford University Press, 2006)

Roskill, Stephen: Churchill and the Admirals (London: Collins, 1977)

Salmon, Patrick: 'British plans for Economic Warfare against Germany', Walter Laqueur (ed), *The Second World War: Essays in Military and Political History* (London: Sage Publications, 1982)

Shephard, Ben: *A War of Nerves: Soldiers and Psychiatrists 1914–1994* (London: Pimlico edn, 2000)

Smith, Michael: 'The Government Code and Cypher School and the First Cold War', in Smith and Erskine (eds), *Action This Day*

Smith, Michael and Erskine, Ralph (eds): *Action This Day: Bletchley Park from the breaking of the Enigma Code to the birth of the modern computer* (London: Bantam Press, 2001)

Stafford, David: *Britain and European Resistance* (London: Macmillan, 1980)
  Churchill and Secret Service (London: John Murray, 1997)
  Roosevelt & Churchill (London: Little, Brown & Co, 1999)
  (ed) *Flight from Reality: Rudolf Hess and his Mission to Scotland 1941* (London, Pimlico, 2002

Strachan, Hew: *The First World War*, Vol. I, To Arms (Oxford: Oxford University Press, 2001)

Taylor, A.J.P.: *English History 1914–1945* (Oxford: Oxford University Press, 1965)

Tomaselli, P.: 'C's Moscow Station – the Anglo-Russian Trade Mission as cover for SIS in the early 1920s', *Intelligence and National Security*, Vol. 17, No. 3 (Autumn 2002)

Thompson, R.W.: *The Price of Victory* (London: Constable, 1960)

Troy, Thomas F.: *Wild Bill and Intrepid: Donovan, Stephenson and the Origin of CIA* (New Haven, Conn.: Yale University Press, 1996)

Verrier, Anthony: *Through the Looking Glass: British Foreign Policy in the Age of Illusions* (London: Jonathan Cape, 1983)

Wark, Wesley: *The Ultimate Enemy: British intelligence and Nazi Germany 1933–1939* (Ithaca, NY: Cornell University Press, 1985)

West, Nigel: *MI6: British Secret Intelligence Operations 1909–45* (London: Weidenfeld & Nicolson, 1983)
  MASK: MI5's penetration of the Communist Party of Great Britain (London: Routledge, 2005)
  with Tsarev, Oleg: *Crown Jewels: The British Secrets at the Heart of the KGB Archives* (London: HarperCollins, 1998)

Wheatley, Dennis: 'Deception in World War II', *RUSI Journal*, vol. 121, No 3, September 1976.

Williamson, Philip: 'Baldwin's reputation: Politics and History, 1937–1967', *Historical Journal*, vol. 47, 1, March 2004

Wilson, Trevor & Prior, Robin, 'Conflict, Technology and the Impact of Industrialisation: the Great War, 1914–18', *The Journal of Strategic Studies* vol. 24, No. 3 (September 2001)

Winterbotham, F.W.: *The Ultra Secret* (London: Weidenfeld & Nicolson, 1974)

Young, Robert: 'Spokesman for Economic Warfare: the Industrial Intelligence Centre in the 1930s', *European Studies Review*, 6, 1976

INDEX